Tony Geraghty was born in 1932 and served as a sergeant in the Parachute Brigade in Cyprus, Egypt and the UK, a part of his education which led him into a successful career as war reporter and defence correspondent.

After an acclaimed period as a journalist with such papers as the *Guardian*, *Sunday Telegraph* and *Sunday Times*, he became a freelance writer in 1981 and as well as his success with WHO DARES WINS he is the author of THIS IS THE SAS, MARCH OR DIE, and BULLET-CATCHERS.

As a reserve RAF officer he flew with the First Nimrod sorties in the Gulf within days of the Iraqi invasion of Kuwait and served as liaison officer with a US military team in Saudi Arabia later in the Gulf conflict.

He lives in Herefordshire with his wife, who is also a writer.

WHO DARES WINS

The Story of the SAS
1950–1992

Tony Geraghty

timewarner
paperbacks

A *Time Warner* Paperback

First published in Great Britain in 1980
Second edition published in 1983
by Arms and Armour Press
Third edition, revised and expanded, published in 1992
by Little, Brown and Company
This edition published by Warner Books in 1993
Reprinted 1993, 1994, 1995 (twice), 1997, 2000
Reprinted by Time Warner Paperbacks in 2002

Copyright © Tony Geraghty 1980, 1983, 1992

The moral right of the author has been asserted.

A CIP catalogue record for this book
is available from the British Library.

ISBN 0 7515 0358 4

Typeset by Hewer Text Composition Services, Edinburgh
Printed in England by Clays Ltd, St Ives plc

Time Warner Paperbacks
An imprint of
Time Warner Books UK
Brettenham House
Lancaster Place
London WC2E 7EN

www.TimeWarnerBooks.co.uk

'As courage and intelligence are the two qualities best worth a good man's cultivation, so it is the first part of intelligence to recognise our precarious estate in life, and the first part of courage to be not at all abashed before the fact.'

From *Aes Triplex*, an essay
by Robert Louis Stevenson, 1881

ACKNOWLEDGEMENTS

Thanks are due to the many friends (old and new), as well as old soldiers and erstwhile companions in parachuting who gave unstintingly of their time and energy in helping me to write this history. Geraghty's 'garnish' apart, it is their sweat that I have recycled.

I must also thank all those mentioned in the Bibliography, but I am especially grateful to the following authors and their publishers for permission to quote brief passages: *The Regiments Depart: The British Army, 1945–70*, by Gregory Blaxland, and *The Special Air Service*, by P. Warner (both published by William Kimber Ltd); *Bunch of Fives*, by General Sir Frank Kitson, *Last Post: Aden 1964–67* by Julian Paget and *Big Boys' Rules* by Mark Urban (published by Faber & Faber Ltd); *Oman, The Making of a Modern State*, by J. Townsend (published by Croom Helm Ltd); *The SAS In Ireland*, by Raymond Murray (published by The Mercier Press, Cork); *Soldier 'I' SAS* by Michael Paul Kennedy (published by Bloomsbury Publishing); *All in a life: an autobiography*, by Dr Garret Fitzgerald (published by Macmillan).

CONTENTS

LIST OF MAPS

ILLUSTRATIONS

Photographs have been supplied by the following:

First picture section: Private collection except Plate 2 (top) Thorn EMI Electronics.

Second picture section: Plate 1 Private collection; Plate 2 Private collection; Plate 3 Tony Geraghty; Plate 4 Private Collection; Plate 5 (top) Mrs J. Lane, (bottom) JAK; Plate 6 Private collection; Plate 7 Private collection; Plate 8 (top) Private collection, (bottom) Bruce Niven.

Third picture section: Plate 1 Imperial War Museum; Plate 2 Private collection; Plate 3 Private collection; Plate 4 Soldier 'I'; Plate 5 Soldier 'I'; Plate 6 (top) Alastair Morrison, (bottom) Joseph Celecia; Plate 7 (top) Imperial War Museum, (centre) Private collection, (bottom) Chilean Information Service; Plate 8 Private collection.

PREFACE

In 1979, the author was invited to write a history of the SAS Regiment in the years following the Second World War. This was clearly an impossible task and therefore an interesting challenge. The result, to the author's surprise a year later, was an awesome commercial success due to the regiment's televised rescue of the Iranian Embassy hostages at Princes Gate, Kensington coinciding with the publication of the book.

In 1983, a year after the South Atlantic conflict with Argentina, the twelfth impression was printed. This contained the first detailed account of the regiment's sombre triumph in that campaign.

Almost ten years later, in a dramatically-changed political landscape, the original book was clearly out of date. This was not only because of events in the Gulf, Ireland, Gibraltar, South America, South-East Asia, Africa and elsewhere during those years, but the collapse of the Soviet empire under the economic burden of its own armament – like an overclad knight falling from his horse and unable to stand up again unaided – rendered preconceptions of recent history instantly obsolete. For example, before the Berlin Wall fell, we could only suspect that many Euro-terrorists were, in effect, surrogate warriors of the Warsaw Pact. We knew that as a fact after some of East Germany's secrets were made public following German reunification. Western hostages in Beirut and elsewhere were released after years of captivity when the terrorists holding them could no longer rely on the ultimate anti-Western shield of Soviet support.

When – if – the definitive history of the Cold War, 1948–89, is written it will become apparent that the SAS, along with a tiny number of other specialists, was fighting it for real. The vast shadow-boxing show between Nato and the Warsaw Pact in Europe was, after all, a war of silent economic attrition rather than an actual military event. (Nato's exercise scenarios always ended at the moment when the embattled West was obliged to use nuclear weapons, after which there was a question mark as big as a mushroom cloud.)

For two generations, the strange theologies of deterrence dominated most military life in the northern hemisphere. Was it to be Mutual Assured Destruction (MAD) or Flexible Response? Strangelove or Machiavelli? With icebags on heads, serious career soldiers were entombed in think-tanks with no more authority than journalistic pundits or men with slide rules calculating throw-weights and Circular Error of Probability. One distinguished soldier eluded that fate. His name was Peter de la Billiere.

In the real world, small brown men with guns were mocking the super-powers by walking through jungle and desert to exercise influence with the throw-weight of a .303 bullet. Brezhnev and others backed them as protagonists in wars of 'national liberation'. The war for living space, for food, for shrinking resources in a world with too many mouths to feed and too many guns will continue regardless of political doctrine.

The SAS uniquely has dedicated itself to this theatre of real conflict during the past forty-two years, rather than the great European conjuring trick. It is a shifting world where experience counts, the risk of disaster is ever-present and the ground rules are few. The SAS should now be seen not so much as a military maverick or a reluctantly-licensed Rottweiler; but more as the shape of armies to come: compact, sophisticated, selective in their targeting and capable in a limited war of controlling immense firepower. It is the military mainstream.

The author has been privileged to know SAS soldiers over the years as fellow parachutists, as drinking companions and as friends and almost equally privileged to write a mere outline of their history.

Tony Geraghty

INTRODUCTION

More than fifty years after David Stirling created a largely mythical organisation described as 'L Detachment of the Special Air Service Brigade' (although the Detachment of fifty-three men – reduced to twenty-two after the first raid – existed, the brigade of 4000 did not) the SAS continues to defy precise definition. It is, more than ever, an established part of the British Army's order of battle at a time when other regiments celebrate tricentenial anniversaries as they await extinction under the latest plan for defence cuts.

Yet the SAS is a regiment unlike others. It is without a permanent cadre of officers; they are borrowed from other units for a three-year tour before being sent back to that sometimes distant organ, the British Army. There are two opposed views about the effect of such a practice: first, it ensures that the SAS does not become some sort of private army; second, it ensures that the SAS becomes NCO-driven to an alarming extent. However, it is a system which has assuredly created the most versatile military formation of this and, perhaps, any other century.

In its golden Jubilee Year, 1991, the SAS held not one reunion but at least twenty in locations as widely scattered as Thailand, Oman, Edinburgh, France, London and, of course, Hereford. At one of the open-air gatherings, young veterans of the war behind Iraqi lines played host to the old-and-bold; to children riding a familiar training aid known as the 'death slide' from a 90 foot tower; to toddlers, amazed by the diver in his gigantic fishtank bearing the inscription 'Please do not feed the frogman'. Those outside the tank were able to play noughts-and-crosses with the figure inside in a teasing, ambiguous experience that epitomised SAS magic.

1

'Look, we are basically, just soldiers', the Commanding Officer of 22 SAS assured visitors to a subsequent open day for those willing to contribute £200 to the welfare fund. This is true most of the time, but as one as one of Stirling's original volunteers recalls: 'There is nothing on my personal file to cover years of my service except that I was "detached".'

To serve on detachment is to be drafted for a time from parent regiment so as to soldier elsewhere, usually in uniform, with some other formation. In this case, the word was uttered with invisible quotation marks around it. Detached to what? To whom? For what?

One boy soldier, a young signaller and likely lad, had received parachute training even before the Second World War started, well before No. 1 Parachute Training School opened at Ringway and long before Stirling's massive climber's frame loomed over his horizon. 'I didn't know who my boss was,' he recalls now. 'I was with the French Resistance in Occupied France. At least I think I was. And that's all I know.'

More recent experience has taught a retired officer, his record also punctuated with blank spaces, that 'the SAS isn't just a regiment like any other'. An ex-trooper, with experience of the Argentine mainland during the Falklands War (Operation Corporate) feels able to justify his silence: 'You are told, "You will never speak about this. You will take the experience with you to the grave." I'd feel disloyal if I were to tell you what happened.'

All armies prefer to operate in secrecy (until they win), and the SAS, having been pitched into an undeclared war against terrorism within the United Kingdom, can never declare outright victory. Yet the regiment does more than wait and watch and shoot it out in politically supercharged little contacts in Ireland. Twice in a decade it has been hurled into larger conflicts verging on general war. Their battle honours read: South Atlantic, 1981; Ireland, Gibraltar & Elsewhere, 1982–1990; Gulf/Iraq, 1990–1991; all of which represents a kind of schizophrenic sandwich, in which the soldier's life is valued (on a scale of one to ten) at a high eight in Ulster or at Princes Gate, but somewhat below zero on the big operations far from home. So great is the difference of style, content and firepower between the two types of conflict that it is necessary, even in this Introduction, to look at them as separate histories.

Terrorism is always within the grasp of any political hoodlum. In an democratic society the political criminal, like any other, has the advantage and, if the violence is intelligently applied, there is always a chance of destabilising elected leaders. This has happened twice in the United Kingdom since the Irish Troubles were renewed. On 10 March 1971, the first handful of British soldiers to be murdered in Belfast included three young soldiers relaxing off duty with local people of their own age. Two were brothers. One was just seventeen years of age. They were unarmed, in civilian clothes, and were betrayed by their youthful, local drinking companions. The triple killing, in revolting circumstances, precipitated a series of political crises, including internment, which brought down the Stormont regime.

An even more spectacular success was the political downfall of Margaret Thatcher. The slide began with the IRA's assassination of her former aide, Ian Gow, MP, on 30 July 1990. In the by-election for his Eastbourne constituency on 18 October 1990 a Conservative majority of almost 17,000 was converted into a Liberal Democratic one of 4550 votes. With the loss of Eastbourne, confidence in Mrs Thatcher within the Conservative parliamentary party evaporated for reasons which had nothing to do with Ireland; but the bomb that killed Gow was the explosive catalyst that began the change. Little more than a year later, she was removed. The IRA had got lucky. But then, as they had so often said of their efforts to murder Mrs Thatcher physically rather than politically: 'We only need to get lucky once.'

The SAS is, in all its essentials, a synthesis of the British Army, a cross-section of the best soldiers in one of the world's most professional military formations, an army in which the doctrine of 'minimum force' has been developed exceptionally well. Soldiers – even SAS soldiers – like to keep it simple. That means having standing orders laid down in anticipation of some crisis. A 'standing operational procedure' (SOP) or 'first immediate action' (1st IA) is typical of this approach. Faced with a continuous military operation on its own doorstep, the SAS has responded by throwing a blanket of total secrecy over all its operations, often unnecessarily covering activities greatly to its credit far from home.

The all-embracing silence was one in which the SAS, like France's army in the nineteenth century, became 'La Grande Muette', the mute giant. In this secret darkness, strange fantasies and half-truths flourished fungus-like and bore their misshapen fruit in the headlines, unchallenged, to pass into the printed or video record, so to remain as a poisoned source for historians. For one small example, some newspapers falsely reported that not only did the SAS parachute into Iraq in 1991, its men jumped while wearing helmets to which claymore mines were attached.

Along with such embarrassing 'friends' in the media, there are the undisguised enemies who come not to praise the SAS but to bury it. This assorted rentacrowd includes journalists who hate soldiers as a political preference, as well as members of the armed forces who suffer from acute professional jealousy, particularly if they have themselves failed to pass the regiment's stringent selection process.

If the regiment can afford to brush off the dandruff of such ill-informed praise, the same cannot be said of the heavyweight criticism of serious academics. Some (such as the distinguished military historian Sir Michael Howard, MC) imply that the SAS was at its best during the general, unlimited war that ended in 1945. Others, endorsing that view, also suggest that the regiment was still a vital tool in the Falklands or the Gulf, where the rules of war rather than the rule of law applied, but that the regiment is entirely unsuited to the finely-tuned, politically-manicured minimum force needed on the crowded stage of internal security, where innocent civilians and terrorists mingle and look alike.

INTRODUCTION

Professor Thomas Mokaitis, an American and author of British Counter Insurgency argues:

> Counter insurgency has little in common with other forms of low intensity conflict except that they are not full scale conventional wars. One unfortunate consequence of this grouping is the use of commandos both as guerrillas and to combat guerrillas. The Special Air Service has been effective in out-of-area operations from Malaya to the Falklands but its use in Northern Ireland has been more controversial. The shooting of apparently unarmed IRA members at Gibraltar raised serious questions about the SAS's ability to adhere to minimum force. Such problems may arise when special forces trained to operate behind enemy lines in an open situation with no limits placed on their use of force find themselves assigned to internal security duty where they must exercise great restraint in a very structured situation. If soldiers generally make poor police then special forces may be the worst police of all.

This beguiling distinction overlooks facts of life and death with which soldiers have been faced in Northern Ireland and elsewhere since 1970: that the IRA, in particular, is often better armed than the security forces as a result of Whitehall's minimum force policy. It ignores the high proportion of arrests (more than two to one) over kills made by the SAS in Ireland as well as those lamentable cases in which soldiers have stepped out of their hides to make a constabulary gesture, only to be summarily butchered by the men they had challenged.

The critics skirt round the legal ambiguity which has surrounded the soldier's role in Northern Ireland since 1969. He enjoys no right other than to make a common law, citizen's arrest. Unlike other citizens, however, the soldier is subject to military law and will be punished by court-martial if he fails as a soldier while carrying a lethal weapon. If he uses his weapon in circumstances which are remotely unclear, he is caught in a trap defined by Voltaire: 'The art of war is like that of medicine: murderous and conjectural.' The SAS soldier (in Northern Ireland) has been made the vehicle for reconciling apparently irreconcilable identities of law enforcer and guerrilla. It has been a rough ride at times and that is acknowledged in this history.

Some SAS officers, not surprisingly, take a robust view of their business which overrides distinctions between one sort of armed conflict and another. Major-General Michael Rose, Commanding Officer of 22 SAS in the Falklands, writing later about that campaign, observed that since 1945, the regiment had 'also gained world-wide experience in limited war operations – most notably through its involvement in counter-terrorist operations in Northern Ireland'.

With the end of the Thatcher years, political perceptions of terrorism – internationally as well as internally – changed remarkably. Only hours after Mrs Thatcher's departure as Prime Minister, the British government restored relations with Syria (a pariah state following its support of a bomb attempt on an Israeli aircraft flying from London) and signed a joint statement accepting Syria's 'distinction between terrorism and national struggle', as well as that country's rejection of 'acts of international terrorism'.

The law governing the use of force by security forces at home was also reviewed. In 1991, less than a year after Mr John Major's unexpected occupation of the highest office, a 'high level interdepartmental committee' representing the politicians, the military and the law was set up to study 'the case for creating new offences relating to shootings by security forces'. (There was no similar hint of a review of the policy of releasing back into the community, without warning, convicted terrorists who returned to terrorism.) As David McKitterick, the Independent's perceptive Irish correspondent pointed out: 'The Northern Ireland Director of Prosecutions, in deciding whether to bring charges against members of the security forces [in cases where excessive force might have been used] is faced with the difficult choice of charging with murder or ordering no prosecution.' By September 1991, twenty members of the security forces had been charged with murder, following killings carried out by servicemen on duty. Of those twenty, nineteen were acquitted and the twentieth was released after serving less than three years of a life sentence. But for the SAS, operating at the sharp end, it is business as usual, maintaining a fitness and readiness to fight.

'One moment, the world is a nice place, calm and quiet and beautiful', one of the regiment's top pistol trainers tells his students in a soft, lilting Irish brogue. The voice hardens as he continues: 'The next moment it is bloody chaos and you are going to die unless you react with total, outright violence.'

His shooting skills, using a new self-loading pistol, are awesome: it takes less than a second to draw the gun and six bullets are fired every second thereafter from the median killing-zone range of seven metres, every round potentially lethal into the heart and head of the man-sized cut-out targets. In this world there is no such thing as shooting to wound or disable or detain for questioning. 'Arrest', in these circumstances, is a permanent and horizontal condition we usually describe as death. Anyone who has survived a terrorist machine-gun ambush, or a bomb exploding under his hospital bed, will recognise the difficulty of fine-tuning the 1st IA to meet the niceties of the law. SAS doctrine recognises the inevitable: that on a battlefield someone will be killed.

The regiment also tries to keep a sense of proportion. In 1977, an SAS major bearing the Arabic nickname Shams (for Sun), beginning a two-year posting to Northern Ireland, decided to live alone and incognito, in an isolated cottage vulnerable to terrorist attack, to avoid the bunker psychology. He had a security problem, however: 'Creeping in and out of my new home . . . stuffing a loaded and cocked pistol down my waist-band was quite the most dangerous thing I had ever done.' He decided to emulate the Roman consul Manlius, woken by geese in AD 390 to warn of a night attack by the Gauls, and bought six geese which regularly woke him, for no good reason, at around 2am. As he later wrote:

All hell let loose. Insistent cackling from the yard; time to get under the bed with the trusty 9mm if I could find it . . .
I remained alert where I lay on the cramped boards, waiting

anxiously for the grey dawn, then slipped the window catches and stole off across the fields. No sign of the 'boyos', who had obviously thought discretion the better part of valour, this time. Early breakfast in the Mess.

For a short time his life was dominated by the geese: the care and feeding of them; marketing their eggs; protecting his protectors against their predators in a private war using rat poison and shotgun. He contrived, in spite of that, to run a highly effective intelligence gathering operation.

David Stirling, as he lay paralysed from the waist down in his hospital bed in Cairo in 1941, scribbling his proposal for a tiny raiding force to replace the disbanded Layforce Commando Brigade, was not thinking of minimum force. It was more a question of getting a bigger bang for a smaller buck. Stirling explained subsequently:

> The main thesis . . . was to plead that many objectives envisaged for Layforce . . . could be tackled by a unit less than one-twentieth the size of the 1600-man establishment of Layforce . . . The minuscule demand on the resources of the Middle East Command and the project's high potential reward decided the C-in-C to authorise me to go ahead. Thus was born the Special Air Service.

A cornerstone of SAS philosophy was to try to score a strategic blow rather than win a specific battle or to hold ground as at Arnhem or Pegasus Bridge on the Orme. In western Iraq, 1991, the regiment succeeded brilliantly in achieving a strategic aim, in pinning down elusive, mobile Scud missiles so as to keep Israel out of the war. (Because the worst did not happen, the achievement was rapidly overlayed by the excitement of a long-postponed ground offensive by Allied armour to liberate Kuwait.)

In the South Atlantic a decade earlier, SAS successes were tactical. The regiment frankly failed in a strategic objective which

Downing Street lusted after, that of hitting the Super-Etendard bombers of the Argentine Air Force and their deadly Exocet missiles on the ground, before they could attack a vulnerable British fleet. The truth is that this objective – given the mobility of the target – could not have been achieved without a large-scale invasion of the Argentine mainland by a huge expeditionary force which Britain did not possess.

In both these big, global operations a new generation of SAS soldiers had to face the stomach-churning switch to the values of a general war in which their own lives were suddenly of less value, politically and militarily, than in Northern Ireland or Princes Gate, Kensington. During the Falklands Campaign, Operation Corporate, an attempt to penetrate Argentine air bases using heliborne SAS soldiers failed because it was clear to the young officer leading them that he could not fly from one enemy base to another undetected, while looking for aircraft that might not be there. The SAS view, vigorously expressed to the author by the Regimental Adjutant Dare Newell among others, was that this was not the point. In wartime, special forces soldiers should expect to be isolated and surrounded by enemy forces as part of their working environment, a view emphatically reaffirmed in the Gulf, and which promoted a joke about messages exchanged between an SAS patrol and its forward headquarters:

'Surrounded all sides by four enemy divisions.'

'Good. You are obviously in the right place.'

The captain involved in the Argentine row left the Army soon afterwards but it was not the end of an increasingly hard confrontation between two equally valid philosophies of war: that which would insist that the Light Brigade got it right at Balaclava and might even have succeeded, and that which rejects such sacrifice. (David Stirling, it is said, did not believe that warfare was the art of the possible, but the art of the impossible.) After the failure of the helicopter mission, a new and even more hazardous scheme was constructed to insert the SAS into Argentine air bases. The squadron commander invited to carry out the operation, along with his sergeant-major, did not think it would work and said so. The argument was never resolved in practice, because the Argentines holding Port Stanley surrendered. Again, however, heads rolled.

During Operation Granby in Iraq, the SAS had to face the same vertiginous switch to the values of a general war in which they were suddenly very expendable. The Commanding Officer of 22 SAS was obliged to live with the knowledge that the government would countenance losses not regarded as acceptable to the public since the Korean War.

David Stirling faced down many enemies, from the Afrika Korps to the British Army's own bureaucracy, but he did not have to cope with the massive pressures of publicity – a new and disorienting dimension to any armed conflict – faced by his SAS successors, a dimension which blends journalism with hi-tech, instant, worldwide communications and public opinion. Had he been faced with ranks of reporters, communicating their fears about the number of body bags he would need (as did General de la Billière and others in Riyadh in 1990) there is little doubt that the orthodox-minded military staff officers at Mid-East HQ would have convinced the British government in 1941 that Stirling, like Byron, was bad, mad and dangerous to know.

In Stirling's war, information was a weapon only in so far as it was an item of specific military intelligence such as an air photograph, concerned with a given target. Since then, information in the general sense of the word has become a weapon of strategic importance, no more so than when it has been given a facelift and converted into that artefact which journalists describe as a 'story'.

Nato's decision to abandon the enhanced radiation warhead, misnamed the 'neutron bomb', in 1978 was a textbook example of the damage journalistic top-spin can inflict upon a sound military plan. The *Washington Post* newspaper achieved what the KGB had failed to do: halt in its tracks a programme to modernise nuclear weapons so as to cut down the number of potential civilian casualties in a European war. Nato's retreat from its own neutron warhead was the Warsaw Pact's greatest Cold War victory, freely handed to it, without breaching official secrecy as such, by the liberal Press. (This is not to advance a case for military censorship in peacetime: merely to point up the way the world has changed around the armed forces.)

Like Nato, the SAS has a problem of information policy which has little to do with military secrets but has everything to do with the way the world has changed around the SAS and other fighting services and the way the regiment's activities are reported. In April 1992, writing in GQ *Magazine* (a manual that devotes fourteen pages to advising its readers 'How To Pull The Chicks') Mark Urban quoted an anonymous, 'recently-departed SAS officer' to the effect that 'The SAS has become Animal Farm – run by pigs'.

When the distinguished Irish lawyer Paddy McGrory – always his own man and no marionette of the IRA – suggested at the Gibraltar inquest in 1988 that the SAS was 'an unholy priesthood of violence', there were probably some fantasists who read the words as the literal truth. The author-priest Father Raymond Murray, in his book *The SAS in Ireland*, invites us to consider 'a sinister interpretation' of the regiment's badge, which is that 'there is in the SAS a warrior elite ethos derived from the Jacobite Freemasons of Scotland and the winged dagger is a vengeful symbol, a survival of a particular grade in their lodge'.

The SAS has become a victim of its own mythology. During the Second World War, the enemy complained that 'such men are dangerous'. In a world in which public gullibility and naive journalism combine with mass communication, the regiment is more vulnerable than ever to damaging theories which are not always discouraged by some of the jokers inside the Stirling Lines stockade.

Another theme is pursued by the journalist Mark Urban in his book *Big Boys' Rules*. In many ways a valuable account of the evolution of the many counter-terrorist agencies created in Northern Ireland, it finds anonymous voices to present the SAS as a once-great elite infiltrated and taken over by a mafia of Parachute Regiment NCOs. To quote an example: 'Non-Para members of the Regiment . . . maintain that the airborne soldiers are more violent, less likely to consider the consequences of force and less likely to propose alternative solutions to problems, than men from other regiments.'

11

It is entirely true that the SAS has had a long love–hate affair with the Parachute Regiment. The Urban version is a variant of a long-held fear, implying penetration from within, by way of the Sergeants' Mess, rather than administrative instruments in Whitehall. After the Second World War, the late Dare Newell, OBE, as SAS Regimental Adjutant (and brilliant backstairs politician) fought off successive attempts, as he saw them, by the Aldershot-based Paras to absorb the SAS. To comprehend the difference between the two it is enough to compare the mayhem wrought by a handful of Stirling's Originals on the Luftwaffe in the Western Desert, 1942 with the gallant tragedy of Arnhem, 1944.

In September 1987, Dare Newell and a wartime SAS veteran, Colonel David Sutherland, published a paper about the regiment's postwar evolution in which they asserted:

> The 1959 success on the Jebel Akhdar followed later by Borneo and Aden in the mid-1960s, established 22 SAS as an important strategic element in national defence. By the mid-1960s, 22 was being seen by many senior Parachute Regiment officers as a potential threat to the future employment of the Parachute Regiment. In particular, the memory of the Jebel Akhdar operation, originally allotted to Para and vetoed by the Prime Minister (Sir Anthony Eden) on the grounds that to employ the elite airborne unit [i.e., the Paras] would be to place too much emphasis on a tribal conflict, was still fresh in their minds . . . They [the Para officers] began a series of manoeuvres . . . to group 22 SAS with the Parachute Regiment in some form of general airborne formation in which, by force of numbers, they would be the dominant partners.

This version does not seem to have been accepted by Colonel John Waddy, OBE, an officer who (like many) served with both units. In April 1988 he identified for the SAS journal *Mars & Minerva*

a disease once endemic in a past generation of SAS officers, which I call 'paraphobia' or a mistrust of the 'maroon machine' . . . I believe . . . that any plans to take over the SAS were . . . the notions of a very few senior officers with previous service in the Parachute Regiment.

The Paras would gain nothing from such a takeover except a heap of problems peculiar to the SAS.

If the Parachute Regiment's role (and, often, its high-profile belligerence) is at odds with the lethal stealth of the SAS, it is still no surprise that about 40 per cent of today's SAS recruits are to be found wearing a red beret. The pool of military talent available to an elite force, recruiting from other arms, shrinks year by year.

The Paras, through the hardships of 'P' company selection, identify many SAS virtues, notably a bloody-minded determination to endure and to think. (Along with generations of Para volunteers the author was taught in the 1950s not to seek answers from others but to 'use your bloody Airborne Initiative'.) Until quite recent times the Paras, like the SAS today, accepted no direct recruits but took the best volunteers from the rest of the Army. In the straitened circumstances of the 1990s it would be surprising if a large number of SAS soldiers did not find their way to Hereford by way of Aldershot.

Yet another line of attack adopted by Urban is that officers, the 'ruperts' in SAS-speak, have all but lost control to a permanent cadre of NCOs who know that the commissioned SAS soldier will be moved on to more orthodox work after three years. Any good regiment needs a strong cadre of NCOs, particularly its sergeants, as its backbone. Equally, it does not expect the backbone to do the thinking. Leadership has been spread around in the SAS ever since David Stirling denounced the 'thundering herd' tendency of the typical British regiment to leave its brains at home and march behind the leader all the way into captivity.

There is more to it than that. As Stirling himself put it:

The SAS brooks no sense of class . . . We believe, as did the ancient Greeks who originated the word 'aristocracy',

13

that every man with the right attitude and talents, regardless of birth and riches, has a capacity in his own lifetime of reaching that status in its true sense; in fact, in our SAS context, an individual soldier might prefer to go on serving as an NCO rather than having to leave the Regiment in order to obtain an officer's commission. All ranks in the SAS are of 'one company', in which a sense of class is both alien and ludicrous.

The four-man patrol module is one expression of a collective SAS wisdom. So is 'blooding' young officers by sending them to battle as mere troopers, as two were in the Gulf. So is the 'wigwam parliament', when the risk is high and there is time to discuss it. (The Rhodesian C Squadron called the process 'think-evil'). Colonel Charlie Beckwith, the American founder of Delta Force, served a term with the SAS in 1961 and wrote later of the initial, cultural shock of discovering this more subtle, diffuse form of leadership:

> I couldn't make heads or tails of this situation. The officers were so professional, so well read, so articulate, so experienced. Why were they serving within this organisation of non-regimental and apparently poorly disciplined troops? The troops resembled no military organisation I had ever known . . . Everything I'd been taught about soldiering, been trained to believe, was turned upside down.

It is easy to be misled by the relative egalitarianism of the SAS, as well as its sometimes macabre sense of humour, which enjoys teasing writers, above all, to believe that NCOs ROOL OK. In practice, the SAS officer, like any other military commander, has to lead from the front and take the blame when things go wrong, as they are likely to do in the highly unstable world of special operations. There has been no campaign fought by SAS soldiers since the early 1960s (at least) from which some officer or senior NCO, or both, have not been returned to their original unit, ending their careers with the SAS Regiment and sometimes with the Army altogether.

If the SAS is unforgiving of any leader who hesitates at the wrong moment even for good reason, it can be the launch-pad for some brilliant military careers. General Sir Peter de la Billiere, a national hero after the Gulf War, is one of many high-flying officers who were shaped by the SAS. Others include Lieutenant General Sir John Watts, Lieutenant-General Sir Michael Wilkes, Lieutenant-General Sir Charles Guthrie, Major-General Tony Jeapes, Major-General John Foley, Major-General Mike Rose and numerous brigadiers and colonels, some of whom have left the SAS to take command of their original regiments.

Others, including Alastair Morrison, David Walker and Ian Crooke, have chosen to leave the Army after SAS service to find adventure or profit, or both, in the freebooting world of private security. Morrison who, with Sergeant Barry Davies, put his boot through the door of a hijacked Lufthansa airliner in Mogadishu and hurled the first stun grenade of a deadly encounter, is now the millionaire boss of Defence Systems Ltd. Walker, running another influential company, is targeted by journalists as a result of his alleged involvement in irregular operations in Central America and elsewhere. Crooke, the man who led a counter-coup in Gambia to the amazement, and finally the gratification, of the Foreign & Commonwealth Office, left the Army and then the UK in a cloud of controversy. The least plausible criticism of such men is that they were dominated by their NCOs, whether from the Paras or elsewhere. Some, like de la Billière, took a strictly constitutional road; others did not. All were winners; all profoundly shaped by repeated tours with the SAS into an awareness of their own mortality. It is a dimension that sets them apart from the majority of their countrymen who have been taught to regard risk as a disease rather than a spiritual purgative.

If society's values change, the SAS does not, though it welcomes innovation. Fitness to fight is one of its immutables. So is the regiment's ability to ride the punches and renew its faith in itself. It is not afraid to declare its own mysticism, one which reflects the hardship of desert, mountain and jungle rather than the closed, secret chamber of a masonic hall. Flecker's verse, inscribed on the memorial clock at Stirling Lines was discovered for the SAS by Padre William Evans as he searched for a regimental collect in 1969:

We are the pilgrims, master.
We shall go always a little further;
It may be beyond the last blue mountain
Barred with snow, across that angry or that glimmering
sea . . .

This mysticism is also up held in the Celtic blessing, rehearsed at the memorial service for David Stirling in the Guards Chapel as IRA mortar bombs descended on nearby Whitehall, and later at Hereford Cathedral when the Scuds had ceased falling impartially upon Jew, Arab and Christian:

Deep peace of the running wave to you
Deep peace of the flowing air to you
Deep peace of the quiet earth to you
Deep peace of the shining stars to you
Deep peace of the Son of Peace to you
And the blessing of God Almighty
The Father, the Son and the Holy Spirit be with you all
evermore.

The SAS philosophy owes more to the Roman general Marcus Aurelius and the Stoics than to the freemasons, a philosophy of the experience of hardship and death as a rocky road to wisdom. As Marcus wrote as he fought his German campaigns around AD 170: 'Disdain not death . . . but wait for it as one of the natural functions.'

This does not imply a desire to jump prematurely into the grave. The regiment's survival experts such as Lofty Wiseman emphasise the will to live as the greatest factor in survival itself, though he has his own, characteristic definition of the great changeover: 'Death', he has said, 'is Nature's way of saying you have just failed SAS selection.'

The Gulf provided epics of individual survival that will not be bettered. The soldier who has lost his trigger finger through Himalayan frostbite and still takes on the IRA in a gun battle is serious about survival. He also perceives death, as in the words of Sir Fitzroy Maclean at the Stirling memorial service: 'Death is only an horizon and an horizon is nothing more than the limit of our sight.'

For some, it is the living on after the action that requires the final reserves of courage. The SAS knows many of them: the one-armed, one-eyed (and still phenomenally fit) veteran who has become a charismatically successful schoolteacher; the paraplegic who converted his once legendary physical aggression from a wheelchair into intellectual overdrive to conquer classical Arabic; only more surgery (the number of operations run into three figures) stands between him and his university place.

Such people are rare, but not so rare in the SAS. Though they would laugh at the notion, or pour beer over the author's head for suggesting it, they set the rest of us a moral example.

In 1992, after meeting Falklands War veterans at the Imperial War Museum in London, journalists were struck by the unashamed idealism of some of the servicemen. It was like an encounter with a living fossil. One of the scribes wrote later: 'We now live in an age of selective cynicism, in which to admit to a strong belief in anything more fundamental than acupuncture is deeply unfashionable . . . These men . . . seemed entirely unaware of the conventions of their age.'

Instinctively, the soldier who makes it in the SAS, often sacrificing the rank and pay he had elsewhere to do so, is not only trying to join a regiment. He is on an escape and evasion exercise from the acupuncture society. Maybe that is why we envy him when he succeeds.

What of the political impact of the SAS throughout these years? Only with the collapse of the Soviet empire after 1989 was it possible to assess the regiment's contribution to the history of this turbulent century. The context was that from 1945 onwards there was an almost universal belief among politicians and others that Marx and Lenin were correct in believing that revolutionary victory was historically inevitable, as if responding to a natural law. Harold Macmillan described it as 'the wind of change'. As Britain withdrew from her colonies, to be followed by the US retreat from Asia after Vietnam in 1972, so did 'wars of liberation' sponsored by Moscow topple one newly independent state after another.

SAS victories in Malaya, Borneo, Oman and elsewhere were discreetly concealed by the British government. In any case, they seemed to be a political aberration, historical freaks resulting from small wars of only local interest in dark, obscure corners of the globe.

With the astonishing disintegration of Soviet Russia the philosophical illusion of historical inevitability was smashed. The IRA and Shining Path (Peru) alone among major terrorist formations still cling to this ideological myth, the Irish because their passionate nationalism befuddles their own natural intelligence. The IRA volunteer is willing to sacrifice his own life, ready to cannibalise his own humanity, in the certain belief that his cause is predestined to win.

But what if he could be persuaded that there is no certain, ultimate victory after all, that there will be no IRA war memorial on which his name will be honoured . . . that, in a word, he has been had? Would he still be happy to mutilate himself for a lost cause? The SAS, uniquely, has shifted perceptions a long way in this direction by holding the line for more than forty years, far away from Ireland, to demonstrate that winning 'small' wars is not a matter of historical determinism, but above all a question of commitment and human willpower.

Part I

The wars they said could never happen again, a long way from home

The Gulf War 1991

The South Atlantic War 1982

Oman 1958–59; 1970–76

Prologue

The Gulf War and the South Atlantic campaign – Operation 'Corporate' – have more in common than mere distance from home. In both cases the government of the day had no contingency plan for the conflict. Major-General Rose, recalling the South Atlantic ten years later, wrote: 'Only two months before the invasion of the Falkland Islands, SAS Regimental Headquarters, who were continually reviewing contingencies around the world, had been assured by a superior headquarters that no scenario could be envisaged where it would be necessary to deploy the SAS to the Falkland Islands.' After the Falklands were liberated, with SAS help, Whitehall's mandarins declared (with that sacerdotal confidence of someone who is about to place another polished toecap into another pile of dog dung) that Europe was still the military centre of gravity and that the Falklands War was a one-off; it was the sort of war we no longer fought and would not – could not – be repeated. Nine years later, it was.

The two campaigns also shared a reliance by government, at the last minute, upon special forces to make good the failures of policy and technology.

There are other similarities. Two dictators, the Argentine Galtieri and the Iraqi Saddam Hussein, were fed diplomatic honey when what was required was a political emetic to dispose of their unworldly ambitions. Both are greedy men, who had been encouraged by Western liberal governments in their folly, and who then snatched territory which was not their property.

What are special forces supposed to do in such a situation? Their role is strategic, directed from the supreme commander's

21

headquarters rather than as part of a local, tactical campaign. Hopefully – using the old weapons of surprise, guile, deception, concealment and, above all, daring – they will be able to strike crippling blows deep inside enemy territory.

Government, caught out in a crisis, its plans (if any) unravelling in public, is human and fallible. It invests great expectations in special forces at such a time. The author concludes that in the South Atlantic, though the SAS commander shortened the war remarkably through psychological pressure on the enemy, the SAS as such was asked to achieve the impossible. In Iraq, 1991, only the nearly impossible was expected, and it was delivered. Some of the same occurred in Oman in 1950 and again in 1970. The stakes were just as high, though there was less publicity at the time. It seemed appropriate to include those earlier SAS campaigns in this section, not least because they demonstrated a consistency within the SAS to pursue a distinctive role, out of the mainstream, when other military careers were dedicated to the essentially garrison life of Nato Europe.

THE GULF WAR 1991

How the plague was stayed from Israel

In January 1991 President George Bush told anyone who would listen that he had grown tired of trying to talk sense to the Iraqi dictator Saddam Hussein. Saddam, the devious product of a sadistic and fearful Arab cabal, had manpower, and nothing else, to oppose the super-power strength of the American giant . . . or so it seemed, as the dictator gloated over the discomfiture of Bush's ambassador to Baghdad, April Glaspie: 'I do not belittle you but . . . Yours is a society that cannot accept 10,000 dead in one battle.'

The equation of US air power v. Iraqi blood sacrifice was always one which would produce a military victory for America. The doubt that nibbled at Washington's cupboard of hi-tech wonders and CIA-polished analyses was whether the victory would be a self-defeating, pyrrhic affair, turning 'friendly' Arab opinion away or worse, provoking the downfall of governments whose oil reserves were still essential to the industrial world. The shrewd political money, then, was on the use that Saddam could make of blackmail, a weapon with which he had more practice than the pistol on his belt. Surprisingly, no one took seriously the mayhem his own military technology might inflict. The use of the Scud missile and its derivatives was there for all to see during the 'War of the Cities' between Iran and Iraq. But Western analysts were sure they had that threat taped. They knew, or thought they knew, they could hit the missile before it got off the launch-pad. They were wrong.

When this became manifest after the initial Allied air strikes on Baghdad, an emotion stronger than concern but short of

23

panic gripped the Western leaders. The problem was Israel. As the American writer Seymour M. Hersh observes in his recent history of Israel's nuclear armoury:

> An American satellite saw that Shamir had responded to the Scud barrage by ordering mobile missile launchers armed with nuclear weapons moved into the open and deployed facing Iraq, ready to launch on command . . . No one knew just what Israel would do if a Scud armed with nerve gas struck a crowded apartment building, killing thousands. All George Bush could offer Shamir, besides money and more batteries of Patriot missiles, was America's assurance that the Iraqi Scud launcher sites would be made a priority target of the air war.
>
> Such guarantees meant little; no Jews had been killed by poison gas since Treblinka and Auschwitz . . . The escalation didn't happen, however: the conventionally armed Scud warheads caused – amazingly – minimal casualties . . .

The escalation did not happen because the SAS, in its finest hour of geopolitical warfare, kept the lid on the Scud threat just enough to deter an Israeli response either with its own ground forces, who were preparing a full-scale invasion of the areas from which the missiles were being fired, or with its nuclear weapons. Had nuclear weapons melted down Baghdad the consequences for world peace would have been incalculable. Yet, as General Schwarzkopf was generously to acknowledge after the war, air power alone could not cope with the threat. Nor could any other formation in the Alliance except the SAS.

The British soldiers doing 'the biz' were – perhaps fortunately – not entirely aware of the awesome burden they were expected to carry, though they knew perfectly well that this was the biggest concentration of SAS effort on the ground since the Second World War. With characteristic impudence, the senior NCOs staged an extraordinary meeting of the Warrant Officers' and Sergeants' Mess in a wadi 80 miles inside Iraq.

This chapter pieces together for the first time the way in which American hi-tech and the British 'Keep it simple' approach

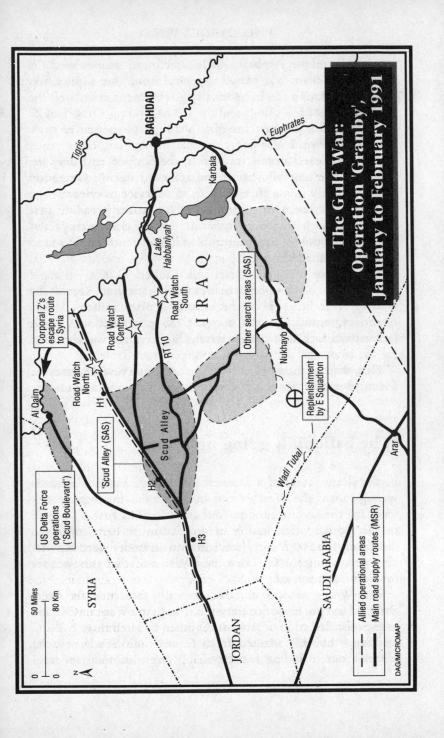

The Gulf War:
Operation 'Granby',
January to February 1991

BAGHDAD

Tigris

Euphrates

Karbala

Lake
Habbaniyah

I R A Q

Road Watch
South

Road Watch
Central

RT 10

Other search areas (SAS)

Corporal Z's
escape route
to Syria

Road Watch
North

H1

Al Qaim

Nukhayb

Replenishment
by E Squadron

Scud Alley

'Scud Alley' (SAS)

H2

US Delta Force
operations
('Scud Boulevard')

Wadi Tubal

Arar

H3

SYRIA

JORDAN

SAUDI ARABIA

50 Miles
80 Km

N

0
0

Allied operational areas

Main road supply routes (MSR)

DAG/MICROMAP

achieved a unique symbiosis. When technical magic failed the unsolved problem was passed to special forces for a quick-fix, high risk solution. In London, the government calculated the risk, made its dispositions and the Commanding Officer of 22 SAS had to face potential losses on a scale not experienced since the Second World War.

In public, even among its friends, the SAS offered only the most oblique hint of what it had achieved during Operation Granby. Safely home after the war, at a service to celebrate the regiment's jubilee, a young trooper of A Squadron read the first lesson. Through his dense Scottish accent, the closing chapter of the Second Book of Samuel rumbled like distant cannon round Hereford Cathedral.

A pestilence was upon Israel and it killed 70,000. An angel stretched his hand upon Jerusalem to destroy it. David the warrior met the angel at the threshing place [where, in the twentieth century, it was not just the corn that was being beaten] and sacrificed burned oxen. 'So the Lord was intreated for the land, and the plague was stayed from Israel.'

This, then, is the story of how the SAS intervened to prevent a limited conventional war deteriorating into a nuclear one.

'The balloon is going up'

In the sleepy quiet of a December Sunday, Saddam Hussein wrong-footed the West's multi-billion dollar intelligence services for the second time in four months. His first success in the art of deception had been on 2 August 1990, when he unleashed 100,000 hungry soldiers into an undefended Kuwait after persuading the CIA that they were massed on the border for show, not for use.

The West's second blunder, exactly four months later, attracted less public notice although it was almost as catastrophic as the miscalculation of August. Saddam ordered three ballistic missiles – hybrids adapted from Soviet-built Scuds – to be wheeled out of hiding for test-firing over 400 miles of Iraqi territory, towards Israel. That was bad enough. Much worse was the realisation, acknowledged by one US Intelligence officer, that: 'We saw no launcher activity. There wasn't any tipoff that a missile launch was coming.'

The event was enshrined in Intelligence lore as Scud Sunday, 2 December 1990. It shattered the illusion, sedulously disseminated at secret Allied briefings, that the Scud was detectable well *before* it left the launch pad. Western misconceptions about Iraq's Scuds piled one mistake upon another. The Allies believed that the missile had to be refuelled every four to six weeks if it was not to become contaminated and potentially hazardous to its handlers. In fact, as the Russians revealed in the nick of time, the 'gestation period' was twice that.

This made it much more difficult to keep the missiles-in-waiting, or in transit, under surveillance. Iraqi forces briefed by US Intelligence during the Iran war in the art of avoiding satellite observation – by using slots of time when satellites were over the horizon – could make some good guesses about when they were safe. When Iraq subsequently became the enemy of the West, Saddam's men used these immune periods. One rueful, expert assessment almost a month after the air war started was that five US satellites could observe targets in Baghdad only 2.5 hours in every twenty-four, though a British expert, Air Vice-Marshal R. A. Mason, would claim later that just two geosynchronously orbiting spacecraft were able to sweep the launch areas with infra-red detectors every twelve seconds. What was certain was that the Defense Intelligence Agency, as one correspondent noted, had come 'to depend more and more on satellites for military intelligence'.

Such Intelligence, even directed against fixed targets, could be deeply flawed. Veterans of the war found it hard to understand how air reconnaissance had failed to spot Saddam's supergun at Jabe Hamryn, north of Baghdad. The fixed barrel raised to the desert sky was 170 feet long. This failure was only the first of many and not the most serious.

The West's first error about the Scuds was compounded by a second. This was that refuelling the missiles with dangerously volatile liquid propellant in a hot climate had to be undertaken in the open and could take up to thirty minutes or more, depending on the ambient air temperature. Saddam cheated the system and prepared the Scuds under camouflaged cover at remote desert locations. Then he brought them out after dark and fired them without delay. The missiles went approximately towards Tel Aviv.

As tactical battlefield weapons, their inaccuracy rendered them useless: the West was correct in that belief, at least. But as instruments to destabilise a fragile diplomatic arrangement in which – above all else – Israel had to be kept out of any coming war, the Scuds' potential was devastating. The Scud factor was to come closer to unravelling the alliance of mediaeval Arab kingdoms and Western, oil-dependent democracies than any other.

As it was, the first of the 2 December 'test' shots was six minutes into a seven-minute flight from a base near Basra when a US satellite detected the flare from its rocket motor. By the time this knowledge was flashed around Allied Intelligence centres, the simulated Iraqi warhead (high explosive?, gas?, nuclear?) was crunching into a vast military zone in western Iraq. Detecting two subsequent launches also relied upon the satellites' infra-red detection of the heat and light emitted by the missile after it was away.

To complete the West's embarrassment, Saddam even delivered an oblique warning in advance that *something* was about to happen. Civil airliners were told to keep out of Iraqi airspace from midnight preceding the test. On the strength of that warning, Israeli Air Force pilots were in the cockpit, engines turning, ready to strike back if Israel were attacked. So were USAF aircraft. When the missiles were detected on a bearing that had not been predicted, senior US officials believed that the war had started. In Baghdad, the chief US diplomat, Joseph C. Wilson IV, received an urgent telephone call from the State Department in Washington. The message was grim and simple: 'The balloon is going up. This is no drill.'

As the sombre implications of Saddam's demonstration of power and resolve sank in, so the telephones also rang out in Washington and Camp David, in London and at Chequers: and as the UK's novice leader, John Major, would admit in due time: 'I lost a lot of sleep over the Scuds. I was always woken once they were in the air.'

Saddam's reading of Western psychology as well as his timing were, as usual, exact. Support in Congress for a desert war was looking flaky, though the British were solidly in favour of hostilities.

When the UN Security Council had approved a use-of-force resolution on 30 November, Iraq fired a test missile in circumstances which were clearly 'declarative'. No attempt was made to conceal the preparations for that test. Now, a month later, the US and its Allies were committed to a deadline. The Iraqis would withdraw from Kuwait by 15 January 1991 or else. An awesome military machine was already lumbering forward in obedience to a computerised exercise played out at Centcom HQ, Tampa, in July. This exercise, Internal Look '90, anticipated by a month the threat to Gulf oil from the north. The computers had been programmed to cover every contingency. Hundreds of thousands of service men and women were in Arabia and hundreds of thousands more were on their way. It was not a good moment to discover that Saddam might, after all, have a handle on the situation.

Hasty orders were flashed to America, Britain and Europe calling for specialised reconnaissance aircraft, but publicly the Allies reacted by hoping that the worst would not happen. Over the next ten days various alibis were found to deodorise the threat. From Riyadh, the English-language *Saudi Gazette* reported: 'US has answer to Scud'. This, it was claimed, was an Army Tactical Missile System targeted by American artillery on Iraqi command posts and supply routes. To be sure, it was a useful counter-battery weapon but events would prove that it was not an anti-ballistic system. US soldiers, meanwhile, were warned that there was no effective defence. The Scuds might even carry poison gas warheads. The soldiers were impressed.

As one Scud 'test' succeeded another, the race to get into NBC suits and gas masks became more terrifying. On Friday 28 December, alarm bells blasted through the companionways of a 1000-bed hospital ship, the USNS *Mercy*, anchored in the

Gulf. A public address system announced: 'A missile has been launched. This is not a drill. All personnel take your emergency stations.'

Throughout the region, similar scenes were enacted on Allied bases including the British headquarters in Riyadh. By now, the Iraqi commanders were switching off the system's Squat Eye guidance radar to reduce the West's chances of pinpointing the missiles and their launch areas. Two US satellites whose infra-red sensors react to heat generated by missiles were re-set to target Scuds. The information they picked up was relayed to an Intelligence HQ in the Gulf, from which Patriot surface-to-air missiles were alerted automatically to the Scud's course and speed. The process took four minutes, paring warning time down to two minutes or less.

Patriot was an untried weapon, originally designed to destroy aircraft. It was known for its high unit cost ($82 million) and complexity. It would save America's face, come the war, but it would not provide a failsafe answer.

Israel meanwhile, promised not to launch a pre-emptive attack on Baghdad but demonstrated that it, too, possessed an intermediate range missile, the Jericho. One of these was fired over the open Mediterranean without warning on 21 December. This was not good news. Saddam might bluff about his weapons of mass destruction. The Israelis, almost certainly, had a nuclear weapon which might just have been refined for use as a missile warhead.

As well as seeking the Scud bunkers and support systems, Western analysts were also working round the clock to guess how many such weapons Saddam now held. They even turned to Moscow for help. The numbers game was complicated by the Iraqis' ability, boosted by European know-how, to build missiles themselves. The fear that this home-made potential generated among the Allies was such that when the war started a single assembly plant near Baghdad was repeatedly hit by Tomahawk cruise missiles fired from the US battleship *Wisconsin* long after the factory had been demolished. (But then, a Tomahawk is only as good as the guidance programmed into its computer. Changing that takes time.)

The best prewar Allied estimate of Scud numbers varied from 400 to 1000 missiles on 30 to 36 fixed sites and perhaps 36 mobile launchers. The true number of mobile launchers was nearer to 200. The mobile launchers were not entirely invulnerable, however. Even in the vast emptiness of western Iraq, Scuds had to be fired from pre-surveyed positions which were usually approached along metalled roads. Someone, soon, would have to discern where and when the Iraqi transporter-erector-launchers passed; a case, almost literally, of 'follow that Scud!'

Allied special forces

For the SAS, the first five months of the crisis had been months of intense frustration. As Britain's leading exponents of desert warfare, they were – by January 1991 – the only ones without a certain role in any war with Iraq. Since August, a forward operating base had been established in the Gulf. Two squadrons – D and G – had carried out intensive exercises in the region, testing men and equipment. One basic assumption – that this conflict would require a lot of desert driving, fighting and survival – was to prove entirely correct, if not for the reasons predicted, as the summer of 1990 shaded into an autumn of military poker between President Bush and Saddam.

The primary function of the SAS, short of an all-out war, would be (like that of the American Delta Force) to rescue hostages. Since the Iranians destroyed the credibility of an American president at home by this device, Western governments had been much exercised by the problem. The British had the largest number of human bargaining chips in play: at least 800 in Occupied Kuwait and another 1000 in Iraq. The dilemma facing the rescue planners was that with hostages dispersed to many locations, the focus of a rescue operation was almost impossible to define. Like President Carter in 1979, President Bush and Mrs Thatcher had to calculate the odds in favour of rescuing enough of their citizens for the affair to be viable.

There are no textbook answers to this inhuman calculation. The rescue of a single child, in some circumstances, might be perceived by a democratic people to warrant the sacrifice of many lives. VIPs are another privileged category. This was the first of many unenviable calculations the SAS and its friends had to make in which the moral gesture had to be weighed against hard military reality. So far as the hostages were concerned, a planning team in London reached the not-surprising conclusion that extracting even a small number would need a lot of manpower, probably a full brigade (say, 4000 fighting men plus another 1500 support arms such as signallers). The bottom line of that sort of calculation belongs to the world of the tar baby. More potential prisoners-of-war, killed, wounded and missing-in-action might be left on the ground than the sum total of hostages brought out.

There were other tasks during this plan-for-anything period. One was to insert an SAS presence into the growing US special forces element of Operation Desert Shield. A captain with long SAS experience joined the American Special Operations Central Command (Soccent) to work alongside 5 Special Forces Group brought from the USA; the amphibious Sea Air Land (SEAL) units; US Air Force special force; the Psychological Operations and Civil Aid (Psyops and Civaid) components. In time, the respect developed for the SAS by key American officers – notably its Air Force commander, Lieutenant-General Chuck Horner – would have a critical influence on the role of British special forces.

If it was clear that there was a hostage problem, it was equally plain that air power would determine the outcome of any war with Saddam. He had – comparatively – endless human resources to throw into a war of attrition. The West could only restore the balance, limiting its own casualties, with its sophisticated command of air weapons. The SAS took special care to bone up on the precise capabilities of, say, the Tornado bomber. Target designation, using lasers, was one clear option. There were others.

Two events in early December marked the countdown to an entirely different type of campaign from those which had been the subject of so much wasted planning. First, the events of 'Scud Sunday', 2 December, brought home to Western planners that there was a dangerous hole in their apparently watertight, sand proof arrangements. Second, the release of the hostages meant that the SAS were also now free to go after less shadowy objectives. The regiment's minds turned to the sort of campaign that Stirling, Mayne and other pioneers excelled at half a century earlier, a free booting desert war of disruption far behind the lines, devastation of the 700-airplane Iraqi Air Force on the ground, attacks on lines of communication and any other mischief that would keep Saddam's soldiers off-balance.

It was an ambitious scheme but for once the SAS was not operating in tiny, penny-packets. The entire regiment except G Squadron was to be committed to the Gulf in the biggest SAS combined operation since the Second World War. In the reorganisation of British special forces after the Falklands campaign, the group now also included the Royal Marines Special Boat Service (SBS) and a small but dedicated (in both senses) team of RAF special forces aircrew. The force assembled in December, with its own signals and headquarters teams, totalled more than 700. Over 300 of these were badged SAS soldiers from the Sabre squadrons, men of A, B and D Squadrons, 22 SAS as well as 15 volunteers from the elite reserve team known as R Squadron, happy to leave their civilian life so as to make up the strength of other teams. There was also a single Royal Marine Special Boat Service squadron.

Most of the men had Christmas at home – just. It was an odd festival, singing carols under the shadow of an avalanche. The order to move came, in most cases, on Boxing Day. SAS wives are accustomed to the pain of sudden separation but this was harder than usual. The stress had lasted for them, like the hostages, for months before the reality of it hit them. Many of the men had joined the work-up in the Empty Quarter and returned home. This second departure, and the sense that not everyone would come back, was especially hard. Once at their Gulf base, the soldiers were denied access to the telephone, and all their outgoing mail was heavily censored.

By 4 January, Britain's special forces group, the largest

team of its kind assembled by the UK since 1945 but still modest by American standards, stood like greyhounds in the slips. Disconcertingly, its mission was still unclear. Front-line reconnaissance was firmly under the control of the US 5th Special Forces Group and US Marine Corps recon specialists. The only fighting resistance to Iraq's occupation of Kuwait was coming from the anarchic, increasingly enfeebled, Kuwaiti Resistance movement.

A week later, one enigmatic event seemed to point to an effort by Western commandos to probe Iraq's defences. A number of Soviet-built MI-8 Hip helicopters flew into Saudi Arabia, escorted by US fighters. At first, the Saudis joyfully asserted these were defectors. A senior Saudi official made a point of calling personally on the Allied Information Bureau in Dhahran late that night to pass on the news. US information officers confirmed this also, only to deny after 24 anxious hours that there were any helicopters. A retired American Delta Force veteran named Lieutenant-Colonel Bill Cowan asserted that the machines had been flown by US special forces in a raid to bring back sensitive front-line radar equipment. A well-placed British source in Dhahran wrongly attributed the operation to the SAS, perhaps because British aircrew flew some of the machines on a mission dense with secrecy. Neither Delta nor the SAS had a hand in it. The risk of compromise was immense. The best guess must be that it was made by some specially composed force to extract Western military advisers trapped in Kuwait, or was, after all, a delegation from Baghdad. It could also have been a group of survivors from a failed attempt to assassinate Saddam Hussein.

The fact of the matter was that even at this eleventh hour, the SAS, the world's most perfectly trained commando force and certainly the great inheritor of a desert tradition, still awaited confirmation from the C-in-C, Norman Schwarzkopf, that it had a role. The Bear was not over-impressed by unconventional warfare. As he told journalists during the phoney war waiting period: 'The Vietnam experience left a lot of scars. I was on the Cambodian border at a time when the rules were that the enemy could attack across the border and beat up on you and do anything he wanted. But when you started to get the upper hand he could run back across the border and you weren't allowed to chase him. That's not my favourite way to fight a war.' He kicked some sand and went on: 'When you go to war, you're going to war all the way. That's exactly where I come from. No more Cambodian border situations for me.'

Special operations over borders in either directions were out of favour with other influential American soldiers, mindful of the gradual, deadly involvement of US special forces in Vietnam in preference to a knock-out punch in the first round, of the Delta Force disaster at Desert One, of the political stink surrounding aid for the Contras and of the less-than-convincing performance of some American commandos during the Grenada invasion.

Even more fundamental was the changed perception of rapid reaction – swift, rapier-like operations in which surprise is the best weapon – a form of warfare in which the Israelis excel. Rapid deployment once meant lightly armed forces who were sometimes sacrificial victims wearing the symbols of airborne or special forces. By 1989, rapid deployment had been up gunned to match the armaments poured into the Third World from the northern hemisphere. As the clever Chairman of the US Joint Chiefs of Staff, General Colin Powell, said at the beginning of the Gulf crisis: 'Light and lethal is good but you also need heavy and lethal.'

To other military minds, Powell's shorthand translated into something more than fire power. It was about the type of fighting man and strategy that accompany main battle tanks and heavy artillery as distinct from the unconventional warrior who is ready to kill at very close quarters if need be, with hands and feet. The shorthand is supremely about loyalty to military orthodoxy. It is a long way from where David Stirling came from. The shared perception of Schwarzkopf and Powell on this issue was to have a significant effect on SAS operations in the Gulf. Ironically it was the senior American airman, General Horner, who would give the SAS its chance.

Even earlier and more persuasively than Horner, the person who encouraged Schwarzkopf (known in Riyadh as the 'Sink' [for 'C-in-C']) to change his mind was the senior British officer in Arabia, Lieutenant-General Sir Peter de la Billière. He was Mrs Thatcher's choice, on the eve of his retirement. As it turned out, she retired first. De la Billière had uniquely reached the general staff without serving as part of the constipated pachiderm that was the British Army of the Rhine or becoming trapped in the passionless atmosphere of Whitehall. He had fought with the SAS in jungle and desert since the 1950s; commanded all three SAS regiments as Director of SAS when the regiment smashed the terrorist grip on the Iranian Embassy in London and throughout the Falklands campaign. He was a lucky general who made his own luck, sometimes ruthlessly. Politicians benefited from his luck and liked him for it. He was the route through which SAS operations were backed up from London.

His successful experience of unconventional warfare was one of the many vivid differences between himself and Schwarzkopf. The other was presence. 'DLB', as his friends know him, is deceptively self-effacing. He embodies Theodore Roosevelt's axiom, 'Speak softly and carry a big stick; you will go far.' His unemphatic manner was another contrast with the larger-than-life presence of an American commander who started his career with a football scholarship, an image that also concealed an unusually high IQ.

If Schwarzkopf was persuaded by his British comrade-in-arms that the SAS should have a role to match its experience, he was equally influenced by two other factors. One bore the label 'Scud'; the other, emerging much later, was the 'rice bowl', that pursuit of military credibility linked to a shrinking defence budget once the war was over. The war-within-the-war during this campaign was the rivalry between air power and an army on the ground. Air had a good war, just as USAF General Michael Dugan said it would, before the White House dismissed him for saying so too publicly.

Reconnaissance preferred to mayhem

To deal with the Scud, a host of new hi-tech solutions had been flown as kites and wheeled on stage. None looked overly convincing. The SAS had proposed an offensive role, but at the last moment this plan changed remarkably. The emphasis would be on reconnaissance rather than mayhem, identifying Scuds and their infrastructure; more particularly, targeting the elusive mobile Scuds for destruction from the air. The best Intelligence assessed the number of such vehicles (known as trailer-erector-launchers) as 15 to 20. It was one of many examples of the fallibility of the gee-wizz technology of satellites. Soldiers do not share the computer industry's philosophy: 'If it works it is obsolete'. As General de la Billière put it later: 'The main lesson we learned with special forces is that you can't beat a pair of eyes on the ground.'

The good news was that the SAS alone would be licensed to cross the line ahead of other ground forces, to try its luck on or soon after D-day, set for 29 January. The regiment would act as an agent for air power, a synthesis long predicted but never given practical expression, yet perceived by some as the way ahead for the SAS in any general war. Britain's special forces were undeterred by the experience of an initial cross-border operation by France's 13 Regiment de Dragons Parachutistes (13 RDP) which, says one expert, 'was in and compromised well before the SAS.'

The SAS carefully considered the option of 'painting' targets with laser-designators on the ground. Theoretically this would direct a compatible air-delivered smart bomb onto its target with total accuracy. The regiment had been studying the potential of lasers for ten years or more. A major set back to that programme was the loss, in the South Atlantic, of its RAF liaison officer Garth Hawkins. Yet in the Gulf, though the teams carried laser, they used it only once, in passing, against an enemy observation post.

Their sudden, last-minute commitment to battle in a vaguely-defined role meant that there had been no time for work-up rehearsals with the US strike aircraft, F15E and A10. Target identification by night would further complicate the process. The SAS, entering a battleground that was like Matthew Arnold's darkling plain, 'swept with confused alarms of struggle and flight, where ignorant armies clash by night', preferred to keep things simple and familiar; indeed on one operation they used a sledge hammer to great effect.

All that was possible, in a rapidly-changing situation, was an arrangement through which SAS patrols would alert their own Riyadh headquarters to enemy movement on a high frequency wave band, while making contact on an entirely different, tactical radio link with the strike aircraft when they arrived in the battle area. The advantage of HF was its near-immunity to interception but HF was also a slow, even cumbersome, system. Too often, events were to move at a speed which required instant contact with a faraway tactical headquarters. Instant contact was usually not available. Combined with failures in signalling equipment, this meant that the soldiers were to find themselves isolated at the very moment when the danger was greatest.

The waiting was not yet over. At their base somewhere in the Gulf, through the first two weeks of 1991, the British special forces counted the days off the calendar. A dying parody of peace negotiations came and went, without result as US Secretary of State Baker and Iraq's Foreign Minister, Tariq Azziz, held a dialogue of the deaf. A senior RAF officer in Britain lost the grand deception plan to a passing car thief in London. The thief was also a patriot and in due course returned the secrets known as 'the crown jewels', but by then the confidence of Americans in their British Allies in Riyadh cooled noticeably. Secrets were less readily shared.

The SAS was warned to be ready to move by the night of 22/23 January in anticipation of a start to hostilities on 29 January. Meanwhile, the rest of the world was hypnotised by President Bush's deadline for an Iraqi withdrawal from Kuwait, 15 January, the date known to the Saudi Press as 'K-Day'.

The SAS was as surprised as most others, including the Iraqis, when the first blows were struck before dawn on 17 January, by soldiers of the US Army's 101st Airborne Division. A British observer, Major-General R. D. Grist, OBE, Director of the UK's Army Air Corps, noted:

> On 17 January at 2.37am, that is 22 minutes before the air war against Iraq began, eight Apaches destroyed Iraqi air defence radars using Hellfire missiles and rockets so that the allied airforces would have two safe corridors down which to fly . . . The helicopters were five to six kilometres from the targets and it would appear that, despite the fact that this was an air defence complex, the Iraqis had no real idea of what was attacking them . . .

It was a moment of military history, the moment when the ground troops staked out more decisively than ever before their claim to low-level airspace above the battlefield. The machine they chose, the Apache helicopter, was one of the most potent night fighting systems deployed by the Allies. Its equipment includes a laser spot tracker and laser range-finder designator to guide its Hellfire missiles; magnified direct optics; multi-power television; forward looking infra-red; night vision goggles; night vision target acquisition and designation – and much else. It can kill tanks in the dark while remaining beyond the range of the enemy's return fire. It was a Prince of Darkness which terrified the Iraqis who were picked off like rabbits by a force they could not see.

Video footage of a typical attack revealed 'Iraqi soldiers like ghostly sheep, flushed from a pen, fleeing their bunkers under a hailstorm of fire, cut down by attackers they could not see or understand, some blown to bits by bursts of 30mm exploding cannon shells.' An Apache pilot of the Army's 6th Cavalry, the 'Knight Raiders', said, 'By God, I thought we had shot into a damn farm. It looked like somebody opened the sheep pen.' Another described his nocturnal attack on a road convoy as 'a duck hunt'.

In this first attack, they destroyed two key command centres each controlling a tunnel of air space with Soviet radars known as Tall King and Spoon Rest. While Tomahawk Cruise missiles and Stealth bombers skewered Baghdad's command centres

('We have a choice of targets in the building: the men's room or the ladies' room,' said Colonel Alton Whitley, commanding 37th Tactical Fighter Wing) 100 other Allied aircraft swept through the 'radar-black' corridors created by the Apaches.

Caught unprepared, Baghdad's air defences could only fire blindly into the night sky. US Air Force officials, expecting to lose between 25 and 40 aircraft on the first raid, lost only one, a Navy F/A-18.

'The Iraqis had no idea what happened to them', a Pentagon briefer said after the Hellfire attack. 'They thought they got hit from above (that is, by airplane) not from below, by low-flying helicopters.'

With Iraq's communications already mauled, and only feebly defended by an air force less visible than Stealth, Saddam's commanders at airfields and other secret bases in the west of the country known as H1, H2 and H3 pressed the start button on a doomsday plan issued personally by the Iraqi dictator before the war began. It was more a gamble than a contingency plan upon which Saddam, with Arab machismo, staked everything. The men at H2/H3 unleashed the Scuds on Israel. Twelve Scuds slammed into the suburbs of Tel Aviv on the second day of the war, by way of Jordanian air space, a fact not lost on the Jordanian government even if the mobs in the streets of Amman were cheering Saddam. Mere chance ensured that Israeli casualties were non-fatal and few. But US Defense Secretary Dick Cheney, like Britain's leader, John Major, was woken by the news. According to *Newsweek*:

> Moshe Arens, Israel's Minister of Defence, was in a rage. He told Cheney that 12 Israeli jets had scrambled after the first Scud attack and were prepared to strike Iraq. He requested that Cheney give him the recognition codes that would allow his fighters to slip past Allied planes without being shot down.

Other demands were that Israel should be given freedom of the skies over Jordan and Saudi Arabia so as to hit Iraq, with air attacks on H2 and H3, followed up perhaps by a full-scale invasion of the area by the Israeli army.

The Americans refused to endorse these schemes as the Israelis knew they would. But it was clear that the Scud syndrome could derail the most perfectly programmed and complex machine created in the history of war, a war pre-programmed by batteries of computers. The Allies responded with sophisticated retaliation from the air, diverting at least 30 per cent of aviation away from the 'real' war so as to stop the Scuds. USAF spokesmen confirmed that their pilots had attacked eleven 'previously undetected mobile missile launchers', hitting six, three of which were loaded with missiles pointing towards Saudi Arabia. But too often, when the air strike went in, there was nothing to hit but a hot 'footprint' in the desert, and many proposed raids were cancelled because cloud obscured the target area.

Even the Bear was disconcerted. On Day Two, 19 January, in his first public appearance after the war began, he grumbled that looking for mobile launchers in the desert was like looking for a needle in a haystack. 'The fog of war is present', he added. 'The picture is not perfect.'

For the SAS this turn of events had an entirely different effect. It finally blew away the ambiguity surrounding its role. The same day that Schwarzkopf found himself in the fog, the SAS was rushed from its holding area to the Forward Operating Base (FOB) at a Saudi airfield in the desert one day's drive from the border with western Iraq. The sudden move, nine days ahead of the original schedule, was made in a non-stop, 24-hour airlift by the RAF's Special Forces Hercules flight in a series of eight-hour return journeys.

Roadwatch patrols

The first joke of the campaign concerned two incoming missiles: a new RSM and the Scud. The RSM, they said, smiled benignly when someone shouted, 'Scud warning!' In his euphoric state he heard only, ''s good morning! . . . RSM.'

If the mission was becoming clear, the details of how to carry it off were left to the SAS itself. The regiment proposed three lines of attack. It would stake out static, covert road watch patrols to report the movement of Scud traffic. Others would then vector F15 strike aircraft onto the Scuds to destroy them. The road watch teams were modest affairs of eight men, to be inserted by helicopter in some desolate spot 140 to 180 miles behind the enemy border, usually without any transport other than desert boots and a strong will.

In parallel, there were to be fighting columns of up to a dozen well-armed Land-Rovers carrying 1.5 tons of war *matériel* each and manned by a half-squadron of thirty men or more. There were four such columns. Their job, when they were finally given the 'go' signal, would be to penetrate one of two major areas in the west, near the border with Jordan, from which the Scuds were launched. This 'Scud box' was a well-defended area of desert about 20 miles by 17–340 square miles – including the motorway linking Baghdad with the Jordanian capital of Amman. Around twelve to fourteen mobile launchers were thought to be in or near the area. Most movement, it was expected, would be by night, for this was no Empty Quarter.

Bedouin came and went, saw what they saw and spoke little. There was a surprising amount of civilian traffic this far west, much of it generated by the fear of Western vengeance on Baghdad. And because this was a critically important military zone, there were Iraqi military personnel of all kinds, from the Scud maestros to the militia: the SAS was to discover there were even mobile Scud decoys, lovingly fabricated in East Germany, complete with their own crews. When life seemed less than usually kind, the British commandos reflected on the good luck that fate had not cast them as drivers of dummy Scuds.

Finally the British Special Forces proposed to cut Iraq's carefully concealed communications links with the outside world. These ran along a complex web of communication towers of a sort familiar elsewhere, known as microwave links, but also, for added security, in dense masses of fibre optic cable buried well below ground, so insulated that even the cunning of the US National Security Council could not bug or tap into them.

As things turned out it was the Special Boat Squadron, an integral part of the UK Special Forces Group, that scored first with Operation Maud. On the night of 22 January two of the RAF's scarce special forces Chinook helicopters lifted 40 SBS men to a spot 'in the middle of nowhere' 40 miles south of Baghdad. There they used electronic detection gear to find an underground communications cable. As the Chinooks waited on the ground, rotors turning gently in neutral, a short sprint away the Royal Marines dug down to the cable, carved out a section of it for analysis in Riyadh, and then blew up the rest.

'As they did so they had a bird's eye view of the bombing of Baghdad', said one of the author's sources. The job took 90 minutes. Still in darkness, under a horizon that glowed theatrically above the Baghdad blitz, the 'Booties' rode triumphantly home. There were no casualties. Their leader, a lieutenant (equating with an Army captain) was later awarded a Military Cross.

It also turned out that there was to be no serious military requirement for the SBS party piece, amphibious warfare. The shortage of helicopters and other back-up – required by the land warfare specialists of the SAS – left little scope for subsequent adventures. In the 'special forces theme park', the SBS had a good secondary role, if not a starring part, in this war.

While the SBS burrowed like termites into Saddam's communications, the SAS was planting eight-man road watch patrols from B Squadron to overlook the three usable roads (MSRs, or Military Supply Routes, in warspeak) that plod from the crowded Euphrates Valley, up an endless desert slope to the Jordanian hills in the west. Scuds were killing and maiming more civilians in Tel Aviv as RAF special forces Chinooks put the watchers down about 20 miles apart on a north-south axis. These were known as the North, Centre and South road watch respectively.

By now, Schwarzkopf's own brief had been changed under the diplomatic impact of the Scud attacks on Israel. It was awesome in its scope. He was expected to limit the conflict by keeping Israel out of the war, preserve the Coalition, particularly its Islamic ingredients (always volatile but never more so than when attacking an Arab brother implicitly to stop attacks on Israel) and to ensure that the Allied (that is, Western) war plan went ahead as planned. Even for a big man, it was a tall order. So that his old regiment should get the message, General de la Billière sent a signal directing that 'all SAS effort should be directed against Scuds'.

Meanwhile the commander of the South road watch nearest the Saudi border, an experienced NCO, decided he would not release the helicopter until he had taken a careful look at the location from which he was to operate. He was not impressed. The gravel plain was a featureless place where any newly dug position would be obvious to a half-alert Boy Scout. Another SAS soldier used the earthy simile, 'as obvious as a turd on a snooker table', to describe such exposure.

The rest of his patrol agreed that to operate from here without wheels would be futile. With great judgement, the leader aborted the operation and returned to base to make his report.

The Central road watch patrol had been placed at its OP area with vehicles but, like the other teams, discovered that concealment in this almost flat moonscape terrain was virtually impossible. The commander, a young corporal, rapidly concluded that the position was untenable. Like others he also found that communications were, at best, intermittent. As a parting gesture, he called down an air strike on two enemy mobile radar systems nearby. The A10s duly arrived and were lined up on the target when the SAS realised they were the target. They snapped a radio signal to tactical headquarters but the signal was not received. Fortunately the air attack destroyed the Iraqi radar and only narrowly missed the soldiers who had inspired it.

Their position compromised, the soldiers signalled that they were 'bugging out', making a hasty but controlled exit. Days and nights passed without further word and anxiety grew for these, as well as other missing men, back at the forward base. There was one report, unconfirmed, that the team was heading for the Saudi border. An SAS major travelled to a frontier post to alert the Saudi National Guard and to remind it not to open fire. At last, after a journey of 140 miles through four bitterly cold nights across the desert, the patrol turned up in the Saudi border town of 'Ar 'Ar, a forward base for US forces.

The first friendly contact was with a Saudi police patrol, which stopped the British soldiers for the very good reason that they were driving without lights. They were airlifted to the forward SAS base, where four were given medical treatment for 'frost wounds'.

The most isolated of the teams inserted on 22 January, Road Watch North, unloaded the Bergens and weapons and watched the chopper depart. Its engine note was engulfed by a buffeting desert wind. Friendly territory was 187 miles away. Other troubles aside, the weather was already the same lethal cocktail of driving wind, rain, sleet and snow that kills soldiers and civilian climbers on the Brecon Beacons in a bad winter.

In this part of the world it was at least thirty years since the winter had been so brutal. Somewhere towards the horizon, the dimmed lights of vehicles suggested the line of the road. They dug in, hunkered down and waited. As Arabian nights go, this was awfully like the Falklands. Another similarity was the absence of wheels.

A grey dawn came and the patrol settled to the aching wait that was punctuated by a few hours' duty on watch, a turn on the domestic chores, a sleep, and another period on watch. The boredom was relieved somewhat by the passage of Allied aircraft on their way back from targets around Baghdad. Occasionally they heard voices, perhaps a dog barking, sounds that told them they were not the only humans at large in this inhospitable patch. Radio transmissions to SAS tactical headquarters were less than perfect. The regiment's signallers noted that on high frequency, words and sometimes whole sentences were lost or corrupted.

On the second day, an Iraqi military convoy moved towards their position over the desert. If this was a bad moment, worse was to follow. The patrol watched, waited, prepared its weapons. The enemy convoy came closer, and then halted, oblivious of the SAS presence. The Iraqi unit was a self-contained entity with its command vehicle and tracked carriers about some business of its own. As covers were taken off a battery of low-level anti-aircraft guns, that business was starkly obvious. The site chosen for an SAS observation position was perilously close to the site also selected by Iraqi staff officers as part of their rapidly growing air defence network.

The SAS team again sent a brief message to its headquarters: 'Enemy triple-A gun now in position immediately to our north.' The arrival of this unwanted presence carried with it more than the risk of compromise. It slammed shut any hope of relief, or resupply or rescue by air unless, of course, the patrol could call down fire virtually on its own position which would destroy the enemy battery but not the patrol.

In the afternoon, what was a clear risk of discovery became a fact. A group of Iraqi civilians attracted to the area, no doubt by the presence of their own military, wandered about and saw a second encampment. The game was up as surely as it had been that day in Aden when a goatherd stumbled upon the sangar concealing Paddy Baker and his comrades.

As the patrol prepared to withdraw amid shouts, fingers pointed by now-excited civilians, the team's signaller tried to be phlegmatic as he sought contact with forward HQ.

It was a time to make haste, deliberately. Once again, headquarters could not read much of the signal. From the corrupted fragments which were received, the message was that the Road Watch North had some kind of problem and might be on the move. One source noted, 'B Sqn Northern MSR Gp reported they had been compromised and requested exfil asp' (military jargon for 'exfiltration as soon as possible'). At the Forward Operating Base, Regimental Headquarters had insufficient information, when it mattered, to know whether the patrol had an enemy contact or a chance compromise.

'Get the gear together. We're moving out!' the patrol commander announced. The men, having read the signs, were already prepared to move, or stowing the last bit of survival gear into the Bergen. As they emerged, heavily laden, from the cover of the hide and made their way downhill, away from the hubbub, the first enemy shots scythed across the 300 metres separating them from the Iraqis. The British soldiers ducked into the dirt, using any fold in the ground as well as their Bergens for cover and started shooting back.

A surprised enemy paused, then started shooting with renewed vigour, using the Triple-A anti-aircraft guns on a trajectory dropped low enough to convert the heavy-calibre weapons into a deadly infantry support role. The Iraqi aim was good. One SAS soldier's Bergen was ripped open by one of the big ack-ack rounds. Totally outgunned, the SAS patrol did the only sensible thing. It legged it, leaving Bergens, principal radio, everything in fact except weapons, belt-kit (water bottle, spare ammunition), minimum food and personal rescue beacons, known by the acronym 'TACBE' (for 'tactical beacon'). The opposition followed but cautiously, deterred by further fire from their dangerous quarry.

An hour after the crisis began, the patrol regrouped in what cover it could find. It was dark now and the bleak fact was that the concealment it gave was the patrol's primary asset. The decision to try an escape to the north was, in characteristic SAS fashion, a collective one. It was, on the face of things, the most sensible course. To the east lay the teeming heart of urbanised Iraq and certain capture. Westward was Jordan, a non-combatant ally of Saddam which was already known to have handed over to the Iraqis an American pilot who had eluded capture before surrendering himself to the Jordanian authorities. Jordan, the behind-the-lines soldiers were told, was a 'No-go' area. To go south would be to march into the arms of the pursuers, though initially, picking up a faint TACBE signal, that is the direction would-be rescuers expected the fugitives to go.

Death in the snow

To the north – or rather, north-west – was the faint hope held out by the frontier with Syria, a member of the anti-Iraqi coalition and the chance of sanctuary. This escape route lay across the MSR, effectively a series of parallel desert tracks. The fugitives crossed these in darkness, in snow, a hue-and-cry still at their tails. In doing so, the team of eight unintentionally divided into two groups, one of five men and the other of just three. A bitterly cold, wet dawn came and the fugitives laid up in scrapes, the countryside around them alive with Iraqi reservists, militiamen ordered to stop them at all costs. The SAS men tried to summon help with their emergency aircrew beacons but no rescue came. An American F15 flying over the area picked up one possible contact and again a Chinook search team prepared to take off. The mission was aborted due to weather conditions more likely to provoke the loss of men than a rescue. The soldiers depending on rescue, meanwhile, could not know that the locations transmitted by their beacons were so vague as to be virtually useless.

By the time dusk returned, the trio had to push one another to resume the march. Back at regimental headquarters, just across the border with Saudi Arabia, an SAS trooper noted that ice was forming on his motorcycle. Out on the windswept Iraqi hills that second night, 26 January, Sergeant Vincent Phillips was lost in driving snow. He died of exhaustion and hypothermia. His comrades lost sight of him during the march. Both turned back when they realised he was no longer with them but he was not in sight. His body was later discovered by Iraqi soldiers and handed to the British authorities in Kuwait immediately hostilities ended. At the point where he was lost his team had covered about 30 miles from its original position.

Later that day, as enemy search parties closed in, the fugitives decided to double their chances of evasion by splitting up even if this reduced each man's odds on individual survival in the desert: an arcane, but typical SAS assessment. One of the pair, a trooper, was spotted by enemy militia and after a brief exchange of fire, finding himself surrounded, he was obliged to surrender.

The last of the trio, Corporal 'Z', got lucky. His navigation was impeccable, the going underfoot was firm and his endurance phenomenal. He was not detected by either the Iraqis or the RAF helicopters still searching for him. After marching for seven nights, wearing only light desert clothing and with just two packets of biscuits as nourishment, he walked across the

Syrian border early on 30 January. During the final 48 hours he was without drinking water. He had covered 117 miles. His achievement is compared by SAS veterans with that of Jack Sillitoe, one of Stirling's Originals. When Corporal 'Z' crossed into Syrian territory he coolly broke down his rifle into its constituent parts and carried it in a small sack, a signal to any soldier that he was not a combatant. Treated with suspicion to begin with, he received increasingly cordial treatment as he neared the Syrian capital, Damascus.

He accepted the warm shower, the civilian suit made up for him even as he bathed and declined the offer of a night around the sights of old Damascus. The British Embassy was pleased to entertain him that night, instead. At the SAS forward base, news of his survival raised hopes for other missing men, which at one stage during the first operations appeared to number 23.

Corporal 'Z' is a tough Geordie whose survival is regarded by the SAS as textbook vindication of the regiment's escape training. His route followed the Euphrates, from whose murky water he was able to obtain enough water to survive. He did not need to repeat the experience of Sillitoe in recycling his own urine but at one point he did try to drink water from a pipe that turned out to be an outlet for some form of industrial waste. At another point on his lonely journey he stripped naked in reeds beside the marshy river and waded through mud to immerse himself and replenish his water bottle. By staying in the valley he avoided exposure to the pitiless windchill that killed Phillips on the hills to the west. In a populated area, he took greater risk of discovery, but minimised that by avoiding all human habitation, travelling by night. With the training and the luck went motivation. His first child was born just before he left Britain for this operation.

Like the other fugitives, he tried to summon assistance with a rescue beacon usually carried by military airmen. It was not a sufficiently precise locator for the searching helicopters to recover him. RAF and US special forces teams repeatedly flew high-risk missions in search of all the men of this patrol. They were never in the area targeted.

'We reached a point where we could not justify the risk to

the search-and-rescue crews without a tangible result', one of the author's sources explains. Like the moral equation implicit in hostage rescue, or the retrieval of Major Delves's party from the Grytviken Glacier, there could be no absolute answer to the dilemma. In this case, intense Iraqi activity and the widespread presence of AA guns raised the odds dramatically against a successful pick-up. The searches were discontinued 48 hours before he appeared in Syria.

Meanwhile the rest of the patrol, the club of five, succeeded in marching all the way to Al Qaim, near the border with Syria and close to the area where American special forces were soon to start work inside Iraq's second main Scud reserve, an area known as the northern Scud box. The nearer the border the five came, the more dense was the cat's cradle of local roads, reflecting longstanding trade between people across the frontier. Nervous Iraqis, fearful of an invasion from that direction, opened fire at any suspect, alien presence. On 27 January the fugitives were only six miles from sanctuary when the inevitable contact happened and a series of gun battles began. Swiss-born Trooper Robert Consiglio, a former Royal Marine, covered the others' withdrawal but was hit in the head and became the first SAS soldier of the campaign to die from enemy fire. He received a posthumous Military Medal.

In the same contact another trooper was wounded in the elbow and ankle and immobilised. As his comrades fought their way out of the trap he was taken prisoner and with him, Sergeant 'B', who was later awarded a Distinguished Conduct Medal.

Two out of the five, led by Lance-Corporal Steven 'Legs' Lane, were still running. The only escape route lay north, across the icy Euphrates river, then in fierce flood and more than 400 yards wide.

'Let's go for it!'

Lane emerged on the far bank in a state of collapse, which is no surprise after what he had endured in the preceding days. His companion, another Lance-Corporal, stayed with him, desperately trying to revive him.

'He was suffering badly from the cold', said the survivor later. 'I helped him to a hut. He couldn't speak. He was incoherent.

His eyes were darting around when he was conscious. He was cold to the touch and in very poor condition.'

As Lane sank deeper into coma, his companion went to find medical help. He attracted the attention of civilians working on land near the hut, knowing that the probable price would be his own loss of freedom and brutal interrogation. He then attempted to escape but was taken prisoner. By the time a retrieval party collected Lane, he was dead, another victim of hypothermia in this most bitter Arabian winter. He, too, was awarded a posthumous Military Medal for his unswerving leadership. His death and his companion's marked the end of the first brave attempt by SAS road watch patrols to act, in General Schwarzkopf's phrase, 'as our eyes out there'.

Mobile fighting columns

If the road watch teams had relied on concealment as their best ally, the four mobile fighting columns were anything but covert. They constituted the biggest overland fighting force put into the field by the SAS since the Second World War. Each column consisted of about a dozen four-wheel-drive vehicles, plus motorcycle outriders. These armadas had their own anti-aircraft and anti-tank missile carriers with, fore and aft, protective .5 Browning machine-guns. Most of the weapons were fitted with thermal imaging night sights and the drivers, aside from the men on two wheels, wore night vision goggles also. The end result was a coherent, mobile weapon able to operate round the clock, rather than a series of separate vehicles loosely gathered in convoy; a force arrayed to defend itself and survive surprise attack. On one spectacular occasion, one column would have to do just that.

Two of the columns – known as Group 1 and Group 2 – were drawn from A Squadron; two more from D Squadron. They were described as 'half squadron groups', the equivalent of 50 per cent of a reinforced fighting SAS squadron. The fighters of A Squadron included a US Army master-sergeant on attachment to the SAS from 1st Special Forces Group.

The columns crossed the border, penetrating immediately into the wilderness of western Iraq on 20 January, three days after the initial air strike, having been delayed by a Saudi National Guard unit on the border which could not understand why they wanted to enter Iraq. There were other obstructions: a berm had been built in the path of one group; another, faced with a track-rod failure on its vehicle, blew up the machine to make sure it would be valueless to the enemy, and walked back.

Even without such complications, initial SAS penetration was limited to 25 miles because of fears that Israel would respond to the battering of Tel Aviv with a full-blown invasion by Israeli Defence Forces to attack the same objectives as those allocated to the SAS and USAF combined. Not only might that cause the Coalition to unravel but there was real risk that some less-than-friendly encounter might occur between two rival teams of Scud-hunters. The risk diminished as 30 per cent of the Allied air effort was diverted to anti-Scud operations and the impact of the SAS in identifying the elusive mobile launchers made itself felt.

The RAF's six reconnaissance GR-1A Tornados, flown from England at the last minute, carried a navigator who edited infrared video recordings of the mission before landing so as to accelerate analysis on the ground. The GR-1 could not itself strike at the launchers. In the shrinking response time, as Scuds were wheeled out and fired in a few minutes, after which the launcher scorched away, the counter-strike was still too late. The risk to the reconnaissance fliers was great. On the night of 18 January, for example, a GR-1A returned from its low level, after-dark operation with a gaping bullet hole in its rudder, and this type of reconnaissance was still perilous towards the end. Squadron Leader Richard Garwood flew 19 missions. His Distinguished Flying Cross citation recorded:

In the last hours of the war, with a possible ceasefire already announced, Garwood . . . accepted an extremely high priority task involving the search for Scud missiles threatening Israel. They were located in an area which was reported to have up to 75 anti-aircraft guns and six assorted missile sites.

It was hardly surprising, given the circumstances, that some articulated lorries on the road between Baghdad and Jordan were soon being hit from the air in the mistaken belief that they were missile carriers. Assessments of the number of mobile Scuds varied from day to day. By 20 January the Allies believed there were between a dozen and fourteen mobile launchers in the southern Scud box, a 350 square mile area (approximately 20 miles by 17) of wilderness in western Iraq. (Israeli estimates were probably higher). As the SAS columns moved deeper into Iraq beyond their initial 25-mile cordon sanitaire, another spoke went into the political wheel. Some of the Allied air barons back in Riyadh, determined to ram home the point that this was a war they could win with little help from ground forces, suggested that the presence of friendly forces in the Scud boxes might blunt their attacks. Others feared that 'friendly' fire could precipitate the 'blue-on-blue' catastrophe, the own-goal, that had seemed possible in the air since the preceding August. To the relief of SAS leaders the US Air Commander, General Chuck Horner, faced down the objections of his own people and gave the British special forces their head.

By 23 January, one of A Squadron's groups was prowling about an open expanse of flat, stony desert between Karbala, south-east of Baghdad, and Nukhaib, about 60 miles from the Saudi border. There was no cover here. As dawn approached, the group moved back to its lair, a camouflaged Laying Up Point (LUP). Two days later another A Squadron team, led by Sergeant-Major J., was able to report a heavy build-up of troops around Nukhaib. In spite of that, J's signaller reported, 'Everything going well'.

A troop from D Squadron, meanwhile, was peering inside road culverts under main roads to check whether these concealed Scuds. The SAS needed information about the Scuds, and quickly. One technique was to snatch enemy soldiers and interrogate them. The removal of Iraqi soldiers, usually after dark, from their posts went without a hitch but 'we invariably found we had on our hands militiamen or low-grade soldiers who knew nothing'. There were also the prisoners-by-chance, those Iraqis wounded and abandoned by their friends in battle, or deserters who were picked up almost incidentally by the SAS.

One of these was an 18-year-old conscript. He was seriously wounded and abandoned. The SAS team gave him first aid (see photograph in the Gulf section and took him along in their vehicle until he could be evacuated as a wounded prisoner-of-war on the next outgoing convoy. One of those who treated him reports: 'His main worry seemed to be about who would pay for the drugs used to help him. We got him into the UK p-o-w "casevac" chain and he survived.'

One especially unfortunate Iraqi group comprised four artillerymen who thought they had chosen the safe option in driving across the desert, thereby avoiding the road and a beating by US A-10 aircraft. Their desert route took them straight towards an A Squadron (Group 1) hideout, 'smack into a sentry position on the approach to a half-squadron laager'. (A laager is a temporary, fortified position, a 'wagon-circle'.) There the British sentries poured Browning machine-gun fire into the vehicle, killing three of the occupants. The event was logged as the first special forces fighting contact of the war.

The survivor – the deputy commander of his gun battery – was the first useful Iraqi prisoner taken by British forces who was not a deserter. He was flown by helicopter to the forward base just across the border and from there to a prison camp, but not before he had passed on information of great background value to the British 1st Armoured Division. Equally useful were the military maps all four Iraqis carried when they met the SAS. These described, to a trained eye, the detailed deployment of an important enemy brigade in western Iraq, near the Saudi border.

The information was promptly shipped back to the Tactical Air Co-ordination Centre, where it justified Horner's faith and enhanced the standing of the SAS cell. Within hours, Allied bombers were striking the positions marked by the Iraqis on their own maps.

On 24 January, four days after crossing into Iraq, the armed columns were pushing their patrols into the Southern Scud box. Their presence, combined with the alarm generated by the discovery and pursuit of the road watch patrols, created something like panic. Though there was to be much action, no Iraqi missiles were fired from the SAS area of operations after 26 January. As someone pointed out to the Israelis at a crucial moment, their own highly skilled special forces could not have done a more effective job.

Having penetrated thus far, the SAS consulted with its Allies in the Joint Special Operations Command, a strategic HQ directed from Washington by the chairman of the Joint Chiefs of Staff, General Colin Powell, and separately with General Schwarzkopf's special forces organisation, Special Operations Central Command (Soccent). The essence of what emerged was an agreement that the British team would concentrate on the task of cleansing the southern Scud box, leaving a second area in the north, near the Syrian border, to US forces. Shortages of helicopters and other technical back-up hardened the SAS conviction that 350 square miles was a large enough operational area for the equivalent of a single battalion 100 miles inside enemy territory.

The blows started to fall in earnest on mobile Scud teams on 29 January when two convoys were spotted and attacked from the air. Even more satisfying was the discovery made by one of the SAS columns of an elaborately camouflaged fixed site which was not an expensive East German decoy. It was the real thing and a salvo of missiles was being fuelled up for a multiple launch. The SAS intervention was just in time to halt a particularly savage onslaught on Israel. The *coup de grâce*, courtesy of the US Air Force, flattened the missile launch area, the adjoining command posts, guidance systems and much else.

The airborne artillery directed by the SAS for such strikes was the F15E strike aircraft flown by men of 336th Tactical Fighter Squadron. The F15 Eagle is a single-seat, 1600 mph machine originally envisaged as the Lord of the Skies, an all-purpose air superiority fighter with greater agility and longer sight than anything yet built. The later F15E, or Strike Eagle, is a predator designed to attack ground targets using a system known as 'Lantirn', an acronym for Low Altitude Navigation and Targeting Infra-Red for Night. It is carried in two pods, one for navigation, the other for laser-targeting. Both are linked to the pilot's electronic helmet visor, magnifying a target fifteenfold. Short of firing laser beams as weapons rather than using them as an aid to missile accuracy, the system is the ultimate in Dan Dare technology, achieving better than 90 per cent accuracy. According to their pilots, the Lantirn-equipped F15E can drop bombs within 10 metres of the target on the first pass even without laser.

Lieutenant-Colonel Steven Turner, the officer commanding the Strike Eagles, was evidently told that it was just simple good luck that the SAS were in the right area at the right time. He informed the US journal *Defense Week* that the British soldiers were moving through northwest Iraq to rescue Allied pilots. 'They were there to provide a number of things such as if someone went down they would provide SAR (search and rescue) but at the same time they were able to turn the tables and be a little more offensive. If they ran across something like the Scuds, they would be able to provide data', he said.

His squadron had fifteen Lantirns. 'It was effective to have someone who was able to provide that needle-in-the-haystack information to pinpoint the exact area', he said. 'We could then come in with our targeting infra-red and find those targets.'

Turner credited the SAS with the intelligence to identify a high proportion of his squadron's Scud kills. 'Maybe one-third', or between twenty and thirty of the mobile Scuds destroyed by his team resulted from such co-operation.

SAS teams were not prepared to leave all the kills in the hands of the airmen. Some Scud launchers were still escaping in the pause that came between their targeting and the air strike, a period known as 'IFECT' (for 'Intelligence Force Employment Cycle Time'.) Increasingly, both launcher and missile were to be destroyed directly from the SAS hide on the basis that 'a Scud in the hand was worth two in the bush'.

The soldiers had brought from Europe a cheaper, more commonplace weapon than the mighty F15E. This was the humble Milan anti-tank missile. It was a last-minute inspiration on someone's part to include this in the war chest. With a range of 2000 metres, Milan enabled the attackers to stand further out of danger than the 1500 metres potentially available from laser designation. Furthermore, Milan is almost impossible to detect in combat because of the reduced flash, noise or smoke usually linked to such weapons. It is wire-guided and therefore not vulnerable to electronic counter-measures. Most important of all, its response-time is immediate, unlike hi-tech airborne detectors.

The armoury also included the M19, used to hurl small but potent 40mm grenades more than a thousand metres. It was to prove particularly useful against soft-skinned vehicles such as trucks.

More action for the SAS teams

The movement of sizeable, armed columns in a sensitive military area could not go undetected for long, particularly since some of the SAS teams were now roving around in daylight. Long before, the Iraqis had erected a chain of early warning stations whose automated sensors were on high observation towers, a modern and effective equivalent of Britain's original 'Home Chain' radar system built for the air battles of 1940. In Iraq, in 1991, all the towers were manned as part of Saddam's own iron curtain. On 28 January, observers in one of them caught sight of unfamiliar vehicles and reported that to their regional headquarters. It did not appreciate the fact just yet, but one of the British columns had been compromised.

Early next morning, the compromised SAS team learned the hard way that its presence was known and resented as a concerted attack by around forty soldiers hit the vehicles in their barely concealed, lightly protected laagers. In what one soldier describes as 'a brisk battle', the Iraqi force charged the SAS position and came close to overrunning it. In the furious shoot-out which resulted, ten Iraqis were killed and three of their vehicles destroyed.

Both sides withdrew in a series of fighting skirmishes and the SAS paused to lick its wounds. Two of its vehicles were unusable. Even worse, a party of seven men was cut off from the main body and posted missing. They included a lance-corporal, gravely wounded by a high velocity round which entered his stomach and punched a hole through the soft tissue, narrowly missing his spine as it passed through.

With a field dressing and morphine to keep him going, he walked with the other six for two nights, making no concession to his wound. On the third day of this adventure, the leader, a corporal, 'liberated' an Iraqi vehicle and completed a clean escape into Saudi territory, only to be halted and arrested at the first Saudi police checkpoint they reached, in 'Ar 'Ar. The police, perhaps understandably, were baffled by the Iraqi number plates on a friendly vehicle, just as regular British soldiers had been suspicious of Stirling's grimy warriors inbound from the wilderness. The wounded man was flown to hospital, his six comrades airlifted back to their forward base in Saudi Arabia to be re-equipped and sent back to Iraq. (One of them, a reservist, died on exercise in Belize in 1992.) The group from which they were separated continued its raids inside Iraq until the end of hostilities.

For the next five days, the SAS started to roam and strike with increasing confidence. A favourite hunting ground was Wadi Amij (also known as Wadi Amiq) which runs west, between two main roads from the Euphrates towards the town of Ar Rutbah. The SAS had another name for it – 'Scud Alley' – and it was the western end of this gully that attracted D Squadron columns in a series of nocturnal stalking expeditions.

On 3 February a team which combined the talents of 16 and 17 Troops, cruising across the desert by day, spotted a mobile Iraqi convoy of fourteen vehicles – Scud transporter-erector vehicles and escorts to repel attack by tanks and aircraft, all under camouflage – parked alongside the trail. As the convoy moved off, the SAS followed, calling an air strike. Four F15s were scrambled but of four strikes, only one hit the target. The SAS team boss, a captain, now hit the convoy with Milan missiles. One launcher and its Scud blew up but there were others which did not. The enemy, responding like veterans, coolly brought their triple-A machine guns into action, forcing the SAS to retreat. Outgunned on the ground, the British leader called on US air power. The F15s swept down yet again but even their firepower was not sufficient to destroy every last Iraqi Scud. If part of the convoy survived, the same could not be said for the morale of Iraq's strategic rocket force, far from the official front line in any ground war . . . or so it thought. Until the SAS exploded in their midst, there had been no military action on the ground except for the Iraqi cross-border attack on Khafji, in Saudi territory near the Gulf coast. That battle had only just ended. The sensitivity of the subject was such that neither side revealed what was happening. The silence by Baghdad spoke volumes about the effect on morale of SAS attacks.

For the SAS, the most disconcerting experience was to come under attack from its principal ally, the US Air Force. While the team that had engaged the Scud convoy returned to its hideout, another column, comprising 18 and 19 Troops, attracted the attention of an A-10 pilot. The A-10 is an inelegant flying machine built round a cannon that fires depleted uranium shells into tanks. The pilot must also navigate, often with map on knee. As a concept, it is a return to the age of Biggles and prone to error. On this occasion the pilot mistook the SAS column of Land-Rovers, neatly parked, bumper-to-bumper, awaiting resupply, for a single long Iraqi vehicle which could be a Scud launcher. The attack caused one minor casualty: a bruised foot. Similar 'friendly fire' caused deaths among British soldiers elsewhere and triggered off a public row in the UK and US after the war.

Next day, 5 February, it was the turn of D Squadron's Group 2, of whom little had been heard, to call an airstrike on a Scud convoy comprising two launchers and four escort vehicles. An hour or so later, part of the same team (Patrol D20) fought Iraqis defending an observation tower. Ten Iraqis were killed, and one vehicle and the enemy control building destroyed without loss to the SAS. Group 2 rounded off a busy day with a firefight around an Iraqi observation post. Three Iraqis were killed and two taken prisoner. Prisoners were becoming an embarrassment. Next day, when A Squadron picked up another two, described as 'conscripts with no useful information', the squadron was ordered to release them. By contrast, a prisoner taken by D Squadron on 7 February who did have something useful to say about Scud operations, was brought out by helicopter and promptly delivered to Soccent. Meanwhile a reconnaissance operation targeted on a likely missile launch site was cancelled because diesel oil in the vehicle to be used had frozen. Next night, this operation and several others went ahead in spite of the weather. D Squadron called an air strike on an important radar installation (code-named 'Flat Face') and a patrol from A Squadron toppled a microwave communications tower. As they were leaving they ran into an enemy force of 'transport troops' and a 40-minute battle resulted.

Yet another ugly little skirmish occurred in the early hours of 9 February, as the A Squadron team, led by Sergeant-Major 'J', probed around a communications centre near Nukhayb. Initially, all that was known back at the forward operations base was that 'three personnel and one Land-Rover are unaccounted for . . . The vehicle has no navigational equipment and had been playing up.' Until now, 'J's team had been running a highly successful, and stealthy, reconnaissance war. It was not until 11 February that the headquarters team learned that 'J' himself was missing presumed killed. As one diarist noted, 'This day started bad, continued bad and ended even worse . . .'

Sergeant-Major 'J' was one of those people known to all armies since the Roman legions marched out: a rocklike presence that was its own guarantee that everything would be OK. If that sort of man is lost it is not just the regimental furniture that is rearranged, there are also ominous cracks in the ceiling. From the two survivors, rescued after some 72 hours in the wilderness, it seemed certain that 'J' was a dead man. They described at their debrief a vicious firefight during which their vehicle was separated from the rest of the force. 'J' was wounded in the groin and seemed likely to bleed to death. In spite of that, the sergeant-major kept his cool and directed his team away from their disabled vehicle on foot. In the ensuing manhunt, the fugitives paused long enough to staunch the blood flowing from the sergeant-major's wound with a tourniquet. The enemy followed, closed twice and twice the two unwounded soldiers fought them off.

After some hours, 'J' couldn't move. Some of the time he was unconscious. In what he must have perceived as his last moment of conscious command, he ordered the other two to make a break and leave him. One of his companions, appalled by the implications of capture by the Iraqis or a lingering death in a freezing desert, offered to act as his executioner.

'Shall I put a bullet into you, sergeant-major?' he asked.

The wounded man, a fluent Arabist, said no thanks. Both knew it was not a unique case. From time to time, in Dhofar and elsewhere, SAS soldiers have been lethally disabled. The last duty of a casualty's partner, in that case, might be to finish the job, a process described with a shudder by one SAS wife, as 'joining the Exit Club'. In rare cases, both men go together, but this is not the Roman army or the French Foreign Legion. The SAS trains its men to believe in their survival. When the moment comes to choose between death now and death briefly deferred, a casualty usually prefers to take his chances this side of the grave. That was what happened this time.

It was 24 hours before an Iraqi patrol spotted the rucksack and the still form lying beside it. Miracles can still happen, and one was happening now. In the brittle, clicking Arabic of the Iraqis, they asked his name.

'Shu ismak?'

'English', he said. 'Inklizee.'

An English prisoner might be worth something in these uncertain times. They decided not to kill him outright. They called their officer. With a humanity that astonished the SAS, he called for a stretcher and a vehicle. The surgery performed on his leg by an Iraqi civilian doctor, trained in Britain, inspired respect for his handiwork among those who treated him later. His patient was interrogated as harshly as the rest, but survived. His reappearance amazed the authorities in England, who cancelled the grim warnings to next-of-kin that he was missing in action. In due time he was awarded a Military Cross, a decoration normally reserved for commissioned officers, last awarded to an NCO in 1965 when another A Squadron sergeant-major, Lawrence Smith, was decorated for operations in Borneo.

Those who were taken prisoner were interrogated with characteristic Iraqi brutality. Some stories about that process, such as the removal of fingernails or torture so extreme that it proved fatal, are untrue. One of the more reliable accounts of what happened comes from Captain Russell Sanborn, aged 28, a US Navy pilot who was also taken prisoner and held in the same sinister building – probably the Mukhabarat Secret Police headquarters at 52nd Street, Baghdad – as the SAS men.

Sanborn himself was 'pushed through a gauntlet of roaring soldiers maybe 100 yards long. There were hundreds of blows', he told a Miami journalist. In an adjoining cell were British soldiers whom he thought were SAS men. Said Sanborn:

> The Iraqis hated the British and I would hate to know what damage they did to these men in their hours of torture. The guards would take them out to the interrogation room one at a time and hours later I'd hear them being dragged back in. I could tell from their breathing and moaning that they'd really been worked on.
>
> The British prisoners never complained but sometimes when the guards were out of the cell area I'd hear them giving each other encouragement. I wondered if they were SAS or some kind of special advance commandos. They were top soldiers of some kind. I looked up to these gentlemen . . . They carried themselves well. After a while, the Iraqis began to hold them in high regard and the interrogations slowed. The British prisoners had earned their respect. They were very tough. I don't know what the Iraqis were doing to them and they never told me.

After their return, there was – of course – a problem of readjustment but it was an SAS problem. Such highly motivated soldiers, trained escapers, find it difficult to distinguish between capture and failure. In some cases it does not seem to have struck them that they faced impossible odds. All have returned to regimental duty.

Problems of logistics

At forward base, the Commanding Officer and others were working on a problem not encountered on this scale since Stirling's war. This was how to replenish and resupply columns operating on enemy territory. In Iraq, hardworked Land-Rovers, Unimogs and motorcycles needed major servicing. In spite of the wonders of the helicopter this was not an operation which could be run from the air. Iraqi low-level anti-aircraft guns were still the greatest threat to all hostile aircraft and the RAF did not yet have the inexpensive equipment to run such an operation in total darkness. The SAS ran its own supply column instead, overland. This consisted of ten 4-ton trucks crewed by badged SAS soldiers and REME mechanics, escorted by teams drawn from B Squadron in six armed Land-Rovers. The caravan was led by a major of considerable Middle East experience. As one observer recorded on 10 February: 'Those who got up early to see the convoy off, watched with mixed emotions; firstly wishing they were part of it and secondly, a feeling of some apprehension. We have yet to name the convoy but some possibilities are the "Wadi–Bottom Wanderers" and the "Cowboy Convoy".' In the event the SAS named it 'E Squadron'. It was two days before the convoy was cleared to cross the border. This it did at 5am on 12 February, arriving at the Wadi Tubal rendezvous, 87 miles inside Iraq, at 4 pm after the meeting place had been scoured for any enemy presence by one of the fighting columns from A Squadron. The convoy then mounted guard over the scene while the columns did their housekeeping. During the next five days a mobile workshop did a roaring trade as the columns came in from the Scud box. Entire engines were replaced. Weapons were stripped and serviced.

Morale – dented on 11 February by confirmation of Sergeant Major 'J's apparent 'death' – was also given a lift when, with a degree of *chutzpah* which should win some sort of award from Mossad, the newly appointed Regimental Sergeant – Major of 22 SAS decided this would be a good opportunity to confirm his elevation at a meeting of the Warrant Officers' and Sergeants' Mess. At noon local time on 16 February a quorum of thirty-three senior NCOs drawn from eight SAS departments convened and the extraordinary meeting began.

Among items on the agenda carried without dissent were a vote of thanks to the retiring RSM; another thank-you to the Christmas party organisers; next mess dinner night arrangements; the provision of a mess washing-machine. Apart from the signatures, added later, of H. Norman Schwarzkopf and Peter de la Billière, the only acknowledgement of the unusual nature of the meeting was a cautionary note from the President of the Mess Committee, recording that 'if he was to be in a nonsense whilst returning to the Saudi border he would be compelled to eat the minutes of the Mess Meeting'.

By now, only Saddam Hussein was being obliged to eat his words. 'E Squadron' returned to Saudi Arabia unharmed on 17 February. Asked how it was out there, the major commanding the column told a friend: 'Piece of piss. I've had more excitement in the Naafi on a Saturday night.' In fact, the journey back was not entirely without incident. The route the convoy followed in and out of Iraq was swept by an RAF Tornado reconnaissance aircraft to check the presence of hostile forces. The column spotted an enemy observation post and used laser for the only time in this campaign to direct an air attack. Air support was required twice before the convoy reached the sanctuary of friendly territory. There, the 'squadron' was disbanded after an existence shorter than any other element in British special forces since Popski's Private Army.

For the fighting columns, as the supply teams got back, it was business as usual. On 18 February a D Squadron patrol spotted an Iraqi hideout in Wadi Hawran which concealed one Scud transporter and seven missiles. US F15s were called in for the kill.

Two days after replenishment, a prowling SAS column came upon a Scud launcher and missile driving out of the Scud box, towards the north-east. This might well have reflected an Iraqi decision to salvage its only credible weapon while it could. By now, some missiles were discovered, after they had landed in Israel, to be armed with concrete 'warheads'.

By moving the launchers back from a forward area endangered by enemy commandos, the Scud commanders, like the Iraqi Air Force itself, hoped to fight another day. The convoy of 19 February was not so lucky. The SAS called down the wrath of the F15, which picked it up as it hurried along the highway. Even better, the godlike perspective of the cockpit revealed a whole matrix of concrete hides and 'revetments'. One F15 missile scored a direct hit. As more accurate hits went in the explosions shook the earth.

Communications system targeted

When the SAS discovered launch sites undamaged by the airmen, it dismantled key components with explosives or, as a cheaper alternative, with sledge hammers. British casualties remained remarkably few, in view of the risks. On 20 February a D Squadron soldier suffered a flesh wound in a skirmish which an uncharitable comrade attributed to 'his wallet falling on his foot from his back pocket'. It would require his evacuation to hospital, protesting loudly, a couple of days later.

If there was one target as important as the Scuds it was the communications system coming out of Baghdad that controlled Saddam's finger on the trigger. Saddam Hussein, consistently underrated by the West even as they were selling him ultra-sophisticated equipment, had been well advised by the CIA among others during his war with Iran, about the importance of secure communications.

The network targetted by the SAS was a mixture of microwave link towers, in which telecom messages of all kinds are transmitted short distances by air waves, and well-buried fibre optic cables able to carry an astronomical weight of data in a tiny diameter. With the aid of good intelligence the regiment concentrated on the fibre optic element in the chain. The line carried Baghdad's orders to the men in the field, immediately responsible for Scud operations. It also ran Saddam Hussein's diplomatic traffic to Amman, to his cousin in Geneva, his ambassadors in Paris and at the UN, sustaining the reality of his control of his big, apparently disordered country.

This credibility was, if anything, a higher value target than Saddam's more clumsy ballistic missiles.

Alongside a main road, the SAS went for the weak point in the system: repeater (relay) stations needed to boost the signal along its way. Hitting these would really hurt, since Iraq, entombed by an effective embargo, had no spares. The SAS blew up seven of these in daylight alongside the old highway between Baghdad and Amman, the Jordanian capital. Bemused civilians on the road heard the explosions, saw the British Land-Rovers . . . and when the cheery demolition men waved so confidently at them waved back. If Saddam's links with the outside world could not be severed completely, then they would be forced up to the surface by temporary repairs, exposed to interception.

On 21 February, as the regiment completed its destruction and started to withdraw, one of A Squadron's fighting columns (initially commanded by Sergeant-Major 'J') was involved in a running battle – 'a series of contacts', said one participant – with an enemy force. In a particularly intense exchange of fire a motorcycle outrider, Lance-Corporal David Denbury, aged 26, from Ponthir, near Newport, was hit in the chest.

One of his comrades said later: 'He called my name. I moved across to him and saw that he had been hit.' Within a few minutes he was dead. Under heavy fire, his body was hauled away and loaded onto a Land-Rover by his friend. The column now extracted itself from a dangerous situation and made for the Saudi border. By now, the Iraqis knew the score and had organised retaliatory mobile teams on stand-by. One of these set off in pursuit of the British column, using heavy machine-guns and mortars.

Yet more communication problems meant that the quarry in this deadly game could not play their trump card, air support. The hunt went on across the desert for 25 miles, a journey punctuated by three separate battles in which the SAS hit back with Browning machine-guns and Milan missiles. There were times, as the column twisted an evasive route home, when it seemed uncertain who were the pursuers and who the pursued.

At last the enemy gave up, having taken casualties and lost vehicles. They, also, had no air support, which made this a very old fashioned combat indeed.

Denbury's loss, at the eleventh hour, was poignant. Of course this was a high risk operation and it was inevitable that some teams would pay a high price. Nonetheless it was a cruel irony that the beleagured survivors of Mirbat, 1972, fared better with a pair of Omani Strikemasters than a team which, in 1991, should have had on call only a few minutes' flying time away the most mighty array of air power the world has ever seen.

He was an Army boxing champion. Denbury's sister Julie said of her 'dashing, blue-eyed, blond-haired and very handsome' brother: 'He boxed for the Army, played football for the Army; now he has died for the Army.' The Army was not unmindful of his sacrifice. He received a posthumous Military Medal to add to the Queen's Gallantry Medal awarded earlier for services in Northern Ireland.

Next day, a routine helicopter mission was flown to recover Denbury's body. The presence of enemy troops meant that D Squadron's casualty of 20 February had to wait. This was somewhat ironic, since the soldier was opposed to his evacuation.

By the time the long-awaited Allied ground offensive to outflank Kuwait began on 24 February, the SAS had already achieved its great strategic objective, that of containing attacks by the elusive, mobile Scuds, so Israel had stayed on the sidelines. The impact of SAS attacks, as General Schwarzkopf acknowledged in a tribute to the regiment, was that 'the principal areas used by the Iraqis to fire Scuds on Tel Aviv were no longer available to them. They were required to move their Scud missile firing forces to the north-west portion of Iraq and from that location the firing of Scud missiles was essentially militarily ineffective.'

When they returned to Saudi territory, the regiment's long range Land-Rovers had covered an average of 1500 miles and the motorcycles 1875 miles. Hulls of fighting vehicles – usually the front offside wings – were decorated with stencilled silhouettes of individual 'kills', ranging from tracked Scud launchers to communication towers. The battlefield area on which they were able to threaten the Iraqis would cover, in Britain, a zone flanked by, say, London and Darlington. The mobile columns had spent between 36 days and 42 days behind the lines. It is no surprise that the Baghdad high command became convinced that it was opposed not by a force of just over 300 men, but a team of 10,000.

By this time, advised by their British comrades-in-arms, US special forces, notably Delta, were also wreaking havoc on Scuds in the so-called 'Scud box north', near Qaim on the border with Syria. (The Americans had another name for it: 'Scud Boulevard'.) A briefing for the *Washington Post* and others on 4 March 1991 revealed that 'A special forces team helped locate and direct US aircraft fire that destroyed 16 mobile missile launchers at several sites in Western Iraq.'

One of those involved in these operations told the author that it was not just missiles that he targeted. 'We had just small patrols out there for weeks, lying low. When we saw a bunch of enemy troops, maybe a company, maybe more, we simply called down an airstrike. We called down an A-10 armed with the Maverick missile. It simply wiped them out.'

At its peak, such activity meant that the Iraqi army was fighting on so many fronts that the very word 'front' was losing any meaning. Deep inside Iraq, in the salt and sand deserts and mountains, no soldier of Saddam Hussein could feel secure for long. Allied special forces rapidly struck from all points on the compass to hit any suitable, sausage-shaped target that showed up on the thermal imager.

Some of the targets proved, after all, not to be Scuds but fuel containers. When those exploded in the centre of a convoy which mixed civilian and military traffic, it was inevitable that civilian casualties resulted, a fact which gave the soldiers responsible no pleasure.

Nevertheless, the soldiers were impressed by the new equipment. A particular favourite among US special forces was the British-made Thorn EMI hand-held thermal imager. Its weight – dramatically reduced to 5kg from the preceding standard of 11kg – gave special forces a chance to carry it anywhere and combine its use with laser targeting. The technical literature reveals that 'the potential of thermal imagers as night sights for missile systems, particularly man-portable anti-tank missiles, was quickly recognised' and acted upon by British forces two years before the Gulf war. Hand-held Magellan satellite navigation aids were also welcomed as an easier alternative to the dangerously slow business of the sun compass mounted on the front of the vehicle. In this desert, in this war, there was no sun anyway.

The sat-nav device known as GPS (for Global Positioning System) is applauded by the SAS as 'a war-winning equipment'. Reasons for the applause went beyond routine navigation, important though that was. Without GPS, RAF helicopters could not deliver vital supplies to a patrol deep inside enemy territory or lift out casualties.

In Riyadh, the Tactical Air Co-ordination Centre – where the regiment was represented throughout – needed to know exactly where SAS patrols were and (unlike Stirling's teams) precisely where they were going, so as to brief Allied pilots on targets they were not to attack. Such pinpoint accuracy was even more vital when the SAS called down air-strikes in the dark 1000 yards or less from their own hides.

US and French commandos wade in

While the SAS fought its near-private, pre-emptive war in remote western Iraq, the main action, an advance through the desert to outflank Saddam Hussein's absurd reconstruction of the Maginot Line, was going like clockwork. It was battle that depended heavily on the dash of commandos of another kind, the American airborne forces of 82nd and 101st, and the French Foreign Legion.

These airborne forces were dropped by a helicopter armada behind Iraqi positions to hit known strongpoints along a 200-mile front that would first by-pass, then envelop, the Iraqi army. Iraq was fooled by a box of electronic black arts into expecting an attack from the Gulf coast to the east, not the limitless desert westward. US Air Force electronic deception had started to test, then to 'spoof', enemy radar with false signals as early as November.

Around 20 February, special forces' air teams rolled parachute-stabilised BLU-82/B fuel-air bombs, also known as 'Daisy Cutters' (weapons which blend the IRA's once-favourite mixture of ammonium nitrate, polystyrene soap and aluminium powder mixed with petroleum, albeit in a larger, 12,000 pound unit) from Hercules transport aircraft at 6000 feet over a Kuwaiti minefield, detonating the whole package, minefield and all from about 7 feet above ground level. The use of Hercules − a cargo and paratroop aircraft − as bomber is novel as well as primitive, but BLU-82/B is a fearsome weapon. As described by Air Vice-Marshal R.A. Mason: 'On impact . . . an initial charge dispersed the explosive mixture over a wide area. A second fuse ignited the gaseous cloud, creating an expanding shockwave seventy times atmospheric pressure and detonating mines scattered below it over a wide area. Such pressure was instantly fatal to any troops in dugouts.'

The Iraqis lost their cool when this hit them and switched on all their radar systems, which were promptly recorded by airborne intelligence gatherers. The initial deception was completed when two US Marine Divisions supported by a heavy armoured brigade breached the massive sand berms guarding the short route to Kuwait. It was a deception plan with the capability to succeed as an invasion in its own right.

Meanwhile in a concealed movement of D-Day proportions, two entire Army Corps including the British 1st Division, with a French division on the exposed desert flank, were smashing their way through Iraq's back door to the west in five columns of concentrated firepower carried on tens of thousands of vehicles. Such an offensive when it works − and this one worked − will be limited only by adequate supplies of fuel and ammunition.

A few commanders have beaten this law of armoured warfare by attacking the enemy to seize his fuel. They include Germany's Afrika Korps hero, Rommel and the American General, Patton. By 1991, tank technology ruled out such a solution. A modern division of US M1A1 tanks consumes 600,000 gallons of fuel each day. To complicate matters further, the fuel is JP-5, a jet engine mixture.

Early in the morning of 24 February, paras of the French 6th Division and US paras of XVIII Airborne Corps descended on As Salman airfield to destroy a battalion of Iraqi mechanised infantry, creating a logistical base for the next wave of ground and air operations. From As Salman, in Operation Cobra, 460 attack helicopters of 101st Airborne struck even further north to land unopposed on the road network astride the River Euphrates, near Samawa.

The same morning, men of 101st swooped on Objective Gold, a staging area in south-western Iraq. The Iraqi army was now cut off from Baghdad and crumbling with each passing hour.

Some of these operations depended on deep reconnaissance by men of 5th US Special Forces Group, two of whose road watch patrols were spotted by the Iraqis in the Tigris and Euphrates Valley. As one official account puts it: 'The missions were predominantly static positions covering main supply routes . . . Two were compromised in their position and were engaged in heavy combat before extraction was possible.'

Yet such behind-the-lines work was not 5 SFG's primary job. Its first priority was to lubricate a unique machine blending Arab and non-Arab forces into a workable coalition. Expert liaison teams went into combat with 108 non-American units. As well as the Arabs, these included French and Pakistani contingents. The teams fed back to Schwarzkopf's headquarters 'ground truth' about 'the location, status, capabilities and intentions of the Arab Coalition Forces during the offensive ground campaign'.

Deployed early in the crisis, in August and September 1990, 5 SFG soldiers jointly patrolled the Saudi border with Iraq and Occupied Kuwait. Its 2nd Battalion 'drilled in contingency plans that bore a resemblance to Custer's last stand'. Saddam paused, fatally for his success and while he did so, the Americans – whose own expertise ranged from linguistics to forward air control –

trained their new allies in everything from basic skill-at-arms to airmobile operations.

Other elements of US special forces units included the US Army Special Forces Command; 160th Special Operations Aviation Regiment and the US Air Force 16th Special Operations Squadron. They lost a combined total of twenty-two men during Desert Storm. Unconventional American units already mentioned included Delta Force, a transatlantic cousin of the SAS, and parts of the US Marine Corps.

Hostilities cease

The sudden end to hostilities caught everyone, including General Schwarzkopf, by surprise. Kuwait was on fire. Saddam Hussein was still in power in Iraq, a potent symbol for Arabia's have-nots. And a substantial portion of the Republican Guard, the core of Saddam's power, was intact, though trapped, in the Basra Pocket. The overriding motive of US policy was to avoid entrapment in another Vietnam. As ex-Defense Secretary Caspar Weinberger observed during the early days of Operation Desert Shield: 'You go in with overwhelming force, you go in very quickly and once its over, you get out. That is a refreshing change from the Vietnam era.'

The policy was given more cynical expression by Senator Tom Harkin: 'The Gulf War was like teenage sex. We got in too soon and out too soon.'

When the Bear received the call from Washington in the ultra modern, underground Joint Operations Centre in Riyadh, he showed no excessive surprise or indignation but by now, his aides sensed when the famous growl was imminent. On the other end of the line was Colin Powell, chairman of the Joint Chiefs, as spokesman for the President. The order was clear and simple: 'Hostilities will cease as of 0800 hrs your time tomorrow.' That would be midnight in Washington on Wednesday, 28 February, after just 100 hours of land warfare.

Schwarzkopf punctuated the conversation with deadpan monosyllables: 'Yes'. 'Right'. 'Understood'. 'I hear you'.

One of the author's sources, present at the time, heard Schwarzkopf saying: 'Sir, you should know that we need another 24 hours to reduce the Iraqi Republican Guard . . . We do not need to go all the way to Baghdad, but the force around Basra is another matter.'

Schwarzkopf himself said on television but subsequently withdrew the comment: 'Frankly my recommendation had been to continue the march. The decision we should stop did leave some escape routes for them [the Iraqis] to back out.'

In spite of claims that ending the war was a military and not a political decision – itself a novel idea in a democracy – it is most probable that Schwarzkopf was overruled and later blamed for halting the campaign prematurely in response to public revulsion at home over the one-sided slaughter of retreating Iraqis. Even the British added their protests. Sir Charles Powell, Downing Street Foreign Affairs Adviser, 1984–91, told a BBC Panorama team five months later that there had been a surprising and unaccustomed 'outbreak of chivalry' on the Western side. Those who were being chivalrous were 'those who wanted to stop'. Invited to include Schwarzkopf among them, he said: 'My understanding is that American military advice would be that it would not be sensible to prosecute the conflict beyond the point at which they said a ceasefire should come into effect.'

British Defence Minister Tom King, in the same programme, said that Schwarzkopf had reported to Washington 'on the situation on the ground' and the President then took that decision [to stop the fighting]. 'He discussed it with the Allies, what he proposed to do, and we agreed with it.'

Some months later, in February 1992, Britain's Prime Minister John Major told a BBC radio documentary: 'All of the Iraqis' fighting troops had effectively left the front line' . . . The people we would have been killing were relatively young conscript troops who were in no condition to defend themselves. A lot of them would have been killed. There would have been a lot more bloodshed if the international troops were to have gone on into Baghdad. At the time there was no mandate for that. At the time there was no will to do that. At the time, the military commanders did not think we should have done that.'

What of Saddam? Some participants, including General de la Billière, 'felt that Saddam would not last more than three or four weeks after the war'. But expert observers, such as Lieutenant-General Leonard Peroots, Director of the US Defense Intelligence Agency from 1985 to 1989, had expected – at least – an attempt to destabilise the Iraqi dictator. Some even hoped that the problem might be solved by means of an assassination, possibly employing non-American surrogates. Former President Richard Nixon, for example, advocated an assassination 'contract' on Saddam.

If Western liberal values prevailed in this crucial eleventh-hour debate it was because the West still did not comprehend the similarity between contemporary Iraq and Tsarist Russia, whose constitution was defined by a German count in 1868 as 'absolutism moderated by assassination'.

Peroots told the veteran BBC reporter, Tom Mangold: 'You know, if Saddam dies under any circumstances during the next few years, the US, rightly or wrongly, will certainly take a share in the blame as will the Israelis. So there will be guilt by association whether there is an association or not . . . though plausible deniability is something we accomplish a lot of things through around the world.'

President Bush's vaccilation about what to do about Saddam *personally* took an interesting turn on 15 February, the day after the Iraqi dictator offered a conditional withdrawal from Kuwait. Bush called on 'the Iraqi military and the Iraqi people to take matters into their own hands, to force Saddam Hussein, the dictator, to step aside.' According to the American writer Gail Sheehy, 'Several senior Iraqi army officers heeded President Bush's public exhortation and made contact with both Sunni Arab dissidents and Kurdish rebels, according to on-site research by Peter Galbraith for the Senate Foreign Relations Committee. But by the time conditions were ripe for elements in the military to join the insurrection, Bush had backed down from his support for a popular uprising.'

Having stoked the fires of revolution among Shi'ites in the south and Kurds in the north, the American President was edging round to the conclusion that Saddam 'had made himself too useful to exterminate'; better Saddam, the known devil, than uncontrolled fundamentalism or Balkanisation of the region into tribal, terrorist mini-states.

British advice seems to have emphasised the risks of destroying the coalition of Arab monarchs and Western presidents if Iraq was humiliated as well as defeated. Preserving Arab dignity (for which Western diplomatists in the Gulf substitute the word 'sensitivities') is an obsession among many Europeans with real knowledge of Arabia.

Aside from the problem of resolve, or lack of it, in the White House another major obstacle to assassinating Saddam was, ironically, the advice his numerous bodyguards had received before the war from a training team supplied by a private British security company. This was part of an extensive transfer of Western expertise to buttress Saddam as a friend of the West in his war with Iran. Saddam had initially hired German advisers from GSG-9 to do the job. When the pioneering Iraqi team made its first daring abseil from a helicopter during training, it depended on a rope which was not securely rigged. One man was killed and several others injured. The event was recorded on video and was fatal to further German involvement in the scheme. A British evaluation team was summoned in December 1983 and continued work through much of 1984.

The programme covered more than Saddam's personal protection. The latest SAS techniques in storming a hijacked airliner were also part of the package. Like Mussolini and other historic targets of assassination, Saddam had learned to keep moving, but to secure the rope himself before swinging to the safety of the next branch.

In twenty years of state terror, the Iraqi leader had also surrounded himself with a Praetorian Guard numbering 60,000, rather more than the formations Julius Caesar required. Even after Iraq's second ruinous war, Gail Sheehy believes, this force remained 'intact and dedicated to only one cause: the preservation of Saddam Hussein'. The benison of Western expertise in this as in other parts of Iraq's war machine did not diminish its efficiency, as the West discovered just before the air war began.

The art of killing a modern dictator is a highlyy technical business. It starts with an intercept of the target's telephone and radio communications so as to anticipate his movements. Saddam, enjoying the benefits of Western training as well as his own youthful experience as an assassin, gave nothing away. In December, when the US National Security Agency attempted to intercept his calls, it discovered that he had virtually stopped using the telephone. Nearly all his orders were relayed at second hand and then after a safe time limit.

Possibly Saddam had discovered that British-made signals equipment supplied to him shortly before the conflict had been rigged like an electronic Trojan Horse to transmit, without Iraqi knowledge, to the secret GCHQ listening post in Cyprus.

There was another, somewhat paradoxical explanation for the West's restraint. This was that although America was at war with Iraq's armed forces, Saddam Hussein had to remain off-limits – in spite of his role as Iraqi commander-in-chief – because of a US legal doctrine that forbids assassination as an act of state policy. 'Assassination' has been redefined, in this context, to mean exclusively the killing of a head of state, in contrast with the Kennedy heyday of CIA plots to murder such opponents as Fidel Castro, the target of twenty-four attempts, one employing poisoned cigars.

And yet, 'We bombed all his palaces,' said one Allied front line planner after the war, 'but he was never there.'

With the Iraqi army defeated, contrasting public figures extolled the virtues of special forces. The 'little men with little guns', were now eulogised in vindication of all ground troops including heavy tank and artillery divisions. Schwarzkopf's praise of commandos – which caught his own information team off guard – was followed by that of John Major and even the Prince of Wales, who seemed to confuse the SAS (not threatened by impending defence cuts) with county regiments which were.

Major, the British Prime Minister, told a group of Israeli businessmen: 'I'll tell you who destroyed the Scuds. It was the British SAS. They were fabulous.'

The commander of the Strike Eagles, Lieutenant-Colonel Turner, added his tribute. The SAS were 'the unsung heroes'.

At the London Guildhall, reviewing a muted parade to commemorate the victory, Prince Charles said: 'It is worth remembering that the classic and exemplary role performed by our Special Forces throughout this campaign, whose valiant and heroic deeds in an extraordinarily harsh environment must remain largely unsung, was chiefly made possible by the very strong sense of regimental identity which has long been the hallmark of their astonishingly courageous exploits.'

The SAS – as a political as well as a military success in the blows it has struck against terrorism – was not under threat. Furthermore it rejected the lumber of regimental tradition, placing its faith in innovation. It was not a regiment in the normal sense. Most of its members were people who had rejected, temporarily or otherwise, attachment to their regiment or corps of origin. One friend of the author's even bridled at the idea of a return to the Parachute Regiment as 'rejoining the British Army'. If one test of a regiment is that it has a permanent cadre of officers, then the SAS fails such a test since the vast majority of its commissioned ranks serve one or two brief tours with special forces before returning home to the Guards, Infantry, Cavalry and so on. The gravitational force that holds the SAS so securely together is the shared experience of high risk successfully overcome.

For the strategists in their colleges the Gulf War demonstrated that a combination of special forces married to air power can provide an answer to a peculiarly Western dilemma: how to win a war with minimal casualties, since casualties incur an instant political penalty at home. France long ago found an answer to the problem by hiring foreign mercenary soldiers – men of talent but also men without a home – to fight her Third World wars.

To rely on technology instead of a Foreign Legion incurs its own penalty. As professors Gene I. Rochlin and Chris D. Demchak noted in an essay on the technological lessons of the Gulf War:

Saddam's Scud missiles are merely a foretaste of what Western expeditionary forces can expect in the future. The US will have to develop ever more advanced weapons, as today's systems are sold abroad. The chimera of a clean, cost-free war carries the potential for military disaster. As the cost of weapons systems continues to escalate there will be pressure to trim back the military budget . . . a tendency to depend increasingly on scarce, individual weapons, on elaborated electronics and computers and on integrated co-ordination of even the smallest details of battle . . . This might lead people to think that wars can be fought with smaller forces and that technology can be substituted for people . . . Without the massive support provided in the Gulf, the next war could be more costly in lives and equipment . . . or assured of success only with continued good fortune or against smaller and smaller enemies.

Immediately after the Gulf War, the British government raised the stakes against the SAS in battle by enhancing the role of special forces while cutting the size of the regular army from which it is drawn. As Winston S. Churchill observed in a letter to the *Daily Telegraph* on 23 July 1991: 'We will end up with the absurd situation of having more MoD civil servants than the entire strength of the British Army.'

That judgement should not obscure the remarkable impact on the political as well as military evolution of the Gulf conflict by a comparative handful of men. Britain's special forces group of seven hundred was unusually large by SAS standards but it was a tiny percentage of the half-million strong Allied expedition. The achievement was properly recognised in the total of fifty-five awards for gallantry and meritorious service (see Appendix C). Of ten Military Medals, three were bestowed posthumously on Corporal Denbury, Lance-Corporal Lane and Trooper Consiglio.

It was General Schwarzkopf, in a generous tribute (see Appendix A) who acknowledged that the only force fit to conduct the first, dangerous operations against the Scud was the SAS. Coming from an American commander not celebrated for his belief in unconventional warface, it was as remarkable as it was fitting.

THE SOUTH ATLANTIC WAR 1982

A military gamble

Argentina invaded the Falkland Islands on 2 April 1982 and the separate British dependency of South Georgia, 800 miles away, the day after. When these events occurred a number of eminent people expressed surprise. It is a rare shock to the British political system that can precipitate the resignation of an entire team of Foreign Office ministers, particularly one headed by such an intelligent Secretary of State as Lord Carrington.

When diplomacy collapses it is the business of the soldier to pick up the pieces. This time, however, the pieces were 8000 miles from home and it was not at all clear how they could be glued together again. For once even the SAS – whose Intelligence staff tend to observe political violence with the professionalism of stockbrokers monitoring world markets – were wrong-footed by the Ministry of Defence. As the Argentines were openly boasting about their intention to liberate the 'Malvinas', alert British journalists were making their way to Port Stanley to watch it happen, and to photograph the event. It was as if Britain's official minds, military as well as civil, were frozen into inactivity by a sense of incredulity. In fairness it should be stated that the Argentine people also seemed surprised – pleasantly so – but surprised all the same. So far as the Foreign and Commonwealth Office was concerned there had been many wolf cries from Argentina before which had come to nothing. Across the road, the Defence Ministry had no contingency plan to recapture the Falklands if they were lost.

As Lord Lewin (a recent Chief of Defence Staff) pointed out

soon after the invasion, twenty years of defence reviews meant that 'opposed landings were excluded from future scenarios'. British forces were expected to operate on the basis of 'red carpet entry' in support of friendly countries which supplied the necessary air bases. By 1982, the concept of an opposed, amphibious landing had long since disappeared under a crushing weight of economic argument. It was a concept which had gone with big carriers, a large surface fleet and a policy of almost worldwide power projection.

The SAS, with its undiluted interest in Third World conflict, was an eccentric exception to the Europeanisation of British defence thinking, tolerated because it added much to national prestige abroad without costing much money. If the regiment suffered any disadvantage in the impending Falklands conflict it was that of being no longer accustomed to working within and alongside larger formations of Nato's amphibious and naval forces in the defence of Europe. Yet despite the fact that the regiment was a prime tool for the job, it was offered merely two places in the initial British response to the crisis. The two men, both divers of G Squadron, joined 2 Royal Marine Special Boat Section at RAF Lyneham in response to a 3am telephone call.

Over the next two days, as the government determined that something had to be done, and swiftly, the SAS role grew. During that time the regiment took a vacuum cleaner through the Ministry of Defence's map department and politely squeezed out of British Antarctic Survey officials every drop of relevant information about the area. But still events were moving too fast for an orderly appraisal of what was to be done.

The Commanding Officer of 22 SAS, Lieutenant-Colonel Michael Rose, first learned of the invasion through a BBC news flash. He immediately told D Squadron to be ready to move. He then telephoned Brigadier Julian Thompson, in charge of 3 Commando Brigade – the spearhead of any British counter-attack – to offer the regiment's services in any forthcoming operation. The day after the invasion D Squadron was assembling at the regiment's headquarters. The following day – Sunday 4 April – the men were given a general briefing about the conditions they were likely to encounter in

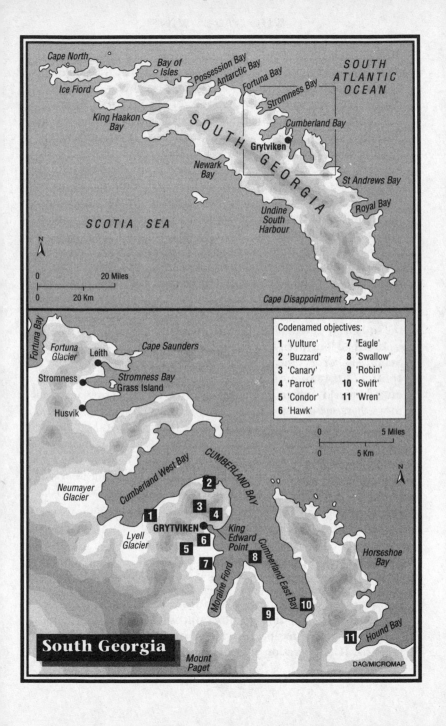

South Georgia

Codenamed objectives:

1 'Vulture'   7 'Eagle'
2 'Buzzard'   8 'Swallow'
3 'Canary'   9 'Robin'
4 'Parrot'   10 'Swift'
5 'Condor'   11 'Wren'
6 'Hawk'

DAG/MICROMAP

the Falklands. 'Just like the Brecon Beacons in a wet winter', was how one officer put it. Another pointed out that the Falklands lie as far south of the Equator as London is to the north. Little, if anything, was said about the infinitely more harsh Antarctic environment of South Georgia; within the space of three weeks the men of D Squadron would learn about that without having had the chance to acclimatise. When they left Britain they did not even know that South Georgia was one of their objectives. Their orders were simply to embark at Ascension Island in the Royal Navy's fleet auxiliary, *Fort Austin*, for an unspecified destination. But then, the SAS is in the business of action rather than acclimatisation.

That same afternoon the squadron's advance party – a small group from Squadron Headquarters – flew out of Brize Norton, Oxfordshire, bound for Ascension Island. The most southerly campaign in the history of warfare was beginning, exotic even by SAS standards. Within another twenty-four hours the rest of the squadron, fewer than 100 men, was also airborne. Their first landfall had long been a British military base leased to the United States Air Force. One of its advantages was total governmental control of communications between the island facilities and the outside world, which were denied to the civilian population on more than one occasion for security reasons. But the island also suffered from a disadvantage. It sits in the centre of the Atlantic just ten degrees south of the Equator and enjoys a warm climate. The SAS and other special forces were going to have to go to war in the wet cold of the Falklands or the numbing blizzards of South Georgia. Ascension was a good place to get away from before it made everyone soft.

Operation 'Paraquat' begins

It was several days before the squadron, commanded by Major Cedric Delves, was able to move out with a battle fleet tailor-made for the rapid recapture of the former whaling base of South Georgia. The operation was originally codenamed 'Parakeet', and was then changed to 'Paraquet' and sometimes, jokingly, to 'Paraquat', a weed-killer. The details of the operation were revealed to those involved only after they had sailed from Ascension Island. While still waiting for this embarkation Delves was ordered to detach just one troop, a force of approximately 25 men, to sail on the mission. He persuaded the Royal Navy to include the whole squadron because, as one of them explained, 'We didn't want to miss a scrap', even if no one knew yet exactly where the scrap was going to happen. One reason for the delay – a matter of three days, during which the squadron lived in a disused school hall – was that Paraquet was already planned in London as a joint affair, with M Company of 42 Royal Marine Commando under the overall direction of Major Guy Sheridan. Sheridan's Royal Marine rank equated with that of an Army lieutenant-colonel.

M Company, about 150 men, is a colourful unit. Its nickname, 'The Mighty Munch', derives from some flamboyant nocturnal activities of an earlier generation during a night out in Singapore. On 9 April, the day the Munch arrived by air, the SAS Squadron embarked in *Fort Austin* and the battle fleet put to sea. It included the destroyer *Antrim*, the frigate *Plymouth*, the fleet auxiliaries *Fort Austin* and *Tidespring*. Also waiting, thousands of miles to the south, was the Royal Navy's Antarctic survey ship *Endurance*, whose captain was one of the few people to hoist warning cones about the forthcoming crisis. Since the Argentine intrusion into South Georgia in March, *Endurance* had hung about in the South Atlantic, conducting a delicate Intelligence war.

Guy Sheridan's assets – his assault force – included about 25 men of 2 Special Boat Section, Royal Marines, as well as the Munch and D Squadron. The SBS has long historical links with the SAS of which, for some years during the Second World War, it was part. Like David Stirling's SAS it was a surviving fragment of General Bob Laycock's disbanded Middle East commando force, specialising in attacks from the sea by canoe and submarine. After 1945, as an élite element of the Royal Marines, the SBS evolved as a maritime and beach reconnaissance unit as well as a force specialising in underwater demolition. During post-war years it had found fewer opportunities than the SAS to practise its skills in operational conditions. True, it had been active in Borneo, Aden, the Gulf and Northern Ireland, in small numbers. The policy decision to avoid all opposed amphibious landings and to discard contingency plans requiring beach-storming had called into question, in some minds, the point of having an SBS at all. In fact it had, and has, a clear-cut place in British defence policy, through which it must concentrate almost exclusively on a potential war in Europe, the 'Priority One' task. This role has deprived the SBS of some of the valuable experience acquired by the SAS elsewhere. In recent years the SBS had played an offensive role as 'enemy' forces in NATO exercises in northern Norway and elsewhere. It had also been given the job of protecting Britain's North Sea oil installations from terrorism. In a sense it was living from hand to mouth, apart from a tiny handful of men working on ultra-secret operations not discussed here. Relations between the modern SAS and SBS during the South Atlantic conflict were to vary from the fraternal to the fratricidal.

The glacier war

As a preliminary to the recapture of South Georgia – a prize much cherished by a politically embarrassed British government – Sheridan and Delves decided that a covert reconnaissance of Argentine positions be carried out on 14 April. Patrols by the submarine *Conqueror* and an RAF Victor found no trace of the enemy's navy. The approach looked good. Delves proposed that D Squadron's mountain troop land on the Fortuna Glacier west of Leith and proceed along the coast via Husvik and Stromness, to Leith itself. Meanwhile 2 SBS would go ashore at Hound Bay to reach Grytviken by way of the Moraine Fiord. Grytviken was the primary objective. On 12 April the SBS men, together with D Squadron's mountain troop, transferred by helicopter to the *Endurance*. Here, for the first time, SAS soldiers began to acquire firm information about the conditions in which they would have to fight. An earlier Falklands brief had said of those islands, 'Winter temperatures are similar to those in Great Britain, but the summer mean is more in keeping with that of Scotland.' This homely analogy did not hold good for South Georgia, the gateway to Antarctica, at the threshold of winter when downslope, katabatic winds propel blizzards at a malevolent 100mph. Mountain Troop had a new 'boss', a young officer recruited from the Green Howards only three months before. Captain (Gavin) John Hamilton was an accomplished climber who had already twice led his troop to the top of Mount Kenya. The approach to the target in South Georgia was essentially a mountaineering problem. The overall task, however, was a military one in an Antarctic environment. Hamilton and his men approached the job with professional military detachment.

Plans of obvious target areas – the settlements at Grytviken, Leith, Stromness and Husvik – as well as the British Antarctic Survey station at King Edward Point were rapidly produced. Maps of the entire operational area were photocopied after a grid had been agreed with the Royal Marines and superimposed upon it. Two SAS troopers worked round the clock drawing finely detailed street and building plans of the five settlements, from original plans provided by *Endurance*'s hydrographer. On the map of Leith, where the original (and illegal) group of Argentine 'scrap-metal' men were thought to be based still, the relevant map noted: 'Red 17 likely to be occupied by "scrappies".' Area 'Red 21' was the hospital. At Stromness even the piggery was marked as such. At Grytviken the British Antarctic Survey's Discovery House – now occupied by Argentine soldiers – was charted room by room. Such geographical details were backed up by carefully drawn moon tables. It was a cool, yet stunning display of the care taken by ordinary SAS soldiers preparing to risk their lives, and the very opposite of recklessness. All the detailed plans were photocopied aboard *Endurance* and a copy was provided for virtually every member of the squadron.

These painstaking preparations reflected an assumption that the main threat to the patrol's survival would come from the Argentine garrison rather than from the environment of South Georgia. Expert advice about the Fortuna Glacier itself was mixed. Few people had first-hand experience to draw upon. The explorer Shackleton had traversed it many years before. It had proved an extraordinarily hard and dangerous journey. Some in the British Antarctic Survey team aboard *Endurance* argued that the glacier was impassable at that time of year because of the weather and numerous crevasses. As one BAS meteorologist puts it, 'The glacier is a wind tunnel hemmed in by mountains and the winds are unpredictable.' Lieutenant Bob Veal, RN, who had led a recent climbing expedition in South Georgia, was against the SAS route. By contrast, a distinguished military climber, a veteran of Nuptse and Everest, who also knew South Georgia, thought the approach was feasible. At this stage, D Squadron was not required to watch Grytviken. That job had been allocated to an SBS team which was to be withdrawn after much effort, frustration and little success. The SAS was interested initially in the other settlements and there was only one approach to these from the enemy's 'blind' side, and that was from the glacier. The route made military sense. Delves and his team decided that the reconnaissance from that side was worth the try. With luck and a fair wind, it could come off . . . In the event, the glacier was to prove a more implacable opponent than the Argentines.

Before leaving *Endurance*, Hamilton's team collected more suitable equipment than the Brecons/Falklands gear it had picked up on its hurried departure from England. Skis, snow-shoes, pulks (man-hauled sledges) and climbing equipment were issued. For good measure this was topped up with lightweight sleeping-bags and waterproof 'bivvy' bags to cover them, and more warm clothing. As things turned out, Mountain Troop was going to need every stitch.

Hamilton's men now moved base again by helicopter to the destroyer *Antrim*, affectionately known as 'the grey ghost' because, as one crewman put it, 'No one knows where the hell we are.' Already aboard *Antrim* was one other D Squadron troop and a compact Squadron Headquarters consisting of Major Delves, a staff sergeant, a senior signals specialist, and Delves's second-in-command, Sergeant-Major Lawrence Gallagher, BEM. Gallagher had risen the hard way, through fourteen years' continuous SAS service. The plans were discussed, the briefings gone over yet again. Hamilton's whole troop would land by helicopter well inland at a point 1800 feet up the glacier to the right flank of the most westerly coastal settlement, Leith. One patrol under Hamilton himself was to set up an observation post above the neighbouring whaling stations of Stromness and Husvik. A second, led by Staff Sergeant Philip Currass, QGM, was to watch Leith – the nearest target – while Sergeant Sid Davidson would command a third patrol which had the delicate job of finding potential beach or helicopter landing zones on the coast of Fortuna Bay. Currass had joined the SAS from the Royal Army Medical Corps ten years before. Davidson had nine years' SAS service. After they left the helicopters they would have to move down the Fortuna Glacier and cross the rubble of terminal moraine – silt, rock and sand – before starting work.

At noon on 21 April three Wessex helicopters attempted to place the troop of 16 men on the glacier. Violent wind combined with dense snow to create 'white-out' conditions. Even for someone standing still on a mountain, as recreational skiers have discovered, a severe white-out can distort the sense of balance as well as direction. In a helicopter the problem is worse: the horizon (when the pilot gets a glimpse of it) jerks up and down like a badly projected film. Twice the helicopters tried to land the troop and twice they had to return to *Antrim*. At the third attempt the men bundled out, some thinking that almost anything would be better than this airborne version of blind man's buff. They were wrong. Things could get worse.

The soldiers landed in a 50mph wind which blew a scouring spindrift of snow into their faces and equipment. Very soon this fine spray blocked the feed trays of the troop's general-purpose machine-guns ('gimpies') and then turned to ice, rendering the weapons inoperable. There was nothing to be done except to get on with it and that is what Mountain Troop did. Sergeant John ('Lofty') Arthy, a Himalayan climber 'who could make frostbite sound exciting', led the arrowhead formation, followed by Corporal Paul Bunker, a free-faller as well as a climber, and another corporal. Each soldier carried about 80 pounds on his body in Bergen rucksacks and as belt kit, and had to take his turn in hauling the pulk. The troop had four of these vehicles and each weighed about 200 pounds.

A choice crevasse

The leaders moved cautiously, probing the ice for signs of a crevasse. One mistake in this situation would be one too many. Yet among determined souls, even a crevasse is not invariably hostile. Hamilton's troop, having covered less than half a mile in an exhausting, five-hour march during which it was halted time and again by white-outs, pushed back by wind and impeded by the inertia of the pulks, found an outcrop in the glacier and a small crevasse which offered some shelter from the relentless wind. There was no time to rest. They would not survive the Antarctic night, which was almost upon them, unless they obtained cover of some sort. To dig a hole was out of the question since there was insufficient snow covering the glacier's impenetrable ice. So Hamilton's men now attempted to erect two small green Arctic tents, each designed to accommodate two men. Even in the comparative shelter of the crevasse the tent poles snapped in the wind and one tent was torn from their hands to be swept away over the mountain. Five men, with sleeping-bags, contrived to insert themselves inside the second tent. They kept their shelter erect, after a fashion, by sitting against the side walls. Every hour, or less, one man had to leave the tent to remove driving snow which, ironically, now threatened to bury them. What of the rest of the troop, those who were outside? 'They kipped under the sledges or stayed in their bivvy bags with their boots on', said one survivor later. 'We all had an uncomfortable night.' This was characteristic SAS understatement. Aboard *Antrim* the anemometer recorded a near storm force eleven wind, but the precise wind strength on the Fortuna Glacier that night was anyone's guess. By the following morning it was clear that Mountain Troop would not survive another twenty-four hours. Reluctantly, the men sent a signal asking to be lifted out.

The weather ruled out any hope of a rescue mission before 10.50am. At 1.30pm three Wessex helicopters – one bringing with it an anxious and determined squadron commander, Major Delves – did reach the troop but then only during a brief, fifteen-minute period of clear weather and aided by both green smoke and a search/rescue radio beacon (SARBE) carried by the soldiers. In continuing high winds which made flight near the ground very hazardous, the helicopters lifted off the men and most of their equipment. Of the three machines, an anti-submarine Mk 3 Wessex fitted with sophisticated navigational gear was leading the convoy with Delves on board. The flight plan was simple enough: follow the glacier down to a landfall, carry on out to sea and return to the ships . . . You couldn't miss it . . . But the capricious, volatile weather of South Georgia was not going to let the SAS off the hook that easily. Within moments of departure, as the Mk 3 swung down in a cautious right-hand descent of about 250 feet, the Mk 5 (call-sign, 'Yankee Foxtrot') following it encountered a white-out. The pilot had just enough time to pull up the nose of his aircraft before it hit the ice at 30 knots. The tail rotor struck the ground first and the machine whirled out of control before skidding to a halt on its left-hand side. Of the seven men on board – six SAS soldiers and the pilot – only one, Corporal Bunker, was hurt. Despite a back injury he climbed out of the main door along with the others. 'The good news,' said one survivor, 'was that the door was on the starboard side and therefore unobstructed.'

The other two helicopters hover-taxied to the crash site and the survivors were divided between them. Dumping fuel and equipment to lighten their load, both helicopters took off in unison ten minutes later. The soldiers now carried only their weapons and belt kit containing ammunition, water and the most basic survival gear. Their Bergen rucksacks, holding food, sleeping-bags, fuel and much else, had to be left.

Again the Mk 3 Wessex, affectionately known as 'Humphrey', led the way. Once again the view from the following aircraft, 'Yankee Alpha', was blotted out within seconds by a pancake of snow. Yankee Alpha hit a ridge of ice running parallel to the edge of the glacier. On impact, the helicopter slewed round and tipped onto her right side. Yet again, miraculously, there were no serious injuries.

Delves, the squadron commander, squatting over a machine-gun in the open doorway of Humphrey, signalled to his fellow passengers that Yankee Alpha was down. At that stage there was nothing the Royal Navy pilot, Lieutenant-Commander Ian Stanley, could do except note the crash site and return to *Antrim* as quickly as possible. Three helicopters had set out on the rescue mission that morning. It was a sombre return for the lone survivor. Back on board the destroyer, the rescued men were taken to an emergency medical post set up in the officers' wardroom. With a half-load of fuel, Humphrey was flown back to the glacier by Lieutenant-Commander Stanley yet again, carrying blankets and medical supplies.

At the first attempt, the rescue team were beaten back by the weather. News of the operation as it now stood – two helicopters lost and most of an entire SAS troop in dire trouble – dealt a body blow to the morale of Downing Street and the Ministry of Defence. For a time, the credibility of Britain's capacity to retake its lost territory seemed finely balanced. The public was not allowed to know what was happening.

A senior Ministry of Defence official described his reactions to author Robert Harris: 'You can imagine how we felt. This was the first real action of the war and it was a terrible reversal. It provoked hideous memories of the American helicopter disaster when they tried to rescue the hostages in Iran. The accident was so sensitive that it was agreed not even to raise it at the morning meeting of the Chiefs of Staff committee. With negotiations with Argentina still in progress, it was thought that news of the disaster might change the mood of the country and the House of Commons. It might even lead to the recall of the task force . . .'

This last view was possibly exaggerated, but for Lord Lewin also, as he later admitted, it was one of the worst moments of the campaign.

By now, those stranded by the second crash had extricated themselves from the wreck, with some difficulty, and were 'making ourselves comfortable'. That is to say, they foraged a survival tent from the wreck, and much else of value from the scene of the first crash. The faithful Mk 3 Wessex, with Ian Stanley still at the controls, refuelled and immediately returned to the glacier. The men on the ice were able to report that they were in good shape and that there were no serious casualties. This information they had to relay by radio. At ground level, visibility was so poor that even Stanley was forced to postpone his latest rescue attempt. Later the same day he flew his seventh sortie over the glacier within forty-eight hours. He landed and watched, apparently impassively, as more and more bodies were crammed into the tiny helicopter. Including his navigator and himself, there were seventeen people on board. This anti-submarine Wessex is designed to carry five people.

With its single Bristol Gnome engine at full throttle and rotors creaking under the strain, the helicopter clawed its way into the sky. But with such an overload there could be no question of a normally cautious, hover-to-land approach to *Antrim*'s tiny flight deck. 'It was a one-shot straight-in landing like the descent of a brick dung store', said one participant later. All the survivors were now assembled and examined. The only evident injuries were a deep gash on Currass's cheekbone, which was stitched; Corporal Bunker's feet (which were suffering from frost nip) and his back, which was bruised. Next, the men of Mountain Troop invited themselves into *Antrim*'s wardroom (the officers' mess) to toast Ian Stanley and his crew and thank them for their bravery. Such behaviour by Royal Navy ratings would be unthinkable. For the SAS soldier, irrespective of rank, it was an instinctive and spontaneous expression of gratitude not to be blocked by naval protocol. (For his flying skill, the pilot of Humphrey, Lieutenant-Commander Ian Stanley, RN, was awarded the Distinguished Service Order. Humphrey now resides on permanent display in the Fleet Air Arm Museum at Royal Naval Air Station, Yeovilton.)

Next day, the Squadron tried again. This time it was the turn of the boat troop to set up viable observation posts. Delves and his team, re-examining the problem overnight, were now in no doubt that the environment was a greater hazard than the enemy, and that a brazen, frontal approach from the sea must be attempted. Five Gemini inflatable boats fitted with 40hp Johnson outboard engines were prepared for the attempt. As a precaution against any technical failure at the last moment, the engines were taken off the boats and started up on test rigs on *Antrim*'s deck. Once the engines were thoroughly warmed up they were re-fitted to the boats. The Geminis, each carrying three men, were then to set off to watch Leith and Husvik whaling stations from Grass Island in neighbouring Stromness Bay. That was the plan.

At the outset, this latest gamble looked good. *Antrim* was lying in Stromness Bay, in darkness, calm water and fine weather, a mere 800 yards from Grass Island. Astonishingly, in view of the care taken to nurse the engines, three of them would not start when the boats were launched. Boat troop now faced an exceedingly tricky choice: to hold off until the engines were serviceable (missing a tide and losing at least twenty-four valuable operational hours) or to use the two functional craft to tow the other three. After a quick discussion between the squadron commander, Major Delves, and the boat troop leader they decided to proceed immediately. They cast off and glided away from the big, grey destroyer into the darkness. Of the two functional Geminis, one was towing two of its disabled companions while the second towed the other.

The main characteristic of South Georgia's weather is its unpredictability, and its unusual knack of generating gale force winds in one spot only five miles or so from an area of total calm. This is partly an effect of the 'wind tunnel' of the Fortuna and other glaciers, decanting a powerful downhill airflow into a local sea area. Just such a wind now hit the Geminis with the force of a torpedo; part of a DSO citation for Delves refers to 100mph katabatic gusts blowing during this part of the operation. Under the impact of the sudden storm, the lines of two of the disabled craft parted and they were scattered into the night.

Three Geminis reached their objective. Of the two others one was found drifting, hours later, by the indefatigable Ian Stanley. Before they were winched into the helicopter one of the three men on board, a corporal, sank the Gemini to ensure that it would not be washed ashore to compromise the operation. The occupants of the second boat, meanwhile, were in an even more desperate situation. They were being carried past the last landfall for thousands of miles when they managed to wade ashore at Cape Saunders. After surviving on the ice for three days, they concluded that it was now safe to announce their position by SARBE. They were right. By now South Georgia had been recaptured and they were retrieved, still fit to fight, by helicopter. Meanwhile Delves, like other SAS squadron commanders before him, could only speculate about the fate of his missing men, and sweat.

While the SAS was attempting to set up its reconnaissance on Grass Island, the Royal Marine SBS team was about to make similar efforts elsewhere. Soon after midnight on 23 April, St George's Day, the marines landed at a spot known as Sorling Valley on Cumberland East Bay. The SBS team's hopes of crossing the bay in Geminis were destroyed when glacier ice, blown into the bay by strong north-west winds, punctured the inflated hulls of the Geminis. That evening the team was plucked off the bay by helicopter and brought back to the ships.

In the event, it was the re-insertion of this team which accidentally started a chain of events culminating in the Argentine surrender. The Argentines knew something was afoot. Radio signals intercepted by *Endurance* included at least one Argentine message suggesting that the British had put a team ashore. This signal the Argentines subsequently cancelled. They certainly knew also of the presence offshore of the mini-task force. Using civil Boeing 707 jets flying from the mainland, 1200 miles away, the Argentines were conducting regular reconnaissance of the area. One of these aircraft passed over South Georgia on 24 April, and on that day a deadly game of hide-and-seek began. The task force, aware that a submarine was in the area, temporarily withdrew to deeper, safer waters where it was joined by the frigate *Brilliant*. The obstinate *Endurance*, meanwhile, did not withdraw but lay quietly in Hound Bay, one peninsula away from Grytviken. Most of the British ships returned to South Georgia during the night of 24/25 April,

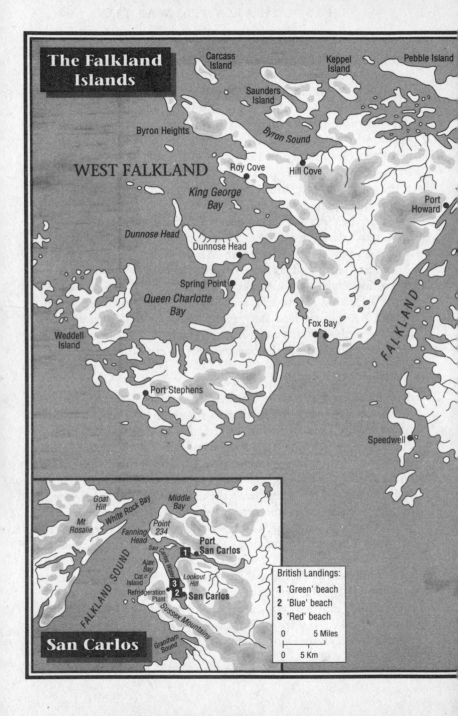

The Falkland Islands

Carcass Island

Keppel Island

Pebble Island

Saunders Island

Byron Heights

Byron Sound

WEST FALKLAND

Roy Cove

Hill Cove

Port Howard

King George Bay

Dunnose Head

Dunnose Head

Spring Point

Queen Charlotte Bay

Fox Bay

FALKLAND

Weddell Island

Port Stephens

Speedwell

San Carlos

Goat Hill

Middle Bay

White Rock Bay

Mt Rosalie

Point 234

Port San Carlos

Fanning Head

San Carlos Water

Ajax Bay

Cat Island

Lookout Hill

Refrigeration Plant

San Carlos

FALKLAND SOUND

Sussex Mountains

Grantham Sound

British Landings:
1 'Green' beach
2 'Blue' beach
3 'Red' beach

0   5 Miles

0   5 Km

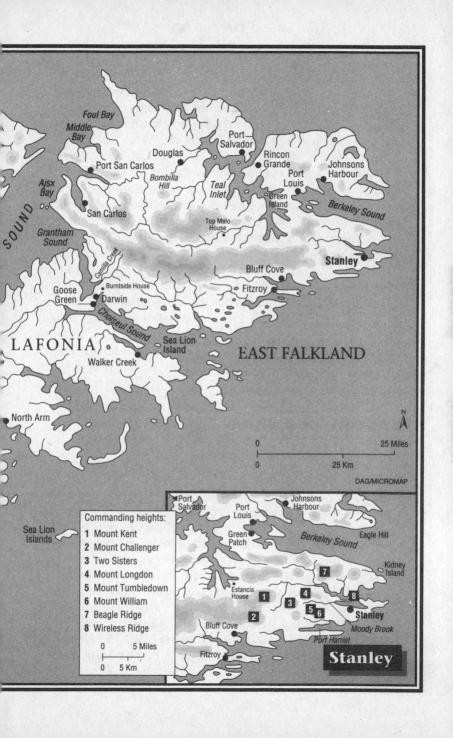

Foul Bay
Middle Bay
Port San Carlos
Douglas
Port Salvador
Rincon Grande
Port Louis
Johnsons Harbour

Ajsx Bay
San Carlos
Bombilla Hill
Teal Inlet
Green Island
Berkeley Sound

SOUND
Grantham Sound
Camilla Creek
Top Malo House
Stanley

Goose Green
Burntside House
Darwin
Bluff Cove
Fitzroy

Choiseul Sound
Sea Lion Island

LAFONIA
Walker Creek
EAST FALKLAND

North Arm

N

| 0 | | 25 Miles |

| 0 | | 25 Km |

DAG/MICROMAP

Sea Lion Islands

Commanding heights:

1 Mount Kent
2 Mount Challenger
3 Two Sisters
4 Mount Longdon
5 Mount Tumbledown
6 Mount William
7 Beagle Ridge
8 Wireless Ridge

0   5 Miles

0   5 Km

Port Salvador
Port Louis
Johnsons Harbour
Green Patch
Berkeley Sound
Eagle Hill
Kidney Island

7
Estancia House
1   **4**
3   **5** **6**
8
2
Stanley
Bluff Cove
Moody Brook
Port Harriet
Fitzroy

Stanley

leaving *Tidespring*, with M Company of 42 Royal Marine Commando, 200 miles to the north.

By a happy coincidence the Argentine submarine *Santa Fe* was tying up in Grytviken harbour that night, unseen by the British, to discharge marine reinforcements for the Argentine garrison. At first light on the 25th the *Santa Fe* put to sea to hunt down *Endurance* or any other Royal Navy vessel in the area . . . and Lieutenant-Commander Stanley, flying his Wessex, was returning to the *Antrim* after dropping the SBS men a few miles up the same inlet at Moraine Fiord. Glancing down at the cold, slate-grey waters of Cumberland Bay, he saw a submarine sitting vulnerably on the surface. Stanley promptly straddled the vessel with depth-charges which caused just enough damage to make it unsafe for the submarine to dive. Soon afterwards, alerted by Stanley, other helicopters – a Wasp from *Endurance* and a Lynx from the frigate *Brilliant* – followed up the first attack with a salvo of missiles and machine-gun fire which punched hundreds of holes through the *Santa Fe*'s conning tower. Leaking oil and listing, the submarine ran for the safety of the British Antarctic Survey station at Grytviken.

The decisive moment

The submarine's unexpected return was accompanied by confusion and panic ashore. As shore-based machine-guns fired long bursts towards the British helicopters, the submarine crew was seen fleeing for cover ashore. Delves, commanding D Squadron, and his Royal Marine colleague, Guy Sheridan, concluded that this was as good a time as any to move ashore in force and seize Grytviken. True, the assault force available was greatly outnumbered by the opposition, but as one observer of the operation explained, 'There comes a moment in any contact or battle when a decisive moment is reached. Delves and Sheridan felt that moment was at hand and whoever seized the initiative would prevail. The Argentines were already demoralised and had no way of taking any sort of initiative. So in spite of the odds against us, we were really in the commanding position.' The odds, none the less, were a formidable two-to-one against the attackers. The Marines' M Company was still 200 miles away aboard *Tidespring*, while marines in the frigate *Plymouth* could not be lifted ashore by the troop-carrying Wessex helicopter because *Plymouth*'s tiny flight deck was not large enough for the Wessex. So the only manpower instantly available for a landing 'in force' was aboard *Antrim*. Most of them were SAS soldiers.

Two troops, one led by Hamilton, plus a headquarters element including Delves and Sergeant-Major Gallagher, hastily put their gear together. This included Nato's new, light-weight anti-tank missile, Milan, as well as the general-purpose machine-gun. Other troops available for the assault included *Antrim*'s own Royal Marine detachment of ten men, a few of M Company, an SBS team and Royal Marine mortar and reconnaissance sections. The total fighting force was just 75 men, equal to about half the Argentine garrison. Thirty minutes before the assault a Wasp helicopter put ashore Captain Chris Brown, a Royal Artillery officer from 148 Battery, whose men are specialist Naval Gunfire Support Forward Observers, plus an escort. The unwieldy title, NGSFO, conceals adventurous commando-trained spirits who took their chances time and again during the South Atlantic conflict to direct the Navy's guns from covert positions in enemy held territory. Just before the Falklands campaign 148 Battery was threatened with dis-bandment as an economy measure.

John Hamilton's men were next to leave, the first patrol being led by Hamilton himself. They flew in the now familiar Wessex Mk 3 from *Antrim* to a flat, grassy area known as Hestesletten, two kilometres south-east of the BAS station. As soon as they had landed, the troops and Squadron Headquarters formed a tight defensive perimeter to await the arrival of Sheridan and his mortar team. From just over the hill, which rose away from their position, towards Grytviken, they could already hear the crump of falling shells as the 4.5in guns of *Antrim* and *Plymouth* put on an intimidating demonstration of firepower. The shells fell all round the Argentine positions, as intended, without hitting any building or causing a single casualty. But the message was obvious: surrender or die.

As the Marine Commandos arrived, Delves and his men moved off, up the scree and over the top. From this position, Delves saw what looked like white flags around the Argentine positions. By radio he advised Sheridan, still in his helicopter, that D Squadron would go forward to investigate, a signal which Sheridan acknowledged. It has been suggested, erroneously, that there was a 'race' between Delves and Sheridan to be first into Grytviken. In fact, what followed was not a headlong dash by the SAS, but an ordered 'advance to contact' in which likely targets were engaged. Hamilton's patrol opened fire at least twice. To the soldiers' left, as they moved forward, loomed Brown Mountain, from which a spur ran across their line of advance, and down to the coast. On top of the mountain a suspected enemy position was hit with a Milan missile fired by Hamilton personally. The 'whoosh' of the Milan was followed by a resonant clang as the missile scored a direct hit . . . on an ancient piece of angle-iron. Soon afterwards, about 800 metres ahead near the coast, the patrol saw brown, balaclava-clad heads moving in the tussock grass. These were hit by SAS machine-gun fire and, at Hamilton's request, by shells from naval guns offshore. The troop, satisfied that a possible threat had been removed, continued to advance towards the ridge, still well ahead of the Royal Marines, only to discover that the 'enemy' in the tussock grass was a tribe of seven or eight elephant seals. 'They were now somewhat the worse for wear', one SAS soldier said later. Another SAS team saw figures moving, then lie still in the tussocks. The recumbent 'enemy' this time proved to be penguins, sleeping contentedly.

From the top of Brown Mountain ridge the SAS men had a panoramic view of King Edward Cove, with Grytviken nestling ahead in the most sheltered corner. They had now been ashore for just over two hours. Outside Discovery House – an L-shaped building erected in 1925 to commemorate Captain Scott – the Argentine flag still flew. But every building nearby was decorated with white sheets. Hamilton's men could also see the submarine *Santa Fe*, berthed alongside the jetty and listing like a harpooned whale. But not a single human being was in sight.

After fifteen minutes, as the Royal Marines occupied positions on the ridge, the Argentine troops finally emerged from Discovery House and formed up alongside their flag. By now the SAS men led by Delves were scurrying towards them along the shoreline of King Edward Cove. On they came, past the wreck of an Argentine Puma helicopter shot down by the defending British marines three weeks earlier, through the deserted whaling station and into the area around Discovery House. There, as Hamilton's troop spread out round the enemy, pointedly covering them with Armalites and machine-guns, the garrison proffered the surrender of Grytviken to Delves. But first, Squadron Sergeant-Major Gallagher lowered the Argentine flag and produced from his battle smock a Union Jack which he ran up in its place, smiling broadly as he did so. Major Sheridan arrived by helicopter to complete, as senior officer, formalities of surrender, and his Royal Marines followed an hour later to take care of the prisoners. (Some weeks later another SAS officer would negotiate the surrender of the Falklands and, again, would leave it to others to complete the formalities.)

Meanwhile there was some urgent cleaning-up to be done around Grytviken. A few of the prisoners who spoke English could not understand how the SAS had avoided casualties. 'You have just walked through a minefield', they explained. Corporal Paul Bunker and Sergeant 'Lofty' Arthy took their Argentine guides over the ground to defuse the mines, and mark their positions. The mines had been sited to oppose a beach landing opposite Discovery House and to protect three mortar pits and two machine-gun positions on a slope behind it, facing Cumberland East Bay. The SAS men were not unduly impressed. The mortar pits were half-full of water and weapons of various calibres had been thrown down haphazardly. From nearby Shackleton House Hamilton's men recovered a large haul of automatic pistols, revolvers and carbines including Israeli-made Uzis. Most of these, like those in the trenches outside, were still loaded and poorly maintained.

Next morning two troops from D Squadron together with an SBS team flew by helicopter into Leith, backed up by *Plymouth* and *Endurance*. After much Argentinian rhetoric about 'fighting to the last man', the Leith garrison – including Captain Alfredo Astiz, who was accused of torturing political prisoners in his own country – surrendered meekly. In London, the *Daily Mail*'s front page headline proclaimed in $1^1/_2$-inch lettering, 'MARINES RETAKE SOUTH GEORGIA'. Leaving M Company on guard, D Squadron was back aboard *Antrim* within 24 hours, and a day later moved by helicopter to the frigate *Brilliant*. It was now 28 April and the Squadron was bound for the Falklands.

Already however, the repercussions of the recapture of South Georgia were worldwide. As the DSO citation for *Antrim*'s captain, Brian Young, put it: 'The importance of this operation to the overall strategy of re-establishing British administration in the Falkland Islands . . . cannot be overstated . . .' In the South Atlantic, the main task force now had a base nearer to the Falklands than Ascension from which to stage future operations. Public opinion in Britain was given the encouragement of a near-bloodless victory, and backing for further bold action swept through the country like a charge of adrenalin. The Argentine government now faced, as never before, the prospect of a fight for the Falklands, and the American administration, having tried to maintain a neutral posture, at last came off the fence with promises of *matériel* (i.e., logistic and supply) support. In London, Prime Minister Margaret Thatcher, announcing the news in person in a chilly Downing Street, squashed all questions with the command, 'Rejoice! Rejoice!'

Strategic stress

While D Squadron was setting the pace in the South Atlantic – a blistering pace which it was to keep up throughout the campaign – SAS commanders elsewhere were working to add to that momentum. As a strategic force, answerable to the overall commander of military operations in London rather than to the local hierarchy in the immediate theatre of conflict, the SAS was expected to come up with its own ideas. Yet it had to be sufficiently flexible to fit into plans as they evolved both in London and within the task force at sea.

Being at the centre of things could be a mixed blessing. Several SAS soldiers, undergoing long-range pistol training in the US, hastily returned from that country bringing with them a supply of American Stinger missiles. The Stinger, a shoulder-fired anti-aircraft missile, has a longer range than its British equivalent, Blowpipe. More important, it is ten pounds lighter. In the battles to come, the numerical advantage enjoyed by the Argentine Air Force was to make any good, light SAM missile worth its weight in gold. On their arrival in Britain, the SAS team had not had time to move the missiles off the tarmac before they were intercepted by a group of senior military planners. All of these, it seemed, had their own ideas about the use of the weapon.

One of those summoned from the US was Staff Sergeant Paddy O'Connor of G Squadron. On his return to Hereford he was given twenty minutes to pack his Bergen before flying to the South Atlantic. He jumped off the Hercules tailgate into the sea to join the task force, murmuring, 'I still don't believe it . . .' It was intended that O'Connor train the SAS soldiers to use Stinger, but his untimely death meant that the men of D Squadron received no instruction in the weapon which, nevertheless, they used to good effect in East Falkland.

An even more puzzled SAS team was a free-fall troop destined to be parachuted into East Falkland to carry out the first reconnaissance patrols there. These men, brought peremptorily under the control of strategic planners outside the regiment, were flown 5000 miles to Ascension Island, only to be sent back to Britain again. They were never dropped into the war zone. The reason for this was that their transport, the RAF's Hercules, could not fly the 8000–mile return journey from Ascension Island to the Falklands without repeated in–flight refuelling. At that time, the Hercules were not equipped with the necessary probes. They were modified within a matter of days, but by the time this had been done the men of G Squadron with the amphibious task force at sea were almost within helicopter range of the islands. The planners now had to weigh the risk of incurring casualties by parachuting men into the windy Falklands against the perils facing helicopter crews obliged to fly 'blind' into enemy held territory. In the event, the men who drew the short straws were the Sea King helicopter crews of 846 Squadron, Royal Navy. This decision, ultimately, had to be a cold and professional one. At the very beginning of a covert reconnaissance mission, casualties, with their concomitant radio traffic and 'casevac' helicopter lifts, which could compromise the operation, were more likely to be incurred by paratroops.

The neatest and most successful long-range initiative taken by the regiment concerned communications. Throughout the conflict – witness subsequent complaints from war correspondents attached to the task force – 'comms' remained a nagging problem for the strategists working in the Kafkaesque underground Fleet Headquarters, the 'Hole' at Northwood in Middlesex. Because of the great distances involved the only rapid and secure link was by satellite. Only one of these, Marisat (for 'maritime satellite') was available to the Royal Navy whose planning, for many years, had been geared to a crisis in the North Atlantic. Traffic on the only available satellite soon swamped the system, and prolonged delays ensued. This was acutely embarrassing since, for domestic and international political reasons, the need to show that the deployment of armed force was being orchestrated from London, was held to be at least as important as successful prosecution of the conflict on the ground. Yet there were times when the SAS, to the puzzlement and occasional pique of some in Whitehall, appeared to have tactical information from the front which was not several hours behind events. Former members of the regiment are still coy as to how this apparent telepathy was achieved. It is believed that it might have been done through the use of miniaturised satellite communications.

Only once do the strategic discussions in London seem to have affected – and then only temporarily – the main thrust of

SAS operations in the field. The departure of D Squadron from England to Ascension Island on 5 April was followed a day later by a regimental headquarters led by the Commanding Officer of 22 SAS, Lieutenant-Colonel Michael Rose, OBE, QGM, and by G Squadron. The HQ team worked aboard HMS *Fearless*, an assault craft designed also to act as a front-line HQ for battles ashore. Rose's team was part of a planning cadre known as R (for Reconnaissance) Group. Ostensibly, R Group would plan the first operations ashore including the initial Falklands landing, subject to the endorsement of its plans by London. The R Group was an integral part of 3 Commando Brigade Headquarters, the land forces HQ, headed by Brigadier Julian Thompson, Royal Marines.

As the Falklands crisis developed the British government orchestrated its pressure on Argentina in an endeavour to avoid a land battle. For land battle, with the casualties it implied, would generate much bitterness and make the long-term diplomatic problem of resolving the future of the Falklands that much more difficult. Such orchestration first required a battle fleet to recover South Georgia, which is not part of the Falklands and is, unquestionably, British territory by any yardstick. This was followed by a larger Royal Navy battle group to enforce a maritime blockade round the Falklands, adding to the pressure without necessarily causing bloodshed. The final option, the use of an amphibious group to reoccupy the Falklands by force, meant keeping that group in reserve on Ascension Island until diplomacy – notably an American shuttle headed by Secretary of State Haig – was exhausted. To commit the amphibious assault force, including *Fearless* and the SAS commander, Rose, to the South Atlantic prematurely could have been unnecessarily provocative. It would, at the least, have exposed the soldiers to greater hardship and uncertainty, and reduced their fitness to fight. The amphibious assault group therefore remained at Ascension Island for about two weeks after the Falklands battle fleet had sailed.

It is clear from other published accounts of the campaign that R Group, aboard *Fearless*, did not enjoy the unquestioning support of either the strategic planners at Northwood or the overall task force commander with the fleet, Rear-Admiral John Woodward. Northwood, for example, promoted the swift recapture of South Georgia as a separate venture from similar schemes prepared by R Group. Woodward, properly anxious about a possible submarine threat to the task force carriers *Hermes* and *Invincible*, put to sea with his battle group on 18 April taking with him most of the men of G Squadron aboard the Royal Fleet Auxiliary *Resource*. As the initial Falklands reconnaissance team, it was not surprising that they should go with this first wave rather than remain at Ascension with the amphibious assault group. But so unexpected was their departure that some of the squadron's vital equipment and manpower was left behind. On orders from Northwood one ship returned to the Ascension Island approaches so that the missing men and materials could be retrieved by helicopter. Meanwhile most of the squadron continued on their voyage south, basking in the sunshine and lulled by a holiday atmosphere aboard *Resource*. ('The wine,' one officer recalled fondly, 'was excellent . . . The atmosphere provided by the stewards very gay.')

During the last week of April, as the battle group bore down upon the Falklands, hopes of using the fleet as an instrument of diplomacy – a show of strength – broke down like a crumbling rock face under the boot of Argentine nationalism and obduracy. By the time the fleet arrived in the South Atlantic it is doubtful whether the Buenos Aires junta could have reached a peaceful settlement even had it wished. It was now trapped by the fury of the street mobs it had goaded with its own political rhetoric devoted to liberation of the Malvinas. So what had started in Britain as a knee-jerk response (even if for good reason, in a just cause) now became a deadly jigsaw puzzle from which several vital pieces were missing. One was the absence of sufficient air cover to repulse a determined, mass assault by the Argentine Air Force. It did not require psychic powers to realise that enemy air power combined with sea-skimming Exocet missiles posed a terrifying threat to Woodward's fleet. The necessary data was available to all in standard works of reference which made it clear that the Royal Navy had no weapon that could be relied upon to defeat the Exocet once it was within range.

Second only to this problem was the absence of hard information as to where in the Falklands the Argentines had concentrated their forces. Cloud cover over the islands rendered satellite reconnaissance data all but useless. In any case, Britain depended for this information on American sources, which meant a significant delay in relaying information to the task force by way of London. As the South Atlantic weather worsened with every day's approach to winter, the imperative need, if the Falklands were to be recovered by force, was for good, up-to-date reconnaissance. Without it any attempted landing could replicate the disaster of Gallipoli. The task of obtaining such information was a classic one for the SAS.

G Squadron goes in

From G Squadron, four four-man patrols went ashore in Sea King helicopters of 846 Naval Air Squadron in the early hours of 1 May. The next night another three patrols went in and the third night, yet another. Simultaneously the first six SBS teams began their task of exploring the most important bays and inlets to identify the most feasible invasion points. Yet the honour of being the first returning British serviceman ashore in the Falklands went – fortuitously – to a Captain Chris Brown from 148 Battery, RA. The first of May is historically memorable as the day on which 'the Empire struck back'. An RAF Vulcan bomber, which had been consigned to the breaker's yard not long before, flew 3500 miles from Ascension Island and back – a 15-hour trip – to bomb Port Stanley at 4am. The attack was reinforced with strafing runs by Royal Navy Sea Harriers and a bombardment of airfield installations by the 4.5in guns of the fleet. Brown was spotting for the Navy's guns from a hovering Lynx helicopter which was obliged to make a forced-landing after being hit by enemy fire. He was on the ground for about ten minutes before the Lynx left, with him on board. The SAS and SBS patrols were obliged to remain ashore rather longer. After a flight of 120 miles from HMS *Hermes*, the teams were placed under cover of darkness up to 20 miles from their final observations posts. First came the men, weapons in hand, boots squelching in the cold, soaking peat, then the Bergen rucksacks, backs buckling under the 100lb load. Welcome to the Falklands . . . The helicopters lifted away, engine noise drowned by the crooning South Atlantic wind, and they were alone in enemy territory. The ration packs were sufficient for about a week, but they were going to have to last longer. It was the familiar SAS problem of weight versus mobility. One patrol, lying low above Port Stanley, was not to be relieved for 26 tense days.

Of these first patrols one overlooked Port Stanley proper and a second, the approaches to the capital. Elsewhere, other patrols watched Bluff Cove (where the tragedy of the bomb attack on *Sir Galahad* and *Sir Tristram* was to occur after D–Day) and Darwin/Goose Green. On West Falkland one team kept an eye on Fox Bay; another, on Port Howard. The siting of these OPs was based upon the meagre Intelligence available from Royal Marines repatriated after the British surrender; from civilians who chose not to live under occupation and from two RAF technicians who wandered about Port Stanley airfield freely for several days after the invasion a month before.

Each patrol's precise landing site was chosen by the team's leader after discussion with his squadron commander, the Intelligence team and the Royal Navy's helicopter pilot. Such discussions, based on the meagre information to be gleaned from a 1:50,000 map, usually took place in the women's lavatory of the *Resource*. This was the only spare room on board and it became G Squadron's floating operations room. The team then flew on the basis of this intelligent guesswork to a spot where, hopefully, the enemy was not. The first part of the route into East Falkland, established as a 'safe' road and never varied much, was from the north across Bombilla Hill and thereafter along any convenient valley, but it was crucial that the outgoing patrol should know precisely where it had been set down. Its navigation on foot thereafter would depend upon a correct initial fix.

Such pinpoint accuracy and, indeed, the whole insertion operation was helped by new equipment which, for once, merited the overworked description, 'Magic kit'. American passive night goggles, issued experimentally to some of the Sea Kings' crews just before they left Britain, enabled them to fly in absolute darkness with complete accuracy and confidence.

With the Sea Kings' departure back to the security of HMS *Hermes*, the isolation of the patrols became acute. The nearest British ground forces in any strength were still hundreds of miles away at sea or 3500 miles distant on Ascension Island. There were no back-up squads, no quick-reaction forces to help any patrol which hit trouble. SAS Captain Aldwin Wight was decorated for his conduct during these operations. His official citation reads:

Inserted . . . at a range of 120 miles, he positioned his patrol in close proximity to enemy positions, cut off from any form of rescue should he have been compromised. This position he maintained for 26 days. During this time he produced clear and accurate pictures of enemy activity in the Stanley area, Intelligence available from no other means, which proved vital in the planning of the final assault. On one occasion he reported an enemy helicopter concentration against which an air strike was directed, resulting in the destruction of four troop-carrying helicopters essential to the enemy in maintaining flexibility and rapid deployment across the islands; a task complicated by the enemy's changing the location of his helicopter holding area each day. In spite of his exposed position . . . his Intelligence reports were detailed and regularly updated. The conditions in which he and his men existed were appalling, with little cover from view or the elements. The weather conditions varied from freezing rain to gale force winds, with few clear days.

The troops approached their task with a canny mixture of caution and daring. The helicopter drop was sometimes made as far as twenty miles from the ultimate destination. As well as Morse transmitters, food, and as much cold- and wet-weather clothing as possible, the men also carried a large quantity of ammunition, which they hoped not to have to use, for this operation was the antithesis of D Squadron's attacking role. For G Squadron, there was no sudden spurt of action to burn off the adrenalin. Instead, just a steady, remorseless build-up of anxiety day by day, with no hope of release.

Costa hypothermia

Once out of the helicopter the patrols' first priority was to get away from the landing zone at a rapid pace, on a compass bearing chosen during the planning stage aboard *Hermes*. After some hours there was a terse, whispered conference to decide how much farther the team should go towards its objective before first light. Well before then, each man had to be concealed in his 'scrape', a shallow trench covered by hessian net, camouflaged with tussock grass or peat. The soldiers quickly learned that to dig more than 18 inches down into Falklands soil is to strike either granite or water. The wise ones lined their scrapes with plastic, but these gravelike holes were never dry and barely secure for observation. Others were to find them even less tolerable. After the main landing, according to Lieutenant-Colonel Malcolm Hunt, of 40 Royal Marine Commando, 'Positions almost on the crest of the hills were filling with more than 2 feet of water. One marine had tried to sleep in his trench despite such discomforts and had to be evacuated by helicopter suffering from acute hypothermia. At one time during that morning his heart had stopped.'

To brew up or cook anything on the tiny hexamine stove was always a risk. By day the Argentines foraged around the perimeters of their own positions on foot or – more effectual – flew over suspect areas in helicopters. From these aircraft any patch of carelessly disturbed soil would be vividly obvious. Cold rations such as biscuits, cheese and chocolate had to suffice most of the day. Daylight hours, on the British clock, were between approximately 10.30am and 6.30pm. On almost every other day these 'daylight' hours were obscured by sea fog. 'We could see the fog coming in off the sea and over Port Stanley', one man recalled. 'Once it rolled in it usually stayed there all day.' After dusk the patrol, now shivering with cold, would move on. Little things, like the slow, painful return to life of numbed feet warming up in perpetually wet boots mattered increasingly as the patrol settled down to a lifestyle and a rhythm of its own.

No one spoke, except in a whisper, and then only when absolutely necessary. It helped that the Argentines built roaring camp fires by night. When these were spotted, a nod of the head, a hand squeezing a comrade's elbow or a silently pointed finger rated as conversation. The residual, unspoken anxiety centred on the minefield risk. Too close to the enemy, one foot placed on the wrong spot in the darkness, could bring crippling injury or death – and jeopardize the operation.

So just how far to go on each leg of the march was always a matter of nice calculation. Each part of the journey was treated as a self-contained operation requiring its own special reconnaissance before the entire patrol was committed to it. In the first days ashore the patrols played it 'safe' – comparatively – by lying up in an OP several miles from the nearest Argentine position.

The sense of isolation was emphasised by news from the outside world which they picked up by tuning their radios at minimum volume to BBC World Service broadcasts. Listening to the discussions about UN Resolution 502 and Haig's shuttle 'while grovelling in the peat watching Argentinians' could be disconcerting. During the first days of the covert reconnaissance operation, as the diplomatic quadrille danced this way and that, some of the more thoughtful SAS men speculated on the status of their mission. There had been no formal declaration of war, although this was assuredly a state of armed conflict. Was it another grey area, similar to Ireland? What if they 'bumped' some Argentines and killed them? What was their position if captured? Then came the news on 5 May of the fatal Exocet attack on the destroyer *Sheffield*. 'That night was the worst', one patrol veteran recollected. 'The news was very alarming. From our point of view it seemed that the task force ships – our lifeline – were there for the picking.' The Exocet attack, 48 hours after the sinking of the *Belgrano*, impressed upon them, as had nothing else so far, that 'we were committed . . . for us, the sinking of *Sheffield* was as good as a declaration of war.'

There was one other potent element in the patrols' isolation; no one knew when they would be withdrawn. The original insertion could not be built around a specified cut-off date or even a precise method of extracting the patrols. Ideally, they would join up with advancing British forces . . . if they landed successfully . . . if they advanced far enough . . . Such monumental question-marks were a nagging reminder that this was not an extended exercise, but the real thing.

After the long march in, the patrol's final OP was established in a less than comfortable hide on a windswept, eye-watering hillside, from which the men of G Squadron, using powerful telescopes, took turns to tabulate the enemy's movements. At the end of such a shift, despite their experience of similar work in Northern Ireland, eyes were redrimmed with fatigue. In clear weather the target was more visible, but so was the OP. In the most sensitive hides even bodily functions had to wait, or be performed with minimum movement. As one man explained, 'Even then, you worried about being given away by rising steam. So you did it very slowly. If your feet got sprayed it didn't make much difference. They were already soaking anyway.'

Transmitting the information, so painfully acquired, in rapid Morse burdened the patrol with the most deadly detection risk of all: that of being 'DF'ed. 'DF' is military shorthand for 'direction finding', a simple electronic method of identifying the source of a radio transmission by taking two co-ordinates on the frequency. The Argentines, according to one specialist who has studied their equipment, were equipped with 'one piece of direction-finding equipment which could locate a transmitter after it had been on the air for a matter of seconds.' In addition to this problem, there was the risk of casual detection by local civilians. On the Falklands the virtual absence of a public telephone system means that everyone routinely listens to his short-wave CB radio. True, the casual listener could not break an SAS code, but he would certainly recognise the emergence of a powerful Morse signal as a sign that something odd was happening. Ultimately, the DF hazard was to cause the death of one SAS soldier and the capture of another. The risk of detection could be diminished by transmitting from a site remote from the OP itself, but this expedient was attended by its own hazard, movement across open country.

The location of reconnaissance patrols near the main population centres of Port Stanley, Darwin/Goose Green, Mount Challenger and – in West Falkland – Fox Bay and Port Howard, increased the risk. The reward was the invaluable knowledge that the Argentines were obviously demoralised, poor at watch-keeping and without defensive positions around San Carlos Water, a proposed beach-head.

Hardest of all, for the boldest spirits, was the imperative that no target, however succulent, was to be attacked by an OP team. So, on occasion, Argentine Pucara aircraft as well as helicopters came and went and the sheep around them could safely graze. Wight's patrol, watching Port Stanley from Beaver Ridge, had to wait for several agonising days before its target was hit by Harrier jets. At dusk, after the initial RAF bombing of Port Stanley on 1 May, the Argentines began moving their helicopters out to the wilderness of Mount Kent and Twin Sisters, west of the town. They could not afford to lose these aircraft, particularly the American Chinooks which could carry half a company of troops in one lift. The machines were the key to a defensive strategy depending upon mobile reserves held in Port Stanley. After sheltering in 'the camp' overnight, the helicopters would return to the capital at daybreak. The SAS patrol spotted them more than once, but were frustrated by communication problems in their efforts to report their findings. On one occasion they counted nine Argentine helicopters including two Chinooks. When, finally, they did get word through, they had the satisfaction of seeing the destruction of two of these big machines and two other helicopters.

Other patrols saw nothing of military significance. This was trying for the soldiers concerned who began to wonder if they were the task force's official bird-watching team, but to the Intelligence analysts 'negative' information, revealing gaps in the Argentine positions, was of priceless value. Finding such gaps, if the recapture of the Falklands was to succeed, was the name of the game.

Among those OPs which did have the satisfaction of being in a 'live' area the price paid in additional stress was enormous. At regular intervals a routine radio signal was expected from every team simply to report that it was on station and secure. One patrol could not risk even that short message for a period of seven days during which its position was surrounded by jumpy enemy soldiers equipped with excellent night sights and DF equipment. It is hardly surprising that after weeks of such pressure combined with lack of normal sleep and food, one SAS soldier was said to be 'in a dreamlike state, almost hallucinating' while others 'some of the fittest men we have, returned weak and looking like old men.' In addition to the effects of stress, most of the men suffered from trench foot, an unpleasant condition not generally encountered in the British Army since the First World War. 'But there's this to be said for it,' one Falklands veteran commented, 'if you're that isolated, no one on your side can interfere.'

Sergeant Joseph Mather was one of those who took the greatest risks. His patrol was watching the Bluff Cove and West Stanley areas for 28 days. 'In a totally hostile environment, with the only protection from ground and air search provided by the skill and stealth of his patrol, the reporting of Sergeant Mather was both accurate and timely', a Military Medal citation records. 'In order to obtain the detail of the enemy disposition he was required to move his observation position to close and often obvious positions to gain the Intelligence required. This he did with great courage and skill knowing that if compromised his patrol could not have been extracted from any predicament caused by enemy action. In addition he communicated his information in an environment where the enemy were known to possess a Direction Finding capability.' Mather's leadership and example, the citation concluded, were in the highest traditions of the SAS and the Army.

The overall impression of the enemy generated by SAS Intelligence reports was that the Argentines were slovenly,

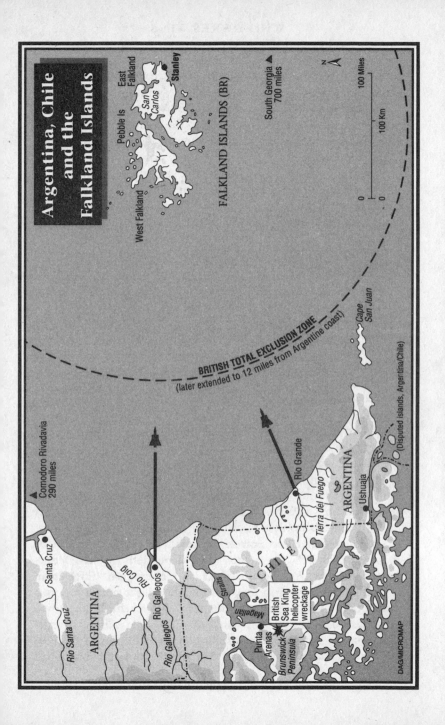

Argentina, Chile and the Falkland Islands

inexperienced and badly-led soldiers. From this evaluation, some in the task force began to hope that once the enemy came under pressure, he would collapse without resistance.

Broadly speaking, this assessment proved correct. Given the numerical odds (12,000 defending the islands against 7000 attacking); the defenders' deep-dug positions commanding the high ground; the stockpile of food and ammunition; their air power, they should have been able to wreak havoc on a lightly-armed, under-strength attacking force. For brief periods the Argentines did fight vigorously. Then, as they started taking casualties, they surrendered or retreated with equal vigour.

SBS in action

The SAS, as usual, were doing things the hard way, regardless of jibes from less intelligent members of other units that the regiment was privileged. As a conscious policy, they decided not to make contact with Falkland Islanders who were potential allies. The SBS came from Britain armed with a list of such people, but decided against using it until the campaign was almost over. SBS men carried out valuable reconnaissance operations on the west coast of West Falkland – the nearest landfall to Argentina – as well as exploring many of the bays and inlets of the main population centre, East Falkland. In this work they had a uniquely useful yachtsman's guide to the islands, lovingly compiled by a Royal Marine officer, Major Ewen Southby-Tailyour. While serving with the Falklands garrison in 1978, Southby-Tailyour had sailed exhaustively. With the start of hostilities his book was classified as a secret document.

SBS reconnaissance patrols operated in similar fashion to those of the SAS, on which they depended for base communications at Ascension Island and elsewhere. Each man carried an extensive armoury: M-16 lightweight rifle (a superior Armalite), M-203 grenade launcher, fifteen high explosive grenades, one 66mm anti-tank missile, 200 rounds of rifle ammunition, smoke and phosphorous grenades, 9mm Browning pistol, and hunting-knife. For observation the team had binoculars, night sight, and tripod-mounted 60x telescope. The load was rounded off with sleeping-bags, quilted trousers in which to sleep, a change of clothes, Arctic dried rations and standard tinned 'compo' ration packs, which require cooking on an individual hexamine stove.

At 1.30am on 1 May one SBS team landed at Eagle Hill overlooking Berkeley Sound. A second was deposited at Johnsons Harbour, farther inland up the same stretch of water. Another two teams were placed on hills overlooking Salvador on the north coast. On the west coast, near the future British invasion site, a fifth squad established an observation post behind the refrigeration plant at Ajax Bay. A sixth concealed itself immediately across San Carlos Water on the Inner Verde Mountains. The following night more teams were set down, including a patrol committed to watching Port San Carlos for seven days. The name of the game was to identify suitable invasion beaches which were not garrisoned by the enemy. After clearing the landing zone as quickly as they could, the SBS men set up temporary bases on their way to their selected OP, checking their position with compass bearings before resting during the daylight hours. Of the four men in a team, three would dig while the fourth, acting as look-out, prowled the immediate vicinity. In one hand he held a fishing-line attached to a rucksack at the camp site. A tug on the line to rock the Bergen was his warning sign.

The SBS took exquisite trouble to make their two-man hides invisible, however temporary these might be. The ideal site was a fold in the ground covered by grass growing to 18 inches or so. From this they carved pieces of turf which were placed carefully to one side as if they were costly hairpieces. Then they dug deeper, putting the peat to one side. At a depth of 18 inches they lined the holes with waterproof groundsheets. Next they built a small earthwork round the hole, using the spare peat, so that the original fold in the ground was now level with the surrounding area. The hide – 8ft long by 5ft wide – was then roofed with chicken-wire stretched taut and pegged down. On top of that was placed a layer of hessian net. Finally grass was stuck in the hessian weave until the hole was invisible and the top 'hairpiece' matched the ground adjoining it. The Roman Army, which prided itself on its civil engineering, would have approved.

The SBS men said, 'We called ourselves "The Interflora Squad".'

Two hides, separated by no more than ten yards, each with a spyhole at both ends, were built for the four men. A third hide was constructed some distance away to conceal food and other stores. Each man knew how many paces and on which compass bearing this hide lay. Food for the day had to be drawn before first light. Immediately afterward the marines brushed upright the grass flattened by their feet, using foam camp mats for the purpose. By dawn they were under cover, invisible to the outside world.

For most of them time passed quickly. As one of them explained, 'There was a lot to do. By day each man was on watch for two hours and off for six. By night, when it is harder to stay awake, we had one hour on watch and three hours off. There's a lot to do during the "off-watch" periods. Cooking takes an hour or so. Everyone chooses his own menu and cooks for himself.'

By night the team moved stealthily across country to its ultimate objective after concealing all traces of the night's lodging. The group assigned to watch Fort San Carlos from Cameron's Ridge, facing the settlement across a narrow lead of water, spent two such nights before they reached their objective. There, luck was with them. A cave created by a rock fall was large enough for all four men, and little more than half a mile from the settlement. Expectantly the patrol waited for some sign of Argentine troops, probably in company strength. But the sergeant leading the patrol was flabbergasted to discover that none were present. 'We saw civilians moving about but the Argentines seemed happy to fly around checking the settlements before they disappeared back to base.'

After dark he examined the bay. 'We were looking for steeply shelving beaches into deep water, free from kelp but sheltered from the open sea, where landing-craft could come in without running aground. But it was no use landing on a beach enclosed by cliffs. An exit point inland was equally important. We found Sandy Bay, a beach just a few hundred yards from Port San Carlos settlement, but out of sight of it behind a headland, and another, secondary beach below Fanning Head. Best of all was the absence of Argentine troops.'

Meanwhile the SBS patrol at nearby Ajax Bay was having a more eventful time. During the team's sixteen-day watch one Argentine helicopter landed only 100 yards from the hide while the pilot got out to relieve himself. Other helicopters also landed nearby, which convinced the men in hiding that they had been spotted. This, as we shall see, was to have some unexpected results. On another occasion a helicopter actually hovered over this hide, the downdraught of its rotors stripping camouflage away. The pilot, preoccupied with the map on his knees as well as flying his machine, did not notice what was immediately below him.

Tho most harrowing experience was that of an SBS corporal and a young Marine who had just joined the unit. They were peculiarly unlucky. The hilltop position chosen for their observation post by the R Group team on *Fearless* was also selected, at about the same time, by an Argentine patrol. The SBS men, moving stealthily in fog, had to choose between challenging the enemy – thereby compromising the operation – or allowing the Argentines to occupy the position, between the two men and the rest of their team. The two, going to ground at a safe distance, inevitably lost contact with their comrades and disappeared. They had no radio. They now followed a pre-arranged emergency drill, moving from one rendezvous to another, waiting at each for a specified time, hoping to be found. Day followed day and they were without food. The patrol's leader, meanwhile, was obliged to withdraw to meet a helicopter pick-up. Then with a fresh team he returned to hostile ground in an effort to find his missing men. By now, Special Force planners believed, it was an odds-on chance that the missing men were dead of exposure, or had been taken prisoner, or were hiding in a barn as clandestine guests of friendly locals. The search for them was concentrated upon the final rendezvous on the emergency list, though the agreed pick-up time there had long since passed. At this rendezvous, a bleak scrape in the peat, the corporal and his companion were found twelve days after the original incident. 'They were a bit thin,' said one of their comrades later, 'but glad to be found. We brought them back to the task force, fed them, debriefed them and sent them back to work.'

The SBS team watching Port San Carlos, meanwhile, reported that the area provided good landing sites with no Argentine garrison to guard them. The area, on 13 May, was 'clean'. D-Day was little more than a week away.

'Prelim' at Pebble Island

The SBS information, although vital to the main landings, was of no relevance to the first British land offensive on the Falklands. As events were to show, the SAS assault on Pebble Island, off the north coast of West Falkland, on 14 May depended almost as much upon good luck as the Fortuna Glacier reconnaissance in South Georgia. With hindsight, both the military and the journalists have tended to see the Pebble Island raid as part of some strategic grand design to soften up the enemy and persuade him that when the main invasion came at San Carlos it would be just the latest in a series of hit-and-run attacks. Like the 'disinformation' on this subject put out by the Ministry of Defence in London the raid did serve the purpose of throwing dust in the enemy's eyes, but it was originally intended by the SAS to have the same effect as a kick in the crutch: a blow not necessarily fatal, but which would certainly demoralise. The code name 'Operation Prelim' matches both interpretations.

When D Squadron first mulled over possible targets in the Falklands the only firm information about Pebble Island suggested that it held a small, isolated garrison of Argentine Army engineers and Air Force technicians working to prepare the airstrip as a dispersal field, a sanctuary for aircraft under attack at Port Stanley. Admiral Woodward, the task force commander, did not like the idea. It would require naval support and put valuable ships at risk. After the loss of *Sheffield* on 4 May, his caution is understandable. But then something happened to invest Pebble Island with a new significance.

A Harrier pilot returning from a raid on Darwin believed he had detected radar emissions from the new Argentine base. A radar system on Pebble Island would certainly identify an approaching invasion fleet, so it had to be removed. Woodward ordered a nocturnal 'elint' (electronic Intelligence) reconnaissance by aircraft equipped to read radar signatures. The operation did not confirm the Harrier's initial suspicion and D Squadron's proposed raid was again vetoed. The SAS persuaded Woodward to change his mind a second time, however, and the operation was finally approved.

Three days later, on 10 May, a reconnaissance team from one of D Squadron's boat troops – the same team which had gone ashore in faulty Geminis at South Georgia – was preparing to land near Pebble Island when severe weather obliged it to stand down for 24 hours. That night aboard *Hermes* the two four-man patrols went over the proposed route yet again: by Sea King helicopter to the remote Mare Rock peninsula on the most north-easterly point of West Falkland. From this delivery point the patrols were to use collapsible Klepper canoes to travel by sea round the Mare Rock headland and set up an OP facing Pebble Island across the fast-running, tidal Tamar Strait. Once they were satisfied that the coast was clear they would paddle across to Pebble Island. From this point they would still have to cover about ten miles to their objective, Pebble Island Settlement's airstrip. They would have to move on foot across a 'moonscape' which afforded no natural cover except for creases of dead ground. It was not a potential picnic. However, the very remoteness of the place led the planners to hope that the Argentines would not patrol it. The briefing finished, some of the men settled down to play cards and Scrabble. Others checked their equipment, yet again.

In practice the first, routine snag was that surf crashing ashore at the West Falkland delivery point completely ruled out any hope of launching the canoes. The boat troop teams climbed back into the helicopter and flew closer to their destination. Now they had to march across a ridge at the end of the Mare

Rock headland, carrying their canoes as well as other equipment. The only way this could be accomplished was by moving the rucksacks first, returning to pick up the canoes so that these, too, could be manhandled to the north shore. Once there they built an observation post and settled down throughout 11 May to watch Pebble Island. They saw nothing but sea-birds. At dusk the canoes were launched into the swirling, icy waters and the teams reached Pebble Island in the comforting safety of darkness.

At first it seemed that, for a change, a D Squadron reconnaissance was going to work as planned. One patrol stayed with the canoes as a firm base, with a radio link back to *Hermes*. The second patrol of four men then marched through the night until it reached the tight neck of land, girded by sea on both sides, which is the settlement. Day dawned, cold and grey above the airstrip. As the sky lightened, two things were dramatically obvious. The first was that there were eleven Argentine aircraft – a squadron's worth – dispersed about 2000 yards from the patrol's position. That was the good news. The bad news was that where the patrol lay and as far away as they could see, the ground was as flat as a football pitch with no protective cover whatever. The Argentine sentries were not alert but they were present. To try to walk away would have been suicidal. Even to crawl out with the bulky Bergens on their backs would have been to risk almost certain discovery. So the four abandoned the rucksacks and slithered away like slow, cautious serpents. When at last they reached dead ground they laid up throughout the day. The only equipment they had now were their Armalite rifles and belt kit containing ammunition and survival gear. That night they marched back to their firm base. Some time in the early hours of the following morning, 13 May, they signalled their findings to *Hermes* and preparations began immediately. The squadron's orders were to destroy all the aircraft and kill everyone in the garrison.

Time was of the essence now. The longer the raid was delayed the greater the risk that the reconnaissance team's abandoned equipment would be discovered. Equally oppressive was the pressure on helicopter time. Between 16 and 19 May the available Sea Kings were committed to a resupply of G Squadron's covert reconnaissance patrols. They had now been living hard for two weeks and resupply could not be put off. Aboard *Hermes*, D Squadron started drawing the weapons and ammunition it would need for Operation Prelim.

For reasons which are not clear, naval planners miscalculated the time it would take to bring the carrier within helicopter range of the target. This in turn meant a late dash into the target area, sailing at speed into a high wind, which ruled out movement on the flight deck. This meant that the helicopters could not be made ready. The result was that only one of the two original objectives – destruction of the aircraft – could be sustained. For the time being the lives of the Argentines manning the garrison were to be spared.

The revised plan of attack had the great virtue of simplicity. Only one troop – John Hamilton's Mountain Troop of about 20 men – would attack the airstrip itself. Another would remain in reserve to deal with any unexpected opposition. A third would seal the two approaches to the settlement. Finally, the remaining Boat Troop men not involved in the original Pebble Island reconnaissance (who were still staked out there) would protect the mortar team as well as the Royal Artillery officer, Captain Chris Brown, who was to direct fire from the destroyer *Glamorgan*. With everyone standing by and ready to board the Sea Kings, the helicopters were still not ready. After an agonising wait of 90 minutes – the worst point in any military adventure – the three 'choppers' whined off *Hermes*'s deck and away into a windswept morning. It was still dark.

Awaiting the raiders at the landing zone 45 minutes later was the Boat Troop captain and his reconnaissance team. Despite the great need of haste, weapons, ammunition and explosive charges were unloaded with fastidious care, and the helicopters departed. Then, in bright moonlight, the captain briefed squadron and troop officers about the target, a mere four miles away. This did not take long, and in absolute silence, the squadron moved off behind him. As well as his own equipment each man carried two bombs for the 81mm mortar, an additional load of 13-pounds. These were deposited at the mortar position.

The teams which were to seal off the settlement, and the one which was to attack the airstrip, were then guided to their destinations by scouts from the Boat Troop reconnaissance team. The Boat Troop captain personally conducted Hamilton and his assault squad to their target.

It was now 7am. According to the original plan this was the time at which the raid should have been concluded. D Squadron therefore had just thirty minutes in which to do its worst. For the squadron to stay longer could have put *Hermes* at risk. She, after all, had to approach within helicopter range for the raiders to be recovered. Ideally, the recovery would be complete and *Hermes*, together with *Glamorgan*, would be turning for safer waters before first light.

At first, Mountain Troop did not tackle its task as an orthodox, text-book demolition job. With so little time to spare the men were at first content to blast away with small arms and 66mm rockets at the aircraft dispersed around them, a process known to soldiers as 'brassing up'. These aircraft were six Pucara ground attack planes, a Skyvan transport and four Beech Mentor trainers. By now, *Glamorgan*'s guns were firing on the Argentine trenches as a diversionary measure. The only response was a sporadic burst of small arms fire from the trenches, on the other side of the airfield.

As it became clear that the opposition was not going to interfere too seriously, Hamilton's raiders moved on to the airstrip proper, within sight of the trenches, and started to destroy the aircraft in a cool, systematic way, using standard SAS high explosive charges and more 66mm missiles. By now, Argentine ammunition and fuel stores were ablaze as a result of naval gunfire. Soon after 7am, one of the troop was hit by shrapnel in the left leg. Staff Sergeant Currass, a veteran 'medic', dressed the wound and the man continued fighting. By now Pebble Island airstrip looked like the scene of a spectacular military tattoo, but one aircraft remained apparently undamaged. Covered by Hamilton, Trooper Raymond ('Paddy') Armstrong, a demolition specialist, went forward and disposed of it. He and his troop captain that night shared the distinction of wrecking at least two Argentine aircraft each, and

Armstrong was promptly nicknamed 'Pucara Paddy'. Neither man was to live to see the end of the campaign.

Silhouetted against the burning aircraft the troop spread out and began to fall back off the airstrip, towards the agreed rendezvous. As they did so a landmine was exploded on command from the Argentine lines. It blew up in the centre of the troop, the blast hurling Corporal Paul Bunker 10 feet. Bunker, a mild-mannered Royal Army Ordnance Corps private turned SAS free-faller, was concussed. Miraculously he and his comrade, hit by shrapnel earlier in the operation, were the only casualties. That man, now faint from loss of blood, was given an escort of two men and told to go direct to the final rendezvous where the Sea Kings were to collect the whole squadron. As this party reached the edge of the airstrip they heard four or five Argentine voices nearby, shouting towards the settlement. The wounded SAS soldier opened fire with a grenade launcher attached to his Armalite rifle, and kept firing until screams told him he had hit his target. So far as is known, this was the only Argentine casualty of the night. As things had turned out, the destruction of military hardware with minimal bloodshed appeared as a model of clinical, constrained use of force, though that had not been the original intention.

At 7.15, Hamilton's troop regrouped and with its wounded moved through the forward rendezvous manned by a captain and Squadron Sergeant-Major Lawrence Gallagher. At 7.30 contact with the enemy was broken off and the rest of the squadron was on its way. At 9.30, right on time, the helicopters returned. First aboard were the injured men, swiftly followed by the exhausted reconnaissance team. No one spoke much during the eighty-minute flight back to *Hermes*. Everyone was trying to come to terms with an SAS raid modelled on the offensive style of David Stirling in the western desert. It was the sort of thing most of them had only read about until that night.

Only later did they learn that the Argentine garrison totalled 114 men, outnumbering the attackers by about three-to-one. The impact on Argentine morale elsewhere was devastating. First, South Georgia had fallen with no more than token resistance. Now a Falklands garrison was unable to prevent the destruction of eleven valuable aircraft. There had been no pursuit, hot or cold, by the defenders after the raid. One senior British officer (not an SAS officer) let it be known that the raid established the 'moral ascendancy' of the British Army even before its main forces were put ashore. Certainly this was the message promptly conveyed to the Argentine occupation army through Spanish language broadcasts by 'Radio Atlantico del Sur', an official British radio station hastily established at Ascension Island. The next time the phrase 'moral ascendancy' was used, was after 2 Para's battle for Goose Green.

The Pebble Island raid also had an odd postscript. On 25 May the destroyer *Coventry* was sunk by three Argentine bombs and 19 of her crew were killed. Task force planners suspected that an American-built mobile ANTPS-43 radar was still functioning at Pebble Island and had guided the Skyhawk bombers to sink *Coventry*. An SBS team, inserted by trawler, spent ten days scouring Pebble Island for the radar, without success. This team counted 120 Argentine service-men at the base and a new attack was planned for 15 June. Two RAF Harriers were to bomb the airstrip, after which 34 SBS men were to wipe out any of the garrison who survived. In the event, the Argentine high command at Port Stanley capitulated 24 hours before this attack and, for the time being, the conflict was over. The SBS accepted the surrender of 112 Argentines at Pebble Island . . . and the SAS Boat Troop captain who had led the original reconnaissance of 10–14 May returned to look for his soldiers' missing rucksacks. They were still where the team had left them. Much later, Admiral Woodward summed up the operation: 'Easily the best example of a successful "All-Arms" special operation we are likely to see in a very long while. A short-notice operation carried out with speed and dash: no dead, one injured and eleven aircraft written off in one hour. Total time from start to finish, five days. Remarkable. But . . . because it succeeded on this occasion, it may be tempting to expect such operations to be feasible in this, or shorter, time scales at the drop of a hat. The time-scale will usually be longer and the assets needed . . . considerable.'

Sea King disaster

The Pebble Island raid had provided the task force with an auspicious beginning to a week which was to conclude on 21 May with the stunningly successful landing of 3000 troops on the narrow beaches of San Carlos, without loss of life. For the SAS it was the week in which it suffered the greatest single blow in its post-war history: the loss of a Sea King helicopter with twenty men serving, in one capacity or another, with 22 SAS Regiment.

While the Pebble Island raid was taking place the finishing touches were being put to the invasion plan. On 13 May, the day when Royal Marine SBS patrols had reported that the proposed beachhead and the hills overlooking it were 'clean', individual assault units were assigned their beaches and places in the order of battle. A sense of expectancy and anticipation, mixed with anxiety, gripped the invasion fleet as it made its rendezvous with the carrier group led by *Hermes* on a flat calm sea on 18 May. Ashore the reconnaissance patrols of G Squadron were still fighting their private, silent war of information gathering.

D Squadron, meanwhile, had been briefed for a characteristically ambitious raid in the area of Darwin/Goose Green. The Argentine garrison had been identified by G Squadron; now it was up to D Squadron to tie it down long enough for the vulnerable landing force to get ashore unscathed a few miles to the north. On 19 May, two days before D-Day, D Squadron moved from *Hermes* to the multi-purpose assault ship *Intrepid* to prepare for this assault. Two hours after dusk, at about 9.30pm, the last elements of the Squadron clambered into the Sea King for the five-minute flight across the half-mile of water separating the two ships. One of those on board described it as, 'a routine flight; nothing exciting about it'. Most of those on the lift were men of John Hamilton's Mountain Troop, including the two men wounded during the Pebble Island raid. They had come from the carrier's sick-bay and were given the first two places aboard the helicopter. Not all the passengers were fully-fledged, 'badged' insiders of the SAS Regiment. Some were specialists attached to the regiment who wore the same beige beret but kept their own, separate cap badges. Nevertheless, they went to war with the SAS and took the same chances. Among them were soldiers of the Royal Army Medical Corps and an RAF Flight Lieutenant, Garth Hawkins. An expert in directing air strikes to support special operations, Hawkins delighted in the vagrant, gypsy life he had discovered with the SAS. The regiment regarded him as one of its own. Finally, there were the helicopter crew: pilot, co-pilot and navigator.

The two wounded men sat up front, on the port side, behind the co-pilot. On the opposite side, almost facing them, was the space from which, for operational convenience, the main door had been removed. As they settled down the rest followed, glad to be on the move after a long wait. To avoid further delays, no one asked for the cumbersome, tight-fitting rubber survival suit which passengers are normally obliged to wear for a helicopter flight over water. One of those on board later told the author that he was wearing ordinary Army boots, socks, a blue boiler suit, heavy-duty sweater, uninflated life-jacket, 'and that was it'.

As the helicopter lifted off into the darkness, *Intrepid* was sailing abreast of *Hermes*, on the carrier's port side. Both vessels were heaving on a rolling sea. The Sea King made a circuit from the stern end of *Hermes*, away out to starboard and then round *Intrepid*. The helicopter was not permitted to land immediately, however, because another helicopter which had touched down on *Intrepid* moments before had yet to be cleared away from the flight deck. This meant that that machine's engine had to be stopped and its rotor blades folded before it could be stowed away. As a result, the Sea King was obliged to make a second circuit.

When it was roughly midway between the two ships, some of those on board heard a double report from the engine. Others felt 'something like a sledgehammer blow' near the front end of the Sea King. At that point the helicopter was between 300ft and 500ft above the sea. 'Then we were in the water, in complete darkness. Everything happened so fast. One moment we were flying, then we were submerged. I told myself not to panic. But there was no way of knowing which way was up or down.

At first I thought, "There must be a way out." I was groping around and thought I was drowning', said one man.

At this point, in fact, the Sea King was still afloat – just – although capsized and becoming engulfed. 'Then someone trampled all over the top of me and disappeared. I thought there might be a chance for me, too. But the person who trampled over me knocked the air out of my lungs. I reached up, trying to find something. Because the helicopter had rolled over, those of us who were sitting on the port side were now nearest the door on the starboard side. When I found something I grabbed hold of it and pulled myself up. In fact it was the main door. But I was still trapped by something. I think it was a life-jacket round my waist. I eventually freed myself and bobbed to the surface beside the co-pilot.

He had a small automatic light on his shoulder and was about 10 feet away. I made my way to him. I didn't have a life-jacket any more and I'm not the best of swimmers. I grabbed hold of his shoulder. He inflated a one-man dinghy so I let go of him and grabbed hold of that. It was capsized, but afloat. Then I found I couldn't move one arm. I was also being sick. I held on as firmly as I could with the good arm and hoped for the best. There were more and more people coming towards us now. It was very dark.'

For another survivor the main recollection of the crash was that he was hurled about in complete darkness, under water. For him the journey to the surface seemed to take for ever. On the surface, vomiting a mixture of seawater and aviation fuel, he noted that the only remaining trace of the big helicopter was one wheel which occasionally broke surface. He, too, swam to the inverted dinghy. Soon ten survivors, including the pilot and co-pilot, were clinging to it. When their improvised life-raft rose on the crest of a wave they could see lights aboard *Intrepid*. These seemed now to be a long way off.

Those wearing life-jackets inflated them and held on more grimly than ever, yet still talked to one another, encouraging the injured not to let go. 'Hold on. Stay calm. They'll come soon', someone said. The aircrew were not going to leave rescue to chance. Somehow they managed to make their personal search-and-rescue beacons work and they fired flares. By the time the first search helicopter found them, hovering a few feet away, its searchlight probing the darkness, most of the survivors were near the fatal point of unconsciousness. The machine circled, flew away and returned seconds later. At first, the helicopter winchman tried to put his rescue loop round one casualty whose shoulder had been dislocated. The man merely shook his head. To release the tenuous hold he had on the raft with his one good arm already numbed by cold would mean the end. Around the raft the exhausted men discussed tersely who should go first. The corporal who was nominated still had the dinghy's painter, wrapped round his wrist. As the helicopter moved away so he dragged the dinghy with him . . . but only for a second. He released the rope in the nick of time.

The survivors had now been in the sea for thirty minutes, far beyond the time anyone could rationally expect to survive in those waters. They could not hope to last much longer. At this moment a small rescue craft from the frigate *Brilliant* found them. As they were hauled inboard several of the survivors collapsed, pole-axed by a combination of shock and exposure. Some were already verging on hypothermia. One SAS soldier, still wearing his bulky belt kit, could not help himself into the rescue craft even to the limited extent of reaching up an arm for help. One of *Brilliant*'s crew, risking his own life, promptly jumped into the water to help the man to safety. He was characteristic of *Brilliant*, a vessel in the thick of every bit of trouble, usually in support of Special Forces operations.

All the survivors, except for the man winched out by helicopter, woke up aboard *Brilliant*. One of them came round after more than two hours to find himself curled up, totally naked, under a hot shower. It was a radical but effective way of dealing with hypothermia, a condition in which the body's core temperature, having fallen to a certain level, will continue to drop fatally unless drastic steps are taken to reheat it. His rescuers put the man into bed, where he lay awake throughout that night. Impressions of his ordeal came crowding back . . . the moment when he thought he was drowning and all he could think of, to stay alive, were 'the wife and kids' . . . the questions, most importantly, how many had been lost? All those who had clung to the dinghy clung also to the belief that somehow, the others would have been picked up. But in the isolated condition of all who have been 'casevacked' out of a military operation they were now out of the mainstream.

Firm information drifted to them only in snippets as they made their way back to Britain aboard *Canberra* (after the D-Day bombings) and the QE-II. What they did not know until much later was that they, the ten who had clung to the dinghy, were the only survivors. The full extent of the disaster reached Britain somewhat faster. Within twenty-four hours reporters in London had been given an outline of what had happened. Aside from speculative reports about SAS reconnaissance patrols, this was the only news about the regiment to reach Britain prior to 6 June. It was to relieve the blow to morale caused to SAS families – which, through mail from home, might have had a knock-on effect upon the morale of SAS soldiers in the field – that the record was set straight. It was done through the medium of war correspondent Max Hastings. In a memorable, pooled dispatch he gave a graphic account of SAS successes.

The precise cause of the Sea King crash, like much else about the South Atlantic conflict, may never be known. It is significant that after the incident a mass of bloodstained feathers was sighted floating near the scene. This, combined with the double bang from the helicopter engine, convinced knowledgeable observers that this was yet another disaster caused by a bird. It is improbable that the bird was – as some inevitably speculate – an unlucky albatross. The Royal Society for the Protection of Birds suggests that the giant petrel, almost as large, with a wingspan of up to 6 feet, was the more likely cause. Flocks of these fly from the Falklands, following ships in search of food.

What is certain is that Hamilton's troop lost a significant percentage of its best men in the crash. The regiment lost two squadron sergeant-majors. Mountain Troop losses from D Squadron included most of the veterans who had played an important part in recapturing South Georgia, and the Pebble Island raid, including Staff Sergeant Philip Curass, Sergeant

Sid Davidson, Sergeant 'Lofty' Arthy, Corporal Paul Bunker and Trooper ('Pucara Paddy') Armstrong. Also killed was the Squadron Sergeant-Major, Lawrence Gallagher, who had restored the Union Jack to South Georgia.

G Squadron's Sergeant-Major, Malcolm ('Akker') Atkinson, a former Grenadier from Barnsley, who had been with the squadron since its formation in Borneo, was another significant casualty. His career spanned twelve fully operational tours and he was a veteran of Mirbat. Other veterans were Staff Sergeant Paddy O'Connor (Irish Guards), the Stinger missile expert and an SAS soldier since 1966; Sergeant W.J. (Taff) Hughes (Welsh Guards); Sergeant P. (Taff) Jones, a former Welsh Guards regimental rugby player, latterly converted to angling, and an SAS soldier since 1975.

Yet another G Squadron casualty was Corporal Willy Hatton, QGM, the regiment's first fully qualified diving supervisor. Hatton was originally a Royal Marine SBS diver who subsequently worked for a civilian company in the North Sea. He then joined the Army and was as successful with the SAS as he had been with the commandos. Indeed he was attached to 2 SBS during the Falkands campaign as one of a small team, including an SAS medic, which boarded and seized the 1400-ton Argentine spy trawler *Narwhal* on 10 May after it had been disabled by an RAF Harrier.

The SAS support arms lost Corporal William ('Paddy') Begley (Royal Corps of Transport), a small, lithe mountaineer; Corporal John Newton (REME) an armourer; Corporal Rab Burns (Royal Signals) signaller and bagpiper; Corporal Steve Sykes, signaller, marathon runner and cross-country skier; Lance-Corporal Paul Lightfoot and Corporal Michael McHugh (Royal Signals). Flight-Lieutenant Garth Hawkins, RAF and his signaller and partner, Corporal Douglas McCormack (Royal Signals) were an inseparable team and they died together. Hawkins, a forward air controller, was about to return to civilian life and had just bought a pub. Finally there was Corporal Edward ('Wally') Walpole, a Greenjacket, who had served as D Squadron storeman for five years and was, albeit unbadged, a regimental character.

In all, the SAS and support specialists lost twenty men. Others in Mountain Troop survived the helicopter crash but were sent back to Britain to recover. They included two of the men wounded at Pebble Island one of whom, still in his twenties, had also survived two successive helicopter crashes on Fortuna Glacier. He is now nicknamed 'Splash'. To replace the Sea King casualties, replacements including 'unbadged' signallers were flown from Britain by way of Ascension Island to join the task force. The last lap of their journey was a parachute drop from an RAF Hercules into the cold South Atlantic. Some of these men were in the water for 40 minutes before they were picked up by the Royal Navy, and were dangerously close to becoming exposure cases.

A beachhead compromised

The most critical reconnaissance of the entire Falklands conflict was in the hands of the SBS. This was proper. As amphibious experts they were the most appropriate people to examine the approaches to the invasion beaches and the tactically sensitive areas overlooking them. Without proper reconnaissance the slow-moving landing-craft, crowded with soldiers, would be sitting ducks. On 1 May, when the first 'advance force' recce patrols went ashore, four possible sites – one on West Falkland – were being considered as invasion beachheads. San Carlos, at that time, rated only third in order of preference. The SBS, with a mere 84 men available and denied helicopter transport at the most delicate phase of reconnaissance, had to land its parties, check each widespread area, withdraw, report exhaustively to the R Group on board *Fearless*, and then land again at the next site. There were not enough men or helicopters to keep all options under continuous scrutiny. The data required ranged from beach angles to the inland going for men and vehicles. It was too detailed to be sent by radio. The information gleaned from a 'simple' beach reconnaissance, one, expert estimates, would require four hours' transmission time. Any signaller staying on the air for a fraction of that time would certainly be 'DF'ed. Despite such difficulties, General Sir Jeremy Moore was later to reveal that 'we worked throughout on allocating fourteen days to special forces' reconnaissance before the main landing.'

On 8 May, about three days before the final choice of beachhead was made, the SBS had to withdraw two teams from the San Carlos area. A third, at Ajax Bay overlooking San Carlos Water, remained hiding among the ferns in front of an abandoned refrigeration plant. On 13 May, when this patrol had been on watch for sixteen days, an Argentine helicopter landed only 100 yards from the SBS hide while the pilot dismounted to relieve himself. Even more daunting, six more Argentine helicopters – two Puma, two Huey, two unidentified – landed on Lookout Hill overlooking San Carlos Settlement. From these machines an Argentine Army search party started to sweep the area, which another SBS patrol had left a few days before. The Ajax Bay patrol, 'thinking their time had come', flashed a radio signal 'in clear' (uncoded) to report that their position was in imminent danger of discovery. For the special force commanders aboard *Fearless*, it was a particularly gloomy moment. Ashore, it seemed, the Argentines and SBS were missing one another as narrowly as characters in a bedroom farce by Feydeau. The British government had vigorously declined to confirm that any of its forces were back on the islands. If the Argentines captured such men, the Junta in its turn would be under no pressure to confirm the captives' existence as prisoners of war. The implications of that grey area were not good. In the event, the SBS men who thought they had been discovered kept their heads down and held their fire. Their brief radio signal, so far as they could judge, went undetected by the enemy and they were safely withdrawn under cover of darkness on 15 May.

On that same day, the R Group planners received a tip which they had to take seriously. This asserted that the Argentines were in a position at Fanning Head known as Point 234 which, the source said, was '4 kilometres north of San Carlos'. This puzzled the R Group analysts. Fanning Head is *14* kilometres north and several kilometres west of San Carlos. The analysts now had to make the best guess they could as to where the

Argentines really were: in the immediate vicinity of San Carlos, where the SBS men had spotted them from Ajax Bay, or almost ten miles away on Fanning Head, overlooking the approaches to San Carlos Water. As one of them put it, 'we knew there were Argentines in the area and said so. We did not know exactly where they were. The analysts' best, and first guess was wrong. Although one SBS officer noted on 13 May, a full week before the landing, that a full enemy company might be either on Fanning Head or Lookout Hill above San Carlos, the truth was that both places were manned. The greatest Argentine strength was in Port San Carlos settlement, immediately overlooking the main invasion beaches.

The vital San Carlos reconnaissance operation was in trouble in other respects. As we have noted, all the teams except that at Ajax Bay were withdrawn on 8 May, when the final choice of beachhead was still three days away. The Ajax Bay team came out on 15 May when the narrow squeaks of previous days made it appear that the team's time was running out. Discovery seemed imminent. On 11 May, once San Carlos was finally chosen as the main landing area, the SBS tried to restore its coverage. But that scheme was stalled by lack of Sea King helicopters to put the recce teams back ashore. The aircraft concerned were by now committed to the SAS raid on Pebble Island. Immediately after that raid, *Hermes*, the Sea Kings' host carrier, sailed away north to meet the amphibious force on its way south from Ascension Island. The Sea Kings went with it.

The SBS now made energetic efforts to reinsert reconnaissance patrols by ship. On 16 May the Ajax Bay OP was reoccupied after a gap of 24 hours. The same day, the frigate *Alacrity* landed another patrol, with a Gunner officer, south of Ajax Bay. During the next twenty-four hours this team marched to a spot overlooking San Carlos Water. It reported no activity in the Port San Carlos area which was, in fact, some miles from its position and the other side of a hill. On 17 May a third SBS recce team, specifically charged to watch Port San Carlos, was to be put ashore from the frigate *Brilliant*, at Middle Bay, well to the north of the target area.

This position is on the opposite side of Fanning Head peninsula from Port San Carlos and screened from it by the mass of the peninsula itself. Approaching the shore in rubber boats, the SBS men needed no psychic powers to perceive that the area was occupied by Argentines. Their camp fires and voices conveyed the message that the approaches to the British landing site had been reinforced. For the team to follow its original orders and cross an enemy occupied hill, risking capture at such a late stage, could have compromised everything. So the Marines, after paddling quietly round the bay for two hours, returned to *Brilliant*. Their judgement was initially criticised by their SBS commanding officer, but applauded by the Brigade chief, Brigadier Julian Thompson.

With little more than three days left before the biggest British amphibious operation since 1944, the R Group knew it had a problem. The enemy had reinforced the landing area, but no one knew exactly in what strength or how extensively. After another 24 hours, with the amphibious force closing on the approaches to East Falkland, the SBS again asked for helicopters to put their recce patrols ashore. Again the request was turned down. The most the SBS could hope for was a minimum number of aircraft to fly a force to Fanning Head six hours before the main landing. At best, the Argentines might be persuaded to surrender without a fight, as at South Georgia. If they did it could repair the Intelligence gap at a stroke. For this reason the SBS team going ashore at Fanning Head was told that live prisoners were more important than dead enemy. The mixture was to be one of sweet persuasion and military muscle, if necessary. The mixture was to prove almost fatal for those who administered it.

The Fanning Head squad was allocated two Wessex helicopters which flew from the destroyer *Antrim*. Because of the need to store one aircraft with rotors folded while the other took off, the first Wessex was obliged to hover above *Antrim* for a long time while the second was made ready . . . So long, in fact, that when the second started flying, the first had to land again to refuel, while the second hovered in its turn and waited . . . All this in foul weather and darkness, just before a sensitive and difficult operation. When, finally, the whole party was assembled it included not only the SBS but also an SAS mortar team, a public-address device known as a 'bullhorn' and a remarkable Royal Marine captain named Roderick Bell, who speaks colloquial Argentine–Spanish. He was later to play a uniquely useful role in partnership with the SAS, in bringing the conflict to an end without prolonged bloodshed.

The operation started with a novel and startling success. Although the helicopters were older than most of the men they carried, one of them, a Mk V, was fitted with a piece of equipment with which police in the Home Counties had been experimenting to search for bodies abandoned in dense woodland. This device, a thermal imager, records the presence of a living or even a recently dead body by registering its heat. The imager can select from an entire apartment block which flats are occupied and which are not. The other Wessex, the anti-submarine Mk III piloted by Ian Stanley, carried the radar required to guide the Mk V through fog, rain and darkness for a 'hoovering' operation over the peninsula. Then, after several sweeps which drew a blank, tell-tale white spots indicating either sheep or men, appeared on the screen. In this, its first use as a war weapon, the imager identified 22 bodies hiding near Point 234. They were Argentines, and, as later became apparent, they were armed with two 106mm recoilless rifles and at least one mortar which could have caused hideous damage to the landing force.

The SBS men and their expert assistants, including a Gunner officer to direct *Antrim*'s two 4.5in guns, were set down about 1000 yards from the Argentines' position. The Mk V Wessex had to make five journeys from *Antrim* before the whole team was assembled. Each time the helicopter touched down on Fanning Head it needed the aid of lights, a highly dangerous undertaking on such an operation. Unlike the Sea Kings, it was not a 'PGN' machine which could see in total darkness. Once ashore the landing force divided into two groups, one to tackle the known position on Fanning Head, the other to sort out the suspect area overlooking Port San Carlos.

It was still dark when the Fanning Head party moved off.

Finding the enemy was not a problem. The team had a man-portable thermal imager. Making non-violent contact with the Argentines was another matter. Bell went forward, unescorted, into the darkness and tried to make himself understood. It is unclear whether all 22 Argentines ever heard his words. A strong wind often obliterated his voice, as he stood calling into the darkness. The first response to his presence was a burst of machine-gun fire which ripped through an SBS man's rucksack at a range of 900 yards. The SBS did not return fire immediately for fear of hitting Bell with cross-fire and because their orders were to give first priority to taking prisoners. But with Bell safely back in the fold this restraint was removed. The first return burst by an SBS machine-gunner killed the Argentine who had started the shooting. Then *Antrim*'s guns were ranged on the enemy position. In the resulting slaughter another eleven Argentines were killed and three wounded. None escaped.

Meanwhile, the second SBS team, a four-man patrol, moved down the coast of Fanning Head peninsula to Port San Carlos beach. The original Intelligence reports, as well as military sense, suggested that any Argentine troops in the area would have taken up positions on the hills above the settlement. The Argentines had not fallen in with this logic. About half a company – some 60 men – were sheltering in the settlement itself when the shooting started on Fanning Head. Alarmed by the noise, they quietly started to pull out and make for the sanctuary of the hills. The SBS team stayed on the beach to await the first wave of assault troops from the Paras and 40 Commando, unaware of the enemy force just behind them, in the village. If the Argentines knew that a British reconnaissance force was only a few yards away, they gave no sign of it. Neither side pushed its luck. As a result, the first wave of troops from the main landing force, Parachute Regiment, were surprised by the evident presence of the Argentines inland about a mile away. When they came under mortar fire from the Paras they beat a hasty retreat but later that morning they scored their first success, shooting down two Royal Marine helicopters as the aircraft escorted a Sea King ferrying ashore a Rapier missile battery. Three out of the four Gazelle crewmen were killed.

'Brassing-up' Goose Green

During that same long night, D Squadron of the SAS was in action again. Its march to attack a 1200-strong garrison at Goose Green was later described by one participant as 'the toughest hike I've ever done with the SAS'. The squadron, depleted as a result of the Sea King helicopter losses little more than 24 hours earlier, flew from *Intrepid* to land east of Darwin/Goose Green. It then began a fighting march of 20 hours' duration. Each man carried at least 80 pounds, mostly ordnance. The purpose of the operation – one of several diversionary raids that night – was to convince the Goose Green garrison that it was under attack from a battalion-size unit of 500–600 men rather than one of one-tenth that number. So the instruction was, 'Noise, firepower, but no close engagement.' To accomplish this the squadron was armed with general-purpose machine-guns, mortars and the American M-203 grenade launcher used at Pebble Island. The anti-aircraft missile, Stinger, was also brought along. This firepower was augmented by the guns of the frigate *Ardent*.

Right on time, from the low hills north of Darwin/Goose Green, the squadron laid down its barrage, pouring Milan missiles, machine-gun bullets and tracer into the Argentine positions. The SAS men were spread as widely as possible and shifted their positions frequently. The Argentines returned fire, but did not attempt to advance beyond the safety of their own perimeter. Meanwhile, 2 Para had landed at the head of San Carlos Water and was now advancing up Sussex Mountain, in the direction of Darwin/Goose Green. At daybreak the SAS broke contact and marched north to meet the advancing Paras. From the rendezvous the Paras watched as the small SAS column came over the horizon and marched down a forward slope. Then from a clear blue sky, the drone of an unfamiliar aircraft engine heralded a black shape which floated in a leisurely, menacing fashion from the same direction as the SAS men. It was a Pucara, the heavily armed, slow-flying counter-insurgency aircraft, specially designed to attack ground forces. The SAS column spread out, melting into the ground, but to the spectators it seemed certain that some of the men they had just seen would never move again. But warfare is full of surprises. From one SAS position a lone figure rose deliberately, something dark on his shoulder flashing towards the aircraft. The pilot seems to have become aware of his mortal peril when it was too late. As his aircraft exploded some of the men of 2 Para stood and cheered, waving their fists as if watching a goal scored at a football game. Robert Fox, a BBC war correspondent, recalls, 'We saw a cloud of blue smoke and a piece of material fluttering like an autumn leaf. Dangling underneath was a body; it was the parachute of a pilot whose Pucara had been shot down . . . by an SAS patrol covering the landing.' The Stinger had stung.

Later the same day, as Argentine Air Force attacks began in earnest, the same SAS soldier tried to add to his bag. From a carefully-selected firing point he released five more Stingers at incoming aircraft. To his disgust, they all missed. Then, with the rest of the squadron, he returned by helicopter to the assault ship *Intrepid*. Neither the missile nor the man could be blamed for the five aircraft which got away. The only man with the task force trained to use Stinger was Staff Sergeant O'Connor, who had died in the Sea King helicopter crash. His training manuals were lost with him. D Squadron was having to learn to use the missile by trial and error. The first-round kill on Sussex Mountain was a lucky shot. The others, fired out of range, fell short.

The squadron's maritime guardian angel did not get off so lightly. As the sun rose, the frigate *Ardent* – isolated from the rest of the fleet in Grantham Sound – came under savage attack from the air. At one stage, eleven enemy aircraft appeared to form a queue to hit the ship. *Ardent* destroyed one Pucara and carried on fighting despite the fact that she was now drifting out of control, her Seacat missile and 4.5in gun disabled together with her propulsion. Finally her skipper, Captain Alan West, ordered his men to abandon ship. He was later awarded the Distinguished Service Cross.

The intervention of both the SAS and SBS had removed three potential threats to the men of 3 Commando Brigade as they came ashore. Some units, discovering their assigned beaches covered by dangerously deep water, were obliged to check the depth themselves with poles before getting ashore where they could. A few blamed such problems on poor reconnaissance. They were unaware of an order from Brigadier Julian Thompson to the SBS to stay away from the precise landing places to avoid compromising them. Both naval and military top brass believed they had enough beach information without adding to the risk of detection at the last moment in an effort to reinvent the wheel. In general, the landings had gone better than anyone could have hoped. Even a hundred determined and well-armed men could have given the landing force a bloody nose, as might the Argentine Air Force have done, if it had struck earlier. But by the time the first air raid began in the 'Bomb Alley' of San Carlos Water on the morning of 21 May, most of the troops were ashore. When the enemy aircraft did appear, they concentrated their attack – as captured pilots told their SAS interrogators later – on warships and not the vital transports, including *Canberra*, whose supplies would sustain the expeditionary force ashore.

There was no good reason for the Argentines' sluggish response to the British landing. Argentine troops had been in Port San Carlos until the early hours of D–Day as well as on Fanning Head. The Argentines there do not seem to have made a convincing job of alerting their headquarters in Port Stanley before they fled. There was no Paul Revere to ride out with the warning, 'The British are coming!' That was our good luck. The landing of a 2400–strong expeditionary force 8000 miles from home on a beachhead already compromised, and with insufficient air cover, needed luck. During the first 24 hours after the landing, five out of eight warships lying in the approaches to San Carlos Water were hit by Argentine bombs. The frigate *Ardent*, supporting an SAS operation, was sunk and *Argonaut* was badly damaged. *Antrim, Brilliant* and *Broadsword* were more fortunate. Bombs which struck them did not explode. During the first 48 hours, eighty Argentine aircraft flew against the fleet, their pilots displaying the reckless courage of nineteenth-century cavalrymen. In that same period, the Argentine Air Force lost seven Mirage and four A-4 Skyhawk jets, three Pucara, one

Chinook helicopter and one Puma. On 23 May, D+2, *Antelope* exploded spectacularly and sank, and *Glasgow* was hit by an unexploded bomb. Next day, the landing ships *Sir Galahad* and *Sir Lancelot* were also hit by UXBs. On 25 May *Atlantic Conveyor* was crippled by an Exocet missile and sank after only one of her valuable cargo of Chinook helicopters, and 14 Sea Harriers had been salvaged. That loss was to have sombre implications for the SAS. The same day, the destroyer *Coventry* went to the bottom. During this period, at least seventeen more Argentine planes, most of them fast jets, were brought down. In the eerie periods of calm between air attacks, the British were piling ashore tons of food, ammunition, Rapier missiles, tracked vehicles and other paraphernalia of an expeditionary force. On the beachhead it was a time to dig in, consolidate and wait.

Overlooking the scene from the chilly heights of Sussex Mountain, the men of 2 Para watched and waited impatiently. They could not advance yet. The SAS were still busy in the area ahead of them, around Argentine-occupied Darwin/Goose Green. The SBS, meanwhile, had established reconnaissance patrols 35 miles ahead of the beachhead, sprinkled along the north coast route to Port Stanley. From well out to sea, they penetrated miles inland along East Falkland waterways. One explored Port Salvador water, and withdrew just before the Argentines retreating from the Fanning Head/Port San Carlos actions arrived there. Another team, from 6 SBS, travelled 30 miles by small boat from *Fearless*, to land and hide at Green Island. From this position they ran close reconnaissance of Port St Louis and Green Patch for a week until the Commando brigade reached them. Soon afterwards, 2 SBS was inserted from *Intrepid* to carry out a careful survey of Teal Inlet. Before 3 Para arrived there the hard way, on foot, the SBS had discovered good news for them. There were no Argentines at Teal.

From the main beachhead the fastest and most direct route to Port Stanley, and victory, was the southerly one across which 2 Para now sat and waited. In time, the British would advance along both coasts. But first, in the south, was a threat which had to be removed.

The island of East Falkland is shaped like an egg-timer which leans eccentrically to the right at an angle of 45 degrees. The 'neck' of the egg-timer is a narrow isthmus on which lie, Darwin Settlement to the north, separated by a few miles from Goose Green Settlement to the south. The isthmus, at sea level on each flank, rises inland to a series of low but easily defended escarpments. The approaches to it from the north, the direction of the main British advance, are screened by a series of low ridges rising to about 300 feet, facing across a valley towards the forward downslope of Sussex Mountain. It is not a place where the element of surprise has much going for it. Yet for the southerly route to be opened up, it had to be taken. The four-man SAS patrol there, responsible for watching an area of about ten square kilometres, had accurately reported the number of enemy fighting troops: 600 men of 2 and 12 Regiments. Twelve Regiment was a hand-picked Argentine mobile reaction force. So long as it remained the Argentines could threaten the British beachhead. It could not be by-passed.

Intelligence controversy

The battle fought by 2 Para to win the isthmus has been graphically described elsewhere and is only summarised here. What should be noted is that the number of Argentine prisoners taken by 2 Para totalled 1100. Another 200 of the enemy were killed. The British battalion's all-up strength for the assault was 450 and its fatal casualties, seventeen. According to the *Sunday Times*, 'The Intelligence was wrong . . . If the true odds had been known, the attack might never have taken place.' The *Sunday Express* magazine team, however, after examining the evidence afresh, concluded that the 'faulty Intelligence' story was a myth generated by the unexpectedly large number of Argentine prisoners. 'Intelligence,' it argued, 'did not predict the hundreds of "extras" – naval, Marine and HQ elements – who were there but who played little part in the battle.' Additionally, as two independent researches show, some Argentine reserves were brought into the settlement by helicopter from Mount Kent a few hours before Goose Green surrendered. These reinforcements were the result of 2 Para's move towards the isthmus being noted (inevitably) by an Argentine observation post the day before the battle. The Intelligence controversy may never be resolved satisfactorily. One of the author's sources is adamant that the true number of Argentines holding the isthmus was reported by the SAS to the Commanding Officer of 2 Para, Lieutenant-Colonel H. Jones.

Colonel Jones, in fact, personally debriefed the SAS reconnaissance teams on board the assault ship *Intrepid* just before 2 Para went into action. It is conceivable that H decided to disregard the Argentine 'extras' in weighing the true military odds, but he died, winning a posthumous VC, and we shall never know. Certainly there were other less celebrated cases in this campaign in which SAS reconnaissance provided information which, it later became apparent, did not reach the front-line soldiers who needed it. The accuracy of SAS Intelligence was degraded by last-minute Argentine reinforcements which might, or might not, have resulted from a Whitehall leak to the BBC suggesting that the Paras were within five miles of Darwin. This was broadcast on the World Service just before the battle began. In one of the earliest contacts an Argentine reconnaissance platoon, taken prisoner by the Paras, revealed that the garrison was stronger than the Paras had expected. According to Hastings and Jenkins, H was furious and demanded, 'What the hell have the SAS been doing down here?' Soon afterwards, as the Paras attacked the enemy-occupied Burntside House at Camilla Creek, the enemy fled leaving two dead. 'Inside, lying terrified on the floor, were four British civilians, two of them elderly women. Once again the soldiers cursed their Intelligence. They had been assured that Burntside House was solely occupied by the Argentines and had raked it ruthlessly with machine-gun fire . . .' These comments, according to a special forces operator who has no SAS connections, are unfair. 'Such reconnaissance patrols,' he believes, 'can only be expected to report that the enemy are present in an approximate strength.'

What is beyond dispute is that the SAS Goose Green reconnaissance team was no less effective than any other as the

Military Medal citation for Corporal Trevor Brookes makes plain. He commanded the OP at Darwin/Goose Green for sixteen days immediately before the main landing. 'His position was most vulnerable at all times and the difficulty of achieving observation of the target necessitated his surviving under the main enemy helicopter route between Stanley and Darwin. Frequent enemy air searches and foot patrols were carried out in the area. He fully realised that no support was available to him, in the event of compromise by enemy action. His courage and leadership in this situation was of the highest order. The accuracy of his reporting was such that a successful air strike was carried out on his information against a petrol installation on the airfield at Goose Green.

'His information was of great value during the preparation for the successful attack on Darwin/Goose Green by 2nd Battalion, the Parachute Regiment. His performance as an individual and a leader was in the highest traditions of his regiment and the Army as a whole.'

Even if the numerical odds had been equal the Goose Green battle was certain to be a bloody affair, with no assurance of success by 2 Para. To attack a well-fortified position of this sort the British needed numerical superiority. 'We reckoned they were about a battalion, so it would be one for one', the Second-in-Command of 2 Para, Major Chris Keeble, told the *Sunday Times*. If so, the tactical odds were still stacked against the Paras. A more professional enemy could have held the bridge, like Horatius, almost indefinitely. This operation, like others before it and since, was part of the great gamble of Operation Corporate.

The Argentines, packed into easily controlled, well-dug defensive positions, had a powerful arsenal: three 105mm guns; four twin 20mm and 30mm Oerlikon anti-aircraft cannon, which were used as battlefield weapons against the Paras; Pucara aircraft carrying napalm; a wealth of mortars, both 81mm and 120mm, machine guns and good supplies of ammunition. The Paras, by contrast, had as heavy support weapons, one 4.5in gun aboard *Arrow* (which jammed as the battalion crossed its operational start line); three 105mm artillery pieces; two mortars and a limited stock of bombs; Milan anti-tank and Blowpipe anti-aircraft missiles. Low cloud disrupted essential helicopter resupply to the battalion and, for most of the time, prevented Harrier jets from flying in support of the troops.

The battalion started its movement along the isthmus – just 400 yards wide at this point – in the dark at 2.30am on 28 May. The battle was to last all day. Almost as soon as the move started, Argentine shells began to explode around the attackers, causing surprisingly few casualties. With dawn at 6am, the Argentines fought tenaciously, trench by trench. Each was cleared at close quarters by the British, using grenades and anti-tank missiles.

On the east side of the isthmus Darwin Hill impeded the advance so badly that H, 2 Para's Commanding Officer, feared that the momentum of the attack was wavering. With his adjutant, Captain David Wood, he led the assault on what proved to be a series of well-concealed machine-gun positions. Both men were killed. On the other side of the isthmus two companies of the Paras led by H's deputy, Keeble, crawled for 1000 yards along the beach in order to outflank the other strong point, Boca Hill. They then hit it from two sides. As this position surrendered so did Darwin Hill, the scene of H's death. Only one strong point now remained between the advancing Paras and Goose Green Settlement. This was School House, to the settlement's immediate north. It was while accepting the surrender of Argentines here – signalled with a white flag – that three of the Paras were shot dead by Argentines in an adjoining trench. None of the defenders of School House was left alive in the fight which resulted. As dusk fell an Argentine prisoner was sent into the heavily defended, but now surrounded garrison of Goose Green, with a formal note from Keeble. This invited the enemy commander to surrender by 8.30am next day 'or take the inevitable consequences'. The Argentine commander, Air Commodore Wilson Pedroza, surrendered. Soon afterwards, 114 civilians who had been kept prisoner in a local community hall for a month were restored to freedom. The SAS was to make good use of the Air Commodore at a later stage of the campaign.

Leverage on Mount Kent

While the Goose Green surrender was taking place, British forces elsewhere were tightening their grip on East Falkland along the island's north coast. In a memorable 26-mile night march, 3 Para and 45 Royal Marine Commando reached Teal Inlet. But it was clear that the two-pronged coastal approach could be imperilled if a vacuum remained at the centre. The vacuum was large: about thirty miles separates Teal Inlet in the north from Goose Green in the south. The centre ground had to be taken and held as a pivot for the whole strategy to work. This task was given to D Squadron which, after its raid on Darwin/Goose Green, had transferred from *Intrepid* to the landing ship *Sir Lancelot*. The main initiative for moving into the vacuum came from the SAS Commanding Officer, Lieutenant-Colonel 'Mike' Rose. He selected an adventurous target for D Squadron. Mount Kent, many miles forward of both coastal prongs, is a 1400-foot hill which dominates the ridges rolling away to Port Stanley. For the Argentine garrison it was vital ground and certain to be defended. So, in spite of G Squadron's small, four-man OP already in the area since 1 May, a full-scale occupation of the area was an audacious move. Rose, studying G Squadron's reconnaissance report that nothing much was happening there, took a calculated decision to start something. He persuaded Brigadier Thompson to support his plan to seize the position.

Initially, Major Cedric Delves, the squadron commander, was put in with a small patrol to verify that the move was possible. This patrol reconnoitred the area and passed back the invitation, 'Come on in. The water's fine!' In fact it was snowing on the mountain and the 'water' was deceptive. On 25 May, Argentina's national day, just 24 hours after Rose's scheme had received approval, another Argentine Exocet missile was sending to the bottom of the Atlantic three big troop-carrying Chinook helicopters and six smaller Wessex. All had been stowed aboard the container ship *Atlantic Conveyor.* For a short journey the Chinook could probably carry up to seventy armed men. The loss of the helicopters was a body-blow to the Army's mobility. One consequence of this was that D Squadron, committed to seizing Mount Kent, would have to dig in and hold it, with limited hope of resupply or reinforcement for an indeterminate period; certainly for longer than originally intended. But, 'Come on in . . . The water's fine' was an offer the rest of the squadron could not refuse. So in they went, led by the new Second-in-Command, Gallagher's successor, to dig in, infantry style, on a strategically vital position 40 miles behind enemy lines. In the Second World War it was the sort of move which would have provoked a massive counter-attack. In East Falkland in 1982 it generated a series of small but deadly skirmishes between the SAS and Argentine special forces.

After one confrontation in the dark, an SAS soldier grumbled, 'Every time we get near an Argy patrol, they leg it . . . We ran into one the other night though. Took two, wounded two, killed three.' On another night an Argentine patrol and an SAS team met unexpectedly, face to face. The Argentine 'point man' hurled a grenade. Simultaneously the SAS lead scout opened fire with an Armalite. The SAS soldier was slightly wounded. The Argentine was killed. 'Our training paid off,' was the regiment's terse comment on this engagement.

Prominent in these nocturnal firefights was Captain John Hamilton, leader of the Squadron's Mountain Troop. An official citation relates: 'His leadership and courage proved instrumental over seven days of continuous operations in seizing this vital ground from which the attack on Port Stanley was ultimately launched. On 27 May he identified an enemy probe into the squadron position and in the ensuing battle captured a prisoner of war. The next night he and his troop successfully held off another enemy attack and by doing so enabled 42 Commando Royal Marines to fly in as planned to reinforce the position on 31 May, an important step in the repossession of the Falklands. On the following day he ambushed another enemy patrol, wounding three and capturing all five members of the patrol.' On the Argentine side, Mount Kent was rapidly becoming a 'no-go' area. One patrol after another was sent to discover the British strength only to return, badly mauled or not to return at all.

Five days after D Squadron's arrival on Mount Kent, the SAS Commanding Officer descended to examine the ground in person. With characteristic panache he brought with him the war correspondent, Max Hastings. Hastings, prevented by censorship from announcing directly that this was another SAS initiative, slipped the comment 'Who dares, wins', into his dispatch as a way of making his point. His civilian presence emphasized the more serious idea which Rose was trying to convey, that Mount Kent was up for grabs. The reason why this should be, according to the Royal Marine journal, is that 'the Argentines had vacated their prepared positions on Mount Kent in order to reinforce Darwin and Goose Green. It was thus important that 3 Commando Brigade should seize this vital high ground which dominated the western approaches to Port Stanley, as soon as possible.'

With Rose and Hastings, therefore, came Lieutenant-Colonel Nick Vaux, commanding 42 Royal Marine Commando. Vaux brought his K Company, with two mortars and three 105mm light artillery pieces. But as they discovered on their arrival, not all the Argentines had left. An intensive gun battle was taking place less than a mile from the landing zone. Soon afterwards, D Squadron's commander, Delves, arrived to explain, 'No problem, boss. There was an Argie patrol up there, but we've malleted one lot and we'll sort out the others in the morning.'

Over the next few days the Commandos consolidated positions on neighbouring Mount Challenger, just seven miles short of Port Stanley, as well as on Mount Kent. D Squadron moved even farther forward to occupy Murrell Heights overlooking Port Stanley across Wireless Ridge. From this position on 1 June, military targets in Port Stanley were bombarded at a time when Argentina's radio claimed that the British were still on the beachhead of San Carlos.

An essential springboard for the final assault on the capital was now in British hands. This almost bloodless victory was marred by one tragic accident when a Royal Marine SBS patrol, not yet familiar with the terrain, overshot a grid reference (marked by a stream) and strayed into an SAS operational zone known as the Green Patch Area. In the exchange of fire which followed the

SBS team leader, an endurance diver and skier, was shot dead. It was one of several battle accidents to demonstrate that in this respect the Falklands campaign was no different from other large-scale military actions. The SBS commander did not blame the SAS for what had happened. In fact, liaison between the two special force units became significantly tighter after this episode, and for a very good reason. As the British hardened their grip on the area around Port Stanley, the fighting battalions needed as much detailed knowledge of the area as they could get. The area includes a lot of water; Rose invited the SBS to attach at least one four-man patrol of scuba-divers to D Squadron. In fact, six SBS men joined first G, and later, D Squadron. The object was to improve the reconnaissance capability of the task force generally, and to explore ways of making underwater attacks on the Argentines through 'the back door' from the north. In the event, there were no scuba operations, but the SBS did link up with the SAS in the last hours of the campaign for one of the most spectacular battles of all.

Meanwhile, both D Squadron and the SBS turned their attention to John Bull's other Falkland Island. From a military point of view, West Falkland had seemed until then to be a sideshow. But since G Squadron's reconnaissance teams had established that there were 800 enemy at Port Howard and another 900 at Fox Bay, plus an unknown number deployed elsewhere, this was not a case where ignorance was bliss. Several ugly possibilities existed and the SAS wanted to lay them to rest. One was that as Port Stanley was under constant threat by the British, an alternative route for supplies and reinforcements to the Argentine garrison might exist on West Falkland. There was also the risk of an unexpected Argentine amphibious or airborne assault against the San Carlos beachhead, mounted from West Falkland.

With the same possibilities in mind, the SBS had inserted its patrols into Pebble Island, Port Stevens, Weddell Island, Dunnose Head, Byron Heights, Carcass Island, Saunders Island, Keppel Island and Sea Lion Island. As one SBS officer put it, 'West Falkland was ringed. It became obvious that most settlements were completely free of Argentines. Our men went down and made contact with the islanders during the night, disappearing into the hills at dawn. During our visits to the settlements, the fatted calf was killed several times over. The islanders were a valuable source of Intelligence. They knew how many planes had flown in, what they carried, and where the Argentines were. It was a well-informed grapevine. Perhaps we should have made contact with them earlier.'

As well as watching and listening, the SBS went on to the offensive on three occasions in West Falkland and in a way peculiarly suited to special forces. By using their observation posts for artillery spotting they were able to bring a barrage of naval gunfire to bear with fine accuracy on the Argentine garrisons of Port Howard and Fox Bay. It was a classic use of such troops as a 'force multiplier' without indiscriminate, excessive force. It was also somewhat risky. One team paddled away from its island OP just before an Argentine patrol came looking for them.

Initially, D Squadron dedicated five four-man patrols to its new operational theatre. Two of these replaced G Squadron teams on 5 June. The new teams quickly discovered that Argentine opposition was more aggressive than anything they had encountered so far. The Argentines' radio direction finding equipment was also in excellent shape.

Fresh from his adventures at Mount Kent, John Hamilton was assigned the hazardous job of watching the Port Howard garrison. For him, the nightmare which haunted all SAS soldiers running these covert OPs was now about to become a reality. An official citation explains that he 'managed to establish himself in a position only 2500 metres from the enemy, from which he sent detailed and accurate reports . . . Shortly after dawn on 10 June he realised that he and his radio operator had been surrounded in a forward position. Although heavily outnumbered and with no reinforcements available he gave the order to engage the enemy, telling his signaller that they should both attempt to fight their way out of the encirclement. Since the withdrawal route was completely exposed to enemy observation and fire' – he was overlooked as well as surrounded – 'he initiated the fire fight in order to allow his signaller to move first.

'After the resulting exchange of fire he was wounded in the back and it became clear to his signaller that Captain Hamilton was only able to move with difficulty. Nevertheless he told his signaller that he could continue to hold off the enemy while the signaller made good his escape, and then he proceeded to give further covering fire. Shortly after that he was killed.'

Hamilton, the survivor of so many tight corners since the beginning of the conflict, from Fortuna Glacier to Mount Kent, was awarded a posthumous Military Cross. As the citation put it, 'Captain Hamilton displayed outstanding determination and an extraordinary will to continue the fight in spite of being confronted by hopeless odds and being wounded. He furthermore showed supreme courage and sense of duty by his conscious decision to sacrifice himself on behalf of his signaller. His final, brave and unselfish act will be an inspiration to all who follow in the SAS.' Hamilton's service with the SAS had lasted just five months.

For his signaller, the odds were equally hopeless. He had run out of ammunition. After a brief pursuit he was seized, disarmed and taken prisoner. He was then confined in the cellar of a sheep-shearing shed until just before the final Argentine surrender five days later. He was not brutally treated. An Argentine officer who had witnessed Hamilton's death paid warm tribute to the courage of both men. But when the prisoner was discovered by a party of Royal Marine Commandos they were convinced he was an Argentine. The signaller, like a number of other SAS soldiers, is not a European. His dark skin made him suspect until an SBS man accompanying the Commandos recognised him and greeted him warmly.

Meanwhile the other SAS teams were still at work on West Falkland and remained so until the end of the conflict. One was particularly busy trying to identify the position of an Argentine observation post on Mount Rosalie, across the water from San Carlos. This position, rather than the mythical radar at Pebble Island, almost certainly acted as the 'eyes' for some of the aircraft raiding British shipping in Bomb Alley. A back-up party to attack this position was actually assembled but then, as the tide of war swept south towards Port Stanley, the scheme was abandoned. Equally disappointed in these last days of the campaign were men of an SAS Squadron new to the Falklands. B Squadron – which had broken the terrorist seige at the Iranian Embassy in London – now parachuted from Hercules aircraft into the Atlantic to take over from both G and D Squadrons, which needed rest. B Squadron's advance party, sent to a quiescent West Falkland, included Corporal Tommy Palmer, secretly decorated with a Queen's Gallantry Medal for storming into a room at the embassy where hostages were held. (Palmer was to die in a road accident a few months later in Northern Ireland.)

The problem facing those who were still where the action was in East Falkland was that it was becoming a crowded little war with scant room for manoeuvre. G Squadron overcame their problem by liberating a civilian motor cruiser. The engine of this craft needed attention, but otherwise she was a vessel of which any Guards officer could be proud . . . given time. The team running her then sailed up Port Harriet water and went ashore within two miles of Argentine-held Mount Tumbledown. They then directed accurate artillery fire on the enemy garrison there for two days. Elsewhere, men of both squadrons were based aboard the landing ship *Sir Lancelot* as a quick reaction force. Some were to take part in the last Commando raid of the conflict. This was an operation full of surprises, even for the SAS.

A dose of psyops

To those who do not know him well, Michael Rose, Commanding Officer of 22 SAS during the Falklands conflict, appears to be a slightly donnish figure whose affability only just conceals an evident shyness. This impression, although it matches his background – a PPE degree at Oxford (where he was a contemporary of Tariq Ali) a brief spell teaching in France and a well-stocked bookshelf – is deceptive. Like all successful SAS soldiers of whatever rank or background he thinks aggressively. He also thinks ahead. He had been fortunate in commanding the regiment when it broke the Iranian Embassy siege in London. That experience had impressed upon him, as nothing else could, the value of talking to the enemy at the right time to soften the opposition's resolve. True, negotiations at the embassy had finally broken down and the affair had ended bloodily. But it might have worked.

Rose concluded that an elegant end to this campaign would be, not a blitzkrieg against Port Stanley – crowded as it was with civilians as well as teenage Argentine conscripts – but a civilised chat to satisfy the Latin sense of honour, followed by orderly surrender. In any case, as Admiral Woodward was to admit later, the British force was 'running out of steam' when the surrender finally took place. A prolonged siege outside Port Stanley in a Falklands winter was not on. Nor could an onslaught of the kind which happened soon afterwards in Beirut keep world opinion half-way favourable to the British case. Much earlier, long before D-Day at San Carlos, the SAS had considered hitting the Argentine high command in Port Stanley with a flying column of the sort that David Stirling loved to lead . . . and had dropped the notion as impracticable. So as the battle continued with tragic losses at Bluff Cove, savage fighting across the crags between Mount Kent and Port Stanley, Rose and his friends worked Jesuitically from the calm of the *Fearless* operations room to corrode Argentine resistance at source. They talked to the opposition leaders.

There are virtually no telephones on the Falkland Islands. Most people chat to their neighbours by radio and those who have nothing to do, eavesdrop on the conversation. It is a well-tried method of boredom relief during the long winter nights. A knowing Royal Marine Yeoman of Signals had already cashed in on this custom. On the long voyage from England aboard *Fearless*, he put together radio gear which would enable him to monitor civilian CB sets in the Falklands and, if he wished, transmit to them. Rose showed great interest in the equipment, and the idea. (This personal experiment in 'sig-int' saved at least one life. A civilian injured during a Harrier attack on Port Howard was evacuated to hospital by the SBS two painful weeks later. His condition was the subject of CB radio chat.) The yeoman-signaller became part of Rose's hearts-and-minds team, this time with a more orthodox SAS military transmitter on board *Fearless*.

As a special concession during the Argentine occupation, the military governor allowed Alison Bleaney, a British doctor in Port Stanley, to conduct a radio clinic for the benefit of people living outside the capital. These transmissions had an Argentine 'minder' who monitored what was said. On 6 June, Dr Bleaney and her minder, a corporal, were astonished to receive a message in fluent Argentine-Spanish from someone claiming to speak on behalf of Major General Jeremy Moore, the British land forces boss. The voice was that of Captain Roderick Bell, Royal Marines. Initially, Dr Bleaney suspected that she was the victim of a practical joker, but the voice went on and on. It was the first of many such calls masterminded by Rose. General Moore, commanding land forces, was only half convinced by Rose's plan but agreed that he should give it a try. Rose, however, was entirely certain that he had the ingredients of a successful 'psyops' campaign, including the senior Argentine officers taken prisoner at Goose Green. The first attempt to make contact, by telephone from Estancia House to Port Stanley, failed because the line was cut. The psyops team then tried by radio.

The British approach was anything but bellicose. Please, Bell asked in Spanish, could the British military command talk to representatives of General Menendez about avoiding unnecessary casualties? The soldier who took this call made no promises, no concessions. But he agreed to pass on the British message. Next day at the same time another call was made. Dr Bleaney told the British officer that no Argentine was willing to speak directly to the British, but they had agreed that she could receive and pass on messages. These were finely tuned by Rose over the next eight days to reflect the growing pressure on Port Stanley and the growing threat to the survival of everyone in the town. To Bell's voice was added that of the war prisoner Wilson Pedroza, but his contribution simply enraged his former comrades.

When the psyops campaign began there was still plenty of

fight in the Argentines. The two main components of British land forces – 3 Commando Brigade and 5 Infantry Brigade – had to battle their way through Mount Longden, Mount Harriet, Mount William and Tumbledown Mountain almost to the gates of Port Stanley itself, where British shells caused a handful of civilian deaths.

Five of these final actions were fought savagely at night against an enemy equipped with infra-red binoculars, more sophisticated than anything the British possessed. The battles required uphill attacks on bunkers with hand-grenade and bayonet, fighting of a kind the British Army had not experienced since the Korean War thirty years earlier.

'A suicide mission'

The SAS, whose covert OPs continued work in this increasingly crowded war until the very end, showed its mettle as a combat unit in the penultimate battle of the campaign. On the night of 13/14 June, the last night of hostilities, 2 Para were assaulting Wireless Ridge, a few miles west of the capital. The SAS volunteered to put in a raid from the sea, at the enemy's rear. This, it was hoped, would take some pressure off 2 Para by creating the maximum degree of confusion. Sentiment as well as tactics played some part in this decision. The SAS has a number of ex-Parachute Regiment soldiers in its ranks and the Parachute Regiment has officers – several decorated for their work in the Falklands – who have served one or more tours with the SAS. As one SAS officer explains, 'When your comrades are storming the hills and you are available, it would be unforgivable to stand around muttering that it was time to hand over to the big battalions. We did what we could in the most effective way possible to assist their success.'

The raid was launched on the seaward end of Wireless Ridge, by way of a narrow strip of water immediately north of Port Stanley. One target was a huge ordnance depot. Initially, helicopters were to be used to carry the assault force. Because of bad weather, four Royal Marine fast power boats known as

Rigid Raiders, driven by men of 1st Raiding Squadron, RM, from Plymouth, were employed instead. These craft were brought from San Carlos water aboard the trawler *Cordella*, put into the sea and taken by the attackers into hiding at Kidney Island. The raid was mounted jointly by two troops from D Squadron, one from G Squadron and six men from 3 SBS. This assault force, about sixty men, was supported by other SAS soldiers who descended from Murrell Heights on the north shore of the harbour approach and laid down a barrage of GPMG and Milan missile fire. The assault was also backed up by the guns of the frigate *Arrow*, but in spite of this, one participant conceded later, 'I think we bit off more than we could chew.' Another unblushingly described the attack as 'a suicide mission'.

To approach their target the attackers had to pass the Argentine fleet auxiliary *Bahia Paraiso*, then berthed as a hospital ship in Port Stanley harbour. Yet as the attackers went in, the crew of the *Bahia Paraiso* turned their search-lights on the Rigid Raiders. The SAS/SBS men now came under a hailstorm of gunfire from several directions. Both the Argentines on Wireless Ridge and in the Port Stanley area, convinced that the frontal sea assault they had always expected was beginning at last, opened up with every available weapon. The most intense flak came from triple-barrelled 20mm Rheinmetall anti-aircraft cannon which were depressed to their lowest trajectory. 'Being on the receiving end of that,' recalls one who got out unscathed, 'was rather like seeing that magical sword-beam weapon in "Star Wars". It was a long, continuous, glowing stream of hot metal.'

Since it was obvious to the attackers that withdrawal was the only alternative to being shot to pieces, they withdrew fast . . . all, that is, except a Rigid Raider which had lost part of its propeller. It could now travel at only two knots. The 'hospital' ship's participation was particularly resented since the British Harriers had taken exquisite care to avoid hitting her. So now, according to an SBS source, the Rigid Raiders on their way back drove straight towards the *Bahia Paraiso*, using her as a shield from the fire directed at them. Some Argentine 20mm rounds smashed into the ship's hull as a result. The Rigid Raiders reached sanctuary just in time. One sank slowly under the men climbing out of her. It was like a scene from a slapstick comedy. The other three vessels were so badly holed as to be beyond repair. D Squadron suffered just three minor casualties; the SBS, one.

Next day, the last of the conflict, it was the turn of an OP manned by G Squadron soldiers to wreak havoc. At dawn, from Wireless Ridge, men of 2 Para watched in disbelief as the Argentines, who had fought tenaciously until now, scurried away, all 'running, running back to Stanley'. They were being stalked by the SAS. In his account published ten years later, Rose wrote:

> A patrol of G Squadron had managed to infiltrate the enemy lines and had established themselves on Seal Point. Prior to, and during the battle of Mount Tumbledown, this patrol was able to call down observed artillery fire from 4 Field Regiment Royal Artillery on the rear of the enemy positions. So great was the carnage caused that on the morning of 14 June, when the Argentine forces were fleeing from their positions, a voluntary halt was called by the patrol to the devastating artillery fire on the retreating enemy.

That same morning Dr Bleaney, adding her voice to the appeals of Bell and Rose, persuaded the Argentine Navy Commander, Captain Melbourne Hussey, to respond. By now white flags were appearing over Port Stanley. Recognising the impossibility of his situation, General Mario Menendez agreed that the negotiators should come in. At 11am on 14 June, the Argentine headquarters called the SAS, inviting it to send a delegation.

Late in the afternoon a British Gazelle, white parachute trailing below it as a truce signal, descended into Port Stanley. Rose, Bell and an SAS signaller climbed out, only to discover that they were an embarrassing distance from their rendezvous at Government House. On their undignified way through hedges and gardens Rose saw a young woman watching him intently from the hospital balcony. Was she Alison Bleaney, he asked. She nodded, surprised. 'You did a great job', Rose told her, and passed on through defended enemy positions.

At first Menendez would concede only a limited surrender. The Argentine could not speak, he said, for the West Falkland garrison. Rose insisted that a half-surrender was no surrender at all. If hostilities resumed, causing unnecessary bloodshed, history would judge harshly the man responsible. In London, thanks to the SAS's unique communications, the negotiations were being monitored almost paragraph by paragraph. The regiment's communications 'net' was used in parallel with the orthodox link by way of *Fearless* to Northwood and then up the normal chain of command. As a result, Rose's outgoing messages went direct to Hereford while London's answers were relayed via Brigadier John Waters, Moore's second-in-command, aboard *Fearless*. Menendez, by contrast, received no clear instructions from a demoralised Buenos Aires. He had to play the negotiations pragmatically to save as much face as possible. But this was like the closing stages of a decisive chess game and both men knew it. Rose also knew that his own High Command would, in fact, have settled at that stage for a surrender of East Falkland alone. The task force, as Admiral Woodward later admitted, was 'in a poor way' by 14 June and 'running out of speed'. The Army was down to six rounds per gun. For this reason, no Press photographs of the occasion were permitted, in case Menendez changed his mind.

Rose, keeping his nerve, persisted. He wanted a complete surrender and he wanted it that day. Menendez, unaware that he had even one bargaining chip, gave way. The surrender would encompass all the islands. But at least his men – 11,313 in all – could be repatriated aboard Argentine as well as British ships? Rose promptly consulted London on this apparently innocuous detail. London, aware that outright victory was within its grasp, was not minded to reduce the Junta's public embarrassment. Menendez's personal defeat as well as his Army's was complete. He would return to Argentina aboard a British ship. But he shook hands, first with Bell, then with Rose. It was now 9pm. The substance of the Argentine capitulation was agreed. A little under three hours later, at one minute before midnight on 14 June, the formal instrument of surrender was signed by Menendez and Major-General Sir Jeremy Moore, the British land force commander. Argentine HQ staff extracted from their stock a bottle of Southern Comfort with which they toasted the end of hostilities. Afterwards, Rose went out and hoisted the SAS Union Jack on the Government House flagpost.

It was all over bar the inquests, conducted alike by two official inquiries as well as by a task force of journalists and MPs. This was right and proper. The gamble of Operation Corporate had paid off, though only just. For the SAS, whose leaders had effectively taken the surrender of both South Georgia and the Falkland Islands, there were no intrinsically new lessons; just the reinforcement of old ones familiar to earlier generations of the regiment. Of these, perhaps the most important was that no military operation ever works as originally planned. Success or failure depends on the skill, intelligence and nerve of the man on the ground. As a Soviet military aphorism pinned above the door of one of the regiment's training offices puts it: 'Train hard; fight easy.'

Those mainland operations

For the historian, however, one tantalising question about the South Atlantic war remains unanswered. Were there, or were there not, British special forces operations on the Argentine mainland? In this account of SAS history the author has tried to be faithful to the facts. But, in reading the entrails of the 'mainland' episode, we enter an area of – at best – intelligent guesswork.

The roll of those who subscribe publicly to the theory that there were such operations is too weighty to be brushed aside without discussion. It includes the writer Max Hastings, Robert Fox of the BBC, John Witherow of *The Times* (all correspondents with the task force) as well as other experts, such as R. J. Raggett, Editor of *Jane's Military Communications*. Enthusiastic investigative teams who argue that there was some sort of clandestine operation in Argentina also include the BBC's Panorama team and the *Daily Express*. In general, the view of this formidable lobby is that a special forces team drawn from, or linked with, the SAS was put ashore to count the Argentine aircraft out from Rio Grande and Rio Gallegos (if not back again) in order to give the task force early warning of impending attack. The absence of such early warning was a crucial factor. Had an Argentine air attack sunk one or both British carriers, the British military operation as a whole would have failed. The reason for such vulnerability was that the Royal Navy is custom-built for a war in the North Atlantic, where it can depend upon land-based aircraft flying from Scotland, Iceland, Greenland, Canada or the US for airborne early warning of enemy air attack. In the South Atlantic, no cover of this sort existed until the conflict was over.

The only tangible evidence that this gap was filled by special forces is the discovery on 20 May of a Sea King helicopter of 846 Royal Naval Air Squadron, burned out and abandoned about eleven miles south of Punta Arenas in southern Chile, a neutral country friendly to Britain and at odds with its neighbour, Argentina. Later a crew of three emerged from hiding after surviving unaided, they claimed, for several days in wild countryside. At a short Press conference the Royal Marine pilot, Lieutenant Richard Hutchings, said: 'We were on sea patrol when we experienced engine failure due to adverse weather. It was not possible to return to our ship in these conditions. We therefore took refuge in the nearest neutral country.' Punta Arenas is about 500 miles from the Falklands and about 200 outside the British Total Exclusion Zone. It is only 140 miles from the Argentine air base of Rio Grande in Tierra del Fuego. It is 125 miles from Rio Gallegos, just across the Magellan Strait. Many air attacks were launched against the task force from both bases.

The helicopter crew received no further official publicity until the Falklands honours list was published after the Argentine surrender, though Panorama asserted that one of the three 'ferried SAS men on active service, has been on a course with the Special Boat Squadron, is a qualified frogman, a weapons expert and a parachutist'. In the honours list, Hutchings was extolled for his skills as a Combat Survival Instructor as well as courage on eight operational missions. Like Hutchings, his colleague Lieutenant Alan Bennett, RN, received a Distinguished Service Cross for skill and courage 'despite the particularly hazardous nature of the missions in which he was involved'. The third survivor of the crash landing, Leading Aircrewman Peter Imrie, was awarded a Distinguished Service Medal for 'several missions in very hazardous circumstances'. The crew was exceptional in that all received high-grade gallantry awards, accompanied by citations that made no mention of the Falklands or South Georgia. Clearly, something happened: but what?

First it is necessary to test the military plausibility of such an adventure. In theory it would be perfectly feasible, given time, for an SAS reconnaissance team to watch an airfield, encode a signal describing preparations for an Argentine air attack and then transmit that information by modern 'burst transmission' in a second or less. The speed of such a message would defy Argentine efforts to pinpoint the source. (SAS teams such as Hamilton's would have had a much better chance of survival if they had carried such sophisticated gear. They did not.) Suitable vantage points exist outside the Argentine air bases, some in mountains suitable to SAS activity. The Argentines did from time to time search the hinterland around these bases, but could not commit sufficiently large forces to do the job thoroughly. Movement by Europeans in the area would not necessarily arouse suspicion, since most Argentines are themselves of European extraction.

There is also evidence that, as the Falkland campaign progressed, air alert warning of a general kind did improve. Robert Fox, with the task force, noted that 'early warning of air attacks improved steadily throughout the campaign and sometimes over twenty minutes' prior warning was given before the Skyhawks and Mirages attacked land targets'. This implies that a Skyhawk, flying into the attack at 550 knots, would be spotted 180 miles away, a performance beyond the limit of any radar at sea level of the type available to the task force. If Fox is correct, therefore, then there must have been some other method of identifying the threat. Fragmented interceptions of brief radio exchanges between the incoming Argentine aircraft, which the task force did achieve, would not have been sufficient for the purpose.

Yet there is a vivid paradox here. A generalised alert was provided, but the Harrier pilots, who hoped to intercept the attackers, never received specific information about precisely where and when the enemy would appear. British Aerospace, sifting official records after the conflict, found that there was 'a lack of *any* advanced warning' of the Argentine attacks. A researcher who interviewed about twenty of the Sea Harrier pilots (roughly half of the total) told the author: 'All the pilots I spoke to deeply regretted that throughout the conflict they had no early warning, and none even hinted to me that there was such warning.'

As a result, the Harriers had to rely on flying standing Combat Air Patrols using one pair of aircraft in the hope of a chance contact, rather than being guided to a planned interception. Because the British carriers were 30 to 40 minutes' flying time east of the Falklands there was rarely more than one pair of Harriers over the islands at any time, apart from those aircraft engaged on missions in support of British ground forces.

This handicap resulted from the fact that the Argentines would quickly disappear from the sight of those watching on the mainland. Thereafter, flying low into the Total Exclusion Zone, they could sweep in at sea level and below radar detection. Max Hastings and Simon Jenkins suggest that intelligence teams on the mainland as well as British submarines reported the enemy's departure from Argentina. 'But at least 50 miles from the Falklands,' they add, 'the Skyhawks and Mirages dipped to sea level – low enough to come home with wings streaked with salt – and vanished from British radar surveillance. This was where the fleet's lack of airborne early warning became critical. The Argentine aircraft only appeared as they weaved between the hills or swung among the inlets on their final approach, often seconds before they bombed.' The aviation historian Alfred Price, who has analysed, with his American colleague Jeffrey Ethell, the Falklands air war from both sides, concludes that if a clandestine early warning system existed, 'I have found no evidence that it had any great effect. It did not make any difference to the way the Harrier patrols were flown.' The brutal reality that this blind spot existed throughout the campaign was reinforced as late as 8 June, only a week before the Argentine surrender, when the landing and supply ships *Sir Galahad* and *Sir Tristram* were hit by an air attack that left 53 dead and 46 injured.

There is another powerful objection to the plausibility of a mainland adventure. This is the risk it created for the credibility of British diplomacy in representing the United Kingdom as an injured party engaged in a minimum force operation of legitimate self-defence. If anything went wrong (and on such clandestine, cross-border operations something usually does) then the cost of compromise or capture of the SAS men involved would be at least as great as any potential gain for Britain if they succeeded. For a start, to quote a special forces' joke on the subject, 'What do we say at the Press conference, boss?' Or, for that matter, the show trial? Support for Britain in the EEC, the source of the French-built Exocet missile, rested on a sanctions policy that was always ambivalent. Sympathy for Britain at the United Nations and – for what it was worth – at the Organisation of American States would have evaporated, opening the door for instant replacement of Argentine losses. UN Resolution 502, calling for Argentina's withdrawal from the Falklands – the diplomatic card that justified the whole task force operation – would have been rendered valueless if Britain could be made to appear to be at least an equal aggressor in this quarrel.

And yet it is a fact that a British Sea King helicopter from the squadron flying British special forces at the time *did* land in Chile and its crew *did* go into hiding after destroying their aircraft. According to the BBC's Robert Fox, the plan was that this aircraft should never have been discovered. It was to have 'ditched' into the sea, to be lost without trace. So if a special forces team was put ashore, where did it come from?

The classic solution of hard-pressed governments in such a situation is to employ special forces that are 'deniable', people whose names – unlike those of regular servicemen in the SAS or SBS – do not appear in the Army, Navy or even the honours lists. Ideally, everything about them including their nationality should be blurred. They are soldiers of fortune who have worked through an intermediary, with no certain knowledge of who ultimately controls their operation. It seems implausible that between the Argentines' successful Exocet attack on the *Sheffield* on 4 May – which took the Royal Navy by surprise – and mid-May, there was sufficient time to recruit and brief a high-grade team of mercenaries (even ex-SAS soldiers), let alone put them on the ground in Argentina. So an intelligence-gathering operation on the mainland had to be performed by SAS or SBS regulars with all the risks this entailed, a risk which even the most dedicated SAS soldier might deem reckless.

This author concludes from the evidence as it stands, including the testimony of Hastings, Fox and Witherow, that the Sea King helicopter that was discovered in Chile had been stripped down to undertake a long range, one-way mission to put an SAS team into the mainland. Such a drastic decision would require clearance at the highest level of government and as such – like the sinking of the Argentine cruiser *General Belgrano* outside the Total Exclusion Zone – would be a political rather than a military decision. As we have noted, the risk involved, when set against the probable military value of the operation, would be hard to justify. An SAS identification of an all-out aerial onslaught at one time by every available Argentine aircraft would have justified the operation, but not even the Argentine Air Force was that reckless.

The author also believes that at least one team was deposited inside Argentina, too far from the target areas of Rio Gallegos and Rio Grande to make sufficient progress on foot remotely possible in the time available. Deposited in some confusion in a remote border area, the team reported that the plan had not proved a practicable proposition and then discreetly withdrew to neutral territory.

The evidence, such as it is, points to an operation that probably failed or one that, if it succeeded, did not affect the outcome of the war. The gamble of operating a vulnerable carrier force without airborne early warning was not a bet that could be hedged successfully through resort to special forces, however brave. For once, the SAS was asked to perform an impossible task, which might explain the conviction among some special forces personnel unconnected with the Falklands that, after the failure of the first team in Argentina, a second was assembled. Some of the men concerned, who had impeccable records, declined to embark upon an adventure they regarded as doomed.

The war ended before their opinion could be tested. The purpose of the new mainland operation was not to gather Intelligence but to destroy the Argentine Air Force Super-Etendard aircraft and their hated Exocet missiles on the ground in a bold *coup-de-main*. Had such a scheme succeeded at an earlier stage in the conflict, before the British expeditionary force landed, it might have been the sort of strategic knock-out blow that politicians (and sometimes, generals) lust after. The British task force would have been able to operate with the same degree of impunity, confident of its air control, that the Allies enjoyed in the Gulf. Other landing sites, closer to Port Stanley, might have been picked off. As it was, such schemes were forever inhibited by the need to keep the British flagship, the carrier *Hermes*, out of danger and over the horizon to the east much of the time.

The author doubts whether such a stroke was ever a reality without risking a large additional force which Britain did not have. Other, better minds, disagree. They argue that the whole point of the SAS in a major conflict, if the prize is worth it, is to take risks which an enemy, regarding as insane, would disregard.

There is a bizarre postscript to this debate. This is Soldier 'I's memoir of life in the South Atlantic,

Back . . . in Hereford, they had outlined a plan to crash two C-130s containing a heavily armed B Squadron on to the runway at Port Stanley with the aim of bringing the Falklands war to a rapid conclusion . . . The airfield at Stanley was ringed by General Joffre's Tenth Brigade, 7000 fighting men and, worse still, the 601 Anti-aircraft Battalion equipped with ground-to-air missiles.

Slow and low, Hercules transports would be easy prey. B Squadron, he says, was stunned. Soldier 'I' proposed an alternative. Why not, he suggested, use a dose of Polaris on the Argentine mainland airbases . . .

OMAN 1958–59; 1970–76

The Sultanate of Muscat and Oman is a place of extremes where, according to a Persian proverb, the sinner has a foretaste of what awaits him in Hades. By day its volcanic rock acquires the heat and airlessness of an oven, generating a nocturnal summer temperature of 112 degrees Fahrenheit at sea level. On the northern mountains in winter, the temperature drops so far below freezing-point that it turns a metal water-bottle into a block of ice. Out of the valleys, the wind is incessant, and turbulence makes air travel a sickening experience. In the south, the summer monsoon brings incessant rain from which there is no shelter on the mountains of Dhofar. Everywhere, at all seasons, wounds fester with appalling speed.

The country is also a political anachronism, an absolute monarchy in a world of popular government, where political dialogue, when it exists, is traditionally violent. But, by an accident of geography, the Sultanate, through its inheritance of the Musandam Peninsula, commands the Hormuz Strait through which passes about 50 per cent of the non-Communist world's supply of crude oil. Successive British governments have concluded that the protection of this strait is vital to the British economy, and successive Sultans have found it essential to rely on British soldiers for their security. It is a delicate arrangement, in which Britain has worked with some success to make the patriarchy of Oman less barbarous while safeguarding the monarchy itself (and one that uniquely defies post-war British policy of abandoning former colonies and protectorates to the wind of change).

By coincidence, a similar political interdependence has characterised the involvement of the SAS in Oman. The regiment has fought two successful campaigns there, one lasting a few months in the winter of 1958/9; the second, a six-year war which ended with the government's victory of 1976. On the first occasion, the regiment had just been included in the Army's long-term Order of Battle and was under pressure to prove that it could function, as it claimed, at short notice outside its now-traditional jungle environment of Malaya. The second Oman campaign began in 1970, at a time when the SAS – never a garrison regiment – had no fighting commitments and when its *raison d'être* was being questioned not only in Whitehall, but also within its own ranks.

Oman I, 1958–59: Mission Impossible

The first Oman campaign had its roots in a rebellion covertly backed by American oil interests and the Royalist Saudi Government in 1954. The revolt against the Sultan at that time was rooted in fertile soil. In 1958, an official from the British Embassy in Beirut reported that in twenty years' experience of the Middle East he had never seen, until he reached Oman, 'a people so poverty-stricken or so debilitated with disease capable of treatment and cure'.

The rebellion was led by three men. They were Suleiman bin Hamyar; Ghalib, Imam of Oman, the 'Lord of the Green Mountain'; and Talib, his ambitious younger brother, the most formidable of the trio. The 'Green Mountain' (Jabal Akhdar) is an elevated, fertile plateau, twenty miles by ten in area, on average 6500 feet above sea level, locked behind sheer cliffs of rock and shale rising to 10,000 feet above a sweltering plain. It has a climate and economy quite different from that of the surrounding countryside: it is almost an Arabian version of Conan Doyle's *Lost World*. On the plateau, Talib had assembled an offensive guerrilla force of 180 sharpshooters supported by about 500 armed tribesmen. There were only twelve known easily-defended approaches to the plateau, and the rebels had ample stocks of modern weapons including .5-inch Browning machine-guns and quantities of mines with which, during raids on the surrounding plain, they blew up 150 vehicles including 18 British Ferret scout cars between March and November 1958. Although short of food and suffering from bombing attacks by the Sultan's air force, they were still a formidable enemy, apparently able to resist indefinitely.

By now, the conflict had already exploded one bit of British mythology about controlling tribes in the Middle East – that it could be achieved exclusively through the use of air power. As Phillip Darby's account puts it:

> The myth had persisted in air force circles that the RAF's air control method was an economical and successful way of dealing with local tribal quarrels. Thus when the Oman revolt broke out the RAF asserted that it could do the job unaided and the government, acting on this advice, authorised rocket and cannon attacks on enemy held forts, and certain other operations . . .
>
> In his statement to the House of Commons on July 23 1957, the Foreign Secretary, Mr Selwyn Lloyd, was categorical that there was 'no question . . . of large scale operations by British troops on the ground'. Indeed, he went on to say that in view of the high temperatures in Oman at that time of year, it would be an example of military futility to seek to employ ground forces in the desert areas.

So much for the received wisdom. The SAS was invoked in October of the following year, through a somewhat complex blend of realpolitik and coincidence. In a sensitive War Office planning post at that time was Major (later General) Frank Kitson, a pioneer of counter-revolutionary warfare since the Mau Mau campaign in Kenya. Kitson's plan for seizing the plateau involved the placing of carefully chosen British officers in positions at the foot of the mountain, with a nucleus of bodyguards and 'a substantial sum of money' with which to bribe local informers. This, it was hoped, would bring about the capture of guerrillas, some of whom would be turned around to work for the government. 'I visualised', wrote Kitson later, 'forming one or two teams of prisoners augmented by some of our own soldiers in disguise.' These groups, he suggested, could then penetrate the plateau.

The Kitson plan was tentatively approved, with an elaboration added by the Director of Military Operations, General Hamilton: why not use the SAS? In the event, the Kitson plan was overtaken by the SAS's own, more direct method of attack. But the notion that the regiment should take on a long-term Intelligence role, anticipating revolution before it actually happened, was one to which Kitson returned in later years, and which the SAS accepted only in so far as it did not change radically its existing role and character. A decade later, in Northern Ireland, some of Kitson's ideas – based, like those of the SAS, on an economic use of small numbers of carefully selected men – bore fruit in the creation of the plain-clothes Military Reconnaissance Force.

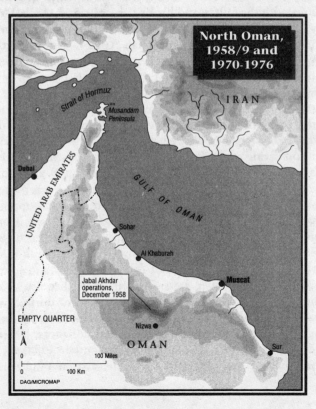

In 1958, however, there were other reasons why the SAS was preferred to one of Kitson's 'counter gangs'. A quick military solution required climbing experts and an assault team that would operate in conditions of ultrasecrecy. Finally, there were indirect political considerations that more orthodox troops (such as Royal Marine Commandos and Parachute Regiment soldiers) would be hard put to meet – a requirement that no serious number of casualties would be suffered, to reduce the risk of adverse publicity at home, and a timetable that would ensure a conclusion before the next UN debate on the Middle East. What it all boiled down to was that the Green Mountain, unconquered since an abortive attempt by the Persians more than 900 years before, had to be taken without British casualties, in weeks rather than months.

Yet another political problem was the delicate question of relations with the Sultan and his British-officered, Arab/Baluchi army. The Sultan's new Chief of Staff, Colonel David Smiley, had been warned by his friend Julian Amery, Under Secretary for War: 'We give the Sultan help; we sometimes give him advice; but we do not give him orders.'

The commanding officer of 22 SAS at this time was Lieutenant-Colonel Anthony Deane-Drummond (an Arnhem veteran who had eluded captivity after that operation by hiding for three days in a cupboard in a German-occupied house). After conferring with Kitson in Oman, he returned to Malaya to gather up D Squadron, under Major John Watts, for the new operation. The squadron was spread around a remote area of the Malayan jungle near the Thai border, still mopping-up the campaign that had kept it busy since 1950. Now it had to retrain and be on the ground in Oman within fifteen days.

The force was brought back to Kuala Lumpur within forty-eight hours, through a series of forced marches and journeys aboard improvised river rafts. It then went through a hectic retraining period lasting sixteen hours a day, during which the favourite SAS jungle weapon, the sawn-off shotgun, was exchanged for automatic rifles and rocket-launchers. When the squadron arrived in Oman early in November 1958, its men learned that of the fifty British troops attached to Smiley's staff, forty-five had been flown to hospital suffering from heat exhaustion, while two others had died of it. Furthermore, the risk of being shot on the slopes of the Green Mountain was such that virtually no Arab would act as guide. Two attempts by the British to seize the jebel in battalion strength had failed.

For the first few days, the squadron pursued its own, energetic reconnaissance programme, and the dangers rapidly became apparent. One corporal – a soldier on temporary attachment from the Royal Army Medical Corps as a specialist – was riding in vehicles which were blown up on the two occasions he left the SAS base; he refused to risk his luck a third time and had to be evacuated by helicopter. Another corporal, 'Duke' Swindells, an experienced SAS soldier who had won a Military Medal in Malaya a few months earlier, was shot dead by a sniper as he walked up a ridge. Given the government's insistence on casualty-avoidance, this was regarded as a very bad augury indeed.

Nights on a bare mountain

Swindells was killed while moving by day. The SAS response was to propose nocturnal movement only, unless the need to do otherwise was imperative. The received wisdom among the Sultan's officers was that the nature of the ground made this impossible, but the SAS went ahead with the new policy anyway, arguing that night had the additional advantage of avoiding the heat and exhaustion of daylight operations. As a result, the squadron was able to move on the mountain with much more freedom. An early episode featured the squadron's commander, Watts, who came striding down a precipitous path, quite alone, as an astonished patrol of the Sultan's armed forces was feeling a tentative way upwards.

The new policy produced a limited success within a few days. Guided by a very nervous local sheik, an SAS troop climbed a steep track, once used by the Persians, on the north side of Jabal Akhdar. In the darkness they reached the lip of the plateau undetected. The track they had followed was punctuated by enemy sangars which, amazingly, were unmanned. At the top, near a twin peak called 'Sabrina', the guiding sheik fell on his knees and thanked Allah for salvation.

The two troops were led by Captain Roderic ('Rory') Walker, who subsequently came to public notice as the Piper of Jakarta during the Borneo campaign. His men occupied sangars 3000 yards short of a strong rebel picquet at Aqbat al Dhafar, and soon came under attack. In one episode, 40 guerrillas armed with rifles and two Brens moved in on a forward slope position held by Sergeant J. Hawkins and nine men. The sergeant ordered his men to hold their fire. When the enemy was only 120 yards away, they let loose a barrage of Bren and rifle fire, killing five men and fatally injuring another four. The attack disintegrated.

In the same area, Walker led an exploratory raid against Sabrina on the night of 27 December. The two troops were detected just before they reached the top. One of them was climbing a rope up a fault in the cliff when the guerrillas above called, in English, 'Come on, Johnny', and opened fire. Walker hauled himself farther up the rope and lobbed a grenade over the top. One guerrilla was killed instantly and his comrades scattered. Walker was over the top now, his men following. In the darkness they killed another eight of the enemy.

Meanwhile, on the south side of the mountain, a small patrol had found a cave used by the guerrillas to guard the main approach to Jabal Akhdar. It was also a main store for weapons and ammunition. Two nights later, two SAS troops moved on it. One of these, under Captain de la Billière, made a ten-hour night march through enemy territory in order to approach the cave from an unexpected direction. It then crept to a point 200 yards from the cave mouth, lined up a 3.5in rocket-launcher, and waited. The only point from which the SAS could open fire was below the cave, and this meant that the rocket crew had to kneel or stand to use the weapon. The same firing-point was, *faute de mieux*, in a natural amphitheatre whose upper slopes were honeycombed by many small caves sheltering enemy snipers. At dawn, as the first of the guerrillas emerged, stretching his sleep-laden limbs and yawning, the soldiers poured a hail of missiles and machine-gun fire into the main cave. Describing the action subsequently, Deane-Drummond wrote: 'Even such withering fire did not cause the rebels to panic or surrender. They quickly dropped into fire positions and returned the best they could. Reloading and firing the 3.5in from the standing position became interesting.' What made it particularly interesting, as well as infuriating, was the failure of many of the SAS missiles to leave the launcher after being fired. They remained unfired but 'active' and had to be extracted immediately and replaced with another round, regardless of the recommended safety drills.

The battle instantly brought down rifle fire from the surrounding hills. Describing the encounter soon afterwards, the journalist Brian Connell wrote: 'Outlying rebel pickets retreated slowly and the SAS picked them off one by one. The rebels still had a mortar firing from a crevice behind the cave, but the SAS had laid on air support. As Venom aircraft came swooping in, one of their rockets made a direct hit. Mortar and men were destroyed immediately. "Right down the chimney!" the SAS shouted as it went up.'

In fact, it was not quite so simple as that. The Venoms were 'stacked' out of sight and sound, awaiting a simple radio signal for an air assault that was to last exactly fifteen minutes, during which the troop was to make an orderly, co-ordinated group withdrawal. This now became a fighting retreat, in which men moved back singly or in pairs, using every scrap of cover available. This lasted rather more than fifteen minutes, and was covered by a .3-inch Browning machine-gun manned by a regimental veteran, 'Tankie' Smith, from the nearest high ground held by the SAS.

As well as D Squadron, the Jabal Akhdar actions now also involved a Life Guards troop acting as infantry, two troops of local Trucial Oman Scouts, a few signallers and REMEs, a total of about 200 men. All shared the same harsh conditions. At night, the men's water-bottles froze. By day, the wind at 8000 feet blew incessantly. It was very different from the jungle, and an environment in which soldiers' lips, and their rubber-soled boots alike, cracked open within days.

Morale, Deane-Drummond asserts, was terrific, possibly

because after Malaya, in which weeks of profitless jungle patrolling were relieved by a few seconds of action, the SAS had now found an enemy who stood his ground and fought. But, in addition to the hardships of the new environment, there were also some spectacular operational muddles. In the first attempt to deliver mortar bombs to the Squadron by parachute, twelve out of seventeen canopies failed to open properly and the bombs they carried exploded among the soldiers, injuring no one.

A game of bluff

By the end of December, it was clear that the squadron's toehold on the north side of the plateau would remain just that unless more men could be brought in to assault it. True, a total of forty rebels had been killed by now, but this had merely stiffened enemy resistance. A full squadron would be required to seize and hold the plateau, while another was essential to maintain pressure on the flanks. And time was against success. Deane-Drummond decided to bring in a second squadron from Malaya and establish a tactical headquarters to co-ordinate the two forces.

Commanded by David Stirling's wartime driver and comrade-in-arms, John Cooper, A Squadron arrived in Oman on 9 January 1959. After less than a week's joint patrolling on the north side of the plateau with an augmented 'troop group' of the incumbent D Squadron, the newcomers were given the task of attacking the twin-peaked Sabrina, at whose centre was the main enemy gateway. This 'training-operation' as Deane-Drummond describes it, was in fact geared to bluffing the guerrillas into believing that this obvious route was indeed the main axis of the British assault; but, although a feint, it required a frontal assault up a narrow track that climbed 400 feet to a strongly-held position. A similar manoeuvre, launched from Tanuf, eight miles from Sabrina, would serve the same purpose. The third element of an elaborate hoax was a confidential briefing given to four local donkey-handlers, who were told that Tanuf would be the main assault route. The handlers, whose animals would carry ammunition, were threatened with death if they disclosed the secret. It was passed to the guerrillas within twenty-four hours.

While these bluffs were being enacted, the enlarged troop from D Squadron, which had taken part in the feint attacks, made a secret withdrawal in the darkness to join the rest of the squadron for the main assault. It was a long march off the mountain to a pick-up point at Wadi Tanuf, from which lorries ferried the men fifteen miles to their rendezvous with the rest of the squadron, and the beginning of another uphill climb. Planning a viable route to the plateau for the main assault on the south side of the plateau had finally become a matter of educated guesswork. The Sultan's Chief of Staff, Smiley, the commanding officer of 22 SAS, Deane-Drummond, and his squadron commanders Watts and Cooper, had all studied aerial photographs of the area. The consensus choice was a climber's route rather than a track, a fine line along a steep ridge extending like a fox's brush into low ground held by the Sultan's men near the village of Kamah. It required a nine-hour climb in darkness, up a 4000-foot slope, for which ropes were needed on one precipitous traverse. Each soldier carried at least sixty pounds weight, most of it ammunition. Behind the SAS Squadron came a troop of Life Guards on foot, and a company of the Sultan's Northern Frontier Regiment, hauling protesting donkeys laden with machine-guns.

This untried route was tested by de la Billière's leading troop. Almost three-quarters of the way up, the troop found just one Browning .5-inch machine-gun whose two-man crew, as Deane-Drummond put it, 'could have mown down the attackers in the moonlight, but they had withdrawn to their cave secure in the knowledge of ten centuries that the jebel was impregnable'. The guardians of the Browning were asleep when the SAS reconnaissance troop found them. They were left to sleep on, with an SAS guard watching over them. Guerrilla picquets on the other side of the plateau, around Sabrina, had now been increased to 100, while the remainder of their force was concentrated at Tanuf.

From this point on, it seemed to the attackers that the way was clear, but it was now almost 3am. Watts, leading the squadron, and the commanding officer, Deane-Drummond, therefore had a choice. They could continue to move a ponderous but well-armed force up the hill, with the risk that it would fall into the text-book trap of mountain warfare, that of being overlooked by the enemy at sunrise. Or the SAS Squadron could cache its heavy rucksacks and make a dash for the top with only a minimum of ammunition. This plan would also, had it misfired, have been fatal – costly in British lives if even a small group of guerrillas lurked unseen at the top, and politically embarrassing. Watts decided on a quick dash. The rucksacks were dumped on a false summit short of the plateau, in what was now a race against the sun, and the main force left to catch up later. With just their rifles and what ammunition they could carry on their bodies, the SAS men slithered down the steep incline leading from the false summit they had reached, to begin climbing once more.

'In the final stages', one of those who took part recalls, 'there was a race to be first on top since the Persians.' The front runners included Deane-Drummond, Watts and de la Billière. They arrived on the unguarded plateau 'absolutely shattered' by their climb, only to be scourged on by Deane-Drummond to advance and consolidate what was still only a tenuous hold on the guerrilla stronghold.

With the dawn came an air strike by Venoms and a parachute supply drop, which apparently convinced the few guerrillas remaining on the south side of the plateau that a full-scale airborne invasion of the area was in progress. Whatever the reason, the guerrilla leaders fled, leaving eight mortars, six heavy machine-guns, twelve Brens, quantities of mines and other ordnance, and a great deal of revealing documentation about the uprising. There was also an Aladdin's Cave, explored that morning by the SAS: a labyrinth full of boxes, which the soldiers opened by torchlight. They contained only clothes, but there were moments when the soldiers wondered if the next box might not just contain something approximating to the Crown Jewels . . . The loot included a 6mm MAB pistol, belonging to one of the guerrilla leaders, which finally found its way to the regimental museum.

For many of those involved, there were more orthodox rewards. Deane-Drummond was awarded a DSO and Captain Walker one of four MCs. The others went to John Watts, de la Billière and Lieutenant Anthony Jeapes. Sergeant Hawkins received a DCM and Trooper A. Cunningham, an MM. Six men, including Cooper, were Mentioned in Dispatches. The comparative lavishness of the awards reflected, not only the military achievement, but also the gratitude of Whitehall for the fact that a highly embarrassing rebellion had been snuffed out, after more than four years of failure by the security forces in Oman. It was, declared *The Times*, 'a brilliant example of economy in the use of force'.

It was also a risky, lucky operation and one that was to have prolonged effects on British defence policy generally. The tide of independence movements in the Third World was already beginning to run counter to the traditional, imperial idea of big overseas garrisons of British forces. Additionally, the new emphasis on nuclear weapons was having an impact on conventional forces available for low-intensity campaigns outside Europe. As Darby cogently points out:

Militarily, the Oman campaign was not much more than a skirmish, but it had important lessons for the policy-makers about the demands of British overseas commitments and the way in which they had to be supported.

This minor operation in the arid wastes of the Persian Gulf, in support of the feudal ruler of a country which had not emerged into the twentieth century, powerfully supported the hand of those ministers who argued for a greater emphasis on conventional forces, and perhaps had more effect on the Cabinet's thinking about defence priorities than all the carefully balanced arguments of the preceding few months.

Even more significant was the decision of the Chiefs of Staff in 1961 'that Britain must be increasingly prepared to intervene in Asia and Africa and that this would be her major military role over the next decade'. The policy from now on, until the 'Europeanisation' embodied in the 1974 Defence Review, was strategic mobility, the 'fire brigade' approach to power projection, the first successful experiment in which was the SAS intervention in Oman in 1958/9.

Oman II: defeat into victory

By the spring of 1970, the regiment had no suitable theatre within which to rehearse its 'training operations'. The classic counter-revolutionary campaigns that had started with Greece in 1944, and continued through to Aden/South Yemen in 1967, were now a matter of history so far as British interests were concerned. Early in 1969, an SAS officer, disturbed by the lack of action, analysed British military history and concluded that since 1830 there had been only one or two years in which the Army was not fighting a war somewhere. It seemed that 1968/9 was one of those years. True, from August 1969 onwards, violence in Ulster required the presence of about 14,000 British troops, but they were there initially as a peace-keeping force, UN style, rather than as counter-insurgency forces. Apart from one brief, unpublicised tour of Northern Ireland as orthodox infantry in 1969, the SAS was now living from hand to mouth: testing new weapons in Britain, testing the security arrangements at the country's newest prison (where they broke out over an 'unscalable' fence in less than two minutes), training special forces and paramilitary police forces of such allies as Iran, and even providing bodyguards for some friendly foreign heads of state. Some men serving with the regiment at that time heard the rumours that afflict all special forces at such periods, that there was no future for them and that the unit was to be disbanded.

It was in this climate that a small group of senior SAS officers decided to turn their attention to one place where their services would be of value. Twelve years after their first campaign in northern Oman, the ageing Sultan Sa'id bin Taimur, the thirteenth hereditary monarch of Oman, now had a much more acute internal security problem in the southern mountains of Dhofar. The regiment's interest in Oman was revived in 1969 when British Intelligence sources reported that an Iraqi-trained guerrilla training team had started work among the primitive tribesmen of the sensitive Musandam Peninsula. As a result, a squadron of SAS soldiers was landed on the peninsula by Royal Marine Special Boat Section Gemini inflatables. One suspect was shot and wounded and one SAS soldier, Trooper 'Rip' Reddy, was killed during a nocturnal free-fall parachute drop into the area (probably the first operational fatality of its kind in the British Army). The drop, by a reconnaissance free-fall troop, was peculiarly hazardous – a 'HALO' ('High-Altitude, Low-Opening') from 10,000 feet with equipment, into a near-vertical 120mph free-fall, to canopy deployment in a depression surrounded by 4000-foot mountain peaks. Reddy became unstable as the heavy Bergen pack he carried shifted. The result was a tangled canopy deployment and instant death. Too late, the SAS discovered that 'the report of enemy activity in the Musandam was the product of the imagination of a grossly inadequate Intelligence Officer and had no basis in fact.' It would not be the first time that the regiment was wrong-footed in this way.

Meanwhile, at the other extremity of Oman, 625 miles away on the border with Marxist South Yemen, the Sultan's disastrous conduct of his country's affairs had provoked a Communist-led guerrilla war and brought his own regime to the brink of extinction. Even within Oman, Dhofar is a faraway country of which the rest of the population knows little, sandwiched politically between Royalist Saudi Arabia to the north and Communist South Yemen. It is about the same size as Wales, with 4000-foot peaks topping an escarpment that rises like a natural fortress from a narrow coastal plain. From June to September, a monsoon wind sweeps off the sea on to the hills, bringing low cloud and fine rain which runs off the hills, to be followed by months of sunshine. As a result, the narrow plain between mountain and sea luxuriates in vegetation, including frankincense. The lower slopes are cut by ravines, thousands of feet deep, through which secret paths wander beneath thick undergrowth. It is perfect guerrilla country, honeycombed by limestone caves where food and guns may be stored for months and in which men may live.

The hill people, perpetually short of water, have always had to fight for existence against their neighbours as well as nature itself, as they move with meagre herds of cattle, goats and camels from one scant grazing ground to another. According to one recent authority, 'the characteristic Omani settlement is a semi-fortified village around a water source', a society in which arms are carried as a badge of masculinity and status as well as for protection. The hill man's ethnic links are with the people of what is now South Yemen, while the ruling Sultan (a client of the British since 1800) is traditionally a remote and contemptible figure, a plainsman living behind palace walls at Salalah, with an escape route to the sea guarded by foreign mercenaries.

How not to win friends

In April 1969, five years after oil had been discovered in commercial quantities, a distinguished British economist, John Townsend, arrived to help Sultan Sa'id begin 'a cautious move forward into the modern world'. Townsend recalls:

> My first meeting with the Sultan had a dreamlike unreality: I met a strange, small old man with a splendid set of Father Christmas whiskers, tended and guarded by burly young men of undoubted African origin who were known as 'slaves'. He gave me, in excellent English, careful instructions as to whom I should meet and what I might say. All the people with whom I was to work were expatriate; I was not to meet any Omanis. 'Our people are not yet ready for development', was the explanation . . .
>
> There was great poverty and disease . . . yet nothing was done because the Sultan would not permit it. No man could leave his village and seek work without the permission of the Sultan. No man could repair his house without the permission of the Sultan. This remote old man, who never left his palace

in Salalah and ruled by radio–telephone through expatriates, had instilled such a fear in his people that very few of them dared defy him and undertake any initiative to improve their lot.

There were no schools, so Omanis who wished to study were obliged to become political exiles. Some did so in Russia and East Germany, others elsewhere in the Middle East. There were no hospitals in Dhofar, and only one road out of the coastal plain. Almost all foreign goods were forbidden, and Omanis were prohibited from dancing, playing music, smoking, wearing sun-glasses, taking photographs or wearing Western clothes. As an official British Press briefing document was later to admit: 'The penalties for disobedience were either flogging or imprisonment.' Such penalties were the minor ones. As one SAS veteran was to discover, Sa'id's collective punishments included the cementing over of water wells with catastrophic results for entire communities. Sa'id, the official brief concluded, was 'a medieval and somewhat despotic ruler'.

Across the border in Aden and South Yemen, left-wing Arab Nationalists had been engaged in a terrorist campaign against the British since 1963. It was inevitable that Sultan Sa'id's regime should also provoke rebellion. Dhofari tribesmen, trained in Iraq, started a sporadic campaign of armed ambush, mine-laying and assassination in 1965, and this led to savage repression by the increasingly isolated ruler. Within a year, the Sultan was the target of an assassination attempt by his own bodyguard, several of whom fired at him from a range of a few feet while he was inspecting them. They missed. It is part of the legend of Sultan Sa'id that he then drove himself to his principal Army garrison (leaving behind a wounded Pakistani palace guard commander) to tell its British commander: 'We seem to be having a little trouble down at the palace. I wonder if you would be so good as to come down?'

Not surprisingly, opposition to Sa'id prospered. Fred Halliday, a left-wing British journalist and academic who has studied the Oman campaign, records:

In the first five years, up to 1970, the British were on the defensive and merely tried to hold out with their ramshackle army and colonial administration. The main tactics used were traditional ones: villages were burnt to punish the populations, corpses of guerrilla fighters were hung up in the main square in Salalah; the mountains were blockaded and Salalah itself was ringed with a barbed-wire fence so that no food could be taken out or weapons brought in.

In November 1967, a year after Sa'id's bodyguard had tried to kill him, the British left neighbouring Aden. Although the hinterland bordering Dhofar became a battleground for two warring factions within what was now South Yemen, it was clear that Sa'id's opponents in the mountains would soon have more room for manoeuvre: the British were, almost literally, off their backs. It is an axiom of guerrilla warfare that a sanctuary and a secure source of war materials, preferably contiguous with the war zone, must be established if the campaign is to succeed. Clearly, the rebels would soon have just this. The war would be lost if something were not done to change Sa'id's disastrous conduct of affairs, and this change occurred soon after the unexpected election in June 1970 of Edward Heath's Conservative government in Britain. Townsend has recounted how the outgoing Wilson government of 1970 had announced that there would be a British withdrawal from the Arabian Gulf at the end of 1971, while 'the Conservative government which followed it was less inhibited about dabbling in the affairs of other states. Both the Foreign Office and the Ministry of Defence were worried that an unstable situation in Oman could well prejudice the smooth withdrawal from the Gulf in the following year:' There was another, more pressing reason for anxiety in London: the flow of oil through Hormuz.

On the afternoon of 23 July, less than a month after Heath's election in Britain, Sheik Braik bin Hamud bin Hamid al-Ghafari, an Omani aristocrat and the Wali (Governor) of Dhofar province, entered the Salalah palace to demand the abdication of Sultan Sa'id. It was an act of courage buttressed by Sheik Braik's knowledge that the Sultan's son and heir,

Qaboos – Sheik Braik's close friend – as well as key British officers in the administration were part of the plot. The Sultan responded to the Sheik's unexpected appearance by snatching a pistol from his desk and opening fire. One round wounded the Sheik, another killed a palace servant and one or two more wounded the Sultan in the foot and stomach. (It is generally believed that the Ruler himself was the cause of all these injuries.) That night, the Sultan agreed to surrender himself to a British colonel seconded to his armed forces, and abdicate. Both Sheik Braik and the Sultan were then flown to a Gulf hospital aboard the same aircraft, separated by a curtain, and the RAF spirited Sa'id away to London where he spent the last two years of his life in seclusion.

Operation 'Storm'

A few months before these events, after comparing notes at the Hereford Headquarters of 22 SAS, three senior officers had spent the Easter holiday weekend of 1970 examining the Dhofar problem and devising a winning strategy. By now the regiment had come a long way from its role as saboteurs during the Second World War. 'Low intensity' operations still involved hard, if unorthodox soldiering, but Confrontation in Borneo and the Vietnam war had shown that a winning strategy, in an age of revolutionary fish swimming in a proletarian sea, was a matter of shaping the perceptions and loyalty of the population at large. By Easter Monday, one of the three had produced a plan for what was to become Operation 'Storm' in Dhofar, the basic elements of which would change the course of the war there. The plan demanded, first, a vigorous but intelligent and coherent military campaign run by soldiers, in which indiscriminate reprisals would be avoided. The other basic elements of the strategy were:

1.   A medical campaign to provide aid for the 50,000 or so people living in the Dhofar mountains, most of whom were then regarded by Salalah as enemies.

2.   A veterinary campaign to improve farm stock, including

the provision of that most scarce commodity, fresh water, as well as skilled advice about husbandry.

3. A coherent Intelligence-gathering operation that would embrace every scrap of knowledge about the opposition (as the rebels were regarded at Hereford) aimed at isolating them and breaking their morale as well as underpinning military operations.

4. A psychological operation to persuade the rebels to change sides, the basic ingredients of which were communication by air-dropped leaflets, offer of amnesty to tribesmen wishing to surrender and an aggressive civil-aid programme that would outbid anything the opposition could afford.

Possibly because Sultan Sa'id was still ruling Oman, such a change of style did not meet with universal approval in 'informed' circles. It was a risk strategy and one that required cunning co-ordination as well as greater discipline among the military leadership in Salalah. For example, the existing use of air power – then consisting of six BAC Strikemasters – was, in the view of one SAS officer, remarkably informal. 'At that time', he noted, 'the Sultan's Air Force operated in an *ad hoc* way. The pilots seemed to sit around the mess in Salalah, then someone would suggest, off the top of his head, "Let's go and hit such-and-such a place." Systematic air support for infantry operations did not really exist.'

The removal of Sultan Sa'id, however, gave the SAS the chance for which it had been waiting. Within hours of the palace coup, a small SAS team (officially an 'information team') was on its way to Salalah, led by the chief architect of the 'win strategy' document. It provided an instant bodyguard for the new Sultan, Qaboos, about which there is a story (possibly apocryphal) that it stood behind a two-way mirror while Qaboos received petitions in his palace. One petitioner was a venerable, bearded figure much given to florid gestures. He did not know that each time an arm swept towards his robe, the trained hands of SAS men behind the mirror moved towards their weapons.

One of the team's first operations was to organise a leaflet drop over rebel territory. Despite some mild mockery from the British Left, which criticised the leaflets' Arabic syntax, and scepticism within the Salalah old guard, and the real objection that only a tiny percentage of the intended audience was literate anyway, the operation produced an unexpected prize. The best military brains among the guerrillas at the time included Mohammed Suhail, a former soldier in the Sultan's British-officered Trucial Oman Scouts. Suhail had been sent to Mons Officer Training School at Aldershot, sponsored by the Foreign and Commonwealth Office. He was a good soldier: best rifle and machine-gun shot on his course, and top of the FCO sponsorship list. On his return to Oman, however, he was disillusioned with the Sa'id regime and joined the opposition in the mountains. The first leaflet, with its offer of amnesty from the new ruler, Sultan Qaboos (himself a British-trained officer), brought Suhail back again to work with the SAS and the Sultan's Intelligence staff, headed by an SAS officer.

The team in Salalah consisted initially of one troop of fifteen men, plus specialists including Intelligence Corps linguists, a doctor, a veterinary surgeon, and a 'psyops' expert to disseminate information among the guerrillas. As a first step to penetrating the community it started a model farm on the outskirts of Salalah, which included cattle and poultry as well as root crops. The SAS even sent a soil sample for analysis by British agronomists, via one of its officers on his way to London.

As it turned out, penetration worked both ways. First, two thoroughbred bulls flown by the RAF by way of Dubai (where they created a commotion aboard the plane, to the alarm of the aircrew) were used to serve Dhofari cows before an appreciative civilian audience. But the SAS's prize cockerels met a less happy fate: local farmers, anxious to improve their stock, smuggled hens into the roost, and these passed on fowl pest to the imported cocks, which died in action as a result soon afterwards. The experience had a deadly familiarity. No regiment suffers so much from exotic diseases as the SAS – eighteen out of thirty-six men on a subsequent Oman operation contracted hepatitis in one hill locality – but the team's vet was undismayed. Asked how he liked working in Dhofar, he replied, enigmatically, that he preferred it to caring for homosexual goats at Harwell.

Only a fortnight after the coup, the SAS team leader was on his way back to London with a long shopping list of unmilitary equipment, including drilling gear with which to dig water wells. The Dhofari hill men and their livestock had been cruelly impeded in their nomadic pursuit of water as a result of both the war and Sa'id's repressive habit of sealing off such wells as there were. Water, above all, was the currency that was to prove decisive in winning friends and influencing people. The SAS took its request to the Army's Chief Engineer, Richard Clutterbuck, who later became an academic scientist specializing in counter-revolutionary warfare. Asked to provide drilling gear to help dissident tribesmen in Oman he replied: 'That's what we're here for.'

At this stage, London would not sanction the use of SAS patrols into rebel territory. Political considerations as well as the need for the soldiers to familiarise themselves with the environment both played a part in the decision. And at this stage, too, a troop of fifteen men was just not sufficient. The politics of Oman as well as Britain made caution necessary. On 20 December 1970, the *Financial Times*'s Ralph Izzard reported from Bahrein that, although SAS soldiers wearing the familiar beret with its winged-dagger emblem had been spotted in Bahrein, Sharjah and Oman, their presence was officially denied at first.

'It is now explained', Izzard continued, 'that this denial was meant to save embarrassment to Sultan Qaboos who ousted his father in a palace coup in July . . . He clearly would not want it to be thought his own British-officered armed forces were incapable of dealing with Dhofar's Chinese-trained guerrillas.

'Services spokesmen maintain that the SAS have been in Dhofar purely for training purposes. They had no contact with the insurgents and no shot was fired in anger . . . Dhofar has special attractions as a training ground because it is partly covered with thick vegetation as a result of the summer monsoon.'

In Britain it was clear that the premature commitment of the SAS to action, with perhaps the risk of large numbers of casualties, would generate publicity that could have imperilled the whole strategy to retrieve Oman's security. In those early days of the campaign, then, the SAS worked at hearts-and-minds, dispensing medical aid in villages on the plain, setting up two- and three-man teams to assist the people in any way that seemed useful. In some cases the soldiers even organised an efficient postal service. Their olive green uniform was non-descript, though recognisably European garb, and cap-badges were not worn. It all helped to ensure that the incomers were accepted by the Sultan's men, expatriate British officers, as well as the locals. Because of the SAS's unique constitutional position in Dhofar, finally answerable not to the Sultan and his military command but to the Ministry of Defence in London, it was a delicate and vital exercise in credibility before military operations could begin.

Meanwhile the amnesty campaign – much criticised by some British soldiers as a double-edged weapon that supplied much war material to the rebels – was reaping a useful harvest of 'surrendered enemy personnel'. The price paid by security forces was that rebel camel-trains moved unmolested in and out of the Dhofar mountains. But the defections were accelerated in September 1970, by a split within the rebel camp between the Communists and Islamic traditionalists, which led to fighting between the two. A British Army brief records that 'the attempted counter-revolution was ruthlessly suppressed by the Communists and resulted in mass defections to the Government'. Between September 1970 and March 1971, encouraged by promises of cash as well as amnesty, a total of 201 rebels surrendered. Some handed over their Kalashnikov AK-47s and were paid an extra bounty of £50. The most useful men were then screened with the aid of Mohammed Suhail, and recruited into irregular counter-guerrilla units known as 'firqas'. (This is an anglicised version of the Arabic word 'firqat' originally meaning 'a party of men'; or 'firaq' meaning several parties. The final Arabic letter 't' is not pronounced). The training, management and leadership of the firqas was one of the most important tasks taken on by the SAS in its role as a British Army Training Team. As the operation got under way, SAS soldiers were sent for intensive, ten-week courses in colloquial Arabic at

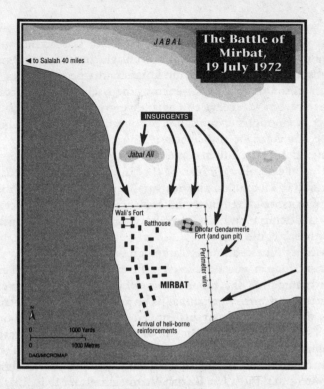

The Battle of Mirbat, 19 July 1972

JABAL

◄ to Salalah 40 miles

INSURGENTS

Jabal Ali

Wali's Fort

Batthouse

Dhofar Gendarmerie Fort (and gun pit)

Perimeter wire

MIRBAT

N

0   1000 Yards

0   1000 Metres

DAG/MICROMAP

Arrival of heli-borne reinforcements

Beaconsfield, before being attached in three- or four-man groups to firqa units in their own tribal areas. One such team was to be involved in one of the regiment's most desperate actions of this, or any other campaign.

In October 1971, two SAS squadrons were committed to Operation Jaguar, to secure their first firm base on the enemy-held jebel around the village of Jibjat. The start point was a former Sultan's Air Force base on the plain known to the soldiers as Lympne. A night march from this position, across a stony desert in hot conditions, laden like mules with machine-guns, mortar, radio and ammunition, was later described by Soldier 'I' as 'the death march'. It was merely the beginning of a bitterly fought advance of fifteen miles into the mountains over a period of almost three weeks. Both sides used heavy machine-guns and mortars. In this battle Sergeant Steve Moores was killed by enemy fire, the first SAS soldier killed in action in this campaign, and two were wounded. Tony Jeapes's account of the action speaks of the ferocity with which the former enemy, firqat soldiers fighting alongside the SAS, battled against their tribal kinsmen still on the enemy side, 'when both sides were close enough to exchange grenades and insults'.

The Battle of Mirbat

On 18 July 1972, the British Army Training Team at Mirbat – a meagre group of ten SAS soldiers, despite its grandiloquent title – was looking forward to the following morning, a Wednesday. On that day, the men, drawn from the Regiment's B Squadron, would fly out of the desolate, barbed-wire enclave they had occupied for more than three months and return to England. They were glad to be going home. Even by Omani standards, Mirbat was not much of a place – a huddle of flat-topped houses and a couple of ancient, stone-walled forts flanked on two sides by the sea, forty miles from the provincial capital, Salalah. Children and insects were numerous, but not much else. More than most wars, this one was a long, grinding spell of boredom punctuated by brief spurts of action. In Mirbat even the 'action' was frustrating: the whistle of incoming mortar bombs or anti-tank missiles fired by an unseen enemy. On 28 May, six mortar bombs had hit the town. On 6 June, another six. Two days later, three 75mm shells. And that, throughout the tour, was that.

The training team – acronymously known as 'Batmen' – had kept busy and alert, training local forces, repairing vehicles and dispensing rudimentary medical care to human beings and camels in the quest for goodwill, while keeping their undisciplined allies in check through a prudent control of the ration stock. Their departure date was well into the monsoon season. It was a time of incessant rain, low cloud and damp clothes, and therefore a time when visibility towards the hostile mountain three miles inland was dangerously limited. The season favoured the Marxist guerrillas of the Dhofar Liberation

Front, biding their time in limestone caves on the mountain, in another important way. It usually made flying all but impossible. In a tight situation, as both sides well understood, the British team might depend upon air supply for ammunition, reinforcement and casualty evacuation, as well as supportive aerial bombardment. On the eve of the team's departure it seemed that no such problems existed. As the soldiers turned into their sleeping-bags for their last night in the 'Batthouse', they could hear the wind screeching in from the Indian Ocean and buffeting past them to rage against the mountain. But that night the guerrillas were also on the move, launching a silent attack on the town to begin the most ambitious frontal assault of their ten-year war against the Sultan and his British advisers. More than 250 of their best warriors had been assembled for this battle, armed with Kalashnikov AK–47 automatic rifles, light, heavy and medium machine-guns, mortars of various calibres up to 82mm, two 75mm recoilless anti-tank rifles and an 84mm Carl Gustav rocket-launcher. As well as ammunition for these weapons, each man carried a profusion of hand grenades. The guerrilla column marched south towards the town and the sea, and then broke into carefully-organised combat groups, each of about ten men, which spread out in a wide arc around the town. Another group made a circular trek east to the beach and then back again along the coast to penetrate the town from that side. Before dawn, the garrison was isolated with no way of escape.

Inside the wire, in addition to the SAS team, was a group of about thirty Askaris from northern Oman, 500 miles away, armed with accurate but slow-firing .303-inch rifles. They served the Sultan's representative, the Wali, as town gate-keepers, searching all who came and went for messages and supplies, including food, that might be going to the enemy on the hill. The Askaris occupied a fort near the water's edge, known as the Wali's Fort. Living in the town itself, armed with FN automatic rifles and light machine-guns, was the local 'firqa'. Nominally its strength was about sixty, but at least twenty of them were somewhere on the mountain on a reconnaissance patrol. The remaining forty were in bed with their wives. Finally, there was another force of about twenty-five men of the Dhofar Gendarmerie, armed with FN rifles and a single light machine-gun, in a second fort just inside the wire. In front of the fort was the dug-out position for a venerable 25-pounder artillery piece of Second World War vintage. The DG Fort dominated the town and Mirbat's only airstrip. It was a vital position. Apart from the artillery piece, the heaviest weapons available to the SAS, at their nearby Batthouse, were a single .50-inch Browning and an 81mm mortar.

About 800 yards outside the wire, on a hill to the north of the town, another eight Gendarmes were on picquet duty. Predictably, it was their position, known as Jabal Ali, that first came under attack. Completely surrounded, it was to have been suppressed in a silent attack, but, as the guerrillas crept up on the position just before 5.30am, the Gendarmes spotted them and a single high-velocity shot rang out. Immediately a 12.7mm Shoagin machine-gun opened fire from a position nearby. In the fight that followed, four of the Gendarmes were killed; the other four escaped. It was the start of a battle as remarkable as that fought at Rorke's Drift.

Guerrilla mortarmen, realising that surprise had been lost, immediately began raining bombs on the DG Fort, the Batthouse and the town itself. Inside the house, Captain M. J. A. ('Mike') Kealy, aged twenty-three, rolled out of his sleeping-bag, slipped on a pair of 'flip-flop' beach sandals, seized his automatic rifle and ran to the rooftop to see what was happening. What he saw was unlike any enemy attack of the war, and Kealy thought it possible that the firing was an appalling confusion caused by false identification of the friendly firqa patrol on its return. In the half-light of a grey dawn he could see groups of armed men running across open ground in front of the Batthouse, pausing to fire at the DG Fort away to his right. Men were also swarming over the picquet position on Jabal Ali: clearly it was already in enemy hands. Kealy ordered the team's only mortar, pre-laid to fire over the picquet to cover just such a situation, to open fire with high explosive and white phosphorous smoke to obscure the enemy's vision. Another of his soldiers, Trooper W., opened up with the Browning, raking the area between the two forts, while others, firing from the roof of the Batthouse, picked off targets with careful precision with FN automatic rifles and a light machine-gun.

As Soldier 'I' recalled in his book:

> We opened fire simultaneously, unleashing a hail of GPMG and .50 calibre bullets at the assaulting Adoo troops. The running figures became a focul point where the red tracer and exploding incendiary rounds converged. . . . Where moments before there had been an orderly advance, parts of the line now faltered and collapsed. Figures staggered . . . but still the Adoo kept coming, wave upon wave over the plain . . .

Kealy was by now profoundly disturbed. A frontal assault of this sort on a government garrison must mean that the guerrillas had assembled an unusually large force and that they probably knew the real fighting strength of the defenders (effectively, about fifty men). He handed control briefly to one of his NCOs, Corporal 'B', while he drafted an urgent signal to the provincial headquarters at Salalah. The message safely away, Kealy prepared for a long, hard day by changing from flip-flops into desert boots.

By now, a well-co-ordinated assault was under way. Guerrilla combat groups moved as though presenting an infantry demonstration of fire and movement back home in Britain, one group advancing under covering fire until it could find dead ground from which to cover those who followed. From the overrun Jabal Ali, above the town, came accurate, considered bursts of heavy machine-gun fire, and mortar bombs were landing all round the DG Fort and the Batthouse. Even more sinister, stray enemy rounds were whistling in from the southern, seaward side of the town, 'overs' which told Kealy and his men that they were surrounded. The battle now became a three-cornered affair. Askaris were firing from the Wali's Fort near the water's edge on guerrillas advancing towards the DG Fort. The SAS mortar team under Corporal 'B' was identifying its targets from the flash of enemy mortars. And from a gunpit close to the DG Fort, an antique, Second World War artillery piece – a

25-pounder – was in use. This gun was manned by an Omani, Walid Khamis, and two Fijian SAS men, Corporal Labalaba and Trooper 'T', who had run to the gunpit through intense fire at the start of the battle. The noise was stunning.

None of this deterred the guerrillas despite the casualties they were suffering. As one group was cut down another replaced it, until they advanced to within a few yards of the perimeter wire. Once there they opened fire on the DG Fort with Soviet RPG-7 rockets and the Carl Gustav. At a range of only thirty metres the Carl Gustav's 84mm armour-piercing rounds had a devastating effect on the fort's ancient masonry: its tower crumbled in a plume of smoke and dust. Throughout the confusion, Corporal 'B' calmly indicated targets for the SAS mortar, the Browning and light machine-guns, using lines of tracer to emphasise his fire orders. He also picked off leading guerrillas with his own rifle. This firepower, such as it was, now turned on the leading group of guerrillas at the wire, manning the Carl Gustav, as it attempted to rush the fort less than a hundred yards away.

Kealy meanwhile was trying to maintain radio contact with the gun crew in its pit in front of the DG Fort and the Wali's men in their fort. Messages from the gun crew were laconic, giving little sign of a situation that was turning from bad to desperate. On the radio, Labalaba's voice, which had been indicating possible mortar targets to the Batthouse crew, announced, 'Enemy now very close. I've been chinned but I'm all right.' It was now about 7am. Within the Batthouse it was almost impossible to hear anything but a steady roar of battle as rounds from the Carl Gustav hissed across the roof to explode just behind the building. Kealy had already asked for strike aircraft at Salalah to stand by, but in these conditions, with cloud almost at ground level, it seemed a remote hope that the Air Force could do much. Now, in the light of Labalaba's last message, Kealy summoned a helicopter to attempt a casualty evacuation.

Both sides had been firing intensively at one another for about an hour. The guerrillas, although they had breached the wire, had not yet taken the DG Fort. Both sides needed to pause to see to their casualties and bring up more ammunition. In the lull that resulted, the firing became spasmodic – so much so that children gathered on the roof of a building behind the Batthouse to watch the action.

Kealy, concerned about the absence of any return fire from the Gendarmerie Fort and its nearby gun position, as well as continued radio silence, now took a brave decision. He would go to the fort himself. This meant crossing about 400 yards of almost open ground under enemy fire. It was also possible that by now the fort had been overrun. Others in the training team volunteered to share the risk, but he took just one man, his medical orderly, Trooper T. P. A. Tobin, to aid the casualties. Simultaneously, Lance-Corporal C. slipped away from the Batthouse, through the town to a helicopter landing-pad near the beach, to guide the machine in as a preliminary to clearing the casualties. Kealy and his medical orderly were en route to the DG Fort when the 'casevac' helicopter clattered in over the sea. On the landing site, the lance-corporal threw a green smoke grenade to indicate that all was clear. But, as the aircraft made its final approach, the guerrillas, reinforced and rearmed in dead ground around the DG Fort, started shooting with renewed ferocity. One of the first targets was the helicopter. Another was the man trying to guide it in. The lance-corporal stayed long enough to throw a red grenade to warn off the helicopter, and then dived for cover. The helicopter whined back into the cloud, its cabin pockmarked by machine-gun bullets.

When the battle erupted afresh, Kealy and his medical orderly were still 350 yards from the fort. From the Batthouse their comrades laid down a covering barrage from the Browning and light machine-guns, as the two men bobbed and weaved their way forward through the smoke, one pausing to fire while the other advanced. Luck was with them and they at last reached the gun position. As Kealy and Trooper Tobin slithered into the gun-pit and peered through the smoke, they found an appalling situation. Walid Khamis, the Oman Artillery gunner, lay on his back seriously wounded. Above the gun-pit on the parapet of the DG Fort, a dead soldier sprawled across his machine-gun. Another dead Gendarme was in the pit itself. Both the SAS Fijians were still fighting. One of them, Trooper 'Ti', was propped against the wall of the bunker, bleeding from serious head and shoulder wounds, still firing his rifle at the guerrillas. The other, Corporal Labalaba, wore a shell dressing on his face to staunch the flood from his chin wound. He was loading and firing the 25-pounder unaided. The gun itself, its shield riddled with bullet holes, had been depressed through 45 degrees to be sighted down the barrel and fired at pointblank range.

Labalaba reloaded the gun yet again as the medical orderly set to work to dress Trooper 'Ti's wounds. From the ammunition bunker, Kealy snapped a terse radio message to the Batthouse calling for an air strike. Before he had completed it, Labalaba was shot dead, and soon afterwards Trooper Tobin had his jaw shot away. (Later in the battle, the same man was to be wounded in the back and hand by a grenade.) The bunker was now being defended by two men, Kealy and the wounded Fijian Trooper 'Ti'. By now, the guerrillas were only thirty yards away, moving on the gun-pit and ammunition bunker from left and right. Both gun position and the fort behind it were being hammered by small-arms fire and shuddering blows from the 84mm Carl Gustav. Kealy, from the right of the bunker wall, picked off first one guerrilla who was about to shoot Trooper 'Ti', then another who clambered out of a ditch towards their position. Trooper 'Ti', still propped up, fired carefully-aimed shots at enemy coming from the left. From somewhere too close for comfort, a light machine-gun fired at the two men, and Kealy felt a bullet pass through his hair. Now came the enemy grenades, which burst near, but not near enough to achieve their intention. One, lobbed right into the gun-pit itself, landed among the dead and dying, but failed to explode. From his position on the left of the bunker the obstinate, brave Trooper 'Ti' asked Kealy for more ammunition.

A hopeless position was retrieved at that moment by the arrival of two Strikemaster jets of the Sultan's air force, hurtling over the scene just above ground level and under a cloud base of only 150 feet. From the radio in the ammunition bunker, Kealy passed targets to the Batthouse: 500-pound bombs on a ditch where the guerrillas had gathered in force and 7.62mm machine-gun fire along the wire only sixty yards from both fort and gun-pit. As the guerrillas retreated, Kealy hastily draped an air identification panel over a body in the bunker to identify his own position to the jets. Even before the first air strike was over, Kealy was also issuing orders to his mortar position at the Batthouse, a few hundred yards away. The mortarman, Lance-Corporal 'H', found that the proposed targets were now so close that he could not elevate the barrel sufficiently by orthodox means. His solution was to pull the barrel up to his chest, lifting the supporting bipod off the ground, and to grip the weapon with his legs before dropping bombs down the barrel.

The battle around the bunker had now been going on for ninety minutes. From the Batthouse, Corporal 'B' directed the second wave of Strikemasters. One of these hit guerrilla machine-guns on Jabal Ali, overlooking the town, while the other made several attacks on the enemy hiding in dead ground near the fort and the wire perimeter. 'There are hundreds of them down there!' an astonished pilot reported. One of the aircraft, seriously damaged by heavy machine-gun fire at close range, cut out of the battle and limped back to Salalah.

While the pressure was off his position, Kealy gave water to the wounded and re-dressed their injuries, then went to fetch the DG Land-Rover inside the fort for use as an ambulance to the heli-pad. He found the vehicle unusable, its tyres and petrol tank holed by grenades thrown over the wall.

If the air strikes had taken the heat off the fort for the time being, it was clear that nothing less than substantial reinforcements could save the situation completely. That they were on their way was due to a fortunate coincidence. Before B Squadron (to which Kealy belonged) could leave the territory, it had to hand over to its successor in Oman. This group, from G Squadron, had arrived in Salalah the previous day. When Kealy's first messages alerted the base, the men of G Squadron were dressed and armed to check their weapons on the firing range. Instead they flew by helicopter, almost at sea level, direct to Mirbat beach. Their arrival at 9.15am almost coincided with the second air strike around the fort. A party of eighteen from the first helicopter lift advanced inland in two groups, wiping out a ridge position held by five guerrillas. The new SAS group was spotted by guerrillas near the DG Fort, who fired at it before starting to withdraw. The tide had turned at last.

From the beach, a second wave of SAS reinforcements, operating in three-man teams, engaged in brief, vicious battles with three guerrilla positions on the southern, seaward side of the town. In another incident the SAS party covering the helicopter landing zone waited in concealment as three guerrillas came closer. They were only five yards away when an SAS officer stood up and ordered them to drop their weapons and surrender. They did so, instantly. It was almost 10.30 before the most seriously wounded – the medical orderly, Trooper Tobin, whose jaw had been blown away, the obstinate and thrice-wounded Fijian Trooper 'Ti', and the Omani gunner, Walid Khamis – could be removed by helicopter. The Fijian insisted on walking into the aircraft. By then, Lance-Corporal 'H', the man who had held the mortar between his legs, had moved from the Batthouse to the gun-pit to aid the wounded in the closing stages of the battle. By clearing Trooper Tobin's windpipe of blood, it seemed that he had saved the man's life; but Tobin was to die of his wounds later. The next group of wounded to be flown out included some of the enemy who had been taken to the Batthouse during the first lull in the battle. By lunchtime it was clear that the position was under control again.

Kealy, whose judgement throughout the battle had been impeccable, now decided to see what could be done to save the original firqa patrol still in the mountains. He took a group of men outside the wire and up to the Jabal Ali area, which had been the first position to come under attack that day. But by now there was no way of knowing whether the patrol had encountered the retreating guerrilla force and if so, where. The firqa limped back later in the day with four men dead and three wounded.

SAS casualties were two dead – Corporal Labalaba and Trooper Tobin – and two seriously wounded; the Gendarmes lost one man killed, one wounded; and the Oman Artillery, one dead. The retreating guerrillas left about thirty bodies and about ten wounded, taken prisoner, but their sources later admitted that the toll was much higher. Factional feuds provoked by the defeat at Mirbat caused further fatalities. Others died of their wounds and these, added to the list of surviving wounded and taken prisoner, left fewer than half of the guerrillas' original elite force unscathed.

When the war ended four years later, one authority concluded: 'The rebel forces never recovered from this defeat and were never able to deploy sufficient forces to mount a similar attack elsewhere.' But in Britain, the battle received no publicity. Gallantry awards made public four years later included a DSO for Kealy, a DCM for Trooper Tobin, an MM for Corporal 'B' and, posthumously, a Mention in Dispatches for Corporal Labalaba. In February 1979, Kealy, now a major, died of exposure while taking part in an SAS exercise in bitter conditions on the Brecon Beacons in Wales (see page 512).

Mirbat was the high point of the SAS campaign in Oman. The guerrillas had lost some of their best men. Worse, they had lost credibility in a warrior society through defeat in open combat when the odds were in their favour. But the decisive effect of the régiment on the war was more diffuse, more subtle than its skill at arms. By the time the war ended in 1976, the combined anti-guerrilla forces numbered about 15,000 men. The SAS commitment most of the time was a single squadron averaging about eighty, and even this figure could vary by as many as thirty more or, more frequently, less. As one of those who had an important role in planning SAS operations in Oman argues, 'It was not our numbers, but our ideas which made a big difference.'

Running the firqa

The action at Mirbat was not the only one of its kind. One potent reason for the success of the SAS was that despite frequent disciplinary problems with the volatile firqas, the irregulars learned from experience that their British tutors would sacrifice their own lives rather than desert an ally in trouble. On 12 April 1974, Captain Simon Garthwaite was killed while trying to rescue a firqa pinned down by enemy fire. Garthwaite's magnetism was considerable: that his SAS soldiers used his Christian name is a measure of their respect for him. A friend who wrote his obituary recorded that Garthwaite was uneasy at formal mess dinners, but at home on the jebel. 'Boots (no socks), shorts, a belt and his rifle were all that he carried . . . He had an astonishing way with local soldiers. They were drawn to him and . . . whatever "the Captain" said, they would gladly do; wherever "the Captain" went, they would follow.'

This does not mean that the firqa technique was an unalloyed success. There were furious debates within the SAS about the problems that resulted from paying some of the irregulars better salaries than the Sultan's regular soldiers, as well as supplying the firqas too generously with automatic rifles, ammunition and blankets. One lobby argued for a 'lean-and-mean' style of management; the other believed that full bellies ensured loyalty. Certainly there was extravagance. At Mirbat during the first end-of-fast festival after Ramadan, the local firqa celebrated by firing 5000 rounds – almost the entire garrison stock – into the air and hundreds of FN rifles disappeared.

There were also chronic problems of command, which depended crucially upon the relationship between the SAS team leader and his tribal second-in-command. According to one British veteran, every firqa experienced a mutiny of some sort at some time, and a few units were disbanded. These problems were least manifest when the SAS leader lived close to his firqa, like Garthwaite, but only one SAS soldier immersed himself so totally in native culture as to dress as a native and speak the language fluently. In general, SAS teams were with the firqa but not of them. They lived and ate apart, preserving their identity, even if the space between the two groups was a matter of yards.

Finally, there was a growing tendency among the irregulars to demand more and more supportive firepower from the regular army and air force before they would go into action, a process that cancelled out their natural advantages of stealth and surprise, and the guerrilla techniques they understood. At its best, a firqa backed by regular military forces worked with a speed and efficiency unique to Dhofar in recovering lost territory. In an unclassified lecture, the operational commander during the final, victorious phase of the campaign, Brigadier (now General) John Akehurst, described how this happened: 'First, the firqa would select a base of their choice. Provided it offered good prospects for land access and drilled water we would mount a largely military operation, perhaps a whole battalion, to capture it. Military engineers would then bulldoze an access track and down the track would come a drill rig.

'Troops would then thin out to the minimum necessary to defend the base with firqa assistance. While the drill turned away, the Civil Aid Team set up a clinic, a shop (with government rations which would be free at first but later sold, though at subsidised prices), a school and a mosque. Engineers would be building a distribution scheme for the water with water-points for humans and troughs for cattle and camels.

'All this probably took four weeks. Water is at a premium . . . and people throughout the tribal area would bring in their cattle . . . The civilians, of course, were in regular touch with the enemy, many of whom were their relations. When they came in for water and other government munificence the firqa talked to them, first to gain Intelligence, but second, to tell them to let the enemy know that they should not interfere with the provision of these good things. The enemy themselves were totally dependent on civilian goodwill and therefore were forced not to interfere.'

Firqa offensives did not always work so smoothly. In January 1975, the Liberation Front was being pressed back towards the border with South Yemen, with a growing intensity of conflict and increasing casualties on both sides. In a catacomb of limestone caves, almost invincibly protected by an ugly, dominating hill, the guerrillas had their main store of weapons and ammunition. It was a natural fortress, the conquest of which initially demanded speed, stealth and local knowledge. On SAS advice, a lightly-armed firqa unit was nominated for the task of spearheading a battalion assault. SAS climbers were on hand to assist in the final stages and, after the caves had been taken, the regiment's demolition experts were to destroy them and their contents. But things did not work out that way. Before the firqa would cross the start line to begin the assault, they insisted upon a demonstration of supporting firepower from aircraft, artillery and armoured cars, and demanded that this be repeated every few hundred yards during the advance. This orchestrated barrage advertised the beginning of the operation: not only was surprise lost, but the subsequent ponderous advance gave the guerrillas ample time to prepare an excellent defence.

During the next two days, under increasingly accurate enemy machine-gun, rocket and mortar fire, the assault ground to a halt. Akehurst recalled in his lecture how the situation deteriorated: 'In an attempt to capture the caves the advance was ambushed by the enemy as it crossed open ground and the leading company lost 13 killed and 22 wounded in less than an hour.' The first to die, in a perfectly prepared ambush, was a British officer who was moving down an exposed forward slope with his company before attempting to cross a gully. This group was now hit by the full fury of well-sited machine-guns and mortars almost immediately above it. Attempts by back-up forces to save the now-isolated vanguard encountered more withering fire, and spectacular bravery was shown by individual officers and SAS troopers to recover the wounded. At dusk on the third day of the operation, the SAS Squadron moved forward to make withdrawal possible for the beleaguered company. Hitting back at rebel positions with accurate GPMG and rocket fire, they kept the enemy's heads down while the remnants of the advance guard fell back. (The SAS officer in charge of this rescue was awarded an MC. One of his troopers became Commanding Officer of 22 SAS in the Gulf War in 1992.)

An operation originally intended to last twenty-four hours now ground on for three weeks, though without occupation of the caves by government forces. What did happen, however, was that the approaches to the caves were denied to the rebels by constant fire from 76mm guns mounted on armoured cars, and were never again used as stores caves. According to one officer involved in the campaign, it was from that point on that the guerrillas began to lose to the Sultan's regular armed forces in straight military battles. Like Mirbat, it was a body-blow to the guerrillas' credibility.

One officer recruited by the Sultan from the original SAS force as a freelance, contract firqa leader, did adopt the tactics of the true counter-guerrilla. Working under the direction of another SAS veteran who was now in charge of Dhofar's military Intelligence, he lived for months on the edge of the Empty Quarter, dressed like his Dhofari warriors and indistinguishable from them. He dropped and collected agents over the border with South Yemen, the guerrillas' main supply base, and in 1972 decided to blow up an army fort at Sinau, eighty miles inside Yemeni territory. The operation was totally clandestine, so much so that if he had been taken prisoner he would have been disowned by the Sultan's hierarchy, most of whom, including the British Commander-in-Chief, had no knowledge of the operation.

With two Bedford trucks each carrying 500 pounds of unstable gelignite, and eighty men, including a party of South Yemeni exiles trained in Saudi Arabia, he arrived unimpeded at the fort, where the small garrison surrendered without resistance. Little more than half an hour was needed to plant the gelignite, still in its fifty-pound boxes, in each corner of the two-storey stone fort, and to link these with detonator cord to a five-minute safety fuse in the courtyard. Having ensured that the engine of his escape vehicle was safely running, the British firqa leader lit the fuse and got out. Just after dusk, a spectacular explosion mushroomed red and orange in the desert sky, destroying not only the fort but also a government shop, garages and a house. The object of such an operation was to divert the resources of South Yemen's army from aiding the guerrillas as these crossed into Dhofar farther south, along the coastal plain. Although the Sultan of Oman was impressed, his British military commanders were horrified. Border crossings are a sensitive political issue for Whitehall. The contract officer at the centre of this adventure transferred to other duties in Dhofar soon afterwards, in charge of another firqa. His direction of the Empty Quarter firqa was taken over by an orthodox SAS team, which also crossed the border, tying up a Yemeni brigade.

The unexpected victory

The end of the war, when it came, was as improbable as an Errol Flynn film. The final assault was to be launched by helicopter at dawn on a day in October 1975. Its object was to seize high ground above a 2000-foot-deep wadi and elsewhere on mountains near the border with South Yemen, while an armoured car-bulldozer column would advance simultaneously from the plain to control the foothills. But, at the last moment, what was to have been a simple diversion became the main pivot of the attack. The diversion was from an isolated, air-supplied mountain-top position held by government troops at Sarfait. Such an attack was, predictably, a kamikaze manoeuvre and both sides knew it. The descent was by steps down a series of cliffs, the first of which was an almost sheer 600 feet. Government troops had tried to break out once in 1972 and they had failed.

Nevertheless, on the night of 14 October the Muscat Regiment probed its way downhill to take the first plateau. There was no opposition. 'We learned later', Akehurst has revealed, 'that the enemy considered anything from Sarfait would only be a diversion and we believe they probably got confirmation of this from the firqa taking part . . . In any event, they decided to do nothing.

'At about midday on the 15th, I sat with Ian Christie, the commanding officer of the Muscat Regiment, and contemplated our unexpected success. I asked him what he thought he would need to carry on down to the sea. After some discussion he decided two more companies. In the next two minutes I threw seven months of planning and 40 pages of operation orders out of the metaphorical window.'

The main attack went in from Sarfait the same night, and by morning the government forces held a three-mile corridor to the sea, cutting the guerrillas' last supply line. From now on, the guerrillas' chief priority was to reach the safety of South Yemen. For many of them it was a long, pitiless march along waterless tracks north of the mountains they had controlled for five years. The war ended formally a few months later with a ceasefire between South Yemen and Oman.

The full story of how the fortunes of this war were swung from the near collapse of government forces in 1970 to their outright victory by 1976 must await the memoirs of the operational commanders. Broadly, it is one of gradual penetration of Dhofari society, in which the firqas, trained and advised by the SAS, reoccupied the mountains using water wells as the ultimate currency of persuasion; and in which increasingly ambitious, orthodox military operations finally required thousands of Iranian and Jordanian, as well as Omani, soldiers to cut guerrilla supplies coming from South Yemen. This was accomplished by building a series of communication barriers, which employed barbed wire, booby-traps, mines and electronic ground sensors. Air and naval bombardment was used to soften up hostile areas before such operations took place, and everything that might aid the guerrillas, including cattle, was removed. The first of these barriers, the Hornbeam Line, covered thirty-five miles and took twelve months to build.

The closer government forces came to the border with South Yemen, the more they came under attack from 130mm artillery fired from within that territory by regular forces. Government helicopters and strike planes were constantly menaced by some of Russia's latest anti-aircraft missiles supplied to the guerrillas. Contrary to even informed left-wing opinion in Britain, the war was not a totally one-sided affair. If it had been, it would not have lasted for ten years.

Was it all worth it? Although the Press reported that the SAS suffered 'scores of casualties', the regiment in fact lost twelve dead during its six-year war. In the light of subsequent events in Iran and Afghanistan, and their impact on Western oil supplies, the strategic importance to British economic interests of winning the war can hardly be overstated. The victory also sustains in office – as Townsend, the Sultan's former economic adviser, points out – a regime in which trade unions are still outlawed and in which strikes, also illegal, 'tend to be settled by the police or the army rather than by negotiation . . . When the apparently infinite cornucopia of material benefits begins to falter, the Omani people may demand more say in their government.'

Certainly the material well-being of the people of Dhofar is now incomparably better than it was in 1970, and the most petty restrictions on personal liberty have been removed. But what if the rebels had won? Townsend, a critic of many of the Sultan's policies from within the regime, does not conclude that life might have been better under a Communist government. The extremism and incompetence of the rebel movement, he believes, was such that it deserved to be defeated. 'Victory for the Popular Front movement would have resulted in a harsh and negative extremism far worse than that of the Sultan, if the example of South Yemen is taken as a guide', is his conclusion. Townsend does not defend Qaboos's absolute monarchy. He asserts that the Sultan can only survive if he realises that he is almost the last absolute ruler, and that the facts of history are against his survival. By assisting that survival at a critical juncture, the SAS helped to buy time for more peaceful evolution within Oman as well as serving the interests of the British, and other Western economies.

Part II

The Irish dimension, the Paddy factor and the legal wilderness

Ireland 1969–92

Gibraltar 1987–88

Prologue

Irish terrorism – Loyalist as well as Republican – presents the armed forces of the UK with a unique problem. This is how to defend the constitution of a democracy, including the rule of law, against well-armed people who simultaneously reject the rule of law but who avail themselves of it when captured. Is it a police task? The police have been tried many times but if they are to be armed on equal terms with the IRA, the most formidable of the Irish terrorist movements, then they would become a para-military force themselves. Is it a job for soldiers? If this were a classic counter-insurgency campaign, civilian rule would be suspended and replaced by martial law. There would be free fire zones, hot pursuit of terrorists to their safe havens and the use of heavy weapons, including air power, after the pattern of most colonial wars. Ireland is not in that category, although terrorist propaganda wishes to persuade the world that it is. Ireland's unique contribution to military evolution is the first campaign in history in which the soldier has required his attorney to be on hand before he can go into action.

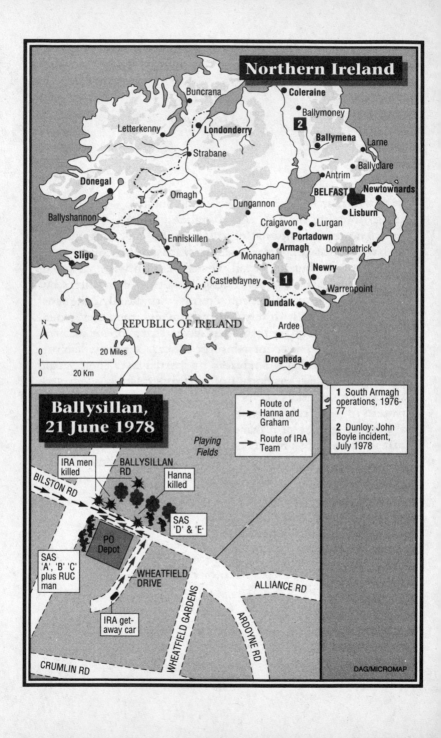

Northern Ireland

Buncrana
Coleraine
Ballymoney
2
Letterkenny
Londonderry
Ballymena
Larne
Strabane
Ballyclare
Antrim
Donegal
Omagh
Dungannon
BELFAST
Newtownards
Lisburn
Ballyshannon
Craigavon
Lurgan
Enniskillen
Portadown
Downpatrick
Armagh
Sligo
Monaghan
Newry
Castleblayney
1
Warrenpoint
Dundalk
REPUBLIC OF IRELAND
Ardee
N
0   20 Miles
0   20 Km
Drogheda

1 South Armagh operations, 1976-77

2 Dunloy: John Boyle incident, July 1978

Ballysillan, 21 June 1978

→ Route of Hanna and Graham

→ Route of IRA Team

Playing Fields

IRA men killed
BALLYSILLAN RD
Hanna killed
BILSTON RD
SAS 'D' & 'E'
PO Depot
SAS 'A' 'B' 'C' plus RUC man
WHEATFIELD DRIVE
ALLIANCE RD
IRA get-away car
WHEATFIELD GARDENS
ARDOYNE RD
CRUMLIN RD

DAG/MICROMAP

IRELAND 1969–92

Section I

There was one brief moment in the long and rancorous history of relations between Ireland and England when it seemed the quarrel was at an end. This occurred on 20 June 1922 when the people of the newly-created Irish Free State, in their first free and democratic election, voted two-to-one in favour of the Treaty with Britain, confirming their independence within the Commonwealth and accepting the partition of the country between a Catholic Ireland of 26 counties and the mainly Protestant, Northern Ireland comprising six of Ulster's original nine counties. The arrangement was not perfect but it was the best compromise the two sides could produce after 300 years of hostility.

The Irish majority endorsing the Treaty (72 per cent) was made the more remarkable by the fact that Sinn Fein, although divided into two factions, for and against the Treaty, made an electoral pact in their efforts to win popular support. The day after the election result was declared, in an action which would symbolise the shape of things to come, the IRA murdered a Northern Irish political opponent (Field Marshal Sir Henry Wilson) outside his London home. The Free State President, Arthur Griffith, denounced the murder with words which would be heard again in one form or another: 'It is a principle of civilised government that the assassination of a political opponent cannot be justified or condoned.'

Three months later, Irish schizophrenia was neatly expressed by Eamonn De Valera, a future president of his country but technically stateless when he, alone among the leaders of the

1916 Dublin Rebellion, was not executed by the British, having been born in the US of a Spanish father and Irish mother. On 10 September 1922 De Valera wrote to Joseph McGarrity, the boss of the IRA in America: 'If the Republicans stand aside and let the Treaty come into force acquiescence in it means the abandonment of National sovereignty . . . if the Republicans do not stand aside, resistance [to the Treaty] means armed opposition to what is undoubtedly the decision of the majority of the people.' (Quoted in Tim Pat Coogan's 750-page history, *The IRA*.)

In the event the IRA showed its contempt for the ballot box by assassinating those who disagreed with it in Ireland as well as London. Among the first victims was the IRA's own founder, Michael Collins. A civil war began and a shoot-to-kill policy as a thug's way out of an argument became enshrined in the traditions of an Ireland free of the British.

In 1937, sixteen years after his revealing letter to McGarrity, De Valera turned back the clock. Five years in power as the Free State's elected leader and boss of a former IRA faction known as Fianna Fail, he introduced a new constitution, later endorsed by referendum. This asserted that the national territory of Eire (the Free State's new name) was 'the whole of Ireland'.

Such territorial claims were fashionable at the time on the part of Mussolini, Hitler and Stalin. (To the end, De Valera respected the Nazis. In 1945 he called on the German ambassador to Dublin to offer his condolences on the death of Hitler.) While he worked on his new constitution, De Valera was also imprisoning his old IRA comrades, sometimes using emergency procedures to do so. So whatever legitimacy he thought he could invoke for his claim to 'the whole of Ireland', it is clear that even he did not accept that this process in its turn legitimised the IRA. Historically, the IRA has been rejected by the Irish people in the vote of 1922 and subsequently by De Valera, the only long-term survivor of the 1916 Rebellion.

Not surprisingly, the IRA has been loath to accept democracy within its own ranks. As the author Raymond Murray, a Roman Catholic priest, reminds us, it was not until 1987 that an 'Army Convention' of volunteers – disguised as an Irish language seminar – met at Navan to elect a twelve-person executive and a seven-man Army Council. In view of this history, it is surprising that the IRA claims a legitimacy equal to that of security forces – including the SAS – to vindicate its actions; astonishing that so many journalists and politicians seem prepared to accept that moral equivalence. That acceptance, a form of surrender to fascism, is the IRA's greatest asset.

The IRA is not the only source of trouble in Ireland to provoke SAS involvement. The repressive traditions of the new Northern Ireland after 1921 did nothing for the cause of political sanity. Theoretically part of the United Kingdom, the province presented its advocates elsewhere with an unanswerable question. That question was: how could it be that in 1968, more than two generations after partition, the Protestant Unionist ascendancy continued through each successive election? Clearly there was something fishy about a democratic process in which one community (the Catholics, rejecting birth control methods as a matter of religious dogma) usually produced a larger juvenile population than the rest, but never expressed that majority once the juveniles reached voting age.

The answer was that to obtain work and homes, Catholics were obliged to emigrate. Discrimination against Ulster Catholics, including tens of thousands who served in Britain's armed services, was a necessary political mechanism to preserve the idea of a homeland for Ulster Protestants regardless of the ballot box. For the best part of fifty years, successive British governments averted their gaze from Northern Ireland. The last IRA campaign spluttered despairingly to a halt in 1962 and the province proceeded unhindered on its wicked way, backed up when necessary by the bully boys of the UVF and other paramilitaries.

This hell's broth, in which two politically sophisticated but extremist groups were beyond the reach of any hearts-and-minds campaign, was to present the SAS with an insoluble problem. The regiment could not hope to achieve the miracle of converting the fundamentalists to the rule of law as it had done in Malaya and Oman. The only other option, it seemed, was military victory but that also, since there was no officially acknowledged armed conflict, was ruled out by a police role, even if the British government was issuing a General Service medal decorated with a campaign clasp that said: 'Northern Ireland'. There have been few 'civil' situations in which so many awards for military gallantry – Military Medal, Military Cross, etc. – have been made.

Ulster's rejection of normal democratic process with the complicity of London produced an explosion of indignation in 1968–69 that had nothing to do with the antique gangsterism of the IRA or dreams of reunification. Those of us who were in Northern Ireland during the civil rights campaign learned that the Catholics (along with enlightened Protestants; trade unionists; ex-service people and even the only accredited Communist Party member prominent in public life) wanted equality of civil rights. It was a fashionable time to launch street protests in a good cause. Something of the sort had happened in Paris and Berlin; in American cities also.

An enlightened Unionist leader, Captain Terence O'Neill, perceived (like Harold Macmillan in another context) that the wind of change required a response. At Christmas 1968, he made public guarantees which went a long way towards satisfying the protesters' proper aspirations. The initiative almost succeeded. Civil rights protest leaders were ready to give O'Neill's programme a fair crack.

Against their wishes, one splinter group within the civil rights movement set out on a protest march from Belfast to Londonderry (Derry to Catholics) in January 1969. A march in Ireland is a political gesture which the British – with their anything-goes philosophy – do not understand. It is a tribal event, catlike in its declaration of territory occupied. The march, organised by Queen's University student members of the 'People's Democracy', was ambushed by Unionist thugs including off-duty police officers. O'Neill's move towards reconciliation was destabilised. The IRA now infiltrated the civil rights movement to provide it with march stewards who carried no guns but were, in the words of a Scottish judge, Lord Cameron, the best-disciplined. IRA women such as Maire Drumm, meanwhile, organised refuges for Catholics burned or intimidated out of their homes in Belfast. It was potent propaganda.

Mavericks and fanatics on both sides saw to it that each time peace was restored in one place, violence broke out afresh elsewhere. The IRA, although split between the advocates of non-violent revolution and the old, unreformed gunmen, would soon learn not only the left-wing politics of the 1960s but the revolutionary agitprop art of violence-as-propaganda, as practised in Paris, Berlin, Algiers and Saigon. The IRA's credibility was not helped by the rescue operation mounted by the British Army in August-September 1969. The British Army, also, was embarrassed to find that in negotiating with 'defence committees' in Belfast it was doing business with what Raymond Murray describes as 'the new IRA'.

Even more toxic was the legal fudge handed to it by the Labour government of Harold Wilson. As Insight's history puts it: 'Labour's legal "minimum solution" entailed that all the civil power's resources must be exhausted before the troops could legally go to its aid . . . That meant the B Specials. And to call the B Specials into Belfast was one move the Catholics were certain not to forgive or forget.' London had cobbled together a doctrine enabling the troops to go in without being under the control of Stormont, as 'common law constables'. A precondition of that manoeuvre was that law and order had to break down before the troops intervened, reopening the long-healed fissure in Irish history. Worse, for the soldier, his actions must be justified by a doctrine of 'equivalent force', enabling him to shoot someone if that person was prepared to do something equally drastic to him. As Insight presciently put it, long ago in 1972: 'It was a solution that was to cause the Army endless problems.' As the proactive end of security, the SAS was to become a notable victim of that legal fudge long after the Wilson government had vanished. It would also be the vehicle for resolving the apparently irreconcilable duties of peaceful arrest and undeclared warfare.

By 1969 in Northern Ireland, civil rights protest had made its point. Could it now make progress, or would it be subverted by the Irish obsession with the past?

J. Bowler-Bell, an American historian of the modern IRA, writes that after the creation of the breakaway 'Provisional' IRA, its Army Council met in January 1970 to

. . . assume the role of nationalist defender, replacing the British Army and pre-empting any Dublin effort; (2) the IRA would shift the nationalist focus to the British Army-as-enemy, thus benefiting from their own provocations and the nature of the military to begin retaliatory operations; (3) these would engender a cycle of provocation-and-response that would permit an offensive IRA campaign. Supported by an emboldened and committed nationalist population, the IRA would then have at long last an armed struggle, bedded in an oppressed people, visible to the world media, and enhanced by a just cause that ultimately would require a united Ireland, a Republic, a culmination of the dream.

The Australian strategic analyst Andrew Selth has uncovered the significant fact that

When the PIRA's first major terrorist campaign began in 1971, the Army Council's first target was to kill 36 British soldiers, believed by the PIRA to be the same number who died in Aden . . . This target was reached in November 1971 . . . In fact, 44 members of the British security forces were killed in the Aden fighting.

Bowyer-Bell finds that Pira's seven-man Army Council 'authorised a move from retaliation to offensive when appropriate' early in 1971. In practice, the IRA's opportunity had been presented to it when British security forces imposed a curfew on the Belfast Falls Road area during the weekend of 3 to 5 July 1970, following an Army raid on a Republican arms dump in Balkan Street. The trouble escalated to become a confused street war in the dark in which some British soldiers shot at others. Four civilians were killed and hundreds of others (including the author) arrested and handcuffed at gunpoint before being taken to an interrogation centre.

The suspicion in Catholic minds that the British Army had changed its stance of protector to enemy was confirmed when journalists were taken in a triumphal convoy around the sullen, still curfewed and shuttered area, on the Sunday morning of that weekend, led by two smiling Unionist Ministers, Captains William Long and John Brooke.

As one RUC officer put it: 'It's a grand day for us.' Next day, in Parliament in London, government spokesmen denied that a curfew had taken place. There had been 'a restriction on movement'.

Long before Bloody Sunday or Bloody Friday, the Falls Road curfew was the seminal event which gave the IRA a street-credibility it had never enjoyed before on either side of the border. Coming a year after an eight-year-old Catholic boy, Patrick Rooney, was killed in his nearby bedroom by .5 Browning machine-guns fired from close range by police armoured cars, this triumphal parade around a smouldering Falls Road made the place as impenetrable, emotionally, as the Crater district of Aden. Until June 1970, the IRA had comprised only a few hundred activists at most. By December the figure was 800 and growing fast. So were fairytales about the SAS.

In his book *The SAS in Ireland*, Raymond Murray (relying upon a newspaper report by Gery Lawless) suggests:

After the Falls Road curfew a decision was taken to send a group of SAS to Lisburn HQ to be attached to the 39th Brigade [sic] . . . After six weeks special training for the Irish situation at an Army base in Honiton, North Devon, 45 SAS soldiers and some members of the Joint Service Intelligence Wing came to Northern Ireland.

They were to form a core of intelligence officers who would prepare the interrogation techniques for internment, help run the MRF (a plain clothes Army team run under the auspices of Brigadier [later General] Kitson and based on his experience in fighting Mau Mau in Kenya) and deal with pseudo gangs.

This version of events is denied flatly by the author's sources, some of them serving in Ireland at that time.

It would not be surprising if the renewed Irish troubles did attract, at an early stage, British specialists in unconventional warfare. The founding fathers of Special Operations Executive, a sort of political uncle of the SAS and the organisation which gave the postwar SAS some of its best talent, had learned their trade in Ireland in 1921–22. By 1970, however, the greater part of the SAS was being drawn into the Dhofar campaign in faraway Oman. The author's sources, serving with the SAS at that time, dismiss the Lawless version as untrue for the very good reason that no SAS soldier, or formation, was serving in the province in any capacity in 1970.

The regiment's orientation was still towards neo-colonial conflicts in the Third World. Not until after the Munich massacre of Israeli athletes in 1972 did the SAS finally get into the business of combating sophisticated, modern urban terrorism with the creation of a Counter Revolutionary Warfare wing. In 1969–70, the SAS decisively missed the Irish ferry. But then, few soldiers expected the renewed Irish crisis to last more than a few months, even if a charismatic street fighter called Bernadette Devlin was raising hell and talking about 'the wrath of the risen people'.

Section II

Yet there was an interlude, odd and inconclusive, which gave the SAS its first taste of the troubles almost immediately order collapsed in the Province. In response to a recall code, 'Free Beer', men of D Squadron drained their glasses in bars near their Hereford base before hurrying to barracks to pick up uniforms and Bergen rucksacks. (The code had to be changed after one irate parent, already angry about her son's drinking habits, construed it as yet another invitation to a bottle party. There was even some doubt about whether she would pass the message on to him.)

The squadron was commanded at that time by Major (later Major-General) Anthony Showan Jeapes. He was better informed than most soldiers about the Province. Immediately before returning to the SAS as a squadron commander, he had spent 1967 as Brigade Major with 39 Infantry Brigade in Northern Ireland. He now led his team, in uniform with regimental cap badges displayed, ostensibly in pursuit of the gun-runners of both communities.

In practice, the IRA were regarded as the less serious threat after their failure to hold off the Belfast firebombers of August when the initials 'IRA', in ghetto graffiti, were translated as 'I Ran Away'. (One irony of that time is that the first warrior to die fighting the RUC belonged not to the IRA but to the British Army. Trooper McCabe, Royal Irish Rangers, was taking home leave in the Lower Falls area of Belfast when the Wilson formula finally allowed law and order to collapse in August 1969.)

D Squadron's first Irish tour, from September to November, was not its most eventful. The soldiers patrolled the countryside between the Glens of Antrim and the Mourne Mountains to establish whether the Protestant operations of 1914 (when the UVF landed 35,000 rifles at Larne to resist Home Rule) might be repeated. The squadron also searched incoming fishing and cargo vessels. No arms were found.

The squadron was based in a Territorial Army drill hall at Newtonards. By chance, the men discovered that the local cemetery held the grave of their greatest war hero, the Irish rugby international Colonel Paddy Mayne. In their best uniforms, they held a ceremonial parade and laid a wreath on his tomb. Then they changed into tropical kit and left for Oman. They left behind an image, teasing yet satisfying to many Irishmen, of the sinister Pimpernel. If such people existed, London might have controlled the escalating crisis somewhat better.

Instead, the British inaugurated the Military Reconnaissance Force (MRF) whose creator, Brigadier [later General] Kitson was Commander of Land Forces, Northern Ireland in 1970–72. A veteran of the campaign against Mau Mau in colonial Kenya in the 1950s, Kitson had devised 'counter gangs' of pseudo-terrorists to penetrate the enemy camp.

It was surprising that the SAS was not used for the clandestine work of running MRFs, some of whose members, like the 'firqas' in Dhofar, were former enemies who had been 'turned'.

The use of the SAS, like that of heavy tanks on the streets, was deemed to be an unnecessary political and psychological escalation. In any event, Kitson had adequate experience and men to create his own 'firqas'. This fact has never inhibited the Irish from blaming the SAS. It is a useful pantechnicon into which to load a lot of paranoia. Some Irish commentators, implicitly recognising this, now distinguish between the 'SAS' and 'the real SAS'.

When the Unionist government of Brian Faulkner persuaded London to engage in a disastrous internment operation in 1971, the Irish again blamed the regiment. Raymond Murray documents one case, that of Paddy Joe McClean. This version suggests: 'When Paddy Joe McClean was being tortured at Ballykelly he saw some of his torturers face-to-face when the hood was removed, bare-chested, tanned, super-fit SAS men in drill trousers.'

We are not told whether their bare chests were tattooed with SAS insignia. Major-General (Professor) Richard Clutterbuck's analysis concludes that British soldiers carried out the arrests though not the interrogations and bore the brunt of the street violence that resulted. In March 1972, the Stormont parliament was prorogued and direct rule from Westminster instituted.

It was after this disaster that SAS soldiers, mainly officers, were posted as individuals to sensitive jobs in Military Intelligence in Ulster. For experience, some were attached to units already serving in the province. They were part of a much larger migration of Intelligence specialists of all kinds, joining a counter-insurgency 'gold rush'. Their world was like that of Gerald Seymour's novel about the undergound war in Northern Ireland, *Harry's Game*, a world of petty but lethal jealousy and division among conflicting agencies, a world of dirty tricks inaugurated by Military Intelligence officers and their superiors.

The MRF was one agency which was conspicuously storing up problems for everyone during the years 1970–72. Occasionally, using IRA renegades as spotters, its Q-car patrols did identify active IRA men and women who could, with luck, be photographed by cameras concealed inside the car boot. Too often, however, MRF operations went over the top, achieving nothing but propaganda for the IRA.

In 1972, two episodes led to the disbandment of Kitson's organisation. On 22 June, a two-man team opened fire from a moving car on men standing at a Belfast bus stop. The weapon they used was the Thomson sub-machine-gun, symbol of Al Capone, the prewar IRA and wartime British commandos. Both soldiers were prosecuted but claimed they had come under fire first. On 2 October, the IRA ambushed an apparently innocuous laundry van in Belfast, killing the driver. His companion, a woman, escaped to a nearby house. In time it became apparent that the Four Square Laundry was no ordinary cleaner. It was an MRF front, collecting clothes in suspect districts for forensic examination. The dead driver and his companion, both soldiers, were natives of Northern Ireland. The Four Square Laundry was a good try, fatally compromised by the unit's habit of using and occasionally losing IRA people who, having been turned once, turned back again.

A new reconnaissance unit

The end of the MRF left an embarrassing gap in the security forces' ability to penetrate the republican ghettos unnoticed. The police, in or out of uniform, worked regular shifts and were mere targets for gunmen. In any case, they had access to Republicans held on remand in the security of some police head-quarters. Some of these suspects, reminded by their damaged kneecaps that they had scores to settle, gave the RUC useful information but this was not always passed on to the Army.

The officer charged with finding a viable substitute for the MRF was a major who had been one of the best (and, his friends suggest, underrated) brains ever acquired by the SAS. He had left the Army, spent two years working for MI6 but did not care for the life and returned to soldiering. This officer – let's call him 'Major Lord' – was not looking for SAS recruits. He wanted men with keen powers of observation, able to take in the details of a living room at a glance and record accurately every detail of what was there. The recruits also needed quick wits and, when detected, even quicker trigger fingers. (One of these was to shoot his way out of an IRA ambush single-handed, killing two men and wounding a third.) Another quality, rare in soldiers, was the ability to work entirely alone on enemy urban territory. The new men did not need SAS physical stamina since they would not be expected to march across desert or jungle, or parachute into Arctic Norway, between tours in Ireland.

The training officer for the new team was another special forces soldier who was still serving with 22 SAS. He warned the recruits that they would not be able to pass themselves off as locals, eavesdropping gossip in Republican bars or clubs. To do so would soon attract impudent questions from, perhaps, a streetwise 14-year-old member of the IRA youth wing. The grown-up hard men tended to appear soon afterward, to be followed by the coroner.

'Think of your car as a diving bell', said the training officer. 'It contains your communications and perhaps a spare weapon. If you leave it, imagine you are taking a lungful of air under water. Don't stay out too long or you will die. Don't assume an Irish accent. If you are challenged you only need two words: "Fuck off".' Some efforts were made, nevertheless, to penetrate Loyalist strongholds, with results that were laughable rather than lethal.

The new reconnaissance unit was given various names. Its official title was 14 Intelligence Company. When the first detachment went operational in Armagh in the spring of 1974 it was given the cover title, '4 Field Survey Troop, Royal Engineers'. Although it shared a compound at Castledillon with a real Sapper unit, it was equipped with unmarked, civilian Q cars and non-standard weapons including the Ingram silenced sub-machine-gun. It was also known as 'Northern Ireland Training and Tactics Team'.

The team was commanded by Captain (Julian) Tony Ball, a rugged and popular character who had served in the ranks of the Parachute Regiment and the SAS before taking a commission in the King's Own Scottish Borderers. As a captain in charge of the

KOSB reconnaissance platoon in 1972 he had set up the Army's first covert observation post in Republican Belfast, relishing the risk involved. Ball returned to the SAS in 1975 before leaving the British Army to command the Sultan's Special Force in Oman. With another veteran of Military Intelligence, Andrew Nightingale, he died in Dhofar in 1978, on the desert road near Thumrait, when a tyre blew out as they travelled at more than 100mph. At 38, he was a lieutenant-colonel, a remarkable record for an ex-Parachute Regiment ranker. He is buried in the SAS plot at St Martin's, Hereford.

His second-in-command in 14 Company in 1974 was Lieutenant Robert Nairac, a Catholic Guards officer and Oxford boxing blue, educated (like the founder of the SAS, David Stirling) at Ampleforth.

It was not long before their new, secret operation aroused the curiosity of others in Northern Ireland's overcrowded Intelligence world. The year 1974 was one in which sharp divisions appeared between the two main non-military Intelligence agencies, MI6 (the Secret Intelligence Service run by the Foreign & Commonwealth Office, never publicly acknowledged) and MI5, the Security Service charged with counter-espionage. The tribal nature of the RUC – wounded by the reforms imposed on it after 1969 – meant that the force's Special Branch was also running its agents with little regard for what the Army wanted.

SAS officers, between tours with 22 SAS but occupying key Intelligence positions at the military headquarters at Lisburn and elsewhere, were especially exposed to internecine rivalries since it was frequently their job to co-ordinate operations against terrorists. The same officers were also a means of friendly, trusting communication between rival agencies when other means failed.

A pecking order emerged. While SAS officers co-ordinated, soldiers from other areas acted as Military Intelligence Officers or Field Intelligence NCOs (Fincos) in liaison with the RUC. Such men and women came from the Intelligence Corps, Royal Military Police and, ultimately, many other sources. The link with each RUC police division was a Special Military

Intelligence Unit, containing MIOs, Fincos and Milos (Military Intelligence Liaison Officers). An MIO working as part of such a unit could find himself torn by conflicting duties to the RUC, Army Intelligence and MI6.

RUC Special Branch, meanwhile, was running its own, secret cross-border contacts with the Irish Republic's Gardai Special Branch. This was a world in which personal chemistry – and trust – counted for everything, combined with a prodigious memory to recall who knew what about whom.

After one upheaval in the power struggle between Five and Six, an MIO known as 'Major Fred', who repeatedly crossed the border in civilian disguise, bearded, wearing dirty jeans and carrying a false driving licence issued in Dublin, claimed that he was told by an SAS major (known to the author) running the Military Intelligence wing at Lisburn: 'We're not working with MI5 because one of our lads has committed suicide. He had done four years and handed over ten first class sources to MI5 who had just taken over and within a week, they'd all had a head job by the IRA, which means they've got a leak in their system.'

The role of the tiny number of SAS soldiers in this gloomy situation has been described as 'cement for disintegrating intelligence'.

The system included Captain Fred Holroyd, a Royal Corps of Transport officer who was the MIO attached to Portadown Police HQ. Holroyd was interested in joining the SAS at that time and became persuaded that 4 Field Survey Troop was 'the spearhead of Kitson's counter-insurgency policy', as well as being an arm of the SAS. He wrote later:

> More ominously, in a cupboard in their armoury was a tray of 9mm Browning pistol barrels, extractors and firing pins which had been . . . declared unfit for use . . . and officially destroyed . . . These parts could be placed in normal issue Brownings, fired, destroyed and replaced with the original 'official' parts. This would make it impossible to connect the weapon with any shooting – there would be no ballistic evidence.

An officer who helped to set up 14 Company at that time dismisses this assertion as 'crap'.

Holroyd also claims, in his book *War Without Honour*: 'It was my role to obtain intelligence, Nairac's to act on it.'

The author's source challenges this also, since 14 Company was set up as an agency to watch and gather information about the IRA, sometimes following one man for months at a time, sometimes collating information gathered by others, while it was the task of the SAS to act on the intelligence when action was necessary. When a member of 14 Company started shooting it was because the IRA had spotted him and often when the terrorist had fired first.

Neither Ball nor Nairac is able to answer from beyond the grave accusations now made about their activities during 1974–75 by Holroyd and others. It is a period of British political history in which the truth about anything is peculiarly elusive. Between the two general elections of 1974 – March and October – a Military Information officer named Colin Wallace was waging an information war against the IRA.

He was also, he claims, engaged with others in a campaign to destabilise the minority Labour government. The allegation of political dirty tricks in London by a minority of ultra right-wingers in MI5 is supported by the testimony of the MI5 veteran, Peter Wright. In 1974, he wrote: 'The country seemed on the brink of catastrophe.'

There was also a specifically Irish nightmare to warp normal judgment. During a raid on an IRA headquarters in Belfast on 10 May, security forces discovered a 'doomsday' contingency plan for counter-attacks on Protestant areas if there were a repetition of August 1969. Army sources described the find as the most significant in five years of trouble. The plan, according to a British Intelligence source, was defensive but Harold Wilson, now back in office, was influenced by an MI5 analysis of the IRA plan as an offensive one that imminently threatened a frightening escalation of the conflict. This top-spin reflected continuing rivalry between MI5 and MI6. The Foreign Office, including MI6, was seeking a political solution which at that time involved secret contacts with the IRA. The IRA played along. MI5 said the terrorists were merely seeking a breathing space, time to regroup. Seizure of the 'doomsday' plan gave MI5 a perfect chance to discredit political contacts.

So well did the scare succeed that an immediate growth in the Army's plain-clothes operations was sanctioned. By March 1978, Mr Roy Mason, as Minister for Northern Ireland, was ready to announce that every Army unit would be training for undercover operations. These were to become known as 'Close Observation Platoons', or 'COPs'. Most units serving their tour in Northern Ireland now have them. But in 1974, as one of those involved put it:

We couldn't get the soldiers trained quickly enough because orientation took time. We had suitable men who had volunteered for twelve months undercover work in Ulster [i.e., with 14 Company] but how could we make them look, talk and think like Irishmen? Two of them attended a Paisley meeting with unshaven chins, wearing scruffy clothes.

Not surprisingly, in view of the Orangeman's emphasis on smart turn-out, they were shown the door. There was more embarrassment when two of the volunteers didn't know the words of a favourite Protestant hymn. I sang with them as loudly as I could, but they weren't even moving their lips. They stuck out like two sore thumbs.

Eventually it was agreed at Prime Ministerial level that SAS soldiers should be sent to Northern Ireland, but not publicly. They were sent on the basis that, although they were members of the regiment, they were 'returned to unit' and immediately posted to plain clothes duties. They were filling a temporary gap until we had trained sufficient soldiers from other units. Meanwhile intensive training of other volunteers took place both sides of the water.

These were turbulent, dangerous times: the anarchy of the miners' strike and the three-day week precipitating the downfall of a democratically-elected Tory government; the creation of a non-elected but potentially neutral power-sharing executive to replace direct rule of Ulster from London; the collapse of that executive under the intimidation of the Ulster Workers' strike and IRA violence including the special horror of the Birmingham pub massacre; the Dublin bombing; an IRA truce through Christmas/New Year 1974–75 during which a top PIRA commander rested from his labours in the sanctuary of the Irish Republic. From whatever side of the political barricade one peered, it seemed that the bad guys were winning. It was also the start of a three-year period in which Jeapes, now a lieutenant-colonel, took command of 22 SAS.

Years after Nairac was murdered while a prisoner of the IRA, Holroyd asserted that Nairac had told him 'quite plainly' that he had crossed into the Irish Republic on 10 January 1975 to shoot the Provisional IRA commander in North Armagh, John Francis Green. The killing had taken place at an isolated farmhouse in County Monaghan. With two NCOs, whom Holroyd does not name, Nairac allegedly kicked in the door of the farmhouse before all three 'emptied their guns into his body'.

Then, instead of fleeing, one of the team took a Polaroid photograph of the body. Nairac, Holroyd continues, 'produced a photograph of the dead man, lying in his own blood – a colour Polaroid . . . I took the photograph from him and asked if I could keep it. I was a keen collector of all such memorabilia . . . Nairac seemed none too happy with this. But he did not ask for it back.'

This macabre story has elements of truth. Although (see below) it is more likely that Green was killed by Ball rather than by Nairac, it is true that the latter was in the habit of retaining photographs of the victims of violent death, obtained from police files. Since Holroyd was the military liaison officer with the local police headquarters, he might have known about that. Nairac, however, was not in the habit of handing to casual acquaintances, even those who were in the same line of business, evidence to incriminate himself in political murder. Holroyd adds: 'As to the Polaroid picture, whose existence has been doubted – I can only say that I saw it, and gave it to the RUC as evidence.'

Elements of B Squadron were deployed to Northern Ireland, a full year before Green's killing, using the too-appropriate codename, 'Operation Cuff'. According to Paul Foot the decision to send the SAS contingent was taken by the Heath cabinet in January 1974. The minority Labour government (Wilson's second administration) elected about six weeks later, was not informed of what had happened, Foot says. This is not necessarily sinister. The end of the MRF left a vacuum in covert reconnaissance at a crucial time. The successor organisation, 14 Intelligence, was still being trained for a uniquely difficult role. About half of B Squadron was sent to fill the gap.

Towards the end of that month, on 26 January, William Black, a former UDR soldier, was shot by security forces using a silenced sub-machine-gun. They had been in hiding, watching a suspected arms cache at a cottage near Tully-West, County Down when Black arrived. He was seriously wounded, and was later awarded £16,500 damages against the British government.

In 1990, Armed Forces Minister Archie Hamilton said that Black was shot 'while threatening the life of a soldier'. The SAS came under suspicion. The soldiers, not trained for an urban anti-terrorist role and fresh from the Omani desert, were not made aware of the legal hazards of their new environment. There was worse to come. B Squadron's contingent was withdrawn abruptly from Ireland some five months before Green's murder after two of its number attempted to rob a bank in Londonderry. Both men were later sentenced to six years imprisonment.

Tony Ball, meanwhile, continued to serve in the Province as detachment commander of '4 Field Survey Troop', with Nairac as his deputy. Only a handful of people know the truth about that time. The author's information is that Ball did cross the border into the Republic more than once, on his own initiative. During one of these expeditions, a few hundred yards into the Republic, Ball snatched a senior IRA man at gunpoint for trial in the North. Some also suspect that Ball shot and killed John Francis Green.

The author's sources do not disagree with the finding of Duncan Campbell, a left-wing investigative journalist, in the *New Statesman* for 4 May 1984, that prior to Green's death:

Ball and Nairac visited intelligence officers in the Armagh area, including Holroyd in Portadown, asking for suggestions of worthwhile Intelligence targets. They told Holroyd that they were under the direct orders of SIS (MI6) and Army headquarters Intelligence staff.

On 10 January 1975, in a remote mountainside farmhouse in County Monaghan, John Francis Green was murdered. Careful planning and good intelligence was evident in his killing, for he had only visited the farm at short notice. The killers waited until Green was alone and then burst in on him, emptying the contents of two pistols into him.

If, in fact, Ball and not Nairac was responsible for unlawfully killing Green, why would Nairac claim falsely that he had done the job? Those operating on the same circuit at that time, in conversation with the author, suggest that such braggadocio would not be out of character. Many soldiers operating on the edge, are guilty at some time of what the SAS describes as 'big timing'.

The IRA ended its Christmas truce on 16 January 1975, six days after Green's murder, blaming the SAS. The political beneficiary of this return to violence was the IRA, which needs the momentum of action if it is not to disintegrate. The truce, or ceasefire, had come about in response to covert talks at Feakle, Co. Clare, between the IRA and moderate Protestant clergy in December 1974. During 1975, the ceasefire was briefly restored. Gerry Adams, president of Sinn Fein, regarded it as a disaster. He said later that Britain 'came as near at that time to defeating the Republican struggle as at any time during the last 14 years'.

One of the church ministers who met IRA boss Daithi O'Conaill at Feakle later revealed: 'O'Conaill told me, "Behind every one of us on the [IRA] Army Council there's a young man with a gun in his hand who still has to make his name for Ireland and write his name in the history books. And when they take over, there will be no more ceasefires".' Nor were there.

In terms of political cause-and-effect, therefore, Green's

murder was a stupendous own-goal out of keeping with the psychological cunning exercised by the SAS in Malaya, Oman and the Falklands. Ball's direct cross-border actions may be seen as part of a grievously misguided effort to impose control on the uncontrollable at a time when others made similar, if less fatal, mistakes.

The actions of both Ball and Nairac fall far short of an all-embracing, right-wing conspiracy against democracy, involving the SAS, implied by Foot and others. The regiment's obituary of Ball describes him as 'a natural soldier and leader who was happiest when the going was rough . . . His energy, personal bravery and keen sense of humour cannot be surpassed'. These are qualities shared by many SAS soldiers but political prudence is not a virtue for which Ball is remembered, even among his own.

In that strange year of 1974–75, there were other events to cause unease about undercover operations. On 8 November, for example, the seizure of the Dublin–Belfast mail train by armed men and its subsequent derailment in the North, near Portadown, was attributed to British soldiers in plain clothes. This apparently hare-brained scheme was no more so than the activities of 'Major Fred', who wanted to offer doctored ammunition to an IRA assassin, so as to kill the assassin rather than the intended victim.

The public had to wait until February 1992 to know for sure that some undercover agents run by Military Intelligence are themselves obliged to break the law to function convincingly. In that month, Brian Nelson, MI's deep throat inside the 'Loyalist' Ulster Defence Association from the late 1970s, was sentenced to ten years' imprisonment for terrorist offences including five murder plots.

What is relevant to this history is that Nelson was the civilian servant of an agency other than the SAS. Since 1976, the regiment has specialised in a different art of undercover war in Ireland. It has left the job of penetration (like Kitson's pseudo-gangs) to others. Many of those who live this dangerous double-life are (like Brian Nelson) native Ulstermen. The SAS, meanwhile, has concentrated on the arduous business of entrapping known terrorists on a battlefield of their choosing, sometimes lying in the open, in concealment for days, nerves stretched, before the sudden explosion of action.

It is hard to judge which is the more dangerous or disagreeable role, the gathering of intelligence or execution of the follow-through. At times, both are equally ambiguous. It is a fact, however, that 14 Intelligence Company has received significantly more medals for bravery than the SAS in Ireland. By the early 1980s, the total had run into three figures.

Section III

The decision to commit the SAS publicly to Northern Ireland was announced, as part of a public-relations coup, by the Prime Minister from Downing Street on 7 January 1976. The regiment would be engaged in 'patrolling and surveillance' in South Armagh. Harold Wilson's statement was greeted by many people in the Province with a certain lack of surprise. Paddy Devlin, an amiable IRA veteran of the 1940s, now a leader of the Social and Democratic Labour Party, reflected the common view: 'It is only a cosmetic exercise. The SAS have always been here.'

In reality what the Downing Street announcement signalled was a change of role from Intelligence gathering to combat by elements of the regiment's four regular Sabre squadrons on rota. The commitment was imposed by the Prime Minister without warning or reference to the Ministry of Defence. It seemed like an about-turn by a government which had taken the view that the regiment's presence would be a political liability. There were just eleven men of D Squadron, just back from Oman, available when the announcement was made on a Friday evening, perfectly timed to grab headlines in the Sunday newspapers. A senior general, highly unamused, telephoned 22 SAS headquarters at Hereford and asked the duty officer what was going on. The duty officer was a young NCO not even 'badged' as an SAS soldier. He could do no more than to promise to find out and call back when he, too, knew.

In Downing Street what mattered at that moment was the impact of the statement rather than its true military implications. Wilson, a clever manipulator of editors, was engaged in a public relations conjuring trick to calm anger in Ireland over the latest sectarian atrocities. During the week preceding the decision, ten Protestants had been massacred in one episode and five Roman Catholics in another. In the area near the border between the Republic and South Armagh, the 'score card' read: British Army dead, forty-nine; IRA dead, nil.

Merlyn Rees, Home Secretary, confessed later that committing the SAS was 'a presentational thing'. It was an extraordinary, almost frivolous way of reaching a momentous military decision, inserting soldiers almost as exotic as the Brigade of Gurkhas – and equally associated with far-off colonial wars – into the heart of a domestic security problem. Once started, the process would accelerate so as to draw the SAS into such military novelties as control of prison riots in Scotland.

In the sixteen years since the Wilson initiative the SAS has killed almost forty Republican terrorists and arrested about a hundred. Others have been killed by 14 Company. Almost all the terrorists were armed or had access to arms when they were stopped. Most of them had been exposed to arrest, trial and imprisonment for earlier acts of political violence. Undeterred by the judicial process, they then chose to take up arms again, sometimes within a few days. By the time they came face to face with the SAS they had chosen to be outlaws. This should be recognised as a legal issue of the first magnitude, since it demonstrates an intention on the part of the terrorist to press on regardless of any warning to stop. The soldier's state of mind – his motivation, in law – will be shaped accordingly.

This selective process, as extraordinary in its way as SAS selection, contrasts vividly with the experience of other soldiers in Northern Ireland. Only one in seven of the 2000 civilians killed in the Province have died at the hands of security forces, which total around 30,000 men and women at any given time. Most soldiers never see an armed terrorist. In February 1992, Mr Peter Brooke, then Northern Ireland Secretary, revealed that up to half of those charged with terrorist offences had no previous 'paramilitary traces'. In other words, they were military virgins.

The SAS soldier, by contrast, knows that at the end of the long wait, 'nerves stretched and personal hygiene forgotten', it is all but certain that he will meet a man at least as dedicated as he is, equally well armed and ready to shoot first. The wait may last for days, fearful of compromise through dogs or children, in a shallow hide, in all weathers. 'The tension becomes unbearable', one ex-14 Company soldier admits.

Urban OPs, inside unmarked vehicles, can be equally testing. An SAS veteran of Mirbat and the Iranian Embassy siege writing under the pseudonym Soldier 'I', described how, in 1976, two youths stopped his car in Springfield Road, Belfast. The hijacker held the door of the car open with one hand as the other was ominously concealed inside his jacket. The threat – 'Get out of the fucking car or I'll blow your head off' – was clear enough but Soldier 'I', easing the safety catch off his own hidden pistol, could not fire pre-emptively. Where was the shooter? 'Show me a shooter, you bastard! Show me a shooter!' Soldier 'I''s companion, Taff, wrested the door from the youth's grasp and flung it open, winding him, before they drove off with a screech of accelerating tyres.

As the Viva roared up Grosvenor Road . . . I sank back in my seat. I looked down at the hand holding the 9-milly (Browning pistol). It was shaking slightly. I eased the safety catch to 'safe' and replaced the copy of the *News of the World*. I could have been the lead story in next Sunday's edition, I reflected, if I'd pulled the trigger. The fame would have been as instant as the hijacker's death.

In spite of the risks, the regiment has kept its own casualties at a remarkably low level. Over the same sixteen-year period just two SAS soldiers (Captain Herbert Westmacott and Lance-Corporal Alastair Slater) have been killed by the IRA. An officer serving on attachment to the regiment, Captain Robert Nairac, was seized as a prisoner by the IRA, tortured and murdered. Some writers (notably the author–priest Raymond Murray) list many more names as SAS 'victims'. Murray identifies 26 shot dead and one drowned trying to escape during the period 1981–87 but – like some of his attributions pre-1981 – he confuses SAS operations with those of 14 Intelligence Company and other covert units, or with the criminal activities of Loyalist terrorists. Murray identifies another 13 Republican activists as people shot dead by the SAS before 1981.

Firepower – limited and unlimited

The biggest controversies – even outrage – have resulted from cases in which the enemy did not meet SAS criteria: a hardened, armed terrorist, undeterred by experience of the legal process, who can be stopped from committing more violence only by a bullet. The exceptions include Dunloy cemetery, 1978 (John Boyle) due largely to an RUC failure to warn innocent people to keep out of the area; and Gibraltar, 1988, when the soldiers were led to believe, wrongly, that their adversary was armed.

Mark Urban, in his book *Big Boys' Rules*, (a phrase not previously known to SAS veterans) finds that the SAS killed twenty-nine republican terrorists between 1976 and 1991. He also concludes that between 1978 and 1987 the IRA had killed at least twenty-four of its own, either by accident or because they were informers.

Other deaths have been caused when the SAS shot innocent people, mistaking them for terrorists (as with John Boyle, the youth killed after he had drawn a rifle from an IRA arms cache in 1978) or accidentally, in the confusion of a gun battle or ambush. Urban nominates six such casualties; Murray, many more. In the author's view the SAS is responsible for five such deaths. These were William Hanna, Belfast, 21 June 1978; John Boyle, Dunloy, 11 July 1978; Frederick Jackson, Portadown, 19 October 1984; Anthony Hughes, Loughgall, 8 May 1987 and Ken Stronge, Belfast, 1 July 1988.

An SAS veteran with long experience of Borneo, Oman and Ireland speaks for many in the regiment in accepting that any unnecessary death is one too many; but he also suggests that by comparison with low intensity conflicts elsewhere, including Oman, the casualty level on both sides has been remarkably limited. At least twelve SAS soldiers were killed and about twenty gravely wounded during the six-year Oman conflict. The number of Dhofari rebels killed ran well into four figures.

London's policy of minimum firepower, rejecting the use of ground or air-launched missiles, mines, heavy machine-guns and armour, has contained the casualty figures to a level which no other government fighting a terrorist movement supplied with funds, explosives and modern weapon systems from abroad and with access to a safe haven has been able to match. Captain Westmacott died while disrupting the ambush of a thin-skinned police vehicle by a powerful M60 machine-gun in IRA hands. It is in that context, the soldiers suggest, that the legal phrase 'reasonable force' should be invoked to judge their conduct. The IRA by contrast does not hesitate to employ huge mines, mortars, missiles and heavy machine-guns. The underdog it is not.

In keeping with the minimum force concept, the SAS killed two men during its first year of operations. The first of these was an unnecessary and unintended death. On 15 April 1976 SAS soldiers helped to arrest Peter Cleary, an IRA 'staff captain' and scrap dealer at his fiancée's sister's home at Tievecrum, just 50 yards north of the border. The regiment had been looking for him for a week.

Early in the evening, a helicopter landing at Crossmaglen was attacked by rockets and machine-guns. When Cleary was found in the house two hours later, he was a desperate man. He murmured to a friend: 'I'm dead. What will I do?' With an SAS escort he was taken to a nearby field to wait for a helicopter. It was now after 11pm and dark. The chosen landing zone was a short sprint away from the sanctuary of the border. One of the SAS team said later: 'There were five of us. We radioed for a chopper . . . All of our men had to be used to hold up landing lights to let the machine down. Cleary was being held by just one chap . . . He grabbed a soldier's rifle by the barrel and tried to pull it away. The soldier squeezed the trigger three times and got him in the chest.'

No Republican will believe it happened like that. To be shot while trying to escape is a cliché out of the book of military atrocities. In this case, the author's sources insist, it did happen like that and that the officer in charge of Cleary was suspected of incompetence. His career, they assert, 'hit the buffers'. The critics conceded, however, that an arrest in these circumstances was impeded by insufficient manpower on the landing zone and a lack of handcuffs.

In his book *Emergency Tour: 3 Para in South Armagh*, Brigadier Peter Morton recalls:

The death of Peter Cleary was the first big controversy involving the SAS since their deployment into South Armagh . . . It showed the SAS's determination and skill . . . Believing their own propaganda, the PIRA was quite convinced that Cleary was cold-bloodedly murdered . . . Naturally the man who shot Cleary was questioned extensively by both the RUC and the RMP Special Investigation Branch which resulted in his being placed under a very considerable strain.

By this time another local IRA terrorist, Sean McKenna, was in custody as a result of an SAS arrest. When he appeared in court he claimed he had been woken in his bed in the Republic by a British soldier holding a pistol to his head. The SAS said he had stumbled, drunk, into one of its patrols. On 14 May, the same day that Robert Nairac (now a captain) vanished, McKenna was sentenced to 25 years imprisonment for 'a whole catalogue of terrorist offences'.

Cleary and McKenna were high on a list of wanted men handed to the SAS on its arrival in the area. Two others were arrested in the Republic, after help from an informer.

On 16 January 1977, just over a year after the Wilson announcement, the SAS scored a peculiarly satisfying victory. Two weeks before, 2 January, Lance-Corporal David Hinds of the Royal Highland Fusiliers had been murdered at Crossmaglen. The IRA does not believe in limited firepower and used a mortar bomb to kill Hinds. The only clue was a car with a black vinyl roof seen in the vicinity and thought to be a scout vehicle for the mortar team.

On 16 January, in the gathering darkness of a Sunday afternoon, the vehicle was spotted again, near the border. An SAS patrol waited as a young man approached its position. He wore a black hood and carried a bandolier of ammunition, as well as a sawn-off shotgun. As one of the patrol rose to challenge the man he lifted the shotgun. The SAS trooper instantly fired several times. The impact of the bullets hurled the gunman backwards.

Simultaneously the soldier came under fire from one or two other unseen gunmen using high-velocity Armalite rifles. The shots, about twenty in all, missed their target as the soldier ducked for cover. At the same time, other members of the SAS patrol fired back, aiming at the muzzle-flash of the IRA weapons. Later, a trail of blood was found, in a dyke beside the road.

The first armed man they had shot turned out to be Seamus Harvey, a labourer aged twenty. He lived nearby at Drummakaval and died less than 200 yards from the site of an ambush in which three British soldiers had been killed just before the SAS arrived. One source claims that two of Harvey's wounds were caused by an IRA Armalite automatic rifle later used to murder a UDR corporal. (The IRA at that time was better armed than the SAS, which did not yet have the Armalite.)

The deterrent effect of such ambushes was impressive. While soldiers and RUC officers continued to be killed regularly elsewhere, IRA attacks in South Armagh virtually ended for a year after Harvey's death. When they were resumed at Forkhill, the first casualty was a local pig.

SAS pressure was maintained during that first year, and afterwards, through intensive patrolling. From time to time, on an unmarked border, soldiers strayed into the South. This happened to soldiers other than the SAS. Men of 3 Para were inadvertently put down in the Republic by an RAF helicopter in May 1976, three weeks after the SAS made the same mistake on the ground. This episode, rapidly inflated into a diplomatic incident, began just before 11pm on 5 May near Omeath, County Louth when a civilian car containing a plain-clothes patrol from D Squadron, driving fast, the navigator relying on a torchlit map on his knee, took a wrong turning near Carlingford Lough. The soldiers had arrived direct from Oman with no chance to retrain for the very different environment of the unmarked Irish border, with its twisting, leafy back lanes and withered signposts. The Q-car was stopped at a police roadblock a mere 600 yards south of the Ulster border.

In spite of appeals to let the patrol return north ('We're supposed to be doing the same job, aren't we?' asked one SAS soldier) the Gardai insisted on taking advice from Dundalk. The affair now escalated into political farce. A second SAS Q-car, searching for the one which was missing, arrived at the same spot at 2.15am, repeated the error of the first and was also detained. Weapons taken from the men included Sterling sub-machine-guns, pump-action shotguns and self-loading pistols.

An SAS memoir recalls how the Garda officer at their subsequent trial in Dublin, described the arrest.

Corporal 'Y', on being told he was in the Republic, replied: 'Jesus, I was hoping to be made up to sergeant but after this bloody cock-up there's absolutely no chance!'

And how did the soldiers react, he was asked, several hours later, as a second four-man team was ushered into the police office to join the men who were arrested first?

'Well, Sorr, they were very pleased because they thought they had come to escort them home. Then the second lot explained that they had come to look for them after they disappeared, missed the signpost and ended up being arrested just like they were.'

'So what was the reaction then?'

'Well, Sorr, they all looked a bit sheepish. Then they all burst out laughing.'

If the SAS prisoners were struck by the absurdity of their situation, Irish eyes were not smiling. In an autobiography published in 1991, the Irish Foreign Minister of the day, Garret Fitzgerald, revealed:

> The armed men claimed to be British soldiers who had strayed unintentionally into the Republic. In the frequent cases of accidental border crossing by members of the security forces it was normal to send them back. Some time previously, however, a man had been kidnapped in this area, taken into Northern Ireland, and murdered. The Gardai wanted a forensic test carried out on the latest intruders' firearms to see whether any of them might have been used on that occasion, and they wished to hold them overnight for this purpose.
>
> In the circumstances, I agreed. The following morning Pat Cooney (the Republic's Justice Minister) told me that the test on the guns had proved negative.

After meeting top officials, Fitzgerald decreed that the men should be released immediately but by now the police commissioner had already charged the soldiers with possession of firearms with intent to endanger life, on the directions of the Director of Public Prosecutions 'who, unknown to us had earlier ordered the Gardai to notify him immediately of any people found with arms in border areas with a view to taking prompt action in such cases'.

The rumpus now involved different perceptions between the Prime Minister Liam Cosgrave, his Foreign Minister and government on one hand and on the other, a newly appointed DPP who was 'very much his own man' who 'stood on his rights'.

> We had to inform the British that the men . . . would, if released on bail, return to face trial. The British reacted with fury. They could not envisage a law officer acting independently in this way . . . They insisted that our contrary view was a politically motivated act by our government. Indeed, Jim Callaghan rang Liam Cosgrave to demand the men's release. But in the end they had to agree to send the

men back for trial, which they did some months later. In the event the soldiers were found guilty only on a lesser charge of illegal possession of firearms, were fined £100 each and released.

For the soldiers, the trial was an edgy experience. A senior SAS officer let it be known that the men would not be allowed to risk their lives travelling in public to Dublin unless he accompanied them, which he did. His presence emphasised the danger as well as regimental solidarity. The journey to Dublin was aboard an RAF transport aircraft. One of the escorts recalled later:

We took off and headed South. I dozed fitfully until the Loadmaster tapped me on the shoulder and motioned me up to the cockpit. 'What's the plan for the approach?' the pilots asked me anxiously. Thinking of the devastating effect a terrorist SAM-7 [missile] might have on our progress, I chose a high/low angle of attack. The aircraft shuddered as full flap was abruptly selected and the nose came down in a screaming dive.

We pulled up just short of the runway and as we ran in, now at very low level, Irish Air Force aircraft joined us at both wingtips. Below, as far as the eye could see, troops of the Irish Army and Gardai Siochana were positioned behind bushes and buildings. They were all very heavily armed.

No sooner had the aircraft come to a stop at the end of the runway than the doors were flung open and we were motioned quickly into a long convoy of Panhard armoured cars, which already had their engines running. The grim Irish occupants were wearing steel helmets and body armour and had spares of both for the two escorts. Spirits lifted. At least the first major concern that we all had had, was being addressed in style and apparently with considerable professionalism.

The entire party was hurried to cells below the courthouse, for its own protection.

The cell door shut with a loud clang and as if to confirm the note of finality, the warder made a great show of flourishing his keys as he turned the lock. Ten members of the regiment and myself were now well and truly banged up and as far as I knew, as I eyed the bars on the tiny window, there was not even one nailfile amongst us.

The first morning of the court proceedings passed quickly and I had time to reflect on the PIRA graffiti on the walls which had welcomed the SAS to their cell. We now returned to these underground cells and my spirits lifted further when a substantial meal was served on trays. The 'Boss' did not even touch his; nor did the others. Instead he motioned to me to get tucked in, which I did. The others watched intently as I stored away the stew and potatoes.

'Aren't you eating?' I enquired politely.

'Maybe in a minute or two,' the Boss snarled, 'after we've seen how you get on.'

'The crafty buggers,' I thought, 'I'm the food tester. Personal security is very hot today.'

After two days of evidence, three judges returned a formal finding of guilt on entering the Republic without permission but rejected the more serious charge (possessing arms to endanger life) as a nonsense. The court was being cleared when the senior judge called, 'Hang on a minute. What about all these weapons here?'

The SAS memoir goes on:

He motioned to the assorted pistols, rifles and sub-machine-guns which lay as exhibits in front of the court. 'When you left your base on patrol in the North last year, you must have signed for all these guns. They'll still be on your signature, so perhaps we should be giving you them back, eh?' He gave the Prosecutor an old-fashioned look. 'So, Mr Prosecutor, you wouldn't object if we gave the boys their weapons back now? . . . But on second thoughts, if the boys picked up their weapons (sigh) you might be charging them with being in possession of weapons again . . . OK boys, off you go. We'll arrange for them to be sent on to you later.'

The RAF transport lifted off across Dublin Bay, banked east and flew direct to Northolt.

Section IV

Legal limitations on a regiment accustomed to the freedom as well as the dangers of the battlefield were soon as acute in the Province as across the border. In response, perhaps, to a warning from one squadron commander about this legal minefield, the SAS soldiers were in due course to be accompanied by members of the Army Legal Service as they made their explanations afterwards of how it came about that an armed terrorist, recently released from prison, declined to give himself up peacefully on a dark night while on 'operations'. In time, the soldiers themselves would accept that their role as 'proactive' defenders of the peace – not passive targets but hunters – could be covered by only one legal formulation.

The Yellow Card procedure, through which the soldier may legally start shooting, does permit the soldier to fire without warning, using 'reasonable force', if this is necessary to save life. By the time the SAS is summoned, that course is frequently necessary, though the regiment itself asserts that the ratio of terrorists arrested outnumbers those shot dead by more than two to one. The number shot is still much greater than that killed by other Army units. The reason for that is simple. The SAS is allocated the hard cases about which there is good, timely intelligence; cases in which an IRA team of perhaps eight hardened terrorists (as at Loughgall in 1987) armed with the latest weapons including Semtex explosive, will only be stopped by defensive firepower carefully tailored for the occasion. If there is time, a warning may be shouted. It is a rough-and-ready procedure but the best that can be devised in an ambiguous conflict once known as no-war-no-peace.

The political rhetoric of earlier days is less heard in the 1990s.

Not since Margaret Thatcher has any national leader spoken about being 'at war' with the IRA. In 1977–78 such sentiments were to be heard more generally, from Harold Wilson to Stormont's penultimate Prime Minister, James Chichester-Clark. It was a time when the IRA in Dublin surrendered control of the campaign to the hard men in the North, whom they had once despised as 'the Belfast mafia'.

The SAS contingent in the Province was also reorganised to put it under a new joint command with 14 Intelligence Company known as Intelligence & Security Group. The boss is often someone with SAS or Intelligence experience. One outstanding commander learned his soldiering with the Foreign Legion paras in the Battle of Algiers and elsewhere.

As the tempo quickened on both sides, undercover soldiers unwary enough to expose themselves to armed killers learned the hard way. Captain Robert Nairac, working for the combined Intelligence & Security Group – effectively on attachment to the SAS as an Intelligence analyst and brain-about-town – pushed his luck and, against orders, adopted the role of 'action man'. On 15 May 1977, without informing his SAS controller, he parked his Q-car outside a Republican bar near the border, and in civilian clothes, tried to pass himself off as a Belfast man who was good 'crack', (or company) and, from a small stage in the bar, a decent singing voice. He had left his Browning pistol in the locked car.

As he emerged from the pub to the darkness of the car park outside, he was set upon by a gang of seven IRA men and savagely beaten. He tried desperately to get the car door open to reach his pistol and when that failed he tried to escape. An executioner was summoned from across the border. Nairac seized the gun but it misfired. He was recaptured, murdered and buried in an unmarked grave. The IRA team responsible were later convicted and imprisoned in the Republic. There the assassin admitted to Nairac's SAS controller: 'Your man never told us anything.' His killers believed that he was a member of the alternative, Official IRA rather than the Provisionals. In 1979, Nairac was awarded a posthumous George Cross.

Less than a year later, on 16 March 1978, at Maghera, David

Jones, a Parachute Regiment lance-corporal serving with 14 Intelligence Company, stepped out of his concealed position to challenge three men in combat dress. The leader of the trio, IRA Volunteer Francis Hughes, immediately shot him in the stomach. In spite of his injuries, Jones shot back, hitting Hughes. Jones's companion, another Para volunteer with 14 Company, was also wounded. Jones died next day, a victim of the primacy of non-violent, citizen's arrest.

Hughes, meanwhile, unable to walk because of leg injuries, crawled into undergrowth. The Army, using tracker dogs, took thirteen hours to find him. When they did so he snarled at them: 'Yu's fucking dogs is no good.' The Army, respecting his endurance if nothing else, handed him to the police. He had killed many people with explosives, including a ten-year-old child. In prison, his aggression turned inward and he died on hunger strike, a hero to Republicans, a psychopath in the eyes of the police.

With the hard cases, came the controversies. The most enigmatic is still the death of Paul Duffy, a 23-year-old carpenter from Carnan, County Tyrone and a low-grade IRA volunteer. Soon after dusk on a Sunday evening, 26 February 1978, after watching a football match at Ardboe, Duffy walked into a disused, rambling maze of empty farm buildings looking for an IRA explosives cache.

As he prowled around the yard, alone and unarmed, he was shot dead. The circumstances were similar to those attached to the 1974 shooting of the Protestant, William Black, which Black survived and responsibility for which is denied by the SAS eighteen years later.

According to Raymond Murray's account of Duffy's death, the IRA man had learned casually, at the football game, 'that explosives brought from Dungannon had been left at a derelict house' and were a danger to two old men. Duffy was not so aroused by this news that he hurried immediately to the area. With a friend acting as driver, he called on a house nearby, drinking Lucozade until some time after 5.30pm. His friend, asking no questions, dropped him off in the dark some 400 yards from the deserted farm.

If that is the whole story, one may take it that Duffy could not know where, in a rabbit warren of disused buildings, in the dark with or without a torch, he was going to discover a casually left explosives dump. He could hardly hope to find arrows set up directing him to 'IRA Ordnance Store'. He would not know how extensive it would be and whether he could move it away safely, single-handed. We do not know whether he was trained in handling explosives to know the difference, say, between stable, easily handled Semtex and unstable gelignite.

Some hours after the shooting, his body was inspected by torchlight by an RUC Chief Inspector and the victim's uncle, Mr P.A. Duffy, a solicitor. Mr Duffy said: 'When I saw Paul's body after the shooting it was clear he had been shot through the forehead from the front with his back against the wall. There is not even the slightest shadow of doubt that he was not even given the chance to surrender . . .'

Mr Duffy saw no weapons or explosives near his nephew's body. The Chief Inspector, however, said he saw a mortar lying 6 feet from the corpse.

The soldiers did not give evidence at the inquest ten months later. Their statements said they had shot Duffy as 'he came out of the house' or 'as he ran across the yard'. These are not necessarily inconsistent.

Mr Duffy's greatest criticism had to do with the legal framework within which, he believed, the Army justified shooting his nephew. This raises the tricky question of how the soldier is to respond if – like Peter Cleary – the prisoner makes a bolt for it. On 7 August 1974, an innocent farm labourer named Patrick McElhone was shot dead by soldiers who had just questioned him, told him to go and then changed their minds. They called on him to stop. He tried to run away. The soldiers (from a line regiment, on their first trip to Northern Ireland) said they shot McElhone as he tried to escape.

The soldier who fired the fatal shots was tried for murder and acquitted. Before the House of Lords, Lord Diplock argued that because there was 'an armed and clandestinely organised insurrection' in Northern Ireland, it was necessary to balance an innocent man's death against the harm that might have been caused if McElhone had really been a terrorist escaping to fight another day. It was a classic expression of the doctrine of the lesser of two evils: sound philosophy but open to the objection that it could be used as a licence by soldiers to shoot any suspect so long as it appeared that he was not going quietly.

Thus Paul Duffy's lawyer-uncle said: 'It will be recalled after the death of Patrick McElhone and the judicial justification given in that case to the shooting of a person when he is trying to escape that I personally pointed out to the Secretary of State . . . the great risk . . . that [it] gave the British Army a free hand to shoot down any person on the allegation that that person was attempting to escape. This is now the third occasion in which the British Army have used that statement in order to justify a killing.'

There was, of course, no general rule permitting soldiers to kill people while trying to escape. The McElhone judgement related to that case alone. As Lieutenant-Colonel Charles Wakerley, Assistant Director of Legal Services for Northern Ireland in 1972–74, told Panorama: 'For twenty years soldiers have been in Northern Ireland with no greater legal back-up than you or I have if we happen to go out of the house on a Saturday morning and witness some altercation on the street. That seems to me to be an absurdity.'

The case of Paul Duffy took another bewildering twist during the author's research for this history. In spite of the fact that the army press office at HQ Northern Ireland took the ususual step of attributing this operation to the SAS in 1978, the author's sources, familiar with the regiment's operations at that time, now say that Paul Duffy's death was the work of 'another organisation'.

They confirm that an SAS surveillance team did kill another IRA terrorist named *Patrick* Duffy in a house used as an IRA arms store at Maureen Avenue, Londonderry, on 24 November 1978, nine months after Paul Duffy was killed. Like Paul Duffy, Patrick Duffy was checking – 'servicing' is the SAS word for it – weapons in store. Patrick Duffy, aged fifty, a father of six, an unemployed fitter and a known IRA man, had borrowed a BMW car for his operation. With an adult daughter and a baby grandchild as cover, he parked the car outside 2 Maureen Avenue. Leaving his daughter in the car, supervising his grandson playing with the steering wheel, he entered the house, nominally unoccupied, but in practice concealing an SAS team.

The weapons were in a wardrobe in a first floor room overlooking the street. Firearms must be cleaned and re-oiled if they are not to malfunction in use, and as Duffy attended to his deadly housekeeping in the gloom the SAS reception party killed him with a total of fourteen bullets. They believe they acted within the Yellow Card rules.

Patrick Duffy was given an IRA funeral, his coffin covered by an Irish tricolour, with an honour guard firing two volleys over the bier. Duffy has been described as a mere auxiliary, but in spite of that his status attracted the presence of Sean Keenan to deliver the graveside eulogy. Keenan, a respected veteran of the 'fifties campaign, had spent years of imprisonment without trial when the author met him in 1969. His survival through the renewed troubles was phenomenal.

In the summer of 1978, under its new management, the IRA decided to wage 'economic warfare', hitting targets to cripple the Province's infrastructure. Such targets were largely urban. The SAS operated exclusively in rural areas. The RUC had made it clear that it wanted no more shoot-outs on the streets of Belfast or Londonderry. Such events were not only bad in themselves. They were also a cruel reminder of the RUC's defeat on the same streets in 1969.

In spite of that the SAS was invoked to deal with one of the first terrorist raids in the new economic warfare campaign. The target was a Post Office transport and engineering depot at Ballysillan Road, North Belfast. The leak from the IRA to Military Intelligence was detailed and accurate. Intelligence officers knew that three or four bombers would attack the target within the next few nights. They also knew that the bombers would probably carry no weapons other than the satchel bombs they were to hurl over the unlit perimeter fence from waste-ground adjoining the target.

Soldiers of G Squadron, on temporary duty with 14 Company's

Belfast detachment, in a hurried briefing with their RUC guide, were not told that the attackers were probably not carrying firearms. The reason for that omission reflects the conflict between priorities of the Intelligence war – a war in which sources must be protected, a war in which a sprat is sacrificed today to catch a mackerel tomorrow – and the shooting war, whose outcome can be measured in milliseconds.

To provide the soldiers or front-line RUC men with an excess of information could compromise fatally a high-grade informer deep inside the IRA hierarchy. For that reason, when an arms search was directed at a particular house, the soldiers might be tipped off only to look in the area around the target. The general, apparently random, trawl that resulted was meant to cover the precise nature of the Intelligence. As one SAS operator puts it: 'We get Intelligence, often vague, certainly not a script.'

The down side of this arrangement was that an insufficient brief to a soldier ordered to stop an armed attack could be fatal to the soldier, or some third party. At Ballysillan, it was a passer-by, a Protestant happily on his way home from a drinking club by a roundabout route enabling him to avoid the risk of passing through a Republican area, who was caught in this rather arcane form of cross-fire.

Just after 11pm on 21 June, five SAS soldiers and a captain armed with Armalite rifles, accompanied by an RUC officer ('our native guide') armed with a Stirling sub-machine gun, hurried into position to wait for the bombers. The rules of engagement, aside from Yellow Card rules, were that the aim of the operation was to stop the terrorists causing damage to life or property at the sub-station and if possible to apprehend the terrorists.

The team split into two groups. Soldiers 'A' (Who was the commander, a captain), 'B' and 'C', together with the RUC man, hid in a garden facing across a lane to the front of the targeted building. The lane, just four feet wide, flanked by the depot wall on one side and a fenced hedge adjoining playing fields on the other, turned at the corner of the building, out of sight of 'A's team. It then led down one side of the depot to the rear of the building where this flanked a cul-de-sac, Wheatfield

Drive. At this end of the lane, in bushes, watching the rear of the depot, were Soldiers 'D' and 'E'.

It appears from the testimony of 'A' that there was 'another observation post' the location of which was not clear, from which Wheatfield Drive was being watched. It was in this cul-de-sac that the IRA getaway car would park. The ambush party did not know how long it would have to wait. In the event, the bombers arrived only an hour afterwards, parking their stolen getaway car in Wheatfield Drive, leaving the driver with the vehicle.

Three of the men then slipped into the lane, passing 'D' and 'E' as they walked in single file towards the front of the building and the captain's reception party. The IRA men were now effectively in a trap.

At least one of them was an experienced terrorist. James Mulvenna, aged 30, had been shot and wounded by soldiers while on a bombing raid seven years earlier. He had served six years in prison and had been out of prison for just a year.

As they rounded the corner at the front of the building, the three terrorists started to throw their bombs over the perimeter fence. The bombs were satchels containing petrol combined with explosive, a type of weapon that had caused twelve horrific 'napalm' deaths at the La Mon restaurant four months previously. The author's sources confirm that the soldiers and their RUC companion, hidden a few feet away in a garden across the lane, opened fire immediately. As one observer put it later, 'It seemed that all the conditions attached to the Yellow Card had been met and their duty was clear. They thought Christmas had come.'

In a subsequent statement, however, one of the SAS men identified as Soldier 'C' claimed that he had shouted 'Stop!' He then 'engaged the men whom I believed responsible for firing in my direction'.

The driver of the IRA getaway car, when he heard the shooting, reversed in a panic, then leapt from the vehicle and ran away. By now, two men on their way home from a Protestant drinking club were walking down the lane in the opposite direction, from the Ballysillan Road, their silhouettes visible to the soldiers. The soldiers' brief was that there were three or four bombers. They had accounted for three. Two of the men (Mulvenna and Denis Brown, aged twenty-eight) lay like rag dolls, legs splayed, chests repeatedly hit by gunfire, alongside the target's perimeter fence. The third bomber, William Mailey, aged thirty, was perhaps twenty yards off to the left, behind a low hedge on the edge of playing fields, his brains spread in a plume across the ground.

As the soldiers advanced from their cover to pursue the 'fourth man', (confusing the terrorist with an innocent Protestant named William Hanna) they fired two more rounds at the heads of the nearest bombers, Mulvenna and Brown, to ensure that they would be no threat. These final shots were close enough to the victims' heads as to cause powder burns and give rise to the suspicion, subsequently, of *coup de grâce* killings. The retreating silhouettes were now shot at. Both dived for cover.

Interviewed later by Army Intelligence and legal officers, the soldiers said they were sure that they had come under fire before they shot the terrorists. When it was pointed out to them that no spent cartridges except their own were found on the ground, one soldier brightly suggested that the IRA men must have been using a revolver, which does not eject the spent cartridge. No revolver was found, either.

Critics of the SAS, some within the RUC, suspected that this sequence of events pointed to gratuitous killing by the ambush party of unarmed men, rounded off by a psychopathic series of head-shots into people who were already dead. Such a conclusion had to ignore the fact that Hanna's companion – a potentially damaging witness of any killing orgy – was handed over unharmed to the RUC.

In Raymond Murray's version the survivor, David Graham, said: 'All of a sudden and without any warning I heard shooting very close at hand . . . I hit the ground immediately . . . I rolled into bushes at the side of the lane. When I heard the voices [with English accents] I shouted, "I'm over here, Mister." . . . I was put against the wall at the side of the lane and searched. I was later taken to North Queen Street police station.'

Graham, frightened but untouched, was released. In a subsequent statement Soldier 'B' said: 'Soldier "C" told Hanna not to move. He then told him to put his hands on his head and as he did so, he made a twisting movement as if to go for a weapon. As I believed he was reaching for a weapon I and Soldier "C" opened fire on this person.'

When an Army investigation team arrived soon afterwards William Hanna, aged 28, lay dead near bushes beside the lane, still wearing his Loyalist tam-o'-shanter. He was a few hundred yards from home.

The soldiers were interviewed by two teams of police officers and the opinion of the Northern Ireland Director of Public Prosecutions was sought. Questions about the soldiers' knowledge of what to expect were central to the issue but not pursued because of an unwritten rule that matters touching upon Intelligence sources inside the IRA were off-limits, in the interests of national security, even to the DPP.

Furthermore, this was an operation approved by the RUC in which one of its own officers had participated enthusiastically. In those circumstances the soldiers were not prosecuted but, as one acknowledges, 'we were frozen out of Belfast for a year'.

So, as it happens, were the IRA bombers, though *Republican News* asserted that 'death is no stranger or deterrent to the volunteers of the Irish Republican Army'. The SAS troop captain in immediate charge of the operation was not invited to extend his tour with the regiment and later left the Army.

One mystery remains about the involvement of the two Protestants, Hanna and Graham. It is clear from the route the survivor Graham says they took (walking from Bilston Road to Ballysillan Road and 'across into the lane which runs onto the Ardoyne Road', en route to Graham's home in Wheatfield Drive) that they were walking down the depot lane in the opposite direction to that taken by the IRA party. In one Press interview, Graham confirmed that they had walked 'halfway down the lane when the shooting started'.

To do so, they had to move through Captain 'A's position unchallenged and might even have passed the IRA men in the darkness of the lane just before the first shots. A civilian witness, 'H', in Wheatfield Drive shortly before, noted the getaway car, the driver still in it, and 'three or four fellas standing about half-way up the walk. They were just standing close together'. This witness walked away and heard shooting. He then saw the getaway car reverse, stop with front wheels on the kerb and the driver escape over a nearby wall.

Were the 'three or four fellas' he saw, an uneasy nocturnal encounter accompanied by grunted greetings, between two Loyalist drinkers walking home and an IRA bombing party on its way to a target? It would be a natural reaction for the uninvolved Protestants to run away as the shooting and screams started behind them. Graham, according to his statement, immediately dived into the cover of bushes flanking the lane at the end of which Soldiers 'B' and 'C' were waiting to halt any terrorist trying to escape from the trap for which they were now the stop party. Hanna's intentions and movements were fatally ambiguous.

The soldiers clearly did believe he was an IRA man, armed and dangerous. Tragically it is possible that Hanna made a similar mistake and thought that the soldiers were IRA terrorists. This is a mixed area, close to the notorious Ardoyne district, a potentially dangerous place for a Loyalist, in the dark, alone, while shooting is going on nearby. The survivor Graham, it should be noted, identified himself only when he heard English voices.

Three weeks after Ballysillan, another civilian was shot dead by the SAS in ambiguous circumstances for which the soldiers got the blame. On 10 July 1978, John Boyle, aged 16, came upon an arms cache hidden beneath a tombstone near the family farm at Dunloy, Antrim. The family alerted the RUC, which summoned the SAS. Some police suspected that the weapons, including explosive, would be used for an anti-Protestant outrage on the Loyalist festival of 12 July. An SAS ambush was hurriedly set up. The RUC promised to alert the family, telling it to keep away from the cache. It did so, but too late.

Two of the ambush team, Sergeant Allan Bohan, aged twenty-eight with six years SAS experience, and a corporal watched as a man they thought to be a terrorist approached the arms cache and drew a rifle from it.

As Bohan said later: 'He stood up . . . turned bringing the weapon to bear on us and I thought our lives were in immediate danger. I fired and he fell and as soon as he fell I stopped. I fired not more than twice and probably once.' As Bohan fired, so too did the corporal. They killed not a terrorist but young Boyle, who had found the arms and now, for reasons never made clear, returned to the hide after a military operation was up and running. The family, Catholics who had done their citizens' duty, did not know that, for the RUC had yet to keep its promise to warn the Boyle family.

Bohan and his companion were charged with murder largely because an autopsy concluded that Boyle had been shot in the back. Such evidence strengthened the suspicion of unnecessary and therefore illegal use of force. Only after the case started did independent pathological evidence demonstrate that this was a dubious conclusion. Having launched its case on the basis that Boyle was shot from the rear, the prosecution found it necessary to float the theory that Bohan may have made a noise deliberately to induce Boyle to turn in Bohan's direction, 'and then you shot him'.

Acquitting the two, Sir Robert Lowry, Lord Chief Justice of Nothern Ireland, criticised them for 'a badly planned and bungled exercise', adding: 'I do not intend to give any currency to the view that the Army is above the general law in the use of weapons.'

This, of course, brought all soldiers into a legal conflict – like the nut in a nutcracker – between the Wilson government's formula, that they were exercising their powers as 'common law constables', while simultaneously carrying weapons as members of the armed services acting in aid of the civil power. The argument has raged ever since.

Section V

It was to be five years before the SAS killed anyone else in Northern Ireland. Differing reasons are offered up for this fact. According to Mark Urban, in *Big Boys' Rules*: 'In late 1978 the Army reviewed its policy on the deployment of SAS troops and ended, for the time being at least, the use of these highly trained troops for mounting ambushes. This followed . . . gathering unease about the conduct of SAS soldiers in undercover operations.' The SAS, he asserts, was 'reined in'.

The author's sources say that if there were such a change of policy, the SAS was unaware of it. The regiment continued at the front end of high risk operations mainly against the IRA, which was now cultivating contacts with Libya which would reap a harvest of death from 1986/87 onwards.

One change which did take place, in December 1981, was a reduction of the SAS presence from a squadron to a reinforced troop. From December 1978 onward, there had been a steady fall in the number of civilian deaths caused by terrorism, reversed when the IRA got its hands on the huge supply of Semtex plastic explosive donated by the Libyan government. The graph virtually started its lethal upward curve, reversing that trend, with the murder of eleven civilians at the Enniskillen Remembrance Day service in 1987. But in December 1981, the total number of people being killed by terrorism was averaging eighty-eight, compared with a total of 467 for the single, peak year of 1972.

Furthermore, the overall strength of the British Army in Northern Ireland was being cut at this time. The Regular Army (excluding the UDR) had 17,250 men in the Province in 1973–74. The figure had dropped to 14,159 by 1978, when the so-called review of SAS deployment was taking place, and was down to 11,114 in 1981 when SAS strength there was actually cut. The figure declined steadily to 9578 until 1990, rising again in the two following years (see Appendix B) largely in response to IRA terrorism. Civilian deaths were back up to 71 in 1991.

It made sense to reduce the SAS contingent stationed in the province in line with an improving situation in 1981. To link a rational decision to dilute Harold Wilson's dramatic (and PR-driven) commitment of 1976 to some changed perception of the SAS role misreads the facts.

If there were no 'ambushes' in the sense implied by Raymond Murray and Mark Urban, there was no lack of action. The SAS arrested around twenty terrorists during the 'reined-in' years. On 2 May 1980 (in the same week that the regiment stormed the Iranian Embassy in London) military headquarters, Northern Ireland, received an emergency call from the RUC. An IRA team armed with a 7.62mm M-60 machine-gun, one of seven stolen from National Guard armouries in Boston, Mass. was lying in wait for any soft-skinned security forces vehicle passing its position on the first floor of a house at 369 Antrim Road, Belfast. There was no time for the normal reconnaissance, the careful overture to most SAS operations.

Led by Captain Richard Westmacott, an SAS patrol made one pass in front of the terrorist position, in a civilian car, before bundling out and storming the front of the building with sledge hammers. The team chose the wrong door and hit the house next door to that held by the terrorists. As they did so, the IRA fired into the street below, killing Westmacott. The M-60 is a belt-fed, high speed and accurate weapon. In all, fifty bullets were fired in two long bursts. The first fusillade was a dozen rounds, the last two of which hit and killed the SAS troop leader.

A stalemate ensued, in which the IRA team of eight men signalled its surrender with a white sheet, but insisted on arranging the formalities with a Catholic priest in attendance. The SAS team, also of eight men, stood by warily until the terrorists were handed over for trial, charged with murdering Westmacott, the first SAS soldier to be killed by the IRA. The men escaped from custody before the trial ended, helped by a pistol smuggled into them. Most of them were later recaptured to serve life sentences though one escapee, Joe Doherty, was lionised by New York as he contested, unsuccessfully, moves to extradite him from the USA.

One version of the story seeping out of the imaginative world of Intelligence proposes that the M-60 was rigged ('jarked' in the jargon) by weapons Intelligence experts to malfunction and present no danger to the SAS. The gun was also allegedly fitted with a concealed, miniature transmitter, enabling Military Intelligence to keep track of it before being replaced in its hide as a poisoned gift to the IRA. Whatever the truth of that, it would appear that the weapon was still capable of causing the first SAS death at the hands of the IRA.

Westmacott would appear to be another victim of the doctrine of minimum force compounded by misapplied optimism on the part of those who claim to have 'jarked' the M-60. If the SAS was discreetly being 'reined in' during a period of police primacy from 1979 onward, then the policy had also given the IRA its first victory over the SAS. As one soldier had noted some time before: 'We define the "Irish Dimension" as the art of letting the terrorist have the first shot.'

It is not a view from which honest Irishmen would dissent. As Raymond Murray, summing up the results of an IRA pre-emptive attack on a 14 Company observation post, in which three men died said: 'Hogan and Martin' (two IRA men) 'realised that surveillance was coming to a point where they would be assassinated by the SAS. It was a matter of who moved first.'

Another life-saving operation during this period, for which the SAS is not granted due credit, is its success in providing emergency first aid to Bernadette McAliskey (née Devlin) and her husband Michael after Ulster Defence Association terrorists had shot them in their isolated home near Coalisland on 16 January 1981. The three unsuccessful assassins were arrested by an SAS team and later imprisoned. Raymond Murray alleges that the soldiers were Paras, that they 'claimed their radio was not working' and 'left without giving medical aid'. He asserts that twenty minutes later, soldiers of the Argyll & Sutherland Highlanders arrived and did give first aid.

The facts are that the soldiers were SAS men wearing Parachute Regiment insignia, put into position the night before the assassination attempt on the McAliskeys on information from the RUC. The nearest feasible hide was in a copse 300 yds away from the house. The soldiers lay in the open overnight, in sub-zero temperatures, waiting for a message that never came. Early next morning the assassins drove at speed to their target and smashed their way into the house with sledge hammers. The author's sources are emphatic that SAS soldiers not only arrested the attackers but also sprinted to the house to give life-saving first-aid to the injured couple as they heard the shots. The condition of Michael McAliskey was grave: he was 'spurting blood' from a severed artery and would not have survived a twenty-minute wait for medical attention. His wife was also bleeding from seven bullet wounds.

The soldiers admit that the operation was flawed by a communications failure between themselves and the RUC, as a result of which the soldiers did not receive the early warning they had been led to expect that the assassins were on their way. Such an alert, part of the plan to foil the attempt, would have enabled more timely intervention. Just over a year later the three attackers, all loyalists – one a former UDR soldier – were sentenced respectively to life, twenty and fifteen years' imprisonment each. The SAS patrol commander was awarded the British Empire Medal.

The affair reminded some students of close protection in Ireland of the death of Maire Drumm, a colourful, vociferous nationalist murdered by Loyalist extremists as she lay in her hospital bed in Belfast in October 1976. On that occasion an SAS screen discreetly placed around the Catholic Mater Hospital was withdrawn shortly before the assassination though on whose orders is not clear. Since the officer in charge of the team later died in Oman it is unlikely that we shall ever know.

The allocation of high-risk ambushes to the RUC was to prove no less controversial than when the SAS was responsible. In a series of episodes in 1982, later investigated by John Stalker and popularly known as the 'Shoot-to-kill' cases, the police killed five known terrorists and one innocent at a time when the victims were unarmed. These actions, like the imprisonment of many terrorists of all kinds during the 1980s, were intimately linked with the use of informers who had committed terrorist crimes themselves. But whereas the misuse of the 'supergrass' at a criminal trial could produce, at worst, an undeserved prison sentence, the use of summary force to 'take out' suspected bombers and assassins was irrevocable and lethal, without the justification that the killing was necessary to halt further, imminent killing. Such a strategy, though not legally classified as murder, implied some rough moral equivalence between the security forces and the terrorists, to the decisive advantage of the terrorists. The SAS, although it trained some RUC men in ambush techniques, was not involved in the 'shoot-to-kill' cases investigated by Stalker and others. These, it should be noted, led to the prosecution and acquittal of some of the police officers involved.

When the SAS again killed two IRA men, on Sunday 4 December 1983, in a field near Coalisland, Tyrone (source of the first civil rights agitation in 1968) it was very much a case of business as usual: a tip-off from an informer relayed to the RUC, after the accidental discharge of an IRA weapon; a request that the security forces provide a team able to handle the long wait beside the arms cache and the dangerous business that would come when the terrorists, armed and alert, also arrived.

The waiting extended over two bitterly cold days. Six soldiers, in pairs, were hiding near the cache, which held an Armalite rifle, a shotgun and other items. The Armalite had killed at least four off-duty reservists, all unarmed at the time. The SAS soldiers also had Armalites. After Sunday lunch and attending Mass, Colm McGirr, a 23-year-old local bricklayer and his friend Brian Campbell, aged 19, a mechanic, were driven to the field, overgrown with thistles, surrounded by a high embankment, ducked under a wire fence and disappeared. McGirr was wearing his Sunday best. There was no question this time of the terrorist weapons having been rigged so as not to fire.

McGirr went to the hide, pulled out the Armalite and handed it to Campbell. That was what the soldiers had been waiting for. Soldier 'A', the NCO in charge, stayed in cover but shouted: 'Halt, Security Forces!' The men had a second within which to do something and they made the wrong decision. 'McGirr,' says Soldier 'A' 'pivoted round, pointing the shotgun in my direction.' Campbell seemed to be running towards the car.

Within the rules of engagement lives clearly were endangered if this continued and the SAS teams opened fire. McGirr was hit by at least thirteen bullets. For Campbell, two were enough to kill him. The driver, guessing what had happened, was wounded but escaped.

The families of both men acknowledged that they were IRA volunteers but claimed, with Republican logic, that their men could have been arrested peaceably. Their deaths were cases of murder, they said. The priest who conducted McGirr's funeral, brother of an IRA hunger-striker, told the congregation: 'There is surely some law of nature which is offended and violated when Irishmen are struck down in their native place by faceless, nameless strangers.'

Raymond Murray suggests that McGirr and Campbell were killed and not captured as part of a public relations offensive to mollify Protestant opinion after masked republican terrorists had fired indiscriminately into the Darkley Gospel Hall, Armagh, killing three people and wounding seven more two weeks before. He also cites James Prior, Northern Ireland Minister, rebutting the suspicion with the comment: 'The SAS have been here the whole time and it happens from time to time they have an opportunity of showing what they can do.' Another notable contribution to public debate at that time came from the newly elected leader of Sinn Feinn, Gerry Adams, who proclaimed: 'The armed struggle must go on.'

In fact, as McGirr's family acknowledged, Colm was held in Gough barracks on a 'Section 11' detention order for three days in the week before he died. They allege that he had been threatened with assassination by the British Army and the RUC. If that is so, he was clearly undeterred by the threat before he drew the weapon from its hide. It would be at least consistent if he were not ready to surrender when he had the gun in his hand.

The argument in this case, as in others, is about whether the game has been played to Irish, rather than British rules: whether the IRA man was given the chance to shoot first. If he was not, it is construed by his community as murder. Such a construction works only if the Republicans can lay decent claim to a political legitimacy they do not have. They are, in fact, the doomed disciples of a lost cause but human nature being what it is, some will blame others for that unhappy condition. On this as on other punishment runs, the SAS stays silent.

Section VI

From the autumn of 1984, after the IRA came close to assassinating most of the British government with a bomb at the Grand Hotel, Brighton, a new pattern emerged from the conflict between the terrorists and the SAS as a result of which the regiment tended to kill many more IRA terrorists. It is unclear whether this was an SAS response to the IRA's increasing confidence, bolstered by huge shipments of arms, ammunition and explosives from Libya, or because the IRA, by setting up increasingly lavish operations, made itself a larger target. If it was the latter, then the mistake was one which had been made from time to time (until they learned better) by other guerrilla forces in Indo-China and Algeria, a *folie de grandeur* which plays into the hands of regular armies. The IRA found itself, probably for the first time in its long career of violence, in possession of more firearms than volunteers once Libyan supplies came onstream.

This, then, appears to be the pattern as it started emerging just before and after the Brighton bomb:

21 February 1984: Three IRA volunteers attacked a covert observation post set up to watch the home of one of the attackers, Henry Hogan, at Dunloy. The post was manned by Sergeant Paul Oram of 14 Intelligence Company and two others. The IRA men hit the OP from the rear, killing Oram. Hogan and another volunteer, Declan Martin, were killed by a back-up team that arrived on the scene within minutes. It was not an SAS operation.

12 July 1984, Ardboe, Tyrone, just before midnight: Four IRA saboteurs were ambushed as they carried incendiary bombs into a kitchenware factory. One of the four, William Price, was

shot dead by the SAS. He was carrying a revolver and self-loading pistol. A second man escaped. Two others, Raymond O'Neill and James McQuillan, were arrested by the SAS.

In view of the repeated allegation that the SAS gratuitously kills terrorists when a realistic option exists to arrest them, it is worth quoting the statement made after the Ardboe contact by Soldier 'D', one of the perimeter stop party: 'A shot . . . which sounded like a rifle shot . . . Then I heard footsteps coming along the road and two persons came into our view from approximately a hundred yards north of our position. I saw one, the first one to appear, had a red pullover on and the other person, who was about five metres behind, was wearing a black jacket. I challenged them and said: "Stop or I'll fire." As soon as I shouted the fellow with the black jacket stopped immediately and put his hands in the air and stood there, the other fellow ran on quite fast. I pointed the rifle in his direction and called again for him to stop but he ran on and made a swing to his left towards some shrubs. I thought he was going to escape so I took two quick aimed shots and on the second shot he dropped to the ground.' Both men were then arrested unscathed. They were later convicted of possessing weapons and sent to prison for nine years.

During a period of less than eight years after the Brighton bomb, from October 1984 to April 1992, the total number of Republican terrorists (IRA, INLA and IPLO members) shot dead by the SAS was twenty-nine (plus one wounded, escaped) compared with a total of nine during the eight years immediately after the SAS was committed by Harold Wilson to a fighting role in the province.

This was a period in which senior posts in the Province were filled by long-serving SAS officers on the way up. In December 1983, about a week after McGirr and Campbell were killed, Mike Rose, commander of the SAS during the Falklands campaign, took over 39 Brigade, covering Belfast, County Down and Antrim. In 1985 Tony Jeapes, another ex-boss of 22 SAS, became Commander of Land Forces, Northern Ireland, just one post below the summit of General Officer Commanding all military forces in the region.

Jeapes's accession to power seems to have caused some hearts to flutter in Dublin. In the spring of 1985, Dr Garret Fitzgerald, the Taoiseach (Head of government) of the Republic, along with others in his government, 'became concerned at the insensitivity of some of the decisions being made in or in relation to Northern Ireland. In mid-April I took some of these issues up with the British Ambassador, Alan Goodison. One such issue was the promotion of an RUC officer who had been in charge at the time of the machine-gunning of flats in Belfast in August 1969.' (This caused the death of Patrick Rooney, aged eight, in his bedroom. Those responsible were never brought to justice.)

'Another was the appointment as Commander of Land Forces in Northern Ireland of an SAS officer, later described to us by a British official as a very good officer whom one would not, however, like to meet on a dark night. We were also concerned about "shoot-to-kill" incidents, in respect of one of which, occurring at about this time, we eventually received from British sources three different, and in our view incompatible, explanations.'

Not even Jeapes, however, could have stage-managed events so that the IRA would launch increasingly suicidal missions with growing numbers of volunteers, to make ready targets in broad daylight.

Section VII

For the regiment, the post-Brighton phase got off to a grim start with the accidental death of an innocent civilian followed by the loss of a dedicated SAS NCO. A week after the Grand Hotel bomb, Frederick Jackson, a 43-year-old businessman, was about to drive away from a haulage company yard in countryside near Portadown just after 8.30am on 19 October 1984 when he was hit by two bullets. One shattered the windscreen; the other punched through the driver's door.

Some distance away an IRA assassination squad in a hijacked yellow van had been intercepted as the terrorists stalked a UDR officer driving to work. The terrorists were chased by the

SAS and started shooting. The SAS fired back. The wrong man died.

On 1 December, a former deserter from the Irish Army, Tony MacBride – fresh home from a Republican propaganda trip to Norway – joined four other IRA men on a mission to mine a culvert under the drive of a restaurant on a country road in Fermanagh. He was the sole member of the team who could drive.

Having delivered the mine (about 1000 pounds of explosives in beer kegs) MacBride parked his stolen van on a nearby slip road to be lookout for the men assembling the bomb and its command wire. He had a radio transmitter and when a police car came into sight, he alerted the bombers with the single codeword, 'One'. The terrorists pressed the firing button but the device malfunctioned. Nothing happened.

SAS soldiers in two Q cars had intercepted MacBride's message. They now quietly cruised into the area and blocked the road. MacBride approached them on foot, trying to bluff it out. The SAS soldiers walked towards him, unaware that they were ready targets for the bombers who were armed and lurking in a drainage ditch beside the road.

Lance-Corporal Al Slater of B Squadron's free-fall troop asked the terrorist: 'What are you doing? Who is "One"?'

As he did so, another IRA man fired at him without warning from a ditch about 10 feet away. A gun battle followed in darkness suddenly illuminated by SAS flares. MacBride was killed. The other terrorists ran for the border. One of these – Kieran Fleming, on the run after a prison break fifteen months earlier – drowned as he tried to swim to the Republic across the swollen River Bannagh. Two more were arrested at a police checkpoint in the South a few hours later.

Slater's obituarist in the regimental journal, *Mars & Minerva*, wrote: 'Despite being hit at point blank range he managed to return fire. The operation was a success, leaving two IRA men dead, a further two captured, recovering 1000 lbs of explosive and saving countless RUC lives.' Nevertheless, the regiment admitted, the loss of Slater – nicknamed 'Mr Angry' – was 'a bitterly high price'. A Parachute Regiment sergeant before he joined the SAS, Slater was known to TV audiences who had followed 'The Paras' series on BBC television as the NCO training officer.

As a trainer, he was happiest with his men out on the Brecons rather than in barracks, where his temper shortened. Those who survived his training were the better soldiers. One Para recruit, a former lumberjack, is quoted in Frank Hilton's book, *The Paras*, as follows:

> What they had been training for in Wales had now become reality . . . relevant to the situation they now found themselves in. Even before they came to Ireland, T. had sung Corporal Slater's praises for what he had done with their section at Brecon. Really switched them on, he had. Really pulled them together and given them the confidence they needed when they went to their battalions. Corporal Slater, said T., was the sort of guy you wanted to be with in Northern Ireland . . . You knew you were in safe hands.

Five days after the deaths of Slater, MacBride and Kieran Fleming, another Fleming – Willie, his cousin – was shot dead in the grounds of the Granta Psychiatric Hospital near 'Derry. With Daniel Doherty, Fleming was prowling the grounds at breakfast time, waiting for a UDR victim to start work. Both men were armed. They encountered a 14 Intelligence Company patrol and were shot dead. This was not an SAS operation.

At the inquest, Mr Brian Kearny, representing next-of-kin, wanted to know whether it was necessary to kill the men. Fleming, part of a fanatical Republican family, had gone to prison earlier in the year for damaging a police car and refusing to pay the fine. The more mature Doherty had served four years in prison in the Irish Republic for IRA membership and possessing explosives. He had emerged even harder, more dedicated to political violence. As the *Republican News* put it after Ballysillan: 'Death is no deterrent.' This was more than rhetoric. It was a statement of fact. It also underscored the British problem in Ireland, that the terrorist sets the agenda, orchestrating violence with propaganda to put the authorities into a no-win situation.

Section VIII

In the early hours of 23 February 1985, five IRA men from Strabane prepared to ambush a police car on a lonely country road. As they did so they were watched by a security forces reconnaissance team. The IRA's intended target never appeared. Three of the gang – Michael Devine, aged 22; his brother David, aged 16 and Charles Breslin, aged 20 – started carrying the weapons back to their hide about half a mile away. It was just 4am. They walked off the road and into a sloping field beside Plumbridge Road, on the outskirts of Strabane and were shot dead. The other two members of the assassination squad fled. One was arrested later and sent to prison.

People living on the adjoining Springhill Estate, woken by the noise of gunfire, said they heard two bursts of automatic fire, then a series of single shots. According to the soldiers, they had made a temporary halt in their patrol and were hiding behind or on top of an embankment adjoining the estate, where the three IRA men lived. When the Devine brothers and Breslin entered, soldier 'A' said he murmured a warning to the others. The intruders heard his voice and 'swung their rifles towards us'.

Soldier 'A' came up on his knee and fired a burst of twenty-five rounds from his HK53 automatic rifle. He then fell backwards down the slope and into the back garden of a house.

'I radioed my base and told them I had a contact', he recalled later. When he got back to the top of the bank he could hear the terrorists shouting to one another. After he had fired again, his gun jammed, so 'I drew my pistol, a 9mm Browning . . . and fired seven rounds . . . towards the gunmen.'

Everyone in the field stopped shooting. With the arrival of the back-up party there were more shots from the direction of the road. When all the shooting had stopped, 'A' moved forward, cautiously. The three intruders appeared to be dead but as a rifle was lying alongside one of the bodies, 'A' picked it up and threw it away, out of reach. The same man's holdall, he discovered, contained 'rocket-type projectiles', a form of grenade launcher. Two other rifles were found on the scene. Both had the safety catches on. One of the weapons had been used thirteen months' earlier to murder a UDR soldier.

One of the back-up team, Soldier 'D', described how he had driven to the scene with police. He heard someone tell him to shoot out the street lights. (Why, was not made clear. Possibly the police feared snipers operating on a Republican estate.) He had fired two bursts of tracer from his HK at the lights, but missed.

The shooting provoked a controversy which has continued ever since. A typical reaction from the local community was that of the Strabane parish priests Father Anthony Mulvey and Father John Farren. They said in a statement: 'If no warning was given and no challenge was offered and no effort made to effect an arrest, then the shooting was murder.'

Gerry Adams, Sinn Fein leader, alleged that after the first volleys, one of the SAS 'gang' had approached the bodies and fired one shot into the head of each. This allegation of murder (or mutilation) by *coup de grâce* was taken up by the journalist Mark Urban. He told readers of the men's fashion magazine, GQ:

Early in 1985, three IRA men were killed in Strabane by three SAS soldiers firing 117 rounds. One of the IRA men was hit 28 times; all had a single shot through the head. A source who served at the time in a senior position at Stormont . . . says there was considerable anecdotal evidence that the SAS had administered *coups de grâce*. Those familiar with the operation allege many inaccuracies given in the soldiers' accounts to a subsequent inquest court.

The message was that an SAS team had murdered helpless men, or mutilated their corpses and then told lies on oath to cover up their crimes.

In *Big Boys' Rules*, Urban – noting that two normally reliable HK rifles had jammed at Strabane – went on:

As the SAS soldiers approached the terrorists they might have drawn their Browning 9mm automatic pistols. A pistol is a better weapon for a *coup de grâce* since it causes less trauma to the target's body when fired very close and poses less of a risk to the firer through the impact of ricochets. Forensic evidence showed that both soldiers did use their 9mm pistols, so they had to give some explanation for having done so.

Urban does not cite the forensic evidence enabling him to reach this conclusion. Soldier C's statement (passed on to this author by Urban) relates: 'I . . . drew my Browning pistol . . . I never fired my Browning pistol.' Soldier B did not fire his pistol, either.

Searching for some rational reason for the unusual indignation provoked by the Strabane shooting, this author finds one significant difference between these Republican deaths and many others. It is one of the rare cases in which two of the IRA dead, the Devine brothers (one of whom was permitted to go into action at the age of sixteen), had not been exposed to the salutary, often ugly business of detention at the hands of the security forces. In that sense, they were 'innocents': they had not yet had their first, unofficially licensed bite at the security forces, followed by some form of legal process and release back into the community. The community from which they came, on whose fields they died, probably knew that.

The most remarkable thing about Urban's account is that it is factually wrong in stating that the soldiers involved belonged to the SAS Regiment. The author's sources are emphatic on that point. There is also reason to doubt Urban's version of the autopsy material. This is important, since it is the only plausible confirmation of *coups de grâce*. In fairness, one should not lose sight of the controversial nature of most military autopsies. Some people still probably question the post-mortem carried out on Julius Caesar by the physician Antistius, who concluded that only one of the twenty-three dagger thrusts suffered by the Emperor – the second one, in the chest – was fatal.

In Urban's version of what happened at Strabane:

> Post-mortem evidence showed that each of the IRA men had at least one shot through the head. Yet their balaclavas contained no bullet holes, leading to suggestions that the soldiers had approached them, lifted off the masks to identify the men and then delivered the fatal shots.

Raymond Murray, by contrast, quotes the veteran state pathologist, Professor Thomas Marshall, as follows:

> Charles Breslin had been hit by at least 13 bullets . . . Charles Breslin's head-wound was caused by a bullet from a high velocity rifle which hit him as he turned away . . . David Devine's head-wound had been caused by a bullet from a high velocity rifle fired from above . . . the bullets would not have been fired under two feet.

In Michael Devine's case: 'A bizarre series of wounds . . . almost defeated interpretation . . . one of the bullets went through the bridge of his nose.'

On that evidence, there would appear to be no autopsy material to support the theory about a *coup de grâce* involving the Browning pistol. By contrast, there is positive autopsy evidence of head wounds inflicted from a range beyond two feet, by high velocity rifle fire. The autopsy evidence matches, with reasonable proximity, what the soldiers said. It is to Urban's credit that he later conceded (in a letter to the author): *I accept that the available evidence does not justify the passage about bullet holes in the IRA men's balaclavas.*

In his book, as in *GQ* magazine, to support the theory he shares with Gerry Adams, Urban cites an anonymous figure at Stormont who 'told me, "One thing one couldn't be sure of after Strabane was whether they were finished off afterwards . . . There was heavy anecdotal evidence that they were".'

As anyone who knows Northern Ireland rapidly discovers, it is a land rich in anecdotal evidence and never more so than when the subject matter is a violent political death. Doctoral theses could be written on the subject, with volumes of material as back-up evidence, starting with the death of Trooper McCabe in 1969. Around Divis Flats the local people were convinced that McCabe had been cut in half by the RUC's machine-guns. So it was reported in the London newspapers. He died, in fact, from a single high velocity round which entered under one cheekbone and exited through his rib cage, a fact which went some way to confirming the story no one believed, except the Reverend Ian Paisley, that McCabe was in the prone position, firing a rifle himself, when he was hit.

When three young Scottish soldiers (Dougald McCaughey, John McCaig, aged 18 and his brother Joseph, aged 17, all Royal Highland Fusiliers) were murdered in sickening circumstances by the IRA on 11 March 1971, it was widely believed that they, too, were the victims of *coup de grâce* mutilation.

Each generation of journalists new to Ireland encounters its first, beguiling dose of anecdotal 'evidence'. The resulting headlines are always powerful. The errors are rarely acknowledged even when (sometimes after exhumation) they have been discredited. But that is Ireland.

If the soldiers who killed the Devine brothers were not SAS men, who were they? Evidence such as the weapons they carried and the role they performed points to membership of 14 Intelligence Company. It is clear from their evidence that they were convinced that their position was compromised. They remembered how the IRA had hit the 14 Company observation post at Dunloy and killed Sergeant Paul Oram, and the murder of Lance-Corporal David Jones, another 14 Company victim, had shown how fatal it could be not to open fire as soon as one's own position was compromised.

The stress of waiting for that to happen, while hoping it will not, is enormous. Some soldiers who have experienced it speak of needing two or three days after an operation to 'come down' from the agony it involves.

If there was no *coup de grâce* at Strabane that February

morning, what gave rise to the story, other than a characteristic desire by Republicans to salvage a propaganda point from a small military defeat? We may take it that Urban's Stormont sources did believe their anecdotal evidence independently of anything Gerry Adams had asserted. The author's view is that the SAS has been saddled with the *coup de grâce* myth ever since Ballysillan. On the battlefield it is not unusual to make sure an apparently dead enemy really is no danger before turning one's back on him. This process is not so much a *coup de grâce*, with its overtones of the duel, but more a *coup d'assurance de tous risques*. At Ballysillan, someone had followed battlefield practice without comprehending the legal implications of it in Ireland, where the use of force is limited.

After Ballysillan, SAS soldiers starting a tour in the Province were told very simply, in words of one syllable, 'Don't do it.' But – witness the legend of Strabane – the myth sticks because journalists and others want to believe in it.

Section IX

The number of IRA dead at the hands of the SAS rose sharply to twenty-seven between 1986 and 1992 as the IRA, becoming ever more reckless in its use of American money and Libyan ordnance, increased the scale of its attacks. Although the purpose of this history is to describe the SAS role, it should not be forgotten that the IRA was killing an ever-growing number of innocent people, mostly civilians, during these years. The victims included the baby daughter of an Anglo-Asian airman in Germany; the German wife of a British soldier and next-of-kin of service people killed fighting Hitler during the Second World War at a service commemorating their loss. In an increasingly degenerate campaign, many of the attacks in Northern Ireland seemed to have had the provocation of a sectarian civil war as their main purpose. Between November 1987 and August 1988, nineteen civilians were killed in Ireland as a result of bungled IRA operations.

The new series of IRA losses began early in 1986 at Toomebridge after a year in which the local Active Service Unit and the RUC skirmished with one another. During May of the preceding year, an RUC reservist and his companion had been shot and wounded. The suspects included Francis Bradley, a Catholic joiner aged 20. Bradley, slightly built and of nervous disposition, was regarded as promising material by the interrogators, looking for the weakest link in the chain. He soon found himself caught between an RUC rock and an IRA hard place. He was arrested and questioned soon after the attack on the reservist; arrested again on 21 October, questioned intensively for three days; lifted once more after fifty-seven shots were fired at Castledawson police station. When he was not in custody he was being followed by police officers. Some, he claimed, were threatening to kill him before Easter.

In spite of the stress he was under he did not go straight home from work on 18 February. Instead he shopped around for some rubber gloves and went to an IRA arms dump. The weapons had been hastily left alongside a shed in a field behind a house overlooking the main Toome road. As in other such cases, the SAS was alerted by the RUC, which felt that its intense surveillance of Bradley was paying off at last. Two mobile SAS patrols in civilian cars were contacted. At around 9.30pm, less than thirty minutes before Bradley arrived at the dump, five soldiers were inserted into a potential ambush position forty yards away behind a hedge. One of the soldiers said later: 'We had been told there were gunmen in the vicinity of the farmhouse and we had been instructed to take up the most suitable positions to apprehend them.'

Soldier 'A', using a night sight, saw a car arrive and two men appear at the back of the house one of whom, who proved to be Bradley, picked something up from the rubbish pile beside the shed. The soldier's statement said: 'He stood up and I saw that he was carrying a rifle in one hand . . . I challenged him by shouting "Halt!" . . . The gunman turned sharply as if to confront me and I saw that the rifle was now in both hands, traversing in an aggressive manner in our direction. I believed that he intended to open fire on me and my colleagues and I fired one aimed shot. Almost instantaneously, I heard a burst of shots fired from my right and I saw the gunman fall . . . The other man [with Bradley] ran off.'

For Bradley this was only the beginning. Soldier 'C' advanced to a point close to the IRA man; the soldier guessed twenty yards; the pathologist guessed ten feet. 'C' then saw that Bradley was still moving and assumed he was still a threat. He fired another burst into Bradley, who was hit by eight bullets including a group of three fatal shots through the stomach. The civil rights campaigner and priest, Father Denis Faul, said the soldiers could have arrested Bradley; instead, they had murdered him. A detailed account of the incident by Raymond Murray reveals that it was to Denis Faul that Bradley had complained formally about police harrassment and interrogation.

The weapons found in the IRA dump included an Armalite and an FN automatic rifle; firearms used in four murders and twenty attempted murders of members of the security forces. One gun was used to attack the police station on 9 December, for which Bradley was questioned and released with a warning after he had provided an alibi. (He was visiting his grandmother.)

Bradley was not a significant terrorist. He was one of the IRA's expendables. But his case is illuminating since it combines many elements of the Irish tragedy: an inadequate young man trapped by forces he cannot control; targeted by police as a potential informer; behaving like a small-time crook when arrested by the police yet claiming the status of guerrilla soldier when on 'active service'; the frustration of RUC officers who repeatedly arrested and interrogated him; the last-minute summons for SAS assistance (which the Army is legally bound to provide) and a briefing (probably by radio, as the team drove to the scene) about unidentified gunmen at an arms cache; the hurried insertion of an ambush party in the darkness; the rising adrenalin on both sides and the near-inevitable, fatal outcome. The bottom line is that Bradley had been arrested so frequently that he had come to regard the process as harrassment rather than as a 'gypsies' warning' that he was playing with fire; but someone was going to use the guns he went to fetch that night, so as to kill.

Some two months later, on 24 April, terrorists planted 1000 pounds of explosives in a road culvert at Mullaghglass, Fermanagh. The terrorists pressed the button as security forces came along but nothing happened. The terrorists withdrew. Next day, a four-man SAS patrol, in two pairs, hid in nearby undergrowth. At dawn next day, after waiting around thirty hours, the soldiers ambushed the incoming bomb team, Seamus McElwain and Sean Lynch. Both carried rifles and were in combat uniform. The SAS opened fire, killing McElwain and wounding Lynch, who lay hidden and bleeding for two hours until a police dog found him. Was he hit, he was asked. He replied: 'I'm riddled.' He recovered, all the same.

McElwain was not a novice. On 14 March 1981 he surrendered without resistance to an SAS team surrounding his hideaway, a Fermanagh farmhouse. Later that year, he was sentenced to thirty years' imprisonment for murdering an unarmed UDR soldier and an off-duty RUC reservist. He escaped from the Maze Prison with 133 others on 25 September 1983. At his funeral, even Martin McGuiness, a Sinn Fein VIP, commented that others in McElwain's boots would have thought of 'going to the United States to start a new life', rather than return to 'active service'.

Forensic evidence suggested that the IRA weapons had not been fired, although in their statements two of the soldiers believed the terrorists were preparing to fire or actually were firing. The hard fact is that the category of terrorist who selects himself for SAS attention is almost invariably a danger to the lives of those who would arrest him, claiming the status of soldier in an army of a republic that does not exist and which has no political legitimacy. Such a 'soldier' opens fire on combatant and non-combatant alike, without warning. His case is covered by the Yellow Card rules aimed at protecting innocent life. An inquest jury blamed the SAS.

McElwain embodied the SAS problem. Arrested by one of the regiment's toughest NCOs in 1981, he broke out of a high-security prison to resume his murderous career until the SAS 'arrested' him a second time, with a bullet, five years later.

Section X

Journalists characterised the Loughgall ambush – in which eight members of a larger IRA bombing team, armed with the latest weapons including new German automatic rifles, were shot dead on 8 May 1987 – as the greatest victory over the IRA in twenty years. Irish nationalists reached back even further to 1921, when Black-and-Tans killed twelve of the old IRA in Cork. That, however, was before the Irish voted overwhelmingly to accept independence plus the separation of six primarily Loyalist counties. The futile IRA attack at Loughgall, North Armagh, was an assault on that democratic decision as well as an RUC police station.

RUC stations ('barracks', in the local idiom) were hit with many forms of unlimited high explosive before and after Loughgall, from RPG-7 rockets to horrendously inaccurate heavy mortars. The working model for the Loughgall operation, using a mechanical digger to ram a huge bomb against the fortified target, had been an assault nine months earlier and five miles away at The Birches, County Tyrone. The building was destroyed. For the much bigger Loughgall operation, Mark Urban suggests, a troop of fifteen soldiers from G Squadron was flown from 22 SAS Headquarters, Hereford to augment the twenty-four men already serving in the Province.

The IRA team seems to have been well penetrated by RUC intelligence. According to some sources, the police undercover surveillance team, E4A, watched the 200 pound bomb being loaded onto the digger a few miles from Loughgall, before it was driven nine miles to the target. Not only was there a security failure but the highly experienced leaders of this raid seem to have changed their minds at the eleventh hour, fatally as it proved, about their plan of attack.

The original plan, according to Raymond Murray, was to repeat the success of an attack eighteen months earlier on Balleygawley police station when the same team tricked and shot their way into the building, killing two officers before blowing up the place. Some RUC men escaped through the back door and it was to ensure no repetition of that when the Loughgall police station was attacked, Raymond Murray suggests, that an IRA unit increased to eight men took part. If this was the case, then the frontal attack which followed, with no attempt to place a stop party at the rear of the building, is one symptom of a last-minute change of plan, or of confusion.

The other sign of wavering judgement relates to the purpose of this attack. The station closed at 6.40pm on Fridays. The attack went in on a Friday at 7.20pm, when the building contained no police officers (though some SAS soldiers were inside, waiting for the onslaught). If the purpose was to plant a bomb in an unguarded building (using a crew of three: the driver of the digger, Declan Arthurs and two youngsters, Gormley and O'Callaghan, to ride shotgun) then the addition of another five men in a van, including two of the most senior and experienced guerrilla fighters in Ireland, was – to coin a phrase – overkill.

If the intention was to destroy the police station and kill policemen, the absence of a stop party at the rear of the building as well as the timing were inept. The leaders of this expedition, Patrick Kelly and Jim Lynagh, could do better than that. Their van was late at the roadside rendezvous with the digger and a reconnaissance car near Loughgall. Was that due to a late dispute about tactics? The possibility of divided command was vividly obvious on this operation. Kelly, in command, was junior to Lynagh, whose very presence seems to have surprised some Republicans. Another member of the team with experience to match his opinions was Lynagh's comrade-in-arms, Padraig McKearney. The leaders were very different personalities: Lynagh the handsome, laughing extrovert contrasting with Kelly, a worrier and rigidly upright man 'who loved his family, his Irish culture, his faith and his country'.

We learn from Mark Urban's account that when the attack finally went in – after a cautious and repeated series of feint passes in front of the building, watched by the SAS – 'Patrick Kelly and a couple of the others climbed out of the van, levelled their assault rifles and opened fire on the police station.'

On an empty building in a Protestant community, needlessly sacrificing the weapon of surprise?

The account goes on: 'It would appear that, unlike Balley-gawley where RUC officers were shot, this fusillade was an act of bravado, as the IRA were not expecting Loughgall station to be occupied.'

In Murray's version, the 'bucket-bomb' team lit the fuse with a Zippo lighter and rammed the defences, the van following with its five guerrillas still inside that vehicle. The two men escorting the digger opened fire. Both groups were then shot to pieces by the SAS. This leaves entirely unanswered the question why the five fighters in the van including the leaders did not dismount before the bomb attack began, to provide a protective cordon round the bombers or create a diversion elsewhere. If this was the sequence, it suggests, yet again, disagreement within the the IRA team about the tactics to be employed.

There is another solution to this sordid little mystery. It is that there had been a row at the last minute which had unsettled the team. Kelly, leading by example, dismounted from the passenger seat of the van alongside the driver, young Seamus Donnelly, and started shooting to announce the beginning of operations. This would finish the argument with a flourish that ends many internal IRA rows, a conversation-stopping coda of automatic fire '*pour encourager les autres*'.

It was a disastrous error. The SAS had ambush positions in a football field opposite the police station; a GPMG machine-gun on high ground overlooking the rear of the building; cordon teams staking out the approach road in both directions and men inside the building. The building was seriously damaged but not destroyed. Three people inside it sustained minor injuries.

The most tragic outcome was the death of one civilian motorist and serious injury to his passenger on the road approaching Loughgall. The driver, Anthony Hughes, aged 37, halted when he heard shooting only to be hit by a fusillade of shots through the rear windscreen from one of the cordon groups. The other casualty was his brother, Oliver, aged 40. The most likely explanation is that the soldiers concerned, surprised by the ineptitude of the IRA attack, believed that the new arrival was an IRA back-up team and fired too promptly. The dead man's widow, Bridget, with three children to rear, was later awarded compensation by the British government in an out-of-court settlement.

The records of the IRA team are a fair indication of the implausibility of believing that they would go quietly when caught with guns and bombs in their hands. Indeed Lynagh was undeterred by the injuries he sustained fourteen years' earlier when a bomb in his car exploded prematurely.

The men in the back-up van were: Patrick Kelly, aged 30, leader at Loughgall and commander of East Tyrone PIRA units, released from prison, 1983, suspected of murdering two RUC officers, December 1985; Jim Lynagh, aged 31, about 15 years' IRA service, former Sinn Fein councillor, suspected of many killings including the murder of Sir Norman Stronge, former Speaker of the Northern Ireland parliament, released from Portlaoise prison, Irish Republic, twelve months before Loughgall, prison record included five years for possessing explosive (his own-goal bomb), three years in the Irish Republic for possessing ammunition, acquitted of murdering a UDR soldier, 1980; Padraig McKearney, aged 32, 15 years' IRA service, Maze Prison escaper, September 1983 while serving 14 years and subsequently 'a key figure in daring and innovative missions', said *Republican News*, prison record included seven years for possessing weapons, 1973, 14 years for possessing a sub-machine gun, 1980; Seamus Donnelly, aged 19, three years' IRA service, van driver at Loughgall, claimed he was threatened with assassination by RUC, but undeterred; Eugene Kelly, aged 25, five years' IRA service, veteran of many operations in the Cappagh area, frequently arrested on seven-day detention orders.

The team on the digger were: Declan Arthurs (digger driver) aged 21, five years' IRA service, left home after repeated spells on detention on seven-day orders, alleged RUC assassination threats but undeterred; Gerard O'Callaghan, aged 29, 12 years' IRA service, convicted, 1980 for possessing weapons, imprisoned for six years but released in 1983 after which, say Republican sources, he 'immediately reported back to the IRA . . . and carried out some of the most daring attacks on barracks and commercial targets' along the border; Tony Gormley, aged

24, six years' IRA service, arrested and interrogated many times, undeterred.

Section XI

After Loughgall the IRA did not resume large-scale, guerrilla style daylight assaults until 13 December 1989, when twelve of its men attacked a roadblock at Derryard, Tyrone, killing two soldiers of the King's Own Scottish Borderers. In the thirty-two months between those operations much had happened to stain Irish history with even more blood: the killing of Farrell, McCann and Savage in Gibraltar; the Loyalist vengeance at their funeral; the lynching of two soldiers in Belfast and many other atrocities.

The SAS continued to ambush IRA hard-liners with deadly regularity. In the early hours of 1 July 1988, in a confrontation similar to Loughgall, an IRA team of three men fired an RPG-7 anti-tank missile at North Queen Street police station, Belfast from the top of a saloon car. As this exploded against the building, it was accompanied by the rattle of automatic fire from an Armalite used by the same team. Inside the building, the SAS were waiting. They fired back, hitting the terrorist car. The terrorists fled, leaving the rocket-launcher, spare missiles and a blood-stained jacket. The other casualty was an innocent taxi driver, Ken Stronge, driving past the scene when an SAS bullet came straight through the terrorist car and hit his windscreen. Mr Stronge, a Protestant, was wounded in the neck and evacuated to the Catholic Mater Hospital where he died three days later of a heart attack.

The subsequent calendar of death from SAS action ran something like this:

30 August 1988, Drumnakilly, Tyrone:
Gerard Harte, aged 29 and his brother Martin, aged 22, with Brian Mullan, aged 25: intercepted and killed while on an assassination mission armed with Kalashnikovs; (Tom

Mangold, for BBC TV Panorama, suggested that the assassins were stalking a civilian lorry driver who was also a part-time soldier and that an SAS decoy replaced him in the cab, at which point the predators became prey; it is certainly true that the IRA fired first and that three terrorist weapons were recovered).

18 April 1990, Kinnego, Armagh:
Martin Corrigan, aged 25, an Armagh bricklayer, profoundly embittered by the murder of his father, Peter, eight years earlier at the hands of a Loyalist terrorist doubling with the Ulster Defence Regiment. Martin Corrigan saw it happen and became consumed by an appetite for revenge. An IRA left-wing splinter group, the Irish People's Liberation Army, found him the perfect killing machine. His favourite weapon was a sawn-off shotgun; his chosen victims, off-duty police or Army reservists. He had already murdered three of them, all in front of their families, when he walked, masked and armed, into the garden of another reservist's home. There an SAS ambush ended his blood feud. The IPLO meanwhile continued a homicidal row with the IRA and another splinter group, the Irish National Liberation Army.

9 October 1990, Loughgall, Tyrone:
Desmond Grew (known as the 'Widow Maker'), aged 37, and Martin McCaughey, aged 23, a former Sinn Fein councillor: shot while moving Kalashnikov rifles from one hide to another. Grew had been suspected of murdering six-month-old Ruthy Islania in Germany; McCaughey, said his friends, was 'determined to fight to the bitter end'.

12 November 1990, Victoria Bridge, Strabane:
Alexander Patterson, aged 31, a member of the Irish National Liberation Army (INLA), a republican breakaway responsible for the violent end of many innocents, including children and a postmistress aged 67. Tim Pat Coogan in his IRA history wrote: 'The INLA is largely financed through robbing banks in Ireland and by Middle East subventions . . . The organisation decided to kill Airey Neave [MP, friend of Mrs Thatcher,

wartime MI9 operator, who was blown up as he left the Commons] because he had been calling for a strengthening of the SAS and UDR . . .' Patterson opened fire on the empty home of a UDR reservist when the SAS intervened. A terse official statement said: 'A house belonging to a member of the security forces . . . was attacked by gunfire. British soldiers returned fire. One man was killed. A machine-gun was found in a car.'

3 June 1991, Coagh, Tyrone:
Peter Ryan, aged 37, IRA specialist in 'close quarter' murder of off-duty policemen; Lawrence McNally, aged 39 and Tony Doris, aged 21: stopped by a hail of SAS gunfire as they drove to their next murder assignment.

16 February 1992, Clonoe, Coalisland:
Kevin Barry O'Donnell, aged 21, an IRA man for four years; Sean O'Farrell, aged 22; Patrick Vincent, aged 20; Peter Clancy, aged 21: all ambushed in a church carpark after they had shot at Coalisland police station with a 12.7mm armour-piercing machine-gun (a heavy weapon not permitted to the security forces) which was bolted to the back of a hijacked lorry. The heavyweight rounds easily penetrated armoured glass on a sentry position at the police base. With the 12.7mm gun the soldiers also recovered three Kalashnikov rifles.

O'Donnell might have been safe, but for his acquittal by an Old Bailey jury only eleven months previously on a charge of possessing two Kalashnikovs found in his car in London. He was then a student of agriculture in Shropshire. He told the jury: 'I don't support the IRA. I come from a devout Catholic family . . . they do not support the taking of life.'

It was the sort of hand-on-heart but deadly blarney that persuaded many an innocent, visiting journalist. For once, revulsion over these unnecessary deaths was directed by leaders of the Catholic community against the IRA. One family refused to permit their son to be buried under the trappings of a paramilitary parade. The veteran civil rights campaigner, Father

Denis Faul, headmaster at St Patrick's Academy, Dungannon, where O'Donnell and O'Farrell were educated, attacked the IRA for using the military tactics of the 1920s to confront a high-tech army of 1992.

'The IRA,' he roundly declared, 'is a crazy outfit and should be disbanded. All they are doing is contributing to the grief of decent families.'

At the Republican funeral of Peter Clancy, the priest in charge, Monsignor Liam McEntegart, said it was 'neither right, just nor moral for paramilitary leaders to send the young man out to die, nor for the security forces to shoot him dead'.

Such sentiments, breathing the fresh air of mature common sense into the Irish hothouse, will not change perceptions overnight. Kevin Barry O'Donnell was known at the Harper Adams Agricultural College in Shropshire as 'mild, courteous and conscientious'. He was also saddled with a Christian name that resonated with the legend of an earlier Kevin Barry, hanged by the British and celebrated in song. Like so many others he was a prisoner of that 'terrible beauty' which the comfortable, middle-class, Hammersmith-educated poet William Butler Yeats attached to the Irish death-wish. The cult is more deadly to impressionable young minds than that of the Goddess Kali. Like that tortured brand of Hindu mysticism, it embraces death as a woman.

In pre-Christian Ireland, the clan chief was 'married' to the earth as well as to one, or more, earthly women. In Irish code language, Cathleen ni Houlihan (proud, even arrogant, Cathleen) is a synonym for Ireland, a young bride whose bed is the grave: the earth itself. In a poignant Irish ballad – later debased by America as 'The Streets of Laredo' – the Bard of Armagh anticipates the moment when 'Sergeant Death in his cold arms embrace me and lull me to sleep' before the Bard finally lies 'by the side of my Cathleen, my young wife . . .' in – where else – the grave.

Not even the sergeants of the SAS can hope to cure such cultural psychosis. They can only do their best in a tangled legal and political minefield which lawyers, elegant in their studies back in England, sometimes describe as a system of checks and balances.

GIBRALTAR 1987–88

Preamble

The deaths of three dedicated IRA terrorists while on 'active service' at the hands of four SAS soldiers in Gibraltar on 6 March 1988 have resonated through the corridors of power (including the corridors linking television studio to news room) more noisily than any other operation undertaken by the regiment in the past ten years. The killings were of no special military importance, save that the world was not deprived of much by the sudden termination of these lives. The bombing atrocity the Gibraltar Three had hoped to commit reflected – at best – a callous acceptance of random, innocent victims which placed the terrorists beyond the norms of human sympathy. They were potential war criminals.

The deaths made an enormous political impact among civilised people for an entirely different reason. This was that they sharpened a suspicion that the SAS, more than most British regiments committed to Northern Ireland, had become what Irish paranoia always said it was: an officially sanctioned 'special assassination squad'. Even some of the regiment's friends made jokes which appeared to confirm this idea. So did others. The journal *Private Eye* published a front cover ('SAS Inquest Shock') in which one soldier asked another: 'Why did you shoot him sixteen times?' 'I ran out of bullets,' was the reply.

It is the unique political importance of the Gibraltar operation that makes a careful, even an obsessively detailed, re-examination of the event an inevitable part of this edition.

Section I: Flavius

The operation to defeat an IRA bomb attack on the ceremonial guard-mounting parade at Gibraltar on Tuesday 8 March 1988 (a popular local spectacle which attracts, among others, school children and tourists) was code-named 'Flavius'. But who was Flavius? The SAS operational commander in Gibraltar told the inquest into the affair that Flavius was 'the Roman magistrate'. Magistrates, of course, express and enforce the rule of law. The historical role model for this magistrate was a distinguished Roman soldier, grandson of a gladiator and a centurion who fought his way to the top, suppressing rebellion, to be hailed by a desert army as the Emperor Vespasian in AD 69. He was no aristocrat. He became part of the ruling elite through force of arms and merit, rather than accident of birth, an 'aristocrat' only in the somewhat Arthurian sense that David Stirling defined the term. Flavius was to the magistracy what Wyatt Earp was to law and order in Dodge City, Kansas, in 1879.

In AD 69, Vespasian took over a Rome scarred by the pyromaniac excesses of the mad Emperor Nero. In AD 1969, as it happened, the British Army intervened to extinguish the petrol bombs of Derry and West Belfast. In AD 70 Vespasian opened, as part of Rome's rebuilding programme, the 'Flavian Amphitheatre', otherwise known as the Colosseum, centre of the public duels between gladiators. The ground rules in Flavius's circus are defined by one contemporary writer as 'a type of combat that has no rules except that the winner is the man who walks away alive'.

In 1970 a resurgent IRA challenged its ancient opponent by killing Gunner Curtis, the first of hundreds, in a form of combat which also had no rules except that the winner was the man who walked away alive.

What happened in the Gibraltar colosseum before an unwitting audience watching from apartments overlooking the killing ground was clear enough. Three warriors from one side, including one woman, lay dead and their four enemy walked away. The difficulties, the questions, the public clamour derived from the IRA's efforts to establish a moral equivalence in the public mind with the security forces *outside* the amphitheatre where the gladiators meet; that and the security forces' vulnerability to public inquiry as part of a process we call the rule of law. The scandal, if scandal there is, has to do with shifting perceptions of legality. Unlike the Roman Colosseum, this circus was governed by rules. The IRA also has an interest in upholding the rule of law, but only when this works to its advantage. Otherwise it has a shoot-(and bomb)-to-kill policy less selective than those of the governments it wishes to destabilise.

On this occasion, the rules were classified 'top secret', addressed by name to the SAS operations officer in charge at Gibraltar and entitled: 'Rules of Engagement for the Military Commander in Operation Flavius.' The complete text is at Appendix H. Their significance is that they act as a bridge between the rule of law as the man-in-the-dock might understand it and the exigencies of the battlefield.

They move from such sentiments as 'You are to operate as directed by the Gibraltar Police Commissioner . . . Act at all times in accordance with the lawful instructions of the senior police officer . . . Not use more force than is necessary . . . Only open fire if . . . he/she is . . . committing/about to commit an action likely to endanger . . . lives' to the more warlike Rule No. 6: 'You and your men may fire without a warning if the giving of a warning or any delay in firing could lead to death or injury to you or them or any other person, or if the giving of a warning is clearly impracticable.'

The SAS had been there before. More than its courage and its habit of shooting to kill if it had to shoot, its experience in the quicksand battleground of a no peace/no war conflict made it a natural choice for Operation Flavius. In 1981, when it stormed the Iranian Embassy in London, it was the credible threat that the building was wired for an explosion that provoked the storm of SAS bullets that killed the terrorists – including one who had apparently surrendered – and appalled some spectators. The Gibraltar briefing, examined in greater detail below, placed deadly emphasis on the terrorists' bomb and the button which any of the IRA team might have used to trigger it at the first hint of trouble. There was even a recent case – that of the Border

Fox, Dessie O'Hare – in which the fatally wounded terrorist had still contrived to shoot back. The resonances of SAS experience recalled Rule No. 6 perhaps more vividly than Rules One to Five, addressed to the SAS as if it were the local constabulary.

Was the suggestion of a radio-activated bomb after all no more than the 'spectacular mish-mash of assumptions' by M15, as the *Guardian*'s careful correspondent, David Pallister, believes? The author's sources (not, let it be emphasised, SAS sources on this occasion) assert that there *was* an event which was the genesis of the Gibraltar ambush and which steered everyone's thinking towards a radio bomb. The notion that there was such a device when this was demonstrably not the case, implies an unusual degree of 'mind-set' on the part of all the security forces, including the SAS. There were solid reasons for their belief.

Soon after the IRA's bombing of the Remembrance Day parade at Enniskillen on 8 November 1987, military signallers in Gibraltar detected a powerful radio tone transmitted on a military frequency. It was traced to the Spanish mainland but the exact source remained unclear. This worried British security authorities engaged in the most secret of secret wars against terrorism, the war of electronics. Ever at the vanguard of new techniques with the help of technology supplied by American citizens and institutions as well as revolutionary regimes such as Libya, the IRA is the most innovative terrorist formation as well as the oldest. It knows its business.

The Enniskillen bomb had been detonated by a simple timer, effectively a form of targeting based upon blind and indiscriminate near-guesswork that murdered twelve civilians including a young nurse. The IRA could do better than that, when it wished.

More precise operations already tended to use a bomb that exploded in response to a signal from a human observer, whether by a command wire leading to a device concealed in culvert or hedge or – as in the assassination of Lord Mountbatten off the Irish coast in 1979, or Sir Maurice Gibson, Lord Chief Justice of Appeal for Northern Ireland on the Irish border in 1987 – by radio signal. Some of the IRA's signal equipment was adapted from such innocent artefacts as model aircraft.

By 1988, British counter-measures designed to jam the bombers' systems had encountered three new problems. One of them was that the terrorists were known to be working to adapt American radar equipment normally used for detecting speeding motorists so as to trigger bombs, but operating on much higher frequencies. Wallet-sized radar sensors costing a mere $125 (£75) in the US and rewired for use as detonators, were to be concealed in target vehicles. To set off the charge, an electronic gun as used by police in estimating a car's speed could be aimed at the target from a distance of half a mile. When the signal was detected by the radar receiver, the bomb would explode.

An electronics engineer specialising in this field believes that the higher frequency of a radar beam – 10,000 megahertz and above – took military authorities by surprise when terrorists used it for the first time to kill eight soldiers and wound another twenty-seven in a coach on the Ballygawley-Omagh road, County Tyrone, five months after Operation Flavius.

The second refinement was described to the Gibraltar inquest by Dr Michael Scott, a lecturer in electronics at the National Institute for Higher Education in Dublin, called as an expert witness by the IRA trio's next-of-kin. Having noted that each side in Ireland was 'involved in a race to produce and counter new technology, a survival of the fittest', he said that a method favoured by the IRA was a hybrid device linking a mechanical clock, such as the timer from a parking meter, to an electrical contact. This would not permit the radio signal to work until a certain time had passed. It was 'an absolutely failsafe way of stopping a signal getting through before the man with the button was ready'.

The third nightmare haunting Gibraltar was that the mysterious signal which had been intercepted shortly before the events of 6 March was not a means of detonating a bomb but of priming it in such a way that the next signal on the same, military frequency – probably from an Army vehicle in the immediate vicinity, engaged in routine signals traffic – would cause the explosion.

Whatever the precise design of the bomb to be planted by the IRA in Gibraltar, the considered opinion of a British military scientist, Dr Alan Feraday, was that it could have been triggered by radio from anywhere in Gibraltar 'or even Spain'. Others were to question his conclusion, but Captain Mark Edwards, Royal Signals, observed in tests he conducted for the inquest that the signal appeared to become stronger as he drove towards the Spanish border on the landward side of the colony's airport, furthest away from the Rock.

Even before the SAS was summoned, three assumptions underlaid the planning of Operation Flavius. These were first, that there was a plot to place a car bomb somewhere in Gibraltar; second, that it would be detonated by a radio or radar pulse, possibly on a military frequency; third, that the terrorists might be able to detonate the weapon from the sanctuary of foreign territory, in this case, across the Spanish border rather than that of the Irish Republic.

The drill in such cases – in soldiers' jargon, the first operational procedure – is well established and has evolved as a result of much co-operation, often covert, among the security agencies of different countries fighting a common, underground war, sharing information if only in the belief that the enemy of my enemy is my friend.

The Gibraltar bomb alert triggered an automatic response first to identify those IRA personalities out of prison but active and absent from their usual haunts. One of the three later shot by the SAS was spotted at Malaga airport as early as 5 November 1987, three days before the Enniskillen disaster.

The threat assessment concluded that the most likely target for the IRA would be an assembly point where the band of the garrison regiment (the Royal Anglian) prepared for the ceremonial parade, the Changing of the Guard. This was (as Police Commissioner Joseph Canepa later reminded the inquest), a public thoroughfare surrounded by buildings including a school, a senior citizens' home, a bank, theatre, shops and houses. School children use the area sometimes and nurses from two nearby convents would be there for the band parade.

The MI5 evidence suggests that the identities of those in the IRA formation – asserting their essentially military character as part of a self-styled Active Service Unit (ASU) – were not established until the eleventh hour approached. This is surprising since the three principals came from Republican West Belfast and at least one of them – Sean Savage – appears to have been under surveillance even before he left home. On Thursday 3 March, three days before he was killed, Savage told his mother that he was taking a break in the rural, Gaelic-speaking area of Galway, across the border. He was going to stay in a caravan there.

In the *Observer* (19 May 1989) the journalist Ian Jack described the anxiety felt by Savage's mother about the fish she had bought for the family's dinner the day after. 'Her son said he would take his share and cook it in Galway', wrote Jack. 'He left soon after, a serious young Irishman (hobbies: cycling and Irish language evening classes) walking down a Belfast street, bound for a healthy weekend in the Gaeltacht. A lie, of course. Savage went to Dublin and from there he flew to Malaga on the Costa del Sol . . .' Savage flew to Malaga by way of Paris with a driving licence, birth and baptism certificate and organ donor card in the name of Brendan Coyne, to hire a white Renault 5 car from Avis. He arrived in Spain at 20.50 hours on Friday 4 March on the same Iberia flight as 'Robert Wilfred Reilly'. Although the real identities of Savage and Mairead Farrell, a woman member of the team, were already known to British (and, one must suppose, Spanish) authorities, an MI5 witness at their subsequent inquest would claim that 'Reilly's' true name – Daniel McCann – was not immediately known.

Other members of the cast were assembling at the same Spanish town that Friday. A woman readily identified by her long and beautiful hair who had flown by Aer Lingus from Dublin to Brussels under the *nom de guerre* of Johnston had subsequently used a stolen British passport in the name of Mrs Katherine Alison Smith (née Harper). But her wristwatch bore the essentially military inscription 'Good Luck. From your comrades in Maghaberry [Prison], September 1986.' This was Mairead Farrell, a former convent school girl from Andersonstown, a young woman with a specially deadly motivation.

The dilemma facing the British and Gibraltarian authorities was to decide at what point to detain the three. It was an issue explored with merciless thoroughness at their inquest by a redoubtable Belfast counsel hired by their families (Mr Paddy McGrory) and journalists from Granada television's investigative programme, World In Action. To move prematurely would, perhaps, leave other IRA teams free to proceed with the bombing. In any case, the members of this ASU were on Spanish territory. While the security authorities there were co-operative, there was no guarantee that the Spanish courts would be willing to hand over three terrorists to a Gibraltar whose government they did not really recognise, or to a UK which depended upon a case of conspiracy as grounds for extradition.

The Spanish police were prepared to treat the affair as surveillance of suspected international terrorists in transit through their jurisdiction; so long as no one was likely to detonate any Semtex on Spanish territory, of course . . . As Gibraltar's Special Branch boss, Detective Chief Inspector Joe Ullger, was later to confirm: 'We provided the Spanish with photographs. We provided them with names . . .' In fact, the names of two false passports as well as the ASU's true identities were sent to Spain, which suggests a very close observation of the trio by a British squad as well as the operation mounted by the Spaniards themselves. British Intelligence was remarkably good. The IRA itself could not be certain that Farrell would join the team until the last minute.

In spite of all that, Detective Chief Inspector Ullger was to argue later that the terrorists 'were not under surveillance: the terrorists were on the loose in Spain'. Furthermore, he added: 'We did not know whether they were coming on Friday or Saturday.' Whenever they came, the plan was to arrest the terrorists with SAS help and then to hold them in custody in 'a military installation' as the local police station was inadequate for such dangerous people. Official Gibraltar was in a state of fear, if not panic. In the light of recent events at Enniskillen, bomb attacks at the British headquarters at Rhinedahlen in Germany and elsewhere, there was good reason for anxiety.

The Gibraltar Three also had a formidable track record of terrorism in their own right. After her convent school, Farrell went on to serve ten years in prison, most of them in Armagh, for planting a bomb in the Conway Hotel, Belfast, in 1976. The *Republican News*, after her death, announced with pride: 'She reported back to the IRA. Her ten-and-a-half years in prison had, as she said herself, strengthened her resolve.'

Another event had hardened her. Her companion and fellow bomber Brendan Burns, Sir Maurice Gibson's assassin, had blown himself up, accidentally, on 29 February. Farrell is said to have broken down when she heard the news and then to have volunteered for the final, critical phase of the Gibraltar assignment in a mood of grim fatalism. Grief seems to have made her agnostic about her own, continued survival. She told one friend that the future held nothing for her but prison or a premature grave.

According to Father Raymond Murray Sean Savage was, at 23, a young man of many talents. 'His activity in the IRA was unknown. He, like Daniel McCann, had been arrested in July 1982 on the word of a "supergrass" but was released after a month. He was an Irish language enthusiast, rambler, cyclist, Gaelic footballer, cook. He was single, did not smoke or drink, rarely expressed political views; he was never seen at Republican functions. His great love for Ireland prompted him to travel the country on bicycle and learn his native language. Both Daniel McCann and Sean Savage were expert IRA engineers.' [This is a somewhat specialised use of the word 'engineer': the victim of an IRA explosion, if he survived, would describe the person who made the device as a bomb-maker.]

McCann, aged 30, a butcher's assistant, came from the Clonard district of Belfast and was known in SAS circles as 'Mad Danny'. He would have been aged twelve when Catholic homes in the area were burnt to the ground by Loyalist neighbours in the hot, angry summer of 1969. He was a dedicated IRA veteran who had led a charmed life. In a long career as an assassin, he had chalked up only one serious conviction – possessing a detonator

– for which he was imprisoned for two years. The *Republican News* would describe him as '. . . a lifelong activist who knew no compromise, to die as he lived, in implacable opposition to Britain's criminal presence in our land.'

The RUC held him responsible for the murders of Detective Sergeant Michael Malone and Detective Sergeant Ernest Carson in the Liverpool Bar, Donegall Quay, near Belfast's Irish Sea ferry terminal in August 1987. The policemen were off duty, taking a glass in an area traditionally regarded – until McCann and his team struck – as neutral ground. Having murdered Malone and Carson, and wounded another police officer and a barman, the hit squad fled in a waiting car. The RUC regarded McCann as an enthusiastic exponent of shoot-to-kill.

IRA behaviour is often an odd blend of military sophistication and political as well as social naivety. An irony of this event is that the IRA team almost certainly underestimated the pervasive nature of the terror they were dedicated to spreading. If they had exercised a more adult perception of the impact of their action upon others, they would not have walked unarmed into the lion's den. Certainly that is not what their British opponents anticipated. Rarely was the element of surprise more complete, or more counter-productive.

Section II: The Briefings

There was much interest at the inquest in the perceptions, the state of mind, of the soldiers. Mr Paddy McGrory, representing the next-of-kin of those who had died, did not disguise his belief that the SAS men, whom he described as members of 'an unholy priesthood of violence' were an execution squad licensed by the British government. In fact what was uppermost in the soldiers' minds was their own anxiety to get it right and to stay alive. These anxieties were throttled back, kept under control by a long-practised professional discipline. Coming to terms with stress is a basic of SAS conditioning.

Overriding everything else was the briefing – or rather, series of briefings – which shaped the soldiers' expectations as well as their knowledge of events. The authorities, as we have seen, were in a state of acute nervousness, building a worst-case scenario of the Irish threat to life as it was known on the Rock. Mr McGrory's perception of events as well as his view of the SAS was conditioned by a personal acquaintance with Paddy Mayne, a distinguished wartime leader of the regiment, and by the self-mockery of 'Who cares who wins?', a regimental parody of its own motto. Mayne, one of Stirling's original guerrillas, operated within the legal limitations, such as they were, of the Second World War, uninhibited by civilian law and civilian police. Himself a lawyer by profession, Mayne would have thrown through the nearest window anyone who sought to lecture him about the virtues of minimum force.

The most important brief was compiled in London by a senior member of MI5 identified publicly as 'Mr O for Orange', a use of military phonetics which, in the political context of Ireland, was unfortunate. Orange, astonishingly, was not in Gibraltar to deliver his critically important message to the troops. He delegated the job to an even more shadowy figure who never appeared at the inquest. At the inquest, Orange explained that members of an IRA active service unit 'are all highly trained terrorists . . . they have received instructions in basic bomb making, using a number of different weapons, and in counter-surveillance and interrogation techniques . . . not petty thugs . . . highly trained, dangerous terrorists.'

The IRA team, Orange claimed, was not under surveillance. 'They were believed to be in the area of Malaga. It was not known which members of the active service unit would come across the border or when . . . There was reason to believe the target would be the Changing of the Guard ceremony, the personnel of the Guard and the band, on 8 March . . . The operation would be a large bomb designed to kill as many soldiers as possible . . . probably detonated by remote control . . . If the means of detonation were indeed a radio-controlled device it was possible that the terrorists might, if confronted, seek to detonate that device.'

Most crucial of all, perhaps, was the advice that 'the ASU

would comprise three individuals, dangerous terrorists who would almost certainly be armed and, if confronted by security personnel, would be likely to use their weapons'.

By 5 March, three days before the assumed date of the attack, the SAS had moved about a dozen men onto the Rock. With them had come a swarm of security people of both sexes, mainly from MI5, augmented by local Special Branch personnel, to act as watchers and an armed reserve. On the evening of the fifth, the SAS tactical leader, Soldier 'E', passed on to his men the knowledge he had obtained from Orange back in Britain. 'I particularly emphasised to my soldiers . . . that at least one of the three terrorists, if not more, would in all probability be armed; and secondly, there was a strong likelihood that at least one, if not more, of the three terrorists would be carrying a "button job" device' [to make the bomb explode].

At midnight, with other elements of the Flavius force including carefully screened members of the local police, the soldiers crowded into an ultra-secure briefing centre (almost certainly deep within the gun galleries of the Rock itself, galleries and caverns which also contained a model of a 'typical Ulster village', where soldiers trained in counter-insurgency techniques). Around fifty people were present at the briefing, run by an advisory group comprising British Intelligence officers from MI5 and MI6; two 'senior military officers' (i.e., ranking major and above) from 22 SAS and HQ Special Forces; the chief of Gibraltar's Special Branch; and the Deputy Commissioner of Gibraltar. This was the team which would advise the Police Commissioner, Joseph Luis Canepa, who was nominally in charge of law enforcement. Mr Canepa's evidence suggests that the group was formed in haste.

When the official objectives of Operation Flavius and the Rules of Engagement were disclosed to the soldiers, it was not by the Commissioner himself. He would later confirm that he had signed an order about Rules of Engagement and the need for minimum force on 5 March before he handed them to four of his senior officers including the head of the Special Branch. Although he did not personally pass the order to military personnel, he understood that 'they and those involved in the shootings would have been aware of the rules.' Later he emphasised that 'The matter was discussed with them and they understood the rules of minimum force and engagement . . . In that order I stated that every effort would have to be made to protect life, to foil the attempt, to make arrests and to take custody of the prisoners.'

There is some uncertainty about the time when the authorities positively identified their quarry. By midnight on 5 March, the night of the major briefing, Commissioner Canepa had been given the names Daniel McCann, Sean Savage and Mairead Farrell. They were said to be 'highly dangerous, on active service, probably armed . . . Armed members of the police force would not be able to cope with a situation like this.' As we have seen, 'Orange', from MI5, was uncertain about which of the trio would actually try to enter the colony.

When the three terrorists were spotted in Malaga, said Mr Canepa, Gibraltar's police were alerted to watch for all of them. In spite of that, it became apparent during the inquest that many policemen had no idea that a high-powered anti-terrorist operation was going on around them. The oblivious ones included Inspector Louis Revagliatte, in charge of routine policing on the Rock at the time. Some, at least, of Gibraltar's thin blue line were uninformed of the danger. Others were misinformed.

No direct evidence was given by the Spanish authorities about their role, an issue addressed in more detail later in this chapter. The absence of a Spanish representative from the Gibraltar briefings meant that both the police under Mr Canepa and the SAS depended upon the Security Services – mainly MI5 – for their intelligence and therefore their perception of the threat. If a Spanish representative had taken part in the briefings it is possible that someone would have asked what Madrid was doing about the huge car bomb then being driven around its territory. Quaintly, the risk to Spanish lives seems to have been ignored by everyone involved in subsequent inquiries, though the issue was to emerge as one of pivotal importance.

If Mr Canepa vividly recalled the level of threat conjured by 'Orange' (a threat so intense that armed policemen could not cope with it) how did the front line SAS team view the issue? Soldier 'E', the young officer commanding the four-man patrol that encountered the terrorists, recalled references during the midnight briefing to the likelihood that the IRA team were armed with guns and a 'button-job' bomb.

The Coroner, Mr Felix Pizzarello, asked: 'So you particularly emphasised these two points to your men?'

Soldier 'E': 'Correct'.

Coroner: 'Had they already been emphasised at the briefing on the night of 5th/6th?'

Soldier 'E': 'Correct. Arrest was the aim of the operation. The plans were for the soldiers to initiate the arrest. This was because of the great danger posed by the terrorists.' The priorities were: arrest; disarm; defuse the bomb. A policeman was to be with the soldiers to act as eye witness and to take any arrested person into police custody.

One of two SAS men who gunned down Savage recalled that the briefings had emphasised that the IRA team were 'fanatical terrorists'. Asked if anything was said about the terrorists' skill-at-arms he replied: 'We were not told they were skilled handlers of guns. We were told they were professional terrorists . . . We were told that . . . all three members could be carrying a device to detonate the bomb' at the press of a button.

On the day the team deployed, 'we were told that the bomb had been planted in the area of the assembly point . . . Once we had decided to effect the arrest, the pistol would be there. We would shout: "Stop. Police. Hands up." Once that was done we would make sure the terrorists were on the floor with arms away from the body.'

Soldier 'F' asserted that they had practised arrest procedures 'in conjunction with the local police force'.

There was one further, crucial refinement built into the briefings. As the SAS commander, 'F', explained, they had been told that the car bomb would be brought into Gibraltar a day or more before the attack. The bombers would not use a 'blocking car' to reserve a parking space in the target area. The IRA vehicle, when it arrived, would therefore be perceived as the real thing: a bomb and nothing but a bomb.

Beyond the fine print of orders drafted in London and polished in Gibraltar by people who sought no direct contact with the SAS enforcers, there was the regiment's own basic rule of engagement, expressed by Soldier C, who fired six rounds into Savage: 'You should go on firing until the terrorist is no longer a threat . . .'

Asked by McGrory if the best way to ensure that was to kill them, 'C' replied: 'Yes, sir.'

McGrory: 'Was it necessary for so many bullets to be fired at this man if the intention was to immobilise him?'

Soldier 'C': 'It was to make sure he could not react back to initiate the button.'

McGrory: 'You have heard the expression, "overkill", I suppose?'

Soldier 'C': 'It was never overkill, sir . . . You use a gun to kill.'

The SAS approach – indeed, that of the Army in general – has been shaped by experience. A sort of case lore has developed over the years. The soldiers at Gibraltar went armed with four magazines each, a total of 48 shots per man, or 192 rounds among the four. The ammunition, a mix of British and French 9mm, used a new, smokeless propellant which emits less smoke and flash than traditional gunpowder. (Civilian witnesses at the inquest, cross-examined by the counsel for the soldiers, told the truth when they said they saw no 'smoke and waste' coming from pistols.)

Since only 27 spent cartridge cases were recovered after the operation, some might argue that this was underkill; that, or the SAS, hyped by a series of misleading briefings, expected at least a detonated bomb and a shoot-out with three armed terrorists. One soldier had in mind a siege, with no other aid on hand to contain it.

In any case, the team concluded, one could not be too careful. Some IRA men had survived after sustaining apparently fatal wounds, including the legendary Francis Hughes who, in 1978, crawled away from an Army ambush suffering from severe leg wounds to survive 13 hours before being captured. Other men would have bled to death. He was nursed back to health and sent to prison. On 12 May 1981 he became the second IRA hunger-striker to die.

Less noticed by non-military witnesses and the media was an important statistic, adduced by a barrister representing the soldiers, Mr Michael Hucker. He asked one of the SAS officers, Soldier 'F': 'Over the last ten years, do you know what the ratio of arrests to kills has been in these operations?'

'Yes', 'F' replied. 'The ratio between arrests and kills is 75 to 25 in percentage terms in favour of arrests.'

The arrests, it is worth noting, included those of the IRA gang that murdered an SAS captain, Richard Westmacott in Belfast in 1980 and then surrendered under protection of a white flag with a priest in attendance. The Balcombe Street surrender was also induced by an SAS presence. In Gibraltar, said Soldier 'B', he would have disobeyed an order from his immediate commander, 'E', if 'E' had suggested killing McCann and Farrell 'regardless of what was being said by others at briefings'.

And yet, as Soldier 'F' observed, the final orders provided for 'the use of lethal force for the preservation of life', as well as minimum force. The degree of force, everyone agreed in the inquiries that followed, had to be 'reasonable'. But what was reasonable depended on the circumstances. What held good for Goose Green or Iraq might be criminal on Salisbury Plain.

When the SAS went to work in the early hours of 6 March, it was burdened with a package of political incompatibles. Had these been military hardware rather than a ragbag of official aspirations and warnings, the soldiers would have more readily identified them as 'rubbish kit' more dangerous to friendly forces than the enemy. The Gibraltar establishment feared a bloodbath on its streets. The soldiers were to avert it. MI5's technicians had warned of a 'button job' bomb which could be detonated instantly. The soldiers were to ensure it did not happen. The law required that they should simultaneously exercise 'reasonable force', shooting not to kill gratuitously but to make an arrest if they were to avoid censure.

It was a fragile, ambiguous situation, a melting cornice of disaster teetering on the point of avalanche, a situation in which disaster was more plausible than happy ending. If the IRA guerrillas had not launched themselves as undercover agents with false passports a la James Bond on a death-or-glory mission; if MI5 had done a better briefing job; if the Gibraltar police had not reacted as if this were the Apocalypse, the outcome might have been otherwise. As it was, the IRA was about to lose three volunteers. The SAS was about to get the blame.

As they wait to go into action, soldiers usually have some time, however little, of private contemplation which takes their unspoken questions beyond the scope of the official briefing. In this case, noting that the law's effect if not its intention over the years had been to present an agnostic face to the death of a terrorist discovered on active service, it would be merely human for any soldier to conclude that he was better off alive and blameworthy rather than virtuously dead. The IRA men at whose hands Westmacott had died had been enabled to escape from legal custody just five weeks later. One of them – Joe Doherty – had become a political celebrity in America, from which the murder weapon had come.

Another case, more clear as a guide to conduct than any of the 'nods and winks' which Mr McGrory and others sought in the Gibraltar briefings, was that of Sir Maurice Gibson, a senior Ulster judge who commended RUC officers brought to trial for killing three unarmed terrorists with 109 bullets in 1982. The police, said Sir Maurice had brought the terrorists 'to justice . . . the final court of justice.'

In such a world, justice has its rough edges. Yet there was at least one voice at the Flavius briefing that sang a more traditional tune. Detective Chief Inspector Joe Ullger, head of the local Special Branch, would tell the inquest that capture and trial of the IRA team was all-important. Intelligence officers at the briefing, he recalled, had said they did not usually give evidence in court. Therefore, the police role was vital.

Section III: The countdown

Farrell arrived in Malaga by air from Brussels on Friday 4 March to be followed some hours later by McCann and Savage, in-bound from Paris. Their movements after that until the last few moments before they died on the afternoon of Sunday 6 March are still disputed. The inquest into their deaths heard one version, from which any Spanish testimony was excluded; investigative journalists from the *Independent* and the *Irish Times* presented an entirely different account, based on Spanish police claims made anonymously eight months after the inquest, and there are irreconcilable differences between the official British and unofficial Spanish accounts.

First, the 'Spanish' version argues that the Intelligence services of both countries had monitored the movements of Farrell, Savage, McCann and two other IRA members using the aliases John Oakes and Mary Parkin for about six months before Operation Flavius; second, that Farrell, Savage and McCann were under surveillance up to the moment they crossed on foot, unarmed and together into the colony; third, that as a result of the killings the location of the car bomb, on Spanish soil, was not traced during the period when those concerned thought it was timed to explode; fourth, that the IRA car that was parked in Gibraltar was known to the British to be a harmless blocking vehicle, driven into Gibraltar by 'John Oakes'. The betrayal of the safety of the people of Spain was the most serious charge.

The *Independent*'s team, Tim McGirk and Heather Mills, wrote on 23 May 1989:

> The Spanish say the close and constant communication between the British and Spanish police forces heightened their sense of betrayal when the IRA trio were killed. One high-ranking officer said: 'The British told us that the IRA had died in a shoot-out, which wasn't true. We couldn't believe they had killed all three of them. Maybe just two. But with them all dead, how in the hell were we supposed to find the car bomb?'

The British version, laboriously built up at the inquest by equally anonymous witnesses, but tested in public by Mr McGrory's probing mind, runs as follows:

In spite of being briefed by British Intelligence, the Spaniards lost contact with the IRA trio in the last, vital hours before they crossed into Gibraltar. Furthermore, a member of the Gibraltar force (who did identify himself publicly) also failed to notice Sean Savage's arrival from Spain in a white Renault 5, the vehicle presumed by the British (and by implication, the Spanish also) to carry a massive bomb. The appearance of the white Renault near the parade assembly area and the meeting there of Farrell and McCann with Savage came as 'a complete surprise'. After that, this version runs, the SAS was responding to a series of unplanned events.

The only direct evidence of border surveillance to emerge from an identifiable official source was that of a junior representative of the local Special Branch, Detective Constable Charles Huart.

The SAS commander at Gibraltar, Soldier 'F', had already asserted that there was no surveillance or early warning from the Spanish side of the border, while 'M', in charge of the MI5 surveillance squad, had told the inquest that there was no co-operation from immigration officials. Huart's evidence offered a different picture. The day the IRA trio died, he was on duty on the Spanish side of the border for seven hours, in an impressive demonstration of Madrid's desire to combat international terrorism. Huart said he sat in an enclosed room beside a Spanish immigration officer, facing a screen onto which the Spaniards projected images of passport photographs and numbers taken from people crossing the border.

The Spanish were aware that Gibraltar police were watching for the IRA gang. Car registration numbers were passed to him by the Spanish officer, who was in contact by telephone with his colleagues watching the cars go through. Huart had been instructed to look out for two men and a woman named as Savage, McCann and Farrell. The Spaniards knew of these people and already had their photographs. Huart was in contact by personal radio with the operations room, passing on details of passports and car registration numbers given to him by the Spaniards. At 3.15pm he was instructed to return to Gibraltar because the IRA team had now been spotted there. He returned by motorcycle and found himself in traffic on Smith Dorrien Avenue where he saw McCann and Farrell carrying newspapers, which they exchanged. Savage was with them.

He instantly recognised the three. He could not have known that they were within a few seconds of death.

The Coroner, Mr Felix Pizarrello, QC, in his summing-up, examined the surveillance phase of Operation Flavius to test a hypothesis, that there was a 'wicked plot' to murder the IRA team rather than make legal arrests. With that in mind, Pizarrello noted: 'When the time comes, surveillance is so bad that the three suspects get into Gibraltar without detection. This suggests that the three have been led into a trap in order to ambush all three. Here evidence of sorts begins to filter into the picture.

'M', the head of surveillance, was unhappy about the situation at the frontier and did not like it, but he said the security people wanted it that way, the security people being O's department.

'The surveillance set is ludicrous. It is set up on the Spanish side with the real names given to the Spanish police, and PC Huart is put into a computer room to check passports which are fed to him by the Spanish police. And, mark it well, he is looking for the true names of the suspects, and only those three names, at a time when the names of Coyne and Reilly were well known. How, it is asked, can it reasonably be expected of three terrorists on active service to use their real names? The reason is because it was intended to let them in.

'That is something Detective Chief Inspector Ullger admitted . . . Having regard to the fact that one of the objects was to prevent the commission of the offence, it is remarkable that no serious steps appear to have been taken at the frontier to stop the [IRA] car from coming in . . .'

The evidence of Ullger, head of the local Special Branch, is particularly significant. He believed that the Spanish and Gibraltar police on the border had the names of two false passports used by the IRA and photographs of all three.

In spite of that, the three entered undetected as did their vehicle, an ostensible car bomb. Although the terrorists were 'not under surveillance', but 'on the loose in Spain', they had to be allowed into Gibraltar so that evidence could be gathered to convict them. Everything was done to detect their entry into the colony, so as to effect their arrest.

That was clear enough, as far as it went. But what about the bomb? Ullger, cross-examined by McGrory, agreed that the security authorities believed that the bomb was to be detonated on Tuesday 8 March and not Sunday 6 March, the day on which, in fact, the three died.

McGrory: 'Don't you think it highly unlikely that if they intended to detonate the bomb by remote control on the Tuesday, they would take the additional risk of bringing in the radio device on the Sunday? It would add to their risk of detection, wouldn't it?'

Ullger: 'That you would have to ask of people who deal with terrorism.'

Section IV: A time to die

Sean Savage arrived in Gibraltar, so the Coroner estimated, in time to park a hired white Renault 5 in the parade assembly area at 12.50 on Sunday 6 March. He wore a sober, pinstripe jacket which concealed a money belt containing £1,660 as well as 1,370 French francs and twenty-six Irish punts. More than an hour passed before the car was firmly identified by 'H', one of seven MI5 watchers, as a terrorist vehicle. Ten minutes after that, at 2.10pm another watcher 'N', confirmed his colleague's recognition of Savage and discreetly reported that to the operations room. The watchers were equipped with concealed radios and were broadcasting on a network dedicated to this operation.

It was 2.30pm before Farrell and McCann entered Gibraltar on foot, through the La Linea gate, to cross the short stretch of flat mainland to the Rock itself. Although Huart and the Spanish police did not see them – well, ostensibly not – MI5 and others did. Farrell, a diminutive 5ft 1in tall figure, carried a leather handbag containing a stolen passport and pages copied from a book entitled *Big Business and the Rise of Hitler*. McCann wore grey trousers and a white shirt. Soldier 'F', the SAS commander, sitting in the ops room, recalled the signals announcing that they had been spotted. Things happened quickly after that.

Other surveillance teams, which should not have expected to go into action for another 36 hours, were hurriedly deployed. Savage's identity was confirmed. Command of the situation was passed formally from the police to the Army. 'H' reported that McCann and Farrell had joined Savage near the Renault but then, as the trio moved away from the assembly area – possibly to spot suitable 'firing points' from which to detonate the bomb – the police again assumed control.

These switches of authority at such a crucial phase of the operation must have provoked anxiety among the watchers, SAS enforcers and police observers alike, though nothing was said publicly about it. After the inquest one newspaper, the *Guardian*, suggested that the Deputy Commissioner, Charles Colombo, disputed the very suggestion that the police had relinquished control so promptly.

Meanwhile the IRA team strolled about the centre of Gibraltar for some time before returning to the assembly area at 3.25pm. There they looked at the Renault. 'H' later provided a highly atmospheric account of the incident.

'When I came to Gibraltar,' he told the Coroner, 'I realised that this was going to be a difficult job . . . It was also a dangerous job. When I observed the three terrorists in the assembly area, they were observing the car. Nearby were some children. One of the three, Danny McCann, was observing the car and then he spoke to the other two, Sean Savage and Mairead Farrell.

'A few words were passed, maybe a joke. As they moved off there were smiles on their faces. I could not say what was said. It was a chilling moment as I felt that these were evil people who were prepared to spill blood.'

Coroner: 'You are assuming a lot of things.'

'H': 'This is what I saw . . .'

As the IRA team started walking back towards the Spanish frontier two SAS soldiers – 'C' and 'D' – followed, with 'H' a few feet behind them. In the control room command again passed to 'F', the SAS commander, but Commissioner Canepa changed his mind once more, resumed control and ordered a further identity check on the three suspects. By now, adrenalin was coursing through the soldiers as they prepared to confront terrorists as dangerous, they thought, as Dessie O'Hare or Francis Hughes, people who had shot to kill at the merest hint or glance of trouble, people who gave their opponents no second, or even a first chance.

There was one other preliminary bit of business. The authorities – possibly due to the Police Commissioner's continued diffidence – checked the Renault 5 where Savage had left it. One of three Army officers on the team was probably not badged as an SAS regular, but was a no less brave explosives specialist of the Royal Army Ordnance Corps or Royal Engineers. This was Soldier 'G'. After a quick discussion with other members of the Commissioner's advisory group, 'G' was 'asked to visually inspect the Renault'.

He checked the vehicle and returned to report 'that in his view, the car was a suspect car bomb. The most distinctive thing about it was that there was an old aerial placed centrally on the roof of a relatively new car.' The terrorists were still walking away north, towards the border.

Commissioner Canepa concluded, 'that we could arrest on suspicion of conspiracy to murder . . . At that stage I signed a form requesting the military to intercept and apprehend the three persons.' The document he signed, by another of the bizarre historical coincidences with which the evidence was punctuated, was 1689, which is also a year celebrated in English history as the glorious revolution to replace the Catholic King James with the Protestant William of Orange.

What more could Canepa do? Should he have evacuated the area? He evidently thought of it but pleaded at the inquest that he did not have the manpower required. In any case, he and other authorities were soon to discover that the Renault contained no bomb. The peculiarity of the aerial remained one of the smaller unsolved mysteries of this operation.

At last, at twenty minutes before 3 o'clock, the police passed operational control to the Army for a third time. Two minutes later, the three terrorists were dead. The sequence of events during those fatal 120 seconds remains controversial because close eye-witnesses offer differing and sometimes conflicting recollections.

One paradox emerges from many thousands of words of testimony. This is that most of the professional witnesses, briefed in advance about what was supposed to happen, averted their eyes at critical moments, while more random spectators gave finely detailed descriptions of each dying spasm.

The junction of Smith Dorrien and Winston Churchill Avenues is a Mediterranean suburban sprawl. Winston Churchill is a north-south oriented dual carriageway, flanked on one side by a six-storey apartment complex called the Laguna Estate. Between estate and road is a Shell petrol station. When Watcher 'H' whispered into his radio to summon the SAS arrest teams, the IRA trio were still together, chatting in the sun near the Shell station. As they did so, the first SAS pair – 'A' and 'B' – took up positions on the same side of Winston Churchill some yards south. McCann and Farrell then started walking away towards the Shell station while Savage moved off in the opposite direction.

He marched purposefully straight towards 'A' and 'B', his shoulder bumping 'A' as he passed. That glancing contact of one male body against another was a turning point in the operation. Until that moment, Soldier 'A', in his 13th year of SAS service, had intended to shout, 'Stop. Police. Hands up,' and then to summon the police by radio while covering the IRA trio with his drawn gun. But now that Savage had thrust past him, splitting away from the others, he believed that the situation was slipping out of control and that the bomb would be detonated unless he did something immediately.

'A' and 'B', like most others on the security team, were using concealed radios. In their lightweight zip-fronted jackets and jeans the kit was a problem. Their pistols, for instance, were observed by civilian witnesses to be stuck in their waist belts in the small of the back. Soldier 'A' had a push-button radio strapped to his wrist and a microphone fitted inside the collar of his jacket. Thanks to the radio, they should have known that another SAS pair – Soldiers 'C' and 'D' – were already trailing Savage.

McCann, ignoring the convention that the gentleman walks nearer the road when accompanying a woman, stuck close to the low wall flanking the Shell garage. Farrell was on his left, nearer the gutter. For some reason – remembering, perhaps, his counter-surveillance training – McCann looked back. McCann, the Belfast butcher's skinny assistant, was later described by London newspapers such as the *Daily Telegraph* as 'an almost deranged killer with a long history of murder behind him'. Soldier 'A' recalled: 'He had a smile on his face . . . He looked straight at me . . . We had literally eye-to-eye contact. We looked directly at each other. The smile went off McCann's face and it's hard to describe; it's almost like McCann had a realisation actually who I was, or I was a threat to him. The look on his face was one of alertness and he was very aware . . .'

Soldier 'A', believing that McCann's personal 'radar' had identified him as a threat, reacted instinctively. His instinct as a fighting soldier was not to make an arrest. He intended to shout a warning. He went for his gun and started shooting. As he told the Coroner: 'I was just going to shout a warning to stop.'

Coroner: 'You were going to shout?'

Soldier 'A': 'Yes, and at the same time I was drawing my pistol. I went to shout "Stop". If it actually came out, I honestly don't know. I went to shout "Stop" and the events took over the warning. The look on McCann's face, the alertness, the awareness of him, he looked at me, than all of a sudden his right arm, right elbow, actually moved across the front of his body, sir. At that stage there, I thought the man McCann was definitely going to go for the button . . . To me, the whole worry was the bomb and the debussing area . . .' 'A's gun was ready-loaded with one round in the breech, the firing pin cocked

At speed in the Iraqi desert (above) an armed SAS Land Rover blazes its way to the next rendezvous, the Union flag flying as a signal to prowling American A-10 aircraft that no 'friendly fire' is wanted. Even at rest (below) the British flag is laid out as a ground-marker to tell US pilots, 'No bombs, please, we're British.'

The Thermal Imaging Gun Sight from Thorn EMI (above)–seen here attached to a .50 calibre Browning machine-gun –was part of a technical revolution expressed during the Gulf War that gave the Allies command of the battlefield at night. Another lodestar of western magic (left), the handheld Magellan Global Positioning System navigation aid. 'Magellan,' one SAS officer told the author, 'was war-winning equipment.'

This Chinook helicopter in desert camouflage (above), part of the burgeoning RAF Special Forces team, flew the Special Boat Service on its only mission behind the lines among its many risky flights. A USAF A-10 'Thunderbolt' aircraft (below) somewhere in Saudi Arabia. The A-10 is a Biggles-age flying machine built around a seven-barrel, 30mm cannon that fires depleted uranium shells through tanks.

An SAS fighting column forms up somewhere behind the lines, between attacks on Iraqi targets. The vehicles include Unimogs as well as Land Rovers, most of them decorated with the stencilled silhouettes of 'kills', including mobile Scuds, communications towers, etc. The firepower of one

of these twelve-vehicle columns included .50 Brownings, lighter 7.62mm general purpose machine-guns, 40mm grenade launchers, Milan wire-guided anti-tank missile launchers and Stinger anti-aircraft missiles. When they didn't work the SAS used sledge-hammers.

In 1991 the SAS fought three enemies: the Iraqis, the desert and Arabia's worst winter in living memory. At the end of each day's patrol the vehicles formed a 'wagon circle' (above) to anticipate enemy attacks. Torrential rain created flash floods (below) which would have stopped a Paris-to-Dakar rally.

A desert Land Rover (above) with general purpose machine-gun in front and in the rear container US-made Stinger anti-aircraft missile. The regiment is the only British formation to be armed with this SAM. The Iraqi major who survived an SAS desert ambush carried an invaluable tactical map (below) revealing the location of enemy units near the Saudi border.

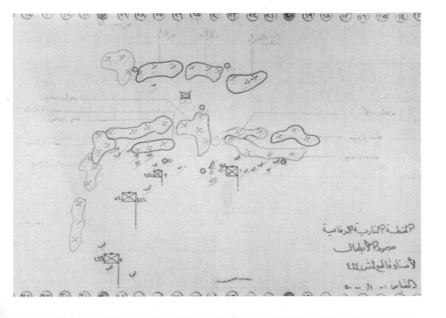

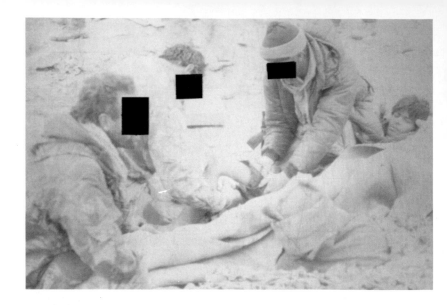

The SAS give their enemy prisoner emergency first aid (above) and put him aboard the next convoy out of the war zone. This SAS team (below) has hit an Iraqi Scud complex. Two Iraqis lie flat, pinioned, as the team leader, gun in hand, questions them in Arabic.

David Stirling (above), founder of the SAS, stands alongside some of his 'originals' on their return from a desert raid 18 January, 1943. The impact of an SAS visit to a Luftwaffe base (below).

An SAS soldier shares a cigarette with an aboriginal Iban tracker (above), an SAS patrol runs for cover from a hovering helicopter (below) and a soldier with well-filled rucksack and rifle (right) is delivered to his patrol area in Borneo.

The SAS were active in the Dhofar region of Oman from 1970 to 1976. A group of SAS soldiers and local allies (left) includes Sergeant Andrew Baxter (centre), and Staff-Sergeant David Naden in the driving seat. Alistair Morrison (below left) and colleague with captured, Soviet-made enemy weapons.

7.00 pm, 5 May 1980 and the eight-man SAS Red Team (above) stands by to abseil from the Iranian Embassy roof. Red Team hits the General Office balcony (centre and below) and storms into the burning building, spare magazines for weapons strapped to wrists and thighs.

The Red Team leader (above), trapped by a defective rope, is in danger of roasting alive as Tommy Palmer works to free him. As they left the burning Embassy, Blue Team soldiers collected some official invitations as souvenirs. An imaginative member of B Squadron 'customised' one (below) after the operation.

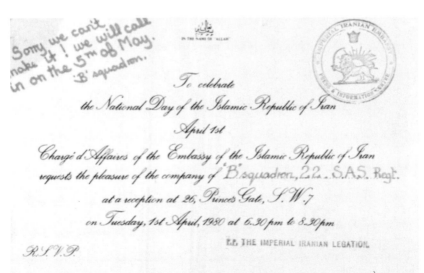

Sorry we can't make it ! we will call in on the 5th of May. 'B' squadron.

IN THE NAME OF 'ALLAH'

IMPERIAL IRANIAN EMBASSY PRESS & INFORMATION OFFICE

To celebrate
the National Day of the Islamic Republic of Iran
April 1st

Chargé d'Affaires of the Embassy of the Islamic Republic of Iran
requests the pleasure of the company of 'B' squadron, 22. S.A.S. Regt.
at a reception at 26, Prince's Gate, S.W.7
on Tuesday, 1st April, 1980 at 6.30 pm to 8.30 pm

R.S.V.P.

E.E. THE IMPERIAL IRANIAN LEGATION

Moment of release at Mogadishu, October 1977 (above) as hostages, aided by SAS men, flee the airliner, inside which a gun battle rages between Arab terrorists and German commandos. Moment of death on a Gibraltar pavement, March 1988 (below) as IRA terrorists Mairead Farrell and Danny McCann breathe their last under the eyes and guns of the SAS.

Chaos on Fortuna Glacier, South Georgia (top) as a heliborne SAS team finds itself trapped by a blizzard. Undeterred, the regiment launches Gemini inflatable craft to try again by sea (centre). Chilean investigators (bottom) examine the wreckage of RN Sea King helicopter after failure of SAS mission against Argentina.

An SAS soldier, armed with a US Stinger anti-aircraft missile, lurks behind a rock near an Argentine-held airstrip in West Falkland (above). An SAS patrol returns to its command shop to de-brief (below). Note sniper rifle silhouette blurred by hessian 'beard'.

back. A life could be measured in the few millimetres between the cartridge head and the firing pin. To complete the job, all that was required was a thumb-flick touch to release the safety catch and a squeeze on the trigger. And so, 'I fired at McCann one round into his back'.

Other shots now followed at a speed which appears to be about three times the accepted maximum fire rate of the Browning HP pistol. (The SAS commander, 'F', argued that his men could fire 'say, six shots in somewhere around three seconds' from each gun: 0.4 second to squeeze the trigger and 0.1 second to reject each spent cartridge case. Jane's Infantry Weapons specifies 40 rounds per minute or one every 1.5 seconds). Soldier 'A's second shot – a single round, unlike the usual SAS pattern of the 'double-tap' – struck Farrell. Then 'A' turned the gun on McCann a second time, 'one to the body and two to the head. He was falling all the time'.

Coroner: One to the back of the head? – Correct.

Soldier 'A' had fired at Farrell, he explained, because she started grabbing at a bag under her left armpit.

Almost immediately, he heard a police car siren. He raised both hands, one still gripping the pistol and shouted 'Police'. He and soldier 'B' were driven from the scene in a police car to report to their officer Soldier 'E' before handing the weapons and unused ammunition to the Gibraltar police.

Soldier 'B', alongside 'A', concentrated his attention on Farrell. He heard 'a garbled shout' from Soldier 'A' as 'A' began shooting. He saw Farrell make a move towards her handbag and he also started firing, putting seven bullets into Farrell and McCann. Why did he start shooting?

'Bearing in mind I did not actually know whether "A" had been shot – all I heard was firing – I opened fire. I drew my weapon as the shots started. You must remember it was all in a split second. I switched fire and turned on McCann because I didn't know whether Soldier "A" had been shot and I perceived McCann as a threat to me and Gibraltar and my comrades.'

As Farrell fell to the ground he shot her again because he could not see her hands. When her hands were away from her body, she was no longer a threat.

As the first bullet entered McCann's body, the third member of the Active Service Unit, Sean Savage, was 120 yards away, walking uphill in the opposite direction along Winston Churchill Avenue, tailed by SAS soldiers 'C' and 'D' and a female surveillance officer from MI5, Miss 'J'. Lurking well in the rear was Watcher 'H'. As Savage turned left into a narrow, tree-lined passageway, all four heard the shooting and the police siren. Savage swung round. Soldier 'C', gun already drawn to arrest him, recalled shouting: 'Stop, police! Get down. Hands above head. Stay still.' At the same time as these words were spoken, Savage 'went down with his right arm to the area of his pocket' adopting 'CQB or Close Quarter Battle stance . . . I fired. I carried on firing until I was sure he had gone down and was no longer a threat [capable of] initiating that device.'

As Savage's body spiralled down he shot the terrorist four times in the chest and possibly twice in the head.

Soldier 'D' was closing in on Savage when a woman got between them. So, 'with one arm I had to move the female away and with my other arm I drew my pistol and engaged Savage.' He fired nine shots. 'Initially I aimed at the centre of Savage's body', he said in a flat, Lancashire accent. 'I fired the first round and carried on firing, very rapid, right into Savage's body as he was turning and fell away to the ground. The last two rounds were aimed at his head. This was possibly inches away from the ground, just before he became still . . . I kept on firing until he was still on the ground and his hands were away from his body.'

Miss 'J' from MI5 said that Savage was 15 feet in front of her when he spun round in response to the shots at the filling station. She was 'petrified' and feared he might trigger a bomb or fire a gun. She went on: 'I felt Savage knew in an instant what was happening. I did not see him after that. I turned around immediately. I did not want to have eyeball contact . . . When I turned away from Savage I did not see anything. I heard a police siren still going. There was a lot of noise in my right ear through my earpiece from the radio. There was a constant buzz in the ear.'

If some official watchers saw nothing, others demonstrated

that they could hear what mattered. Several civil police witnesses said they heard warnings shouted by the soldiers before they started shooting, even when the soldiers themselves were unsure about the sort of warning they had uttered. Those who swore on their oath that they heard the warnings to McCann and Farrell included PC James Parody, off duty in his flat overlooking the Shell station; Officer 'P', a member of the police back-up squad and his colleague Officer 'Q'.

Five police witnesses and one civilian said they heard the police car siren before the shootings began and witnessed the reaction of the terrorists – described by one of them as 'hyperactive' – to the sudden arrival of what must have seemed like a police posse. Civilian testimony was less helpful to the authorities. For example, Mr Stephen Bullock, a barrister and his wife were walking on Smith Dorrien Avenue when they witnessed the deaths of McCann and Farrell. They heard a police siren followed a split-second later by gunfire and saw McCann reeling back with his hands above his shoulders. Two men with guns in their waist belts were peering from bushes at Smith Dorrien Avenue. 'As the shooting stopped,' recounts Bullock, 'they both suddenly turned and ran in the direction of the Landport Tunnel out of my sight, and within a matter of seconds there was another very, very long burst of shooting', a fusillade which signalled the death of Savage.

Mrs Josie Celecia, overlooking the Shell station from her bedroom, heard shots, saw a man and a woman on the ground and heard more shots as two men stood beside the couple, one man with arms extended forward. She saw no gun but she, too, heard a police car's siren and saw the car as it passed the Shell station. After another round of firing, the two men standing beside the couple got into a police car.

Mrs Carmen Proetta said that from her flat overlooking the scene, she saw two people shot while they stood with their hands up. The couple were shot again as they lay on the ground. Mrs Proetta's husband Maxie, recalled Carmen's words in Spanish as they watched it happen: 'Lo estan rematando' ('They are finishing them off.')

Evidence about Savage's death was given by Kenneth Asquez,

309

a 20-year-old bank clerk, and subsequently retracted. In the first version, he saw a man wearing a black beret with his foot on the throat of a bleeding man who lay near the Landport Passage (tunnel). Black Beret allegedly held up an identity card and shouted, 'Stop! It's OK. It's the police' . . . before firing three more shots into his victim. Cross-examined by McGrory, for the IRA's next-of-kin, Asquez admitted he had made it all up.

By now, the Asquez fantasy had been exercised by a leading television documentary film team in their programme 'Death On The Rock' and elsewhere. Its net effect was to polarise witnesses into two camps and to diminish the credibility of evidence critical of the security authorities including the SAS. Yet there were sounder witnesses whose evidence remains disturbing, such as that of a woman named Diana Tracey. She was walking towards the Landport Ditch when two men ran towards her. As they approached, one shot the other with a pistol carried in the left hand. The victim, she said with quiet certainty, was shot in the back and without warning.

In any investigation into a violent death the most eloquent witnesses are sometimes the victims. With the expert help of a good autopsy their bodies can reveal much. In this case, powder burns on the clothes of the IRA dead told forensic scientists that the guns had been fired at a minimum range of 3 feet in the case of Farrell and 4 feet in Savage's case. Fabric fibres on Farrell's clothes revealed that she as well as Savage had travelled in the white Renault. But it was the pathologists' evidence which caused the greatest stir.

Professor Alan Watson, the Scottish specialist who examined the corpses on behalf of the British government, is also a magistrate: clearly, no lover of terrorists. He found that Savage had been hit by at least 16 bullets which caused 29 injuries in something 'like a frenzied attack'. There was evidence that four bullets had been fired into the terrorist's head from above. Watson told a BBC reporter: 'It looks to me as though he was probably shot down and then, whilst on the ground, other shots were put into him.'

Farrell, shot three times in the back and four times in the face, died of two wounds in the heart and one in the liver.

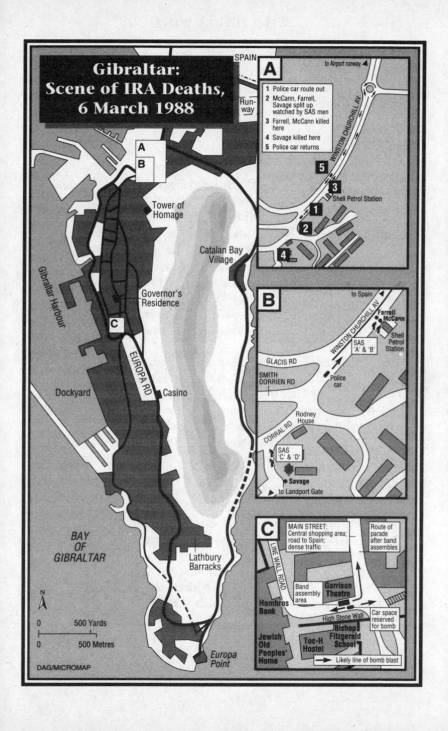

Gibraltar: Scene of IRA Deaths, 6 March 1988

SPAIN

Runway

Tower of Homage

Catalan Bay Village

Governor's Residence

Gibraltar Harbour

EUROPA RD

Dockyard

Casino

BAY OF GIBRALTAR

Lathbury Barracks

N

| 0 | 500 Yards |
| 0 | 500 Metres |

Europa Point

DAG/MICROMAP

A

to Airport runway

1 Police car route out
2 McCann, Farrell, Savage split up watched by SAS men
3 Farrell, McCann killed here
4 Savage killed here
5 Police car returns

WINSTON CHURCHILL AV

5

3

Shell Petrol Station

1

2

4

B

to Spain

Farrell
McCann

WINSTON CHURCHILL AV

SAS 'A' & 'B'

Shell Petrol Station

GLACIS RD

SMITH DORRIEN RD

Police car

Rodney House

CORRAL RD

SAS 'C' & 'D'

Savage

to Landport Gate

C

MAIN STREET: Central shopping area; road to Spain; dense traffic

Route of parade after band assembles

LINE WALL ROAD

Band assembly area

Garrison Theatre

Hambros Bank

High Stone Wall

Car space reserved for bomb

Bishop Fitzgerald School

Jewish Old Peoples' Home

Toc-H Hostel

→ Likely line of bomb blast

Both these organs were 'pulped' and her back was broken. McCann was shot twice in the back and twice in the head. Both sets of wounds were equally lethal. One head shot had 'smashed his skull'.

The verdict

For the first six hours of private deliberation the Coroner's eleven jurors could not agree upon a verdict. Felix Pizzarello had advised them in summing-up that the soldiers were legally entitled to use 'only . . . such force as is legally necessary'. There were three possible verdicts, he suggested: unlawful homicide; justifiable homicide; an open verdict. Another 90 minutes passed before the divided jury returned a nine-to-two majority in favour of lawful killing. It was hardly the 'total vindication' claimed by the soldiers' lawyer, Michael Hucker or the 'clear and conclusive finding' identified by the Ministry of Defence.

Armchair experts were as puzzled and as divided as the jurors. The *Daily Telegraph*'s Defence Editor, John Keegan, a noted military historian, suggested that the SAS Regiment's 'anti-terrorist element, perhaps continuously recruited from within the Army, ought to become a government anti-terrorist force under the control of the Home Secretary'. In effect this would make counter-terrorist teams into 'super-cops' similar to Germany's GSG-9, France's GIGN or – in an earlier phase of political gangsterism – America's G-men.

In so far as the SAS Regiment could express an opinion it did so through its Colonel-in-Chief, Field Marshal Lord Bramall, who wrote to the *Daily Telegraph* after the verdict: 'Those [terrorists] who proclaim they are on "active service" and engage in a war must realise that the law, even in a free society, can, under certain circumstances, allow them to be dealt with exactly as if they were in such a war.'

On 14 November 1988, when the row about the Gibraltar shootings was at its height, Mrs Thatcher, as Prime Minister, told the annual banquet of the Lord Mayor of London: 'Those who choose to live by the bomb and the gun and those who support them cannot in all circumstances be accorded exactly the same rights as everyone else.'

Nowhere was the greyness of the grey legal area encompassing such operations better illustrated than by the position of the SAS team after the operation, but before the inquest. The soldiers unquestionably acted under orders. To challenge these too vigorously (as members of B Squadron discovered during the Argentine mainland operations of 1982) would be to invite return-to-unit and other trouble. Hypothetically, such disobedience could even lead to a drumhead court-martial and execution by firing squad. But with the appalled discovery that the Gibraltar terrorists were unarmed when they died, the manner of their deaths became one for a civilian inquiry. The soldiers' legal status mysteriously changed from the military to the civil and a grateful government left it to the soldiers themselves to decide whether to give evidence.

As one anonymous Cabinet minister put it: 'No political decision has been taken. We will give them every support we possibly can . . . and make it clear what our advice is. At the end of the day, they will have to take the advice of their lawyers, but they are entitled to make up their own minds.'

At the official level, Whitehall argued that it was concerned for the soldiers' safety in view of risks to their anonymity, even behind a curtained screen as they gave evidence. This placebo ignored the public policy issues resulting from the original decision to use SAS soldiers as policemen as well as armed agents of the state.

By making it a *personal* decision on the soldiers' part, the government distanced itself from its legal responsibility as neatly as Pontius Pilate. There are other precedents. In Algiers in 1957 the paras of the French Foreign Legion were authorised to impose their own rules to halt a burgeoning campaign of urban terror including indiscriminate bombing. The legionnaires did not care for this 'bulot des flics', this 'coppers' job'. They did it nevertheless and crushed the Casbah terrorists by methods which appalled French public opinion. France promptly blamed the soldiers rather than the government.

The SAS soldiers, in the light of the public flak they had suffered in the months following the shootings, were anxious not to let their case go by default. At the inquest, Soldier 'D' emphasised: 'All the soldiers from "A" to "G" appeared here because they wanted to appear here. They wasn't told; they wasn't press-ganged to come here. We came because we wanted to come here and we wanted to give our evidence. We wanted to get the story right.'

This was brave as well as honest, but for many people Gibraltar remains – witness a divided inquest jury and expert opinion – an enigmatic affair from which contradictory lessons might be drawn.

The SAS credo, drawn from James Elroy Flecker's *Hassan* contains a vision of pilgrims crossing the last horizon. To most SAS soldiers it implies the last barrier of fear, the fear of death.

The world as Flavius knew it

After Gibraltar, one or two SAS veterans wondered whether this exploration of the unknown had acquired a new dimension. Were the soldiers also cast as pilgrims in a journey across legal horizons to discover a viable new doctrine with which a democracy may defend itself against the scourge of political terrorism while still, somehow, remaining constitutional, answerable to the rule of law and untainted by state terrorism?

May democracies defend the constitution from *outside* the constitution? Perhaps. Since 1984 the US government (following Israel's example) has employed a 'presidential snatch option' to claim worldwide jurisdiction over terrorists and drug traffickers acting against America on foreign soil. The government of Britain – which has no written constitution but a series of recognised unwritten conventions – has revived and extended the royal prerogative, a legal means permitting the government of the day to deny the courts access to state secrets. This was invoked in 1988 in the 'Shoot-to-kill' cases involving the RUC. Patrick McAuslan, Professor of Public Law at the London School of Economics, suggested in 1988 that 'officers of the security services could even be empowered to kill their fellow citizens, for one aspect of the royal prerogative is the defence of the realm . . .'

In contemporary Britain, the constitution still provides – in theory – for a separation of powers among three equally legitimate authorities: Parliament; the courts and the Crown. If one element dominated the others, democracy would cease. It was all very different, and much simpler, in ancient Rome, where just two power centres – the Senate and the Emperor – coexisted and occasionally quarrelled, at which point the army intervened.

One teasing question about Gibraltar is its codename, 'Operation Flavius'. This might have been chosen by computer, as many are. If so, the computer had a superb sense of irony as well as history. Whom did the SAS commander, Soldier 'F', have in mind when he spoke of 'Flavius, the Roman magistrate?' As the historian Dr J. M. Roberts observes in his *History of the World*,

> If there was confusion and indecision at the centre, then the soldiers would decide. This was what happened during the first great burst of civil war to shake the empire, in the year of the Four Emperors, AD 69, from which there emerged [Flavius] Vespasian, the grandson of a centurion and far from an aristocrat. The first magistracy had passed out of the hands of the great Roman families.

In spite of a torrent of words and inquiry, the enigma of Gibraltar remains intact. Was the Gibraltar Flavius a historical abstraction or did he really exist? In 1988, he seemed an energetic sort of ghost. The original model, the Mark I Flavius, was one of the first and most successful Roman generals to put the boot into the native Celts in Britain. Under the Emperor Claudius, he commanded the 2nd Augustan Legion drawn from the Rhine Basin, during its drive west, into the heartland of Celtic Britain around AD 43–47. The massacre of defenders of a fort at Maiden Castle, Dorset, after he had overrun the Isle of Wight is identified as one of his thirty victories in which some twenty enemy strongholds were taken. By Roman standards he was just as well as brave. His biographer Suetonius quotes his dismissive comment about military grandeur, 'Personally, I am content to be a man.'

Flavius Vespasian was also, in his younger days in Crete and North Africa, a quaestor: that is, a magistrate, just as Soldier 'F' said he was, or a judge in a murder case as some dictionaries suggest. Gibraltar (known as 'Calpe' when it was one of the two legendary pillars of Hercules in Greek mythology) had been part of the Roman empire for more than two centuries when Flavius became a magistrate just across the water in North Africa. It is entirely possible that he also operated in Gibraltar. Certainly, when he became emperor, he revealed a keen interest in Iberia. Though he introduced a form of civil rights into Spain in AD 74 it is also true that his life symbolised a military view of justice rather than a civil one.

There is one distinguished SAS soldier who might have bestowed on this operation its historical imprimatur, its code-word and even some of its planning. The commander concerned applies his formidable knowledge of Roman – and other – history to contemporary military problems. His regimental origins are close to Flavius's most celebrated military success against the Celts in Britain. He is a specialist in counter-insurgency, as was Flavius, happy to quote Pliny the Elder, the Roman geographer who was Flavius's distinguished contemporary, or Pompeius Falco, (Governor of Britain, AD 118–22) during the rebellion against Hadrian. ('The idea of the towers in South Armagh,' he told the author, 'could be considered merely an extension of Pompeius Falco's initial concept of building towers on Hadrian's Wall, to use as patrol bases against the Caledons and northern tribes . . .')

The same officer held a key position in Northern Ireland at the time Operation Flavius began. By a quirky coincidence, the Gibraltar Three died on his birthday. He neither confirmed nor denied his possible authorship of Flavius, since 'the Gibraltar cull' was still too contentious.

In Ireland in the twentieth century, the story of Operation

316

Flavius acquired a postscript belonging peculiarly to that gothic world of continuing Irish horror, where – to coin a phrase – frenzied killing has become the norm.

On 16 March 1988 the Gibraltar Trio were buried at the Republican Milltown cemetery in Belfast when a Loyalist fanatic killed three mourners and injured another fifty in a gun and grenade attack before he was overpowered, arrested, and later sentenced to life. Three days later, at the funeral of one of the dead mourners, two British soldiers who strayed into the path of the cortege were lynched and murdered. Aside from the technology, this was the world as Flavius knew it.

The enigmatic Spanish connection

Throughout the debates that raged around the Gibraltar operation one paradox overshadowed British credibility and honour. This was that before and after the inquest of September 1988 the UK publicly affirmed its belief in Spain's reliability as a comrade-in-arms against terrorism but (exclusively in the inquest context) alleged that the Spanish authorities had lost track of the IRA terrorists during the crucial hours before they entered Gibraltar. This was advanced as the reason why the SAS team could not know whether the bombers were armed or not and – not being granted the benefit of a doubt – had to be stopped by a hail of bullets.

This was the sequence:

1. British Intelligence, forewarned of the Gibraltar plot, placed a handpicked team on the Rock, including the SAS, to await the arrival of the IRA bomber: the team of eleven, including two women, was finally assembled at the Rock Hotel on Friday 5 March 1988 though two of the party had been in residence since 19 and 25 February.

2. The three terrorists entered Gibraltar on 6 March 1988 and were shot dead by the SAS; the Rock Hotel party checked out the same evening.

3. On 7 March in the House of Commons, the British

Foreign Secretary praised the Spaniards for their surveillance as did others including the 'father' of the House, Sir Bernard Braine.

4.   Later that day, Spanish police found the IRA's car bomb in an underground carpark at Marbella, Costa del Sol, 30 miles from Gibraltar: it contained 145 pounds of powerful Semtex high explosive and an unattached timing device preset at 11.20am, the time at which the Gibraltar guard-changing ceremony took place. The Spanish police alerted a junior member of the Gibraltar force to the find immediately.

5.   On 9 March an official Spanish communique said that surveillance over the IRA terrorists 'had been maintained until they went to Gibraltar'.

6.   On 8 August 1988 Chief Inspector Tomas Rayo Valenzuela of Malaga Special Branch delivered his testimony about the surveillance operation before a Malaga judge: this document, according to reliable Press reports, was sent to the Gibraltar Coroner soon afterward by way of the UK Embassy in Madrid.

7.   The inquest, it is alleged, received an alternative version of Valenzuela's statement: an unsworn, English-language summary of what Valenzuela told a Gibraltar policeman, Manolo Correa.

8.   The inquest heard from British witnesses including the SAS commander 'F' (on 9 September) that despite intelligence that the IRA three were in Malaga, Spain, they were not under surveillance, although the success of the operation depended on spotting the terrorists as they crossed into Gibraltar.

9.   A few hours after this evidence, a Spanish Interior Ministry official told the *Independent* newspaper: 'When the terrorists entered Gibraltar, the British authorities on the Rock obviously knew they were coming. The British would only have known this if there had been surveillance on the Spanish side.'

10.   On 24 September another Spanish version of events, that of a Spanish Interior Ministry spokesman, Augustin Valldolid, was submitted to the Coroner through an American journalist named Harry Debelius. Such manoeuvres almost certainly reflected Spain's endeavours to present the facts as it knew them

while simultaneously avoiding the concession of recognising British legal sovereignty over Gibraltar.

11. Meanwhile British security authorities were energetically preparing for two VIP visits to Spain: the first, by the Prime Minister Mrs Thatcher on 21–22 September, while the inquest was taking place, and the second, by the Queen and Duke of Edinburgh, lasting a week from 17 October. Threat evaluations for these visits were made by officers of the Royal Protection Group, the Special Branch and MI5 in conjunction with Madrid, while much of the security during the visits was left to Spain. The lives of the British monarch and Prime Minister were in the hands of people who were perceived from Gibraltar to be – at best – unlucky in handling such matters.

12. During Mrs Thatcher's trip, journalists covering the tour, benefiting from unattributable but official guidance, emphasised the strong co-operation between the two countries in the fight against terrorism. In the *Daily Telegraph*, Robert Fox reported: 'The Spanish government has firmly backed proposals made by Douglas Hurd, the British Home Secretary, at the Trevi Group of EEC Ministers . . . for better methods of keeping watch on suspects and arms and ammunition moving through Europe.'

13. On 14 March 1989, just over a year after the deaths of the terrorists, twenty-two Spanish police officers received citations for their part in the surveillance operation preceding the deaths. Miguel Martin, president of the Professional Policeman's Union (the SPP, equivalent of the British Police Federation) said: 'When the IRA crossed into Gibraltar, the Spanish police were able to tell the British who they were, when they had entered the Rock and what their target was. What we weren't certain of is whether their explosives were already inside Gibraltar.'

Martin also claimed that Spain had alerted the British authorities as early as November 1987 to the presence of McCann and Savage on Spanish soil. Britain had immediately sent one of its top Intelligence operators from Belfast, from the RUC's undercover surveillance team, F5, to advise the Spaniards.

Evidence that someone was lying about Spain's role is circumstantial, but no more circumstantial than, say, the evidence against the Birmingham Six who went to prison for their alleged role in an IRA bombing atrocity. The Coroner, Felix Pizzarello, did not entirely discount the possibility of a high level conspiracy to kill the three terrorists. 'Little as it is, it is there', he commented.

Was the SAS part of such a plot or were the soldiers misled by the security services? Those who did the shooting were assuredly told, as a matter of fact, that there was a bomb in the Renault although Soldier 'G', who made a hasty examination of the vehicle, simply regarded it as 'suspicious'.

Soldier 'F', the SAS commander on the spot, when asked by Mr McGrory whether the IRA team could have been arrested on the Spanish border, replied: 'If there had been an indication of both the car and the type of car and the movement, intended movement and detailed movement of the terrorists, then the area of the border and the airport would indeed have been the preferred area to make the arrest.'

Savage, he said later, had driven the Renault across in a matter of ten or fifteen seconds. He had not been identified. 'The border guards only had a very short time . . . to make a possible identification of someone driving a car who was not known to them.' The siting of that surveillance team, he added pointedly, was not his responsibility.

At another point, Soldier 'F' said in evidence: 'We were also told that no surveillance operation was being carried out on the Spanish side of the border.'

The Coroner suggested that if there were some sort of plot, then Soldier 'F' must be part of it. Yet there is no evidence to show that 'F', or other members of the SAS team, had any reliable sources of information independent of the Foreign Office, MI6 and MI5.

When the *Independent* newspaper invited the Foreign Office to express its views about the awards given to Spanish policemen for their surveillance of the terrorists, that department declined to comment. The only available text appeared to come from the Foreign Secretary, Sir Geoffrey Howe, himself. In his parliamentary statement the day after the shootings, Sir Geoffrey said that a dreadful terrorist act had been prevented. He was sure that the House would share his relief and extend its gratitude to the Spanish authorities.

The author's researches in Gibraltar after the inquest turned up an intriguing solution to these contradictions. This was that Spanish security *did* shadow the IRA team, but sent its reports to London rather than direct to Gibraltar because of the continuing dispute over the Colony's status. The Spanish intelligence was then relayed from Britain to British security authorities in Gibraltar. Security sources on the Rock suggested that a communications breakdown between London and Gibraltar at a sensitive moment led to fatal confusion. The same sources insisted that the original plan was to arrest the IRA trio on the road to Spain, where it crosses the Gibraltar Airport runway, and then bundle the terrorists aboard an aircraft bound for Britain.

Part III

Origins – Jungle and Jebel

Malaya 1950–59

Borneo 1962–66

South Arabia 1964–67

Prologue

For most Europeans the period between 1945 and the Cuban missile crisis of 1962 was a slow reawakening from the nightmare of total war, a time to emerge from the bomb shelter to the novelty of sleeping in a normal bed, undisturbed by high explosive. Only the most dedicated soldiers still had stomach for a fight. In 1947 the moribund SAS was coyly reconstituted under the cap badge of the Artists' Rifles, a Territorial Army regiment. In 1950, as Communist guerrillas (some trained by wartime veterans of Special Operations Executive) started their jungle war, Brigadier Michael Calvert, boxing blue, Chindit and wartime SAS commander, raised the Malayan Scouts to fight the guerrillas on their own terms. In 1951 Tod Sloane, a 6ft 2in 18-stone officer of the Argyll & Sutherland Highlanders, took command of the Malayan Scouts (SAS) which now combined the two elements of a reborn SAS. It was the beginning of a history that fused colonial counter-insurgency, of which the British had much experience, with the surrogate battles of the Cold War. The outcome was not clear until the collapse of the Soviet empire and the defeat of its last rogue client, Saddam Hussein's Iraq, in 1991.

MALAYA 1950–59

The inauspicious beginning

Like Don John of Austria, the visionary leader of the last crusade against the Saracens, the post-war Special Air Service was 'risen from a doubtful seat and half-attained stall'. The regiment had been disbanded at the end of the Second World War, together with the Army Commando, Popski's Private Army and other esoteric 'mobs for jobs'. And, when a special jungle force was raised for the long counter-terrorist campaign in Malaya, it owed more to the experience of Wingate than to Stirling. It was through a series of accidents that it became the SAS.

During much of the Malayan campaign the new unit's structure, style, and discipline were very different from, and inferior to, the ultra-professional force into which it subsequently evolved. Hard drinking, indiscipline, the 'fragging' of officers, as well as some good soldiering, all characterised those early days and it would be a long time before the regiment would live down the reputation it had acquired. (The uninitiated should know that the word 'fragging' is derived from 'fragmentation grenade', originally the US M26 sometimes used by American conscripts against their own officers in Vietnam.) But even in retrospect, it is surprising that the regiment got off to quite such a bad start, combining as it did some of the best that British Special Forces had created during the Second World War. That this did happen was due to the speed and ferocity with which the Malayan Emergency built up, leaving insufficient time for selection and training, and the fact that the war was for the hearts and minds of people, rather than for territory. Such a war, at that time, was not one for which the wartime SAS had equipped itself.

No one who knew Malaya was surprised that it contained Communists. A small Communist Party had existed in that prosperous land since the 1930s. What caused the damage was the arming of Communist guerrillas during the war against the Japanese, without thought for the possibility that these guns might be turned on the British after the war. That this had not been foreseen is neatly shown by the presentation to the Communist guerrilla supremo, Chin Peng, of an OBE in the Victory Honours, and his participation in celebrations in London after the war. The justification for arming Peng and his underground army was that until the atom bomb was used against Japan, the Far East campaign offered no short-cut to victory. To assist the guerrillas in Malaya and elsewhere, the Special Operations Executive (SOE) sent a number of adventurous spirits into the jungle, some of whom had aided the partisans of Greece and Albania. One of these was the Regimental Adjutant of the SAS, Major C. E. (Dare) Newell, OBE.

Newell and his comrades were part of a cryptically-named organisation called Force 136. In January 1945 he parachuted into Johore Bahru to meet with two British members of the Underground who had remained after the fall of Singapore. When, a few months later, Japan surrendered, the Japanese commander in Malaya, General Itagaki, did not believe it. Newell and his friends were ordered to remain in hiding until a member of the Tokyo Royal Family was brought to Singapore to persuade Itagaki that the war really had ended. By now, there were at least 4000 British and captured Japanese weapons in the hands of the guerrillas. If there was a moment when the Communists could have seized power in Malaya, this was it. The iron grip of the Japanese had been broken and the British had not yet returned in force. But the chance passed and the war ended with two gains for Chin Peng, in addition to his OBE. One was recognition of the Malayan Communist Party – withdrawn after the Emergency and whose restoration was to be a sticking point in negotiations to end the campaign against the

British – and the other, a large part of the abandoned Japanese arsenal in the area.

In 1948, at a time when the gains of Mao's Communism confirmed in the minds of Chinese elsewhere their innate superiority over other races, a Communist convention was held in Calcutta. The British had left India and Burma, and had started to rule Malaya at one remove through a new Federation. The Calcutta conference seems to have inspired the Malayan Communists – most of them members of the Chinese community – with the belief that if Mao could defeat the superior Western-backed Nationalist Chinese Army in a protracted guerrilla war, they could follow his example in the jungles of Malaya itself. There were also internal stresses in the Communist movement in Malaysia following the defection of its secretary-general, which made it necessary to reunify the movement through an anti-colonial offensive.

Soon afterwards, 1200 wartime guerrillas returned to the jungle in ten 'regiments', only one of which was not exclusively Chinese. Long-hidden caches of weapons were dug up, degreased and prepared for the new offensive, and a clandestine support group among non-combatant Chinese, known as the Min Yuen, came into being to supply food, money and information. Between April and June 1948, the offensive began. Following the advice of a long-dead Chinese soldier, Sun-Zu, 'Kill one, frighten a thousand', foremen and other key figures in rubber plantations on the west coast were publicly executed by groups of armed Chinese, who lectured the horrified spectators about their war against imperialism before melting back into the jungle.

At breakfast time on 16 June, it was the turn of Europeans to become ritual victims of the new order. Three young Chinese cycled into Elphil Estate in Perak and shot dead a fifty-year-old British planter, Arthur Walker. A few miles away, Ian Christian and his manager, Mr J. Alison, were bound to chairs and similarly murdered. Only the day before, Christian had called on an old Gurkha friend, Lieutenant-Colonel J. O. Lawes, to borrow a firearm because he sensed imminent danger. Lawes later recalled: 'I lent him an old Luger of my father's and said that I would try and bring some recruits out to the Estate pig-shooting the following weekend . . . We were sitting on a volcano which was to erupt much sooner than expected.'

The Emergency – limited in its scope – was declared the same day, and thenceforth the war escalated rapidly from terrorism to jungle battles against regular soldiers of the six Gurkha battalions, many of whose troops were in poor shape. Three shiploads had arrived from India without boots or shirts; they included a large number of untrained recruits, many of whom were found to have tuberculosis.

The security forces now faced a tactical dilemma. Should they merely react to events and strive to protect the towns and plantations, or try to pursue the 'bandits' to their bases? Inland Malaya, as they knew from the campaign against the Japanese, was a guerrillas' paradise – mile after mile of slippery bamboo on the mountains, while in the valleys a canopy of trees rising above 200 feet obliterated the sun, reducing daylight to twilight. Below the trees, endless swamp. The first priority had to be defence of the towns, but as a gesture to offensive campaigning, an *ad hoc* group of veterans from Force 136 and a few volunteers from the regular army battalions was cobbled together in July 1948 into something known as the Ferret Force. Almost simultaneously, the first of forty-seven Dyak trackers from the Iban tribe – small, lithe tribesmen with high-pitched voices, who killed with blowpipes and removed their victims' heads as trophies – were imported from Borneo.

Ferret Force did not last long, because the services of the civilians and regular officers in it were needed elsewhere, but its exploration of the jungle revealed how great was the need for such a group. During its first offensive operation, in which it led in a battle group of Devons, Seaforths and Inniskillings from Singapore, as well as two Gurkha battalions, it had uncovered twelve permanent guerrilla camps. These were not primitive hides. They included lecture halls and accommodation for up to 200 men, and this only three months after the murder of Arthur Walker.

By March 1950, the Communists – now known as 'CTs' (Communist Terrorists) – had exacted an appalling toll on

Malaya. A total of 863 civilians, 323 police officers and 154 soldiers had been killed. The CT had also suffered severely (1138 killed, 645 captured, 359 surrendered), but there was no sign of an end to the war, or even a pause in their campaign.

'Win the aborigine'

In Hong Kong at this time, a British staff officer who was an acknowledged expert on guerrilla warfare was observing events in Malaya with growing impatience. A hard-drinking, hard-fighting idealist, his name was J. M. ('Mad Mike') Calvert and he was something of a legend. A physically tough character who had won a double blue at Cambridge, he had given up a commission early in the war in order to join a Scots Guards ski battalion destined for Finland. His wartime service included three years in Burma, much of that time behind Japanese lines. Calvert then commanded the SAS brigade in north-west Europe from December 1944 until it was disbanded in November 1945.

One day in 1950, General Sir John Harding, Commander-in-Chief of Far East Land Forces, called Calvert to confer about the explosion of terrorism in Malaya. The two men talked for some time, and Harding then instructed Calvert to produce a detailed analysis of the problem, with options for its solution. During the next six months, Calvert interviewed most of those conducting the campaign, covering 1500 miles, as he put it, 'unescorted along guerrilla-infested roads and only ambushed twice'. Much of his time was spent with the infantry patrols trawling through the jungle in a usually profitless hunt for an invisible enemy. This study, Calvert told the author, later formed the basis of a controversial new strategy named the 'Briggs Plan' after the Director of Operations, General Sir Harold Briggs, who put it into effect.

To isolate the guerrillas from the rest of the population, Briggs decided that 410 'villages' – many of them shanty towns inhabited by Chinese squatters – should be uprooted

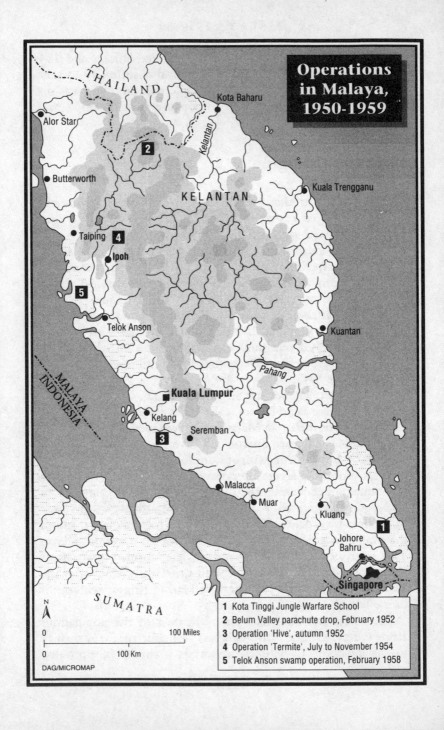

Operations in Malaya, 1950-1959

THAILAND

Kota Baharu

Alor Star

Kelantan

Butterworth

KELANTAN

Kuala Trengganu

Taiping **4**

Ipoh

5

Telok Anson

Kuantan

MALAYA
INDONESIA

Pahang

Kuala Lumpur

Kelang

3

Seremban

Malacca

Muar

Kluang

1

Johore
Bahru

Singapore

N

SUMATRA

0   100 Miles

0   100 Km

1 Kota Tinggi Jungle Warfare School
2 Belum Valley parachute drop, February 1952
3 Operation 'Hive', autumn 1952
4 Operation 'Termite', July to November 1954
5 Telok Anson swamp operation, February 1958

DAG/MICROMAP

and their occupants moved to new, fortified villages. In June 1951, Briggs followed this with an equally ambitious plan to deny food supplies to the guerrillas. Both schemes demanded a uniquely stringent control of people and food, and over the next eight years they finally destroyed the guerrilla movement.

Another proposal contained in Calvert's study was the creation of a special military force to live in the jungle, denying the 'bandits' any sanctuary or rest. Calvert argued that British troops should be able to survive in such an environment for much longer than the seven days then regarded as the maximum for an orthodox infantry patrol. Linked with this was the suggestion that the key to winning the jungle war was the trust of its indigenous aboriginal population. Two months after submitting his report to Harding, Calvert was instructed to create the 'special force' he had in mind. He called it the Malayan Scouts (SAS), with the object of converting the Army to the idea of a series of special forces raised locally whenever they were needed, with a geographical identity linked to the SAS.

Calvert now began an intensive drive to organise and recruit the new regiment. His own retrospective view is that, in spite of acknowledged shortcomings, he was creating a foundation on which others could build, and that to be too fastidious in his choice of soldiers at such a time would almost certainly mean that the unit would never be formed. He had presided over the disbandment of the wartime SAS Brigade and he was determined not to lose this opportunity to resurrect the concept. Invitations were posted to units throughout the Far East for volunteers to join him and no particular criteria were laid down for selection. Some of those who responded were useful veterans of SOE, SAS, Force 136 and Ferret Force; others were men who were simply bored and whose units were happy to see them go elsewhere. One group consisted of ten deserters from the French Foreign Legion who had escaped by swimming ashore from a troopship conveying them to the war in Indo-China. Calvert, working from the premise that 'the best is the enemy of the good', accepted them. The consensus within the regiment in later years was that this approach was unwise. Another profound difference between Calvert's thinking and the consensus was Calvert's theory that any special force (such as the 'Black and Tans') could be disbanded more readily than an established regiment of the line if this became expedient.

There were other pressures on Calvert at this time. Detailed administrative work was necessary at the regiment's first base in Johore. A two-month training programme had to be started in the same area. Simultaneously, rapid results were expected from the regiment's first operational area in Ipoh, hundreds of miles away. Such a task, combined with the search for more recruits, required the attention of four senior officers, but Calvert recalls that for many crucial months he was obliged to run things unaided. Despite the circumstances, however, a surprising amount was achieved in a short time. (Similar pressures were felt by the Gurkhas, many of whose new recruits were committed to the war half-trained.) The first priority, as Calvert saw it, was manpower. In search of this, he travelled 22,000 miles in twenty-one days, including a trip to Rhodesia which led to the creation of C Squadron from 1000 volunteers in that country. From Hong Kong he brought Chinese interpreters and counter-guerrillas, who had served with him in Burma, to join his Intelligence staff.

Another source of men was a squadron of SAS Reservists and Territorials (many of whom had served under Stirling) which had formed up in 1947 as 21 SAS Regiment. The genesis of 21 SAS was a compromise between those in the War Office who thought there would be a continuing need after Hitler's defeat for clandestine special forces such as SOE, and those who did not. From the argument there emerged a Territorial unit commanded by regular officers, of whom Lieutenant-Colonel B. M. F. Franks (a 'Terrier' before and after the Second World War) was the first. There is a conflict of recollection about the circumstances in which this contribution to the Malayan Scouts, the original B Squadron, was sent to join Calvert's force. According to the official regimental history by Philip Warner, the reservists were initially sent east in order to participate in the Korean War (which started in June 1950) and, when this scheme was abandoned, the men of 21 SAS were diverted to Malaya; but Calvert has since told the present author that he had simply asked for a squadron from the reserve and knew nothing of the Korean plan.

The force that now began to emerge as the modern SAS comprised three disparate elements: Calvert's original group of 100 volunteers (A Squadron); the Reservists from Britain (B Squadron); and the Rhodesian C Squadron. Training, as devised by Calvert, was directed at realism combined with domestic familiarity, with live rather than blank ammunition. To become familiar with grenades, for example, recruits ran between monsoon drains – narrow, concrete channels four or five feet deep – in the base area and, on a given order, they would leap for cover while one man threw the grenades. To learn jungle stalking, as Warner records, 'two men armed with airguns and wearing fencing masks would crawl towards the centre of a piece of scrub about 100 yards long. The aim was to shoot one's opponent before being shot by him.' Rifle practice, using live ammunition on *ad hoc* ranges such as the base football pitch, also took place.

Calvert's operational strategy in Ipoh, meanwhile, was to penetrate deep into the jungle with heavily laden patrols of up to fourteen people, including Chinese liaison officers and local police as well as the Malayan Scouts, to establish a firm base equipped with a radio. From this, smaller groups of three or four men would explore a large area of jungle so thoroughly that they could set up ambushes confident in the knowledge that they were covering guerrilla approach routes. Calvert recalls one such patrol, led by Lieutenant Michael Sinclair Hill, which remained in the jungle for 103 days, a remarkable feat at the time. When Sinclair received a message from the RAF asking the SAS not to invoke supportive bombing missions on Sunday, so as to give aircrew time to rest, Sinclair Hill responded: 'Tell us when it is Sunday.'

Other SAS innovations at this time, according to Calvert, were the creation of primitive clinics from which penicillin was distributed to cure aborigines of the skin disease, yaws; river patrols employing inflatable craft supplied by US special forces; and the first use of helicopters (initially flown by the Royal Navy) for resupply of troops in the jungle. Under

Calvert, the regiment also evolved some startling methods of clandestine war fare. One of these resulted from the discovery that local prostitutes were demanding payment for their services in bullets and grenades, rather than cash. This 'currency' was then passed to the enemy. Calvert's men were promptly used to pose as clients in order to supply self-destroying ordnance including hand grenades fitted with instantaneous fuses (to kill the users) and exploding bullets which, when fired, served the same purpose. Jungle food stores were booby-trapped and secret dead letter boxes supplied with notes and even government money addressed to Communist organizers, some of whom were then executed by their own side. It is not known how many enemy were killed during this inaugural phase of the post-war SAS. Fatal casualties among Calvert's own men during his command totalled four: a police officer; a Chinese auxiliary; an SAS soldier who was killed while staying with an aboriginal group, and another who died in a jungle fire-fight. Three others were presumed dead after a prolonged silence about their fate. But, Calvert revealed, 'they were found again living in a village on the east coast, where they had been having a bit of a beano. They had a good excuse. One of them had been wounded.'

By the time the first cadres of A Squadron were completing their initial operational tours in the Ipoh jungle, the other two squadrons were beginning their training in the Malayan Scouts base at Johore. The image of those first A Squadron veterans is still a subject of controversy within SAS circles. The disciplined, cohesive group from 21 SAS and the even more orthodox soldiers from Rhodesia were unfavourably impressed, to put it mildly, by what they found. Calvert himself, in an interview with the author, confirms that the London group was 'shocked to the core; maybe we went too far'.

There are opposing accounts of why this was. A faithful report, thirty years later, can only recount both versions. That of the newcomers was that orthodox discipline was manifestly absent; that there was too much drunkenness, and that the use of firearms in the base area was reckless. Calvert argues that such an impression is misleading and unfair, and reflects the incomprehension about jungle conditions of soldiers whose orientation was European. What the newcomers saw, he asserts, were recruits undergoing hasty battle training in realistic conditions; and the first operational veterans being deliberately encouraged to unwind therapeutically after weeks of hard living in the jungle. If anyone was shocked, Calvert believes that this was because, by the standards of jungle warfare to which he had become accustomed over the years, some of the newly-arrived reservist officers were, as he puts it, 'a bit soft'.

The truth was probably a combination of all these things. The pioneers of A Squadron were a hard, rough bunch, including some men who were totally unsuitable for special forces as well as some who were dedicated, professional soldiers by any standard. They included a senior NCO, formerly a boxing professional and Chindit, who occasionally dispensed justice with his fists in preference to the more orthodox, if bureaucratic, procedure of putting an offender 'on orders'.

Differences of leadership, selection and training style were resolved through the accident of Calvert's return to England about two years after his initial discussion with Harding. Calvert was invalided home suffering from malaria, dysentery, hookworm and the cumulative stress of twelve years' intensive soldiering. By then, as he later told the author, he was a 'very sick man'. But, whatever the criticisms, he had the satisfaction of knowing that he had resurrected the SAS.

The unit was taken over in late 1951 by Lieutenant-Colonel John Sloane, an orthodox infantryman who had been second-in-command of the Argyll and Sutherland Highlanders in Korea. He had no special forces background and no jungle experience, but he did know about good order and discipline. By now, as a result of Calvert's intensive recruitment campaign, the SAS had four squadrons in Malaya – A, B, C and D – plus a full headquarters. Sloane persuaded various officers who had thoughts of leaving the SAS – Dare Newell, later to become Regimental Adjutant, among them – to stay for a period of reorganization during which the regiment was withdrawn from the jungle. As a result, old habits were relearned: weapons were kept clean, and basic administrative matters affecting soldiers' welfare were brought up to date. Some, though not all, of the regiment's 'cowboys' were returned to their original units. Ultimately, according to the assessment of one expert, half of those recruited in Malaya would be disposed of in this manner. The remainder were excellent soldiers.

At this time, one of Calvert's best officers, Major John Woodhouse (later to command 22 SAS), prepared to return to England to set up a selection process better suited to the regiment's needs. A former Dorset Regiment officer, he was not much interested in drill and uniform, but where battle discipline was concerned he hated sloppiness. When a soldier accidentally opened fire with a rifle, Woodhouse removed the weapon and handed the soldier a grenade from which the safety-pin had been removed. 'Carry that for a week,' he said, 'until you've learned how to handle a rifle.' If the modern SAS had a founding father, it was he.

Outside the jungle there was important work to be done. Much of this was connected with the controversial strategy of the new Director of Operations, Lieutenant-General Sir Harold Briggs, the planning of which owed much to Calvert. But in the short run, the use of the SAS to assist the Field Police Force at jungle forts and in 'jungle edge' patrols meant that Calvert's original concept of deep penetration had been put into cold storage.

Return to the jungle – by parachute

In February 1952, shortly before Woodhouse went to England, where he was to remain for three years, the regiment returned to the jungle by parachute. The purpose of the operation was food denial. In some areas the guerrillas were already beginning to suffer from the effects of Briggs's policies and had started to grow their own crops. To do this in the jungle, however, they had to fell trees in order to create clearings which would admit sunlight. Such clearings could be spotted from the air and were therefore vulnerable to attack. One of them was at a spot near the Thai border known as Belum Valley. While

Gurkhas, Royal Marine Commandos, Malayan police and two squadrons of SAS approached the site on foot, an SAS squadron of fifty-four men parachuted into a confined drop zone near the area. It was assumed that some men might land in the trees, but it was hoped that their canopies would snag the branches firmly enough to belay the men safely; with this in mind, the planners gave the soldiers 100 feet of rope each and some good advice about tying knots. In fact, there were no parachuting casualties on this occasion and thereafter, 'tree-jumping' became an SAS speciality. Later experience would demonstrate that serious injury to someone on the drop would occur almost invariably, and the technique was abandoned at the end of the Malayan campaign.

While it lasted, such parachuting produced some good newspaper copy. The *Straits Times* described an operation that, for most of the men involved, was their first experience of tree-jumping. 'They knew that if they landed in bamboo it would splinter, and cut them deeply; rocky or boulder-strewn areas, bomb blasted areas, spiky and weakened trees could smash their necks and bones. Aboard the aircraft, they joked and laughed for a few minutes after take-off. Then there was silence. Some slept, others read; a few glanced out of the windows, fixing their eyes on the jungle. All faces were stern. Ten minutes to go. They checked each other's gear. One man munched an apple; another sucked an orange. A voice said, "Dropping Zone, two minutes to go." Then, "Stand up. Action stations." A crew member stood near the door, tapping paratroopers on the shoulders, yelling "Right, right, right", as each approached him in turn and prepared to jump.' Major John Salmon, second-in-command of 22 SAS, explained later: 'When you are in the doorway, you're scared. You have to conquer the butterflies. There's no turning back, so when you feel the tap on your shoulder you don't hesitate. Next thing you know, you are floating through the air and it's one of the most wonderful feelings in the world; then you see the trees coming. You are coming down beautifully, steering for the middle of the trees. The hot air makes you swing violently, as if a giant had caught hold of you. You let the air spill out of the 'chute and look for a good, healthy tree. Sometimes you make that spot; often you don't. It's hard to tell until you are a few feet away. When you hit a tree you don't know whether you will stay there or not. Often the branch snaps, you hurtle down, smashing into branches on the way, until you finally come to a halt. If it holds you, then you know you are safe.'

The first man out on that operation, acting as 'drifter' to discover which way the wind was blowing, was Sergeant Ken Kidd, a veteran of more than 300 descents, but still wary of tree-jumping, nervous of the odds-on chance that he would 'find himself-dangling in a tree top with his spine or ankle broken'. Kidd 'spun into a tree and he was lucky. His feet and body smashed into the branches and the 'chute caught. He was 150 feet above the ground and all he could see through the branches and leaves was the thick undergrowth of the jungle. Above him, the Valletta aircraft kept circling. Now it began the first run in over the dropping zone. Inside the plane the green light flashed again above the door and the first stick of three steel-helmeted paratroopers was ready. Each seemed to half run, taking what looked like a hop, step and jump, and disappeared. The 'chutes opened 750 feet above the ground; 30 seconds later they were engulfed by trees, looking like jellyfish feeling their way into the depths of the sea.' On the ground, Kidd grinned with contentment. 'You need a lot of luck,' he said, 'but I would rather jump into trees than fly a plane. It's like anything else: you get used to it after a while.' Not everyone was so comfortable. Swinging from the top of one tree was Leon Harris, a thirty-three-year-old Australian who had just completed his first tree-jump. 'He shook so much 150 feet above the ground that it took him some time to get a cigarette into his mouth. At the foot of the tree, members of a ground party yelled, "Come on, Aussie" and Harris, securing his abseil mountaineering pack, called, "Advance, Australia fair. I made it. Here I come. Sydney or the bush".'

On another, similar operation, an SAS officer found himself dangling from a tree below which prowled an armed guerrilla. The officer was unable to reach the valise he had carried down, which held his rifle, and could only pray that the guerrilla would not look up. The episode led to a popular demand among some SAS soldiers for a supply of automatic pistols to cover that risk in future.

One of the first parachuting casualties was the man who succeeded John Sloane as Commanding Officer in 1953. Lieutenant-Colonel Oliver Brooke suffered a complicated leg fracture which required months of hospital treatment in England. Like Sloane, Brooke was a good regimental officer with no experience of special forces but, in contrast to the methodical Sloane, Brooke was a rumbustious, extrovert bachelor, quick to lose his temper, equally ready to bury the hatchet. His command of the SAS began eventfully.

In the officers' mess the night before Brooke formally assumed command, he and Newell were standing in a group, drinks in hand, in animated conversation. It was late. A number of NCOs and men from B Squadron who had celebrated too enthusiastically in the nearest town were returned to the camp by the Royal Military Police. At about the same time, some of the sergeants decided to 'frag' the reception going on in honour of the new Commanding Officer. They did so by setting off an explosive charge which blew down one wall of the mess. The table, around which Brooke, Sloane and Newell were standing, took off and landed some distance away. To Newell's surprise, Brooke did not appear to notice what had happened, but continued talking in an even, measured way. Next morning, having assumed command, Brooke took the unusual step of holding a disciplinary hearing on a Sunday, and ordered the return to their units of origin of a Senior NCO and sixteen other soldiers. They were out of the regiment, and out of the camp, before lunch. (Surprisingly, the rejected men were among those who had formed the original, disciplined cadre from B Squadron, now diluted by newcomers.) This exemplary reaction had its effect, and discipline started to improve.

The effect of Briggs's policies of food denial and political isolation was to drive the CT deeper into the jungle. The security forces were therefore obliged to pursue the enemy there, which gave the SAS its second chance to prove its value. Armed with shotguns and the new Patchett carbine – an early version of the Stirling submachine-gun – they formed the spearhead of deep jungle operations in Pahang and Kelantan, entering by helicopter and parachute. Within the theatre as a whole, the SAS now constituted one of seven major units from the UK. There were also seven Gurkha battalions, one African and one Fijian, as well as eight indigenous Malay battalions.

While more orthodox units concentrated on harrying the Johor rebel committee, the SAS was making its first serious contact with the aboriginal tribes of the interior. Gregory Blaxland's masterly history of the post-war British Army explains that, 'The protection of the jungle-dwelling aborigines of the Seman and Sakai tribes' was the task. 'These scrawny little people had been completely at the mercy of the rebels and had been forced deeper into their service as the policy of food denial developed.

'Now the Special Air Service arrived by helicopter in groups of 15 and began to win over these nomad tribesmen, staying with them 13 weeks before relief.

'They built landing strips to enable them to market their supplies and brought them medical and engineering aid. Villages were turned into fortresses, in which police posts and even artillery were established. Much depended on the few lone persons who stayed to sell them the idea of self-defence. It was all part of the battle for hearts and minds.'

Resupply by helicopter, after its introduction in this role in 1954, presented peculiar problems. The noise generated by these machines was not conducive to security, so the SAS decided at one stage to try moving its bulk supplies into the jungle by elephant. On paper it looked like a good idea: the beasts were quieter than helicopters and not necessarily out of place in certain types of jungle. However, a thicket of bureaucracy had to be penetrated in order to arrange insurance for the animals. Only when this had been accomplished was it discovered that they would not enter the selected jungle anyway. It is one of the few recorded cases where even the SAS had to admit defeat.

Hearts, minds and head-hunters

For several months, the phrase 'hearts and minds' had reverberated around Malaya. Its author was the new, energetic Military High Commissioner, General Sir Gerald Templar. Asked in June 1952 whether he had sufficient troops, he had replied, 'The answer lies not in pouring more soldiers into the jungle, but rests in the hearts and minds of the Malayan people.' In fact, this was an admirable summary of the essence of SAS philosophy at the time, and has been so ever since. As one of the regiment's planners of the successful Dhofar operation was to put it years later, 'It was not our numbers but our ideas which made a big difference.' It was also the concept which Calvert had dreamed of when forming the Malayan Scouts.

Such politico-military operations were not so popular with more orthodox troops. For two months during the autumn of 1952, for instance, two battalions of 2/7th Gurkha Rifles, D Company of the 1st Fijian Infantry Regiment and two SAS squadrons were enmeshed in Operation 'Hive' around Seremban in Negri Sembilan. The history of 2/7th summarises what happened:

> Op Hive was designed to saturate a selected area with troops so that the terrorists' mode of life would be completely disrupted. A concentrated programme of police checks on roads and New Villages was planned in detail with the aim of driving the bandits back on to their jungle food dumps where they would be forced to eat up valuable reserves. Then the military units would move in to specific areas where it was hoped, by intensive ambushes and patrols, to force out the terrorists once more into the open or into the many 'stop' (ambush) positions, established on recorded and likely tracks in the jungle surrounding Seremban . . .
>
> A lot of men were required to close the chinks in the jungle, many more than were available . . . to search for about 100 bandits, hiding in an area exceeding 600 square miles . . . Only 16 of the enemy were killed and in the opinion of one or two officers, not all this total was directly attributable to

'Hive' . . . General Sir Gerald Templar visited the Seremban Operations Room during 'Hive' at a time when he was under considerable pressure from other districts to end the Operation so that troops could return to their normal duties. He was suitably impressed by the food denial aspect of the Operation and, with a typically terse 'Stick to it', he allowed the Operation to follow its planned course.

The impatience of the troops was understandable. But what they were learning was that there were no soft targets in the deep jungle. According to one estimate, 1800 man-hours were expended on patrol for every contact made with the enemy: the man-hour/kill ratio was even more daunting. In spite of this, there was competition among all units for a high body count, the greatest score being that of 1/10th Gurkhas with 300. The SAS, a late starter, 'scored' 108 during a nine-year period, which was the sort of return most infantry battalions achieved in one-third of the time. The SAS, however, was learning its fundamental role in life, a dual one of Intelligence gathering and perception shaping. Its real achievements, then and later, were much harder to quantify, and not dramatic enough to win medals: it was 1953 before the regiment achieved its first Mention in Dispatches, and late in 1957 before the first Military Cross and Military Medal were awarded to it. What is of more significance, perhaps, is that between 1951 and 1953, when the SAS started to penetrate hearts and minds in the jungle, casualties among British forces dropped sharply.

From 1953 onwards, the SAS was living more and more in the jungle during a series of long operations. Simultaneously, it was deeply involved in training Iban trackers in the fundamentals of modern soldiering. The head-hunters were now formally recognised as a locally raised unit of the British Army, the Sarawak Rangers. (So, at this stage, was 22 SAS: unlike the Territorial SAS, it was not yet part of the permanent Order of Battle.) The Rangers were issued with rifles which they sometimes used with more enthusiasm than effect.

Typical of the operations from 1954 onward, when the

enemy was becoming concentrated in certain identifiable areas of wilderness, was Operation 'Termite'. It lasted from July to November, and began with heavy bombing of the jungle by RAF Lincolns – an indiscriminate use of air power which was as likely to kill aborigines as Communist guerrillas, and one which the SAS regarded as counter-productive. (The mistake was not subsequently repeated in Borneo.) Two SAS squadrons, a total of 177 men, then parachuted into jungle clearings created by the bombs. That clearings had to be made in this way attests to the number of casualties suffered by the regiment in its attempts to perfect 'tree-jumping'. Even then, the drop generated four casualties. Such casualties were occurring not just as a result of the unpredictable behaviour of parachutes as they were 'bounced' by the thermal effect of air above the trees: the technique of abseiling out of the trees was also proving defective. In theory, the soldier detached himself from his parachute, lashed a long webbing strap to a branch, and descended safely to the ground. The webbing bulged at intervals, where it had been stitched, and therefore snagged at high speed as it travelled through D rings on the soldier's harness. As a result, three men were killed and one seriously injured taking part in Operation 'Sword' in January 1954, one of the deaths occurring after a soldier in great pain had cut away from the harness and fallen 150 feet.

In addition to the SAS, four infantry battalions took part in Operation 'Termite'. It resulted in the death, capture or surrender of only fifteen rebels, but, as Blaxland records, 'the gain was in the conversion of the aborigines to allies'.

Between 1955 and 1956, there were critically important changes in SAS organisation which at last set the regiment on a winning course. The formidable John Woodhouse returned to active campaigning as a squadron commander under a new commanding officer, Lieutenant-Colonel (later Lieutenant-General) George Lea. Lea wasted no time in weeding out officers who were not good enough for the SAS, and several were sent back to their original units. He was a large, tough character – 6 feet 4 inches tall and weighing sixteen stones – and had no time for the quaint customs of earlier days. (He was horrified, for instance, to learn that a sergeant who had hit the medical officer escaped with a reprimand and an order to shake hands with the officer he had struck.) Lea acquired good officers and promoted the best of those whom he inherited, such as John Cooper, who had started his career with Stirling in the desert. The new intake included Captain Peter de la Billière and Major Harry Thompson, red-haired and, like Lea, a big man, from the Royal Highland Fusiliers. Thompson would go on to become second-in-command of the regiment in Borneo, where he died in a helicopter crash. This team was the core of the regiment during its three most hectic years in Malaya.

Another decisive change was the replacement of the Rhodesian C Squadron with an equivalent group from New Zealand. The Rhodesians were tough, hard and willing; their leader, Peter Walls, would ultimately command all Rhodesia's armed forces after UDI; but some were also colour-conscious to a degree that was not helpful in the task of seducing aboriginal sympathies from the Communists. They were also peculiarly vulnerable to jungle diseases. The New Zealanders, by contrast, included a fair sprinkling of adaptable Maoris who made excellent trackers. Their presence in the SAS also encouraged the first Fijians serving in Malaya to transfer to the SAS. Most important of all, however, was the recognition that SAS soldiers could not be selected and trained in haste. The New Zealanders were hand-picked and given a thorough grounding in jungle warfare in Malaya's Jungle Warfare School before they went operational.

In the same year, 1955/6, the SAS in Malaya was further reinforced by a squadron drawn from the Parachute Regiment in England, known as the Parachute Regiment Squadron, and commanded by Major Dudley Coventry. By 1956, five squadrons totalling 560 men were operating in the jungle, and the number of people killed by the guerrillas had fallen to about half a dozen per month. From now on, the military problem was the pursuit of the estimated 2000 CT thought to be still at large to their increasingly remote bases, which now more resembled sanctuaries than launch-pads for offensive operations. It was a time when the skills of the hunter – concealment, tracking, endurance, coolness and lethally-accurate snap shooting – were at a premium, and the time when 22 SAS came into its own.

The soldier who personified these skills at the time was Sergeant Bob Turnbull, a gunner from Middlesbrough, who combined a quick intelligence and good ear for foreign languages with the grinding determination of a human bulldozer. Turnbull befriended an Iban tracker called Anak Kayan, and achieved an eye for spoor as accurate as Kayan's own, reading the splayed toe-prints of the aborigine for what they were; the terrorist footprint, which invariably revealed cramped toes that had once known shoes; and spotting a fine human footprint imposed by the more canny walker on an elephant footmark in an attempt to blur the trace.

Turnbull once followed the tracks of four men for five days until he spotted the hut they were occupying. He then waited for an impending rainstorm to arrive, correctly guessing that the sentries would then take shelter, and drew to within five yards of the hut before killing the four guerrillas sheltering there. On another occasion, he pursued a notorious guerrilla leader called Ah Tuck, a man who always went armed with a Sten carbine, ready cocked. When the two men finally encountered one another in the bush at a range of twenty yards, Ah Tuck died still holding his unfired weapon.

According to one officer who served with him, Turnbull used a repeater shotgun with such speed and accuracy that it would 'fill a man with holes like a Gruyère cheese'. (The shotgun, its use perfected by the SAS for close-quarter battle, has ever since been the subject of intensive study by US as well as British forces.) One officer who went on his first jungle patrol with Turnbull was unwise enough to insist that the sergeant act as back-marker to an Iban tracker and the officer himself. When this trio encountered a guerrilla, Turnbull instantly fired over the officer's shoulder and had disabled the terrorist while the officer concerned was still reminding himself of the drill for such situations, 'First, safety catch off . . .'

The hunt for Ah Hoi

One of the last major guerrilla hunts, near the Malacca Strait Coast in Selangor, was also one of the hardest. In February 1958 thirty-seven men (drawn from B and D Squadrons) led by Harry Thompson parachuted into a swamp covering an area measuring about eighteen miles by ten. Some veterans insist that this was the Telok Anson Swamp; others, with equal certainty, say it was at Sekinchang in Kuala Selagnor. The object of this operation was to kill or capture two groups of terrorists led by Ah Hoi, also known as 'The Baby Killer', after his murder of an informer's wife. She was pregnant. His accomplices held her down on a table while he slashed at her with a knife, before an audience of horrified villagers. Ah Hoi was now hiding in the swamp.

One B Squadron veteran, Roy ('Pud') Rice recalled a first light drop from a Beverley aircraft into bush some twelve miles from the edge of the swamp. Trooper Jerry Mulcahy suffered a serious spinal injury from this tree jump and had to be evacuated before the military operation began.

By now, the accumulation of casualties from this type of parachuting was such that no training jumps were permitted. As one veteran of the Telok Anson operation put it, 'You just got out of the aircraft and hoped to God you would land safely in the top of a tree.' One man, Trooper Mulcahy, was unlucky. He hit a tall tree, but his canopy did not catch the branches. The canopy collapsed and he dropped like a stone into the tree roots, breaking his back. The squadron's first task was to fell some trees so that a helicopter could evacuate Mulcahy. The clearance thus created was just enough to allow the aircraft's rotor blades to miss the foliage, but it was impossible to land because of the swampy terrain. Somehow, the pilot kept the machine hovering, with one wheel on a log, while the stretcher was taken aboard.

The initial search for Ah Hoi was led by de la Billière in a ten-day trek along river banks and through iron-brown water, the depth of which varied from shin to neck-height. The parts of the body that were submerged were the prey for leeches, the more enthusiastic of which could consume half a pint of the victim's blood before being detected; those areas not submerged were the target for the malarial mosquito and other insects. Each night, the patrol slung hammocks in the trees and enjoyed temporary respite from the swamp. A stay of more than one night made it worth the effort to construct a raft as a sleeping platform.

De la Billière's troop found several camps recently vacated by the terrorists, sites littered with the shells of turtles which the 'bandits' had eaten. Ah Hoi's men, it seemed, knew that they were being pursued. It is possible that the helicopter evacuation of Mulcahy had alerted them. De la Billière's route across the swamp followed the dominant feature of the place, the Tengi River. He reported his progress by radio to Thompson each evening, but made no contact with the enemy, who were now apparently heading up-river towards the centre of the swamp. Simultaneously, a second troop under Sergeant Sandilands was moving on a compass bearing in that direction also, picking a cautious way through the swamp during the hours of darkness, noses alert for the smell of guerrilla cooking fires, ears straining through the cacophony of bullfrog croaks for the sound of a human voice. By day, Sandilands and his men put out sentries and slept.

Finally, at dusk on about the seventh or eighth day, soon after they had resumed the march, Sandilands' troop spotted two of the enemy about seventy yards away across a stretch of open water. Sandilands and a corporal eased themselves into the water to get closer, floating a log before them to conceal their approach. They opened fire from about fifty yards, killing one of the men. The other disappeared. Next morning, the troop cautiously followed a four-mile trail to a freshly-abandoned camp.

Thompson now tightened the cordon round the guerrillas by moving his men to a point on the River Tengi miles upstream from the point that de la Billière had reached, before the two groups started closing towards one another in a pincer movement. Simultaneously, a huge military and police cordon was thrown round the swamp perimeter and barbed wire was laid along the coast, with a notice warning anyone who crossed it that he could be shot on sight. With the need for secrecy eliminated by the Sandilands contact, helicopters now flew daily missions to replenish SAS stocks of food and clothing and to scan any open spaces of water for signs of Ah Hoi. It was now twenty days since D Squadron had dropped into the swamp, and all the men were suffering from prickly heat and other infections. Thompson's legs, ripped by thorns and mildly infected, were a mass of ulcers.

Two days after the cordon had been imposed, a diminutive, emaciated woman in an olive green uniform emerged from the jungle and approached a security forces checkpoint in a paddy-field. She was taken before a Special Branch officer and identified herself as Ah Hoi's messenger, Ah Niet. Ah Hoi had a proposition for the security forces: a payment of £3500 by the government to each of his team and amnesty for those already in prison.

Ah Niet was told there would be no deal: Ah Hoi had a choice between surrendering within twenty-four hours, or death in the swamp where soldiers were already waiting for him. And if they failed, the RAF would bomb Ah Hoi out of hiding. Ah Niet, just 4 feet 6 inches tall, dissolved gnome-like, back into the jungle. Thompson, alerted by radio, flew with a troop of his men to a paddy-field and at dusk, shining torches, Ah Hoi and some of his men emerged. A contemporary account by Brian Connell reported, 'He was still arrogant, still ranting that the Reds would win in the end.' Given the choice of prison or exile in China, he initially chose China, then changed his mind, but was packed off to China all the same.

Ah Niet, meanwhile, led Thompson back into the swamp to make contact with another group of Ah Hoi's men who were ready to surrender. She led the way, swimming in total silence, 300 yards from a police post. It was her favourite entry-point and she had used it undetected for years. She was appalled at the amount of noise generated by the soldiers as they followed her. They did not find the remnant of the Ah Hoi band partly because Ah Niet's considerable strength now failed her. She was suffering from beri-beri, a vitamin deficiency disease. They emerged to surrender forty-eight hours later.

Whitehall jungle campaign

While the SAS was fighting on the ground to establish a reputation as a credible military force, a jungle war of a different kind was going on in Whitehall. In the long term, it was of even greater importance to the future of the SAS – if it had one – than Malaya. Argument about the role of special forces had been smouldering since 1945, and it had found early expression in the compromise function of 21 SAS, the volunteer Territorial regiment. Even this creation was regarded with hostility in some parts of the military establishment, which was suspicious of a 'private army' whose methods and objectives it did not understand.

Efforts to ensure the SAS a permanent place in the post-war regular army also hit opposition from officers who had a chip on their shoulders about the unit, either because they had been rejected for SAS service or because someone of, say, the rank of major had been treated to that terse form of advice – usually two words, of which the second was invariably 'off' – which SAS soldiers express when faced with obtuseness by higher authority. Such episodes should have no part in long-term military calculations, but armies are human organisations and some soldiers nurture grudges. It is also fair to say that some of the critics had a more substantial case, based on their contacts with the Malayan Scouts. The same men who had been company commanders in Malaya during those early days of 1950 to 1952 were staff officers in Britain by the time the political debate about the future of the SAS reached its climax between 1956 and 1957.

Another element in this domestic quarrel concerned relations between the SAS and the Parachute Regiment. The first SAS selection courses of post-war years in Britain were set up by Lieutenant-Colonel John Woodhouse in the autumn of 1952 at the Airborne Forces Depot, Aldershot. This was the home of the Parachute Regiment, an elite force for which, in those days, prior service with another unit followed by prolonged and stringent selection was required. Formal entry into the regiment, marked by the award of parachute wings and red beret, took place only after parachute training. The SAS, by contrast, trained for parachuting after acceptance.

There were other, more profound differences. The SAS emphasised individuality while the Paras, despite their advice to 'use your Airborne Initiative' to solve otherwise insoluble problems, were still much closer to orthodox traditions of infantry discipline. These differences, added to the mixed reputation of the Malayan Scouts, generated an attitude by the Paras towards SAS men that was at best patronising and at worst downright derisive. While they awaited posting to Malaya, SAS soldiers were used exclusively for menial, fatigue duties.

In the longer term, the SAS pioneers were disturbed by a possible takeover of their fledgling unit by the Paras. According to one account, the SAS Colonel Commandant of the day, General Miles Dempsey, accompanied the SAS course organiser, Woodhouse, in an abrasive discussion with the Parachute Regiment's depot commander, Colonel Pine Coffin, during which Dempsey apparently said, 'I hope it is clearly understood that there is no question of the SAS being taken over now or in the future by Airborne Forces.' In spite of that, attempts to absorb the SAS into Airborne Forces continued until about 1962.

In Whitehall, the long-term problem of the regiment's survival particularly concerned Dare Newell and the very few others who were not under pressure to survive the next twenty-four hours in the jungle. That the SAS did survive to fight another day during that critical decade before 1957 was the result of a committee of inquiry into the role of special forces, headed by a Lieutenant-General. This group soberly evaluated the impact of all the private armies of the Second World War, including the Long Range Desert Group, Lovat Scouts, Popski's Private Army, SAS, Paras, Commandos . . . even, it is jokingly suggested, the Royal Corps of Tree Climbers.

The committee found that there was a requirement in a general European war for two types of special operation behind enemy lines – in so far as mobile, modern warfare would have 'lines'. One was for long-term, deep penetration; the other, for short-term, shallow penetration. The first role, the committee found, would be most appropriately performed by the Special Air Service, the second by Royal Marine Commandos. By 1955, the range of officially-proposed SAS targets deep behind enemy lines in a general war, embraced everything from the kidnap of 'important enemy personalities' to 'attacks on important industrial targets invulnerable from the air'.

In 1956, a new Prime Minister, Harold Macmillan, appointed Duncan Sandys as his Defence Minister to clean up some of the mess generated by the Suez operation and Britain's changing world strategy. Sandys was to 'formulate policies to secure substantial reductions in expenditure and manpower' in all the armed forces. For a start, National Service conscription would be abolished gradually. This meant long-term planning for a much smaller army of professional volunteers. In the subsequent debate about which regiments should survive, the advocates of the SAS relied heavily on the findings of the earlier special forces report as a document untainted by partisan calculations. Several former Directors of Operations who liked the flexibility inherent in the SAS approach to war, backed up this argument.

On 24 July 1957, the Army Minister, John Hare, announced the cuts, and many familiar cap badges were to disappear through regimental amalgamation. The SAS survived, though only just, to become part of the permanent Order of Battle, but the regular 22 SAS Regiment was to be reduced from four squadrons to two. Implicit in this decision was the belief that the SAS would not be engaged in continuous campaigning around the Third World.

In the short run, with the end of the Malayan campaign in 1959/60, it was not difficult for the regiment to make the required cuts. Of the four squadrons serving in Malaya, one had come from New Zealand, to which it returned. Another was a Headquarters squadron. All the original British 'Sabre' (combat) squadrons – A, B and D – were well below their nominal, established strength. B Squadron was disbanded and its men absorbed by the other two. In Rhodesia, C Squadron was reduced in strength for several years. When it was raised again as the Rhodesian SAS Regiment, it continued to exist separately from the British 22 SAS both before and after the Rhodesian unilateral declaration of independence in 1964, at which point it became a 'lost legion'.

Although the SAS had won the first round in the battle for political survival, its existence continued to be questioned for several years. In Malaya it had justified itself, if perilously late in the day. What it now had to do was demonstrate that after nine years of jungle warfare it could function elsewhere. After all, the aboriginal Sarawak Rangers were also good in the jungle . . . Briefly and brilliantly, in a politically sensitive environment, the SAS would make its point in Northern Oman within days of leaving Malaya.

BORNEO 1962–66

The camouflaged victory

The jungle war between Indonesia and Britain euphemistically described by both sides as 'Confrontation', lasted four years. It was fought by a mixed Allied force, never greater than 28,000 men, including Gurkhas, Australians and New Zealanders, in an environment no more tractable than that of Vietnam. The enemy was a professional army well versed in jungle warfare, which sought to destabilise the fledgling Federation of Malaysia, of which some Allied territory was part, through clandestine guerrilla warfare and terrorism. When that did not succeed, the Indonesian government turned to all-out invasion, including airborne attacks on the Malay Peninsula.

The conflict ended in September 1966, with the clear-cut, unequivocal defeat of the invaders. Historically, however, the victory was mistimed. It occurred during a post-imperial epoch of British history – at home, the British were mesmerised by the hedonism of the Beatles, Flower Power and the Swinging Sixties – as a result of which it remained entirely uncelebrated, its architect acknowledged only through the award of a bar to his existing brace of DSOs until three years later, when he received a belated knighthood. Walker's friends attribute this enigmatic behaviour by Whitehall to the General's fierce opposition to a scheme of drastic cuts in the Gurkha force, of which he was the Brigade Major-General.

In keeping with such a low profile success, the role of the SAS was also discreet to the point of invisibility. The regiment's task was a classic one of deep penetration and Intelligence gathering across enemy lines, in which combat usually implied that something had gone wrong. This did not happen often. To express journalistically the problem of reconstructing this campaign, there was no story because man did not bite dog: things went according to plan most of the time. Having obtained early warning from SAS patrols of Indonesian attacks, the Allies were able to hit back with mobile reserves from the roads, waterways and the air, as well as creating ambushes in the jungle.

To measure, objectively, the success of the SAS in Borneo is rendered even more difficult by the regiment's characteristic neglect of archives and records until about 1970, and a traditional aversion to 'gong-hunting'. (This attitude, let it be said, is not due to excessive modesty, but more a sort of military existentialism: the important thing, in the SAS, is to be there when it happens, and then get on to the next operation.) There are, however, some historical hints about the regiment's silent contribution to a muffled victory. The first overall commander there, General Sir Walter Walker, rated the value of a few SAS soldiers equal to a thousand infantry, not because they had equivalent firepower, but because their Intelligence gathering and ability to shape civilian perceptions could save that number in battles won without a fight. Even Whitehall was happy. It was able, perhaps uniquely, to fine-tune offensive operations to achieve a precise political outcome as a result of SAS reconnaissance.

During the three years preceding the Borneo operations, the regular SAS had been learning for the first time to live through a period when it was not involved in active operations. Since the end of the Malayan campaign in 1959 and the intensive, but brief, intervention in northern Oman in the same year, there had been much discussion in the SAS about whether its future lay in Europe, or in Britain's shrinking share of the Third World.

'Third Worlders' v. 'Europeans'

The regiment was effectively divided between the 'Europeans', who felt that the long-term future of the SAS, politically as well as militarily, lay in finding a deep penetration and reconnaissance function with NATO forces; and the 'Third Worlders' who suspected that this course would smother the SAS under the bureaucracy of the British Army of the Rhine. Better, they said, to forage for an immediate place in a real campaign than play games in a mock war on the North German plain. Some had joined the SAS to escape from precisely this fate.

Influential people outside the regiment, however, were beginning to question its cost effectiveness. Some in Whitehall, thinking aloud, wondered whether it would be a good idea simply to absorb the two SAS squadrons into 16th Independent Parachute Brigade. A lack of knowledge among senior Army officers about what the SAS was supposed to be doing, and the skills it had acquired, did not discourage such thinking.

By the autumn of 1962, at about the time of the Cuban missile crisis, it seemed that the 'Europeans' had won the argument. The regiment was now retraining with the United States special forces for its new role and the long-term, hypothetical operations that implied. Its commanding officer, Lieutenant-Colonel John Woodhouse, had been a pioneer of the Malayan days, and had made a special study of Communist philosophy. As a result of this he encouraged the process, evolved by the Chinese, of continuous self-criticism. Among the 'thinking bayonets' of 22 SAS there was criticism anyway, but Woodhouse institutionalised it. The decisive moment for setting the new policy in concrete apparently came when the Director-General of Military Training, Lieutenant-General Sir Charles Richardson, visited SAS teams training in the USA. The men were learning foreign languages and advanced field medical training of a kind unthinkable in Britain. Stray dogs collected for destruction were anaesthetised before being killed. Gunshot wounds were then inflicted on the animals, which SAS 'bush doctors' learned to repair with basic surgery. Richardson, a pragmatic Royal Engineer, was impressed by the unique potential of 22 SAS and, within two months, Ministry of Defence clearance was given for the regiment to be re-equipped and modernised. Even more important was the change of political climate in Whitehall. In orthodox military circles the SAS was suddenly 'kosher'.

But Woodhouse, the Commanding Officer, was also at that time a convert to the 'domino' theory about Communist expansion in south-east Asia at a time when Vietnam was succeeding Malaya as the principal battleground of Asia. So he was hedging his bets and encouraging some of his men to learn Thai – on the basis that Thailand, a fellow member of the South East Asia Treaty Organisation, might come under attack next. By doing so, Woodhouse also satisfied some of the aspirations of the 'Third Worlders'.

On 8 December 1962, however, simultaneous guerrilla attacks were launched against police stations, government offices, a power-station and other strategically important centres in the Sultanate of Brunei. Brunei was one of three British dependencies in Borneo; the others were the colonies of North Borneo (later Sabah) and Sarawak; all were relics of nineteenth-century paternalism. These territories, extensive though they were, represented only one-quarter of the island. The rest belonged to Indonesia, whose head of state, President Sukarno – irreverently nicknamed 'The Mad Doctor' by British troops – had been inspired by the Japanese example to dream of unifying south-east Asia under his leadership.

The Brunei revolt, although a home-grown product, had been carefully fertilised by Indonesia. In response, a hasty, shoestring military operation launched from Singapore by Gurkhas, 42 Royal Marine Commando and the Queen's Own Highlanders, freed European hostages taken by the rebels and restored order in the coastal towns within a few weeks. But it was clear that a new jungle campaign was about to begin. The only question concerned the form it would take. Another Malaya? A Kenya? A Vietnam?

Woodhouse, scenting action, called on the Director of Military Operations at the Defence Ministry in London. The commanding officer of 22 SAS wanted the regiment to have a place in Borneo. His most persuasive argument was that in addition to the perfection of its jungle warfare skills during the painful, formative years in Malaya, the regiment could provide for this new campaign the uniquely valuable service of reliable, long-distance Morse communication on the radios with which it had now been issued. As the Gurkhas were to discover to their cost on one disastrous occasion, Borneo's jungle atmospherics could be so bad that the normal procedure of standing-to – that is, preparing for action at the main rear base – every time an outpost failed to make its daily broadcast, had to be dropped. Woodhouse, as it happened, had been studying the problem of long-distance communications in the context of the European, nuclear role. He was very persuasive.

Three days later, accompanied by a signaller and some of the new radios, he arrived in Brunei. Walker had gladly accepted the offer of an SAS squadron for the campaign because he was then short of helicopters and, as a Gurkha who admired SAS parachute operations into the Malayan jungle, he believed that the SAS would be just the thing for use as a mobile, reserve company of infantry. Woodhouse, with vivid memories of the casualties that had resulted from Malayan 'tree-jumping', to say nothing of the loss of security caused by the need to evacuate the casualties, shuddered inwardly. He explained to Walker that the SAS was not trained for orthodox infantry tactics even in the jungle, and that a company of, say, the Parachute Regiment would be more suitable for the task. He went on to expound the SAS's peculiar value in Borneo. These were men who could operate in pairs, or alone if necessary, living among the tribes, speaking Malay – of which enough was known in Borneo to make it a lingua franca – and, most important, providing an Intelligence and communications network in the blank areas of Walker's knowledge. Like any sensible commander, Walker was worried about these blank areas. He 'bought' Woodhouse's proposition and, within three days, 22 SAS was flying to Borneo, the old hands slinging hammocks wherever they could find space in the aircraft, conserving their energy for the conflict to come.

One of the first people with whom they made contact was a British surveyor, Tom Harrisson, who had led an underground tribal resistance movement against the Japanese during the Second World War, and who had now raised his own aboriginal force to cut off the surviving rebels as they fled inland from Brunei towards the sanctuary of Indonesia.

The regiment also renewed old friendships with veterans of the Sarawak Rangers, Iban tribal trackers and head-hunters brought to the Malay Peninsula in the 1950s as teachers and pupils of the SAS during that campaign. As pupils, the Iban had learned something about modern soldiering and firearms from the SAS; as teachers, they had given the regiment a feeling for tracking an enemy in the jungle, silently and invisibly. Few of these Malayan veterans were still living their old life as hunters in the Borneo jungle – some had even taken to driving taxis – and in most cases their jungle sense had deteriorated. But the SAS proceeded anyway to regain its own former expertise and self-reliance in conditions that others, even the Gurkhas, sometimes found almost impossible.

The 700-mile front

When the SAS arrived in Brunei in January 1963, the revolt had been extinguished, but Intelligence reports as well as Sukarno's public speeches made it clear that Indonesia's campaign of subversion was not to be confined to Brunei. Sabah in the north-east and Sarawak, stretching east-west across the island, were equally at risk. As Blaxland explains:

> The frontier lay open and unmarked across 970 miles of wild and mountainous country, over which raids could, and undoubtedly would be made without warning at any point, and the coastline was very much longer and just as vulnerable. The total area to be protected was slightly larger than England and Scotland, and there were only five battalions (including the Royal Marine Commando) available, controlled by a brigade headquarters at Kuching and another at Brunei, and with the need for a regular system of reliefs over an interminable period, there was no immediate prospect of any great increase.

In an effort to fill the gap, SAS teams from A Squadron, usually between two and four men, were staked out across

700 miles. Each team was responsible for a 10,000-yard front sited to block most of the obvious approaches from Kalimantan, as Indonesian Borneo was called; these generally consisted of natural faults in the mountain ridge, which lay across the centre of Borneo like a quiff, and down those jungle motorways, the rivers.

It would be clearly impossible for these minuscule teams personally to watch over such an area. The trick was to arrange matters so that the jungle tribes would act as scouts for the SAS teams, who would be the reporting centre for each locality. In an environment in which as little as five miles a day might be an ambitious tactical movement, a spoor even a day old was valuable information for a defence force equipped with helicopters. Basically, therefore, it was the mixture as before, in Malaya: the hearts-and-minds business to yield information; airborne assault plus familiarity with the jungle to follow it up.

But this was a very special environment. As Blaxland describes it:

> The interior was a roadless confusion of jungle and rivers . . . Innumerable village settlements or kampongs were to be found, either by the river or on a hillside, from which tribesmen of many varieties primitively tilled the land around them or went hunting for fish, deer, baboons, porcupines or the ever-pervasive snakes.
>
> They lived in longhouses which were made of attap wood, had foetid interiors and were apt to creak balefully on the stilts that had kept them out of the water for decades. The Iban of Sarawak . . . were small, cheerful and indolent people, who neither cut their hair nor dressed above the waist, regardless of sex, except when attired in ceremonial finery, which was worn for visiting soldiery who would be primed with rice-wine and invited to do a solo dance.

There was no question here, as in Malaya, of forcibly transplanting populations into new, fortified villages. In any case, most of the tribespeople were well-disposed towards the

British. For the rest, the troops had to rely on charm, quick wits and little else – the weapons of non-violence. Styles varied. One of the Gurkha regiments, with more men than the SAS, concluded that 'the old system of giving salt, tobacco, sugar and beads was wrong for Borneo. Tact, courtesy and, above all, infinite patience and human understanding were needed . . . Bartering of a minor nature continued non-stop . . . It was also important to uphold at all times the dignity and prestige of the local headman. One way of accomplishing this was by allowing him to take the salute at "Retreat".' At ceremonial dances, some British officers achieved a *succès d'estime* by performing the Twist.

Nearer the mountainous border, the SAS approach was to move into the village, cautiously and sensitively, and to live there for five months or more. Tom Pocock, in his biography of General Walker, recounts how 'at first some of the SAS men were sent up-country in civilian clothes; an unexpectedly difficult task because the shirts and jeans on sale in Borneo shops were cut for diminutive Chinese figures, not hulking British troopers'. But disguise was quickly discarded as unnecessary, and the patrols wore the usual jungle green denims and soft brimmed hats with a yellow band for identification.

The first step towards penetration was to build a secret hide in the jungle within walking distance of the selected village. Having kept the place under observation long enough to ensure that neither guerrillas nor Indonesian regulars were already established, the soldiers would walk in, smile, and make contact. Sometimes conversation was possible through the medium of Malay; sometimes a basic sign-language evolved. When this failed, as one veteran wearily recalls, 'they would sit and look at us, and we would sit and look at them'. This entertainment was somewhat one-sided, since the soldiers were probably the first Europeans most of the villagers had seen. On a good day, the SAS patrol would be invited into the animal closeness of the collective longhouse and offered rice-wine and food, before taking their leave to sleep in their hide (basha), endeavouring to conceal the trail as they went.

The next day they would be back. Their message was that evil men from across the mountain were coming, and that the soldiers were there to protect the village. This, when finally comprehended, did not always fill headhunting tribesmen with awe. So, to close a growing credibility gap as well as to rehearse essential reinforcement tactics, A Squadron's commander, Major Peter de la Billière, devised the 'step-up' technique. For this, a full infantry company would be warned to be ready to move by helicopter to a remote forward location for a demonstration of quick deployment and firepower. On the day set for this exercise, the SAS soldiers would explain to the villagers that although the soldiers were only two in number, they had many friends, other warriors who could descend from the sky to their aid. It would be particularly helpful if the necessary space could be created for the flying soldiers to land safely. The tribesmen, who are adept at removing large trees with small, flexible axes, were fascinated by the prospect of such entertainment, and a helicopter landing zone was rapidly carved out of the jungle. The soldiers then radioed the message, 'Bring in the step-up party now!' About fifteen minutes later the helicopters would appear, loaded with business-like Gurkhas armed with sharpened kukris as well as modern firearms. The show usually brought the longhouse down.

Gifts of portable radios, simple medical aid and other favours rapidly ensured that the SAS team became an institution in the community, though with one exception, its aid rarely achieved the elaboration recorded by 2/7th Gurkhas whose native protégés 'made endless requests for trips to outlying kampongs (villages), movement of rice, planks, children, old people and pigs by helicopter . . . The locals came to rely more on the soldiers and airmen than on the civil administration . . .' One young and rich SAS troop commander expressed this hearts-and-minds offensive by flying out, at his own expense, hampers of Christmas food from Fortnum and Mason's exclusive London store to supply the nomads in his part of Borneo. Another unique contribution to village life was made by an SAS soldier of Romany origins, 'Gipsy Smith'. A natural improviser, he constructed a waterpowered generator to provide the only electric light in thousands of square miles. For his next trick, he dismantled his Bergen rucksack and converted its metal frame to a still for making alcohol.

The message that accompanied these diversions was always the same: danger lay on the other side of the mountains and one day it would move closer. The villagers must help themselves by staying alert for anything unusual seen in the surrounding jungle, particularly the characteristic mark of a rubber-soled boot. Could the villagers select one of their number to be a link-man with the soldiers? They could.

By now the SAS team would have its own quarters on the edge of the village, broadcasting daily reports to Squadron Headquarters. The team might be augmented by one or two members of the local police field force. Regularly the team would make a circular tour of the area, lasting up to five days, visiting a series of villages. Like village policemen, they moved on foot. Unlike village policemen they moved unobtrusively, in single file, the lead scout of the patrol followed by the commander and his radio operator, with a gun carrier at the rear playing 'tail-end Charlie'.

Only towards the end of this first five-month tour did something happen to remind even the SAS that the threat about which they had been preaching was real. In the early hours of Good Friday morning, 12 April 1963, a force of thirty guerrillas surrounded the police station at the border town of Tebedu in West Sarawak. After a brisk battle, in which a police corporal was killed and two others wounded, the raiders looted the bazaar.

When the news reached the local military HQ, a troop of Royal Marine Commandos was sent to the scene. The raiders had disappeared back into the undergrowth, leaving leaflets which purported to show that the action was a manifestation of the earlier revolt in Brunei. Later evidence was to sustain the intelligent guesses made at the time that the raid was probably led by Indonesian regulars.

At a remote border kampong known as Rundun, a four-man SAS team was preparing to hand over to a relief group from D Squadron. When the Tebedu attack took place, two of the soldiers from this group had already started the twenty-five-mile journey to the rendezvous, more than a day's march away, in order to guide their successors. Meanwhile, the remaining pair had received an urgent signal from the squadron's operations room, telling them of the Tebedu affair, instructing them to stay at their location and to dig in. This phrase, conjuring up as it did, a vision of divisions massed on the Marne, caused some merriment. The team's reaction was: 'What, both of us?'

From now on, the war followed an inevitable course. More troops and helicopters were summoned to Borneo, and a search of towns in Sarawak brought to light plans by the Clandestine Communist Organisation (CCO) for Malayan-style terrorism. The police began the confiscation of the 8500 licensed shotguns circulating among the Chinese community. There were more cross-border raids from Indonesian soil, and a night curfew was imposed on Sarawak during which the security forces could open fire without prior warning.

On the long, unmarked frontier there could never be enough men to achieve total security. But the success of the SAS in creating a defensive Intelligence network among the tribesmen encouraged General Walker to create, with the help of the SAS and others, the indigenous Border Scouts. This was a controversial decision, if only because experience in Malaya had shown that, while it may be expedient to arm tribesmen and train them as guerrillas in time of crisis, they are impossible to disarm when the crisis is over, with disastrous results for long-term internal security. A more short-term consideration was the role the Scouts would fill.

Inevitably, perhaps, the tribesmen, trained as Border Scouts by the Gurkha Independent Parachute Company in basic weapon-handling and battle tactics within three short weeks, more closely resembled orthodox infantry than the SAS pupils, who were encouraged to think of themselves as the eyes and ears, rather than the fists of their allies. As one Gurkha regimental history acknowledges: 'Although the use of the Scouts in this way involved border kampongs and longhouses in the defence of their own country and kin, their suitability for employment in defensive static positions was limited.'

The unsuitability of the Scouts for this sort of warfare, even under the overall command of such an experienced jungle hand as Lieutenant-Colonel John Cross, became tragically apparent in September 1963. At Long Jawi in Central Borneo, thirty miles from the border, the Gurkhas had established a Scout post consisting of twenty-one locals, two Police Field Force signallers and a six-man Gurkha team headed by a corporal. Just before dawn one day, a well-equipped company of Indonesian regulars fell upon Long Jawi. The signallers were killed as they tried unsuccessfully to summon aid. The raiders looted the village, destroyed it by fire, and withdrew.

The Gurkha HQ attributed radio silence from Long Jawi to bad atmospheric conditions until, four days later, one Border Scout and two surviving Gurkhas reached the headquarters, 'weak and exhausted, but with weapons spotlessly clean, and able to give a first-hand account of the battle'. Gurkha ambush parties were flown into the area, and during the next month most of the Indonesians were hunted down, sometimes in ones and twos, after their escape craft had been shot to pieces by Gurkhas waiting on the river banks. Vengeance had been exacted but the lesson, that such warfare was a matter for professionals, was not lost on Walker and his advisers. More SAS soldiers were needed, and urgently, in the border area. Meanwhile, on Walker's orders the role of the Border Scouts was changed – no more paramilitary work, and exclusive concentration on Intelligence-gathering activities.

Squadrons restored

As a long-term measure, Whitehall approved the restoration of the two SAS squadrons that had been axed at the end of the Malayan Emergency four years earlier, in 1959. John Watts, one of the regiment's most experienced soldiers, started work in England soon afterwards to raise a new B Squadron – for which recruitment teams toured BAOR – while the Parachute Brigade's Guards Independent (Pathfinder) Company was sent to Borneo to learn something like an SAS role on the job (as was the 2nd Battalion, the Parachute Regiment). Later, the Guards Company would provide the nucleus of the new G Squadron.

Also from Britain, the Headquarters of 22 SAS arrived to occupy a position overlooking the palace of the Sultan of Brunei. This building was known as the Haunted House: during the Japanese occupation it had been used for interrogation by Tokyo's Gestapo, and it was popularly believed that the spirit of a young European woman, a victim of torture, lingered there.

Almost coinciding with the attack at Long Jawi, a series of political events elsewhere generated SAS reinforcements from New Zealand and Australia. Less than two weeks before the attack, Sarawak and North Borneo (Sabah) were granted independence, and they promptly joined the Malaysian Federation. (The event was celebrated in the Indonesian capital, Jakarta, with a mob attack on the British Embassy, where the stone-throwers exposed themselves to a withering barrage of bagpipe music played by an SAS officer there, Major Roderic Walker, as he marched back and forth in front of the embattled building.) Since Malaysia was a member of the South East Asia Treaty Organisation, the Australian and New Zealand SAS regiments each sent a squadron to Sarawak, the Australians responding to a visit by Woodhouse to their Perth headquarters early in 1964. As in Malaya in the 1950s, the New Zealanders – possibly because of the number of Maoris in their ranks – were to produce the best jungle trackers the SAS ever had.

This extra manpower enabled the next British squadron on tour in the island – D Squadron, fresh from training in West Germany and Norway – to concentrate its efforts on the shorter frontier between Indonesia and Brunei, which had chosen to remain a British protectorate rather than join the new Federation. The efforts of D Squadron, as Philip Warner's official history of the regiment records, had tangible results: 'Several brisk engagements, including one in which nine out of a party of 21 rebels were captured, and the remainder fled, leaving most of their weapons and ammunition behind.' But fundamentally, in the autumn of 1963, it was the mixture as before: long days in the villages, longer marches between them, for five months. An anonymous contributor to the regimental journal, *Mars & Minerva*, described it thus:

> Four men, living as members of the longhouse itself for months at a time, watch, listen, patrol and report . . . Day by day, the sick come for treatment, the women bring presents of fruit and vegetables, the men to gossip and bring news, the children to watch, silent-eyed and the leaders of the community to discuss their problems and to ask, and offer advice. The patrol slips as easily into the primitive rhythm of the day and season as the people themselves. Soon the cycle of burning, planting, weeding and harvesting becomes part of [the soldier's] life itself, and customs, rites and celebrations as familiar as the Cup Final or Bank Holidays at home . . .
>
> Here a strong patrol of five or six men will train ten or twenty times that number of tribesmen in counter-terrorist warfare. In each camp a simple longhouse houses the Scouts; a similar, but smaller version, their instructors. The daily programme is long and arduous, though the syllabus is basic and directly related to the skills required to be taught.
>
> The patrol embraces all responsibilities for its charge: training, administration, discipline and morale. The language difficulty is ever present . . . pantomime is popular and some are skilful exponents of the art. Helicopter training without helicopters is a useful test piece. Throwing live grenades presents other problems, but no pantomime is necessary . . .

December 1963, this military idyll came to an abrupt halt when 128 guerrillas struck at the prosperous area of Tawau on the coast of Sabah, destroying a force of the Royal Malay Regiment in its own base twenty miles from the border. True, the raiders were all subsequently killed or taken prisoner by 1/10th Gurkhas, but the identification of twenty-one of the enemy as regular Indonesian Marines confirmed that this was no longer a routine counter-insurgency campaign.

Walker, the military supremo, himself characterised the year 1963 as one 'which began with the end of a revolution and ended with the beginning of an undeclared war'. Within a few weeks there were to be other, similar attacks. In January 1964, the British SAS Squadron moved back to the sensitive, unmapped mountain border of central Sarawak, known as the Third Division.

Cross-border operations: 'Those bloody ghosts'

It was not long after this that the regiment started to mount its first cross-border reconnaissance missions, which would ultimately identify the camps from which the Indonesian regulars came and the exact routes they followed to their targets in Malaysia. Such operations were – and are – ultra-sensitive politically as well as militarily, normally requiring approval from the Prime Minister in London. In this case, such operations marked the decisive turning-point of the war in Britain's favour.

The first cross-border patrols were gentle, shallow probes over the ridge into Indonesian territory by four-man groups unaccompanied by local guides. The men carried exactly the same equipment and weapons that were being used in Sarawak. If wounded and taken prisoner, the men themselves, as well as their headquarters, would attribute their presence in Indonesian territory to a simple map-reading error. In the circumstances it would be a fairly plausible cover story. As Pocock puts it: 'The SAS was, as usual, a law unto itself and on reconnaissance missions would sometimes penetrate into what was certainly enemy-held territory.'

Another element in almost all SAS operations in Borneo, to which particular emphasis was now given across the border, was Woodhouse's policy of 'shoot-'n'-scoot' (to break contact with the enemy as soon as possible) whenever contact occurred. Woodhouse, as he admitted years later, was strenuously influenced by his own experience in a ten-man reconnaissance section during the Second World War, when only he and one other returned from a single operation. It had not been easy to find volunteers to replace the lost men.

In Borneo, conscious that he had only two operational front-line squadrons totalling about 120 men, Woodhouse was not going to allow heavy casualties to destroy the morale or the credibility of the regiment in London at such a time. 'Shoot-'n'-scoot' was not popular with the SAS, and both officers and men said so; but there was much to recommend the policy for cross-border operations. As Woodhouse explained subsequently: 'There was a tendency in military circles to fear that the SAS would suddenly take matters into their own hands and that the first news of this to reach the top would be that 200 Indonesians had been shot up in bed. I used to emphasise that it was more important, for that sort of reason, that we should be seen to obey orders than anyone.'

The success of the first patrols into Kalimantan led to something more ambitious. The SAS was given the task of finding the exact river routes used by the Indonesians to move men and equipment up to the border. The recce patrols counted the boats and the men in them, mapped suitable areas from which the boats could be ambushed on the river bank, and quietly walked back over the mountain ridge to Sarawak. Next, the patrols were asked to find the kampongs and bases from which the boats had come. This was an ambitious undertaking which, if it went wrong, could not be dismissed as a mere map-reading error. By now, the first squadron commander to take part in the patrols had given much thought to the preparation of his men. By temperament a man who prefers to resolve problems before they arise, he typically organised random urine and blood tests to ensure that they were taking their prophylactic doses of Paludrin to avoid malaria. For these deep penetration patrols, he took men to the airport to weigh their Bergen rucksacks on the only available scales before they flew by helicopter to the jungle entry-point. If a rucksack weighed an ounce more than fifty pounds (later reduced to thirty) something had to come out, for the emphasis now, unlike the situation in Malaya, was not upon how much a human being could carry, but how far he could travel and function as a soldier carrying the minimum of equipment. As one of his officers remarked: 'You can't go head down, arse up when you are in close proximity to the enemy.'

It was also decreed that nothing be left in enemy territory to betray the presence of British troops: no casualties who might be identified; no spent cartridge cases; no cigarette stubs; no identity discs, photographs or letters from home; not even the heel print of a standard British military boot. So the deep penetration patrols were equipped with the Armalite rifle, which had several advantages. It was the perfect jungle weapon – portable and powerful – and, although circulating in considerable quantities around the world, not standard issue to the British Army. Irregular footwear was preferred or, if this were impossible in the Borneo jungle, sacking or hessian was placed outside the boot to blur all marks indicating its origin.

Above all, the job was one for soldiers who were natural navigators and men who had a feel for the country, with one complete tour of Borneo duty under their belts. It was no time to get lost, since no rescue would be forthcoming. Furthermore, the only certain way to find the Indonesian bases was to follow the spoor left by the enemy's raiding parties. The reconnaissance groups had to be superlative trackers.

Having arrived at their destination, the SAS 'moles' were expected to establish not just the location of the base and its approximate strength but also to draw the most detailed sketch maps of the place they could. This meant penetrating the kampongs in which the Indonesian soldiers lived, without alerting sentries or dogs, and then slipping back to the blessed cover of the deep jungle.

When they finally emerged into friendly territory after three weeks or more, their uniforms sometimes hanging in rags, their appearance often appalled Allied troops. One, recollecting the emaciated condition of these military apparitions, said afterwards: 'They looked like bloody ghosts left over from the war against the Japanese. And they said nothing, nothing, except: "Hello. Hold your fire. We're British".'

Loss of body weight was inevitable when the men were obliged to live on dehydrated rations yielding 3500 calories per day instead of the recommended level of 5000. Upon their return, some men had to be debriefed (one day); allowed total rest (two days); and briefed for the next patrol (two days): a total of just five days in which to eat like hamsters and replace some of the lost weight before another trip across the border. After three of these patrols, most of the soldiers were so worn out that they needed recuperation in England. It was not surprising that Whitehall's attempts to extend SAS tours to six months or more – to reduce travel costs – were fiercely and successfully resisted by the regiment's commanding officer.

The navigation for these operations was achieved through careful scrutiny of air photographs, cultivation of a photographic memory for such features as ridges and rivers and the compass bearings on which they ran, as well as a finely-tuned sense of distance walked to calculate a dead reckoning of mileage covered by reference to time-on-march. Tracking required the knack of seeing, as if they were motorway signposts, traces of human urine, crushed grass, muddied river crossings, bruised moss and broken bark on exposed tree roots. It required also the knowledge that fallen leaves, when brushed aside at the right spot, could reveal a perfectly shaped boot-print impressed in the soft earth beneath.

The recipe for concealment was that which General Walker had laid down for the Gurkhas when in ambush: 'No chance . . . if he smoked, chewed gum, washed his hands with soap, cleaned his teeth, Brylcreemed his hair, whispered or coughed. In ambush, a man is lying in wait for a dangerous, hunted animal whose sense of smell and eyesight can be phenomenal.' The nerve needed for these clandestine operations could not be taught. They involved a form of stress that scarred even the most stable SAS soldiers in some way. After they had experienced weeks of silence and near-silent communication, their comrades noticed, on their return to England, that some veterans of the Borneo patrols could not break the habit of whispering to each other, even when exchanging a joke in the men's room behind their favourite Hereford pub.

Such labours bore fruit a few months later in mid-1964 when, faced by increasingly bold attacks from the Indonesian side, General Walker sanctioned counterstrikes, first by artillery, then by 'killer' groups drawn from the best infantry battalions and led by SAS guides.

These were known collectively as 'Claret' operations and were hardly less sensitive than the reconnaissance that preceded them.

An offensive with golden rules

'Claret' operations were governed by what were colloquially known as the 'Golden Rules' and they were graded Top Secret. The initial penetration depth permitted into Indonesia was 5000 yards and this was increased, for certain specific raids, to 20,000. The objective, according to Brigadier E. D. ('Birdie') Smith of the Gurkha Rifles, was: 'to pre-empt any likely build-up or attack, to harass by ambush and patrols the Indonesians, and to induce them to move their camps back and away from the border . . . Initially, the guidelines were:

a. All raids had to be authorised by the Director of Operations (General Walker) himself.
b. Only tried and tested troops were to be used – in other words no soldiers were to be sent across . . . during their first tour in Borneo.
c. Raids were to be made with the definite aim of deterring and thwarting aggression by the Indonesians. No attacks were to be mounted in retribution or with the sole aim of inflicting casualties on the foe.
d. Close air support could not be given except in an extreme emergency . . .'

For a time, Smith explains, only Gurkha battalions could be used for offensive cross-border operations in addition to SAS soldiers, and no unit was to mount more than one raid at a time. Finally, 'Minimum force was to be the principle used rather than large-scale attacks which would have incited retaliation and risked escalation, turning the border war into something quite different, costly in lives and fraught with international problems.'

The guides for these raids were usually (though not invariably) provided by the SAS, who found them almost relaxing after the nervous isolation of the earlier reconnaissance. As one SAS veteran said: 'Having done your recce, and crept around and done all the sneaky bits, when you came back as part of a Gurkha company you felt as safe as houses in the middle of their perimeter: all those little brown men with GPMGs going out in all directions to set up listening posts . . .' Safer, yes, but on windless, silent days in the jungle, no less stealthy, as the history of 2/7th Gurkha Rifles reveals: 'No rifleman was allowed to eat, smoke or unscrew his water bottle without his platoon commander's permission. At night, sentries checked any man who snored or talked in his sleep. Whenever the company was on the move, a recce section led the way, their packs carried by the men behind. Because of the long approach march, each man carried six days' basic rations together with various lightweight additions and a small reserve in a belt pouch.'

The effect of the raids was often devastating. At one Indonesian Army camp, the enemy were breakfasting on roast pig when the Gurkhas arrived. In thick undergrowth, the patrol brought rocket-launchers, grenade-throwers and machine-guns into position. Then, as the regimental history records:

> The happy camping scene by the river was shattered as a 3.5-inch rocket flared across the water and exploded among the breakfast party. The hut disintegrated in a ball of flame, the men hurled in all directions . . .
>
> As two assault platoons moved in to clear the camp they contacted a number of totally naked, panic-stricken enemy rushing from it. These were quickly dealt with and, covered by fierce fire from the support group, we assaulted the base. Resistance had ceased, but a number of dead lay scattered about the camp and blood was everywhere.

Unaccompanied SAS units also began to attack enemy approach routes. According to Pocock's account, once formal government approval was received for such activities, the SAS, 'instead of watching and counting', would be given permission to begin interdiction: ambushing tracks and rivers and setting booby-traps where it was known that only raiders would pass. Sometimes their ambushes would be sophisticated affairs with electronically detonated Claymore mines catching an enemy party's front and rear, while the SAS troopers' automatic fire raked the centre. Because the essence of SAS activity was speed of movement and reaction, they called themselves 'The Tiptoe Boys'. The ambush parties hit and vanished, leaving the counter-attack to find nothing but apparently empty jungle.

The impact of such operations was not always so one-sided. On both the reconnaissance and offensive patrols things could, and did, misfire. An Australian SAS trooper was gored by an elephant while in Indonesian territory. His companion bound his wounds and made him as comfortable as possible before starting a two-day trek for help from a Gurkha camp. The wounded man had died by the time he was found. Unusually, the body was recovered by helicopter. Deaths on such occasions usually meant the removal of all identification from the body and quick burial in an unmarked grave. In another episode, a 22 SAS sergeant who had contracted the jungle disease leptospirosis was lucky to survive his 20,000-yard march home while suffering from a 105-degree temperature and other symptoms.

Inevitably, SAS reconnaissance groups were occasionally ambushed by the opposition despite all precautions. As a veteran of the Borneo patrols explained: 'The man who is stationary in the jungle has the tactical advantage. We sometimes found it necessary to spend as much as twenty minutes in any half-hour period sitting and listening, and only ten minutes on the move.' Only once was an SAS soldier taken prisoner. A wounded trooper, seized after an ambush, was never seen again, but the regiment subsequently learned from local tribesmen that he had been tortured so appallingly that he died before his captors could 'break' him. There were also some near-misses. Two SAS men had to be winched by helicopter out of the jungle so quickly that they were carried, still dangling from a rope, through the treetops for much of their journey. One of the men lost his rifle in the process, and a search had to be mounted to recover the weapon.

The Lillico patrol

One of the best-documented cases of such an escape, recorded in the regiment's journal *Mars & Minerva*, describes what happened to a patrol from D Squadron in February 1965.

A small 22 SAS patrol was moving down from a ridge on a jungle track towards an old Indonesian border terrorist camp. The camp had been discovered the day before and appeared as though it had not been used for six months.

As the leading scout, Trooper Thomson, ducked under some bamboo across the track – there was a lot of it in the area – a movement attracted his attention. He looked up and saw an Indonesian soldier six yards away to his right, just as the latter fired a burst at him. Several other enemy opened fire simultaneously.

Thomson was hit in the left thigh, the bone being shattered, and was knocked off the track to the left. He landed in a clump of bamboo two yards away from another Indonesian soldier lying concealed there. As the latter fumbled for his rifle, Thomson picked up his own, which he had dropped as he fell, and shot him.

'The second man in the patrol, the commander, Sergeant E. Lillico, was also hit by the initial bursts and had collapsed on the track, unable to use his legs. He was still able to use his rifle, however, and this he did, returning the fire. Meanwhile the remainder of the patrol had taken cover.

Thomson, unable to walk, hopped back to where Sergeant Lillico was sitting and joined in the fire fight. As he had seen Thomson on his feet, Lillico was under the misapprehension that he could walk and therefore sent him back up the track to bring the rest of the patrol forward, and continued to fire at the sounds of enemy movement.

As Thomson was unable to get to his feet, he dragged himself along by his hands and, on arriving at the top of the ridge, fired several bursts in the direction of the camp . . . The enemy withdrew . . .

During the remainder of the day, Thomson continued to

drag himself towards where he expected to find the rest of the patrol. He had applied a tourniquet to his thigh, which he released from time to time, taken morphia, and bandaged his wound as best he could with a shell dressing.

Lillico, meanwhile, 'pulled himself into the cover of a clump of bamboo, took morphia, bandaged his wound, and passed out . . . The remainder of the patrol had decided that the best course of action was to move to the nearest infantry post close by and lead back a stronger party to search the area. This they did, starting back towards the scene of the contact late the same day.'

The following morning, Thomson continued to crawl back towards the border, and by evening he had covered 1000 yards, or about half the distance involved. He was found by the search party just before dusk, carried to a clearing next day and evacuated by helicopter.

On the second day, meanwhile, Lillico had dragged himself to the top of a ridge, 400 yards from the scene of the action. At about 3pm, he fired signal shots to attract the attention of any friendly search party. Instead, the shots attracted more enemy troops, one of whom climbed a tree about forty yards from the spot where the sergeant lay quietly in the scrub. Twice during the day, Lillico had heard a helicopter overhead, but because of the proximity of the Indonesians he did not disclose his position. In the evening, the helicopter returned for the third time that day, identified Lillico's signal, and winched him to safety about thirty-six hours after the action. Lillico was awarded the Military Medal and Thomson was Mentioned in Dispatches.

The superior sergeant-major

It was not only the small parties that hit trouble. From May to October 1965, Squadron Sergeant-Major L. Smith ran the SAS operations room for an area of the Sarawak border 382 miles across, the longest battalion front in Allied Borneo. Such a task, as the historians of 2/7th Gurkha Rifles point out, had not been the responsibility of any SAS rank below that of captain during post-war years. Smith, they reveal, was 'entirely responsible for mounting SAS patrols, maintaining liaison with battalion commanders and for the considerable work involved in mounting and running the patrol operations. He personally led several dangerous and exacting operations when detailed preliminary reconnaissance reports were needed.'

As a result of one of these patrols, a Gurkha company of forty men set off to ambush Indonesian water traffic. Instead, it ran into an Indonesian company of 100 men marching along the same track beside the river. A confused, close-quarter battle followed in which grenades, machine-guns and Claymore mines were used. Smith had not accompanied the patrol beyond an advance base position because of a cough which might have compromised the operation. But 'he had realised that something had gone wrong, so he had worked out a complete fire plan for the (artillery) gun support' and, as the first survivors straggled in, 'brought down a very close-in defensive fire which helped the Gurkhas to make a clean break'. As one Gurkha said later: 'Without his help we would have been faced with a running battle back to the border.'

Now it was discovered that some of the Gurkhas were missing. About thirty-six hours after the initial contact a New Zealand gunner captain who had been with the patrol walked into the forward base with the news that he had carried or dragged a wounded Gurkha sergeant-major through 6000 yards of dense jungle and swamp, an heroic achievement. SSM Smith now led the recovery party and, as the Gurkha history records it: 'In the jungle, SSM Smith was a tower of strength. He found a suitable winching zone, brought in the helicopter and supervised the lashing onto the stretcher of the wounded man. Had the evacuation been postponed further, the injured man would undoubtedly have lost a leg . . . He was discharged from hospital without even a limp.'

Slowly but surely, towards the end of 1965 the Indonesians were forced to abandon their front-line bases, conceding control of the border to the Allies. Nothing had been said publicly by either the British or the Indonesians about the 'Claret' operations, but within Indonesia Sukarno was rapidly becoming discredited among his military commanders and the common people, who were finding the price of his dreams of glory exorbitant.

The British, meanwhile, were making plans to undermine the regime by spreading the guerrilla war to other parts of Indonesia including, if it were expedient, Sumatra and Java. Plans for these operations embraced such external Intelligence agencies as MI6 as well as the SAS, but they were overtaken by events. In March 1966, Sukarno was reduced to a figurehead by his military top brass.

The last invader

The last Indonesian invasion, by fifty soldiers into a Sarawak border area near Brunei, ended disastrously for them. An Indonesian coffee-tin label put a Gurkha battalion on their trail. At the first contact, the invaders fragmented into small parties which were assiduously pursued for many weeks. Their leader, a charismatic figure named Lieutenant Sumbi, who had boasted that he would seize Brunei Bay and the Shell oil installations, was captured on 3 September, three weeks after Indonesia had signed a peace agreement with Malaysia.

With the end of the war, General Lea, the SAS officer who had been Allied military supremo during the final, victorious phase, was promptly knighted. Walker, meanwhile, became the only general to be made an honorary member of the SAS. As the Army's historian, Blaxland, wrote:

Thus ended what must surely rank as the British Army's neatest achievement during post-war years. What might so easily have been an interminable embroilment in the jungle, the kampongs, the villages and towns, with an ever-swelling flow of blood and hate, had been brought to a happy end in little more than three years.

This had been achieved because the Army had won the

confidence of the inhabitants and gained complete mastery over a brave and tough, if not very ably led, enemy. They had combined kindness to the defended with aggression against the attackers, two virtues not always regarded as compatible, and it had all been done with a lack of self-advertisement which must have had a deflating effect on the enemy . . .

The total number of British casualties was 19 killed and 44 wounded, while the Gurkhas had lost 40 killed with 83 wounded. The Indonesian dead numbered 2000.

SOUTH ARABIA 1964–67

The lost cause

What happened to the British Army in Aden, a territory which later became the Soviet satellite of South Yemen, is a well-documented example of how soldiers are obliged to continue fighting for a lost cause when their political masters attempt the impossible feat of leaving a colony, while at the same time remaining there. The abortive Suez operation of 1956; the emergence of Nasserism and its dissemination via the hot-gospel broadcasts of Cairo Radio; the 'shotgun marriage' of the South Arabian Federation between 1959 and 1963, linking the feudal, tribal sheikdoms lying between Yemen and the coast with the urban area of Aden Colony; the establishment of Britain's Middle East Command Headquarters in 1960: all these had generated intense local opposition to the British presence before the SAS arrived.

Most inauspicious of all, the hereditary ruler of Yemen, the Imam, was overthrown in a left-wing, Army-led coup in September 1962, which was instantly consolidated by the arrival of Egyptian troops. Recent evidence suggests that the Soviet KGB, aided by their British agent Kim Philby, had a hand in this. The new republican government in Yemen promptly called on 'our brothers in the Occupied South' – Aden and the Federation – 'to be ready for a revolution and for joining the battle we shall wage against colonialism'.

What now occurred, in effect, was a war by proxy between two colonial powers: Britain on one side and Egypt, backed by Soviet Russia, on the other. The battleground was the whole of that desolate, mountainous territory lying between the Gulf of Aden and Saudi Arabia. In Yemen itself, the deposed Imam eluded his would-be assassins. During the next eight years or more, his Royalist guerrilla army was aided by the Saudis and stiffened by a mercenary force largely composed of SAS veterans using secret bases in the Aden Federation, an operation that enjoyed discreet official backing from Whitehall.

In the Federation, meanwhile, two distinctive campaigns were fought out simultaneously. A tribal uprising took place in the Radfan mountains adjoining Yemen, while in Aden State the British faced their first campaign of sustained urban terrorism. One of the paradoxes to emerge was that in Yemen an SAS 'old boys' team was part of a guerrilla force, while a few miles south in Aden's hinterland their successors in the regular regiment were striving to suppress a guerrilla campaign.

But the most significant battle, as usual, was the one for credibility. What were British intentions? Who would go and who would remain to run the country if the British left? There were many brave pronouncements from Westminster along the lines of 'No surrender', even when in July 1964 a Conservative government set 1968 as the target date for the Federation's self-government. That promise of independence was accompanied by an arrangement that Britain would retain her bases in Aden and not desert the tribal rulers with whom she had maintained protection treaties since the nineteenth century. There were other reasons why Britain should keep her bases in the area. It was a time when shrinking British forces were still expected to maintain global commitments, particularly east of Suez. The Borneo campaign had started, unexpectedly, only a year before. Britain had important bases in Singapore and Hong Kong, so Aden was a strategically important staging-post as well as a port of regional importance (as the Russians would later demonstrate in their Ethiopian campaign of 1978). In October 1964, Mr Harold Wilson's Labour administration swept to power on the promise of a society transformed by 'the white heat of technology' and other instant miracles. Within eighteen months, in February 1966, the new government announced a total evacuation deadline of the Aden base to coincide with Independence. In March

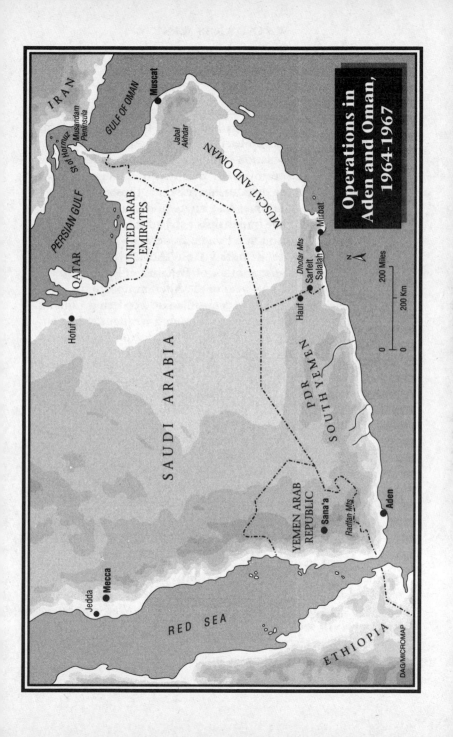

Operations in Aden and Oman, 1964-1967

IRAN

Muscat

Musandam Peninsula

St of Hormuz

GULF OF OMAN

PERSIAN GULF

UNITED ARAB EMIRATES

QATAR

Jabal Akhdar

MUSCAT AND OMAN

Mirbat

Dhofar Mts

Sarfeit

Salalah

Hofuf

Hauf

SAUDI ARABIA

PDR SOUTH YEMEN

N

200 Miles

200 Km

YEMEN ARAB REPUBLIC

Sana'a

Radfan Mts

Aden

Mecca

Jedda

RED SEA

ETHIOPIA

DAG/MICROMAP

1967, the evacuation deadline was advanced to November of that year.

These decisions destroyed the credibility of British promises in Aden, and had the lethal result of nullifying the hearts-and-minds campaign that elsewhere had proved to be a more potent peace-making force than bullets. Nor, as events turned out, did a precipitate British evacuation bring more freedom to the people of Aden, despite the promises of Cairo Radio. 'Liberated' Aden became a drab military dictatorship in which those questioning the regime, such as the Chief Magistrate of the Supreme Court, simply disappeared. The Imperial British had at least doffed their caps at democracy through a limited franchise.

Britain's decision to withdraw from Aden also accelerated the guerrilla war against another of Britain's allies, the Sultan of Oman. During the final year of the Aden campaign, in 1966, Marxist rebels in a remote Adeni sultanate bordering Oman's warlike province of Dhofar, were supplying weapons to Dhofari tribesmen, effectively opening up a third front against the British. In Aden, the Irish Guards were used to attack the Dhofari bases with a spearhead provided by B Squadron of 22 SAS. This textbook infantry operation, a frontal attack, quite opposed to SAS methods, ended with the successful escape of the Dhofaris.

The ubiquitous Major John Cooper, the retired SAS officer who had served as a freelance soldier in Oman before joining the Royalist guerrillas in Yemen, took a more sophisticated interest in this extension of the war. From time to time he would appear at Aden's Intelligence centre, for which he carried a permanent pass, to scrutinise photographs of known terrorist leaders. A friend of those days recalls: 'At the time, John was based partly in Oman, partly in Yemen.'

The British left Aden on 29 November 1967. The political beneficiaries of the war were, quaintly enough, Israel, whose secret aid to the Royalist cause in Yemen tied down 60,000 of Egypt's best troops during the 1967 Six Day War; and Soviet Russia, which took over the base facilities in Aden. It can be argued that the secret war in Yemen also helped to prevent an Egyptian or Marxist takeover in Oman and other Gulf states.

The significance of this prophylaxis would emerge only years later, after 1978, when the Iranian revolution and the Soviet invasion of Afghanistan plunged the world into turmoil.

Punishing the Radfan

The Emergency was declared formally in December 1963, after a grenade had been hurled at the High Commissioner, Sir Kennedy Trevaskis, and several Federal Ministers as they prepared to fly to London for a constitutional conference. The ill-defined frontier with South Yemen, across which Egyptian, Yemeni and Adeni nationalists were bringing weapons (including mines left in Egypt by the British), was then closed, at least on paper. But the border tribesmen, for whom guerrilla warfare was a way of life, were still supplied with money and rifles by Yemen, and a battle now began for control of the scorching, almost waterless Radfan mountains in which there were no roads.

Yet in April 1964, when A Squadron of the SAS arrived there, the strength of opposition and the general scale of the problem was simply not comprehended by the British. One eminent officer, who had served with Aden's Federal Regular Army (FRA) as an Intelligence officer shortly before returning to the territory as officer commanding A Squadron, candidly admitted later: 'We did not appreciate the intensity of the violence of the tribal reaction to our presence. I expected a few dissidents to poop off a few rounds and then go home again . . . So often, we underrate our enemy.'

Between the Emergency declaration in December and the arrival of the SAS in April, there had already been one attempt to subdue the Radfan area by a combined force of three Federal Regular Army battalions of Arabs with small numbers of British tanks, guns and engineers. Officially, this operation was described as 'a demonstration in force', but as Julian Paget's analysis of the Aden affair explains: 'There was no long-term plan as to what was to be done once the military task was completed; there were no plans to prevent further subversion, to finance development of the area or to initiate an intense "hearts and minds" campaign.' The real objective was punitive, and this in an area already in a rebellious mood and steeped in the tradition of 'an eye for an eye'. Paget records: 'There were many local officials, with a profound knowledge of the Arabs, who believed strongly that any attempt to subdue the tribes by force was doomed to be a waste of time and effort.'

The FRA battalions did occupy parts of the Radfan mountains for a few weeks, at a cost of five dead (one of them a British company commander) and twelve wounded. Then they withdrew to perform the even more important task of guarding the frontier. The tribesmen promptly reoccupied their former hill positions and began attacking traffic on the Dhala road linking Aden and Yemen. Meanwhile, Cairo and its puppet regime in the Yemeni capital of Sana'a announced the FRA's withdrawal from Radfan as a resounding defeat for the imperialists.

The Federal government (a mixture of tribal rulers and Adeni merchants) now sought more substantial British military help, despite the misgivings of that government's own Ministers responsible for internal security, who believed the deployment of British troops in so hostile an area would simply make matters worse. Not for the first time, however, the lessons of colonial history were forgotten. The British had first tried to bring the Wolves of Radfan – the Qotaibi tribe – to heel in 1881. From a desk in Aden, sixty miles away, they had declared the tribe nominally subject to the Emir of Dhala, a town on the ancient trade route linking Aden and Yemen. Until then the tribesmen had regarded it as their right to extort payment from travellers using the road, a protection racket deodorized by its antiquity. For years afterwards, the British sent punitive columns trudging into the inhospitable mountains, regiments lost to memory such as the Dublin Fusiliers, Sepoys, Bombay Grenadiers and Outrams Rifles, and they never entirely subdued the hill warriors. Throughout the 1930s, control (such as it was) was left to the RAF, which bombed the rebels from time to time.

In January 1965, in a study of the Radfan tribesman's character, Mr Harry Cockerill, a wartime SAS veteran who was already working in Aden when the regiment arrived there, wrote: 'He will never surrender in battle and will endure shocking wounds, crawling away to die on his own rather than seek aid from his enemy. His territory is such that a few men can hold up a battalion. He is fanatically independent, a local saying being "Every tribesman thinks himself a Sultan". Unless a settlement is made that will allow him his independence . . . the Qotaibi . . . will take to the hills and it will all start again.'

In response to the Federal Government's request, a mixed force of brigade strength plus a squadron each of RAF Hunter ground-support aircraft, Shackleton bombers and Twin Pioneer transports, as well as about ten helicopters, was rapidly cobbled together. The vaguely worded order to this force from the General Officer Commanding Middle East Land Forces, Major-General John Cubbon, was that it should 'end the operations of dissidents in the defined area'. This was subsequently refined as 'to bring sufficient pressure to bear on the Radfan tribes (a) to prevent the tribal revolt from spreading; (b) to reassert our authority; (c) to stop attacks on the Dhala Road'.

The troops were not deliberately to fire on areas containing women and children; villages were not to be shelled, bombed or attacked without a warning to the inhabitants by leaflet to move out. But once the troops came under fire, retaliation could include maximum force.

Exercise into reality

At the time this plan was being constructed, the SAS Regiment consisted of only two squadrons, A and D. A Squadron was resting and retraining after five months in Borneo, and D Squadron was in Borneo. As it happened, A Squadron had already arranged to train in Aden during May and June as a refresher in desert warfare, and its commander, who was in Aden to prepare the ground for this exercise, suggested using his men for the Radfan operation a month earlier than the proposed exercise. His offer was promptly accepted.

A top priority 'flash' signal was sent to Britain to obtain

the necessary permission from the Ministry of Defence. The squadron's commander, having returned briefly to England, composed and typed the unit's manual of standard operational procedures for the forthcoming encounter – a tactical 'bible' – during the flight back to Aden with the rest of the squadron. For security reasons, families were told that the squadron was exercising on Salisbury Plain.

The men arrived at Khormaksar, the RAF base in Aden, just two weeks before they were to spearhead the Radfan offensive. Two weeks was also the period normally allowed for acclimatisation to temperatures up to 150 degrees Fahrenheit; the SAS, as usual, ignored this requirement and drove immediately to a hastily-prepared base at Thumier, sixty miles from Aden and just thirty miles from the hostile Yemeni border. The same night, the squadron moved into the nearby Radfan mountains for a twenty-four-hour proving patrol. In the darkness there was an exchange of fire with a group of armed men who were, in fact, British soldiers. One SAS trooper was slightly wounded. It was to avoid just such elementary failures of communication that this early patrol was mounted, but the episode was an augury of worse to come.

SAS officers discovered that Intelligence concerning the strength of the opposition was negligible. As one of them said later: 'In those early days of the Radfan campaign, no one knew anything about what would be needed. They didn't know whether there was water up in the hills, or anything about the people.' The improvised group that was to re-enter the Radfan now consisted of two battalions of locally raised FRA infantry; 45 Royal Marine Commando with B Company, the Parachute Regiment, temporarily under its command; a troop of Royal Engineers; a battery of the Royal Horse Artillery armed with compact 105mm howitzers and a Royal Tank Regiment squadron equipped with Saladin armoured cars.

As an opening move, it was decided that two hill objectives code-named 'Cap Badge' and 'Rice Bowl', should be seized from the rebels during the night of April. These were key points in the area because they dominated the camel routes from the Yemen as well as the only two fertile areas of the Radfan. The plan was that the Royal Marines should march seven miles from Thumier on the Dhala Road into hostile territory, to climb and hold 'Rice Bowl', the most northerly objective. Meanwhile the Para company was to be dropped near the foot of 'Cap Badge'. Both groups knew that to be caught in the valley after daybreak, when the guerrilla picquets had taken up dawn positions on the heights, would be suicidal. Equally dangerous would be an attempt to land the Paras on an undefended and unmarked drop zone. The job of establishing such a DZ was traditionally that of the Paras' own independent pathfinder company, but this time the task was allocated to the SAS.

The Edwards patrol

On 29 April, as dusk approached, nine men of 3 Troop led by Captain Robin Edwards set out in armoured cars, leaving the road and making their way up the steep-sided Wadi Rabwa. Edwards, a recent recruit from the Somerset and Cornwall Light Infantry, was a brave and conscientious young officer who had contracted poliomyelitis immediately after passing the SAS selection course. His determination made him fit enough for service with the regiment twelve months later. Since arriving in Thumier, his troop had fired on a nocturnal camel train that had refused to halt: two Arabs had been killed and a third taken prisoner. Edwards's anxiety that he might have made a mistake was relieved only when local military Intelligence identified the prisoner as a much-wanted guerrilla leader. Edwards's men were mostly veterans of Borneo and Malaya, physically hard by any standard. The exception was the troop signaller, a slightly-built young ex-sapper named Warburton, who was already suffering from severe stomach pains, about which he did not complain, when the patrol left Thumier.

The patrol had to cover roughly eight miles to reach its objective and had about twenty-four hours within which to accomplish this. Intelligence reports suggested that opposition in the hills would not be serious if the patrol moved discreetly. In the event, the opposition manifested itself from the beginning.

As the armoured cars nosed their way up the Wadi Rabwa, away from the Dhala Road, they came under continuous rifle and machine-gun fire. In such terrain the cars could not move at more than a snail's pace, and it became increasingly likely that the vehicles would soon be forced to halt.

Making a virtue of necessity, the patrol dismounted while the armoured cars' gunners replied to the fire from the hills. By moonlight, each man hoisted his sixty-pound pack on to his back and slipped quietly into the shadows. Even after nightfall here, it was like a warm summer's day in England, the heat stifling the airless, rocky bottom of the wadi.

Each soldier carried four magazines for his self-loading rifle, a total of eighty rounds, plus a bandolier of the same ammunition and 200 rounds of .303-inch for the patrol's Bren light machine-gun. The radio, and enough water for each man – a one-gallon container and four water bottles per head – were other essential items. The squadron's commander, an old Malaya hand, pre-ferred mobility to firepower on such occasions, and the weight carried was a compromise between two conflicting priorities. For the same reason, the Officer Commanding had stressed that ammunition was to be conserved jealously if contact with the enemy did occur. As things turned out, it was sound advice.

Despite these routine problems the Edwards patrol was in good spirits. It had ducked away from the opening battle unseen and was now tramping with quiet assurance through dunes and rocks, up Wadi Rabwa. Off to the right loomed the dark, sinister mass of the 3900-foot Jabal Ashqab. It soon became clear, however, that young Warburton, the signaller, was in poorer shape than his comrades. Possibly he was suffering from a mild form of food poisoning. Gradually, he fell back and the patrol waited for him. Edwards and his two sergeants, L. and Tk., decided to put Warburton in the centre of the file and redistribute the loads so that the radio, weighing forty-four pounds, would be carried by someone else. But after an hour or so Warburton was again struggling to keep up, and the patrol was now becoming dangerously divided.

At about 2am, Edwards and his men paused to consider the situation. According to the original plan they should be in hiding on the objective before dawn at 5.30am. They were then to lie concealed until dusk, when they would secure the drop zone perimeter and identify it with torches and an Aldis lamp for the Paras' night descent. In fact, it was now clear that they would not be able to reach the proposed DZ that night at their present rate of progress. Dead reckoning suggested that they were still about three miles away. To be caught in the open after sunrise would not only make them soft targets for the ubiquitous snipers on the hill-tops, but would also compromise the entire operation.

Despite all these niggling problems, there was also cause for optimism. From the point they had now reached, Edwards and his men had a downhill journey to their objective, and there would be ample time to cover the remaining ground at dusk on the morrow. They were now almost at the top of the highest ridge on Jabal Ashqab, though short of the precipice rising to the summit. Best of all, there were two ancient stone sangars (rock-walled firing-points built by local tribesmen) in which they could hide without attracting attention. As one veteran later joked, for the SAS to have built something without local 'planning permission' would instantly have attracted attention among hill people to whom every stone was familiar. The overwhelming logic of these factors was to halt in the sangars and give Warburton a chance to recover. At 2.30am in his headquarters tent at Thumier, the squadron commander listened carefully as Edwards explained all this by radio. Edwards was apologetic, but felt there was no alternative.

At dawn, the patrol reviewed the situation. It was, it discovered, only about 1000 yards above the hamlet of Shi'b Taym, a meagre collection of mud-and-stone houses. From the village, armed picquets tramped up the hill some distance from the soldiers' position to begin the long day's watch. Later, a group of children passed below, chanting 'Allah yansir Nasir!' (God make Nasser victorious!) Still the patrol went undetected. All was quiet now, and it seemed as though Edwards's gamble was succeeding.

At about 11am however, the patrol saw a herd of goats approaching, following a small wadi only a few feet from their position. The animals were in the care of a herdsman who shouted directions to a woman coming towards the sangars from the village. Almost certainly he was asking her to watch out for strays from the herd. Edwards, without moving from concealment, softly called to the soldier who was covering the herdsman's approach: could the goat-herd be seized silently without a fuss? Out of the question, the look-out replied; the herdsman's companion would see it all. There was nothing for it now but to hope that by some miracle the herdsman would not spot them. If he did . . . Suddenly they all heard the Arab's voice raised in alarm only a few yards away, shouting to his companion with new urgency. The game was up. As he turned to flee, a single high-velocity shot rang out from the SAS position. It was a desperate means of buying time and the only one available to the patrol.

The woman vanished, and armed tribesmen were soon on the scene. They were taking no cover as yet, apparently thinking that the shot might have been an accidental discharge, but determined to establish where it had come from. The soldiers, knowing that a battle was inevitable, decided to reduce the odds against them. As one survivor said later: 'We thought we might as well put a few away while we had the advantage.'

The tribesmen ducked into cover, crawling behind the boulders, still trying to locate the source of the shots echoing across the hillside. It was some time before they succeeded in this. Their solution was to observe the whole sweep of the hill from the ridge top about fifty yards away from the sangars, and twenty feet higher. Edwards had anticipated this and a crude but effective link was created between the patrol and two pairs of RAF Hunter ground-support aircraft. Under Edwards's control, Warburton passed directions by radio to the SAS second-in-command, Major Mike Wingate Gray, at Thumier, where the messages were amplified by use of a civilian transistor radio. The major relayed these instructions by field telephone to the RAF Brigade Air Support Officer, Squadron Leader Roy Bowie, in another tent at Thumier. Bowie, telephone in one hand, microphone linked to the Hunters in the other, repeated the fire orders.

As the first rifle shots struck the sangars from the top of the ridge, about two hours after the herdsman's death, the first pair of Hunters roared down to deliver withering bursts of cannon fire on the enemy position. The tribesmen scuttled back down the hill to the comparative safety of the rocks, and kept off the ridge for the rest of the encounter, which meant that they could not dominate the sangars. Equally, the SAS patrol had no means of escape. For the time being, it was stalemate.

The conflict which ensued was a tense, cold-blooded sniping duel in which the tribesmen fired from a range of only fifty yards at anything they could see – an elbow, a boot, the top of a skull. The Arab sharpshooters were good; even when their bullets scored no direct hits, they sent fragments of granite into the faces of their opponents whenever the British peered over the rock walls of the sangars. As a result, no member of the patrol escaped entirely unscathed. As each carefully aimed round hit their position, the men of 3 Troop called to one another: 'Anyone hurt?' 'Anyone see where that shot came from?' – 'No. They keep changing their positions.'

Overhead, the Hunters wheeled and dived with one eye on the identification panels originally intended for the DZ, and now spread on the ground between the two sangars. One veteran of this operation later recalled: 'We developed the air link to a point where we were getting messages up to correct the aircraft's course on its run-in to strafe the guerrillas.' The beleaguered troop also called down artillery support which one officer later described as 'fairly continuous and intense at times'.

Towards mid-afternoon, the SAS men noticed that the Hunter strikes were becoming less effective; the enemy was becoming more numerous and was creeping closer. The battle was being fought on the east side of Jabal Ashqab, which now began to cast a long shadow, first over the sangars, then over the hostile boulders below them. It was clear to both sides that by dusk the British patrol would lose its air cover completely. Until then, the guerrillas would bide their time. Their quarry was not going to escape, and there were blood-debts to collect . . .

At about 4.30pm, Lance-Corporal 'Paddy' Baker was wounded for the first time. He was inside the larger of the two sangars, but enemy sharpshooters spotted one exposed leg and fired. Two bullets hit him in the left thigh, causing severe flesh wounds from which blood began to flood. He called to the troop commander, Edwards: 'I've been hit, Boss.' From outside the sangar the voice of Trooper Bill H., with a bantering third person reference to himself, added: 'William's been hit as well!' Both men were lucky. Although the tribesmen were armed with accurate .303-inch rifles, their bullets were refills – old shell cases filled with a homemade charge whose velocity was insufficient to penetrate bone. Bill H. later discovered that the round that struck him had creased his back, leaving a wound like a whiplash across his shoulder blades.

The patrol 'medic' threw Baker some extra field dressings. As he strapped up the wounds, Baker thanked his donor then asked caustically: 'But is this the best you can do after all the expensive medical training you've had?' Even as he made the joke, Baker was discovering that his injured leg would no longer support him. In this situation, the injury would be fatal unless he could make the leg function again by dusk . . . As he lay there he kept testing the leg against the sangar wall. While he was doing so, a sniper's bullet grazed the inside of his uninjured right leg. His left leg recovered strength only a few minutes before the guerrillas attempted to rush the sangar. Two of the tribesmen reached the wall and attempted to push it over. This was unwise. Baker, armed with a rifle, and Sergeant Tk., with a Bren gun, rose simultaneously. The tribesmen were still looking puzzled as the sergeant killed them both with short bursts from the Bren. One even attempted a gesture of 'Salaam', as if surprised that his enemy was a white man instead of an Arab soldier.

It was now almost dusk, and from the Thumier base the squadron commander spelled out what they already knew, that air cover would have to be called off very soon. Edwards told his men, spread around him in an area of about fifteen square yards, that the original plan to mark the Paras' DZ had now 'gone for a ball of chalk'. They would have to break out just after dusk and make their way back to Thumier; there would be no intermediate rendezvous. By radio they requested an artillery barrage on the sangars at 7.30pm, by which time they would have left the scene. All these plans were discussed with the squadron commander and contact with base ended with his acknowledgement: 'OK. Good night – and good luck.' For the major there was now nothing to do but sweat out the longest night of his life. He had tried to arrange a rescue of his beleaguered patrol by sending in another troop by helicopter, but the aircraft had been badly shot-up before it reached Edwards's position and had been forced to limp back to base.

At the sangars, Edwards's troop now smashed everything it could not carry, including the radio. From a separate Morse set the soldiers extracted the vital crystals that controlled the set's operating frequencies. Each man carried only his weapon and belt equipment, consisting of water bottle, ammunition pouches and emergency rations. By this time, some of the patrol were still inside the larger sangar, while others had dispersed to the rocks outside. Those inside, the focus of enemy attack, were Captain Edwards; the signaller, Trooper Warburton; Lance-Corporal Baker; Sergeant Tk. and Trooper 'Darkie' B. Hiding among the rocks were Sergeant L.; the wounded Trooper Bill H.; Lance-Corporal 'Taffy' B. and Trooper T. This party would give covering fire to Edwards and the rest as they stormed out, through the rocks and down the hill. Edwards's group, in turn, would then take up positions from which to cover the retreat of Sergeant L.'s party.

There was a final, absurd formality before the breakout began. Edwards, conscientious to the last, and aware of the squadron commander's insistence on routine preventive medicine, asked all within earshot: 'Has everyone taken his Paludrin?' It provoked some wry grins.

Now it was time to go, but as the party rose, ready to move, one man lay quite still in a corner of the sangar. Warburton, the signaller, was dead. He and his A41 radio set had been hit several times. 'All right, we're coming out now!' shouted Edwards. As the four men clattered clumsily down the slope, they were the target of a barrage of small-arms fire from the surrounding rocks, much of it from two large boulders immediately below them. Baker, in the lead, fired back with his rifle. From somewhere behind him, Sergeant Tk. was also blasting the hostile rocks with a Bren fired from the hip. Captain Edwards was between these two and 'Darkie' B. was back marker.

The leading man, Baker, lurched forward as fast as his injured leg permitted, then paused and turned to see whether the others were still with him. As he did so, a new fusillade of shots whistled past him and struck Edwards, who seemed to spin round under their impact before crumpling to the ground. The guerrillas concentrated their fire on Edwards now, and the combined force of their bullets pushed his body sideways across the slope. Baker and Sergeant Tk. continued their advance to a point fifteen yards beyond that of their covering party, and took cover themselves. Edwards lay silent and lifeless. There was nothing they could do for him.

The three survivors from the sangar – Baker, Sergeant Tk. and 'Darkie' B. – now called the original covering party to follow them. They did so stealthily, gambling correctly on the chance that the guerrillas would still be watching the sangar for any survivors. As the whole group tip-toed away at an angle to the valley, they heard a fire-fight continuing around the sangar where, in the gloom, two concentric rings of tribesmen were now shooting at each other. The patrol was least at risk so long as it kept to the high ground. This it did, following the contours of the hill as it swung round to overlook Wadi Rabwa and the road home. They had not gone far when the prearranged artillery barrage smashed on to the sangars. But by then – as later, grisly events were to demonstrate – the tribesmen had also retired, taking the bodies of Warburton and Edwards with them.

As shock and fatigue set in, the march back to Thumier took on a nightmarish quality in which the men's judgement and perceptions were becoming distorted. The two sergeants, with Lance-Corporal 'Taffy' B., 'Darkie' B., the medical orderly, and Trooper T., led the way, with the two wounded men, Baker and Bill H., following some distance behind. After some time, the patrol paused while 'Darkie' applied fresh dressings to Baker's still-bleeding wounds. He also cut away four old dressings which were now flopping round Baker's ankle. (Baker had been dimly aware that something was impeding him, but he was unable to comprehend what it was.)

The men resumed the march, struggling up and down the steep walls of minor gullies near the top of the hill, which fed the main wadi below them. The moon rose, and Sergeant L. called another halt. Barring their path, he fancied he saw a group of Arab tents. If the soldiers were challenged, should they fight? Bluff it out? Or what?

They decided to climb even higher to elude this latest threat. Below the 'tents' lay the main wadi and a track which was the direct route home. It was an enticing prospect, but fraught with the risk of an encounter with guerrilla picquets. Only when they had skirted the mountain for some distance near the summit, always marching south-west, and had examined the 'tents' from another angle, did they discover that the tents were rocks.

Farther still round the hill, the seven men struck a goat track which was going in the right direction, and they trudged slowly along it. Again, Baker and Bill H., the two wounded, fell back. Then Bill heard, or thought he heard, someone following them. Both men paused and glanced back. Some distance away a figure in white was padding quietly along the track in their wake. The two soldiers huddled behind the nearest bush, rifles slippery with sweat as they unlocked the safety catches. This time it was not a false alarm. The man in white was an Arab and there were three others following him in single file. Only the quiet tread of boots, as the rest of the SAS patrol continued on its unwitting way, broke the silence.

As the pursuing Arabs reached the bush, Baker and Bill H. rose, stepped on to the path and kept shooting until the four men went down. Baker, his rifle magazine empty, continued squeezing the trigger, bewildered – by shock, fatigue and loss of blood – that the gun no longer functioned. After some seconds of careful thought, he reloaded with a new magazine. By now, the rest of the patrol had halted, and the voice of Sergeant Tk. was inquiring: 'What's going on?' Baker replied: 'Hold your fire!' The two back markers, concerned that their comrades might inadvertently shoot them, hobbled even higher up the hill and approached the rest of the party in an arc. As they did so, Sergeant Tk., satisfied that they were safe, trained his Bren back up the path and fired three short bursts along it to discourage further pursuit. For some time they waited in ambush positions, but there was no sound except the groans of their dying enemies.

At last the patrol moved off again, even more cautiously, every man glancing back from time to time. An hour later, the back markers, Baker and Bill H., were certain that they were again being followed. Again they set up an ambush as their comrades marched on. This time the pursuers seemed to be guerrilla picquets from the ridge above them. These two were killed in a carbon-copy of the previous ambush.

It was now about 2am. The men had been under extreme pressure for thirty hours or more, but the patrol followed the same drill as before, setting a careful ambush for any follow-up party, waiting, and then continuing the march. The soldiers were now far enough away from the scene of the original contact to make it reasonable to drop down towards the main Wadi Rabwa. From there to the camp was only a mile or so, but this, too, was fraught with danger. If they approached on foot, as someone suddenly recollected from the pre-operation briefing, they would certainly be fired on by the Arab FRA sentries at Thumier. So they walked, drunk with fatigue, down to the wadi itself, to hide and rest until daybreak. At the bottom of the hill they found a stream. No one had any water left, most of the patrol having shared what they had with the two wounded men. So, ignoring an order not to drink from an unpurified source, the men slaked their thirst, hid in the scrub, and waited. Baker sank into unconsciousness.

At first light the patrol moved on again, their faces cut and bloodied by rock fragments from the sangar, the limbs of the wounded rebelling against further movement. After half an hour in the buzzing heat of the wadi, they heard the sound of salvation – the rumble of a Saladin armoured car as it foraged up the slope towards them. A radio message flashed back to the Thumier base, retailing the good news in terse, signaller's jargon. Now the wounded men, Baker and Bill H., were hauled into the vehicle for the last mile home. (Baker was to be awarded the

Military Medal for his part in the operation.) The other five survivors marched back, grim-faced. No one spoke much. They had survived and, for the time being, that was enough. But the reverberations of the SAS skirmish at Shi'b Taym were to echo far beyond Aden.

The main operation in the hills, of which the Edwards patrol had been an essential preliminary, was restructured to seek more modest targets. Instead of a lightning strike at the 3700-foot Al Hajaf hills in the centre of the dissident area, which dominated two watered, cultivated valleys, the Paras and 45 Royal Marine Commando had to fight and climb their way in, peak by peak. Eventually, six major units required five weeks to subdue the area, after which the inhabitants were banished.

While this operation was still in its early stages, a few days after the loss of Edwards and Warburton, a strange and macabre Intelligence report about the fate of the two bodies reached the GOC in Aden, Major-General John Cubbon. Soon afterwards, on the evening of 3 May, Cubbon held a crowded press conference at which he was asked about a Radio Taiz Yemeni propaganda broadcast claim that the heads of the two dead soldiers had been put on public display 'in the Yemen'. The broadcast was confirmed in Aden soon afterwards by two camel-herders who had seen the display. According to *The Times*, Cubbon replied: 'We have reliable information of their decapitation and the exhibition of their heads on stakes in Yemen. If this is true, I must express, on behalf of all three Services in South Arabia, our deepest sympathy with the relatives of the men and their regiments.' The timing of the question and the answer were unfortunate. Not only were the next-of-kin unaware of the deaths, but, like other families of A Squadron, they had been led to believe that the men were on a routine exercise on Salisbury Plain.

At government level, meanwhile, the row was only just beginning. The republican government in Yemen, denying its own propaganda broadcast, now denounced the decapitation story as 'a British lie'. In Taiz, the US Embassy, which handled British interests in the absence of UK diplomatic recognition of the republicans, investigated and issued an ambiguously worded statement to the effect that there was 'absolutely no truth to the rumours that the heads of two British soldiers had been exhibited there'. In context, 'there' could mean the whole of Yemen, or merely the city of Taiz. A row in the British House of Commons followed, during which Labour's front-bench spokesman, Mr Denis Healey, accused General Cubbon of relying on 'scanty evidence' for his claim. But, as Julian Paget's study recorded, on 13 May, ten days after the Press conference, 'a patrol of the Federal Regular Army found two headless bodies buried in a shallow grave in the area of the SAS battle. The FRA patrol was itself fired on by some 25 rebels, but drove them off by artillery fire. The bodies were recovered and identified as those of Captain Edwards and Sapper Warburton; there was no sign of the heads.'

A Squadron returned to Britain on schedule a few weeks later, the object of intense Press interest. Thereafter, like the regiment's other squadrons (D and the re-emerging B), it served in Aden for a few weeks during retraining periods between each four-month stint in the Borneo jungle. These episodes in Aden did not amount to a consistent and continuous campaign. Yet, even if accidentally, they served a number of useful technical purposes which signposted the regiment's future evolution through the Dhofar war of Oman to counterterrorism in Europe. In the Radfan, where the guerrilla war smouldered on until the British withdrew in 1967, SAS soldiers were regularly exposed to desert and mountain operations for the first time since the Second World War.

'Keeni–Meeni' in Aden

By way of contrast, in the foetid alleyways of Aden itself the regiment had its first taste of urban terrorist warfare. Hitherto, nearly all its fighting experience since its post-war resurrection in Malaya, had been in the jungle. The urban campaign in Aden, so different from the guerrilla tactics of Radfan and beyond, was also the launching-pad for clandestine plain-clothes operations later adopted by more orthodox regiments.

True, the originality of Major (later General) Frank Kitson in Kenya's Mau Mau campaign – where 22 SAS made a brief appearance – had produced the pseudoterrorist 'counter gangs', a mixture of former terrorists and loyal tribesmen led by British officers disguised as natives. It was true also that the same technique was used subsequently in Cyprus to create undercover 'Q' units. Here too, British officers performed a clandestine role. But when the major commanding A Squadron of the SAS in Aden set up a Close Quarter Battle Course for a selected group of his soldiers, he knew that there was no hope of 'turning round' Arab terrorists. Britain had announced her intention to leave the territory, and this extinguished any hope of active support even from her traditional friends in the area. So the new SAS units had to function more like the 'Q' squads of the Palestine Police. These had been started by Roy Farran, a veteran of the wartime SAS, and were manned largely by others from the same source. However, it was also remotely possible that, if some terrorists could be taken alive and interrogated, some break in the total, silent security surrounding Nationalist operations might be achieved.

The basic concept in Palestine and Aden, quite simply, was to blend into the local scenery and seize on targets of opportunity. The men chosen for this undercover work were those who most closely resembled Arabs. In the matter of pigmentation the SAS Fijians had, so to speak, a head start in spite of their height. But others who had the sharp, hooked nose and high cheekbones of the Semite looked equally plausible if they were well-tanned and dressed as natives. Such undercover operations were known in regimental jargon as 'Keeni-Meeni' jobs. 'Keeni-Meeni' was originally a Swahili phrase to describe the sinuous, unseen movement of a snake in the long grass. It also became a synonym in Africa – and later, via the slave trade, in the Arabian Gulf – for undercover work. British soldiers picked it up during the Mau Mau campaign in Kenya and subsequently in Aden.

The next criterion of selection for 'Keeni-Meeni' work was the ability to draw the heavy, thirteen-round Browning pistol from the folds of an Arab futah, and fire it with perfect accuracy. Farran had taught his men the then unorthodox triangular firing posture known as the 'Grant-Taylor Method', and required them to be able to put six rounds through a playing-card at fifteen yards. The early SAS 'CQB' Course at Aden was not very different.

The 'Keeni-Meeni' squad of about twenty men operated from various centres in Aden, finally settling in 1966 on Ballycastle House, a block of flats formerly used as married quarters in the military complex at Khormaksar. From this centre they slipped out in twos and threes to make their way to the high-risk warrens around the Crater and Sheikh Othman districts.

Their main quarry was the group of skilled, Yemeni-trained assassins who were steadily suppressing the meagre Intelligence that was reaching the British authorities by the simple, bloody expedient of killing Special Branch officers and their contacts. Sometimes the SAS men would take with them a comrade dressed in Army uniform, or European civilian clothes, for use as bait in areas where the assassins lurked. Others used the idea, notably Major H. M. Tillotson of the Prince of Wales's Own Regiment of Yorkshire, who won a Queen's Recommendation for Brave Conduct because of his skill at this risky game.

Within the SAS it is felt that little of tangible value came out of the experiment except the acquisition of new experience and knowledge. But there were some contacts. A pair of Fijian troopers sitting in a civilian car in Sheikh Othman saw two Arabs approaching them with weapons drawn, ready to fire. The Fijians leapt from the vehicle, drew their pistols and killed the terrorists so quickly that the latter had time only to aim, but not fire, at the soldiers.

Occasionally, the 'Keeni-Meeni' patrol did arrest a terrorist. One was seized as he was about to hurl a grenade. Such attacks became increasingly frequent during 1966 and 1967, and parties of British schoolchildren were a favourite target for these 'Cairo Grenadiers'. This time, the grenade-thrower was picked up and taken back to SAS HQ at Ballycastle House for interrogation, but he was unwise enough to make a break for it as they arrived, and was shot dead. Later, the man was identified as a corporal in the Federal Regular Army, one of a growing number of terrorist converts among the local police and armed forces.

As in Northern Ireland five years later, the popularity of undercover patrols out-paced the elaborate training and co-ordination required for such delicate work. After an SAS plain-clothes patrol led by the redoubtable Fijian, Corporal Labalaba, had opened fire on a group of armed 'Arabs' in Sheikh Othman, seriously wounding at least two men, it was discovered, too late, that the Royal Anglian Regiment had put its newly-formed Special Branch Squad into the same area. Through the usual channels, the SAS had done its best to avoid exactly such a disaster, for unlike other regiments it was not committed to any given 'parish'. Against this tragedy, however, must be set the Anglian undercover squad's success. During a single, six-month tour, a ten-man team from the regiment's 3rd Battalion captured 105 grenades, five automatic weapons, three pistols, two rocket-launchers, an impressive collection of bombs, ammunition and explosives, and fourteen terrorists including two members of the Cairo-backed FLOSY (Front for the Liberation of Occupied South Yemen) organisation.

Back to Radfan

Meanwhile, those SAS soldiers who did not participate in the lethal 'Keeni-Meeni' games around Aden city spent a harsher time among the baking mountains near the Yemeni border, speculating cynically about the fleshpots the luckier 'urbanites' allegedly were enjoying. On a clear night, from the Bakri Ridge, one could see the lights of Aden, fifty miles away or more . . . But in the hills there was the compensation of a more traditional hunt – a world of Hemingway rather than of Le Carré.

The presence of British soldiers in the Radfan mountains, following the initial operations of April 1964, had now ceased to be a novelty. Efforts to halt the flow of arms and guerrillas from their Yemeni bases in the north, as well as to control the war in the hills, made it inevitable and public. What still distinguished the SAS penetration was its covert nature.

The regiment's task was somehow to create observation posts from which enemy movement could be observed silently and invisibly. It was a classic reconnaissance task aided by the terrain, but hindered by the climate. The heat in the mountains could wring, with alarming speed, the last drop of sweat from any living creature, however robust, leaving it dehydrated, exhausted and, if water were not supplied in time, dead of thirst. Medical experts fixed the minimum daily intake for British soldiers at two gallons per day, which meant laborious supply by helicopter and consequent disclosure of the OP position. The SAS overcame this problem in a variety of ways. Occasionally they would move into an overt position with an orthodox unit, remaining in concealment with extra rations for many days after the position had been ostensibly evacuated. They learned to conserve the water they carried inside their bodies by minimal movement during daylight hours, sneaking down to a local stream by night to replenish their stocks. But, even after dark, the exertion of foraging for water invoked the law of diminishing returns because much of what was collected had to be consumed on the way back. As a way of life, it was hard enough to make even the Borneo jungle seem alluring – one veteran describes the jungle as 'a gracious living' when set against life in the Radfan.

From their secret eyries, the soldiers directed artillery fire on to suitable targets. Time and again, guerrilla patrols, moving discreetly along the apparently safe route of some obscure wadi, had to scatter for cover as the hiss of incoming shells told them, yet again, that they were being stalked by an invisible foe. The tribesmen's reactions combined the fatalism of Islam with superstition: the guns, they assured one another, were new weapons devised by the diabolic British, guns with eyes 'which always seek you out, wherever you go'.

At the same time, the tribesmen took advantage of any target they spotted. One SAS attempt to transport men by helicopter on to Bakri Ridge, overlooking the forward base at Thumier, led to a heavy exchange of fire between guerrillas on the ground and the helicopter, which had been equipped as a gunship. That patrol had to be aborted.

Not all SAS personnel up-country were perpetually in the mountains. At least one officer of the regiment became a temporary Political Officer, advising the local tribal rulers and calculating the political implications of individual military operations. His companion, a dogged bodyguard, also drawn from the regiment, was never seen without his rifle; as a result local tribesmen nicknamed him 'Abu al-Bunduq' (Father of the Rifle). Both soldiers were fluent in Arabic.

A friendly early warning

The nearer the projected withdrawal date came, the more essential were the SAS patrols, to give early warning of attacks on the main forward base at Thumier. The guerrillas, in their turn, now occasionally received early warning of SAS movements in the hills from Arab officers of the Federal Regular Army; they knew that, when the British left, their own lives would depend upon a record of co-operation with the rebels. On such occasions, the FRA advised the guerrillas to keep clear of any area where the SAS was operating, but they were seldom heeded.

In one of the last actions in this area, men of A Squadron were patrolling at Dhi Hirran, near the Yemeni border north of Thumier. Below them, a patrol from 1 Troop saw dissidents moving along the bottom of the wadi. The tribesmen, who were equipped with a British Land-Rover, were dedicated Sha'iri supporters of the Egyptian-backed FLOSY movement. The SAS team called down an RAF Hunter strike in one of the last offensive British air operations in Radfan. Politically, the effect of this action was to force FLOSY to merge locally with the more Marxist NLF, which had now almost taken power quite openly in the regional capital of Dhala, and would soon do so in Aden itself, after a bloody internecine battle at which the British would be spectators.

By now, the only major, cohesive British unit which dared to operate at strength outside the shrinking perimeter around Thumier was 45 Royal Marine Commando. Just before dusk on 17 June, only nine days before the final British withdrawal from the Radfan, an SAS observation post spotted three armed men moving along Wadi Bilah, about fifteen miles south-west of the base. The 45 Commando historian, David Young, records: 'Within ten minutes the fully kitted stand-by Troop, Nine Troop (Lt Phil Robinson), was embarked in Wessex helicopters prior to heading for the scene . . . The Troop Sergeant, Sgt John French, takes up the story:

'"We leapt out of the choppers, having placed out two picquets – in case they tried to run away – and as we got out we saw the three men dashing up a low hill about 200 yards away. One stopped and fired at us. We were right out in the open and as there was such a din going on, I blew my whistle and told the lads to adopt a kneeling position for firing. This they did and two dissidents were killed outright, a great achievement as it is a most difficult position to fire from. The third ran over the crest of a hill slap into the picquet commanded by Cpl McLaughlin and was shot at 30 yards range. Throughout the entire engagement, only 80 rounds were expended, a fantastically small amount for three kills."

'At half past five, Nine Troop re-embarked in the Wessex and by 5.32 they were back in Habilayn (Thumier) with three dead dissidents . . . This was the last occasion on which 45 Commando was to be able to show its outward aggressiveness in the Radfan . . . For the last few days, the unit was literally fighting a rearguard action.'

The handover of Radfan to the Federal Regular Army (soon renamed the South Arabian Army), on 26 June 1967, occurred immediately after Israel had crushed the Egyptian Air Force in a pre-emptive air strike of her own, and then destroyed the Egyptian Army in the field during the Six Day War. In Aden, the effect of the Egyptian defeat was to make Arab Nationalists almost mad with grief and hurt pride. Some smashed radio sets and televisions as they disseminated the bad news. For the British, what had been a long dying cause was now assuredly a lost one. It was not a situation likely to help military morale.

As Julian Paget, in his careful study of the Aden affair points out: 'It was difficult to find a political or national cause that was worth dying for. But there were other causes . . . for which the soldiers were happy to fight and die, and the chief of these was their Regiment.' Of no one was that more true than the politically, militarily and geographically isolated patrols of the SAS during those last days in the Radfan. Some months after Independence, in the spring of 1968, Harry Cockerill visited Thumier. There he discovered 'a few Brits' assisting the operation of the airstrip by the South Arabian Army. They included, inevitably, a recently 'demobilised' SAS officer.

Part IV

The war on your doorstep (or, smile for the camera)

Munich massacre to 'killing house'

Mogadishu 1977

London (Princes Gate) 1980

The hot Cold War and other campaigns
Afghanistan
Gambia 1981
Thailand/Cambodia 1980–90
The new opium war
Liberia 1990
Ethiopia 1991
Peterhead Prison 1987

Prologue

From 1968 – the year of chic student revolution in Europe and North America – the world changed dramatically. Learning from such thinkers as Marcuse and Sartre rebels of all kinds, with and without a cause, harnessed the media to pressure elected government and used cheap international travel to turn the world into a gigantic, if dangerous, playpen for adolescent Rambos. In time, the Warsaw Pact (notably East Germany) combined with delinquent Arab regimes to provide the wild ones with training and grown-up weapons.

The SAS was slow to respond to Euroterror. It took notice only after the Munich massacre of 1972. As usual, the regiment learned quickly. At Princes Gate, Kensington, in May 1980, a team from B Squadron stormed the Iranian Embassy in an operation which caused the world to hold its breath. It was the first time the 'freedom fighters' (in this case, Iranian Arabs backed by Iraq) were decisively beaten. By the time an SAS team freed a hostage at Peterhead Prison, Scotland, in 1987 the regiment's role as sheriff for the free world was reaching into some unlikely corners.

This section of the history attempts to describe the transition from the last days of the Cold War (as fought by the SAS in the Third World) to the new, uncharted territory beyond.

MUNICH MASSACRE TO 'KILLING HOUSE'

On 5 May 1980, when an SAS counter-terrorist team abseiled from the roof of the Iranian Embassy at Princes Gate, London to halt the murders (then in progress) of twenty-one hostages, they had the sort of worldwide television audience that terrorist propagandists lust after and sometimes – as in the Munich massacre of Israel's Olympic athletes – obtain. (Or, rather, could obtain in the Cold War heyday, when the covert support of the now defunct Warsaw Pact was the bedrock from which to mount such spectaculars.)

In London, the SAS high-profile success rebounded on terrorists, propagating the then-unfashionable idea that democracy could defend itself if it had to. As at Entebbe in 1976 and at Mogadishu and Assen, Holland a year later (all successful hostage-rescues) the propaganda of the deed reinforced the credibility of the rule of law rather than the law of the jungle. The even greater public success of the SAS at Princes Gate remains the greatest coup of them all more than a decade later. It hauled the SAS out of its closet of secrecy and created instead a high-profile, up-front bogeyman with which to intimidate the intimidators.

The origins of the regiment's urban counter-terrorism can be traced back to the 'Keeni-Meeni' period in Aden (which in turn, perhaps, owed something to the experience of the SAS veteran Roy Farran in Palestine). Although the regiment's founder, David Stirling, had laid it down that for most operations, including those behind enemy lines, the SAS would operate in uniform, the regiment discovered that the urban terrorism of the 1960s was one in which there were no clear lines. If the enemy was to go to war in civilian clothing, then the SAS could do the same. Then, as now, the overwhelming priority was that the undercover soldier had to be as near perfect as any human could be in the use of firearms to minimise the risk of killing innocent bystanders.

The Aden affair ended in 1967, after which, until the SAS went to war in Dhofar in 1970, it had no active campaign to fight. The Commanding Officer of 22 SAS at that time therefore offered the services of his best marksmen to the British government to train bodyguards for overseas heads of state who were thought to be at risk and whose removal would not promote British interests. 'There were hundreds of them, as it turned out', one veteran of the period recalls. 'We went all over the world in their defence.' It was a potent invisible export which yielded Whitehall a rich harvest of goodwill as well as military intelligence. In the 1980s and 1990s the Royal Military Police handled routine close protection of UK diplomats serving in such hotspots as Beirut. When the danger level was particularly high, the SAS still provided its all-embracing cover, from electronic intelligence to resuscitation. Such cases included Sultan Qaboos, Ruler of Oman, during the delicate days immediately after the palace coup through which he ended the disastrous reign of his father, Sultan Sa'id bin Taimur.

Simultaneously, in Hereford itself, a special house was constructed to train marksmen in the perilous skills required to shoot assassins or kidnappers in the close confines of a room without hitting the VIP to be rescued. The house is formally known as the Close Quarter Battle (CQB) House and less formally as the 'killing house'. Over the years, as part of a low-profile programme of public education, the SAS has entertained many people influential in public life, including editors, to the CQB experience. The risk, like the ammunition, is real. One SAS soldier has been killed accidentally, but the idea has been copied around the world. By 1992 there were 100 CQB houses.

In the beginning, each six-man bodyguard training team on its return to England would train others in the practical lessons learned at the sharp end of the job overseas. To maintain the momentum a Counter Revolutionary Warfare (CRW) Wing was created, commanded by a single officer whose task it was to keep international developments in his field under constant review. But in 1970–71, as a result of the regiment's commitment to Dhofar, there were no longer enough SAS soldiers to act as the world's best bodyguards. The training was scaled down. The CRW Wing was less important to the SAS now that it had a real war to fight. As things turned out, this almost total change of emphasis was a mistake.

In fact 1970 was the year which did nothing for Britain's reputation as a hard target for terrorist blackmail. It was the year in which a Palestinian woman hijacker, Leila Khaled, was allowed to fly home from London as part of a collective European surrender to international terrorism. Worse was to come. In September 1972, seven Palestinian terrorists took over a dormitory at the Munich Olympic Games village occupied by Israeli athletes. The terrorists' organisation, Black September, then demanded Israel's release of 200 imprisoned Palestinians. Israel refused to give way. The West German government, however, did assent to safe passage for the gunmen and their hostages out of the country. At the airport, as the party was about to leave, German security forces fired on the terrorists. In the battle that followed, all the hostages, five terrorists and one police officer were killed. These grisly events were watched by a worldwide television audience estimated to be 500 millions and the image of the West German government was profoundly damaged.

Other Western governments were alarmed by the implications of Munich. They noted that, through the magnifying glass of television, public opinion tended to blame governments rather than terrorists for a violent end to hostage-taking. Equally alarming, it was borne in upon most of them that no Western country had military people trained to the degree of sophistication necessary to defuse a massive psychological warfare threat of the sort mounted by a few well-trained 'civilians' who were already acquiring more operational experience of sieges than any security force. West Germany responded by creating the GSG–9 (border police) anti-terrorist squad under Ulrich Wegener. The French took similar action. In London, Prime Minister Edward Heath directed that a new, specialised unit be created. The Ministry of Defence ordered the SAS to take on this job and the Counter-Terrorist team was born.

The regiment was now given the resources it needed to create a small, permanent anti-terrorist team available at short notice to deal with hijacks and sieges anywhere in the United Kingdom. There was, and is, an orchestra of exotic equipment available for such missions, ranging from parabolic directional microphones to thermal imagers capable of identifying those apartments in a particular building which are occupied and which are not. But at the end of the road, when all the cunning of 'gee-whizz' technology has been exploited, the central problem of a siege is appallingly crude: to save hostage lives by killing the terrorists holding them, if that is necessary.

Weapon training

The SAS solution is to train its close-quarter marksmen to an extraordinary degree of skill, honing their reflexes in action as if they are tennis stars being groomed for the men's final at Wimbledon. The training starts by being terrifying, produces competence, then confidence and finally, something approaching boredom in some cases as a result of the sheer repetition of CQB training.

Second only in importance to the skill of the men is the armament they employ. As Dobson and Payne argue in *The Weapons of Terror*, such is the velocity of modern firearms that 'the up-to-date bullets of law and order, when used without care, not only travel further [than required] but they strike in the cause of the terrorists they are seeking to overcome.'

In other words, excessive firepower will result in a propaganda victory for the terrorists, even if the security forces win the military engagement. And since terrorism is primarily about shaping popular perceptions as part of its psychological warfare, the more important battleground is not the individual siege but the one fought in the pages of newspapers, on our television screens – and ultimately in our minds. For all these reasons, low velocity and accuracy are the desiderata of anti-terrorist weapons for use in cities. Reliability is equally important, since a weapon prone to stoppages is worse than useless. So what is required is a weapon that fires rapidly, precisely on target and at low velocity, hitting the intended target without penetrating one body and striking another. A dramatic illustration of this philosophy in action occurred when the joint SAS/GSG–9 team burst into the hijacked Lufthansa airliner at Mogadishu: every terrorist was wounded in the first quick burst of gunfire, but the ensuing battle continued for eight minutes. A woman terrorist was wounded nine times, and survived after medical treatment in custody.

Initially, the SAS/CT team armed itself with the American Ingram submachine-gun, but on automatic fire it tended to spray bullets too liberally over the target area, with ominous implications for innocent hostages. Eventually, the regiment chose the Heckler & Koch MP5. Experiments in West Germany, where the weapon is made, had led to the accidental discovery that a certain non-German bullet could yield unparalleled accuracy among such weapons, and stoppages caused by the new bullet were cured by redesigning the magazine, making it curved. The weapon was used in action by the SAS for the first time at the Iranian Embassy siege. The other firearms carried by the team include the thirteen-round Browning automatic pistol, a reserve weapon that lingers in the SAS armoury partly as a result of the experience of an officer in Malaya in parachute harness, weaponless, while an armed guerrilla prowled around immediately below him. The heaviest firearm used is the Remington shotgun, to blast the lock from a door to a room known to be occupied by terrorists. Also carried are plastic explosives and concussion grenades – 'flash-bangs' – which are magnesium-based and have the shock effect of paralysing the enemy during the vital first five seconds of an encounter. CS gas grenades can be used if surprise has failed to overcome an adversary. Both the 'flash-bang' (an SAS invention) and CS carry with them the risk of causing an explosion or a fire or both. In an assault such as that which took place at the Iranian Embassy, team members wear protective gas-masks throughout the attack, so that if they use CS they will not need to waste time donning masks after the assault has started. Finally, the team is equipped with a variety of specialised motor vehicles and aircraft, enabling it to travel with its equipment at short notice anywhere in Britain.

At the same time as this re-equipping was taking place, the regiment explanded its CRW Wing to a permanent cadre, or cell, consisting of one officer and four instructors to be responsible for all aspects of training in hostage rescue, bodyguard work, Intelligence gathering about terrorist techniques, and so on. The Counter-Terrorist team, at that time comprising about twenty men and drawn on rota from the four operational Sabre squadrons, was deployed in earnest for the first time in January 1975, when a civil airliner was hijacked at Manchester by an Iranian armed with a pistol which later proved to be a harmless replica. The whole affair turned into black comedy after the hijacker was persuaded that he had reached his desired destination (Paris) when in fact he was at Stansted Airport in Essex, where the SAS awaited him. The only casualty was a soldier bitten by a police dog as he left the aircraft. The hijacker was sent to prison.

Reputation induces surrender

The next time the SAS were summoned to a siege, the mere knowledge of their presence was sufficient to induce the terrorists to surrender. In December 1975 a four-man 'Active Service Unit' of the Provisional IRA was trapped by Metropolitan Police officers in a flat in Balcombe Street, Marylebone, in London where they held the occupants, a nervous middle-aged couple, hostage. Through the wonders of fibre optics, it was possible for a controller at Scotland Yard to monitor what was happening in the flat from minute to minute. The terrorists had a transistor radio and, when the BBC announced that the SAS were on the scene and standing by to take over the building, the terrorists surrendered. But the revelation that the soldiers were on the scene, successful though it was, focused public attention on who is in charge of such a situation: the police or the military authorities? The legal situation that has evolved to meet such a case is an effective British compromise.

In an exclusively criminal enterprise, such as the seizure of the Spaghetti House Restaurant in London in September 1975, total operational control remains with the local police chief, who has armed officers under his control. However, if a siege is an exercise in terrorism, i.e. an attempt to coerce government for political reasons, then direction of the affair is in the hands of a government committee known as COBR (for Cabinet Office Briefing Room). This is chaired by the Home Secretary, and includes junior Defence and Foreign Affairs Ministers, with advisers representing the police, MI5 and the SAS. Thus, the regiment has a direct channel to the top of the decision-making pyramid as well as operational links on the scene with the police, who remain in tactical control during the negotiating phase. This is as it should be, since the SAS is stringently subject to the rule of law, for which the police are responsible. The Army's counter-terrorist teams are reminded of this by a litany of ground rules, more elaborate even than the 'Yellow Card' governing the rules of engagement for soldiers in Northern Ireland. It travels with the team for display in their tactical operations room near the scene of the siege.

True, there might be some practical advantage in a more organic arrangement through which, say, the SAS handled negotiations as well. But, as things stand, the team members know that they are on scene in exactly the same way as military bomb-disposal squads might be elsewhere, as military aid to the civil power. Politically, they are not merely neutral, but 'neutered' also. There is another reason why the SAS – even in the view of the regiment itself – should not be in the driving seat at an earlier stage of the siege. This is that the use of force, albeit minimum force, is only one of several options open to government in defusing the situation. The others range from total surrender to terrorist demands, in the style of the Austrian and past West German governments (as well as the British in the case of Leila Khaled), to a measured response that permits, say, a limited draught of publicity but nothing else. Interestingly, there are cases, still hypothetical in Britain though not elsewhere, where government might advocate a violent solution to break a siege, but where expert SAS advice might be that this would be unwise – counter-productive, even. It cannot be overstressed that the contemporary SAS is an acute intrument of psychological warfare, and is keenly aware of the political content and ramifications of the violence it can inflict. Most media men, for whom violence is an exotic and vicariously exciting beverage (along with group sex and drug addiction), usually fail to comprehend that the SAS does not share their perception of risk and violence. Like experienced drinkers, the SAS has learned the wisdom of avoiding intoxication, particularly if the party is attended by moralistic outsiders who are likely to accuse the regiment of excessive violence, while using the excitement generated by that violence to improve newspaper circulation or television viewing figures.

MOGADISHU 1977

When the SAS CT team goes into action outside the United Kingdom, where political control is in the hands of the host government, different considerations apply. In October 1977, four Palestinian terrorists – two men, two women – joined seventy-nine normal passengers on a Lufthansa flight from Majorca. The cursory baggage checks there enabled the terrorists to smuggle an assortment of weapons aboard the aircraft, which they then hijacked. The principal object of the operation was to force the West German government to release the leaders of the notorious Baader-Meinhof gang, a team of chic middle-class revolutionaries then in prison in Germany. For good measure, the hijackers threw in a demand for a £9 million ransom. The hijack occurred six weeks after the kidnap of Hans-Martin Schleyer, a powerful West German industrial baron; his release, like that of the Lufthansa hostages, was conditional upon freedom for the Baader-Meinhof team, and he was still imprisoned when the Lufthansa place was seized.

Such was the crisis of credibility faced by the Bonn government that much normal administration was being paralysed by the need to manage the crisis. As so often before, government was in a 'no-win' position: a surrender to terrorism would damage belief in government's ability to govern; a hard line, if it resulted in hostage deaths, would provoke a storm of protest from society's professional humanitarians. The terrorists knew they were on to a good thing since, until that time, most captured terrorists had obtained freedom within one or two years as a result of such blackmail by their comrades outside. (The unfashionable Moluccans tended to be an exception to this rule.)

A wild aerial journey followed the Lufthansa hijack around various places in the Middle East and the Horn of Africa. Soon after it began a German minister travelled to London, accompanied by a member of the GSG-9 team, to seek British help and, in particular, liaison with the authorities of Dubai where the hijacked aircraft was about to land. (A member of the United Arab Emirates, Dubai has close links with Britain.) Initially, the purpose of the Germans' visit was to ask Whitehall to use its good offices with the UAE ambassador in London to ensure diplomatic clearance for GSG-9 to go into action in Dubai. As a subsidiary objective, the GSG-9 representative thought that his SAS opposite number might have equipment that could be useful in breaking into the aircraft. The Germans had not appreciated that the SAS knows the Persian Gulf intimately and that, for example, Dubai's elite presidential guard is trained and led by former SAS soldiers. During the London conversations, therefore, it became clear to everyone that an SAS liaison team on this operation would be a decided asset, and such a plan was instantly endorsed by the respective premiers, Callaghan and Schmidt. The two men selected for the job were Major Alastair Morrison, OBE, MC, an SAS veteran and then second-in-command of 22 SAS, and Sergeant Barry Davies, BEM, commanding the counter-terrorist teams' sniper group. Taking a specially crated collection of 'flash-bangs' they left immediately for Dubai.

They arrived to discover that GSG-9's leader, Wegener, and two of his men were being kept 'under escort' in the international airport's VIP lounge – in the politest possible way – while the hijacked airliner, with its hostages, stood on the scorching tarmac. Morrison and Davies sorted out this bureaucratic nonsense, and then set about training the Dubai Royal Guard in the basics of siege-breaking with a view to providing a back-up for GSG-9, whose main force was then in a pursuit aircraft in Turkey. But, before this elaboratae scheme could be put into operation, the Lufthansa airliner flew on to Aden. Obstacles might have been placed on the Dubai runway to delay the hijacked aircraft's departure, but at that point the terrorists could threaten the hostages effectively while the security forces could not convincingly match that threat. In such a case, the golden rule is that government must be able to 'put its money where its mouth is' if it is going to arrest, or even contain, terrorists, or pay for its failed bluff with hostage lives. So the Lufthansa plane, refuelled and replenished, took off, followed by another aircraft carrying Morrison, Davies, Wegener and his two aides. For a time, the hijacked airliner enjoyed sanctuary at Aden, while, for some hours, the Morrison–Wegener group flew in the vicinity seeking permission to land on the same airfield, but this was refused. Aden, now capital of the Marxist People's Democratic Republic of South Yemen, contained numerous East German and Soviet advisers, whose governments declined to put pressure on their Arabian client to assist GSG-9.

By now, Morrison and Davies had become *de facto* members of Wegener's team, and they stayed with him when the hunt moved from Aden to Mogadishu in Somalia, where the German commander was joined by the main body of his force after a flight from Turkey. The whole rescue party got together just twelve hours before the rescue attempt. The role of the SAS men would be to throw the 'flash-bang' grenades at the start of the operation if peaceful persuasion did not work. The Germans were in earnest about a peaceful solution: their pursuit aircraft carried the ransom – £9 million in cash – in a large metal box. But at Aden, the captain of the hijacked airliner, Jurgen Schumann, was murdered by the terrorist leader, 'Captain Mahmoud', after he suspected Schumann of secretly communicating with the security forces. The Lufthansa airliner flew on to Mogadishu, where Schumann's body was thrown from the plane. For many hours prior to that it had lain on the floor of the aircraft, in full view of the terrified hostages.

From the moment the pilot's body was hurled on to the Mogadishu runway, there was no hope of a peaceful end to the siege and, five days after the SAS team joined Wegener, they threw their 'flash-bangs' from each side of the aircraft to signal the assault. The attack plan, composed by the SAS team, was one in which fortune favoured the bold. The assault team entered the aircraft through the emergency doors set above the wings on each side of the fuselage, kicking in the doors as the 'flash-bangs' exploded. Once inside, they had to tackle terrorist gunmen at the front and rear of the airliner. Aviation fuel as well as duty-free alcohol scattered by the terrorists inside the aircraft might have exploded, but it did not. During the eight-minute battle inside the aircraft, the terrorists rolled two hand grenades towards the assault team, but these exploded harmlessly beneath padded passenger seats. The hostages, strapped in their seats, were below the line of fire being exchanged between the terrorists and the raiders, and three of the four terrorists were killed. Later, their leader was identified as Zohair Akache, a professional assassin serving the Palestinian extremist Wadi Hadad. That he was operating on this occasion on behalf of the Baader-Meinhof group was a vivid illustration of the organic nature of international terrorism in the 1970s. Within hours of the Mogadishu battle, the terrorist leaders who had hoped to be set free as a result of the hijack – Andreas Baader, Gudrun Esslin and Jan-Carl Raspe – committed suicide in their cells. And, six days after the rescue the kidnapped West German industrialist, Schleyer, was found shot dead in the boot of a car.

Confirmation of the SAS involvement in the Mogadishu operation came immediately after the rescue from Prime Minister James Callaghan, then in Bonn with Chancellor Schmidt. In front of television cameras Callaghan told Schmidt: 'It should have been Dubai.' But even if the venue was changed, the event added new lustre to the SAS reputation, and it was good for Britain's relations with Europe. Within Germany, an agonising political crisis had been resolved. And a secret agreement among West European governments to co-operate in the war against terrorism – made eighteen months before at the time of the Moluccan siege at Assen in Holland – was given operational reality for the first time.

Inside a terrorist's mind

The event was also to have momentous implications for the role of the SAS in future years. The CT team was still little more than twenty strong and in the light of the political crisis generated by expert terrorism within West Germany, the Callaghan government took the significant step of authorising a substantial increase in the British CT force. From now on each SAS squadron was committed in turn to the CT role on rotation, between tours in Northern Ireland and training missions abroad. The implication of that decision was that Britain was now a potential SAS operational zone in a way not previously contemplated. The squadron dedicated to CT would spend a prolonged period undergoing refresher training in the necessary techniques under the guidance of the permanent CRW Wing. During this British tour – 'the war on your doorstep', as one SAS man called it – the squadron would then work up to the monthly siege-breaking exercise, usually in a new environment each time, followed by a prolonged debriefing, or 'washup'. At the end of the tour, the same squadron would remain on stand-by and assist its successor squadron's retraining in the role. The wisdom of this decision only became apparent two years later, when the scale of the problem at the Iranian Embassy was within the compass of a squadron (about eighty men) but far beyond the capabilities of the original team of twenty. Yet again, the SAS had made one of its unique evolutions into a new role to meet a need that others could not satisfy.

The period between Mogadishu and the embassy siege was one in which London became a battleground for various Middle East terrorist groups in conflict with the Israelis and with one another, and during which – in July 1978 – Britain had to expel eleven Iraqi diplomats because of their involvement in terrorism. In Hereford, meanwhile, the increased emphasis on CT was accompanied by more funds and improved training facilities which, as one veteran put it, 'moved out of the world of Heath Robinson in the late sixties to superb equipment in the late seventies'. Details of those new facilities are secret, and rightly so. In general terms, however, it may be said that they train the SAS teams to enter a terrorist stronghold by a variety of means and, once inside, to distinguish instantly between terrorist and hostage (unless, as happened in the Iranian Embassy, some of the terrorists neither fight nor surrender but pretend to be hostages). In the 'killing house', now furnished with a television and pictures on the walls, dummies representing terrorists and hostages are moved from place to place. The CT team is divided into two specialist groups, the assault group who enter the building, and the perimeter containment group, snipers who provide a cordon sanitaire around the scene. The assault group members have to be able to burst into a room in pairs and instantly fire two pistol rounds or short, controlled bursts of automatic fire – the 'double tap' – into each terrorist, aiming for the head, without causing injury to their fellow team members or the hostages. Each two-man team has its own room to deal with and each man has his own arc of fire so that, once one room is cleared and the next squad has followed through, the possibility of an 'own goal' or battle accident, is drastically reduced. The use of balaclava masks, first introduced in the Aden days for certain operations, assists the process of instant identification in action while in Britain; and it also ensures that any SAS soldier accused of murder (for, unlike the terrorist, he subjects himself to the rule of law) will go on trial without the encumbrance of a jury that has identified him from newspaper photographs. In an age when the camera is ubiquitous, and terrorist resources enjoy the sophistication of government backing in Iraq, South Yemen, Libya and Lebanon, the mask also assures the future anonymity of SAS soldiers. Over the years, the dissemination of CT training throughout the regiment means that most CT men have been prepared for the sniper's role on the perimeter as well as the assault role, greatly enhancing the mutual comprehension of SAS team members. Such is the stability of the regiment that the same small group will work together for years. Two of those who stormed the Iranian Embassy in London fought together at Mirbat in 1972, and one was decorated for his courage there. The SAS team at Mogadishu were among those who flew to the relief of Mirbat.

What the SAS does not attempt to do is to assume control of the negotiations with the terrorists. (There are, as have been explained, good constitutional reasons for this.) Negotiating the release of hostages has become a technique for specialists, which the SAS studies carefully, but is not best qualified to practise. The aim of such negotiations is to ensure the release of the hostages, alive, but not at any price. Thus, the terrorists have to discover, once the siege starts, how far their demands are 'real' in the sense that there are some things no government could guarantee. Pressure on the Dutch government by Moluccan extremists to arrange that a part of another country – Indonesia – should be granted independence from that country over which Holland has no control, falls firmly into the category of total unreality. In practice, most terrorist sieges over the years have been aimed at securing the release of other terrorists from lawful imprisonment and, in general, it is a form of blackmail that has succeeded. At the other extreme from total surrender is the style adopted by the Israeli and French governments, the full frontal assault technique, which affords the terrorists no scope for manoeuvre. This gung-ho approach to the siege problem carries with it the lamentable by-product of dead hostages, which is politically dangerous.

Both the New York Police negotiators (whose motto is 'We bore them to death') and the Dutch security forces have pioneered the middle road of substitute, or surrogate, achievement through the use of one subtle negotiator. His is the voice on the telephone which, in a psychological sense, gets into bed with the terrorists, referring to the two sides – terrorists and negotiators – as 'us' or 'we', and the government and its security forces as 'them' or 'they', the outsiders. This Machiavelli gradually persuades the hostage-taker that if he kills any of his prisoners it will damage the terrorist cause. After all, the argument goes, the terrorist has commanded maximum media coverage for his grievance. Give it more time for the public to digest the lesson, Machiavelli continues, and meanwhile come out peacefully with clean hands to win respect by facing a bourgeois court. The argument is a seductive one for a terrorist who is trapped along with his hostages: it provides the terrorist with all the benefits of martyrdom without the unpalatable corollary of death, a bit like Mark Twain's description of attending his own funeral and being quite overcome with grief. But terrorists also read Mark Twain and much besides, and some of them have

PhDs. Even the comparatively rustic Iranian Embassy terrorists had apparently equipped themselves with tranquillisers to help sustain the stress they were about to face.

The clever ones now add to the pressure on democratic government by launching their assaults at election time, when government is peculiarly vulnerable to the pressures of public opinion, which in turn is influenced by the media. The Dutch government, faced with such a siege during an election in 1977, learned that to 'play it long' in this way became intolerable. The result, after days of negotiation, was a quick, brutal military solution using Air Force jets as well as Marine Commandos. SAS observers in Holland, noting that the terrorists could run a siege at two locations simultaneously (a village school and a commuter train) took note and fine-tuned their tactics accordingly.

Yet another psychological factor is the so-called 'Stockholm syndrome', when a strong emotional bond is established between hostage and captor in joint opposition to the rescue team. Part of this intoxicant is the hostage's emotional dependence on his new 'parent', expressed as a child-like requirement to seek permission even to go to the lavatory. Through various academic studies it has become axiomatic that after a few days, the syndrome will assure the survival of the hostages so long as the security forces do not accidentally precipitate a massacre by frightening the terrorists. But, as the murders of numerous European hostages in the Congo in the 1960s demonstrated, the assumption underlying the Stockholm syndrome is a life-saver only if the terrorists share the same cultural values as the negotiators. Cultural assumptions about the sanctity of human life are part of the fabric of Western, democratic and essentially Christian society.

The SAS training scenario does not rely on the essential good nature of the terrorist, though the regiment accepts that – to put it at its meanest – public opinion will demand a convincing effort to end a siege peacefully before unleashing the soldiers. Still, it is worth noting that the training scenario also assumes that a hostage will be murdered *after* prolonged negotiations, during which, if the academics are right, the Stockholm syndrome should have started to produce results. Indeed, to judge from the treatment of the Iranian Embassy hostages by the SAS immediately after they were rescued – as Sim Harris put it, 'thrown from one man to the next, no compassion, no thought of minor injuries and then tied up' – the doctrine also assumes that some hostages might actually try to help their former captors.

Basically, the British style of negotiation appears to be a pragmatic blend of the Dutch and Israeli styles: to negotiate in good faith on issues that are negotiable so long as there is no blood-letting; to continue to negotiate to buy time once the murder of a hostage has taken place. The SAS adds its own garnish to that. The regiment prepares a plan, however crude, for an *immediate* assault (or, 'Emergency Response') if it is summoned to a siege, in the belief that there are some situations where pessimism and prudence go hand in hand.

LONDON (PRINCES GATE) 1980

With the wisdom of hindsight it is possible to identify the end of the Iranian Embassy siege in London on 5 May 1980 as more than a spectacular victory over international terrorism. It was also an opening skirmish in the war about to be waged by the Iraqi dictator, Saddam Hussein, against his neighbours. The six-man team which held the embassy and more than twenty hostages for six days was trained in Baghdad, issued with Iraqi passports, supplied with weapons brought by diplomatic bag from Baghdad and controlled by an Iraqi army officer who flew home the day the siege began.

The terrorists came from the embittered, impoverished Arab minority in an Iranian province just across the Shatt-al-Arab river border with Iraq known as Khuzistan. It is the centre of Iran's richest oilfields around Abadan and includes its largest port, Khorramshahr. In February 1979, the Shah of Iran (an ally of the West) was overturned by the fundamentalist revolution of the 76-year-old Ayatollah Khomenei. His zeal stirred his fellow Shia Muslims in Iraq as well as in Iran. Less noticed in the West was the almost simultaneous emergence of another dictator a few months later. Saddam Hussein, an old-fashioned Mafia politician, finally got his hands on the Iraqi presidency in mid-July, just six months after the Ayatollah's return from exile. In March 1975, Iraq had ceded the eastern half of the Shatt-al-Arab boundary to Iran. In 1979, Saddam wanted it back.

With the emergence of two new, opposed power blocks in the cockpit of the Gulf, events moved fast. In September, Iran's Revolutionary Guard seized the American Embassy in Tehran taking 53 diplomats as hostages. Meanwhile Iran's oil pipelines in Khuzistan were sabotaged by agents of Baghdad.

It seems plausible that Saddam chose London for an embassy seizure as a result of the political pay-off resulting from the Iranian victory over America in Tehran and on the world's TV screens. By reaching out to Western soil to stage his own spectacular, Saddam was raising the stakes even higher. The prize was a convincing show of leadership for the rest of the Arab world.

The first phase went surprisingly well. Each man was given £725 in cash and sent to the British Embassy to pick up a visa to visit the UK ('Purpose of visit: Medical treatment') using new Iraqi passports and mugshot photographs taken in a downtown photo-cabin. The object of their mission, they were told, was to publicise the plight of Arabs in Iran and to demand the freedom of 92 political prisoners held in Iranian prisons.

The first of the passports was issued in Baghdad in February. The party's Iraqi controller, Sami Mohammed Ali (passport No. F443373 and described as an official of the Iraqi Ministry of Industry) persuaded the men that they would be on their way home as heroes after a siege lasting only twenty-four hours. He himself arrived in London with four of the six on 31 March and rented two apartments in Western London.

The terrorist life had its compensations, even if the men were asked by the landlord to move because of the number of prostitutes they entertained. They were in London in time to see uncensored, televised reports of the Desert One disaster in April. The US Delta Force, a cousin of the SAS, left eight dead amid the burning hulks of helicopters in the failed attempt to rescue American hostages in Tehran. From where an Iraqi terrorist-in-waiting stood, it was a good omen.

The night before the siege began, Sami Mohammed Ali delivered their weapons: two Skorpion W263 Polish sub-machine-guns, three Browning self-loading pistols, one .38 Astra revolver and five RGD5 Soviet-made hand grenades. There was also a lot of ammunition. Before they left Baghdad they had been shown plans of the embassy. They were briefed also on the number of hostages to expect: twenty-five staff plus a British police officer. All were to be taken as hostages and a programme of demands issued to the British government.

Just twenty-six hours were to be allowed to pass before they were to kill their first hostage. Subsequently, according to their script, the murder rate would be one hostage every hour.

On the morning of 30 April, a few hours before the operation began, Sami was back at the apartment, collecting the men's passports and arranging for their belongings (suitcases filled with Western consumer durables) to be sent back to Baghdad. Sami himself flew home the same morning.

It seemed, on the face of things, as if their confidence was justified. The embassy was guarded by just one avuncular constable, a placid, middle-aged man who kept his topcoat buttoned, his pistol in its holster out of sight and his cap squarely on his head. This was London-the-Open-City in spite of IRA and other terrorist outrages over the preceding six years. The appearance of passivity at No. 16 Princes Gate, just across the road from the tranquillity of Hyde Park, was deceptive. There was an iron hand inside the woollen police glove but it was kept out of sight most of the time, 150 miles away at SAS Headquarters, Hereford. The Iraqi terrorists were not to know that the regiment had been practising the use of lethal force at very close quarters for the preceding seven years, or that one of their number could be struck down by an SAS sniper lurking in the park.

Should the siege-breaking attack be aimed at a sealed fortress (technically tough but politically convenient, in that the area around the fortress can be sanitised to exclude journalists or allies of the terrorists) or a mobile target such as a convoy?

The regiment's contingency plans, code-named Operation Pagoda, involved an entire squadron, known as the counter-terrorist team, to be on constant stand-by. The core of the operation was a command group of four officers plus a support team (an officer and about twenty-five men) ready to move at thirty minutes' notice. A second fully-equipped team replicated the first, on a three-hour stand-by until the first team had left Hereford. A third team could be composed from experienced SAS soldiers if necessary. The close-quarter support teams were backed up by sniper groups to pick off targets from outside the terrorist location and specially trained, military medical teams to rescue and resuscitate the victims.

The SAS plans were carefully constrained by the doctrine of police primacy. By a neat coincidence, the Iranian Embassy alert coincided with preparations for a joint exercise with the Northumbria Police Force. The people and equipment were all in place at Hereford, ready to move, less than three hours distant by road when the crisis began.

If the terrorists had a timetable of murder and an agenda for blackmail, the SAS also had its own prescriptions in waiting. The basic scenario for its joint exercises anticipated to a remarkable extent the way events would actually develop at the embassy. It went something like this:

1. Terrorists seize hostages and incarcerate themselves in a building, an aircraft, a railway train, a bus or aboard a ship.

2. The police negotiate in good faith, offering media coverage of terrorist demands as a bargaining chip, a substitute or surrogate achievement for the terrorists' declared aims.

3. The terrorist demands are directed not at the British government but a foreign one over which the British have no control.

4. The negotiations start to crumble when terrorists threaten to kill a hostage and shots are heard from the siege area. Later there are more shots and the contemptuous public exposure of a victim's body.

5. A timetable of executions is announced by the terrorists and the SAS assault follows.

6. As soon as the siege is over, police investigators and forensic scientists move into the stronghold to reconstruct exactly what has happened during the brief period of military control of the area. The investigation includes forensic autopsies on the victims and ballistic analysis of the rounds fired, matched with the weapons employed.

Day One. The siege begins

The Iraqi terrorists' first rendezvous was a spot inside Hyde Park, near the Albert Memorial, opposite the Royal Albert Hall. It was a cold morning. They wore anoraks for comfort as well as to conceal their sub-machine-guns. At the embassy a few hundred yards away PC Trevor Lock was grateful for the cup of coffee slipped to him by the embassy's official doorman. Lock was drinking this in the tiny lobby between the main doors giving access to the street and an inner pair of special security doors that led to the main entrance hall. In 1977, during the Shah's reign, the SAS had been asked to advise the embassy about its security. The security doors, all but impenetrable without explosive charges, resulted from that advice.

The Iraqis moved as a pack towards the outer door. As the policeman opened it, the first man in fumbled inside his anorak, trying to extract the gun. Simultaneously he bumped into Lock and a struggle began. As they wrestled, Lock slammed the outer door closed and sent a half-strangled warning on his personal radio to his headquarters at New Scotland Yard.

One of the terrorists left outside drew his Browning pistol and fired three shots through the glass panel of the outer door. A shower of glass blinded Lock just long enough for the attackers to force the door. As they scrimmaged into the lobby they tore his radio away. They did not know he was still armed.

Inside the main entrance hall, the terrorists announced their presence by loosing off automatic fire into the ceiling. At the back of the building the embassy's charge d'affaires, Dr Ali Afrouz, jumped from the first floor window in an escape attempt, landing on a pavement. He was knocked unconscious by the fall and hauled back inside the building by his captors. His colleague, Fahad Gity a counsellor, was more lucky. He clambered out of a window on the fourth floor and entered the building next door through an adjoining window. Two women on the staff, quiet as mice, tiptoed to safety through the back door of the building into the extensive gardens.

In spite of these defections, the terrorists' haul of hostages was impressive: fifteen Iranians and one British citizen employed by the embassy; PC Lock, bleeding profusely from a facial wound; and five visitors, of whom four were journalists. The security door was slammed shut, the hostages bundled into a small first floor office. Afrouz could not stand because of a leg injury suffered in his unsuccessful leap for freedom. A Press officer, Mrs Frieda Mozafarian, began a series of fainting fits combined with noisy spasms. Lock's face continued to bleed. After ninety minutes, the terrorists made their first contact with the outside world, a telephone request for a woman doctor.

The SAS was only a part, if a vital part, of a vast, regularly-exercised machine that now clicked into gear. By 3pm the Home Secretary, William Whitelaw (no stranger to earlier rehearsals for this sort of crisis) was presiding over a top level crisis-management team known as COBR (pronounced 'Cobra' and representing the Cabinet Office Briefing Room). Its function was to lay down basic guidelines for the police (and, if necessary the Army) to follow. The essence of the policy was summarised as 'No surrender'. The affair could end peacefully with the release of the hostages and the surrender of the hostage-takers but there would be no safe-conduct for terrorists out of the country.

If Saddam's men were hoping for a replay of the release by British authorities of the Palestinian terrorist Leila Khaled in 1970, then their luck was out. Times had changed. The new mood was expressed by the Metropolitan Police chief Sir Robert Mark at Spaghetti House in 1975: 'We made it plain that the gunmen were going only to a prison cell or a mortuary.'

Day Two

In 1980, police negotiators given the sensitive job of talking to the terrorists did not put the position as coarsely as that. In boring detail and very slowly, they addressed irrelevant issues as if they were negotiating matters of substance. Over the next few days their agenda would include food, medical attention, communications, access to the media and the involvement of the ambassadors of friendly Middle Eastern states. Meanwhile, a trickle of ailing hostages was released and could give the security forces vital information about the number of terrorists, their weapons and their state of mind. The slow burn approach enabled the police and MI5 to plant listening devices inside the building and the SAS to get its act together.

'Basically,' said one participant later, 'we were facing a fortress situation here. You have to bear in mind that this was a big mid-terrace building on six floors (four above the ground) with fifty rooms, easily defended at front and back because of the open spaces on either side of it; twenty hostages and six terrorists who got increasingly jumpy as time went by, moving the hostages from one room to another.'

The teams sent from Hereford came from B Squadron, which had only just taken its turn on the counter-terrorist rota, to the annoyance of D Squadron, which had just finished its stint. As an opening move, the SAS insinuated one Pagoda team (identified as the 'Red Team') into the Royal College of Medical Practitioners building next door. (An alternative location was the Royal Albert Hall a few hundred yards away to the west.) This consisted of a captain and twenty-four men including Corporal Tommy Palmer, later killed in Northern Ireland. To dodge the Press they were smuggled in by civilian furniture vans in the early hours of Day Two, 1 May. They completed the trip with a stealthy movement over walls and rear gardens into their location, known to them as the Forward Holding Area (FHA).

Red Team's task, directed by the Commanding Officer, Lieutenant-Colonel Mike Rose and their squadron commander, a Major, was twofold. First, they had to be ready for an assault on the embassy at ten minutes' notice if the killing started. This was the 'Immediate Action Plan': a crude and risky game of hide-and-seek, in which the soldiers would have to break in through the upper windows and clear the building, room by room, with CS gas and firearms in the hope of reaching the hostages before all were murdered. Such a plan was completed within one hour of the Pagoda team's arrival. The second job was to prepare for the 'Deliberate Assault Plan', to be launched at a time chosen by the SAS, when – hopefully – the terrorists would be exhausted and the location of the hostages known.

Meanwhile, Intelligence about the situation inside the embassy was piling up. The regiment's Intelligence cell, aided by a member of the embassy staff, was fabricating a model of the building and a Home Office psychiatrist was monitoring the terrorists' mood. Something like a full-scale model of the embassy's key rooms was being constructed at Regent's Park Barracks, with walls ingeniously made of hessian and an embassy caretaker on hand to describe the layout.

Day Three

As the Deliberate Assault Plan became more defined its most important elements were fed into the Immediate Action Plan, the scheme to storm the building as a prompt response to any murders. This meant that for the Red Team the learning process was non-stop. Since their own lives depended on getting it right, the soldiers studied every photograph, drawing, report and other scrap of information fed to them about the people next door with rapt attention. As each new terrorist deadline approached ('Broadcast our message by 1300 hrs or else . . .') the Reds also had to get into their fighting equipment and out onto the roof to prepare to go into action, on a radio message, at four minutes notice. They were stood down repeatedly. The Blue Team arrived at the FHA at 3.30am on Day Three, Friday 2 May, by the same circuitous route pioneered by Red. By that time, Red Team had been on continuous duty for twenty-three hours, screwed up time and again for the imminence of action, and stood down again. Not surprisingly, later in the operation, as it became manifest that there would be no peaceful outcome, the Director, SAS, Brigadier Peter de la Billière insisted that once he and his men were committed, there should be no last-minute change of mind. However, half-way through the crisis, all was as quiet as the grave as Blue Team (one captain and twenty-four soldiers) took over the responsibility for the Immediate Action Plan. Red Team caught up with a little sleep.

During those first two days, a key development had been the evacuation of the BBC Television News organiser Chris Cramer, with severe stomach cramp, at 11.20am on Thursday 1 May. Cramer could confirm that Lock still had his gun; that there were six terrorists, not five as initially believed; that each terrorist carried two hand grenades as well as small arms. The great unresolved question was whether the terrorist claims to have the building wired up for a doomsday explosion, were true.

Just before 5pm that day the terrorist leader Awn Ali Mohammed (*nom-de-guerre*, 'Towfiq', police codename, 'Salim') telephoned the negotiators with a new programme. It appeared that he had dropped his demand for the release of prisoners in Iran. Now he wanted a bus with curtained windows to carry his men and the hostages to an airport where the British captives would be released; an aircraft to fly the rest of the party including the Iranian hostages, to the Middle East. The ambassadors of Iraq, Algeria and Jordan as well as a Red Cross representative were to be present during the transfer. The SAS started examining alternatives to a fortress attack.

Next morning, possibly regretting the implied weakness of his changed objectives, Awn – a twenty-six year old Baghdad-born merchant – appeared at a second-floor window with the embassy's cultural attache, Dr Abdul Fazi Ezzati. Pointing a gun at the man's head, the terrorist shouted down a message. Unless his demands were broadcast, a hostage would be shot. Ezzati thought his time had come. He reeled back to the room where the other captives were held and there he collapsed in a fit, foaming at the mouth.

In subsequent negotiations, Awn was increasingly jittery, repeating his demand for safe conduct out of the country with a bodyguard of ambassadors. Inside the building some of the six women hostages (held in a room separate from the men) complained of noises in the wall. This was the sound of a technical support team quietly drilling holes for pinhead microphones and, hopefully, tiny fibre optic camera lenses also.

Lock and another male hostage, the Syrian journalist Mustapha Karkouti, came to listen and offer a masculine opinion. Lock, with total conviction, identified the sound as that of a London mouse.

Though it was not obvious at the time, that Friday morning was a turning point in the operation, the moment when any hope of a peaceful end to the crisis (never a likely outcome) finally evaporated. The Home Secretary, Mr Whitelaw, with Douglas Hurd, representing the Foreign Office and the Police Commissioner Sir David McNee, discussed their next move. According to one informed source, they chose 'a policy of maximum patience' which excluded any capitulation to the terrorists' demands, but which also ruled out any pre-emptive SAS assault before a hostage was murdered.

The effect of this decision was to leave the initiative with the terrorists. It was also a policy of psychological attrition which depended on maintaining an appearance of negotiation. The culture from which the terrorists came virtually ruled out any hope that they would surrender peacefully. The irresistible force was moving steadily towards the irremovable object.

At 8.15 that evening an embassy secretary, Mrs Hiyech Sanei Kanji, was set free bearing another message. The terrorist demands must be broadcast or 'a hostage will be killed'. Meanwhile the strategy of maximum patience was endorsed by the Prime Minister, Mrs Thatcher.

Day Four

Next day – Saturday 3 May, Day Four of the crisis – the British government did approach the Arab ambassadors, but only to try to persuade them that they should help convince the terrorists to give up peacefully. The ambassadors insisted instead that the British government should give way and allow the terrorists safe conduct out of the country. It was an impasse.

At a meeting of COBR late that night Brigadier de la Billière tried to settle the argument about whether the terrorists would surrender peacefully in any circumstances. Drawing on his own knowledge of Arabia he emphasised to William Whitelaw that such an outcome was very unlikely. At Regent's Park Barracks, Army engineers had now completed a full-scale model of each floor of the embassy. For eight hours, the assault parties of both Red and Blue teams had been able to rehearse the detailed choreography of their moves inside the building. Within the embassy, as one terrorist stood guard over the hostages, trying to stay awake, the others prowled restlessly, guns lifted, expecting an attack through wall or ceiling at any time. On the roof, the SAS assault teams were gently laying out their abseil ropes.

Day Five

Throughout Sunday 4 May, the police negotiators were told to discuss a deal with the terrorists linking the release of hostages to some sort of intervention by the ambassadors. In fact, there was no serious hope that the negotiators could deliver a deal on such a hypothesis. The ambiguity took its toll. One of the police team, showing strain, had to be replaced. New people were added to the team.

The tension almost boiled over inside the embassy also during that claustrophobic Sunday afternoon. The cause was trivial. The terrorists mischievously sprayed subversive slogans on the walls of a room where the Iranian hostages were kept. The row, audible through the hidden microphones, led to yet another stand-by on the part of the SAS. But that evening, there was a windfall of intelligence for the authorities when the Syrian journalist, Karkouti, was set free because of his failing health. He was the fifth hostage to come out peacefully. He revealed that Awn's authority over the rest of his team – uneducated men in their twenties – was fading. They had expected the siege to last only twenty-four hours.

Red Team, meanwhile, was now practising its abseil techniques from the roof of Peel House, a police residence in Pimlico.

Day Six

At 9am next day, Monday 5 May, COBR met again. Whitelaw turned the screws on the terrorists a notch further. He let it be known that what he called the 'ambassadorial phase' had passed and a firm line would be taken throughout the day. The only concession to the terrorists was that an Imam from the Regent's Park Mosque could be given access to the embassy as a mediator.

Lieutenant-Colonel Rose, commanding 22 SAS, was able to offer some good news and some less good news. The Deliberate Assault Plan would now require two hours' notice to succeed. By 5pm, given the progress of preparation and training, both plans (Immediate Action and Deliberate Assault) would merge into a response time of a few minutes. The Deliberate Assault Plan, of course, was that which gave the maximum chance of surprise and the best hope of hostage survival. The not-so-good news was that even if all went as intended, the best chance of saving hostage life was no more than 60 per cent of the total. Often, the odds were much bleaker.

Just two hours after this assessment and six days after he led his team into the embassy, Awn's self-control finally disintegrated. He warned Lock that unless there was a prompt answer to his demand for the ambassadors to come into the negotiations, a hostage would be shot in half an hour. Lock and Sim Harris, alarmed at the changed atmosphere, sensed danger and warned the police negotiators. They were told to take careful note of the BBC News at noon. The radio bulletin contained nothing new.

Abbas Lavasani, the embassy's chief Press officer, had volunteered to be a martyr after the bitter row with Awn about the terrorist leader's anti-Khomenei graffiti the day before. He was led out of the room where the male hostages were held and down to the ground floor to be tied to a chair. Lock, in a macabre conversation, described the scene for negotiators. The negotiators, playing for time as usual, said the ambassadors would meet at 5pm. Lock and Harris were conducted back upstairs to rejoin the other hostages. They heard three carefully spaced shots; then silence. Awn, looking pale, entered the hostages' room and said he had shot Lavasani, but neither the hostages nor the police outside could believe that the killing had started. There was no sign of a body and they hoped Awn was bluffing. One of the few key players who believed the killing was for real was the SAS commander, Lieutenant-Colonel Rose. He sensed that the timing was right for such an event.

An hour later, COBR was again in session to be told by Mr Whitelaw that in the absence of any proof that a hostage was dead it would be disastrous to react as if this had happened. The crisis managers now had to find a route out of a minefield of doubt and death, against the clock. Awn, with Lock in attendance at the window, had accepted the 5pm deadline for a meeting with the ambassadors. Whitelaw, still suspecting a bluff, asked the COBR team what would be the position if, by 5pm, the terrorists had produced proof of murder.

It happened that SAS preparations for a Deliberate Attack would be complete by 5pm. From that hour onward, the assault could be launched with minimum delay. De la Billière said that his men would have a better chance of success if they were given the go-ahead before nightfall, at 8.30pm. What was vital, even imperative, was that between the time a corpse was produced and the start of the SAS assault, the terrorists should be fed a cover story to keep them happy and off-guard. He had one other point to make. This was that the soldiers, once committed, should be left to get on with their job. If the Deliberate Assault was approved and then halted at the last moment it would be – he used characteristic understatement – 'not good for morale'.

Whitelaw steered a middle course. He kept in place the emergency cover, through which the police would pass control to the SAS at short notice if multiple murders started inside the embassy. Otherwise, the Home Secretary wanted to take further counsel with the Police Commissioner. He would also inform both the Prime Minister and the Defence Minister at 'the moment of decision'.

Many unpleasant imponderables remained. Was there a body? Might a demand for proof of Awn's claim actually provoke a murder that had not happened yet? Should the ambassadors be brought into play and on whose terms? Sir David McNee, Police Commissioner, was one of those who wanted the ambassadors present and on parade in good time or failing that, clear guarantees that they were coming. Since he did not believe anyone had been killed he was not in favour of pressing too hard to call Awn's 'bluff'.

The 5pm deadline passed and for half an hour or so nothing happened. Then Awn telephoned the negotiators. He still wanted to see the ambassadors. If they did not come, another hostage would be killed after 45 minutes and both bodies thrown onto the street. The negotiators kept him talking. Would he speak to the Iranian Consul-General by telephone? Would he meet the Regent's Park Imam?

Whitelaw, anticipating events, had just spoken to Mrs Thatcher and she approved his dispositions. Her shrewd politician's mind reminded all concerned, however, that the West could not afford a repeat of Desert One. Just before 6pm, the Home Secretary convened a meeting representing the Foreign Office, Defence Ministry and SAS. The sense of that meeting was that the end-game was close. If there was unambiguous evidence that hostages had been murdered then the Deliberate Assault Plan would be put into effect. Blue and Red teams went onto a ten-minute stand-by. Though he did not know it, Awn's hand was the last brake on an SAS assault. Nothing would happen unless he proved that he had killed a hostage, as he claimed and appeared to be killing others. He was about to make the one mistake that would bring the fragile negotiations crashing down into anarchy and death.

The Imam appeared and there was a brief, spirited argument in Arabic. Soon after that, three more shots were heard inside the building. Another short pause, and the embassy's front door was cautiously opened, a masked face peering round it. Two men were at the door, their shoes crushing the broken glass in the lobby. They were tugging at something heavy. Then they turned back into the building and pushed the object into the street. The corpse of Lavasani lay like a sack of flour on the cold pavement.

Awn telephoned the negotiators ten minutes later, bleakly

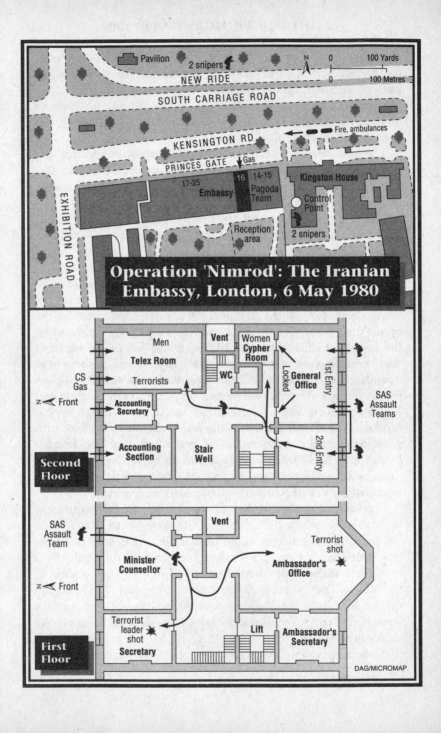

Operation 'Nimrod': The Iranian Embassy, London, 6 May 1980

announcing that he had shot 'a hostage' and giving permission for stretcher bearers to collect the body. In the minds of the security authorities the suspicion now grew that Awn had killed not once but twice. They did not know that the shots they had just heard were a fatal bluff on Awn's part. The police pathologist had not yet had the chance to confirm that the body had beer. dead for hours rather than minutes. Three minutes after Lavasani's remains were picked up, Sir David McNee telephoned COBR to say he was committing the SAS to action. At 7.07pm, Lieutenant-Colonel Rose formally took control and passed this on to Major 'Lysander', the tough, media-hating Para commanding B Squadron. The die was now cast.

'Hello. This is John, the police negotiator. Is "Salim" there?'

Awn Ali Mohammed ('Salim'), had brought the telephone upstairs from the ground to the first floor to be closer to the hostages. Just before he shot Lavasani, Awn had moved fifteen of the male hostages out of a vulnerable general office at the back of the building, on the second floor, to the telex room at the front, overlooking Princes Gate and Hyde Park. The four women captives were kept in the cypher room adjoining the general office on the same floor. PC Lock and Sim Harris had by now won the status of virtual trusties in this private prison. They were invaluable as a means of converting Awn's less than perfect English into something meaningful.

The authorities outside, depending on outdated information from the released hostage Mrs Mosafarian, believed that the male captives were still to be found in the general office. This was now locked and barricaded as well as empty.

As he took the latest telephone call, Awn kept Lock and Harris nearby.

'Salim,' said the police voice, 'listen carefully, please. We want to talk about the bus.'

'Bus? What bus?'

'The bus that will take you to London Airport.'

'Oh yes, the bus to the airport.' Awn, eyes moving restlessly from telephone to hostages to the ceiling, thought he could hear noises that did not sound right. He suggested, without much conviction, that PC Lock – whom he called

'Mr Trevor' – should be the driver; that they wanted a thirty-six seat coach.

But in answer to other questions he said: 'I will speak later.' His voice was abstracted, the flat tone of a man who is at the end of his tether.

On the roof, Red Team's abseilers were poised like black crows, masked and armed. Behind walls at ground floor and garden level, Blue Team soldiers waited with explosives and ladders, each team netted into the radio frequency that would enable it to strike the moment Awn's attention was sufficiently seduced by the voice on the phone. In an apartment block at the rear of the embassy and at a camouflaged position in Hyde Park, at the front, SAS sniper teams peered through telescopic sights, their gun barrels rock-steady on bipods.

PC Trevor Lock, with inspired timing, telephoned the negotiators again. He asked for the bus to be brought along as a matter of urgency, since 'the people here expect an attack any minute'.

'Let me speak to them.'

Awn was on the line again, excited. So were his companions. They darted from room to room, aware of the noises around them. Awn made another effort at telephone diplomacy.

'There are noises', he said. 'Suspicious, strange noises.'

'No suspicious noises, Salim', said the voice of the police negotiator soothingly. As he spoke, an explosive charge blew away the reinforced skylight roof originally protected on SAS advice.

Mike Rose and B Squadron's commander, 'Lysander', had covered every possible angle; or so they thought. Their detailed Deliberate Assault Plan, complete with diagrams describing the lay-out of each room, was focused on an elegant, single objective: 'To rescue the hostages in the Iranian Embassy.'

Red Team was to clear the top half of the building, from second to fourth floors. Blue Team was to tackle the lower half from the basement/garden upward to the first floor and handle evacuation procedures.

Red would drop two abseil teams, each of four men, in separate waves from the roof, down to the second floor balcony at the back of the building. Once on the balcony they would break in through three big windows. To attack the third floor, another group would descend from the roof by ladder onto a sub-roof at the rear, known as the lighting area. At fourth floor level, yet another group would blast a way in through the skylight, direct from the roof.

Blue Team was given charge of the basement (garden) level along with the ground floor and first floor. Theoretically, all that was required was an explosive charge to put in the french windows overlooking the ground floor terrace at the back; with a similar bit of surgery on the front, first floor balcony window leading to the Minister's Office. Access to that balcony was not a problem since it adjoined the balcony of the building in which the SAS had been working and living for several days.

The only uncertainty concerned the explosive power needed to demolish the toughened glass installed on SAS advice. A special frame, matching that of the window frame to be demolished, was tailored to carry the explosive. At the critical moment, it would be carried from balcony to balcony and lifted on to the target like a jacket fitted onto a tailor's dummy. Blue Team also had responsibility for firing CS gas canisters into the rear second floor windows at the beginning of the attack – the main focus, wrongly directed as things turned out – of the hostage rescue. The same team would hold an undiplomatic reception party in the garden afterwards.

The whole operation was to be orchestrated, out of sight of the journalists, by a command group operating from a sixth floor apartment overlooking the rear of the embassy.

Red Team's operation did not go according to plan. At the radio signal 'Road Accident', the attack groups started moving quietly into position. At 'Hyde Park' the abseilers hitched themselves to the rope, ready to start their descent. Their signal to drop at speed to the balcony below was 'London Bridge'.

The team leader travelled only 15 feet before his rope (a replacement, not used in the earlier trials) snagged in its harness. The men following him tried to set him free and in doing so, broke a window. It was a clanging, unplanned noise, sufficient to compromise the operation. The squadron commander, recognising the inevitable, snapped over the message, in clear speech, on all operational frequencies: 'Go!' 'Go!' 'Go!'

They went. The SAS still had a surprise left. A carefully tailored explosive package had been gently lowered from the roof to dangle just above the glass roof of the stairwell. As this was detonated the whole building shuddered with the force of it and some of the roof collapsed. From ground positions in front of the embassy, snipers fired CS gas canisters into the second floor. Soldiers storming into the building from the roof hurled gas grenades down the stairs below the lighting area to the second floor landing.

At ground floor level, the plan to blast a way through the rear french windows had to be abandoned because of the risk of injuring or killing the Red Team leader, a Staff Sergeant still trapped on his rope high above. He was shouting to his team, instructing them to cut him free. Blue, denied the use of explosive, used sledge-hammers instead. The windows collapsed after about thirty seconds.

At the front of the embassy, the four-man party attacking the first floor clambered from the adjoining balcony next door so as to blow their way into the Minister's Office in a scene captured by television. (One of the men later described it as 'the world's most crowded balcony'.) To their horror, the lance-corporal and trooper leading this assault saw the BBC man Sim Harris staring at them from the other side of the glass.

'Get down! Get back!'

Harris did so, in the nick of time. While the soldiers were still putting their plastic charges in place, a terrorist armed with a sub-machine-gun appeared at the second floor window of the telex room immediately above them. The man flung the window open and hurled a grenade down. He had forgotten to draw the detonating pin and the grenade bounced harmlessly away. That was the terrorist's first mistake. His second was to expose himself at the window long enough to become a target for the SAS sniper hiding across the road in Hyde Park. The sniper, Sgt 'S', hit the man with a single round. The terrorist staggered back, dropping his gun. That single, brilliant snap-shot is held to have saved the lives of fifteen hostages trapped in the telex room.

As the balcony charge blew in the first floor window, the assault team hurled in a 'flash-bang' stun grenade as a follow-up. This ignited the curtains. The four men hauled Harris out of the room to the balcony and told him to stay where he was. Harris heard himself shouting: 'Go on lads, get the bastards!' Two of the soldiers – Trooper 'Py' and Lance-Corporal 'McA', searched the room as Lance-Corporal 'McD' and Trooper 'Pa' charged onto the landing beyond. There they heard shouts from an adjoining office, that of the Minister's secretary and entered to discover Lock struggling with Awn. Lock was in pain, his eyes burning but he knew that Awn had a grenade as well as a firearm and would use them. He had drawn his own gun and put it to his opponent's head but could not bring himself to kill 'in anger'. The lance-corporal thrust his brawny Scots muscle into this melee like a rugby player diving into a scrum. He detached Lock, pushing him away with the shouted warning, 'Trevor, leave off'! As Awn tried to regain his balance, the lance-corporal fired a long burst of automatic at his head and chest. His companion did the same. Awn, hit by fifteen bullets, died instantly and became the martyr he had hoped to become.

Just across the landing, towards the rear of the building, 'McA' and 'Py' tried the door of the ambassador's office. It appeared locked but suddenly it was thrown open from within. The soldiers were confronted by Thamir Mohamed Husein (*nom-de-guerre*, 'Abbas'), aged twenty-one, described on his passport as a farmer. He was holding a Browning pistol. 'Py' immediately fired at him. The bullet pushed Abbas back into the room. The SAS pair threw a stun grenade after him. The blast threw Abbas even further back. 'Py' fired a second time at Abbas, who vanished into the recesses of a room now blacked out by smoke. Somewhere in that gloom, the soldiers knew, was a wounded, armed man with nothing to lose by killing them. They went after their quarry.

As they entered the room, 'McA' felt himself choking. CS gas had penetrated his mask. He staggered outside, coughing.

'Anybody got a light?' 'Py' shouted into his throat mike.

Staff Sergeant 'T', from the Blue Team, on his way up from the ground floor, had a torch bolted to his HP-5 sub-machine-gun. With him as their guide, Py and two other soldiers moved cautiously into the ambassador's office, feeling their way forward, the torch sweeping the darkness like a blind man's stick. Then they saw a hand, a face, and a gun. Abbas was half-lying on a large, luxurious sofa near the bay window that overlooked the garden. He gestured with his pistol and the shooting began again. This time he was hit by twenty-one bullets and he did not survive.

At the rear of the building on the floor above (the second floor) Red Team was still having problems. Four abseilers had reached a balcony outside the big General Office where, according to their briefing, most of the hostages were held. They smashed the glass and hurled stun grenades. The room was empty, locked and barricaded, but piled with inflammable material which was now ignited by the grenades. The men stormed inside nevertheless to force the door. On the outside wall just above them, the team leader, a staff sergeant, was still trapped in his harness. Worse, flames from the fire were now roaring out of the General Office window and starting to burn his legs. He could avoid being burned only by kicking himself in an arc away from the wall but each time he swung back again, he was back into the flames.

At last one of the second wave of abseilers, still on the roof, cut him loose and he fell through the flames, onto the balcony. Not in the best of tempers, he followed the others into the General Office where they tried to break out by blowing the locks apart with gunfire. The locks gave way but the doors, barricaded from the other side, did not.

One of the four, Tommy Palmer, decided to try an alternative route. Palmer, a pugnacious Scot, had just been transferred to B Squadron as a result of a 'conflict of personalities' elsewhere. He retreated to the balcony, then reached across to an adjoining window ledge. From here he could see inside the room where Shakir Sultan Said (*nom-de-guerre*, 'Shai' – the Arabic word for tea), aged twenty-three, a terrorist who claimed to be a mechanic, was striking matches to set fire to paper piled up in the room. Had he looked up he would have observed the SAS soldier, vulnerable on the window ledge, as a perfect target.

Palmer smashed the window and hurled in a stun grenade. Said, pistol in hand, ran out of the room. The SAS soldier aimed his Heckler/Koch sub-machine-gun from the hip and pulled the trigger. The gun, in action with the SAS for the first time, jammed. Cursing, the soldier drew his Browning pistol and went after the man. Said got as far as the telex room, off to the right across the landing, where most of the male hostages were imprisoned.

What happened next was described by the British hostage Sim Harris. In the book he wrote with Chris Cramer, he recalled that the terrorist Feisal, tallest of the group and its second-in-command, with Ali and Makki ran into the room as the SAS assault began. They were quickly followed by Said as he fled from Palmer. Using his sub-machine-gun, Feisal swept the cowering hostages, as they huddled together, with bursts of automatic fire while one of the others fired his pistol at the unarmed captives. As well as killing Ali Samad-Zadeh, the terrorists hit the embassy's medical adviser Dagdar with six bullets. Dagdar would survive, after a fashion, with months of intensive medical care. Afrouz, another of the diplomatic staff, was hit by two bullets one of which passed through his right thigh. Others were uninjured but only through exceptional luck. One man owed his life to the 50p coin in his jacket pocket that stopped the bullet.

Having helped in the murders, Ali, youngest of the gunmen (real name, Fowzi Badavi Nejad) dropped his pistol in panic and squirmed in among the hostages. Feisal also dropped his weapon and emptied his pockets of ammunition. Said, Palmer's quarry, and the last to enter the room, stood his ground, finger crooked inside the pin of a grenade.

The SAS soldiers heard the shots and screams of the victims as they charged towards the room. They had every reason to respond as their CQB training required. It was ironic that in the seconds left before they burst into this real killing house, it was the hostages who started to throw the firearms that had just been discarded by the terrorists out of the window into the street. Palmer, pistol in hand as he chased Said, was the first rescuer into the telex room. He gave the door a kick and turned the corner, crouching, gun raised. His eyes fixed on the figure to his left, grenade in hand, and he fired instantly. It was a single round aimed at the head. The bullet entered Said's skull below the left ear and exited through the right temple, killing him outright.

The staff sergeant and his three men had now emerged from the General Office and followed the sound of shooting to join Palmer. The staff sergeant, in spite of the pain of his burns and the ominous spread of smoke around them, systematically organised a search of the people in the room. Corporal 'G', one of the SAS soldiers, staunched Dagdar's wounds with a field dressing. Nearby lay Samad-Zadeh, beyond the reach of first or last aid.

The survivors included Ron Morris, the British chauffeur on the embassy staff. He also recalled later that the terrorists opened fire on the hostages as the SAS assault began, 'then they panicked and threw some of their guns out of the window . . . and just sort of wormed their way in among us'.

In fact, as the rescuers were discovering, the opposition was still armed with grenades.

The SAS now started to identify the 'worms', still wearing combat jackets so as to separate them from the innocents. In the telex room there was an odour of fear even stronger than the acrid smoke of burning fabric and the smarting attack of CS.

The hostages were bundled out, down the stairs to the waiting reception party to be identified: terrorists, if any, to the right; hostages to the left. As the last hostage was being moved out, the Red Team searched the suspects. One of them – later identified as Makki Hounoun Ali, aged twenty-five, a Baghdad mechanic – did not remotely resemble a hostage. There was a surly wariness about him that did not fit the defeated, bovine acceptance of the others.

'Lie down', one of the soldiers told him. The man did so, his arms outstretched.

'Who are you?'

'Student. I am student.'

A second SAS soldier searched the man, pushing his legs open, squinting into the suspect's crotch. He could see metal, something that resembled a pistol magazine. There was also a holster tangled up in the trousers. Makki suddenly changed his position, drew his arms in towards his body and started to turn over. The staff sergeant immediately fired into the man's back, killing him. The body collapsed forward again. The soldiers turned it over and found a hand grenade as well as the magazine.

While this was happening, the second suspect, Feisal – the afro-hairstyled machine-gunner – slid away into the smoke and the darkness where he waited to mingle with the freed hostages on their way down the stairs to safety.

The voices of the women hostages from the nearby cypher room, crying for help, reminded the staff sergeant's men that they had yet other responsibilities. The women were brought to the telex room, rapidly checked for wounds and weapons and told to make their way down the stairs. The staff sergeant's burns – serious enough to require intensive medical care later that night – were punishing him with double-vision. As he started to follow the hostages, he fainted. His comrades called for the special medical team and a stretcher.

Members of Blue Team who had cleared the basement and ground floor now met up with the rest – Blue and Red – from the upper storeys to form a chain along which hostages were passed ('virtually thrown', said one later) from hand to hand. It was still in the minds of the soldiers that somewhere, the terrorists might have hidden an explosive charge as their final response to this attack. Among the men in the chain was Soldier 'I', a veteran of eighteen years' SAS service. He was about halfway down the main staircase linking the first floor to the ground when he heard sounds of a scuffle above him and a shouted warning.

In the published version he wrote with the help of Michael Paul Kennedy, he says that the hostages 'stumbled down the stairs looking frightened and dishevelled. One woman had her blouse ripped and her breasts exposed . . . "This one's a terrorist!" The high-pitched yell cut through the atmosphere

453

on the stairs . . . A dark face, ringed by an afro-style haircut came into view; then the body, clothed in a green combat jacket, bent double, crouched in an unnatural pose . . . He was punched and kicked as he made his descent of the stairs . . . He knew he was close to death.

'He drew level with me. Then I saw it – a Russian fragmentation grenade. I could see the detonator cap protruding from his hand. I moved my hands to the MP5 and slipped the safety-catch to "automatic".'

The presence of his own comrades in the line of fire denied Soldier 'I' the chance to shoot the terrorist without risking their lives also. 'I raised the MP5 above my head and . . . brought the stock of the weapon down on the back of his neck. I hit him as hard as I could. His head snapped backwards . . . I caught sight of his tortured, hate-filled face. The sound of two magazines being emptied into him was deafening. As he twitched and vomited his life away, his hand opened and the grenade rolled out.'

The pin was still safely in its housing. If the terrorist was carrying it to kill himself, the SAS had just saved him the trouble. The man was identified as Shakir Abdullah Fadhil (also known as 'Jasim' and 'Feisal'), aged twenty-one, born in Baghdad and another 'Ministry of Industry Official'. The autopsy indicated that he had been hit by thirty-nine bullets from at least four different SAS guns.

Other members of the team recall that three members of Red Team, at the top of the stairs, were watching Feisal and almost simultaneously spotted the grenade. Corporal 'McD' and others shouted a warning from the top of the stairs and soldier 'I' pushed the terrorist down the stairs. As he reached the bottom, they agree, he was shot dead by Blue Team members.

For some time after that, more shots echoed through the building as the SAS team blasted away locks to check other rooms. The fires had taken grip of the top of the building now, and the hostages, having been removed with expedition (if with some lack of diplomatic politeness) were bound and secured with straps on the lawn behind the embassy. The only terrorist to survive lay among them and was promptly identified by other survivors, including Sim Harris. The terrorist, Nejad, (also known as Ali Abdullah) was later arrested, tried and given life imprisonment for manslaughter. Sim Harris, as he lay on the rear lawn, bound like the rest, told another survivor: 'Think yourself lucky you have just been rescued by what must be one of the crack squads in the world.' Later, in an interview with a BBC colleague, he ended his account: 'Thank you, SAS, for saving my life.'

This was a faint reflection of the emotional scenes that occurred immediately after the operation, in the SAS tactical headquarters at Regent's Park Barracks. The wife of PC Lock, reunited with the husband she had so nearly lost, thanked the SAS soldiers who had saved him, again and again. Home Secretary William Whitelaw, who had advised the Prime Minister earlier in the day to sanction the use of the SAS, was also on the scene, his tears of joy and relief totally undisguised.

The SAS were also relieved. This was the first time they had fought a battle on Britain's own doorstep. If it had gone wrong, the political and public backlash would have been calamitous. In all the circumstances, one burned soldier and another whose thumb was severely mangled by a bullet wound, were a modest price for crowning seven years' preparation with such success. It almost made the publicity tolerable. Later, after the inquest and the trial of the surviving terrorist, there was media disquiet at the force used. But as de la Billière said at the time, the object of the operation was to rescue hostages.

To do so inside a burning building which – the terrorists claimed – had been wired for an explosion was not a place, nor was this a time, to wonder whether the rescue tactics would be acceptable to journalists. Later analysis (See 'Princes Gate Hostage Rescue' timetable, Appendix F) showed that the success was, in the words of Wellington, a close run thing. The Immediate Action Plan, with a predicted hostage survival rate of no more than 10 per cent at times, was the potential first option throughout much of the siege. The Deliberate Action Plan, greatly improving the survival odds, was the available first option only during the last two hours of the crisis, in the nick of time.

Nevertheless, the deterrent effect of Operation Pagoda was incalculable. No similar event occurred in the United Kingdom for more than a decade afterwards. In an increasingly violent world, London was off-limits to one kind of international terrorism.

At the end of that memorable day, someone at the tactical headquarters at Regent's Park Barracks suggested that the party, which included the Prime Minister, should watch the television recording of the rescue. Everyone, including the Prime Minister, agreed that was an excellent idea. In the darkened room, as the set came to life, there was a cheerful, impudent shout from one of the CRW team: 'Sit down at the front and let the rest of us see it.' Glowing with contentment, Mrs Thatcher sat down, cross-legged, on the floor. It had been a good day for the SAS and an even better day for Britain.

The Queen personally decorated five of the SAS heroes. Four (including the Commanding Officer, Rose and Trooper Palmer) received the Queen's Gallantry Medal. The staff-sergeant who ignored his wounds until he fainted from the pain received the George Medal. So, too, did PC Trevor Lock.

On 4 February the following year a Westminster Coroner's jury considered the deaths of the five terrorists and ruled that their deaths were the result of justifiable homicide.

THE HOT COLD WAR
AND OTHER CAMPAIGNS

For some soldiers the Cold War was hot, fought in a hot climate on surrogate battlefields from Latin America to South-east Asia between disciples of Brezhnev's doctrine of national 'liberation' (wearing a red star) and client regimes of the West. Only in Western Europe did the guns stay silent during this forty-five-year conflict.

Until the end of the 1970s, it seemed that the Communists were winning. In parallel with America's ignominious withdrawal from Vietnam in 1975, lifting the last US citizens from the roof of an abandoned embassy in Saigon, other non-aligned states were succumbing to the spread of Communism like victims of chicken-pox in a boarding school dormitory. One expert assessment is that this was a decade in which armed revolution brought fourteen left-of-centre governments to power.

This was not all. From 1970 the pervasive power of international terrorism spread as radical Arab countries hosted gangs of aerial hijackers, safe in the knowledge that they could appeal to the Soviets if the West made a frontal assault on their home bases. It was a cost-effective, versatile and highly successful, if indiscriminate, form of warfare which found expression in the British Isles, later by courtesy of Libyan supplied Semtex, and still manufactured in Czechoslovakia for IRA use after the Soviet empire had collapsed.

For the warriors outside Europe, from Cuba to Kampuchea by way of Angola, it was the special forces of both sides which alone represented the super-powers. The SAS, fighting counter-insurgency wars in Malaya, Borneo and Oman between 1953 and 1976, scored a unique series of wins.

For the West as a whole, however, the outlook was bleak

throughout the 1970s. In January 1979, Islamic fundamentalism had overturned the stability of the Gulf with the downfall of the West's client, the Shah of Iran. In the same month, the predatory Communist regime of Vietnam seized Pol Pot's equally bloodthirsty Cambodia. In March, the democratic premier of Grenada, Sir Eric Gairy, was toppled by another acolyte of the hard left, Maurice Bishop, in an armed coup. In July, Nicaragua fell to the Sandinistas. In November, the US Embassy in Tehran was seized and 100 embassy staff taken hostage. In December, a calamitous decade for the West ended with the Soviet invasion of Afghanistan. This time, it was the regular Red Army, not the Cubans or other auxiliaries, who were extending the empire and threatening Gulf oil supplies.

Both Presidents Carter and Reagan encouraged the CIA to arm the Afghan resistance, the Mujaheddin, to fight a clandestine, guerrilla war. In that operation, as the French political scientist Olivier Roy argues, 'plausible deniability' was a top priority until, in 1985, the CIA fed deadly accurate, shoulder-fired Stinger anti-aircraft missiles to the Afghans. The advantage enjoyed by the helicopter gunship against the Afghans was tipped on its head and with it, the balance of the whole campaign. Until then, the Mi-24 ('Hip') combat helicopter had been a potential war winner, indeed during the first year of the war, the Kremlin had increased the supply to their troops in Afghanistan from sixty to 300.

Afghanistan

This Western victory, the first sign that the tide was turning in the Third World, was achieved by the CIA's Afghan Task Force, based in Langley, with some shadowy assistance from British mercenaries. The Russians were eventually defeated. As Roy points out: 'A staff of around 100 CIA officers, no American citizens killed or imprisoned, no retaliation against US interests and the nominal expense of $2 bn over ten years: these were relatively low costs for one of the most important post-World War II conflicts.'

He adds: 'France and the UK cultivated direct contacts with the Mujaheddin and although it has never been acknowledged, a certain amount of direct military support was given by the two to certain field commanders.'

In one colourful preliminary to the Stinger's successful counter-attack a team of British mercenaries, including one or two SAS veterans, penetrated Afghanistan on behalf of the US Defense Intelligence Agency in 1980–81. Their task was not to fight but to bring back samples of the titanium armour on the Soviet Hips. The team was hardly subtle in its approach. When machine-guns proved ineffective as a cutting tool on a crashed gunship, one of the mercenaries returned to Hereford to buy a mechanical saw.

The presence of another former SAS regular soldier, working alone for months as a documentary film maker, provoked further speculation that the British were not uninterested in the fate of what was, after all, a former protectorate. The soldier emerged with a brilliant account of the action for television but almost too weak to carry his camera.

Less fortunate was Andy Skrzypkowiak, a volunteer serving with 21 SAS (VR), operating as a video cameraman in Afghanistan to cover such battles as the destruction of a Soviet fuel convoy by Ahman Shah Massoud's irregulars on the Salang Pass highway in 1984: he became a victim of internecine tribal warfare. His obituarist, David C. Isby, wrote later: 'Andy was killed in October 1987 in the Kantiwa area of Nuristan . . . caught in the fighting between Massoud and another resistance party, the Hezb-i-Islami' (Party of God) which was 'grabbing journalists covering Massoud'.

Gambia 1981

For the SAS, the new decade brought other successes, notably the regiment's storming of the besieged Iranian Embassy in London in May 1980 (described in detail in the previous chapter). Perhaps the most novel, yet characteristically cheeky stroke was

Crooke's Counter Coup, or the story of how one SAS major, the second-in-command of 22 SAS, plus two NCOs flew by Air France with an undeclared cargo of guns, ammunition and high explosive to restore democratic government to a former British colony on the Atlantic coast of Africa.

It is a basic rule of politics in much of the Third World that a ruler should never take a holiday abroad. President Sir Dawda Jawara, of Gambia, took a gamble and travelled to London for the wedding of Prince Charles and Lady Diana Spencer on 29 July 1981. While the choir sang the anthem in Westminster Abbey, 400 armed Marxists backed by the Cuban expeditionary force in Angola and encouraged by Libya, seized key points in the Gambian capital, Banjul. French-trained paras descended from neighbouring Senegal, to seize the airport, but at a military headquarters outside the capital the rebels were holding thirty hostages including Sir Dawda's first wife and her two children.

Next day, the Foreign & Commonwealth Office telephoned SAS headquarters at Hereford, inviting the regiment to send a reconnaissance team to Gambia. Major Crooke, a dedicated special forces soldier who declined the staff college option and quit the Army as a lieutenant-colonel, was the senior duty officer during this apparently quiet period. With his Commanding Officer's approval Crooke assigned himself and two others to the task.

They flew first from Paris to the adjoining territory of Dacca, arriving there on 2 August. There they met the deposed President and were briefed on the situation in Gambia. One manifest gap in their equipment was a portable satellite transmitter from which to make direct contact with London or Hereford. Crooke turned this situation to his advantage. If communication with the home base was slow, his decision-making was not.

On the face of things, the overall military position was not so bad. The Senegalese had retaken much of the country. One friendly company controlled the capital, Banjul; another, the key Denby Bridge. The main airport, Yundum, was the Senegalese operational headquarters and they also commanded the main road linking the airport to the coast. The less-good news was that the rebels held a large swathe of territory on the coast including the UK High Commission, the US Residency, the Gambia Field Force military depot, Bakau, a middle-class residential area and numerous hotels including the Sunwing. The township gave its name to a potential combat zone in which 400 Europeans were held hostage: the Bakau Salient. In all, eleven VIPs were captives inside the police depot tailor's shop. They included six of the President's children and his brother. Imprisoned in garages elsewhere in the depot complex, another 83 hostages included two Gambian ministers and a senior government official. In the Medical Research Centre, near the British High Commission, the rebels were holding the President's principal wife, Lady Thielal, plus her child.

Crooke's team carried out a series of reconnaissance missions, some after dark, and discovered that the road to the coast, down one side of the salient, was effectively unguarded and open to penetration. The majority of the rebels were now clustered round the Gambia Police Field Force depot. The depot faced the sea, across the main coastal road, a few miles up the beach from the unguarded route they had discovered. Crooke began to see possibilities here of a route to the enemy stronghold that would be as stealthy as a bare foot on a sandy beach.

First, however, he wanted a team more impressive than himself and two others on which he could reasonably rely when the shooting started. He was given command of about 100 Senegalese soldiers and put them through a quick training course the purpose of which was to make them confident enough not to leg it when the moment came to fight. Simultaneously, he outlined his proposed assault to the Senegalese and Gambian leaders: a fast drive to the beach, a sharp right turn short of the sea and a night march over the sands to Bakau.

For reasons which are unclear – *amour-propre*, perhaps – the Senegalese rejected Crooke's plan. Next morning, in broad daylight, they began a clumsy, unco-ordinated move on foot and in vehicles, along the only main highway to the rebel area. Though the enemy's response was a non-event, the manoeuvre was a potential disaster. It stalled before it had gone far, as a result of simple confusion.

Crooke, meanwhile, armed but in civilian clothes and with his two NCOs calmly drove through the rebel lines to the Medical Research Centre. There were only four enemy sentries. With a little encouragement from the hard-looking visitors, they gave up their weapons. Soon, Lady Thielal and the child were on their way to the British High Commission and sanctuary.

For the rest of that day, the opponents lay up and watched for a move on the part of the other side. Crooke conferred again with the Senegalese and came up with another plan. Could he borrow a few armoured cars, please, together with the 100 Senegalese soldiers he had trained? The Senegalese obliged. Crooke does not have a reputation for subtlety. On this occasion, leading a cavalcade of armoured cars, he stormed through the no-man's-land between the last friendly roadblock and the beach, along a coast road that led past the High Commission and, a mile further on, the Field Force (and now rebel) headquarters.

Crooke's cavalcade, which he personally led and conducted, was a demonstration of firepower with all the guns at his disposal, right outside the enemy building. Panic, when it spreads among soldiers – even brave soldiers – is an extraordinary phenomenon, defying reason, throwing away victory in a blind urge to run away and hide. Panic spread in response to Crooke's percussion band. The rebels fled through the back door. Crooke led a charge through the front.

'We're here!'

In response to hostage voices, the rescue team ran through the building and its outbuildings, smashing locks, getting the innocents out. They need not have hurried. This was not the Middle East or Ireland. There were no booby traps or snipers. The enemy had fled. When, in time, the Foreign & Commonwealth Office heard the news, it was delighted by the outcome even if it did not entirely approve of the practical interpretation the SAS had attached to the phrase 'military advice'. In a two-day operation (5 and 6 August) Crooke had overturned a coup. He and his two aides flew back to the UK on 9 August, little more than a week after setting off from Heathrow.

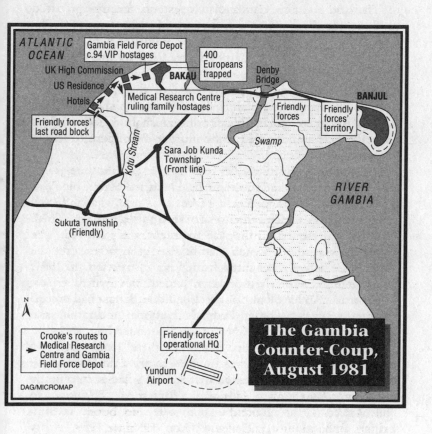

ATLANTIC
OCEAN

Gambia Field Force Depot
c.94 VIP hostages

400
Europeans
trapped

UK High Commission

BAKAU

Denby
Bridge

US Residence

BANJUL

Hotels

Medical Research Centre
ruling family hostages

Friendly
forces

Friendly
forces'
territory

Friendly forces'
last road block

Kotu Stream

Sara Job Kunda
Township
(Front line)

Swamp

RIVER
GAMBIA

Sukuta Township
(Friendly)

N

Crooke's routes to
Medical Research
Centre and Gambia
Field Force Depot

Friendly forces'
operational HQ

**The Gambia
Counter-Coup,
August 1981**

Yundum
Airport

DAG/MICROMAP

Thailand/Cambodia 1980–90

In 1985, in the last chapter of the surrogate Cold War, an SAS training team of one officer and six rankers was sent to Thailand to train Cambodian resistance groups prepared to fight the Vietnamese occupation of their country. The scheme had the blessing of the Prime Minister Mrs Thatcher following the invasion of Cambodia by Vietnam in 1979, when a dangerously expansionist (and Communist) regular army crushed the bloodthirsty power base of the Khmer Rouge, another left-wing dictatorship. Even by Asian standards, the Khmer Rouge is remarkable for its lavish body count. It is generally held responsible for the murder of millions of fellow Cambodians.

The political sensitivity of the SAS role at a time when any Western intervention could be identified as a Cold War initiative, dangerous to world peace, was not what inflamed the controversy which came to surround this operation. There was never any question that the regiment was involved. The argument was about which Cambodian groups resisting the Vietnamese actually benefited from SAS instruction. In 1991, a few months after the operation ended, the Armed Forces Minister Mr Archie Hamilton disclosed that Britain had trained insurgents of the Khmer People's National Liberation and another group, the Armee Nationale Sihanoukienne.

Critics of the SAS argued that since these groups shared a common aim with the Khmer Rouge – to drive the Vietnamese out of Cambodia – it followed that the SAS had been training the Khmer Rouge also. This was a logical fallacy known to philosophers as the undistributed middle. Mr Derek Tonkin, British ambassador to Thailand from 1986 to 1989, acidly pointed out in June, 1991: 'The three resistance factions have spent most of the past twelve years in mutual recrimination.'

Partly as a result of the SAS's efforts, the Cambodian people had a non-Communist option, other than the Khmer Rouge, for their future government after the Vietnamese withdrew in September 1989. Towards the end of the Second World War, many other countries had experienced the war-after-the-war, a contest between resistance groups fighting over the spoils of victory. UK intervention in Cambodia and Thailand, based on that experience, was aimed at ensuring that the ultimate winner was not the Khmer Rouge. In spite of that was it true, as some journalists alleged, that there was some linkage, or co-operation, between the teams trained by the SAS (the KPNLF and ANS) and Khmer Rouge?

Ambassador Tonkin argued: 'In 1990, there were isolated reports of local tactical co-ordination, notably between ANS and Khmer Rouge troops. These reports, though few and far between, caused concern in the United States. They were thoroughly investigated both by the administration and openly in Congress. The conclusion was reached that there might have been a few instances of military liaison between local commanders but overall there was no evidence of strategic planning and central command and control.'

Although the SAS teams had been withdrawn by the time these incidents were reported, it did not diminish the wrath of the critics. Dr Peter Carey, a tutor in Modern History at Trinity College, Oxford, detected a link between the type of weapon most frequently used by the Khmer Rouge and SAS instruction. He claimed:

The Khmer Rouge's most devastating weapon is a Chinese-made anti-personnel device . . . known as the 'wind mine' . . . virtually undetectable . . . Today Cambodia has what is probably the highest percentage of disabled inhabitants of any country in the world . . . There are now at least 100,000 amputees, blinded and disabled people in Cambodia out of a population of 8.5 million . . .

The US and its allies have been so concerned with driving out the Vietnamese that they never fully understood, or perhaps minded, that the guerrilla coalition they supported in order to achieve this aim might lead eventually to the return of the Khmer Rouge. It was a policy which at its worst, from 1985 until 1989 when public opinion forced a termination of the contract, saw British special forces on the border providing training in mine warfare and demolition techniques to the army of Prince Sihanouk – until recently the West's symbol of legitimacy in the guerrilla coalition. It is hard to imagine a more despicable and irresponsible use of the SAS in recent history. The Khmer Rouge use of mines is part of a long-term strategy to regain power . . .

Dr Carey then returned to the theme of the 'wind mine' as a main source of civilian casualties yet to come. It is clear from his own account, in the *Independent*, that the Khmer Rouge depended on China, not the UK, as the source of this material. He does not specify the type or source of the ordnance allegedly linking the the SAS with future Khmer Rouge victims.

SAS soldiers familiar with the operation, which had been running since the early 1980s, say that it covered basic weapons training and jungle tactics. 'There was nothing we could teach the locals about mines', said one. 'In fact, they could teach us a thing or two.' They also believe that this was a politically useful operation but not one which was militarily decisive.

Claims unproven and unprovable abounded during the controversy. The UN as well as the SAS was targeted. The writer William Shawcross, always his own man and an authority on Cambodia, reported that the UN Border Relief Operation in the area had demanded public retraction by journalists of a claim that one of its warehouses was being used by the Khmer Rouge.

In 1991, two British military advisers alleged to have trained the Khmer Rouge at first hand to plant mines that maimed and killed Cambodian civilians successfully sued the journalists involved for libel and were awarded damages. The journalists' counsel, Mr Geoffrey Shaw, QC, read a statement reported as follows in the *Daily Telegraph*:

> The defendants now accept that neither plaintiff has ever trained Khmer Rouge or any other guerrillas and particularly not in mine-laying or any other military techniques which would be directed against civilians. Neither plaintiff would ever contemplate any such thing and would refuse to do it if ordered.

The new opium war

The collapse of the Soviet Union first as a super-power, then as a coherent political entity after 1985 marooned a generation of military strategists whose futures had seemed assured (and whose minds were dominated by) the threat from Eastern Europe known as Priority One. Unique among Britain's regular armed forces, the SAS had preserved wider horizons, through military training teams in the Third World, through the extraction of British and friendly nationals from hotspots in Africa and elsewhere and even occasional forays into a shooting war on the side of a useful ally.

It was natural, when the British government loyally followed the United States in perceiving drug addiction as the new *strategic* threat requiring a military response as part of the New World Order that the SAS should be first in line to take on this latest, mainly jungle war.

In practice, this was an old fashioned commodities war tricked out in a glitzy new uniform. Between 1840 and 1842, Britain prosecuted a highly successful strategic campaign against China to restore Britain's lucrative trade in opium, exported from India under UK protection. Perhaps it was some folk memory in the corridors of the City of London that prompted articles in the *Economist* and *Financial Times* proposing the 'decriminalisation' of some drug misuse. However, as contemporary opium and its derivatives, heroin, cocaine and crack, combined with inner city deprivation to make many American cities no-go areas, President Reagan and then President Bush took up the challenge to abolish this particular sin.

The global scale of drugs production, from Colombia to the Golden Triangle of South-east Asia by way of Pakistan and the Caribbean, meant that the warlords and drug barons controlling it needed permanent private armies. In some territories, notably Peru, elected governments lost control of vast areas of their country to revolutionaries arm-in-arm with drug barons. An American observer, Rensselaer W. Lee III, notes that in the border area of north-west Burma, Laos and Thailand, such armies include remnants and descendants of the Second World

War 3rd and 5th Divisions of the National Siamese Army and the Burma Self-Defence Force. The opium warlord Chang Chi Fu had 'an army of 10,000 fully equipped with the latest weaponry' to protect the growing areas and escort the product to market.

The British commentator Frank Gregory writes:

The anarchy caused by the drugs cartels in Colombia is well known and during 1985–1990 the drugs dealers killed 2011 members of the police and armed forces and caused them to suffer 3384 wounded . . . Britain and America have supported vigorous action in the Caribbean because, as a US official said, 'the Caribbean is a strategic area for us, and the threat is not political subversion, but its subversion by narcotics trafficking'.

In 1989, in response to a worldwide appeal for help from a beleagured Colombian government, the Prime Minister Mrs Thatcher personally directed the SAS to make a contribution. The insertion of the regiment's training teams into Colombia from the autumn of 1989, served three purposes. It provided realistic jungle experience for Britain's special forces. It added a symbolic touch to the UK's moral support of Bush's moral crusade. (In that sense, it was similar to the attachment of Alastair Morrison and Barry Davies to the German GSG-9 team in October 1977. Prime Minister James Callaghan had just reached an understanding with his European partners for a common front against international terrorism. In Colombia, the SAS was again the vehicle for giving practical clothing to the political abstraction.) Finally, the regiment contributed indirectly to a critically important victory in the war against the powerful Medellin cartel.

The British soldiers primarily trained a force exclusively dedicated to the drugs battlefield, the Anti-Narcotics Police. In December 1989, having just completed his SAS training, a captain now attached to another internal security force, received a tip-off that a notorious cocaine baron, Gonzalo Rodriguez Gacha ('El Mexicano') with his son and a team of bodyguards could be found at home. Gacha had been held responsible by

Colombia's President Virgilio Barco for the assassination of the Liberal Party's main presidential candidate, Luis Galan, in August 1989. Gacha lived in style, as befits someone who has declared war on his own government. Home was a large ranch a few miles from Pacho, north of Bogota. As a former judge in that area, Antonio Suarez, acidly noted shortly before the tip-off: 'We always knew when he was home; his big ranch was suddenly surrounded by armed troops – on guard duty.'

This time, security forces raided the big ranch but the bird had flown. Then the Captain (let us call him Hero) had a lucky break. His helicopter, scouting the area, spotted a speedboat on the shore of a lake and a group of men beating someone up. The helicopter landed and seized the party at gunpoint. They were Gacha's people, to be sure, but Gacha himself was not present. He was hiding up in a villa further along the lakeside. Captain Hero promptly organised a combined operation to take the villa, involving the helicopter, ground troops and a team in the speedboat, which he led in person. There was a hectic gun battle before the villa was seized but again, Gacha had vanished into adjoining woodland. It was at this point that Hero applied the basic jungle training he had just received from the SAS. He carefully examined a map of the area and used the helicopter to put a stop party, including himself, into a classic ambush on the most likely escape route. He got it right. This time there was no escape. Gacha, with his son Freddy and five remaining bodyguards, were killed in a storm of machine-gun fire.

It was the biggest boost for months to the credibility of President Barco and a blow to the cartels' myth of invincibility. Half a ton of documents seized in the follow-up operation made 'embarrassing reading for authorities in the Isle of Man and Hong Kong', according to one source. In Panama City, US military sources claimed that US Drug Enforcement Agency officers co-ordinated the hunt for Gacha and that 'a team of Special Forces led Colombian drug forces on the raid'.

The same sources asserted that 'American troops were directly involved in the fire-fight that resulted in Mr Rodriguez Gacha's death . . . The operation is regarded by US planners as a model for future attacks against the drug cartels.'

The SAS said nothing, as usual, though it approved privately of Hero's operation as 'a textbook job'. But from some of their pupils in Colombia, a clear picture emerged of the style of training the British soldiers offered. Like Woodhouse's teams in Malaya and every operation since then, the British removed the slings from their own rifles and from those of their allies. They were then carried ready for immediate use rather than as potential souvenirs for an enemy to retrieve after he had killed the soldiers to whom they were issued.

The journalist Timothy Ross went on patrol with one of the teams hunting for another notorious drugs baron, Pablo Escobar, in Antioquia province. He discovered a characteristic SAS environment: a rain forest, complete with temperatures in the 90s, painfully high humidity, scorpions, fevers, dysentery, poisonous snakes 'and a very hostile local peasantry'. He reported:

> The SAS have given a series of intensive courses in jungle warfare and such specialist areas as combat intelligence. They are much admired by the Colombians for their physical resilience . . . The corporal said, 'The sun burned the skin off their faces but they led us off on patrol exercises at such speed that we were begging for water. 'No,' they said, 'keep on, only five minutes rest every hour . . . Don't stop, shoot as you move' they drilled into us . . .
>
> Some of the men believe the SAS style of tactics should be applied more radically and daringly and complain that dropping in troops from helicopters gives Escobar warning with their rotor noise.

During the year before SAS training contributed to Gacha's death, British mercenaries had been in Colombia, some to train members of Gacha's private army. An ex-SAS veteran, Peter McAleese, told a television reporter that he had trained 'a number of Colombians' in military tactics and skill-at-arms. He confirmed that another British mercenary (with no SAS links), David Tomkins, 'handled the explosives side'. The British team was paid off in 1988 and an Israeli squad moved in, prior to the assassination of the presidential candidate Galan in August 1989. An Israeli supplied weapon was used to murder Galan.

In a revealing aside, the television reporter David Leigh asserted that McAleese believed that he was in Colombia to train people to 'assault Communist guerrillas in the hills'. If so, it was a neat illustration of the degree to which the mercenaries' 'political correctness' had failed to keep up with a fast-changing world. In Angola, Rhodesia and southern Africa, McAleese and others could claim that they were part of the hot Cold War. Their plausibly-deniable operations, through appropriate cut-outs, were sometimes funded (as in Angola in 1976) by the CIA. In Colombia, however, the drug barons were the bad guys and the special forces of the Western world were on the other side of this new war. The regular SAS was about to start training regular Colombian government forces with that in mind.

It was a complex little conflict which spilled across unmarked jungle frontiers into Brazil and attracted regular and mercenary soldiers from all over the world. Not only were SAS personalities thrust into this exotic campaign; two-man RAF dog handling team was sent from Nottinghamshire to Ecuador with six RAF dogs for use in sniffing out hidden cocaine stocks. Royal Navy ships and RAF Nimrods played a part in monitoring drug cargoes as they approached the US coastline.

Liberia 1990

When the Ayatollah's mobs overran the US Embassy in Tehran on 4 November 1979, making prisoners of fifty-two of the staff for 444 days, they dealt a deadly blow to President Jimmy Carter's hopes of re-election and demonstrated the continuing potency of a form of blackmail which belonged to the Middle Ages. Other Middle East groups revived the custom. In Beirut, Islamic Jihad seized Western hostages such as Terry Waite and held them for years as bait in a political trap. Saddam Hussein constructed a human shield of innocent Westerners in Iraq in 1990 to deter an Allied air assault.

This trade in expatriates did not go unnoticed by Western security agencies. They discreetly made contingency plans, reflecting each emerging crisis around the world, to answer the question: 'What if some of our people were caught up in this?'

The first British prime minister to raise the issue was James Callaghan in May 1978, when 1000 Katangan irregulars stormed into Zaire from their exile in Angola to seize the border mining town of Kolwezi. Some 2500 Europeans, most of them French and Belgian, were at risk; many were already hostages and some dead. The French government promptly dropped the 2nd Foreign Legion Paras into the rebel area to restore order.

Callaghan's question, from Downing Street to the Ministry of Defence, was: 'What could we have done if the European hostages had been British?' The answer: 'Very little, Prime Minister. We have only one parachute battalion currently fit to parachute and that is on counter-terrorist duty in South Armagh.'

The solution, short of having a very large rapid deployment force with a worldwide airlift capability, was to anticipate the trouble before it got out of hand. Hundreds of contingency plans, involving various agencies, were developed (and are regularly updated still) to secure the evacuation of British and friendly nationals out of harm's way. Incidents in which the extraction is a calmly ordered one, in good time, are classified as 'Service-Assisted Evacuation' operations. The departure of British citizens from Cyprus, courtesy of the Army and RAF, after the Turkish invasion of 1974, would be in that category. A 'Service-Protected' evacuation, by contrast, is one in which the crisis has taken a dangerous turn. Such operations, because of the risks involved, are yet another job handled often, though not invariably, by the SAS. In some instances, rescues have been carried out jointly with US special forces, or by one nation on behalf of the other.

In June, 1990, as order started to crumble in the African state of Liberia, more than 2000 US Marines took up positions aboard four warships offshore. There they remained, as a civil war developed and Liberian soldiers drove stolen cars round the capital, Monrovia, firing weapons in the air and extorting money from civilians. On 5 August (as it happened, three days after Saddam Hussein invaded Kuwait) 225 Marines went ashore to evacuate US Embassy and technical staff. The UK, meanwhile, sent a single Royal Marine officer, who led a highly successful road convoy of British citizens across the border to Sierra Leone, as well as an SAS team to guard British envoys.

Ethiopia 1991

An equally useful diplomatic operation was the SAS rescue of the surviving twelve members of the Ethiopian royal family just twelve hours before rebels seized control of Addis Ababa in May 1991. Four were children under five years of age. The rest were descendants of the late Emperor Haili Selassie, imprisoned by the Marxist dictator President Mengistu in appalling conditions for fourteen years. They had been released from close confinement and under house arrest for two years when Mengistu fled to Zimbabwe. A few days later, an SAS team was summoned to bring them to the sanctuary of the British Embassy. The refugees included Sarah Gizaw, Duchess of Harar (widow of the Emperor's favourite son), three of her sons, two of the Emperor's granddaughters and other relatives including Princess Zuriashwork and her grandchildren.

Though the movement of the refugees went smoothly enough, in a single convoy, it was across a city torn by gunfire. The Russian hospital in Addis was treating more than 400 gunshot casualties in a period of two days as the rescue mission went in. One of the casualties was Mohammed Amin, a Visnews television cameraman who lost an arm in an explosion. He was immediately evacuated to the hospital in Addis and given emergency treatment.

The Addis rescue almost coincided with the regiment's success at Coagh, Northern Ireland, on 3 June in stopping three notorious IRA assassins. It was another week in which the SAS saved more lives than it took.

Peterhead Prison 1987

In parallel with adapting its role to a changed world overseas, the SAS found itself in some unexpected situations in the UK also. One such was the Peterhead Prison siege in Scotland in October 1987. It was to lead to a rescue remarkable even by SAS standards. The story has not been told before.

Fifty dangerous prisoners, some serving long sentences for multiple murder and rape – men with nothing to lose – seized control of the prison's 'D' Block. Once they had got the riot out of their system, the majority gave themselves up, but a hard core of four or five men continued to resist. They held as hostage a 56-year-old prison officer with one kidney who needed drugs and medical attention to stabilise his condition. His worsening state, day by day, put the authorities under unenviable pressure.

The hard core group retreated into the roof space high in one corner of the building and roosted behind barricades, threatening to cut their hostage's throat if any attempt was made to take them. With regular rooftop performances they could ensure that their appeal to television and microphone would give them an audience beyond the prison governor.

The stalemate continued for almost a week, during which the prison authorities invoked the help of Grampian Police. The police adopted a gradualist approach, their special reaction team armed with all that was necessary, remaining one side of the barricade, the prison rebels the other, constantly watched through fibre-optic lenses and other special security equipment.

During the preceding months, there had been a series of prison disturbances in Scotland. The Peterhead stand-off, however, was dragging on a little too long. The stalemate might make sense on the spot but not in the larger world outside, particularly in Whitehall and Downing Street. After urgent talks between the Scottish Office, headed by Malcolm Rifkind and the Home Secretary, Douglas Hurd, another two-man advisory team was sent at police request from Hereford. The men set off by helicopter at about 10pm and arrived at the prison in the early hours of the following morning. Their remit was not to break the siege directly but to offer advice to the responsible civil power, the local police force. The police believed that the task was one for the SAS. Their legal right to seek military assistance was copper-bottomed. Under the rules laid down for Military Aid to the Civil Power (MAC-P) a soldier breaks the law if he refuses to aid the civil police when they ask him to help. More generally, police forces know that they have the right to call on military power via the Whitehall bureaucracy if order breaks down to a point where they cannot control it.

The use of military power – with its implication of military *firepower* – within the realm, directed against British citizens has been an emotive topic for years. It still conjures up memories of 1911, when Home Secretary Winston Churchill used the Scots Guards with Maxim gun to suppress armed anarchists in London's East End; after which the Worcester Regiment opened fire on rioting rail strikers in Wales and 50,000 troops prepared to move on London or Liverpool, where three warships were also brought to bear from the Mersey.

In the great French student revolution of 1968 known as 'Les Evenements' rioters controlled much of Paris until the CRS riot squads used CS gas to clear the streets. The British view has always been that aside from Northern Ireland, resort to such a high profile of official force is alien and politically dangerous. As a result, Britain does not have the benefits of a 'Third Force' specialising in civil commotion which goes beyond normal police control, yet falls short of armed insurrection.

The only military team with experience of precisely targeted violence available at the time of Peterhead, and for long afterwards, was the SAS. British police forces, although armed with CS by 1987, were unready to use it in an enclosed space or at all, if possible.

One of the SAS Regiment's most enduring characteristics is its lack of inhibition about going for the heart of a problem without agonising. Peterhead was a task for a small, swift snatch squad using the weapons of surprise and speed plus a puff or two of CS (technically smoke rather than gas) to keep the opposition subdued during the few minutes required to retrieve the hostage.

The prisoners' prisoner, the advisory team noted, was the only bargaining chip left to a tiny handful of rioters still holding out in an area under continuous electronic surveillance.

While the discussions continued, the SAS advisers arranged for carefully calculated explosive charges to be attached to various entry points into the wing. There was no need to make a hole in the roof. The prisoners had done that themselves as a way of reaching their television audience. The main assault line proposed by the adviser would require balance and cool nerve: it involved an exit through a skylight, a rope-assisted descent down a steeply pitched roof to a rain gutter followed by a walk of some yards, in the dark, unroped, with a drop of around 80 feet to the yard below if anything went wrong. This was perceived by the SAS team as an entirely normal procedure; the police were not convinced.

There were more negotiations through the government's crisis management group, COBR, in London with the Director of Special Forces, an SAS brigadier. Five days into the crisis, late on the night of Friday 2 October, a regimental response team flew by Hercules to an airhead some miles from the prison. They brought their standard weapons – HK MP5 sub-machine-guns and Browning pistols – though this was not a task for which firearms would be needed. Their adviser, already on the scene, had arranged for a supply of police staves around 4 feet long instead.

It was well after midnight when the aircraft touched down north of Aberdeen. First light was only a few hours away and the unblinking gaze of television would then resume. The condition of the hostage was getting no better. Somehow, the rescue squad had to be inserted into the prison unobserved; break the deadlock, achieve a clean rescue and get out, still unseen by media and prisoners, by dawn.

The team first moved from the airhead by prison bus to the prison gymnasium. It was 4am. There were two hours of darkness left. From London, COBR had given final assent to an SAS operation. They were now committed.

Briefings were pared down to essential details. The snatch squad of four men would make the hazardous journey from skylight to prisoners' roof-hole, by way of the gutter. Back-up teams would blast a way into the floors below on each side of the building and follow through to close any escape route. Once rescued, the hostage would be brought out to the care of a reception party which included a resuscitation team. Another group would receive the surrendering prisoners with handcuffs.

At around 5am, wearing CS masks and armed with their staves, the four-man assault team eased open the skylight and hauled themselves outward. It was a slippery, wet sort of morning to be on the tiles, or slates, of a Scottish prison. To walk the length of the gutter in the dark, with vision dangerously limited by a gas mask demanded a superhuman balance.

With the 'good, solid Victorian' gutter creaking slightly under his rubber boots, the point man moved gently forward, aware that if things went wrong at this stage he could find himself dangling, like Buster Keaton, on the end of a very precarious hold indeed. Yet things were OK, he assured himself. He was nearly at the prisoners' hole now.

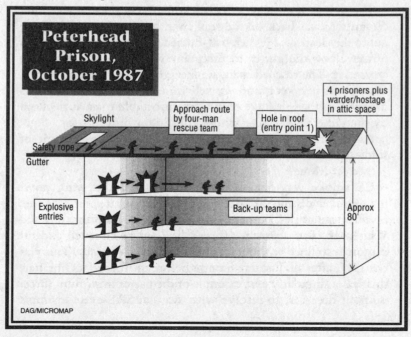

Peterhead Prison, October 1987

4 prisoners plus warder/hostage in attic space

Skylight

Approach route by four-man rescue team

Hole in roof (entry point 1)

Safety rope

Gutter

Explosive entries

Back-up teams

Approx 80'

DAG/MICROMAP

Things were not entirely OK. Across the yard to the right, the prison's B Block held several hundred men – and not all of them were sleeping.

'Watch out, lads! They're coming after you!'

The voice that bellowed across the echoing space between the two buildings was one of the prisoners who had, in all probability, given himself up earlier in the siege. Before the lights could come on, before other voices joined the clamour, the SAS point man had reached the hole. So too, almost at the same moment, did one of the prisoners. The soldier thrust the 'flash-bang' stun grenade into the space separating them and as the prisoner staggered back, the soldier followed it up with a smouldering CS cartridge, then swung his legs over the void and dropped inside.

One man threw a punch before the CS got to him. Soon those inside the roof were coughing and spluttering uncontrollably, eyes streaming. Small explosive charges around the building swept aside the barricades and announced the arrival of the follow-through teams.

The first of the rescue squad, who had tested the walk along the gutter, was back on the roof by now, hauling the hostage out to the clean air. He then half-carried, half-dragged the prison officer along the gutter to the point where the skylight rope crossed it. The rescued man, weakened by his ordeal as well as illness, was in no condition to help himself up the rope. He was dragged up the last stage of his uncomfortable road to freedom by the same SAS soldier who had brought him this far.

As at Princes Gate, the rest were propelled along a line of soldiers.

'Move! Move!'

CS smoke was oozing round the rest of the wing now, tickling eyeballs and throats beyond the immediate combat zone, reviving memories, perhaps, of hard nights in Ballymurphy and Whiterock. But a prison officer's life had been saved and his captors restrained without loss of life or serious injury. This was not 1911, after all. Just five months before the furore at Gibraltar, this was a singularly neat example of the use of minimum force, without firearms, to resolve what was, in SAS eyes, a simple problem. The job had taken just six minutes from the moment the first soldier slipped through the skylight to the moment when the hostage, his face marked with cuts, was reunited with his family in a secure, guarded area.

A few legal formalities – Scottish legal formalities, this time – had to be observed. Statements were given to the police, explaining, justifying what was done and how. The soldiers slipped away to their bus and their waiting C130 after just ninety minutes on Scottish soil. Even for Scots on the team, it was long enough – given the circumstances. They were home in Hereford in time for a second breakfast, in time to hear all about it on the morning radio news. There was little to see on television, though the Scottish Secretary, Malcolm Rifkind, stood up to say that the prime reason for ending this siege by force was concern at the 'disgraceful maltreatment' suffered by the hostage.

The operation had an extraordinary postscript. Learning from experience, the Prison Department of the Home Office started training selected prison officers in the art of breaking sieges. Some were trained by the SAS. Yet the government was slow to use such a team when faced with a colourful riot which destroyed much of Strangeways Prison, Manchester, in 1990. The governor, Brendan O'Friel, wanted to retake the prison by force on the second day but was overruled by the Home Office. An inquiry by Lord Justice Woolf later criticised the decision not to storm Strangeways, asserting that the prisoners would have soon surrendered.

The bill presented to the nation for a 'non-violent' scenario that ran on for twenty-six days was the premature death of three people, 194 non-fatal injuries, virtual demolition of a prison at a cost to taxpayers of £100 millions and loss through sickness or retirement of fifteen prison officers.

Somewhat further down the scale of public disasters was the appearance before a court in Alloa of a prison governor trained by the SAS who retained CS cartridges without authority. In December 1989 the *Independent* newspaper reported that Mr Gordon Jackson, governor of Glenochil Prison, central Scotland, was put in charge of a special unit in the prison service to deal with hostage incidents after several sieges. He was trained by the SAS Regiment to break up such sieges with the minimum of injury and force.

During a training demonstration in England in May, 1988, he received 23 "wax like" rounds which could be fired to open doors without injury, together with seven live and two CS cartridges. He took these back to his office and left them in a locked cupboard. In September 1989, Mr Jackson was convalescing after a heart attack and the ammunition was discovered.

His counsel said that Jackson, a former soldier, had twenty years of exemplary service in Scottish prisons. He had believed that his 'special remit' allowed him to possess the cartridges for training purposes. Sheriff Robert Younger admonished the governor. As he said, no one suggested that the ammunition had been collected for any sinister purpose.

Part V

Death on the mountain

Everest 1981–88

How to select an elite

Prologue

Everest is still a tough number. So is Selection. That is why they are combined in this part of the history.

DEATH ON THE MOUNTAIN

Calculated risk

One evening in 1968, the British Rail signalman responsible for a stretch of track across the Firth of Forth, including the Forth Bridge, noticed something odd about the Edinburgh-to-Aberdeen express. The train was not particularly crowded, but three men appeared to be riding on top of it. The signalman took the sensible course of stopping the express, but not before one of the three had fallen from it, killing himself in the process. Subsequent inquiries revealed that all three men were volunteers in the Territorial SAS. They had become bored with the journey and started speculating about the possibility of climbing out of the train on one side, scaling the roof, and re-entering the carriage by way of a window on the other side. Their misplaced enthusiasm for this impromptu initiative test resulted in a bet worth £1.10s. and, after the inquest, some adverse publicity for the regiment.

It was, of course, a reckless little adventure, which shed light on the lack of mature judgement of the lieutenant, sergeant and corporal involved. But it was also a reminder that the man whose judgement is entirely mature will tend not to gamble with either his money or his life: he will be a pillar of society, but entirely useless if society, to its surprise, requires the services of people who take risks. In a society in which risk-taking is only vicariously respectable (within the evidently fictional world of James Bond), the real climber, potholer, parachutist or hang-glider is regarded with suspicion. More numerous casualties in the familiar and sedentary environment of motor accidents go almost unremarked, while the schoolteacher who

485

seeks to take a party of children for a walk across calm hills is required to produce something called a Mountain Leadership Certificate.

Interestingly, it was a Labour government that recognised how, within the armed services, the calculated risk has value as military training as well as its own, intrinsic worth. In 1964, as part of the withdrawal of military forces from the Third World for concentration in Nato Europe, the Prime Minister, Harold Wilson, suggested in a memorandum to his Minister of Defence, Denis Healey, that adventurous training be incorporated within the framework of official defence activity. This would enable service people on expeditions to enjoy the same pay and preferment as if they were on more routine duty elsewhere and, if hurt, to enjoy the same benefits that would follow a battle injury. Not surprisingly, SAS soldiers had not awaited the reassurance of Whitehall that Adventure was a Good Thing before finding out for themselves. The decision of one SAS officer, posted to Aden, to sail there in his own small boat was so routine as to raise only the most passing comment. After all, the same man had planned to ride home on a Lambretta motor scooter, until he was distracted by bitter fighting on Jabal Akhdar. (The journey home would have taken him from Malaya to Britain.)

The regiment also pioneered high-altitude free-fall parachuting in Britain in the early 1960s. The military value of such techniques has yet to be proven beyond all reasonable doubt, but as an existential, life-enhancing experience it is the stuff that dreams are made of. No doubt there are smart intellectual explanations for such behaviour, that the artificial creation of a risk, and its resolution, are a source of security for insecure people, in the same manner that detective stories resolve anxieties among the less adventurous. But this misses the point that, in the detective story, there are no loose ends, no maverick, unpredictable factors. A real adventure is full of them.

There is an apocryphal story concerning a group of SAS free-fallers engaged in a night drop over Salisbury Plain . . . at least, that's where they thought they were. Uncharacteristically, their navigator placed them in the wrong spot as they left the aircraft at something over 20,000 feet. The leader, a small light gleaming from his helmet, went out first with the others following on each flank, rather like a flight of geese. The jump was technically perfect and the men landed in a compact group, but, as they foraged in the darkness, it became apparent that they were not where they should be. They decided to ask, and approached a modest, suburban bungalow. They marched up the front path, between rows of pansies, the leader in the van, his light still gleaming, and knocked on the door. It was answered by a slight, elderly woman wearing hair-curlers and a dressing-gown. 'Good evening, Madam,' the leader said. 'Could you tell us where we are?' The woman's eyes darted along the line of strangely dressed figures. 'Earth!' she said, and shut the door.

Mid-air rescue

The basic and almost foolproof method of parachuting, used by armies since the 1930s and civilian novices still, is the use of webbing strap attached to a strong-point in the aircraft at one end and the parachute pack at the other. As the jumper leaves the aircraft, several yards of the strap – known as a 'static line' – pay out until the pack is removed from the parachute, which then opens. Well, usually.

On 17 September 1967, at a civilian sport parachute centre in the Midlands known as Halfpenny Green, thirty-six-year-old Sergeant Michael Reeves of 22 SAS was enjoying a weekend's 'fun jumping'. He was also acting as jump master for a group of novices, a familiar enough task for an experienced man, involving leaning out of the machine on its final approach to the drop zone and shouting corrections to the pilot to bring it over the correct spot. Once there, Reeves gave the instruction 'Cut'. The pilot cut the engine to diminish slipstream, and Reeves told the novice to get out of the plane, ready to go. The man did so and, on Reeves's shouted order 'Go!' he fell away. Only this time, instead of flying two seconds later beneath a normally-opened canopy 2500 feet above the ground, he was spinning on the end of a static line. For some reason, this had not functioned as expected.

The aircraft flew on over an increasingly urban area. Reeves leaned out of the plane again, and signalled to the alarmed pupil who, fortunately, remembered the emergency drill he had been taught and placed hands on helmet to indicate that he was conscious and aware. Reeves knew that, for the novice to survive, he would have to land under a normally-inflated parachute canopy; furthermore, that if the novice were to avoid descending on to a railway line, main road or factory roof, the landing must be back on the drop zone. He hurriedly consulted the pilot, and advised him to fly back over the drop zone and keep circling it until the problem was solved.

Reeves solved it by climbing down the static line, a knife in his own, free-fall parachute harness ready for the first stage of the rescue. Having reached his man, Reeves wrapped two legs and an arm around him, and signalled to the aircraft that all was well. They had climbed somewhat now, to give the two parachutists more height, and therefore more time, to accomplish a uniquely delicate operation. Having satisfied himself that they were back over the drop zone, Reeves sawed away at the static line, never releasing his fierce hold on the pupil's body. At last the line parted and they were falling, curling backwards as they did so. Reeves already had his hand on the man's chest-mounted reserve parachute. He grabbed the handle and pulled it away with ferocious urgency, then held on to the novice's body again. The white reserve canopy swirled past both of them and cracked open.

Both men might have landed safely under that one canopy, a similar model of which was to support an entire Cessna aircraft and its occupants in a near calamity a few years later. But the combined weight of the pair would certainly make for a hard landing. Furthermore, the way their bodies were linked would rule out an orthodox landing role, with consequent risk of a broken ankle, or a broken back, or worse. So, although they were now perilously near the ground, Reeves released his hold on the novice and hurtled away again into free-fall. He allowed a few seconds to pass, creating adequate space between himself and the other man, before opening his own main parachute. This, of course, was a free-fall 'rig', opened by the jumper by removal of the ripcord handle from the harness. Reeves's own canopy opened only a few seconds before he hit the ground. They were inside the official drop zone and Reeves did a neat, text-book landing roll. It was an exceptionally cool performance, requiring impeccable judgement, acknowledged through the award of a George Medal.

Between the recklessness of the Forth Bridge episode and the controlled courage of Halfpenny Green there is a spectrum of non-military adventurous stories involving SAS soldiers, which have become part of regimental folklore. The regiment tends not to be good at organised ball games: it shines in tests of endurance, illustrated by Warner's account of the feat of Trooper T. McLean in rowing alone across the Atlantic in seventy-two days.

'He landed', Warner recounts, 'at Blacksod, County Mayo, on 27 July 1969.' His diet on the voyage was sardines, curry and tea. McLean, who was appropriately named 'Moby' and was twenty-five at the time of the 2500-mile row, had been an orphan since the age of two, and, perhaps because of that, had developed a high standard of self-reliance. 'He certainly needed it, for the weather was stormy all the way and once he woke up in the night in mid-Atlantic to find the boat swamped and sinking; he had another very narrow escape when he ran onto rocks off the coast of Ireland and took $1^1/_2$ hours to get off. As soon as he landed he sprinted 200 yards along the beach because he felt a bit stiff and wanted to get himself properly fit again.' It is also likely that this was McLean's way of celebrating the fact that his feet were on dry soil once more.

What such episodes demonstrate is that a number of SAS soldiers would be exceptional people outside the military world as well as within it. Nothing could more completely lay the left-wing myth that they are really 'café-society gangsters', whose heroism is really a carefully-manicured propaganda exercise shrouded in military security for the wrong reasons, than the Everest climb of 1976.

A climbing machine

The expedition was set up by the Army Mountaineering Association (AMA), a club open to all soldiers, including those of the Women's Royal Army Corps. The selectors were not SAS people. They chose the team on the basis of climbing experience, age – no one younger than twenty-five – and temperamental suitability for team-work in adverse conditions. It was led by an ex-paratrooper, Lieutenant-Colonel Tony Streather, as a joint-venture with the Royal Nepalese Army backed up by a group of Sherpas. Interestingly, not only did two SAS NCOs emerge as the summit team, but the four-man support party for that team, which assisted in their subsequent rescue, included another SAS soldier, while one of the expedition's two doctors was a former SAS medical officer, a veteran of Oman. Of the twenty-seven British servicemen taking part in the climb, only the Parachute Regiment, with four representatives, was as numerous. Since the Parachute Regiment is still (in theory at least) three times numerically stronger than the SAS, the relative contribution of the SAS to the expedition was phenomenal.

The plan to climb Everest was conceived at an AMA annual general meeting in October 1971, but it was to be almost five years before the Government of Nepal was prepared to allow the soldiers to make an ascent. During that interval, the team made practice climbs in Britain, the Alps and the Himalayas. In 1975, the soldiers made an attempt on Nuptse, 25,850 feet and the lowest peak in the Everest triangle, generally considered to be a more difficult climb technically. The leading pair on that climb were near the summit when they fell to their deaths and subsequently two more men were killed on a particularly treacherous traverse. It was an unhappy beginning.

During both the rehearsals and the 200-mile walk-in from Kathmandu to the Everest base camp, two men emerged as clear starters for an attempt on the summit. They were Sergeant John ('Brummie') Stokes, BEM, and Corporal Michael ('Bronco') Lane, BEM. Stokes had joined the SAS from the Royal Green Jackets and Lane was an ex-gunner. They had climbed together for ten years. Although not the most accomplished technical rock-climbers in the party, their combined endurance added up to what one of their companions later described as 'a climbing machine'. Everest, in any case, is not a mountain for the elegant, balletic rock-climber. It is a monstrous, baleful challenge to human endurance.

In a book devoted to the expedition, *Soldiers on Everest*, the Scottish correspondent of *The Times*, Ronald Faux, describes Stokes and Lane during a rehearsal climb in Wales, as follows:

Somewhere on that Welsh weekend, out on the frozen Carnedds and hammering themselves implacably through the bitter winter day, were Brummie and Bronco, two figures around whom quite a mythology had grown in my own mind . . . Even case-hardened paratroopers spoke of them with unqualified respect and although they were always regarded as a pair apart, one never somehow thought of one without the other; it was their self-sufficiency and unquestionable strength which made them the perfectly acceptable, a-political summit pair . . . Regimental security overwhelmed them with Victorian reserve. At the sight of the camera they would slink away or regard the photographer with a cold stare. Was I going to cover the first conquest of Everest by anonymous men standing victoriously on the summit with their backs to the camera? There was no need to worry . . . An oxygen mask on top of three months' growth [of beard] and snow goggles are perhaps the most daunting disguise.

During the march-in, the Stokes-Lane team were invariably up and away before anyone else. Their occasional habit of sleeping in the open, as part of the hardening process, was not adopted by the rest of the team.

Climbing Everest requires sustained co-ordination by a team manager to keep a flow of food and oxygen moving up the mountain, with the obvious difficulty that the greater the number of men required to put essential supplies where they are needed, the faster the consumption. Above 20,000 feet, even the fittest and strongest climber finds his legs crumbling beneath him and his mind disintegrating into a soporific nightmare. A gnawing cold that hacks away at the body's core heat makes sleep seem the only sensible thing, but it is the sleep of death. Even the most perfect human calculations, however, can be crushed with Olympian brutality by the mountain itself. Capricious changes of wind and temperature, and radical movements of the earth itself, creating and closing fissures, generate risks that cannot be calculated. One member of the expedition, an experienced Royal Marine climber, simply walked from his tent at Advance Base Camp (about 21,800 feet) into a deep crevasse on one of the 'easiest' sections of the climb. Major Henry Day was dropped on the end of a rope into a hole as inhospitable as a deep freeze to recover, with considerable help from some Sherpas, the dying man. On another occasion a Sherpa was 'projected into the air like a paper pellet from a ruler when a crevasse closed as he was crossing it on a ladder which sprang free'.

The AMA route lay through the Khumbu Icefall, a place of avalanche and crevasse, and then by way of a series of camps hacked out of the snow to the South Col, a plateau 26,200 feet high, before ascending a massive ridge to the South Summit at 28,750 feet, and thence to the main summit itself, 29,028 feet above sea level. The first pitch, through the Icefall, was led by a party of eight, including the SAS team, on 27 March, and Camp I, 2000 feet higher up, was established one week later. Already, the hazards were emerging. Pat Gunson, a REME captain and one of the best climbers in the party, found himself swinging thirty feet above an ice wall when a crevasse opened beneath him. Above Camp II (Advance Base Camp) at 21,800 feet, the going was exhausting, and the daunting task of leading was spread among the team. As one group worked itself out, it was brought down the mountain for more routine tasks, including the movement of more stores.

An early casualty on the higher slopes was a Gurkha corporal, who developed a prolapsed intestine, complicated by piles, at Camp III, 22,800 feet. An operation had to be performed on the spot, and this was handled by Philip Horniblow, the ex-SAS doctor, assisted by Stokes, a qualified medical orderly.

Recounting this episode, Faux writes: 'Philip's surgery, carried out in a tent at 23,000 feet, must surely rank as the highest operation ever performed, although as he admitted when he struggled into the open, hands dripping with unpleasantness, "I'm not sure I'd get my fellowship with that one".'

Camp IV was established on 29 April after a remarkable feat of endurance by several of the team, including the expedition's organising secretary, Major (later Lieutenant-Colonel) Jon Fleming of the Parachute Regiment and his partner, Captain Sir Crispin Agnew, of the Royal Highland Fusiliers. At about 23,500 feet, they moved the summit gear required by Stokes and Lane, as well as their own equipment, without oxygen, each man carrying a fifty-pound load.

During the second week of May, two summit teams totalling four men, plus a small support group of six, reached the South Col and, on 14 May, with Lane and Stokes lightly laden and blazing the trail, the first summit pair, with their support group of four, started climbing towards the site of Camp VI at 27,600 feet, the last one before the summit. It was a weary and difficult climb up the South East Ridge, over loose rock covered by powdered snow, a climb that forced even Fleming to pause between each step to breathe oxygen. On the return to Camp V that day, Fleming writes that he could remember hardly anything of the final thirty minutes and 'the final shallow slope up to the Camp site very nearly defeated me entirely'. Waiting for him was the second assault team, Lieutenant John Scott (Parachute Regiment) and Pat Gunson; and a second pair in support, Captain Philip Neame (Parachute Regiment) and another SAS climber, Lance-Corporal Steve Johnson. Stokes and Lane were now on their own. All they required was twenty-four hours of calm weather to complete the climb.

Camp VI was about 1400 feet from the summit and it was about 3pm when the support team – consisting of a lieutenant-colonel, a brace of majors and a flying officer – withdrew, leaving the sergeant and the corporal to enjoy the privilege, as well as the hazards, of the last pitch. That night, however, a storm started blowing, which continued throughout the following day, and it was thirty-six hours after their arrival at this final launch-pad before Stokes and Lane were able to emerge from their tent. They were climbing, roped together, by 6.30am and praying that the weather would not worsen again. If it did, the risk would be more than that of failure to reach the summit.

On the 55-degree approach to the South Summit they found, to their disgust, that the snow was not firm, but loose, powdery and resistant to swift movement. They had expected to reach this point after ninety minutes; the journey required six hours. At the South Summit, they paused and considered their position. It seemed sensible to turn back at 2pm. The alternative might be to succeed with a late assault on the summit and failure to reach the sanctuary of Camp VI before dark. Neither man was seeking posthumous recognition as an Everest climber. Before leaving the South Summit they cached two half-full oxygen bottles to await their return. They now had just one full oxygen bottle each for the last 300 feet of climb, working with increasing urgency to cut steps into the ridge before them.

Two o'clock arrived and they were not yet on the top of Everest. In fact, they had still to overcome the last technical obstacle before the summit, a thirty-foot wall of rock known as the Hillary Step. The account written by Faux and Fleming describes how, 'at the foot of a slight chimney, the two men stopped for a "Chinese parliament". "Do we go back?", inquired Bronco. "No way", replied Brummie.' The account goes on:

Bronco turned to the pitch and 45 minutes later both men were on the final slope to the summit. Suddenly there was nothing ahead, but a simple mound of snow like any other mound of snow. It marked the summit of the world. There was a quiet tumult of elation and satisfaction; they had made it and the expedition had put them there. It was a fine achievement; a few footprints to mark years of planning, hope and grief for the five people who had died in the attempt to put soldiers on the top of Everest, a few footprints which would soon be wiped away by the wind and which summed up the glorious inconsequentiality of mountaineering.

The two soldiers paused just long enough to take photographs, and then began the return march. It was 3.10pm and they knew that their chances of reaching Camp VI before nightfall were diminishing. The light seemed to be fading long before they got back to the South Summit. On the way, in an effort to speed the progress home, Stokes removed his snow goggles. It was to prove an almost fatal error. Furthermore, his temporarily enhanced vision revealed approaching cloud, and therefore worsening weather. They were far beyond help here. Even if they had carried a radio to link them with the rest of the team, it would be practically useless because there was no helicopter in Nepal capable of reaching them at this altitude.

The point at which they had cached the oxygen bottles on the South Summit was 1000 feet above Camp VI. In rapidly gathering gloom, and near exhaustion after fourteen hours' climbing above 28,000 feet, they stumbled upon the half-full bottles by the sheerest chance. Both men now knew that they were not going to reach the tent that night. To make the attempt in the dark, in their condition, was the road to certain disaster. The alternative they now faced – a night in the open – offered the remotest hope of survival so long as the weather did not get too bad . . . After all, it had been done successfully twice before, once by Doug Scott and Dougal Haston the year before, and in 1965 by an equally expert American team. But more, much more often, the gamble had failed. Stokes took the decision for them both. Removing his oxygen mask, he grunted through the ice hardening on his beard and face: 'We'll have to stop here and dig in somewhere.' Slowly and silently, like two drunken men, they staggered back and forth slowly clawing pawfuls of snow out of their survival hole. They were too tired for serious reflection that this was more likely their own grave they were digging in this benighted place. Like Scott during that final, doom-laden walk across Antarctica, they concentrated only on the job in hand . . . 'Stick-it . . . Stick-it . . . Stick-it . . .'

It is a profound mystery, even to the two men concerned, that they did not drift away that night into the long, endless sleep of death. The instant they huddled into the hole together they were engulfed by a mind-drugging cold. It seems almost certain that it was watchfulness for the other's welfare that kept each man alive. First one nodded towards oblivion, then the other, and each time it was the urgent pummelling of his companion that staved off unconsciousness.

Alive, but snow-blind

There was a moment that night when it seemed that Stokes was dying. His eyes no longer focused, and presently he lost his sight completely. According to Faux's account, Stokes's laconic description to his companion was to the effect that 'some bastard's been sandpapering my eyeballs'. To stay conscious in these conditions was bad enough if the eyes stayed open and aware, but eyes closed by snow-blindness -- which was what was happening -- monstrously reduced Stokes's ability to rouse himself from the temptation to let go, and lapse into deadly slumber. Lane fed his companion oxygen from his own bottle, and Stokes started to revive despite the fatigue and the onset of blindness. Miraculously, he produced from the depths of his layered clothing a piece of unpalatable-looking fudge. They shared it and felt better, despite the numbness that had now seized fingers and toes.

At about 3am the wind changed and started blowing directly into the snow-hole. They retaliated, blocking the entrance with rucksacks. Only two more hours to dawn, and they were in with a chance of survival after all. But they knew that they could no longer move without external help. The only place from which they could expect this was Camp V, on the South Col, about 2500 feet below them. In bad or even merely mediocre conditions, that could be a full day's climbing away. In their hole, Stokes and Lane staved off the implications of that, and tried to conserve their energy and the rapidly dwindling oxygen supply. At least the sun was now shining on Everest. It was a cracking day for climbing, Lane assured his companion. Stokes was in no position to disagree. He was now entirely blind.

The alternative summit team, led by 'Big John' Scott, found them at 9am. Now began a perilous recovery operation, initially involving Scott and his climbing partner Gunson, as far as Camp VI. By 10am, alerted through a radio message infinitely more optimistic than anyone had expected, the mountain was alive with activity. The imperative need now was to get Stokes and Lane back into an environment in which the insidious damage of frostbite and gangrene could be minimised.

From Camp V, on the South Col, the summit support party consisting of Johnson and Neame climbed urgently to assist the casualties down the steep, powder-snow gully that led from Camp VI. This accomplished, the next day the entire party set off downhill from the South Col, bound for Camp IV, at 1.15pm, but it was a bitterly painful climb down. On one exposed traverse, those accompanying Stokes had to place his feet in the holds and they were travelling at only 100 yards an hour. The operation to bring them down to base camp, where a helicopter waited to fly him to hospital in Kathmandu, required four days. For the later stages of the journey off the mountain, he was on a McInnes stretcher, though he had to negotiate one ice-fall, painfully, on foot.

Both Lane and Stokes were to lose several toes as a result of their determination, and Lane also lost the terminal phalanges of his right hand. Both men learned to climb again in Wales in spite of these disabilities, and in 1979, Lane was awarded a Military Medal for his military work in Northern Ireland.

One incident, quoted by Faux, encapsulates better than anything the spirit of these men. On the way down, 'Big John' Scott and 'Bronco' Lane were met by Jon Fleming, the Parachute Regiment major who had been involved in the organisation of the expedition from the beginning, and from whom the overall leadership had been whisked away by the organising committee at the last moment, after the Nuptse expedition. In the comfortable surroundings of the Army Staff College at Camberley, they had explained to Fleming that they saw him as 'a potential summit man; to lead the summit assault, perhaps'. At the foot of the Lhotse Face, just below Camp III, 'Bronco' hugged Fleming. 'Jon mate,' he said, 'we did this for you – to avenge last year.' Last year had been the year of Nuptse, a year of tragedy for the Army climbers, and Nuptse had been the reason advanced by the committee when they changed the Everest leadership for the need to strengthen the team, as they saw it. But, as Lane saw it, Nuptse was not just a tragedy, it was also an unspoken contract.

Return to Everest . . . again and again

SAS parties made at least four more attempts on Everest during the 1980s. In 1981, an expedition including former soldiers of 22 and 23 SAS (the TAVR unit descended from the MI9 escape specialists) and the New Zealand SAS made the attempt by the West Ridge. The party spent four nights at 25,500 feet and went higher at times without oxygen but was beaten back by intense cold and winds gusting to over 120mph. One of the team, Paddy Freaney, wrote later: 'For long periods . . . we just clung to the slope with our ice-axes to prevent being blown away and for hours, Russell Brice (New Zealand) and I could not see one another even though separated by only a short length of rope.'

In 1984, an attempt to put a regimental team up an untried route ended in a disastrous avalanche which killed a G Squadron soldier, Tony Swierzy and gravely injured another, Sergeant Andrew Baxter. 'Bronco' Lane and 'Brummie' Stokes were accompanied by fourteen men from Mountain Troop, soldiers drawn from the regiment as a whole. In August 1983, more than six tons of rations, equipment and stores were shipped to China to await the team's arrival in March 1984. Yaks carried much of this to the base camp at Ronbuk Glacier Morraine, at 18,000 feet. A team of four, with Brummie as camp manager, moved up to an advance base camp at 20,300 feet at the foot of the North Face.

Bronco later wrote:

With each successive load carried up to the site of advance base, we were acclimatising well and feeling stronger . . . The first 3000 feet of the route we knew to be where the technical problems lay and following the rotten ropes (but not using them) left by a Japanese expedition of three months previous, the team each day would climb and 'fix' an average of 800 feet.

By 2 April our progress had been very good. We had acclimatised well and were ahead of our planned timetable. The front runners had pushed fixed rope out to 22,850 feet

At 0615 on 3 April the five occupants of Advance Base were in the process of rising and preparing for another day of climbing and fixing rope on the face towards Camp 3. One of the climbers was outside his tent and witnessed a 400-yard frontage of ice serac [pillars of ice into which a glacier breaks on a steep face] start to tumble towards him. The crash triggered off powder snow avalanches on both Mount Everest and Mount Changtse. The whole mass poured down the glacier, completely devastated the camp, carrying it along some 300–400 yards. Each and every man was hit by debris and tragically, Corporal Swierzy was killed outright by large ice blocks. [It took two days to evacuate the wounded to the Rongbo Road-head.]

On 5 April, at 1100 hours, Corporal Tony Swierzy was ceremoniously buried on the central Rongbuk Glacier near to where he died. A memorial stone has been carved and placed near the base camp.

In 1986, a team led by the veteran Brummie Stokes was repulsed from the unclimbed North East Ridge. In 1988, Harry Taylor (ex-22 SAS) and Russell Brice (NZ SAS) reached the pinnacles on the ridge (the first climbers to do so) at around 26,000 feet though weather denied them the formal triumph of the final, well-trodden extension of the ridge to the actual summit. Nevertheless, they had done what five earlier expeditions had attempted and failed.

In May 1993, Taylor – now aged thirty-three and one of Britain's leading mountaineers – became the first man to climb Everest from the Nepalese side without oxygen. He spent three nights at high altitude without oxygen, coming near to death in a temperature of minus 35°C, an endurance feat that was itself a record. His solo, summit climb lasted twenty-four hours. He returned exhausted and overdue but triumphant to Camp 4.

HOW TO SELECT AN ELITE

In his study of military elites, Roger Beaumont argues that such forces tend to suffer from what he calls the 'selection–destruction cycle'. The most able volunteers are selected for the most hazardous missions and suffer higher casualties than other units as a result. Governments, he believes, like such forces because they reinforce belief in the myth of controllable, rationally waged war. Moreover, in an age when the citizens' army is being replaced by professional forces raised from volunteers, 'one might ask if Western leadership outside the neutral countries has not gotten into the habit of killing off the flower of its youth rather than risking the political feedback that might come from casualties suffered by the generally raised forces. In Vietnam, even relatively few losses toppled the Johnson Government. In a cynical vein, in view of that experience, it seems that the best balance of military forces in a society with anti-military values and an elected government, would be the use of elite forces and of conscripts and/or recruits from politically impotent elements of the population.'

The motivation and selection of SAS regulars is much misunderstood in a society whose feelings about the military community are at best ambivalent. The anarchist fringe, aware of the SAS's special role in counter-revolutionary warfare, has a vested interest in purveying a sinister image of the regiment. Elsewhere, civilian incomprehension and suspicion are reinforced by the secrecy surrounding SAS activities and by the minority-mindedness of SAS men, which springs from their self-imposed isolation not only from the community at large, but also from the rest of the British Army. For psychological as well as security reasons, the regiment has a feline appetite for walking alone, discouraging the interest of outsiders including even ex-members of the regiment. Yet if Beaumont is right, the regiment serves democratic society in a unique fashion by nominating itself as the elite military group willing to take risks that others, comfortable in their suburban semis, prefer to experience from the safety of a seat in the Odeon cinema (or, for that matter, the author's study). When hostages are seized in Balcombe Street or at Las Palmas to begin an enforced journey to Mogadishu, society needs such men as surely as it needs surgeons and public health officers.

The reason why

Why soldiers volunteer for SAS duty is as complex as the motivation of those who take part in such risk-sports as climbing and parachuting. The initial stimulus may be nothing more noble than adrenalin addiction. But for all dedicated risk sportsmen there is a learning curve: to overcome fear is to gain a self-respect, self-possession and freedom unique in a secure, but increasingly claustrophobic, society bound by no doubt necessary rules. To win acceptance among a group who have found the same road to self-respect is to join a community and achieve an identity not attainable in the fragmented isolation of urban life, the world of the 'electric light' people.

From time to time, SAS men are scrutinised by psychologists (one of whom was evacuated from Malaya some years ago in a state of collapse). The resulting conflict of cultures – the one expressing itself by action rather than talk, the other dedicated to intellectual abstractions – does not shed much light on why soldiers volunteer for such service except, perhaps, to destroy the myth that all SAS soldiers are incorrigibly immature personalities seeking to 'prove' themselves. Most of those who are finally accepted are in their late twenties with several years' hard soldiering behind them. Good judgement in spite of stress and fatigue is one of the most important characteristics sought by the selectors, and that quality is rarely compatible with immaturity. The chimera of trying to categorise the SAS soldier in the compartmental world of the psychologist emerges from Peter Watson's exhaustive study of such matters, *War on the Mind*. He reports: 'The psychologists [who test SAS recruits] look for those who, on the tests, are: above average in intelligence; assertive; happy-go-lucky; self-sufficient; not extremely intro- or extraverted. They do *not* want people who are emotionally stable; instead they want forthright individuals who are hard to fool and not dependent on orders. The psychologists do acknowledge that occasionally, with the SAS, there are problems of too many chiefs and not enough Indians.'

What finally links those who pass a rigorous selection process is a dedication to soldiering as such. 'We are a bunch of misfits who happen to fit together', is how one member of the regiment puts it. In an anti-military culture it is an adequate working definition.

If there is a multiplicity of reasons why individuals volunteer for SAS selection, there is little doubt what the regiment is seeking. In 1955, Major Dare Newell drafted a paper that still embodies the regiment's basic philosophy. Newell explained: 'Selection is designed rather to find the individualist with a sense of self-discipline than the man who is primarily a good member of a team. For the self-disciplined individualist will always fit well into a team when teamwork is required, but a man selected for team work is by no means always suitable for work outside the team.' Volunteers, Newell recorded, were assessed for their reactions to loneliness, to unusual situations when tired, and their attitude to Army life in general. The last criterion, apparently banal, seeks to weed out those who mistake the comradeship between officer and man in the regiment – in which Christian names, or 'Boss', are sometimes substituted for Sir – for a relaxation of discipline; to exclude also the tough who 'is seldom at home on his own and without an audience . . . soon loses interest'.

The essential qualities needed for soldiers who were to work for weeks and perhaps months in isolation were initiative; self-discipline; independence of mind; ability to work unsupervised; stamina; patience and a sense of humour. What they represent cumulatively is a spiritual toughness rather than a physical superiority over other troops, and in that sense the pun that an SAS trooper is one of Nietzsche's gentlemen is not far from the truth. Yet, as those who have served with the regiment's fighting squadrons are aware, one of the paradoxes about SAS troopers is that they are not loners in the sense that, say, an espionage agent must be: they cling to the tribal security of a small, four-man patrol with total loyalty. Like all soldiers, they are essentially gregarious, but they function best in small, family-sized groups that do not swamp individuality. Because of the intimacy of SAS operations, the most important factor of initial selection is the subjective judgement of the regiment's instructors as they observe the candidates. They are looking for people they could live with, basically compatible souls who are not rigid loners, manic teetotallers or fanatics of any kind. The comment, 'I don't like him' is probably sufficient to ensure a candidate's failure even if he passes other criteria of selection.

Phasing selection

The selection course for the full-time, regular 22 SAS Regiment, based at Hereford, is a prolonged and elaborate business, best understood if its outlines are first sketched in. It begins with ten days' fitness training and map-reading on the Brecon Beacons – let us call it Phase I – in which the volunteer is one of a group of about twenty men. This is followed by another ten days in which he is engaged in long cross-country marches in the same area, alone. This period – Phase II – culminates in a forty-mile endurance march to be completed within twenty hours, in which the soldier carries a fifty-five-pound Bergen rucksack and a ten-pound rifle, and in which he may travel alone or with other volunteers, as he chooses. Phase II is known as Selection with a capital 'S' because, when it is over, those who are not suitable and have not left the course voluntarily are returned to their units.

The survivors are then sent for fourteen weeks' continuation training: Phase III, during which they are still being tested for their suitability as SAS soldiers. Phase IV is the standard Army parachute course (low-level jumping employing static-line parachutes that open automatically as the jumper leaves the aircraft, a technique that has not changed much since the Second World War). Finally, the candidate faces combat survival training (Phase V), including escape and interrogation methods. Some men are rejected on the final day of this exhaustive process. For the rest, a tiny proportion of the original volunteers, the hand-over of a new beret and cap badge marks acceptance into the regiment. In SAS jargon, the volunteer is now 'badged', though recognition of this fact by his new comrades may well depend upon his performance on a live operation. (The Rhodesian SAS – still unofficially described as C Squadron – used operational experience as an integral part of its official selection system during the long guerrilla war in Zimbabwe–Rhodesia. So, sometimes, does 22 SAS.)

The volunteer's induction is followed by Phase VI, specialist training in one of the regiment's basic skills – Morse signalling, linguistics, field medical care, use of explosives, pistol shooting – combined with tactical assignment to one of four sixteen-man troops skilled in boat work, climbing, long-distance overland navigation in Land-Rovers, or free-fall parachuting. By the time this 'postgraduate' course is completed, the volunteer has been with the regiment for almost two years and he is at last a trained SAS soldier.

His first tour with the regiment is for a period of three years, after which, if he is still fit for service, he can remain for another three years, and so on. In a sense, therefore, only a tiny cadre of permanent staff are the true insiders. For everyone else, the ultimate disciplinary sanction is RTU – return to unit of origin.

Volunteers begin their phase of the prestige and agony of SAS service at a peak of fitness; for many of those who have been engaged with the operational 'Sabre' squadrons, it ends with health impaired by exotic disease or physical injury, or shattered nerves. No one remains unchanged by the experience of SAS service.

The 'Sickener' factor

At the beginning of this selection process (until recent years) each cadre of volunteers was greeted by the regiment's commanding officer at Hereford, or by his second-in-command, with a mordant welcome to the effect that 'It's nice of you all to come along; I don't suppose most of you will be with us for more than a few days'. In fact, Phase I is now intended to achieve two things: to provide simple fitness training to ensure that potentially suitable people will not fail the course because they have not had time to get into sufficiently good physical shape and to induce the 'passengers' – those seeking a break from the boredom of garrison duties in Germany and elsewhere – to drop out as quickly as possible. The first objective is accomplished by cross-country marches in which the distance covered, carrying pack and rifle, increases each day. The weight carried also increases from a basic twenty-five pounds. Until recently, this was clinically dispensed through an issue of numbered bricks from the SAS quartermaster's store; more recently, this policy has been changed so that the make-up weight comprises more useful items such as additional food or clothing. A veteran of the brick-carrying era recalls that his greatest moment of training was when he was ordered to return his bricks – which, in fact, simulate stocks of ammunition – to the store.

For some candidates, basic tuition in map and compass work must also be covered during this first phase. The SAS is dedicated to movement on foot across country, and good navigation is as important as sight itself. Since the only people permitted to join the SAS from civilian life must be members of the regiment's voluntary, part-time Territorial squadrons, the majority of the candidates are already regular soldiers. Volunteers from the Guards and Parachute Regiment, who are numerous, require little tuition in basic navigation, but there is always a surprisingly high number of SAS men whose soldiering began in the various corps (Signals, Engineers, Transport, etc.) and who have to learn almost from scratch to read the contours of a hill rather than a road map. The end result is that the SAS contains quick learners with a bewildering assortment of individual skills. At this stage also, the candidate begins to learn something of the SAS approach to security. Map references should be memorised, never written. Even the map must be re-folded along its original seams so that it could not betray the soldier's ultimate destination to an enemy.

Disposing of 'passengers' was traditionally accomplished by at least two exercises conducted during Phase I, coarsely described as 'Sickener I' and 'Sickener II'. Sickener I, for example, has been known to include the Mud Crawl, in which the volunteer is invited to immerse himself in a gully containing not only mud, but also a liberal quantity of rotting sheep's entrails. There were other, less colourful, disincentives. At the end of a fifteen- or twenty-mile march, the tired volunteers would arrive at a rendezvous only to see the lorries awaiting them drive away empty. Candidates would be told that it was necessary after all to march another ten miles. At that point, several more people would decide to drop out of the course. Those who stuck with it would find that the transport was waiting, after all, only two miles away. Another ploy, introduced during combat survival, was to order the candidate to carry the contents of his Bergen pack from the penultimate rendezvous to the final destination without the aid of the rucksack itself. 'The sickener effect could be quite dramatic,' one veteran recalls. 'On my course we lost 40 volunteers out of 120 during the first weekend.'

During the 1970s, however, the emphasis of basic selection has turned away from this approach towards a positive incentive to succeed. Even the word 'sickener' has vanished from regimental vocabulary. To some extent this change came about because of a growing need for SAS soldiers, as a result of events in Oman and Ulster, and the growth of urban terrorism in Britain. But it also reflected a change in the nature of British society itself. The young men who volunteered for SAS service after the late 1960s were no less fit or courageous than their predecessors, but they had grown up in an environment in which hardship and rejection were less familiar, and therefore more likely to demoralise. The SAS discovered that the generation of the 1980s had to be educated in the ways of adversity before it could begin to learn to cope with them. One of the architects of selection puts it like this: 'We reached the conclusion that the soldiers coming forward did not have the same stamina as the wartime and immediate post-war soldiers. Those latter, the product of the lean pre-war and wartime years, were accustomed to a much harder form of life than those from a welfare state background. We decided, therefore, that our approach to the physical side of selection had to be adapted to the class of man available. This is not to suggest that "little Tommy is not the man his father was", but simply that Tommy has to be shown what his body can put up with if it has to. One of our greatest difficulties was to persuade the older NCOs and warrant officers that this was not a lowering of standards.'

One basic rule is that the SAS volunteer is never more than an arm's reach from his rifle while in the field. One man who walked twenty yards to a lake to wash, leaving his rifle behind, received an instant sickener. 'Do twenty press-ups,' an instructor shouted at him. The man was about to begin when the instructor added: 'No, not there . . . in the lake.' After the victim had waded into the water and performed his task he was ordered to get up again and rejoin the group. 'I can't,' he replied desperately, 'I can't get up. I'm stuck in the mud.'

Among officers who volunteer for SAS selection, the sickener factor, though no longer known by that name, is still apparent. For a week before the beginning of the basic course, they are taken on long and tiring marches round the hills, then brought back to the Hereford base to be given Staff tasks – for example, calculate the amount of fuel and ordnance required to move a troop to a particular objective and demolish it, and produce a plan for the operation. The officer must then present his plan to a conference of veteran SAS troopers and NCOs, who will treat it with derision. 'You must be joking!' 'Where were you trained, the Boy Scouts?' are not responses young lieutenants have been taught to expect from other ranks. For some it is a punishing emotional experience. The officer's reaction to such criticisms will be carefully noted. Of one who failed the course it was recorded: 'He is a good officer and a wonderful person, but he is not SAS material.' The most insidious sickener is the inducement to give up the course without loss of face.

Even before a man arrives at Hereford he is officially told that it is no disgrace not to be selected. The SAS itself is also genuinely concerned not to destroy the self-confidence of men it will reject, for they would be valuable soldiers in more orthodox units.

Phase II of selection begins in the early hours of the morning when the volunteer joins others in a routine muster parade and clambers into the three-ton lorry as usual. But this time, instead of starting the march with a group he is turned out alone at an isolated spot and given a map reference as his next rendezvous. If he is not very alert the lorry has departed before he has properly woken up. It is raining and he wonders whether he heard aright the six-figure number gabbled at him as the vehicle disappeared. Orthodox soldiering is essentially a gregarious, mutually-supportive activity, and this sudden isolation is a shock. He has yet to discover that to cover the route up to Pen-y-Fan and down again three times by different routes within the time set for the exercise, he will have to jog much of the way. In the rain, his Bergen gets heavier as it absorbs moisture.

This situation is one in which it is easy to brood upon the unfairness of the world. After getting lost once or twice, thereby adding to the distance to be covered, the volunteer arrives at the first rendezvous wet from the knees down after penetrating a bog, and soaked by his own sweat. The instructors sit drinking tea, apparently immersed in complacency. Until the seventies, it was normal for an instructor, with feigned solicitude, to say: 'You look all-in, mate. Hop in the back of the truck and get your feet up.' The wise volunteer knew that even to pause to consider the proposal was to invite rejection from the regiment. To remove his pack at that moment was to ensure failure, even if his resolve weakened only for a matter of seconds. So, with a forced smile, he would reply: 'Piss off. I've got better things to do', and continue his journey. Today, the solicitude is probably genuine and the volunteer, far from being seduced into abandoning the march, will be reminded: 'Only another ten miles. You've come more than half way. Stick with it.' Furthermore, the trucks waiting at the end of the march will not mischievously disappear. Not all rendezvous are simple check-points. At some of them the candidate will be required to perform an unexpected task, such as stripping and reassembling a weapon he has not seen before – the physically maladroit are a liability in a section fighting its way out of an ambush – or, perhaps, prove powers of observation by answering questions concerning a dam or railway line he has passed en route.

The endurance march

As the course continues, the volunteer finds that his judgement is becoming eroded by lack of sleep. Each day begins at about 4am and ends with a briefing at 10.30pm or later for the next day's exercise. The effect is cumulative over the whole twenty-one days, and it is at the end of that period that the selectors subject him to the endurance march. One of those who passed the course recalls that 'it is a test of strength, stamina and sheer will power: a real bastard. People worry about it and rightly so. Nothing that has gone before compares with this. Most people who are fairly fit can keep going for eight or twelve hours. This goes on for 20 or more. I took 21 hours which was regarded as rather wet.' By now, only the most determined candidates remain on the course, but it is likely that at least four to six more will be broken before the day is out. The minimum distance to be covered over mountainous terrain is forty miles in twenty hours. (Until recent years, the target was forty-five miles in twenty-four hours.) Allow for map-reading errors, bad luck, bad weather and bad judgement, and the distance may be considerably longer in fact.

The endurance march caused one fatality in 1979. Three others – two of them Territorial volunteers – died during preliminary marches over the next twelve months. Before this, only three volunteers had died during the twenty-three years that the initial selection course had existed, and one of those had suffered from a rare heart condition. Through a tragic irony, the first victim of 1979 was not a novice bidding for a place in the regiment, but the hero of Mirbat, six years before, Mike Kealy, now a major. In the early hours of 1 February 1979, he joined thirty recruits as they set off from Talybont Reservoir in conditions made treacherous by darkness, snow and ice underfoot and with visibility reduced to only a few yards by freezing rain, sleet and snow. Even on a fine summer's day, the forty-mile route would have been a formidable proposition for an experienced hill walker. That day, as events were to demonstrate, it was virtually impossible.

Though the men moved off in two parties, each of about fifteen, they were soon spread out across the hill in smaller syndicates of two or three men. To be completely alone made it harder, slower and therefore colder to walk on an accurate compass bearing in what one SAS officer later described as 'minimal visibility'. Two men, after all, could take it in turns to act as markers for one another if no other landmark were visible. A solo walker might be limited to the uncertain procedure of getting his 'fix' on a patch of bare snow a few yards in front. A further hazard faced the solo walker. To move too slowly in such conditions carried with it the risk of increasing cold in a biting wind, and with it the insidious onset of exposure, which hacks away at good judgement long before it reduces bodily warmth to a dangerously low level.

Kealy chose the loner's way. To some extent this was inevitable: he was not part of that selection course, though he had twice participated in the shorter, twenty-mile marches during the preceding three weeks. Also, he was a comparatively senior officer, somewhat older than almost any other participant, and regarded by them with awe blended with the suspicion that he might be one of the selectors. But why should he participate at all? After all, he had been in the regiment for years and had a record of rare distinction in Oman. A sergeant in charge of the course explained later: 'He wanted to come on the endurance march to see if he could still do it in the time.' Now thirty-three, Kealy had been in administrative work after service in Northern Ireland, and was returning to operational duties to command his own squadron. To an outsider, what may seem uncommonly like menopausal recklessness was, to him, common prudence.

He had to be fit enough for the next operation in any climate, and the only way to be sure of that was to demonstrate it to himself.

Yet in other respects his judgement was questionable. He had made up the back-pack weight of his Bergen to fifty-five pounds with bricks, and was not equipped with the waterproof storm suit issued to the novices. Once on the hill in driving rain, his smock and trousers were quickly soaked, causing a rapid loss of body temperature. At the weigh-in preceding the march, his pack was overweight and a brick was removed. Others on the course made up the correct weight with additional clothing and food. They did not carry bricks. And, though Kealy had gloves in his rucksack, he chose not to wear them. One of the survivors of the exercise found it necessary to wear two pairs, and he was still driven off the prescribed route because of cold.

Initially, Kealy moved fast, passing the first man to leave, Trooper E. But, after an hour or so on top of the ridge, this trooper and four or five other candidates overtook him. By now, conditions were so bad that, despite their foul-weather suits, they decided to get off the ridge and into the shelter of the valley below. As they turned off the original route, Kealy shouted, 'You're going the wrong way!' 'In a sense, we were,' Trooper E. later admitted. 'The major just went on his own and that was the last we saw of him.' By the time this group reached the shelter of a barn in the valley miles below and some hours later, one of their number was suffering from exposure.

Back-markers in the party later found Kealy staggering in the snow, and stayed with him when he finally slumped into a sitting position. But he threw away the gloves given to him by one man, and allowed a jacket placed over his shoulders to blow away, insisting that he was 'all right'. Further offers of help made him so angry that the two novices with him concluded that it was better to walk in front of Kealy and lead him off. He stumbled after them. Then they lost him completely in the darkness. Wind filled in the tracks Kealy made in the snow and after a fruitless search for him lasting well over an hour, the cold drove the two novices down the hill to shelter. At 9.30am, less than seven hours after the march had started, a captain and a corporal taking part in the march spotted what they thought was a rock protruding from the snow. As they got closer they saw that it was Kealy. He was unconscious now, but a feeble pulse could be detected in his neck. Hurriedly, the two men dug a snow-hole and slid the unconscious officer into a sleeping-bag. The corporal also entered the snow-hole and remained with Kealy in an attempt, almost literally, to breathe life back into him. The captain, meanwhile, set off to raise the alarm. For the corporal, it was to prove a long vigil.

By the time the alarm had been raised, several more hours had passed. The first message to reach Brecon Police Station, inviting general police assistance, was timed at 1.55pm. The police contacted the Army only to be told that it would be sufficient to put the local civilian mountain rescue team on stand-by. Nevertheless, a police inspector made his way by road through thick fog to the SAS rescue HQ some miles away, only to be told, politely but firmly, that military authorities were organising the search. The Army did not wish to duplicate matters by using police or civilians. In the event, it was 4.30am the following day, nineteen hours after Kealy had been found unconscious, before his body was lifted off the hill by helicopter. The corporal who had stayed with him, trying unsuccessfully to transfer the heat of his own body to that of the dying officer, survived the ordeal.

The SAS major in charge of the rescue, identified at a subsequent inquest under the codename 'Foxtrot', explained that when the alarm was raised about Kealy's problem other soldiers were still missing. The exercise was abandoned. Attempts by helicopter to reach the position where Kealy lay were defeated by bad visibility. Foxtrot was concerned about the loss of not just one man, however important, but possibly several. His first priority was to account for missing men and to direct those still on the hill, including instructors at prearranged rendezvous, to come down. Furthermore, there were both Army and RAF mountain rescue teams at large. 'I had advice from an experienced mountaineer', Foxtrot told the Coroner, 'that it was unwise in those conditions to put too many men on the hill at the same time.' The only oblique criticism of

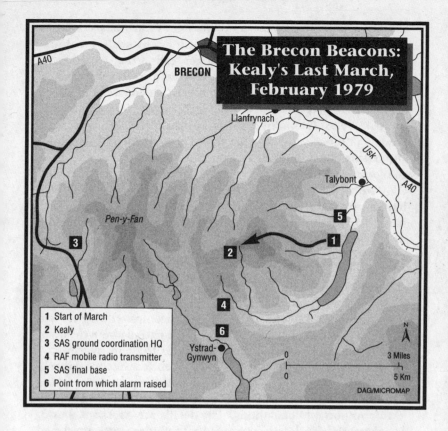

1 Start of March
2 Kealy
3 SAS ground coordination HQ
4 RAF mobile radio transmitter
5 SAS final base
6 Point from which alarm raised

this strategy came from the Coroner, who asked whether it would not have been opportune to invoke assistance from the local civilian mountain rescue team, who knew the area well. Foxtrot's answer, in effect, was that he had not discarded this idea, but that it was overtaken by events in a complex situation.

It is highly likely that another factor at work was SAS determination to keep the problem 'in the family' without external aid (but not for political reasons or because of misplaced 'macho'). What makes the regiment unique is its unswerving belief in self-reliance, in the soldier's ability as an individual to complete his task unaided, if necessary, in the frightening isolation of hostile territory in wartime. In such a culture, more readily comprehensible to a generation that experienced the Second World War than to those who have succeeded it, a commissioned officer enjoys no special privileges. Indeed, as an article by Major Dare Newell, OBE, in the SAS regimental journal, *Mars & Minerva*, once explained: 'SAS operations require an officer, carrying the same kit as his men, to outshoot and outmarch them under most unpleasant conditions, without the company of other officers and those comforts that normally alleviate the officer's lot.' Regimental philosophy would also have shaped attitudes about the weather conditions that night. It is an article of faith in the SAS that its soldiers will operate in any part of the world, in any climate, without pause for a period of acclimatisation. As Watson's study reveals:

At the end of 1972, a contingent of the Special Air Service . . . left its headquarters in Hereford bound for Malaya on a continuous 22-hour flight. Half a dozen psychologists had gone out before, armed with basic information about the men, collected in Hereford in the weeks prior to their journey.

On arrival in Malaya . . . the men were continuously monitored doing various combat and support tasks. As a result of these tests the psychologists were able to come to two important conclusions. The details are classified, but in general the psychologists found that the men who performed best on the first couple of days after the flight were by no means the men who performed best later on . . . Second, the psychologists found they were able to predict how well men would perform in a tropical climate on the basis of several psychological tests given in rural, and normally chilly, Hereford. The tests themselves are secret, but the results have now been put into effect in the selection of British SAS men who may have to serve abroad at short notice.

Subsequently, Watson concludes that the best way to organise military 'fire brigades' would be to have specialist units that can travel and fight immediately for some days, to be withdrawn when the follow-up troops are ready to take over and 'this may be the way the British Special Air Service operates'. Certainly the notion of instant readiness to fight anywhere in the world is fundamental to SAS thinking. It is known, somewhat euphemistically, as 'environmental training', and there seems little doubt that it was with this in mind that Foxtrot allowed the endurance march to proceed on the Brecon Beacons the day Kealy died.

Kealy's death, caused by exposure, disorientation and hypothermia, probably could have been prevented if he had observed basic survival drills. So, too, could the second death, that of an exceptionally fit corporal who was a candidate for selection. This man ignored, or overlooked, instructions to stay away from a short cut on the day's route – the summit of Pen-y-Fan – on an August day when 60mph gales were destroying the Fastnet Yacht Race. Like Kealy, he became soaked by driving rain, suffered exposure and died of hypothermia, although the still-air temperature in the valley was a tolerable, if chilly, eight degrees Centigrade. The third death, in the autumn of 1979, was that of a Territorial volunteer taking part in a march on the Pennines during a week's selection course, who appears to have been swept away in the dark by a rain-swollen river. A common factor in all these cases is that the victims were regarded as being entirely capable of completing the course; all, however, could be said to have been over-confident of their ability to beat abnormal conditions. The fourth death, in March 1980, again occurred in extremely cold conditions. The soldier concerned, a Territorial, collapsed and died soon after passing through a check-point at which instructors felt the bodies of all candidates for signs of abnormal cold. This man appeared to be warm and was marching strongly.

Recruits who have completed the endurance march on time and who pass the initial three-week selection course for the regular SAS are gathered in a barrack room to discover that bad news rapidly succeeds the good. They are being allowed to proceed to continuation training, they are told, but only on sufferance, and it is by no means certain that they will be finally accepted into the regiment. There is no cause for self-congratulation at having come this far. With that deflating message, they are allowed to take a long week-end's leave. It is not unusual for them to sleep all the way home.

Initial selection lasts three weeks. Continuation training – a refinement of selection – is an elaborate process spread over nearly four months. Much of this time is spent learning basic soldiering – fieldcraft, target reconnaissance, weapons-training from pistol to 81mm mortar, ground-control of air and mortar fire – because such a high proportion of those so far selected are not infantrymen. The course also includes an introduction to the use of explosives for demolition and sabotage, with tuition in the use of the standard SAS charge; four or five days devoted to field first-aid training; a language ability test; a 1000-yard swim in shirt and trousers; and a variety of initiative tests. There was a time when, on paper, these involved planning a bank robbery or raid on some other local target in Hereford, but after one such plan was left in a restaurant, with embarrassing results, the practice ended. Each short course ends with a test. 'The object of such tests', explains one former SAS soldier, 'is to weed out the total idiot who was fit enough and lucky enough to get through initial selection.'

Subsequently, as men specialise after acceptance into the regiment, they develop a high degree of expertise in one or more of these techniques. The search for a quick learner, which is what this part of selection is about, is a change of emphasis from the regiment's early post-war years, the years of Malaya, when the accepted philosophy was: 'Head down, arse up and march from one end of the jungle to another until you find the enemy.'

The first post-war SAS selection course in Britain was a simple one-week affair conducted in Snowdonia by Lieutenant-Colonel John Woodhouse, to check basic stamina and map-reading ability. During the course, he suffered an attack of malaria with the result, as he later recalled, that 'my endurance was more severely tested than that of the recruits'. In 1954, he submitted himself to selection, and passed.

Combat-survival/interrogation

One of the most testing and controversial elements of continuation training is a three-week, combat-survival course at
Exmoor, in which candidates are stretched psychologically as
well as physically. The point of such training is to prepare men
to fight a guerrilla war behind enemy lines. Much of the course
is run by a Joint Services Interrogation Unit staffed by SAS and
other personnel. It is preceded by a special period of training at
the regiment's Hereford base. Both courses are a mixture of
tuition in living off the land – identifying edible seaweed and
fungus, learning trapping techniques to procure game or fish
– followed by a realistic application of these lessons, in which
the student spends several days and nights on the moor, being
hunted by soldiers from other regiments. Cunning candidates
have been known to pass some of this time comfortably as
unofficial guests of people living on or near the moor.

The Exmoor course contains the usual 'sickener' element.
Devices include a variant of the numbered brick, a five-gallon
jerrycan of water to be carried over long distances. To eliminate
the possibility of cheating, the water is dyed and the Jerrycan
checked by instructors.

At the regiment's Hereford base and, subsequently, on the
Exmoor course, SAS candidates are also subjected to interrogation of a kind that, to judge from the testimony of those who
have passed the course, does not differ from the treatment about
which terrorist suspects complained in Ulster in 1971, and which
was studied by the Compton Commission. Already-exhausted
soldiers have been subjected to physical hardship and sensory
deprivation, including the use of a hood placed over the head for
many hours, white noise and psychological torture. The object
of these techniques is to force the combat-survival students
to reveal the names of their regiments and details of the
operations on which they are nominally engaged. Not all those
participating are SAS candidates; Royal Marine Commandos
and Parachute Regiment soldiers also take part. The difference
is that for the SAS nominee to break is more than a chastening
experience: it means he has failed to win a place in the regiment.

Those who fail at this stage are often the men who seemed best fitted to the physical rigours of the earlier selection process on the Brecon Beacons.

The experience of one successful candidate in recent years is that three periods of hooded interrogation occur during the two interrogation-resistance courses: a half-hour 'nasty'; an eight-hour period and finally, during the Joint Services' Exmoor Course, one of twenty-four hours interrupted only for periods of exposure to bright electric light while facing the interrogation itself. In one instance, hooded SAS candidates were hurled from the back of a stationary lorry by their over-enthusiastic captors, members of an infantry regiment, on to a concrete road as part of the pre-interrogation, softening-up process. One man suffered a broken arm as a result. A successful candidate on that course, who was still intact, recalls that he then spent eight hours sitting manacled in a puddle as a preliminary to questioning. During another period of interrogation, he was hooded and shackled to a strong-point in a room in which white noise and coloured, flashing lights were used. After some time, guessing that he was alone, he contrived to remove the hood and regain a sense of reality. 'I looked around and there were all these flashing lights', he said later. 'It suddenly seemed ridiculous to me. But until then it was a bit unnerving. Some people get frantic in there. I think there is a limit to how long you can stand it. After 24 hours you begin to wonder if they are on your side. At the time, while it was happening, I was told that the "treatment" would go on much longer and I was almost cracking.' At Hereford, as both victim and interrogator, he took part in more refined psychological brutality during a preliminary combat-survival course run exclusively for the SAS. Candidates were tied to a wooden board and immersed in a pond for up to twenty seconds before being recovered to face the same questions: 'What did you say your regiment was? What did you say you were doing?' One who survived this test later told his interrogators that he realised no one intended him to drown, but he did fear the possibility of a miscalculation, or that things would simply get out of hand.

An SAS interrogator with 'a Machiavellian turn of mind' so arranged matters that hooded captives thought they were about to be attacked by 'a perfectly lovable Labrador'. In an adjoining room, meanwhile, they could hear a beating taking place followed by the sound of vomiting and running water. The victim of the beating was an old mattress; the groans and vomiting were simulated by the interrogation team. An even more elaborate charade involved the use of a railway truck in an old siding, part of a disused ordnance depot. 'We had these guys handcuffed to the rails. By this time they were disoriented and tired. What they heard was a voice shouting from a distance, "Get those men off the line!" The other guards then went through a pantomine. "Bloody hell, there's a train coming. Get the keys!" The prisoners could feel the vibration of the truck approaching. As it got closer one of the guards shouted, "It's too late. Jump!" In fact, the wagon went past them quite harmlessly on an adjoining line into the siding. Among the prisoners, reactions differed. Some positioned their hands so that the wagon wheels would cut the shackles and set them free. Some got themselves into a position where they would have lost an arm. Others went berserk and ended up lying across the rails. But every one of them thought that this was a real emergency and that we had made a monumental cock-up.'

The perception of another, older SAS veteran is that the account given above places undue emphasis on physical brutality. According to this source, the interrogation experts (who include at least one former captive of the Chinese) regard such brutality as counter-productive in breaking a prisoner's will. Furthermore, he adds, candidates are carefully briefed beforehand about what to expect from the interrogators. 'My experience was that the Exmoor course emphasised psychological vulnerability,' he said. In practice, in his case, this 'psychological' approach meant his being left naked in the snow for several hours before interrogation by a panel which included a woman. The size of his penis, much reduced because of the cold, was the object of sarcastic comment. This veteran, a particularly hard man, added: 'I wasn't always certain who was being trained: us or the interrogators. I think it was a bit of both, really.' What is undoubtedly true is that, in action, the most successful SAS interrogators in Oman and elsewhere are those who have used guile and elaborate bluff to penetrate captives' defences. Brutality, they believe, simply strengthens the will to resist.

Peter Watson's study concludes that neither sensory deprivation alone, used experimentally, nor simple physical brutality will break a victim during interrogation. He also points out that there is an inevitable difference in the climate of interrogation practised by friendly forces, and the real thing. 'So far as controlled laboratory experiments are concerned, there can be little doubt that, by itself, SD is not as horrendous an experience as has been painted. But of course there is a large difference between the laboratory situation and SD when used as part of "hostilities".' In the latter case, 'the captor-captive relationship is entirely different, the role of uncertainty and fear is magnified, and attempts to get people to talk will be far more assiduously pursued'. Watson also finds that 'the experience of captivity is far more disorienting than the experience of sensory deprivation, but together they are lethal. To counter them, soldiers have to have training in both. The world's armies are probably more aware of this distinction than non-military scientists.'

The two combat-survival periods – the preliminary SAS course at Hereford and the Joint Services course at Exmoor – end with a solemn, all-ranks dinner representing tastes acquired during this time, including seaweed, frog, hedgehog and rat. On one occasion, following total failure to obtain sufficient hedgehog in the wild, rats were collected for the feast from an Army veterinary establishment. 'What do you want these for, then?' the SAS messenger was asked when he arrived to pick them up. 'To eat, of course,' was the reply.

As well as resisting interrogation – or at least, coming to terms with the grim reality of it – combat-survival training also teaches escape and evasion. In winter exercises it is a long-standing military joke that the SAS man may be identified as the one who walks *backwards* across a patch of snow. The Joint Services Escape and Evasion course devotes a short time to lectures and demonstrations by police dog-handlers on eluding the dog by wading in water or through a farmyard where the scent will mingle with that of more pungent animals. SAS men are also taught how to kill a war dog, a skill some of the regiment's soldiers used to remarkable effect during an exercise in friendly Denmark several years ago, to the outrage of the dog-handlers concerned.

The handful of men who complete the process of initial selection and continuation training – estimates of this number vary between five and seventeen out of every hundred – are welcomed into the regiment by its commanding officer or second-in-command, and handed the beige SAS beret and cloth badge bearing the famous winged dagger.

Further education: HALO, etc.

The new recruit is now ready for intensive specialist instruction. He can opt to serve in any one of four tactically different troops which make up each of the regular regiment's four active-service Sabre squadrons. These are equipped for high-altitude free-fall parachuting; amphibious operations from small boats, canoes or even submarines, in ways similar to the Royal Marine Special Boat Section (though the ultimate purpose is different); mountaineering, including rock-climbing, ice and snow work; and overland missions by custom-built Land-Rover. The last group, known as the Mobility Troop, traditionally functions in the desert and is trained to use sun compass, theodolite and astro-navigation. Many SAS soldiers, who would serve in Norway or Denmark in a European war, must also learn how to use cross-country skis and other techniques of winter warfare. One squadron regularly sends men for training in Northern Norway.

As practised by the SAS, free-fall parachuting is more than usually hazardous and totally different from the basic static-line techniques used by the Army since the Second World War. A six-week HALO ('High-Altitude, Low-Opening') course of about forty descents in Britain, and at Pau in France, drastically introduces recruits to the art of free-fall stability, with an initial descent from 12,000 feet, or about sixty seconds of unimpeded fall, after only three days' ground training. The basic task is theoretically simple: to remain stable in a face-to-earth, starfish posture, with the body's centre of gravity at about solar-plexus level. This is achieved by arching the back and placing the limbs symmetrically so that air pressure on them is uniform. After leaving the aircraft, the jumper will accelerate for the first twelve seconds of fall – about 1480 feet – to terminal velocity of 120mph.

The danger of this 'deep-end' method of training is that a novice can easily become unstable in the air by losing the symmetry of his position. If he starts an uncontrolled tumble at the moment when his parachute begins to open, there is a risk that it will snag on some part of his body, producing a 'horse-shoe' malfunction, instead of deploying unimpeded from the launch-pad of his back. The civilian sport jumper, by comparison, makes a first free-fall of no more than three to five seconds before opening his parachute in conditions of perfect stability, well short of the radical air pressures presented by terminal velocity. What is more, an expert civilian will expect to perform all the manoeuvres the sport involves – loops, turns, rolls, tracking – from about 7000 feet, and it is unlikely that he will often leave the aircraft above 12,000 feet, which is the height at which the SAS novice begins his parachuting.

The HALO course progresses to train the soldier to jump from 25,000 feet or more, by day or night, using oxygen, carrying a rifle against his body and an inverted Bergen pack slung across the back of his thighs below his main parachute harness. Because he carries so much equipment – the load may be 110 pounds – the SAS soldier's freedom to correct his posture in free-fall, so as to preserve basic stability, is severely limited. For example, the unencumbered civilian normally opens his own parachute with his right hand, while the left hand and arm compensate for this loss of symmetry by reaching out directly in front of the helmet to 'grab air'. The SAS soldier, burdened as he is, dare not attempt this manoeuvre except as an emergency drill. For this reason, his parachute is equipped with an automatic opening device. The risks of disaster escalate if, for any reason, the load being carried shifts during free-fall. It was because his Bergen shifted that an SAS trooper, 'Rip' Reddy, became the first British soldier to die during an operational free-fall descent in 1970. Because the load may vary on each descent, the aerodynamic problem of one jump will also differ from that of the last jump, or the next.

There are other peculiar hazards. As the exit height increases, so ice on goggles and chest-mounted altimeter becomes an acute problem. (So does the risk of frostbite.) The SAS soldier, if he is not to jump blind, must learn to rub the ice away with his gloved hands. Again, to preserve symmetry/stability he must use both hands simultaneously, at which point he will tilt head-down before recovering the basic starfish posture. And, because he jumps as one of a group, the risk of mid-air collision is significant. For some exercises, the canopy opening height is also reduced well below the usual 4000 feet (at which height the distinctive crack of canopy deployment is inaudible on the ground). In Norway and elsewhere, the soldier will travel into a valley in a 120mph free-fall with the walls of a mountain on each side of him. He must also learn to stay with the group. To close a gap he will have to manoeuvre across the sky in a tracking posture – arms and legs in a delta position, posterior raised – so as to make progress laterally as well as vertically.

Why use free-fall? Theoretically, it should enable a small party of men to leave an aircraft well away from their ultimate destination and to elude detection by radar. The radar cross-section of a human descending at that speed would resemble that of a bird, detectable only to an unusually experienced radar operator in ideal conditions. Jump suits made from radar-absorbing material further reduce the risk of detection. Behind a mountain screen, as in Norway, it could be the perfect, silent way to infiltrate a reconnaissance or sabotage party across enemy lines. So far, however, the handful of operational free-fall descents made by the SAS has not encouraged anyone to believe that free-falling has many advantages over the use of helicopters. Even the sound of helicopter engines, it is claimed, can be minimised to a point where it does not betray an operation. Meanwhile, free-fall parachuting, as well as being a tactical option, is also regarded by the regiment as 'a good character builder'.

In its most dangerous form, free-falling into the sea is practised by the boat-troops, specialists in diving and other maritime
skills, who do not always use boats. In 1970, the regimental
journal, *Mars & Minerva*, described how 'the boat-troop, in
their rubber suits, flippers, containers and parachutes waited
nervously by the door of the Argosy aircraft for the green light
and their "leap" into the sea. They all started as the voice of their
favourite RAF parachute jumping instructor, Tommy Atkinson
(who supervised the exits), rang in their ears: "One more point,
lads. At Suez, we had some casualties in the aircraft door whilst
waiting to jump. So now, I have orders to simulate this sort of
thing by practising just such an eventuality as you make this
jump." An amazed boat-troop looked goggle-eyed at Tommy
as he made this statement, all frowning with concentration.
"What I propose to do", continued Tommy, "is to punch
every third man in the ear as he leaps from the aircraft." . . .
The boat-troop parachutists descend lower and lower, swaying
through the dusk on their parachutes towards the inky blackness
of the sea. Good grief, it really is black! The boat-troop dropped
into a large oil-slick and emerged like Kentucky Minstrels.
There were some who thought that this might have been one
of Tommy Atkinson's tricks. He was that convincing . . .'

On one occasion, 'the boat-troop Sergeant (a willing pupil
of Atkinson) regarded the free-fall troop seriously as he briefed
them for their annual swimming test in the cold, mid-winter
Mediterranean Sea. "If you have any worries," he said, "raise
your fists above your head and shout. My boys are in the
Gemini pick-up craft and they will be with you almost instantly.
Incidentally, I should warn you about the basking sharks that
occasionally appear in the Med at this time of the year. Mind
you, a man has not been taken here for about seven years, but
just keep your eyes open." The free-fall troop had suddenly
taken a new interest in their swimming. Some smiled in ridicule
but nevertheless they all took a good look around as they
jumped from the Gemini into the sea. Some five minutes had
passed. All were swimming steadily towards the shore. Colin
had drifted away from the others slightly, but was swimming
well enough. Suddenly he felt a movement in the water close

to him. With blurred vision, he peered under the water and sensed rather than saw the black shape flash past his legs; felt something sharp groping at his calf. His frantic cry of "Shark!" and consequent action were all that the books had ever portrayed. He was practically standing on the water. The rest of the free-fall troop promptly developed that gregarious spirit and formed an instant, protective, hysterical cluster in the water. The black shape, and yes, a fin were seen by all. Frenzied shouts. Why the hell were the pick-up party so slow in reacting? They seemed to be doubled-up over their boats . . . Then, as a note of hysteria crept into Colin's voice, Bob, the boat-troop's ace diver, emerged alongside him. In the Geminis, the boat-troop laughed and laughed . . .'

Signallers and surgeons

Within each troop (one officer and fifteen men), whatever its tactical role, every soldier has to acquire one or more of the specialist skills needed when the troop or its standard sub-unit, the four-man patrol, is functioning on the ground. Communication is of such importance that a gifted signaller will be particularly cherished by the regiment. The SAS is one of the few elements of the British – or any other – armed forces still using high-speed Morse. Not only does this make for better security, but there are technical reasons why Morse can be more readily transmitted 1000 miles across rough terrain than voice. The SAS basic signals course lasts three months. The need for a medical specialist well-versed in emergency first-aid and basic surgery, taught to SAS soldiers in this country and the United States, does not require a qualified doctor to satisfy it. If the situation is critical, a doctor will be flown or parachuted to the scene and the casualty will be evacuated. A good 'bush doctor' will know whether such assistance is imperative. He will also weigh against that need the risk that the turbulence and noise inherent in a casualty evacuation may 'blow' the security of a secret operation. The patrol 'medic' is also valuable in dispensing simple medical care to civilians and their farm stock in a primitive environment as part of SAS policy to gain the co-operation of the indigenous population. For the same reason, at least one man of the four needs an adequate command of the language of the war zone to which he is posted. Such courses are intensive and may be tailored specifically to SAS needs. They are held at the Royal Army Education Corps School of Languages at Beaconsfield. For historic reasons, Malay and Arabic have been most regularly taught to SAS soldiers, but more recently European and Scandinavian languages and Russian have become equally important.

Certain fighting skills are also developed to an awesome level of ability. Among these, the use of the automatic pistol in close-quarter battle (CQB) is the most impressive. The object of this six-week course, for which a minimum of 1200 to 1500 bullets per man is provided, is to teach the soldier to burst into a room ostensibly occupied by several armed men and to kill or disable all of them with aimed shots from a thirteen-round 9mm Browning. It is assumed that each target must be hit in the chest by two bullets from up to twenty yards. The technique developed by the SAS in its specially-constructed 'CQB House' at Hereford, is to move continuously, rolling over and over on the ground if necessary, without pausing to fire accurately. Instant magazine changes and clearing jams in the pistol are also included in the repertoire. The ultimate effect of this training is deadly, as guerrillas and terrorists in Ireland, Aden and elsewhere have discovered. In a city or a crowded, hijacked aircraft, such training also minimises the risk of innocent casualties that the enormous velocity of modern firearms makes all too probable.

The use of explosives is a basic tool of all SAS soldiers and forms part of the early continuation training. More advanced techniques taught to specialists in this field include the creation of booby-traps, knowledge of a wide variety of explosives and the use of sophisticated timing and trigger mechanisms.

The troop to which the SAS novice has now been assigned is part of a larger unit known as a squadron, of which 22 SAS, the regular regiment, has four. Each squadron consists of four troops plus a squadron commander (a major), a second-in-command, a sergeant-major, quartermaster and clerks – a total seventy-two men and six officers. Theoretically, the novice is not basically proficient until he has exercised with the whole squadron, though fighting actions involving an entire SAS squadron are rare.

At any one time, parts of the squadron may be dispersed all over the world in small 'team jobs', either training friendly forces or on highly secret operations, often concerned with counter-terrorism in friendly states. But one complete squadron of 22 SAS is always on instant stand-by at Hereford, gear packed and a codeword, signalling an alert, memorised. Readiness is routinely tested, and men are extracted from their beds or their favourite pubs at unsocial hours. Some years ago the code was 'Free Beer!' As it echoed through the Hereford bars many of their regular customers left: back at Bradbury Lines barracks they collected their Bergens and assembled. 'This time it's for real, lads,' they were told. 'We're going to Ireland.'

Research and Intelligence

Also based at Hereford are other SAS groups, whose work is even more specialised. They include a separate signals squadron, an operations research group (evaluating new equipment and weapons), operational planning and Intelligence (colloquially known as 'The Kremlin') and a training wing that runs selection courses and prepares men for counter-revolutionary warfare. Within this complex structure, a variety of exotic skills flourishes, ranging from 'advanced lock neutralisation' (safe-breaking) to expertise in foreign firearms.

The soldier who emerges from this extraordinary training – perhaps the most varied and intensive military education anywhere in the world – does not stand out in a crowd. He tends to be a European, of medium height – only members of G (for Guards) Squadron are taller than average – of lean, athletic build (greyhound rather than bulldog), somewhat hirsute, and distinctly wary in the presence of strangers. A minority of

SAS soldiers grow a luxuriant, cavalry moustache verging on a parody of stage whiskers. The custom is a relic of the days of jungle warfare of the early 1950s, when most men wore beards and – ordered to shave on their return to England – retained as much facial hair as Queen's Regulations permitted. The SAS trooper's background is probably working-class, but he has learned to value such journals as the *Economist* as an aid to understanding the conflicts in which he might be involved at any time. (A junior Labour Minister, having been introduced, at his request, to a 'typical trooper', later accused his Hereford hosts of substituting an officer in disguise. The suspicion was unjustified.)

Within the SAS family, where the trooper's weaknesses as well as his strengths are public knowledge, he shares a ribald humour that mocks everything and almost everyone. It is a world in which the sonorous regimental motto 'Who Dares Wins' is transmuted into the plaintive question, 'Who cares who wins?'

A prolonged period of active service with the SAS involves great stress. The regiment is well aware of this and, not wishing to waste valuable human resources, defies Beaumont's 'selection-destruction cycle' by regularly posting troops from tough operational jobs to less exacting posts in training or abroad, to operational research and elsewhere, where the latest experience of active duty can be fed back to those preparing for such work. Over a period of years, therefore, service with the regiment is a sort of roundabout, from training to operations and back again. But in career terms, what is the cumulative effect?

Pay and preferment

In an age when counter-revolutionary warfare has become the most common form of armed combat, expertise in internal security in all its manifestations is a marketable commodity in and out of the British armed forces. In the short run, however, the soldier who volunteers for SAS duty does not always help his orthodox military career. The effect on non-commissioned ranks can be particularly detrimental. A Guards sergeant earning, say £5000 per annum basic will be reduced, like all other ranks, to Trooper (the equivalent of private soldier) on acceptance into the SAS. During his first year of SAS service, he will continue to receive the same pay as he had before joining the Regiment; after that, like the rest of his comrades, he will be paid as a corporal, about £3650 basic per annum. However good a soldier he is, he may never achieve the same rank he had while serving with his parent unit, because 22 SAS, with a total strength of about 750, is not large enough to offer such preferment. Most volunteers treat the problem as another, permanent manifestation of the sickener factor, as well as a symbol of their commitment to soldiering for its own sake, and of their esprit de corps.

Young officers, by contrast, improve their position marginally by winning their SAS spurs. Most who come in as troop commanders are junior or senior lieutenants. As SAS troop commanders they are promoted to captain. Thereafter, it is not unusual for them to engage in a series of cross-postings between the SAS and their former regiments, with no loss of promotion. But the higher they reach up the ladder outside the SAS, the more difficult it becomes to return to the regiment with the same rank. There are, for instance, about 200 brigadiers in the Army as a whole, but only one who commands the SAS Group (regulars and TA volunteers) based in London. At least one senior officer, Colonel David Smiley, is on record that he declined command of the three SAS regiments and left the Army in 1961 because, as General Bob Laycock, SAS Colonel Commandant at that time, explained to him: 'I know how you feel, David, but in fact the War Office simply isn't willing to pay a brigadier.'

There is also in the higher echelons of the British Army a traditional scepticism about 'funnies'. Their elitism, independence, apparent informality, and special role out of mainstream operations in large-scale warfare, all make them a caste apart. This factor can act as an intangible blocking mechanism to officers' later promotion. Some, because they are supremely expert soldiers, do return to former regiments, such as the

Green Jackets, to command a battalion with the rank of lieutenant-colonel after, say, a period at the Camberley Staff College. But many others find orthodox soldiering too tame and restrictive after a life of dangerous freedom with the SAS. Some of the best men, having become majors, quit the British forces altogether after SAS duty, to seek their fortunes as soldiers, or in some similarly risky occupation, elsewhere. The process was lucidly described by one officer who did this some years ago.

One of the hardest things to assimilate, when you first join, is the dedication of the average Trooper. He is in the SAS for love, not money, nearly always sacrificing what he could attain materially elsewhere . . . A troop is the most idealistic institution you can imagine. The troop comes before anything . . .

The Achilles heel of the SAS is administration. Soldiers come to the Regiment, often at great self-sacrifice, and serve it well. Operationally, they are well taken care of, but self-advancement and career planning leaves a lot to be desired . . . Officer recruitment is an aspect of regimental life which needs drastic revision . . . Perhaps the very excellence and freedom enjoyed with the SAS has caused many Regular officers to leave the Army at the end of their SAS tour, unable to face life in a battalion or regiment again.

I could not have lived a more full life than the one I have been lucky enough to experience for the last four years. Britain, I feel, does not fully appreciate what a superb weapon she possesses in her armoury. If wise, she will look after it well.

The last word (By a former officer of 22 SAS Regiment)

22 SAS is a unique regiment. Many facets combine to mould this uniqueness, not least the type of operations it conducts, for it is truly an operational regiment, engaged 365 days of the year, as heavily committed in peace as it is in war and always drawing from both old and new concepts to see it through its daily operational life.

Working at the highest level, by definition its operations involve significant political input in terms of goals to be achieved, parameters of employment and, naturally, the implications of both success and failure. Of necessity shrouded in secrecy, it is only over a period of time that facts become known; indeed some operations are never made public. Others, by osmosis, do enter the public domain but by then the political aspects are either forgotten, not fully understood, or are accorded little importance.

The regiment also does not help itself to be understood. It is a forward-thinking organisation wherein the end of a particular operation is frequently marked by speedy reorganisation and immediate preparation for the future. Whilst considerable care is taken to learn from both success and failure, general details of past operations can consequently become blurred.

Given the variables, it is hardly surprising that many authors fail to understand either the regiment or its operations. Indeed, it can take some years for its own officers to understand fully the SAS psyche and *modus operandi*. Taken at face value, some believe this learning curve is detrimental and results in the undue prominence of the Sergeants' Mess. But this is flawed logic, for it ignores the old and proven adage that the backbone of any good regiment is the Sergeants' Mess. Similarly, in time of war SAS officers are expected to lead from the front, those failing to do so being relieved of their command. In courageous contrast, the gallant deaths of John Hamilton and Richard Westmacott, among many others, bear witness to this tradition.

The regiment does not lend itself easily to analysis. Indeed, much of what has been written about it can best be described as speculation. We are our own worst enemy, necessarily cloaking everything in secrecy and having little time for the historical perspective. Whilst many authors have attempted to describe 22 SAS, its operations and regimental ethos, few have succeeded. Previous military knowledge or trusted sources are of little help to a prospective author. Far more relevant is a wider understanding of the political and military environment in which we operate, as well as of the type of soldier who volunteers for SAS service.

APPENDIX A
THE GULF

On 9 March 1991, little more than a week after the Allied victory in the Gulf, the Commander-in-Chief, General H. Norman Schwarzkopf, sent the following Letter of Commendation to Sir Patrick Hine, British Commander of Gulf Operations based at RAF High Wycombe, via Lieutenant-General Sir Peter de la Billière, British Forces Commander Middle East in Riyadh:

SUBJECT:
Letter of Commendation for the
22d Special Air Service (SAS) Regiment.

1.   I wish to officially commend the 22d Special Air Service (SAS) Regiment for their totally outstanding performance of military operations during Operation Desert Storm.

2.   Shortly after the initiation of the strategic air campaign, it became apparent that the Coalition forces would be unable to eliminate Iraq's firing of Scud missiles from western Iraq into Israel. The continued firing of Scuds on Israel carried with it enormous unfavorable political ramifications and could, in fact, have resulted in the dismantling of the carefully crafted Coalition. Such a dismantling would have adversely affected in ways difficult to measure the ultimate outcome of the military campaign. It became apparent that the only way that the Coalition could succeed in reducing these Scud launches was by physically placing military forces on the ground in the vicinity of the western launch sites. At that time, the majority of available Coalition forces were committed to the forthcoming military campaign in the eastern portion of the theater of operations.
  Further, none of these forces possessed the requisite skills and

abilities required to conduct such a dangerous operation. The only force deemed qualified for this critical mission was the 22d Special Air Service (SAS) Regiment.

3. From the first day they were assigned their mission until the last day of the conflict, the performance of the 22d Special Air Service (SAS) Regiment was courageous and highly professional. The area in which they were committed proved to contain far more numerous enemy forces than had been predicted by every intelligence estimate, the terrain was much more difficult than expected and the weather conditions were unseasonably brutal. Despite these hazards, in a very short period of time the 22d Special Air Service (SAS) Regiment was successful in totally denying the central corridor of western Iraq to Iraqi Scud units. The result was that the principal areas used by the Iraqis to fire Scuds on Tel Aviv were no longer available to them. They were required to move their Scud missile firing forces to the northwest portion of Iraq and from that location the firing of Scud missiles was essentially militarily ineffective.

4. When it became necessary to introduce United States Special Operations Forces into the area to attempt to close down the northwest Scud areas, the 22d Special Air Service (SAS) Regiment provided invaluable assistance to the US forces. They took every possible measure to ensure that US forces were thoroughly briefed and were able to profit from the valuable lessons that had been learned by earlier SAS deployments into Western Iraq.

I am completely convinced that had US forces not received these thorough indoctrinations by SAS personnel US forces would have suffered a much higher rate of casualties than was ultimately the case. Further, the SAS and US joint forces immediately merged into a combined fighting force where the synergetic effect of these fine units ultimately caused the enemy to be convinced that they were facing forces in western Iraq that were more than tenfold the size of those they were actually facing. As a result, large numbers of enemy forces that might otherwise have been deployed in the eastern theater were tied down in western Iraq.

5.   The performance of the 22d Special Air Service (SAS) Regiment during Operation Desert Storm was in the highest traditions of the professional military service and in keeping with the proud history and tradition that has been established by that regiment. Please ensure that this commendation receives appropriate attention and is passed on to the unit and its members.

H. NORMAN SCHWARZKOPF
General, US Army
Commander in Chief

The commendation now decorates one wall of the Officers' Mess at 22 SAS Regiment's Herefordshire headquarters.

APPENDIX B
SAS CASUALTIES 1950–92

To stay alive, in SAS parlance, is to 'beat the clock'. This derives from the tradition of carving on the regiment's memorial clock at Hereford (a collapsible, portable structure) the names of those killed in training or in action. The clock was erected soon after the regiment occupied its Hereford base in 1980. Each year, the list of those who did not beat the clock grows longer.

Malaya

Tpr T. A. Brown	1950
Pte G. A. Fisher	1950
Tpr J. A. O'Leary	1951
Sgt O. H. Ernst, Rhodesian SAS	1951
Cpl J. B. Davies, Rhodesian SAS	1951
Tpr F. G. Boylan	1951
WO2 W. F. Garrett	1951
Cpl V. E. Visague, Rhodesian SAS	1952
Tpr A. Fergus	1952
Major E. C. R. Barker, B.E.M.	1953
Tpr J. A. S. Morgan	1953
Tpr E. Duckworth	1953
Lt P. B. S. Cartwright	1953
Tpr B. Watson	1953
2/Lt F. M. Donnelly-Wood	1953

Lt (QM) F. S. Tulk	1953
Cpl K. Bancroft	1953
Tpr F. W. Wilkins	1953
Cpl P. G. R. Eakin	1953
Lt J. C. Fotheringham	1953
Lt G. J. Goulding	1954
L Cpl C. W. Bond	1954
Tpr B. Powell	1954
Tpr A. W. Howell	1954
Tpr A. R. Thomas, New Zealand SAS	1956
Tpr W. R. J. Marselle	1956
Lt A. G. H. Dean	1957
Cpl A. G. Buchanan, New Zealand SAS	1957
Tpr R. Hindmarsh	1968

Malaysia

Tpr N. P. Ollis	1969

West Malaysia

L Cpl R. Greenwood   1967

Oman (Jabal Akhdar)

Cpl D. Swindells, M.M.   1958
Tpr W. Carter   1959
Tpr A. G. Bembridge   1959

Borneo

Maj H. A. I. Thompson,
    MC   1963
Maj R. H. D. Norman,
    MBE, MC   1963
Cpl M. P. Murphy   1963
Tpr A. Condon   1964
Sgt B. Bexton   1964
Tpr W. E. White   1964
Pte G. H. Hartley   1964

Brunei

Sgt E. Pickard   1973

South Arabia

Capt R. C. Edwards   1964
Tpr J. N. Warburton   1964
Tpr J. Hollingsworth   1966
Tpr M. R. Lambert   1966
Tpr G. F. F. Iles   1967
L Cpl A. G. Brown   1967

Ethiopia

Cpl I. A. Macleod   1968

Oman (Musandam)

L Cpl P. Reddy   1970

Oman (Dhofar)

Capt I. E. Jones   1971
Sgt J. S. M. Moores   1971
Tpr C. Loid   1971
L Cpl D. R. Ramsden   1972
Tpr M. J. Martin   1972
Cpl T. Labalaba, BEM   1972
Tpr T. P. A. Tobin   1972
L Cpl A. Kent   1974
Capt S. Garthwaite   1974
Tpr C. Hennessy   1975
L Cpl K. Small   1975
Sgt A. E. Gallagher   1975

France

Maj R. M. Pirie   1972
Sgt S. H. Johnson   1978
Cpl F. M. Benson   1978

Northern Ireland

S–Sgt D. J. Naden   1978
Capt H. R. Westmacott   1980

UK

Cpl K. Norry   1962
Cpl R. Richardson   1965
Tpr P. C. O'Toole   1965
Tpr J. Hooker   1965
L Cpl J. R. Anderson   1967
L Cpl A. C. Lonney   1968
WO1 E. T. Nugent   1968
Cpl R. N. Adie   1968
Tpr C. P. Martin   1968
WO2 J. E. Daubney   1974
Maj M. J. A. Kealy,
    DSO   1979

South Atlantic

Capt G. J. Hamilton	1982
WO2 L. Gallagher, BEM	1982
Sgt P. P. Currass, QGM	1982
Sgt S. A. I. Davidson	1982
Sgt J. L. Arthy	1982
Cpl P. Bunker	1982
Cpl E. T. Walpole	1982
Tpr R. Armstrong	1982
SSM M. Atkinson	1982
S-Sgt P. O'Connor	1982
Sgt W. J. Hughes	1982
Sgt P. Jones	1982
Cpl W. J. Begley	1982
Cpl J. Newton	1982
Cpl R. Burns	1982
Cpl S. Sykes	1982
L Cpl P. Lightfoot	1982
Cpl M. McHugh	1982
Flt Lt G. Hawkins, RAF	1982
Cpl D. McCormack	1982

Northern Ireland

Cpl T. Palmer, MM	1983
L Cpl A. Slater, MM	1984

Belize

L Sgt L. Cobb	1983

Everest

Cpl A. Swierzy	1984

UK

Sgt R. Abbots	1985
Sgt A. Baxter	1985
S-Sgt J. Drummond	1986
Tpr G. Worrall	1990

France (Mt Blanc)

Tpr R. P. Arnott	1986
Tpr S. J. Windon	1986

Botswana

S-Sgt K. J. Farragher	1986

Far East

Cpl P. Hill	1988

Iraq

Sgt V. Phillips	1991
Tpr R. Consiglio, MM	1991
Tpr S. Lane, MM	1991
Tpr D. Denbury, MM	1991

TABLE 6
Force levels and casualties Northern Ireland

Year	Army Force Levels (as at 1 Jan) Regular	UDR	Total	Deaths Security Forces	Civ	Tr'rst	Total
1969	2,926	0	2,926	1	10	2	13
1970	7,245	3,326	10,571	2	13	10	25
1971	10,410	4,151	14,561	59	61	54	174
1972	14,349	6,741	21,090	146	223	98	467
1973	17,250	9,098	26,348	79	129	42	250
1974	15,827	7,816	23,643	50	145	22	217
1975	14,654	7,676	22,330	31	196	20	247
1976	14,454	7,793	22,247	52	224	21	297
1977	14,262	7,616	21,878	43	59	10	112
1978	14,159	7,812	21,971	31	43	7	81
1979	12,727	7,761	20,488	62	48	3	113
1980	12,636	7,425	20,061	26	45	5	76
1981	11,114	7,431	18,545	44	52	5	101
1982	10,885	7,350	18,235	40	50	7	97
1983	10,375	7,026	17,401	34	37	7	78
1984	9,294	6,929	16,223	27	25	11	63
1985	9,180	6,468	15,648	29	20	4	53
1986	8,912	6,508	15,420	24	33	4	61
1987	9,920	6,535	16,455	27	54	13	95
1988	9,645	6,364	16,009	39	45	8	94
1989	9,695	6,312	16,007	21	37	2	60
1990	9,578	6,208	15,786	27	45	4	76
1991	10,354	6,043	16,397	19	71	4 ★	94
1992	10,464	6,014	16,478	0	32	5	37 †
			Total	913	1,697	368	2,978

★ To 31 Mar 1992.
† Excludes two terrorist deaths in UK.

APPENDIX C
OPERATION GRANBY:
HONOURS AND AWARDS

22 SAS Regiment

Distinguished Service Order	1
Military Cross (including one award of MC to warrant–officer)	3
Distinguished Conduct Medal	4
Military Medal (three posthumous)	10
Order of British Empire	1
Member of British Empire	3
British Empire Medal	2
Mention In Dispatches	15

264 SAS Signals Squadron

Member of British Empire	1
Mention in Despatches	3

Headquarters, Directorate of Special Forces

Order of British Empire	1
Mention In Dispatches	1

Special Boat Service

Military Cross	1
Mention In Dispatches	2

Royal Air Force Special Forces Flights

Distinguished Service Order	1
Distinguished Flying Cross	1
Distinguished Flying Medal	1

Member of the British Empire   1
Mention In Dispatches   3

N.B.   Medals awarded for bravery in action, listed above, are: Distinguished Service Order; Military Cross; Distinguished Flying Cross; Distinguished Conduct Medal; Distinguished Flying Medal; Military Medal plus, in some cases, the oak leaves which indicate a Mention In Dispatches.

Meritorious service awards placed for military activity other than on the battlefield, listed above, are: Order of British Empire; Member of British Empire; British Empire Medal; Mention In Dispatches.

APPENDIX D
SAS OBITUARIES

Operation Corporate

Captain G. J. Hamilton, MC

John Hamilton joined 22 SAS in January 1981. He joined D Squadron and commanded 19 (Mountain) Troop until his death in action on West Falkland on 10 June 1982.

An accomplished mountaineer, he took 19 Troop to the summit of Mount Kenya twice earlier this year.

John was an officer such as to leave the stamp of his personality on all that he did, and a lasting impression remains with all of us who served with him.

His bravery and skill during the Falklands operations were an example for all.

It was his troop that first landed on South Georgia. Having been forced to withdraw by blizzard conditions, they were involved in two helicopter crashes during their recovery. Despite this setback, it was only a few days later that he led his troop into Grytviken, the culminating moment in the defeat of Argentine forces in South Georgia. Again, during the Pebble Island raid he was in the fore. He personally destroyed four Pucara ground-attack aircraft. On Mount Kent his skill and direction contributed directly to the successful ambush of enemy patrols. Throughout these engagements he displayed a valour that he surpassed only in his last action.

His observation post above Port Howard was discovered by a strong Argentinian patrol. Despite being heavily out-numbered he engaged the enemy and conducted a spirited fight for some considerable time on ground offering little protection. Early in the fight he received fatal injuries. John's courage and professionalism during this action won the praise and admiration of the Argentinian Commander.

WO2 Lawrence Gallagher, BEM

Lawrence joined the regiment from 9 Squadron Royal Engineers in January 1968, joining Boat Troop (17). His mild, gentle and relaxed manner earned him the nickname 'Lofty'.

About 1970 he was detached to IOSF in Bad-Tolz, where he made many American friends. It was he who raised the Union Jack first when South Georgia was recaptured (the Argentinians, who were trying to surrender to him at the time, were told to wait).

Because of his strength and physique he was good at most sports, but never used his size to gain unfair advantage. He was impossible to upset, both on and off the sports field.

His honest, straightforward attitude earned him the deserved respect and affection of juniors and seniors alike.

Sergeant Philip Preston Currass, QGM
(Royal Army Medical Corps)

Phil joined 22 SAS in 1972. He was greatly interested in moun-taineering and it was not surprising that on completion of his selection and continuation training he elected to join Mountain Troop.

Here, amongst kindred spirits, he quickly established himself, not only in the mountaineering field, but also as an enthusiastic soldier.

He saw active service in Dhofar, completing a number of operational tours, later serving in Northern Ireland.

His efforts and enthusiasm earned him the award of the Queen's Gallantry Medal.

He and his troop, along with the rest of the squadron, found themselves operating in South Georgia in the very type of terrain they normally chose to climb in! He survived two helicopter crashes on South Georgia.

He was with the squadron on the raid on Pebble Island. Phil's memory will always be with us, but more especially when in the hills.

24057552 Sergeant Sidney Albert Ivor Davidson

24057552 Sergeant Sidney Albert Ivor Davidson, known by his friends as 'Sid', joined 22 SAS in 1973. He served first in B Squadron, joining D in 1975, becoming a member of Amphibious Troop. He served both in Dhofar and Northern Ireland. During his time with the troop he became an expert on amphibious training, especially canoeing, eventually becoming an instructor in this field.

Sid was renowned for his professionalism, expertise and coolness in difficult situations, and was transferred to Mountain Troop where he again showed his versatility. He and Mountain Troop played an important role in the South Georgia operation where he survived two helicopter crashes. He took part in the successful attack on Pebble Island.

Sid's easy going, understanding attitude combined with his experience and professionalism will be missed by all his friends and colleagues.

Sergeant John Leslie Arthy (Welsh Guards)

'Lofty' came to the regiment in 1975 and joined 18 Troop (Mobility). In 1977 he transferred to Mountain Troop (19) and was renowned for his climbing skill and boundless enthusiasm. He could make frost-bite sound exciting.

After completing the German Alpine Guides' course in 1979 he was chosen to go on the AMA 'API' Expedition to West Nepal. He was on the summit attempt, which reached 300 feet from the top, but was beaten by driving snow. Later the same year he was on another AMA Expedition, this time to China and Jiazi, where he and another member of the regiment climbed

Tshiburongi (5928 metres).

He served with the regiment in both Ireland and Oman and his troop were responsible for the destruction of 11 Argentinian aircraft on Pebble Island a few days before the helicopter crash in which he died.

Like most big, modest men, Lofty was cheerful and good-natured, and had that rare gift of being able to pass his confidence on to those around him. His climbing skill will be sadly missed in the troop, the loss of friendship and soldiering ability will be felt by the squadron and the regiment.

Corporal Paul Bunker (Royal Army Ordnance Corps)

Paul joined 22 SAS in August 1976 and was posted to 16 Troop, the Free-Fall Troop, where he proved to be a keen parachutist and a more than able and well-liked member.

He joined 19 Mountain Troop in May 1979 and proved to be an extremely capable climber.

With 19 Troop he served in Northern Ireland, West Virginia, Florida, Bavaria and the Falklands.

His troop was the first back onto South Georgia. They landed on the Fortuna Glacier, but their tents were destroyed by a blizzard. During the recovery the following day, two helicopters crashed with the troop on board. A few days later it was Paul and his troop who spearheaded the British attack on Grytviken. He was again in action on Pebble Island when the troop helped destroy 11 enemy aircraft.

Paul will always be remembered. His humour, strength and mild manner are a legacy that will long endure.

24110456 Corporal Edward Thomas Walpole (Royal Green Jackets)

Wally joined 22 SAS in 1977 and, until the night of 19 May 1982, when he died in the tragic helicopter crash, he served with D Squadron as Squadron Quartermaster-Sergeant's Assistant.

During this time his mild manner, endless patience and untiring devotion to his duties won him many friends through-out the regiment and particularly in D Squadron who will recall that whenever they needed anything Wally never let them down. He was a friend who will be sadly missed.

Trooper Raymond Armstrong (Royal Green Jackets)

Paddy joined 22 SAS in 1979. His personal fitness, determination, strength of character and sense of humour stood him in good stead and during his time in D Squadron, Paddy met many people and quickly made a lot of friends. His success on specialist courses reflected his constant resolve to do a job well.

In the Campaign in the South Atlantic, both on South Georgia and the Falkland Islands, Paddy took part in all the D Squadron operations. On Pebble Island, in particular, his skill and professionalism in placing and initiating explosive charges that destroyed a number of enemy aircraft earned him the nickname 'Pucara Paddy'.

His death in the helicopter crash was a sad blow to all.

23969493 SSM Malcolm Atkinson

Malcolm Atkinson or 'Akker' as he was known to his friends, joined G Squadron 22 SAS in 1966. His career spanned 12 fully operational tours in Malaya, Borneo, Aden, Oman and Northern Ireland, a record quite exceptional, even for the regiment.

Akker will be remembered for his exemplary professional standards, his good humour and his capacity to listen and then advise in the most patient and logical way. In spite of his formidable experience, as SSM of G Squadron he remained as always utterly approachable. His greatest and most unselfish concern was always the welfare of his men whether at a personal, social level or in ensuring that the training and preparation for operations by his squadron were relevant, exacting and designed to give the greatest fulfilment to those involved.

It was while he was supervising the movement of equipment vital to the operation of his squadron on the Falkland Islands that the helicopter in which he was travelling crashed. The loss of such a character, who had given so much and for whom a continuing and successful career was assured, is inestimable.

Staff-Sergeant P. O'Connor (Irish Guards)

Paddy came to 22 SAS in 1966. He was quick to impress on his arrival. A man of immense character and good humour, possessing an ever-present twinkle. He was a true professional, never afraid to speak his mind and always adopting an intelligent, honest, determined and responsible approach to his work.

He served with us in South-Arabia, Belize, Northern Ireland, Dhofar, Norway and the United States. He was a specialist Signaller, skilful free-fall parachutist and a qualified Norwegian speaker. It is particularly tragic that Paddy, like others killed in the same crash, should lose his life in such a pointless and wasteful way.

He will be very sorely missed by his many friends in the regiment.

24076141 Sergeant William John Hughes (Welsh Guards)

'Taff' joined 22 SAS in October 1972.

For three years Taff proved his utter reliability, complete application to his duties and a preparedness to work uncomplainingly for long hours. In 1975 he came to G Squadron as the Storeman, bringing with him all the attributes already described but also an irrepressible sense of humour. He soon became an invaluable and respected member of his squadron, completing in the course of the next seven years, a total of 12 squadron moves on operational or training tasks. Successive Squadron Quartermaster-Sergeants speak of their great good fortune in having Taff, with his great knowledge of accounting, equipment procurement and capacity for hard work, as the linch pin of squadron administration over this period.

No request was ever too much trouble. Totally uncomplaining, his loyalty to his squadron and concern over his responsibility towards its welfare was absolute. On the night of 19

May 1982, while supervising the Cross Deck Movement of the Squadron Stores, the helicopter in which he was a passenger crashed. Taff was killed. He will be most sorely missed by his Squadron and many friends.

24154752 Corporal William Clark Hatton, QGM

Willy joined G Squadron 22 SAS as a member of the Amphibious Troop in July 1978 with whom he served until his tragic death in a helicopter accident in the South Atlantic on 19 May 1982.

His zest for life and inexhaustible enthusiasm were ideally suited to the varied tasks of an SAS Sabre Squadron. He became the first fully qualified diving supervisor in the regiment. His foresight and inspiration in diving skills were largely responsible for the resurgence of interest and expertise in diving within his regiment. He was present with his Squadron on four operational tours in Northern Ireland when his vast depth of experience in that theatre was of quite inestimable value. He spearheaded the involvement of the regiment in the Falklands Crisis with a short attachment to the 2 Special Boat Section. He was instrumental, during this attachment in the success of the capture of the Argentine 'Spyship' *Narwhal*.

Willy, with all his attributes, his personality and personable companionship, achieved the undisputed respect of his Squadron and all those in the regiment who were fortunate enough to have served with him. His loss has been a cruel blow.

Sergeant P. Jones (Welsh Guards)

'Taff' Jones died in the helicopter crash whilst serving in the South Atlantic. The loss of such an outstanding personality has been deeply felt by all the members of G Squadron.

From the start of his military career, at the age of 15 as a Junior Soldier, his strong open and cheerful character brought him immediate recognition. Whether playing rugby for the Welsh Guards or as a young Lance-Sergeant with the Guards' Parachute Company, his intelligence, sound commonsense and ever present humour backed by endless energy and enthusiasm constantly shone through.

In 1975 Taff joined 22 SAS. During his time in G Squadron it was typical that he never missed an operational tour. When the Falklands Campaign started he was one of the first from the regiment to go out. As one of the most experienced divers in the regiment he had added to an already wide experience which promised him an exceptional future. There was also the ever buoyant, sociable friend and dedicated fisherman as well as professional soldier. Whenever and wherever possible the rods would appear and Taff would disappear fishing. We will greatly miss his direct and cheerful spirit.

24122095 Corporal William John Begley
(Royal Corps of Transport)

Bill Begley joined 22 SAS in 1978 and soon opted to try the Selection Course, which he successfully completed in August 1979.

'Paddy', as he inevitably became known to his friends, was small in stature but large in heart, humour and determination. His modest, unassuming demeanour concealed a durable, quick-witted character always striving to achieve the highest professional standards. His conduct on operations or training exercises was always immaculate. In his three years with the Squadron his contribution to operational tours, his conduct as an experienced mountaineer and not least as a devoted family man, has been an example to us all.

Paddy had an assured future. This makes the tragedy of his loss in a helicopter accident in the South Atlantic all the more poignant. He will be most sorely missed by his Squadron and many friends.

24386053 Corporal John Newton
(Royal Electrical and Mechanical Engineers)

John Newton joined the Infantry Junior Leader's Battalion at Shorncliffe in 1975. His intention had always been to become a member of the Parachute Regiment. However, because of an injury sustained during his Para Selection Course, this was not to be and in 1977 he transferred to the Royal Electrical and Mechanical Engineers. The excellent grounding provided by the IJLB had served to increase his interest in weapons and so his choice of REME was most natural giving ample opportunity for him to exercise his instructional flair as well as becoming master of their maintenance and repair.

In 1980 he joined 22 SAS and soon became an invaluable member of the team of armourers who support the regiment. His good humour, discretion and above all his professional expertise confirmed for him a position of deep respect with those Sabre Squadrons with whom he worked. Exercises in Greece and Kenya tested his skills of improvisation to the complete satisfaction of those he was supporting. Just prior to the Falkland Crisis he qualified as a Parachutist.

His time at Hereford allowed him full rein for a variety of sporting activities, including rock climbing, free-fall parachuting, cricket, squash and regular turn-outs for the regimental and local rugby teams. He was a founder member of the Hereford Army Gun Club.

On the night of 19 May during a routine cross deck operation in the South Atlantic, the Sea King helicopter in which he was travelling crashed. His loss, with all his potential, zest for life and excellent prospects for the future was the cruellest of blows. He will be sorely missed by his great many friends in 22 SAS and throughout the Army.

24369281 Corporal Rab Burns

Rab joined the Army Apprentice College at Harrogate as a Radio Telegraphist in September 1975. He completed his training in August 1977 after a successful two years during which he was promoted to A/T L/Cpl. In September of that year he was posted to 244 Signal Squadron (Air Support) at RAF Brize Norton. He volunteered to serve in Hereford in March 1979, and successfully completed the Signals Selection Course. After a short period he was then posted to G Squadron and during his time with the SAS was awarded the GSM for service in Northern Ireland. Rab was a quiet but happy person with a passion for the bagpipes and was a gifted piper. He will be much missed by his friends.

24256419 Corporal Steve Sykes

Steve enlisted originally into the RAC Junior Leader's Regiment in September 1972 where he served for a year. During this period he became interested in communications and at his own request was transferred to the Army Apprentice College, Harrogate, in May 1973. In 1975 he completed his training as a Radio Telegraphist and immediately volunteered for service with the Parachute Brigade. Unfortunately at this time the Army was being reorganised and after service with his new unit, for only two months, 216 (Parachute) Signal Squadron, was disbanded and he was posted to BAOR to serve with 604 Signal Troop in Munster. Steve still hankered after parachute training however and in February 1978 was accepted into the Signal Squadron after undergoing Signals selection. Steve was awarded the GSM for service in Northern Ireland and gained the distinction of being top student on his RTG Al course in January this year. He was a keen parachutist, a cross-country skier and runner and ran in the SAS Regimental Marathon in September 1981. He much deserved his recent promotion and as a cheerful steady worker will be greatly missed by his friends and contemporaries.

24442111 Lance-Corporal Paul Lightfoot

Paul enlisted in August 1977 and followed in his father's footsteps when he chose both the Army Apprentice College at Harrogate and the trade of Radio Telegraphist. After completing his apprenticeship in August 1979 he was posted to 11 Signal Regiment where he volunteered for 264 SAS Signal Squadron, successfully completed the signals selection course in October 1979. During his time with G Squadron he gained the GSM for service in Northern Ireland.

Paul was a cheerful and popular young man who enjoyed his job and was keen to pass the SAS Selection, towards which goal he was training hard physically.

24398223 Corporal Michael McHugh

Michael enlisted in the Army in August 1976, when he was sixteen. He joined the Royal Signals Junior Leader's Regiment at Warcop and after a year's training was posted to 8 Signal Regiment at Catterick and completed trade training as a Radio Telegraphist in February 1978. He volunteered for service with 264 SAS Signal Squadron and completed the Signals Selection Course in June 1978. During his time with G Squadron he was awarded the GSM with Clasp for Northern Ireland. Michael was a very fit young man and an excellent down-hill skier. He had a cheerful personality, was popular with his Squadron and will be sadly missed by all who knew him.

Flight-Lieutenant Garth Hawkins, RAF

Garth first worked with the regiment in Canada in 1979. By 1982 he had served with all Squadrons, both in UK and overseas, and had extended his considerable influence to the TA as well.

Instinctively one knew that his genial bulk, infectious grin and unkempt appearance suited him well for work with special forces. What may not have been so apparent for those who worked alongside him, was that in addition to being a brilliant expert in his own field, and a patient but exacting instructor, he was also a keen and gifted cricketer and footballer, who was always the last to leave the clubhouse after any party. Somehow he also found time to be a pub owner, property dealer, dog lover, car enthusiast, gardener, builder and musician. He was also an intensely devoted family man.

Garth was a larger than life character who commands all our respect for what he gave to the regiment. He will be sorely missed both professionally and personally.

Corporal Douglas McCormack (Royal Signals)

Doug McCormack was Garth Hawkins' signaller and partner. Wherever Garth's hatless figure appeared the faithful Doug would not be far behind, driving the Land-Rover, operating the radio set, cooking the meal, taking Dougal or Biggles for a walk, or paying for the next beer. The two were inseparable and had intense loyalty and respect for each other, and were perhaps a supreme example of a special forces team in action.

Doug was also an intensely devoted family man and private individual with many hidden talents. Few of his rank or age group for example are German linguists.

His life's ambition was to join 264 (SAS) Signal Squadron, and ultimately the regiment. Tragically he died alongside members of both, having volunteered yet again to be with Garth.

Subsequent regimental obituaries:
A Squadron

Staff-Sergeant Jim Drummond

Staff-Sergeant Drummond joined the SAS in June 1981 from the Royal Signals. He served for three years with 3 Troop before returning to the Royal Signals to complete his Yeoman of Signals course. He became Yeoman of Signals in A Squadron in 1984 and was killed in a night free-all accident at Salisbury Plain, 3 June 1986. Drummond was married with one son and came from Hereford. Described by his comrades as 'professional . . . a perfectionist . . . warm-hearted'. His catchphrase, 'looking good', lived on in the regiment after him.

Sergeant Vince Phillips

Sergeant Phillips joined the SAS Regiment in August 1982 from the Royal Army Ordnance Corps where he had served with both the Para and Commando Logistics battalions. He served in 4 Troop, where he was renowned for his outstanding physical fitness. Sergeant Phillips died of exposure while evading capture in North-West Iraq in January 1991. Originally from Swindon, he was married with two children.

Trooper David ('Shug') Denbury, MM

Trooper Denbury joined the SAS Regiment in February 1989 from 9 (Para) Squadron Royal Engineers. He served in 3 Troop and Northern Ireland where he was awarded the Queen's Gallantry Medal. He was killed on 21 February 1991 during an ambush of a convoy in North-West Iraq. He was awarded a posthumous Military Medal for his part in the action. Denbury was single and came from Cardiff. His death was keenly felt as he had made an unusually deep impression during his short time with the SAS.

B Squadron

Staff-Sergeant Kieran Joseph Farragher

Joe Farragher, born 13 August 1946, was awarded his green Commando beret in 1964 while serving as a Gunner with 29 Commando Regiment Royal Artillery. 'Big Joe', as he became known, joined the Special Air Service Regiment in February 1973 and was posted to 9 (Mountain) Troop. He served in Oman, Northern Ireland and the Falklands, at his calmest when the going got toughest. He died in a climbing accident on Tsodilo Hill, Botswana on 23 February 1986.

Lance-Corporal Alastair Slater, MM

Lance-Corporal Slater was born on 25 June 1956 and joined the SAS Regiment in August 1982, having been a Sergeant with 1 Parachute Battalion. A military perfectionist, he served with 7 (Air) Troop and soon became known as 'Mr Angry' among his many close friends. He was killed in action on the night of 2 December 1987 during a gun battle with the Provisional IRA while serving in Northern Ireland. His dedication and bravery earned him a posthumous Military Medal. He was single and originally came from Leicester.

Corporal Paul Hill

Corporal Hill joined the Parachute Regiment in September 1977 and served with A Company, 3 Parachute Battalion, until he passed SAS selection in January 1982. He became a member of 6 (Boat) Troop, where he quickly became an experienced and confident diver. He was also a good military free-fall parachutist. He died from heart failure while serving in the Far East in October, 1988. It is said of him that 'he enjoyed life in the fast lane'. His speed and enthusiasm are still missed by the squadron.

Trooper Robert Consiglio, MM

Bob Consiglio was born on 13 April 1966. He joined the Royal Marines in April 1983 and served with 40 Commando. He joined the SAS Regiment in February 1990 and served with 9 (Mountain) Troop. He was killed in action on 27 January 1991 during the Gulf War, after surviving numerous gun battles with the enemy. He died providing covering fire to help those with him to avoid capture and was awarded a posthumous Military Medal. He was single and came from Bognor Regis.

Trooper Steven ('Legs') Lane, MM

Trooper Lane was born on 3 July 1963 and served with 9 Parachute Squadron Royal Engineers before joining the SAS Regiment in February 1990. He was posted to 8 (Mobility) Troop. During his short time with the squadron he acquired a reputation as a reliable and valued member of the team. He died of exposure and exhaustion during the Gulf War after a marathon attempt to elude capture in Northern Iraq.

Corporal Tommy Palmer

Born 16 October 1950 and reared in Scotland, Tommy Palmer joined the Army on 17 February 1970 and served initially with 33 Field Squadron Royal Engineers. He did not complete basic SAS selection on the first attempt in 1973 due to an injury. Later the same year, he was accepted for SAS service but was then sent to the Parachute Regiment for basic parachute training. He returned to SAS for the combat survival phase of selection. This he passed in the summer of 1974 and was posted to 18 Troop, D Squadron, with which he served in Dhofar, Northern Ireland and elsewhere. He was posted to B Squadron, for disciplinary reasons, in time for the Princes Gate siege, in which he was burned. He ditched his burning clothing, ignored his wounds and went back into the building. He was awarded a Military Medal, one of five of the Iranian Embassy team decorated personally by the Queen for exceptional bravery. He died in a road accident when his car overturned on a motorway near Lurgan, Northern Ireland, on 8 February 1983.

D Squadron

Trooper Graham Worrall
Graham Worrall, born 30 October 1961, came from Greasby, Cheshire. On 24 May 1978, aged 16, he joined the Army and later the Parachute Regiment. In February 1989 he passed SAS selection from 2 Parachute Battalion and joined 16 Air Troop. While serving with the Parachute Regiment he served in the Falklands and was wounded in action. On 24 May 1990, while motorcycle training in the Hereford area, he was killed in a road traffic accident. He was married with one child and is buried in the Regimental Plot at St Martin's Church, Hereford.

Trooper Robert P. Arnott
Bob Arnott was born in Perth, Scotland on 28 December 1955. He enlisted into the Army on 29 August 1973 and joined the Royal Engineers. He passed SAS selection in January 1986 and joined 19 Mountain Troop. With Trooper Stewart Windon (see below) he died on 26 June 1986 while climbing the Aiguille du Chardonnet, Mont Blanc, in the French Alps. Trooper Arnott was married without children. He is buried alongside Trooper Windon in the Regimental Plot at St Martins Church, Hereford.

Trooper Stewart J. Windon
'Stu' Windon was born in Colchester on 22 September 1956 and enlisted into the Parachute Regiment on 18 December 1972. He passed SAS selection and joined the SAS from 3 Parachute Battalion in October 1985. He was posted to 19 Mountain Troop. He died in the climbing accident which killed Trooper Arnott on Mont Blanc on 26 June 1986. Trooper Windon was married without children. He was a keen footballer. He is buried next to Trooper Arnott.

G Squadron

Captain H. R. Westmacott

Richard Westmacott was the son of a distinguished Royal Navy officer. He completed his education at London University and joined 2nd Battalion, Grenadier Guards in February 1974. He served in Hong Kong as a platoon commander, then as Assistant Adjutant, Guards Depot, where he was known as a soldier who pursued military excellence. He was on his first SAS tour as a troop commander when he was murdered by the IRA in Belfast on 2 May 1980.

Lance-Sergeant Leslie Cobb

Lance-Sergeant Cobb (Grenadier Guards) was born at Cambridge on 12 August 1955 and joined the Army at the age of 19. After passing his basic SAS selection course early in 1983, he died on 15 March of heat exhaustion during subsequent jungle training.

Sergeant Raymond Abbots

Ray Abbots, born 8 January 1951 at Henley, joined the Army in 1969 and served with 4 Royal Tank Regiment, Royal Armoured Corps. He passed SAS selection on 12 January 1973. He saw operational service in Dhofar, Oman and at the Balcombe Street Siege in London in December 1975. Nicknamed 'Growler', as a result of his intolerance of inefficiency, he also generated affection as a result of his integrity, kindness and generosity. He died in a training accident at Hereford on 15 January 1985.

Corporal Antony Mark Swierzy

Tony Swierzy was killed in an avalanche high on the north face of Everest, on the Rongbuk Glacier, on 3 April 1984 during an attempt by an SAS team to climb to the summit of the world's highest mountain. Born 16 June 1956 at Longport, Staffordshire, he had served with 59 Independent Commando Royal Marines before his acceptance by the SAS Regiment in 1977. His body was ceremoniously buried on the glacier two days later. A memorial stone has been carved and placed near the base camp.

Sergeant Andrew David Baxter

Andy Baxter, born at Grimsby on 3 August 1955, died of a brain tumour in Hereford on 12 August 1985. It is believed that his illness resulted from, or was accelerated by, the impact of ice and rock in the same avalanche which swept away Tony Swierzy during the ill-fated Everest expedition the year before. A natural soldier – Junior RSM at the Junior Leaders' course, RAC Centre, Bovington – he went from the Blues and Royals to the Guards Independent Parachute Company and finally, in November 1975, to the SAS. Andy Baxter was a member of the squadron's Mountain Troop and saw active service in Dhofar, Oman.

Staff-Sergeant David John Naden

Born on 18 February 1947, David Naden joined the Royal Signals in 1962 and served with that corps in Germany, Norway and Malaya. He passed selection on 28 July 1969 and was posted to 23 (Amphibious) Troop. For administrative reasons, his parent unit was changed from the Royal Signals to the Scots Guards. His SAS service included Dhofar and Northern Ireland. He held the General Service Medal with Dhofar and Northern Ireland clasp. He was a staff-sergeant, SAS, when he died on 7 June 1978 in a motoring accident at Shanalongford Bridge, near Londonderry.

R Squadron

Lance-Corporal MDR Richards

Mark Richards, aged 29, was killed in a live-fire accident on a range in Belize, a jungle training area, on 23 June 1992. As a member of R Squadron – the first-line reserve used to augment 22 SAS Regiment – Corporal Richards saw active service in Iraq with A and D Squadrons. He was one of the survivors of the battle of 28–29 January 1991 80 miles inside Iraq when a patrol was almost overrun. He was with the group that reached the sanctuary of Saudi Arabia 44 hours later. He returned to Iraq soon afterward. Richards was unmarried and a farmer in Gwent when he was not on SAS service. He passed SAS selection in December 1989.

Founding Fathers

Colonel Sir David Stirling, OBE, DSO

Died 1990, aged 74. Educated, Ampleforth College; Cambridge University (and Newmarket Racecourse). Active service, Scots Guards, Layforce Commando. Founded L Detachment, SAS, 1941 in Egypt while still suffering grave injuries from experimental parachute jump. As the 'Phantom Major' of the Desert War he became a legend. Taken prisoner 1943 but his international force of strategic raiders, including British, French, Belgian and Greek soldiers, enjoyed a phenomenal success throughout the rest of the war. Stirling, after four escapes, was placed in close confinement in Colditz. He devised the regimental motto, 'Who Dares Wins'. Described by Major-General Laycock as 'one of the most under-decorated soldiers of the war,' Stirling was finally knighted in 1990.

RSM Bob Lilley

Died 14 August 1981. One of Stirling's Originals, served with L Detachment as well as founder member of 8 Commando. Active service from Western Desert to Norway by way of Sicily, Italy, France and Germany.

Colonel Brian Franks

Died 1982. After service with the Middle East Commando, he commanded 2 SAS after resignation of Bill Stirling, to disbandment, 1945. After the Second World War he was instrumental in forming the Regimental Association through which the postwar SAS was reborn. He was Colonel Commandant of the SAS until 1980.

Lieutenant-Colonel William Stirling

Died 1983 aged 71. Brother of founder David Stirling. After the capture of his brother David, he formed 2 SAS, 1943, following prolonged service with Scots Guards and Commandos. Quarrelled with high command when it tried to use SAS inappropriately and had to resign but (said David later), 'he won the argument'.

Colonel Ian Lapraik, DSO, OBE, MC, TD

Died 15 March 1985, aged 69. Qualified lawyer (Glasgow) and international runner, joined Cameron Highlanders, 1941; Middle East Commando; SBS, June 1943; wounded six times; captured three times, always escaped. Hon. Colonel, 21 SAS (VR) 1973–83.

Major Dare Newell, OBE

Died January 1989 aged 71. Regimental Adjutant, SAS Regiment, known as 'Mr SAS.' Served with SOE in Albania, 1944 and Force 136 Malaya, 1945. Commanded SAS squadron in Malayan Emergency (MID). Selection and training officer of SAS in MoD, a post from which he defended the SAS against its enemies in Whitehall.

RSM G.R. (Bob) Turnbull, MM

Died 1 February 1989. Served 20 years with 22 SAS. Shot dead Communist gunslinger Ah Tuck in 'blink-of-eye' jungle contact at 20 yards during Malayan Emergency; killed four terrorists single handed in another close-quarter, shotgun battle. From November 1974, was a dignified usher in the Palace of Westminster.

Major-General J.B.M. ('Tod') Sloane, CBE

Died 1990, aged 77. First Commanding Officer of 22 SAS. (CO, Malayan Scouts, 1951). Active service, (Argyll & Sutherland Highlanders) India and Burma during Second World War. Korean War 1950–51.

APPENDIX E
THE SOLDIER'S LEGAL MINEFIELD

The only formal guidance a soldier receives before he opens fire in Northern Ireland is contained in a document known as the 'Yellow Card' (because it is printed on a plastic card in that colour). The correct name is 'Instructions for Opening Fire in Northern Ireland'. It tells the soldier:

General Rules

1. In all situations you are to use the minimum force necessary. FIREARMS MUST ONLY BE USED AS A LAST RESORT.

2. Your weapon must always be made safe: that is, NO live round is to be carried in the breech and in the case of automatic weapons the working parts are to be forward, unless you are ordered to carry a live round in the breech or you are about to fire.

Challenging

3. A challenge MUST be given before opening fire unless:
   a. to do so would increase the risk of death or grave injury to you or any other person;
   b. you or others in the immediate vicinity are being engaged by terrorists.

4. You are to challenge by shouting 'ARMY: STOP OR I FIRE' or words to that effect.

Opening fire

5.   You may only open fire against a person:
  a.   if he/she is committing or about to commit an act LIKELY TO ENDANGER LIFE, AND THERE IS NO OTHER WAY TO PREVENT THE DANGER. The following are some examples where life could be endangered, dependent always upon the circumstances:
       (i)   firing or being about to fire a weapon;
       (ii) planting, detonating or throwing an explosive device, including a petrol bomb;
       (iii) deliberately driving a vehicle at a person and there is no other way of stopping him/her;
  b.   If you know that he/she has just killed or injured any person by such means and he/she does not surrender if challenged, and THERE IS NO OTHER WAY TO MAKE AN ARREST.

6.   If you have to open fire you should:
  a.   fire only aimed shots;
  b.   fire no more rounds than are necessary;
  c.   take all reasonable precautions not to injure anyone other than your target.

In practice, during 22 years of trouble in which around 320 people were killed by security forces and 22 soldiers prosecuted, the rules put the soldier into a situation in which he was likely to break either the civil criminal code, as a result of opening fire, or the legal duty imposed on him as a soldier to shoot when instructed.

In the autumn of 1991, a British government review body began examining alternatives to the existing legal options, a charge of murder or nothing. 'As the law stands,' the barrister Anthony Jennings noted in the *Independent* on 27 September 1991, 'murder charges against members of the security forces almost invariably end in not-guilty verdicts.' (The acquittal rate was 91 per cent). Some of the cases, most notably the death of Patrick McElhone (not at the hands of the SAS) in 1974 produced controversy rather than case law, though in 1977, Lord Justice Gibson compared the soldier's situation to that of someone in a sheriff's wild west posse. 'The posse shoot their man if need be . . . Shooting may be justified as a method of arrest.'

Alternatives to a charge of murder in such cases might include using excessive force or failing to comply with official guidance. They would not necessarily make 'reasonable force' less lethal than it is already. In a situation in which terrorists use modern missiles, land-mines, mortars and heavy machine-guns against undefended civilian targets, military lawyers might well argue that the security forces' use of high velocity automatic rifles and self-loading pistols is less than reasonable.

The SAS, as the Irish section of this book observes, has a special problem in that it is chosen as the proactive enforcement agency against terrorists whose record, almost invariably, has demonstrated their immunity to any deterrent short of lethal force.

That knowledge, in the mind of the SAS soldier, must shape his motivation. Whether lethal force is criminal depends, in the last analysis, on the intention of the man who exercised it. The soldier's dilemma is that the institution he represents shapes the policy, while it is the soldier personally, as an individual citizen, who is legally responsible if the policy goes wrong. So it was that the soldiers involved in the Gibraltar shootings were left by Whitehall to decide, as individual, private citizens, whether to give evidence to the inquest. The institution, meanwhile, can always defend itself with the magic wand of Crown Privilege if the going gets sufficiently rough.

There is a line from Kipling to summarise this nonsense. For once it concerns not that universal British soldier Tommy Atkins, but the whimpering soul of a late Berkeley Square resident named Tomlinson. Poor Tomlinson confesses to only one peccadillo in his former, colourless life, that 'I borrowed my neighbour's wife to sin the deadly sin'. The avenging angel explains that the collective nature of the offence is no mitigation: 'For the sin ye do by two and two ye must pay for one by one!'

APPENDIX F
PRINCES GATE HOSTAGE RESCUE TIMETABLE, 5 MAY 1980

5pm   Deliberate Assault Plan ready after days of intensive local preparation and seven years' rehearsal.

6.45pm Body of Abbas Lavasani, Iranian Embassy Press attache, dumped on pavement. This convinces Home Secretary and police that terrorist claims to have killed a hostage is not a bluff. Shots fired inside the embassy shortly before exposure of the body are a bluff, however, which has the opposite effect of what the terrorist leader intended.

6.58pm Home Secretary, William Whitelaw, authorises a military assault to end the siege and rescue the surviving hostages.

7.07pm Metropolitan Police formally hand over control to the Commanding Officer 22 SAS Regiment, Lieutenant-Colonel Michael Rose.

7.08pm Rose delegates control to Major 'Lysander', commanding the Pagoda squadron.

7.23pm SAS assault begins prematurely after Staff-Sergeant leading Red Team abseil is trapped in his harness.

7.28pm Hostages begin to leave the embassy after six days' captivity.

7.40pm SAS assault completed: embassy cleared of terrorists, casualties and hostages. Building now on fire.

7.53pm SAS Commanding Officer formally hands control back to Metropolitan Police.

APPENDIX G
MEDIA MYTHS ABOUT
THE SAS

Contrary to reports in the *Sun, Sunday Times, Independent On Sunday*, and elsewhere there were no SAS operations in Baghdad or Basra during Operation Granby; no parachute operations by HALO or otherwise; no use of the 'dune buggy' Light Strike Vehicle or its American equivalent. No soldier, with or without parachute, landed with a Claymore mine on his helmet. The SAS did not take part in any *coup-de-main* operation against any airfields known as 'Ali' or by any other name. No SAS soldiers were recruited to work as mechanics for the Iraqi Republican Guard. None penetrated Baghdad, Basra or elsewhere disguised as a fruit seller to plant a homing device for Allied bombers. No significant use was made of laser target designation devices for Allied bombers.

No SAS captive interrogated by the Iraqis had fingernails or toenails torn out, mercilessly or otherwise. None was beaten on the soles of the feet with wire flails. None was pounded on shins or knees with metal bars. None was tortured by having electrodes attached to him. No RAF Chinook helicopter landed in a minefield while setting down an SAS team in enemy territory, though a decoration was awarded for an incident involving a Chinook but not the SAS, after the ceasefire.

The SAS did not train the Kuwaiti Resistance and did not take any part in operations in the Kuwait Theatre of Operations. The SAS did not begin Gulf operations 'as soon as Iraq invaded Kuwait', or in November 1990 or on 16 January 1991 [as the *Observer* asserted a year later] but subsequently. (See main text.) Contrary to the *Observer*'s report that the impact of the SAS on the war was negligible, both General Schwarzkopf and General

Sir Peter de la Billière are on record applauding the SAS success. (See Appendix A). As de la Billière put it in his analysis for the *RUSI Journal* (Winter 1991): 'Their prime operational task was to counter the threat of Iraqi Scud missiles. This objective was achieved with outstanding success . . .'

As in the case of the Falklands conflict, some journalists seem to have based their reports on intelligent speculation, rumour, special forces' gossip, guesswork and earlier Press stories, all without the collateral of a verifiable source. The *Sunday Times*, as part of its Falklands coverage, published an inaccurate report that seven SAS soldiers were secretly held prisoner in Argentina. The report, published in the face of denials from London and Buenos Aires, caused much distress to the widows of SAS men lost in a helicopter crash off the Falklands. Some of the bereaved women were falsely led to hope that their men might be alive after all and at first refused to accept death certificates prepared by the regiment at its Hereford base.

APPENDIX H
RULES OF ENGAGEMENT

TOP SECRET
RULES OF ENGAGEMENT FOR THE MILITARY
COMMANDER IN OPERATION FLAVIUS

For the personal attention of [Soldier F.]

OBJECTIVES

1. These instructions are for your guidance, once your participation in Operation Flavius has been duly authorised. You are
to issue orders in compliance with these instructions to the men
under your command.
2. You are to operate as directed by the Gibraltar Police
Commissioner or by the officer(s) designated by him to control
this operation.

Should the latter request military intervention, your objective
will be to assist the civil power to arrest members of the IRA, but
subject to the overriding requirement to do all in your power to
protect the lives and safety of members of the public and of the
security forces.

COMMAND AND CONTROL

3. You will be responsible to the Governor and Commander-in-
Chief, through his Chief of Staff, for the way in which you carry
out the military tasks assigned to you. You will act at all times
in accordance with the lawful instructions of the senior police
officer(s) designated by the Gibraltar Police Commissioner to
control this operation.

USE OF FORCE

4. You and your men will not use force unless requested to do so by the senior police officer(s) designated by the Gibraltar Police Commissioner; or unless it is necessary to do so in order to protect life. You and your men are not then to use more force than is necessary in order to protect life; and you are to comply with rule 5.

OPENING FIRE

5. You and your men may only open fire against a person if you or they have reasonable grounds for believing that he/she is currently committing, or is about to commit, an action which is likely to endanger you or their lives, or the life of any person, and if there is no other way to prevent this.

FIRING WITHOUT A WARNING

6. You and your men may fire without a warning if the giving of a warning or any delay in firing could lead to death or injury to you or them or any other person, or if the giving of a warning is clearly impracticable.

WARNING BEFORE FIRING

7. If the circumstances in paragraph 6 do not apply, a warning is necessary before firing. The warning is to be as clear as possible and is to include a direction to surrender and a clear warning that fire will be opened if the direction is not obeyed.

AREA OF OPERATIONS

8. Under no circumstances are you or your men to enter Spanish territory or Spanish territorial waters for the purposes connected with Operation Flavius, nor are you or your men to fire at any person on Spanish territory or Spanish territorial waters.

BIBLIOGRAPHY

PART I: INTRODUCTION

Aureluis Antoninus, Marcus 'Meditations' (translated by A. S. L. Farquharson, Introduction by R. B. Rutherford), Oxford University Press, 1989

Beckwith, Colonel Charlie A. Retd., US Army and Donald Knox. *Delta Force* (The inside story of America's super-secret Counter-terrorist Unit), Arms & Armour Press, Lionel Leventhal Ltd., 1984.

Mokaitis, Professor Thomas R. 'A New Era of Counter-insurgency', *Journal of Royal United Services Institute for Defence Studies*, London, Spring 1991, and 'British Counter Insurgency', *Small Wars and Insurgencies*, Vol, 3 December 1990.

Murray, Raymond. *The SAS in Ireland*, The Mercier Press, Cork, 1990.

Newell, Major Dare, OBE and Colonel David Sutherland. 'SAS Postwar Evolution: The Formative Years, 1954–64', *Mars & Minerva*, September 1987.

Rose, Major-General Michael. 'Advance Force Operations: The SAS'. Contribution to *Ten Years On, the British Army in the Falklands War*, National Army Museum, London, 1992.

Stirling, Colonel Sir David. 'The Special Air Service' (from *The World History of Paratroopers* by Pierre Sergent), Soc. de Prod. Litteraire, Paris, 1974.

Urban, Mark. *Big Boys' Rules*, Faber & Faber, 1992.

Waddy, Colonel J. OBE. Response to 'SAS Postwar Evolution', *Mars & Minerva* Letters, April 1988.

Also consulted:

Cowles, Virginia. *The Phantom Major*, Collins, London, 1958.

Farran, Roy. *Winged Dagger*, Collins, London, 1948.

PROLOGUE

Hersh, Seymour M. *The Samson Option: Israel, America and the Bomb* Faber & Faber, 1991.

Rose. Op. cit.

Salinger, Pierre with Laurent, Eric. *Secret Dossier – The Hidden Agenda Behind the Gulf War*, Penguin Books, 1991.

THE GULF WAR

BBC TV Panorama (Tom Mangold), 'America's Secret War', 26 March 1991;

Grist, Major-General R. D. 'The Future of the Armed Helicopter', *Journal of the Royal United Services Institute for Defence Studies*, Summer 1991:

Mason, Air Vice-Marshal R. A. CB, CBE, MA. 'The Air War in the Gulf', *Survival*, May/June 1991 (International Institute for Strategic Studies).

Newsweek, 18 March 1991. 'The Secret History of the War'.

Rochlin, Gene I. Demchak, Chris C. 'The Gulf War: technological and organizational implications', *Survival*, Op. cit.

Sheehy, Gail. 'How Saddam Survived' – *Vanity Fair*, August 1991.

Taylor, William J. Jr and Blackwell, James. 'The Ground War in the Gulf', *Survival*, Op. cit.

Other public sources consulted:

Allen, Charles. *Thunder & Lightning – The RAF in the Gulf: Personal Experiences of War*, HMSO.

American Forces Information Service, 15 October 1990 to 11 January 1991; 'Early Bird' round-up of US Press coverage; files of *The Washington Post; Daily Telegraph; The Times; Daily Mirror; Independent; Observer; Hereford Times; Navy News*;

BBC Radio 4, 'The Desert War', written and presented by Mark Laity.

Bonds, Ray (ed.) *The Modern US War Machine: An encyclopedia of American military equipment and strategy*, Salamander, 1987.

Bramall, Field Marshal Lord, *et al.*, *Britain's Gulf War: Operation Granby*, Herrington Kilbride plc.

British Aerospace. *The Gulf War* and other publications June 1991. Panavia Aircraft GmbH; 'Tornado Report No. 6', June 1991.

British Government Defence White Paper, June 1991.

Defense & Diplomacy, July/August 1991.

5th Special Forces Group (Airborne) in Desert Shield/Desert Storm, Chapter XXXVIII Special Forces Association 1991, USA.

Hiro, Dilip. *Desert Shield to Desert Storm: The Second Gulf War*, Harper Collins.

JAK – Behind The Lines: Fifty Years of the SAS (limited edition published privately by the Special Air Service Regimental Association).

Roberts, John. 'Oil, the Military and the Gulf War of 1991', Journal of the Royal United Services Institute for Defence Studies, Spring 1991.

Simpson, John, *The House of War*, Hutchinson, August 1991.

Porter, Jadranka, *Under Siege in Kuwait: A Survivor's Story*, Victor Gollancz, London, 1991.

Wratten, Bill, Air Vice-Marshal (Air Commander, British Forces Middle East) *et al.*, 'Desert Air Debrief' *Aerospace, Journal of the Royal Aeronautical Society*, June 1991.

THE SOUTH ATLANTIC

Fox, Robert. *Eyewitness Falklands: A Personal Account of the Falklands Campaign*, Methuen, London, 1982.

Harris, Robert. *Gotcha! The Media, the Government and the Falklands*, Faber & Faber, London, 1983.

Hastings, Max and Jenkins, Simon. *The Battle for the Falklands*, Michael Joseph, London, 1983.

Sunday Express Magazine Team. *War In the Falklands*, Weidenfeld & Nicolson, London, 1982.

Sunday Times 'Insight' Team. *The Falklands War, the Full Story*, Andre Deutsch, London; Sphere Books, London, 1982.

Washington, Linda (ed.). *Ten Years On: The British Army in the Falklands War*, National Army Museum, 1992.

OMAN

Clutterbuck, Professor Richard. *Guerrillas & Terrorists*, Faber & Faber, 1977.

Darby, Phillip. *British Defence Policy East of Suez, 1947–1968*, Oxford University Press, 1973.

Halliday, F. *Armed Struggle in Arabia: Counter Insurgency in Oman*, The Gulf Committee, 1976.

Jeapes, Major-General A.S. *SAS: Operation Oman*, William Kimber, London, 1980.

Kennedy, Michael Paul. *Soldier 'I' SAS* – Bloomsbury Publishing, 1989.

Kitson, General Sir Frank. *Bunch of Five*, Faber & Faber, London, 1977.

Smiley, David and Kemp, P. *Arabian Assignment*, Leo Cooper, London, 1975.

Townsend, J. *Oman: The Making of a Modern State*, Croom Helm, London, 1977.

Other works consulted:

Akehurst, Major-General John. *We Won A War*, Michael Russell, 1982.

PART II: IRELAND, 1969–92

Bowyer-Bell, J. 'An Irish War: The IRA's Armed Struggle, 1969–1990', in *Small Wars & Insurgencies*, Vol 1., No. 3., Frank Cass & Co., London, 1990.

Coogan, Tim Pat. *The IRA*, William Collins & Son, 1989.

Dillon, Martin and Lehane, Denis. *Political Murder in Northern Ireland*, Penguin, 1973.

Fitzgerald, Dr Garret, *All in a life: an autobiography*, Macmillan, London, 1991.

Foot, Paul. *Who Framed Colin Wallace?*, Macmillan, London, 1989.

Hilton, Frank. *The Paras*, BBC, London, 1983.

Holroyd, Fred and Burbridge, Nick. *War Without Honour*, The Medium Publishing Co., Hull, 1989.

Kennedy, Michael Paul. *Soldier 'I' SAS* op. cit.

Morton, Peter, *Emergency Tour*, William Kimber, 1989.

Murray, Raymond. *The SAS In Ireland*, Mercier Press, Cork, 1990.

Selth, Andrew. 'Ireland & Insurgency: The Lessons of History', in *Small Wars & Insurgencies*, Vol. 2 No. 2.

Urban, Mark. *Big Boys' Rules* op. cit.

Wright, Peter and Greengrass, Paul. *Spycatcher*, Heinemann, Australia, 1987.

Other works consulted:

Barzilay, D., *The British Army in Ulster*, Vols. 2 & 3, Century Services, Belfast, 1973–1978.

Devlin, Paddy, *The Fall of the Northern Ireland Executive*, Paddy Devlin, Belfast, 1975.

Kenny, Anthony. *The Road to Hillsborough*, Pergamon Press, 1986.

GIBRALTAR 1987–88

Ellicott, Dorothy, *Our Gibraltar: A Short History of the Rock*, Gibraltar Museum Committee, 1975.

Roberts, Dr J. M. *The Pelican History of the World*, Penguin Books, 1980.

Suetonius Tranquillus, Gaius. *The Twelve Caesars*, translated by Robert Graves with an Introduction by Michael Grant, Penguin Books, 1989.

Other works consulted:

Burne, Jerome. *Chronicle of the World*, Longman, 1989.

Cottrell, Leonard. 'Vespasian and the Second Legion' in *The Great Invasion*, Pan Books, 1951.

Salway, Professor Peter, *Roman Britain*, Oxford University Press, 1981.

Smith, William, *A Classical Dictionary*, John Murray, London, 1878.

Taylor, A.J.P. *English History, 1914–1945*, Oxford University Press, 1965.

PART III: MALAYA 1950–59

Blaxland, Gregory. *The Regiments Depart: The British Army, 1945–70*, William Kimber, London, 1971.

BORNEO 1962–66

Pocock, Tom. *Fighting General – The Public and Private Campaigns of General Sir Walter Walker*, Collins, London, 1973.
Smith, E. D. *East of Katmandu* (History of 7th Duke of Edinburgh's Own Gurkha Rifles), Leo Cooper, London, 1976.
Walter, General Sir Walter. *The Bear At The Back Door*, Foreign Affairs Publishing Co., 1980.

SOUTH ARABIA 1964–67

Barthrop, M. *Crater to the Creggan: The Royal Anglian Regiment, 1964–1974*, Leo Cooper, London, 1976,
Paget, Julian. *Last Post: Aden 1964–67*, Faber & Faber, London, 1969.
Young David. *Four Five: 45 Commando, Royal Marines, 1943–71*, Leo Cooper, London, 1972.

Works also consulted:

Harper, S. *The Last Sunset*, Collins, London, 1978.
James, H. D. and Sheil-Small, D. *A Pride of Gurkhas*, Leo Cooper, London, 1975.

PART IV: THE WAR ON YOUR DOORSTEP

Greenwood, C. *Police Tactics in Armed Operations*, Arms & Armour Press, London, 1980.
Gregory, Frank. *'Can Military Force Defeat Drugs Trafficking?'*, in *Small Wars & Insurgencies*, Vol. 2 No. 1, Frank Cass, London.
Kennedy, Michael Paul, Soldier 'I', op, cit.
Lee, Rensselaer W. III. 'The Latin American Drug Connection' *Foreign Policy*, 1985–86.

Roy, Olivier. *The Lessons of the Soviet/Afghan War*, Adelphi Papers 259, IISS/Brassey's, 1991.

Shaw, Jennifer. *et al. Ten Years of Terrorism: Collected Views*, (Introduction by Tony Geraghty), RUSI, London, 1979.

Tonkin, Ambassador Derek. Letter to *Daily Telegraph*.

Other works consulted:

Adams, James. *Secret Armies*, Hutchinson, 1987.

Clutterbuck, Professor Richard. *Guerrillas & Terrorists*, Faber & Faber, London, 1977.

Dobson, Christopher and Payne, Ronald. *The Weapons of Terror: International Terrorism at Work*, Macmillan, London, 1979.

PART V: EVEREST 1981–88/HOW TO SELECT AN ELITE

Beaumont, Roger. *Military Elites: Special Fighting Units in the Modern World*, Robert Hale, London, 1976.

Fleming, John and Faux, Ronald. *Soldiers on Everest*, HMSO, London, 1977.

Watson, Peter. *War On The Mind: The Military Uses and Abuses of Psychology*, Hutchinson, London, 1978.

INDEX